Why Access? Why The Revolutionary Guide?

Access is the PC-based relational database from Microsoft. With full support for the novice programmer, Access is also packed with features, add-ins and wizards that can help professional developers leverage their efforts.

With The Revolutionary Guide to Access, you can take your software into the professional realm, and that means Client/Server technology! As a developer, you will be taken through the implementation of many cutting-edge technologies. Backed up with a wealth of source code on the accompanying CD-ROM, the Revolutionary Guide's practical approach will soon have you producing first-class applications.

Carrying on the Revolutionary Series tradition, this guide gives developers the code, tips and tricks that they are crying out for. Aimed at the status of 'Industry Bible', this series will soon become an invaluable tool in your cross-platform development efforts.

What is Wrox Press?

Wrox Press is a computer book publisher which promotes a brand new concept - clear, jargon-free programming and database titles that fulfill your real demands. We publish for everyone, from the novice through to the experienced programmer. To ensure our books meet your needs, we carry out continuous research on all our titles. Through our dialog with you we can craft the book you really need.

We welcome suggestions and take all of them to heart - your input is paramount in creating the next great Wrox title. Use the reply card inside this book or mail us at:

feedback@wrox.demon.co.uk
or
Compuserve 100063, 2152

Wrox Press Ltd.	**Tel:**	**(312) 465 3559**
2710 W. Touhy	**Fax:**	**(312) 465 4063**
Chicago		
IL 60645		
USA		

The Revolutionary Guide to Access

Stephen Wynkoop

Wrox Press Ltd.®

The Revolutionary Guide to Access

Published by Wrox Press Ltd. Unit 16, 20 James Road, Tyseley, Birmingham, B11 2BA
Printed in the USA

ISBN 1-874416-39-7

Trademark Acknowledgements

Credits

Author
Stephen Wynkoop

Technical Editor
Graham McLaughlin

Series Editor
Gordon Rogers

Technical Reviewers
Alex Homer
Michael Gilbert
David Sussman

Managing Editor
John Franklin

Operations Manager
Gina Mance

Production Manager
Deb Somers

Book Layout
Eddie Fisher
Greg Powell
Lee Kelly

CD Authoring
Darren Gill
Chris Ullman

Proof Reader
Pam Brand

Cover Design
Third Wave

For more information on Third Wave, contact Ross Alderson on 44-21 236 6616
Cover photo supplied by The Telegraph Colour Library

CD-ROM Credits

At Wrox, we try to give you the maximum value from our titles. In addition to the source code, PIM and text viewer on the CD-ROM, we have included some professional level tools. These tools are supplied for your experimentation from various sources who are willing for you to use and enjoy them. Please acknowledge that some of the software supplies is shareware, and if you intend to continue using it after testing, please follow the instruction supplied with the software concerning registration.

We would like to thank the following for their co-operation in keeping the software flowing:

The UK Access User Group
Andrew Couch and Couch Consulting
Dan Madoni and Paul Nielson Computing
Dave Schlosser
Chris Patterson
Ken Getz
Paul Litwin
Ken Stambaugh
Nicholas Couch
Monte Slichter
Michael Mee
Stan Leszynski

A full list of contributors is available on the CD-ROM.

About the Author

Stephen Wynkoop started programming in Pascal, Basic and other more proprietary and obscure languages. In recent years, a focus on the Microsoft environment has enhanced experiences in the Visual Basic, Access and Office Integration platforms. Stephen is a Senior Technology Consultant at MIDAK International/USConnect, a Microsoft Solution Provider in Tucson, Arizona, where he helps in focusing on bringing leading edge technologies to bear on large development projects for their clients. He has worked in many different development environments since the early 1980s and is currently working closely with Microsoft on many soon-to-be-released projects and products. Shephen lives in Tucson with his wife, Julie, and their two children, Brennan and Caitlin.

Acknowledgements

First and foremost, many thanks to my wife, Julie, for helping me with the endless revision cycles, the prodding to keep going, and making sure all the pieces fit together. Also, thanks to Wrox Press for extending me the opportunity to work with such a great group of people. It's truly amazing the level of effort and number of people involved in putting out a book of this nature, and I appreciate everyone's help!

Dedication

To Julie - Thank you for everything you've done and continue to do to make everything possible. Here's to The Rose!

SUMMARY OF CONTENTS

CONTENTS

Introduction

Welcome to the Revolutionary Guide To Access. This book has been developed to give you, the developer, an edge when you develop Access applications that take advantage of some of the leading edge features available today.

This guide picks up where the Beginner's Guide to Access 2.0 ended. The Beginner's Guide covers the development environment, aspects of setting up Access and many other items necessary for your successful use of the Access system. In this guide, we'll be introducing you to technologies ranging from OLE and OLE Automation to Integrating Mail in your applications.

This introductory section serves as an overview of the various chapters, their format and some overall information about the programs provided with the guide.

Who Should Read On?

As with all technical books, it is important that you understand the level of writing as well as any assumptions that we have made of you. This book is most definitely a developer's script. It covers subjects that basic databases don't need to incorporate.

We have assumed that you have a good grasp of Access Basic, and therefore we won't go over the syntax of the language, but we do cover some of the important functions and keywords when they come into play.

For the later chapters, you will need access to a back-end server based database if you are to get the most out of the sections: SQL Server is recommended. For Chapter 14, you will need access to Microsoft Mail in order to make use of the PIM's messaging facilities. You may also find it useful to get hold of a copy of the Access Developer's Toolkit as well as a copy of Access itself.

If you fall into the majority of these categories, please read on, and enjoy the treasure trove of resources that is The Revolutionary Guide To Access.

Chapter Layout

In each chapter, we'll be providing introductory information detailing the content of the chapter. We've used as many screenshots as possible and have explained the operations so you have a good understanding of what is going on. In each chapter, you'll find the following sections:

What's Covered in This Chapter

This section lays out, at a superficial level, what topics will be included in the chapter. This section will generally include a bulleted highlight list outlining the topics and some basic ideas about why they are useful.

How This Chapter Impacts Our Application

As the guide works with the different software samples, we'll often be referring to the sample application, a Personal Information Manager or PIM. This PIM is provided, along with all pertinent source code, on the CD-ROM accompanying this book.

Later in this introduction we'll cover some of the functionality provided by the PIM and how it is presented throughout the book. In the Impact section of each chapter, we'll detail how the examples we show will be implemented in the sample application. In those areas where it's not feasible or practical to include an applicable function in the PIM, separate databases will be used to provide the source code.

Introduction

The Introduction to each chapter goes into a greater level of detail to show what the focus and direction of the chapter is.

Comments and Suggestions

At the end of each chapter, there is a section that provides additional insights into the technology, as well as any other information necessary to enable you to put into practice the information presented in the chapter. In addition, the Comments and Suggestions will indicate what is coming up in the next chapter or chapters.

Overall Book Layout

The Revolutionary Guide to Access is broken into several broad-sweeping groups of chapters. While each chapter provides information on specific techniques, code samples, toolkit applications and other items, there will be a general theme for a group of chapters.

Program to Program Communication

The overall approach of these sections is to show how applications can work together in the Windows environment. These sections highlight many of the technologies that play key roles in the Windows, Windows NT and Windows '95 environments.

Chapter 1: Applications Working Together

New OCX's and OLE objects are powerful leverage to your Access applications. This chapter covers not only OLE objects in a generic sense, but also the OLE Custom Controls included in the Access Developer's Kit. The chapter also serves as an introduction to the Dynamic Data Exchange and Network Dynamic Data Exchange capabilities of the Windows environment.

Chapter 2: Object Linking and Embedding

In Chapter 2, we delve into the different ways you can use OLE in today's environments. OLE Server and the use of methods from other applications is covered. We'll also present information on the Registration Database and what it's used for, how it's updated and what all of the information maintained by it means.

Chapter 3: Implementing OLE in Your Applications

Chapter 3 continues by showing you how to work with compound documents and OLE Server applications, and how you can write Access Basic functions that will easily attach to, and work with, other applications. This chapter gets into the technical aspects of activating objects and what the differences are between OLE and OLE 2.0.

Chapter 4: Implementing OLE Tools In Your Applications

In this chapter, we provide some specific, re-usable code modules that allow you to work with MSGraph, Word and Excel. The examples provided will give you a foundation from which you can build other routines to add to your applications.

Chapter 5: Dynamic Data Exchange

DDE is the older standard of communicating between applications in the Windows environment. Since OLE is still relatively new on the market as a standard, many applications support the older, previously more prevalent DDE environment before they support OLE. In this chapter, we'll show how DDE works and how it translates into the NetDDE, or Network Dynamic Data Exchange environment.

Applications Development in the Access Environment

In these sections, we'll be presenting information that will help advance your system to the next level of design and functionality. These chapters will help you not only define components of your system and how they can be optimized, but also show how to migrate an existing application to a Client/ Server environment as painlessly as possible.

Chapter 6: Optimization Using Transactions and Referential Integrity

Chapter 6 introduces many different ways that you can put Access to work for you. We've included information on rules and triggers and how they work, setting up relationships, and more. For each of these, we show how you can allow Access to handle the database transactions while your application takes responsibility for the user interface and presentation of information to the user.

Chapter 7: User Interface Design

In this chapter, we look at some of the considerations and theory behind designing good user interfaces. We've provided lots of examples of different ways of presenting information to maximize screen real estate. We've also covered the creation of custom menus and toolbars to provide functionality for your users.

Chapter 8: Advanced Access Wizards

You can do amazing things with the different wizards provided with Access. New wizards are being introduced on a regular basis and many of these provide capabilities that can save you many hours of development time and headaches. Wizards can also be extended and modified to more closely suit your needs. This chapter explains the different ways you can do these types of modifications.

Chapter 9: Developing Production-Ready Applications

Chapter 9 includes information on how to use the Setup Wizard included with the Developer's Toolkit. In addition, different techniques for error handling and creating your own add-ins is included. A sample add-in, an INI File Manager, is reviewed and built in the different examples provided as part of this chapter.

Chapter 10: Using SQL in Microsoft Access

The Structured Query Language forms the basis of many database packages so is vital information for anyone who wants to get the most out of their databases. This chapter provides a gentle introduction to the language and shows how it can be used in your Access Basic code routines.

Larger System's Design Issues

Client/Server technologies are a key direction in mainstream applications in the systems developed today. In these chapters, we'll be covering information on how to work in mixed database environments, how to use ODBC to minimize the impact of different systems on your application and much more. In addition, the recently released Microsoft Access Upsizing Tools are covered, providing insight into how the Upsizing Wizard and SQL Server Browser work.

Chapter 11: Using ODBC or Jet Data Sources

ODBC is a standard that can make your development of database systems much more feasible. Using ODBC, you can connect to data sources that are varied and of different proprietary formats. You can even complete updates across databases without regard to their original format. We'll provide information on conversion techniques, how to attach databases to the Access environment and how to manually move a system from Access to Microsoft's SQL Server.

Chapter 12: Using the Microsoft Access Upsizing Tools

Late in 1994, Microsoft released the Microsoft Access Upsizing Tools. Consisting of a SQL Server Browser and an Upsizing Wizard, these tools provide an automated means of converting your applications from the Access environment to a SQL Server environment. We'll provide information on what is happening behind the scenes with these tools and some additional information on how to use these tools and environments to their fullest potential.

Chapter 13: Designing Client/Server Systems

Chapter 13 shows how you can break apart your Access-based system, making feature and function-sets that are most likely to be optimized in the Client/Server environment. This chapter provides the background information and techniques that you'll need in order to effectively set up client server systems.

Chapter 14: Creating Mail-Enabled Applications

Did you know that you can use mail to send data, as well as messages, across the network or around the world? In Chapter 14, we'll show how you can use the MAPI interface to allow two Access systems to 'talk' and exchange information. We'll go through the many ways that you can implement messaging in your application, including how to automate the process of sending messages. In the sample application, we provide a custom in-box and allow for custom message classes to help streamline the processing of different types of messages. This chapter explains all of these techniques and more.

Chapter 15: Application Development Considerations

In this chapter, we provide information on some of the finishing touches that you can add to your system. Specifically, we look at how to optimize your system development using multiple databases. We also cover system security, encryption techniques and considerations when implementing a production application.

Chapter 16: And Finally, How About...

The final chapter includes some little routines and tips that we've included in the sample databases and PIM application, but haven't covered in detail in other chapters. We look at several areas of interest including the IIF() function and Domain functions.

About the Sample Code and Files on the CD

The CD-ROM accompanying this book includes the code from all examples and applications shown in this book. The only exception to this rule are those items copyrighted by other individuals or companies. The wizards and OCXs, Access Developer's Kit, upsizing tools and Office Developer's Kit are examples of these items.

You are free to use, implement and customize all source code, databases and reference materials included with this book. Please be aware of and respectful of any copyrights, trademarks or other protected materials that are included on the CD. We've tried to include as much material as possible for your reference and hope that it proves useful in your development efforts.

For a full listing of the contents of the CD-ROM, see **CONTENTS.TXT** on the CD, but for a taster, see the inside front cover of the book. For instructions on how to install the CD, see the **README.TXT**, also on the CD.

How to Use This Book

This book uses several stylistic conventions, which together with the overall layout, are designed to make the transfer of information from the page as easy and trouble-free as possible. Below is a listing of the styles used in the book, together with a definition of what they mean.

This is code that appears in the text: **DDEInitiateAll()**, while text that appears on the screen looks like this: [Event Procedure].

```
All full listings of code look like this
and important snippets of code appear in this format
```

```
If we refer to the general syntax of a function or command,
it will look like this.
```

This style is for really important notes on the current topic

while this style is for general points of interest.

If we have an **important concept** to cover in a section, the title will be highlighted, and if you should use the keyboard at any time, keystrokes appear in *italics.*

Hopefully, the styles in this book will help you to get the most out of this book.

Other Reference Materials

As we've mentioned above, please refer to The Beginner's Guide to Access 2.0 for more information on the Access development environment. The Beginner's Guide presents information on Wizards, toolbars, customizing the environment and many other aspects of the Access development system.

You may find the following items of additional assistance:

- The Microsoft Office Developer's Toolkit
- The Microsoft Access Developer's Toolkit
- The Microsoft Access Upsizing Tools
- The SmartAccess Newsletter

and last, but not least, you can access CompuServe, in the MSACCESS forum and receive peer-to-peer assistance, help from Microsoft support personnel and gain access to a lot of useful tools and Add-ins.

Let's get started!

CHAPTER

Applications Working Together

The philosophy behind Object Linking and Embedding, Dynamic Data Exchange and even the outdated SendKeys is the same: the spread of data across application boundaries. This concept has been cultured and developed over the last few years until now we aren't confined to simply sharing data. Now we can share the functionality that software designers have implemented in applications throughout our own work. Share data, share methods, cut development time and cut costs.

What's Covered in This Chapter

In this chapter, we will cover the following concepts:

- Overview and terminology of Object Linking and Embedding
- Basics of using other applications' functionality to your own
- Using Custom Controls in your application (OCX's)
- Overview of DDE
- Overview of SendKeys

This chapter will also show how to use the new OCX controls for Access 2. The installation of these new objects is outlined in detail, together with some suggested uses of each. Although these features are not implemented in the accompanying application, the specifics of using the custom controls in your application are included along with sample code.

Chapter 1

How This Chapter Impacts Our Application

This chapter serves as the foundation for the coming chapters as they relate to the application that accompanies this book. The information in this section is very important as you begin to work through these technologies in your applications. Examples of how these capabilities are incorporated in the application are included throughout.

Introduction

With recent Windows development tools and applications, Microsoft has begun introducing modular information 'objects' into the Windows environment. These objects are shareable programs or data that are built to be referenced and used by several different applications on your system. The implementation of these items is known collectively as the Object Orientation of the Microsoft Windows environment. More simply, these components are known as being object oriented.

How exactly does object orientation work, and what does it offer your applications? If you think of a stapler, it has one function that it does very well. It connects together pieces of paper. It doesn't care if it's stapling an annual report or a two-page memo; you can still use the same stapler in either case. The goals are the same for the objects available in the Windows systems being sold today. For example, if you:

- Want to work with a graph, use MSGraph
- Want to work with numbers, use MS Excel
- Want to work with equations, use the MS Equation editor
- Want to work with text, use MS Word

and this is just a very short list of the available tools. We will go into more detail on the various components that could already be a part of the operating environment on your system. The point being made here is that you don't need to re-invent the stapler, just the material that passes through it.

Using The Object Oriented Philosophy

Using this technology, you can implement systems that provide not only increased functionality, but also the same look, feel and operation as the applications that are already in use. As you implement production applications, this ability becomes increasingly important.

There are several different ways to allow your application to share information with other applications. Object Linking and Embedding (OLE) is a means of inserting an object, be it a spreadsheet, a textual document or any other informational item in your application's workspace. Then, depending on the object, you can edit it using the application that was used to create it, often without leaving your own.

A typical example of this might be a case where you want to include spreadsheet functionality in your application. You can implement a Microsoft Excel object on your form or in your database table and allow your users to use Microsoft Excel to edit and maintain the object without having to re-create a spreadsheet package:

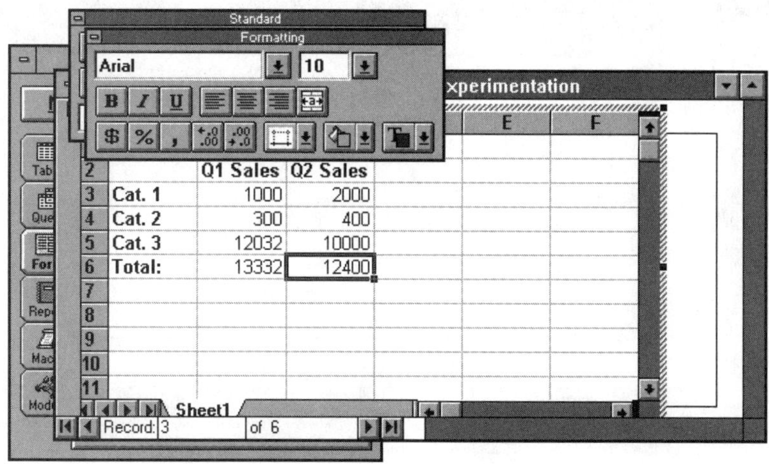

Editing An Excel Object On An Access Form

In the example above, the Access form has been created to allow the user to embed an object. When the user double-clicks on the object, Excel steps in and displays the two floating menu bars, 'Standard' and 'Formatting', and changes the look of the object on your form to look and operate like the Excel spreadsheet environment.

> *Note that in-place editing is a feature of OLE 2. OLE 2 capabilities are new to Microsoft Excel 5 and Word 6. In versions prior to these releases, the application is started as if you had started it from the Program Manager. The object you are editing can still be edited. It just won't be in-place, or within your Container application, which in this case is Access. We'll cover more on in-place activation later in this chapter.*

In the following example, you can see how Word implements the in-place editing as well. Both of these applications integrate well within your application, allowing the user the added functionality of both, without the need for a single without a line of code:

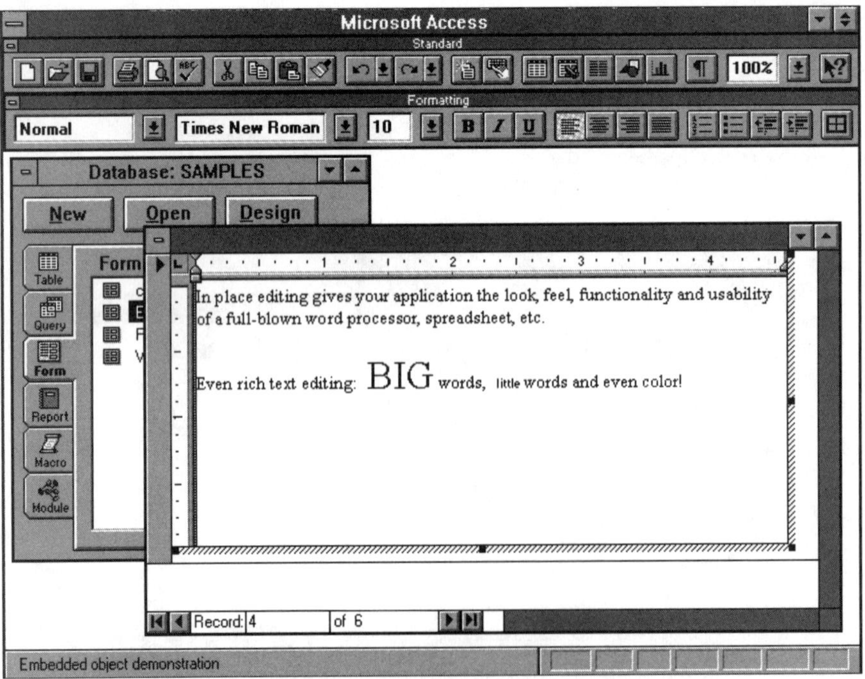

Using Word's Functionality As A Formatted Text Box

As you can see, the functionality can really give your applications a boost, without having to re-invent a word processing system, a spreadsheet or any other components that you may need.

As we work with OLE in this and the next few chapters, we will refer frequently to Microsoft Word and Microsoft Excel. This is simply because they are some of the most widely used applications that support the use of OLE and they represent the most likely candidates for use in demonstrating this technology. The techniques explained in this chapter will work with any embedded or linked object, as well as with any available OLE Automation Server.

Object Linking and Embedding

OLE is implemented with a Container and Server relationship between your application, the Container and the application providing the added functionality, the Server. Your application will maintain the 'hooks' into the Server application and will enable it to be called as needed to update the OLE object.

Object linking and embedding is used to link your application to the functionality contained in another application. For example, when you insert a spreadsheet into a Microsoft Word document, you are implementing an OLE link between Microsoft Word and Microsoft Excel. When you double click on the spreadsheet, Excel is used to edit the object. Using OLE, you are able to allow specialized applications to work in their area of specialization, Word for text or Excel for spreadsheet or grid work.

Using OLE has several benefits. It allows you to leverage your development effort using these tools, as well as giving your users the benefit of using applications that they are already familiar with. This cuts down on development, training and support times. Using OLE within your application can greatly enhance its capabilities.

When you installed the programs included with this book, you were prompted for a subdirectory for the programs. If you specified a subdirectory other than C:\WROX, the SAMPLES database will be there.

For an example of an OLE object, open the **SAMPLES** database, located in the C:\WROX subdirectory and Open the Paintbrush Demo form. The following screen is shown:

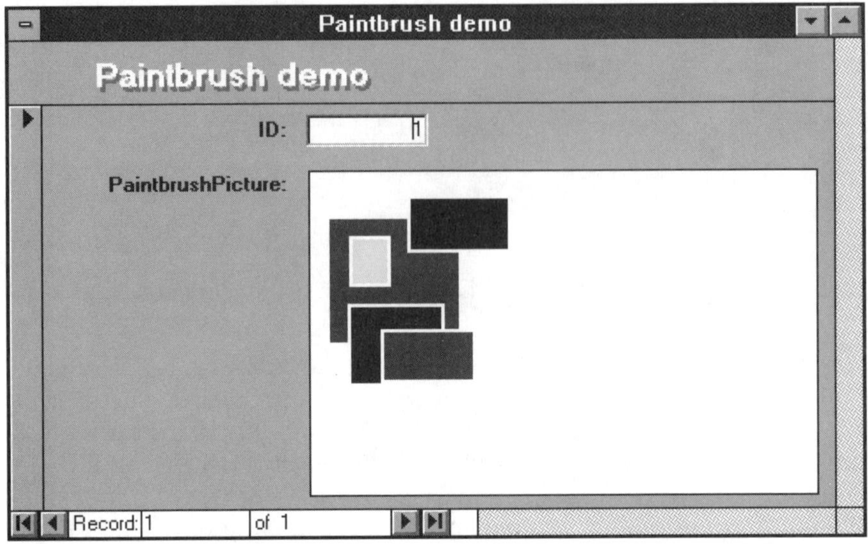

In this example, the Paintbrush picture is saved in the database, but you can edit the picture by simply double-clicking on the picture. Access will load the Paintbrush application and allow you to make changes to the picture. Your changes will be saved back to the database when you either close the Paintbrush application, or choose Update from the Paintbrush File menu.

OLE Object Activation

There are two different types of activation of an OLE object. With the first implementations of OLE, objects resided in your Container application, but were edited externally. A good example of this OLE 1.0 based implementation is our Paintbrush demonstration above. When you double click on the Paintbrush image, the image is loaded into Paintbrush, but the Paintbrush editor runs completely separate from your application; it doesn't provide for in-place activation.

The common examples throughout this exploration of OLE Automation use the current versions of Word and Excel, version 6 and 5 respectively. These versions support the features we discuss in this chapter, such as in-place activation and OLE Automation Server capabilities.

Versions of these products that are released in the future will also support these technologies. However, it should be noted that version 2.x of Word and earlier, as well as version 4 of Excel and earlier, only support the OLE 1 implementation. This limits their use as in-place activation servers and also prevents their use as automation servers.

In-Place Activation

The newest method, as well as one of Microsoft's major goals of OLE2, is in-place activation. This means that the Server application doesn't actually start a whole copy of itself to enable the editing requested. Rather, the Server application just steps into your application and takes over the editing right there on your form while the user does the work. When the user is done, control is automatically returned to your application.

OLE extensions come not only in the form of complete applications, but also extensions to the Access environment. As a simple example, you may need to create a file selector object as shown below:

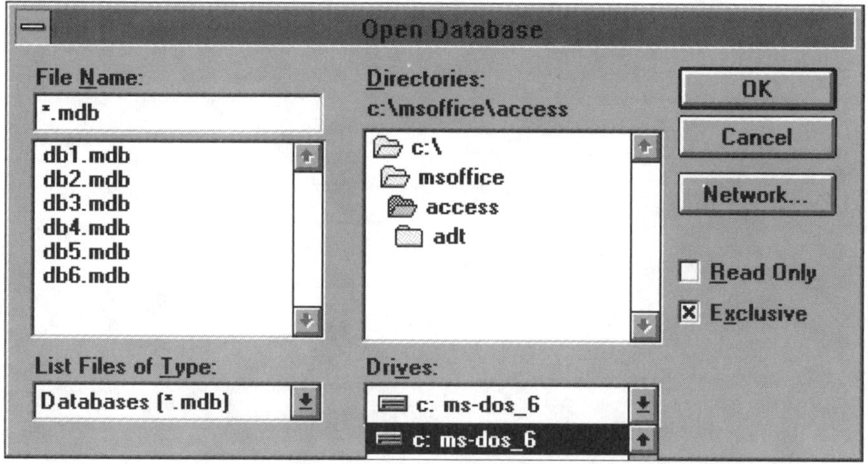

A Common Dialog Box Specializing In File Selection

This could be done as an OLE object and then used in other applications. This is an example of OLE Automation and is accessed as an 'object' by your application, completely separate from your application. You make references to

OLE Automation objects much the same as you do to other Windows DLL functions, with one exception. You create a reference to the object, then set properties and induce actions associated with the object as needed, as opposed to calling specific functions within the DLL and interpreting the results. This is explained in more detail later in the chapter.

The Differences Between Linking and Embedding

OLE objects are implemented in two different ways; linking and embedding. The technology behind OLE is the same in both methods, although the implementation you use will be determined by the specific application. This depends on whether the actual information, such as the document or spreadsheet, is stored within your application or is external to it.

Object Linking

Object Linking allows your application to establish and maintain a link or hook into another object. This might be the case where your application has a linked spreadsheet. In this case, the spreadsheet would be located on disk, separate from your application. This allows the spreadsheet to be modified outside your application.

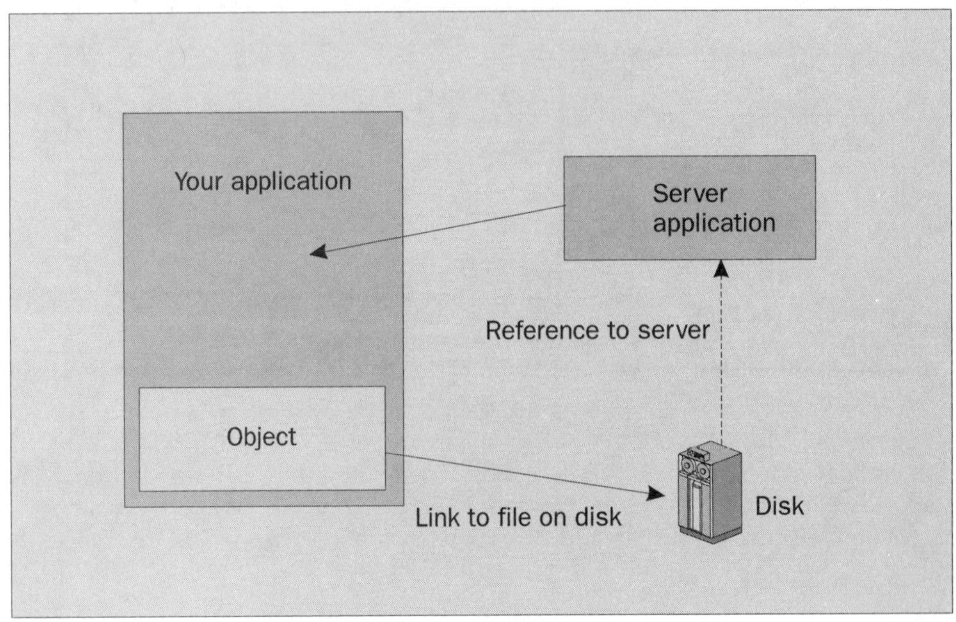

A System Representation Of A Linked Object

This shows that your application is really only responsible for accessing the object on disk. Through the Windows Registration Database, Windows will determine the Server application responsible for maintaining the object and will automatically load it when the object is activated. Your application is not actually storing the contents of the object, only the link to the object within your application or database. When the object is edited, it is actually being changed externally to your program and the data in the object is also saved externally.

> *The Windows Registration database is in the file* **REG.DAT,** *which can be found in your* **WINDOWS** *subdirectory. Be sure not to delete this file or even move it from this directory. It contains vital information required for the proper functioning of your system.*

This is the best way to implement an OLE object that may be changed by the user from outside your application. It will ensure that the object displayed in your application will retain changes made by the user as it will always be referring to the object on disk.

Linking will allow the object to be maintained by both your application and any other applications that are linked to it. For example, if your object is a document, you will be able to update the object within the Access program, while at the same time being able to edit it externally with the word processor used to create it originally.

When you link an object, you will notice that the Insert OLE Object dialog informs you that a picture of your data is being inserted in your database at the time the link is established. This gives a user visual feedback on the object, while allowing the hot link to the file on disk.

One of the biggest drawbacks to Linking is the fact that if the file on disk is moved, the link to the object is not automatically updated. You will need to maintain links manually within Access. From the Edit menu, choose Links to modify path and file name specifications for linked objects.

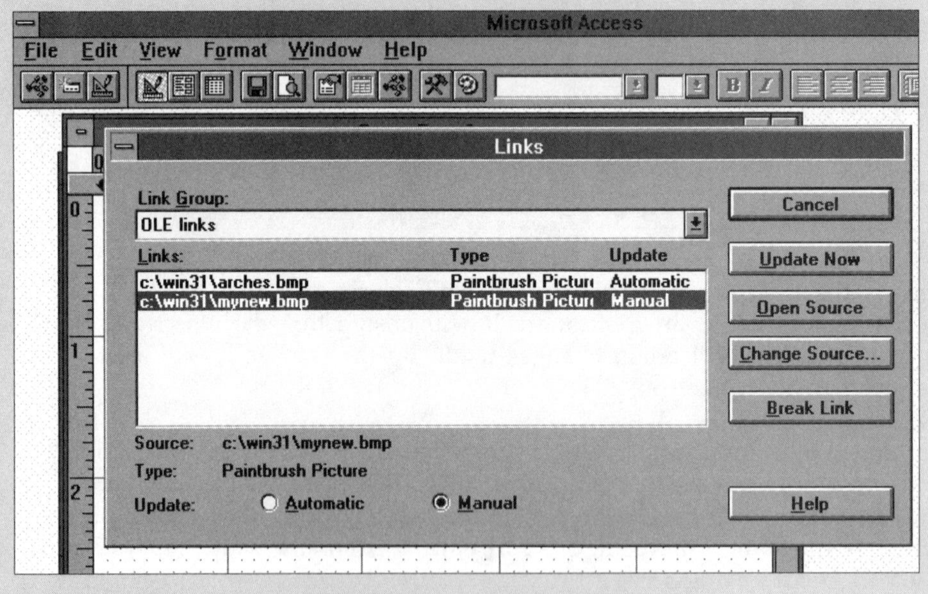

Maintaining Your Object Links

By highlighting the link you want to change you can select the Change Source... button and specify the new location of the linked file.

Object Embedding

Embedding an object in your application requires a slightly different tack as the actual contents of the object are stored in your applications database rather than in a separate file, as is the case with Linking. This might be the case where you define a field in your database table to be of type 'OLE Object'.

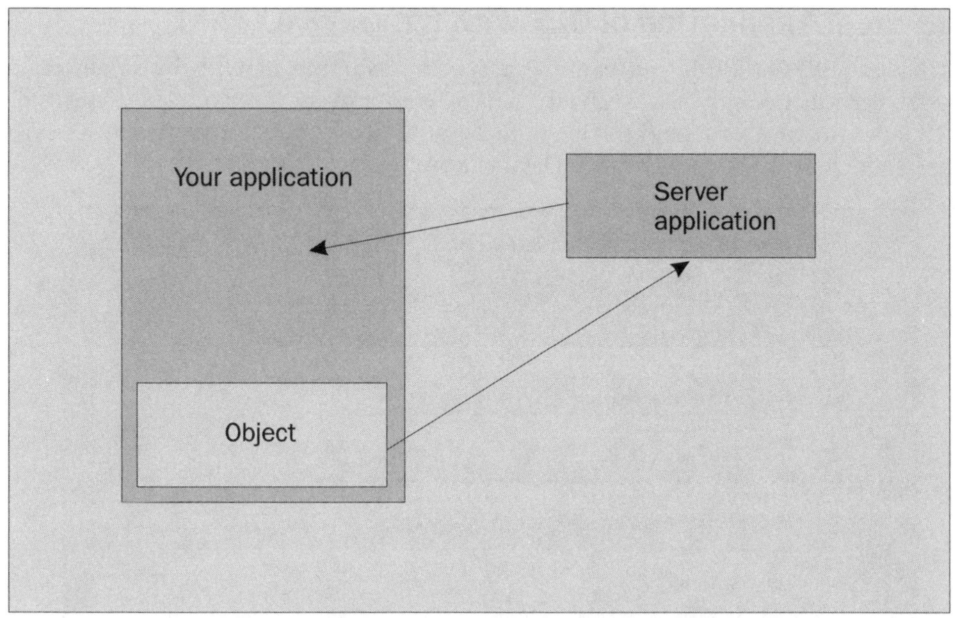

A System Representation Of An Embedded Object

One of the real benefits of embedding is that you can more readily exchange your Container object with other systems by exchanging the Access database (MDB) file. Since all of the objects are physically located within the Container object, you will not have to worry about additional files to pass to the external system to ensure that it has access to the embedded objects.

Additionally, if you only want to view the contents of an object, but not necessarily edit it, embedding means that you don't have to use any additional filters to display it. If you Insert a Picture... in Word and specify Link to File but don't specify Save Picture in Document, then Word will have to import the picture each time you display it. This requires the use of a filter specific to the object you are displaying; for example, a TIFF or BMP import filter. If you embed the picture, the representation of the picture is saved in your Word document, saving this step. Another positive side-effect of Embedding is that you don't have to manually maintain the links to files on disk as when Linking.

The downside to embedding is that if the original object changes on disk, for example by another user or application, there is no automated way of updating the contents of the object within your Container application. You will have to update the contents manually, possibly by re-pasting the object into your application.

Practical Application of OLE within the WROX PIM

Within the WROX PIM, you can see a specific example of OLE by reviewing the Notes functionality for a given contact, company or project. The notes are maintained as a Word object. The figure below shows what the screen looks like when you open the Contact Details form:

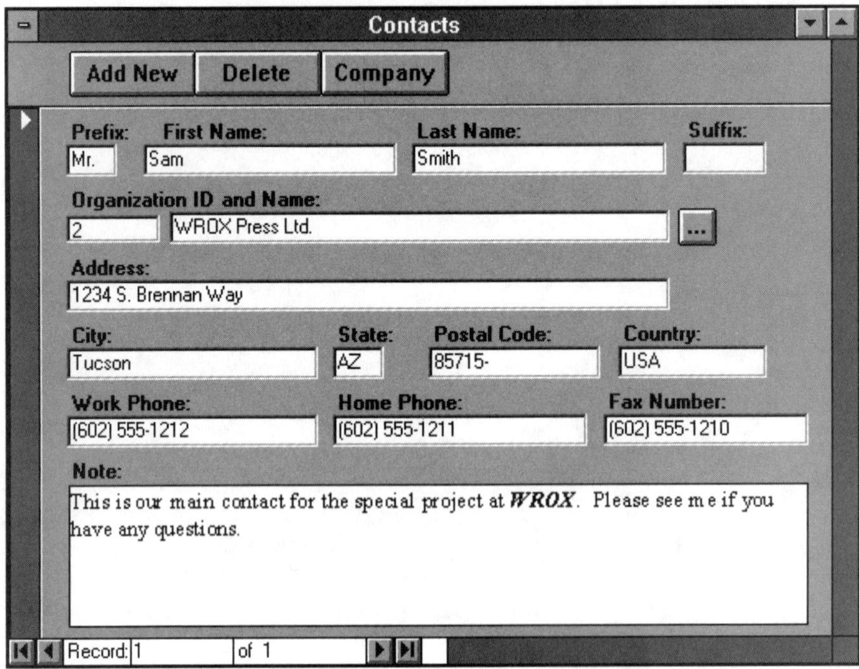

> *If you are starting the PIM for the purpose of reviewing the example code, be sure to hold down the shift key when you load the database. When you start Access, Open a Database, select the Contacts database and press and hold down the shift key when you load it. This will prevent the main selection screen from coming up and will allow you to work with specific forms.*

From this screen, the user can edit the information about a contact. The standard name, address and phone information is here, along with a Note box. This is an OLE embedded object, specifically a Microsoft Word 6.0 Document. Double-click on the note box and you will activate Word and the floating menu bars 'Standard' and 'Formatting' will appear. You can edit the contents of the note in-place within the Access application.

This is just a taste of what is ahead in working with the sample application. In the following chapters, we'll go into all the details behind implementing OLE objects and the different things that are going on behind the scenes in an effort to make sure the user is insulated from potential problems

OLE Automation

OLE Automation allows your application to implement or call the functionality of an external application. OLE Automation object information, such as where to find the application or the class ID of the application, is found in the Windows Registry.

To review your registration database, you can run the Windows REGEDIT program. To see the verbose listing of the commands in the registry, use the / V parameter or specifically, REGEDIT /V. You will see the screen below with the entries specific to your system:

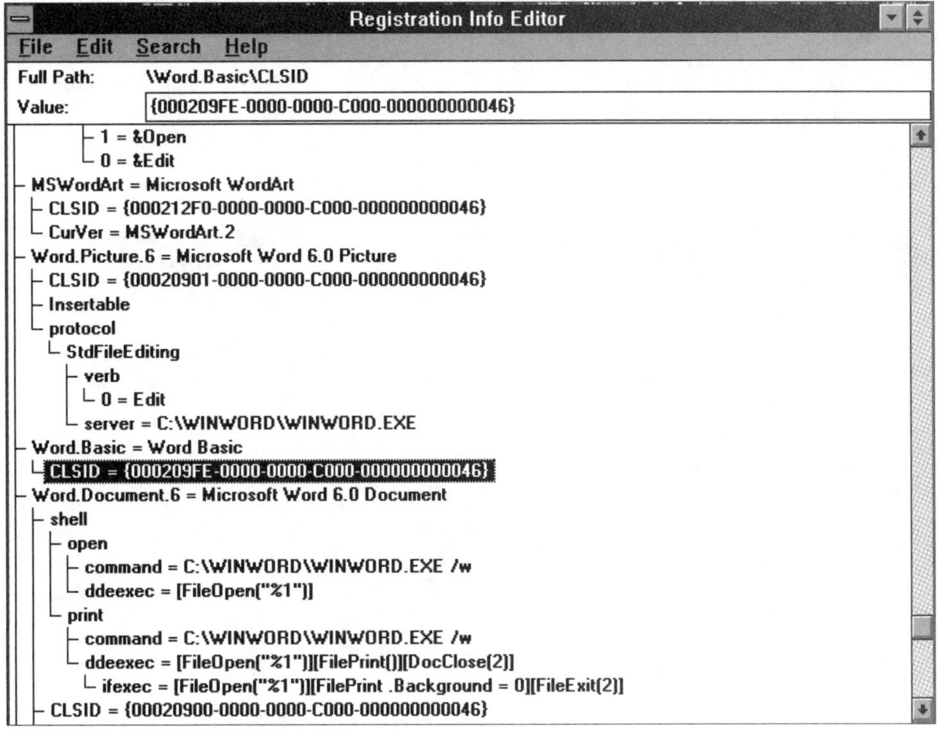

An Example Of A Registration Database As Seen By REGEDIT /V

Reviewing the Registration Database, you will also notice DDE commands, location of files, different capabilities of the programs, as well as other registration information. The Registration Database is the way that Windows keeps track of all this information. The Windows operating systems (Windows, NT and Windows '95) are all moving toward keeping more information in the Registration Database and less information in the .INI file format. This provides better security and increases control over the different configurations that may be required on your system.

If you are at all uncertain, you shouldn't edit entries in the registration database directly. Doing so may cause some applications to operate improperly or to cease functioning altogether. In spite of all these warnings, it can be helpful to review this information when trying to determine what systems will serve as automation servers to your application. We will go into more detail about the registration database and what the different entries mean in a later chapter.

OLE Automation Example

One example of OLE Automation could be the use of Word to print some text. The **SAMPLES** database contains a Word Automation program that shows exactly how to use this function. Open the **SAMPLES** database and open the Word Automation form. The following opening screen is shown:

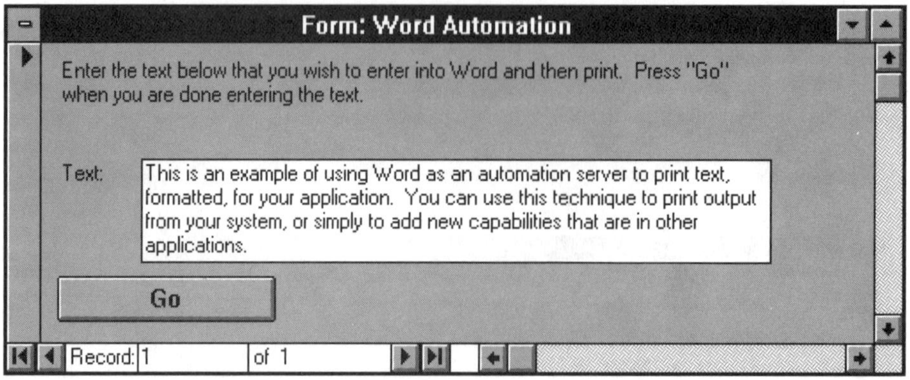

Using Word As An OLE Automation Server

Enter text into the space provided and click on Go. Access will activate Word in automation mode and pass several different commands to the application. Behind the scenes, we are activating the Word Basic OLE Automation Server and calling the various functions to open a new, temporary document, insert the text and print it before finally closing the document. You won't see anything happening on screen, but provided you are connected to a printer, you should get a printout of the text. We'll look more closely at the construction of this form in Chapter Two.

The commands used in calling Word are all Word Basic commands. You can call any Word Basic command from your Access application by simply activating the Word Basic OLE Automation Server. For more information about the commands available to you from Word, choose Help, Search for 'WordBasic', then choose 'WordBasic Help'. This is also true of other applications that provide support for these types of capabilities, one excellent example being Excel.

What are the Differences Between OLE and OLE Automation?

It's important to understand how OLE and OLE Automation differ. OLE is used to embed an object, or a reference to an object, in your application. A typical example of this is the case where you embed a spreadsheet within a document. As explained above, the actual location of the information in the embedded object varies based on whether the object is embedded or linked to the Container application.

OLE Automation allows you to call upon the functionality of another application from within your own, simply by the setting Properties and executing Actions. Visual Basic's .VBX add-in functionality is an example of an early form of OLE Automation. Though the VBX architecture is not global in nature, it serves to add further functionality to Visual Basic applications. Everything from single use objects like custom outline controls to full featured objects like spreadsheet controls can be provided by the VBX model.

For additional functionality demands in Access, OCXs are new to the development environment. They provide enhanced or improved functionality tools for your program. Typically, an OCX doesn't stand alone, but rather provides enhanced functionality as a tool for your applications. In our example of using Word as an automation server above, the routines wouldn't do much if there was not a means of getting text out to the Word automation object.

Think of OLE objects as richly formatted and editable objects that you may want to save as informational objects in your database. OLE Automation is an extension to the programming environment, generally only accessed by programming through your modules and event code.

Examples of Using Components of Other Applications

Several different applications ship with your system that allow you to implement them as either OLE Servers or OLE Automation Servers. For a comprehensive listing of these programs, you could review the Registration Database, but for an easier method, open the Samples database. Open the Paintbrush Demo form in design mode, then choose Edit and Insert Object. The resulting dialog box indicates the various programs installed on your system that support OLE interfaces:

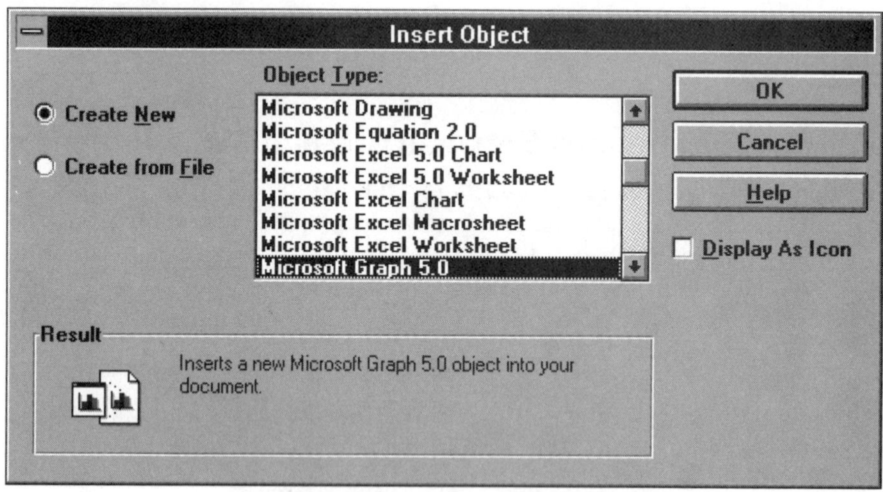

Looking Into Your System's OLE Capabilities

If you select the Create from File radio button, you can specify a link to an existing object that resides on disk in a file. This allows you to implement the 'linking' portion of OLE.

There are several different aspects of OLE that are important to understand prior to beginning work with OLE objects and Servers. Here are a few different terms, considerations and points to be aware of with OLE:

Programmable Objects OLE Servers are programmable objects. You control their functionality with Properties, much the same as the properties associated with the forms and other objects that you work with from within Access. OLE Servers act and react on the information and parameters you provide them.

Action

Actions tell the OLE Server to do something. Just as it sounds, Actions indicate exactly what is to be done with the object. Common OLE actions are Create_Embed, Create_Link, Update, Close, Delete, Save_to_file, Read_fm_file, Insert_obj_dialog, Paste_special_dialog, Fetch_verbs, Save_to_OLE1_file, Copy, Paste and Activate

Verb

Verbs tell the OLE Server what to do when it is Activated. Verbs include Print, Save, Display and so on. Verbs can vary from Server to Server.

Examples of Where to Use OLE Automation

As you have seen, you can embed OLE objects as fields within your standard Access tables. When you create a field in a table and specify the Data Type as 'OLE Object', you tell Access that an OLE object will be stored in that field.

Using OLE Automation takes a bit more planning. You first need to determine what functionality you actually require. For our example, we wanted to have Word print out the text entered in the box. In the example, it was presented very simply, with no direct benefit in using Word for the task. Consider a situation where you want to insert the name and address of a business contact into a form letter in Word and have the document printed out for you. This is a great way to use Word to print a letter for you, allowing Word to manage the margins, printing and any other formatting details.

OLE Automation can be very useful in situations where:

- You have unique hardware interface requirements and you want to minimize the work required to work with the hardware. In this case, you can write an automation server to talk to the hardware, taking care of the handshaking required and requiring your program only to set up certain properties and use certain verbs.
- You have a requirement to have a programmatic tool be available and look and operate the same across development environments. Perhaps you have a company security database that all users must login to. In this case, you could have an OLE Server that provided the user with the login user interface. It can then get the user ID and password from the user, validate it against the corporate database and then return a success or failure to the calling program, whether it be Visual Basic, Access, VBA or even Word Basic.

- You need to implement a spreadsheet-type control in your application.
- You need to implement fancy user-definable printing in your application.
- You want to display Graphs, using Microsoft Graph.
- You want to allow the user to edit a drawing in place, using Microsoft Draw.
- You want to allow the user to access equations, using the Microsoft Equation Editor.

The list goes on and on. Think about the different things you want to do that are not readily provided by Access. If they exist in other applications that you have on your system, there is a good possibility that with either OLE or OLE Automation you will be able to use their services from within your applications.

OLE Custom Controls

OLE Custom Controls, often referred to as OCX controls, are new to the Windows environment. When Visual Basic was introduced, it brought with it a concept of Visual Basic custom controls, or VBXs. These VBXs brought an unprecedented capability to extend the development environment.

The challenge with the traditional VBX is that it is not readily compatible across development platforms; that is, you can't easily use a VBX in Visual Basic *and* Access *and* Visual C++. This was a great drawback to the VBX implementation as, with many projects, cross platform development is a necessary reality. This meant a different look and feel, or operation, for components of an application.

Enter the OCX. OCXs are compatible across platforms, and even within applications that are automated and use the standard. As is always the case, applications will have to be updated to include the added capability of using the OCX technology, but Access 2.0 already provides this capability. Visual Basic and other environments are soon to follow.

OCXs for Access are available from several different sources, but today most prevalently from Microsoft. The Microsoft Access Developer's Toolkit provides three OCXs for use in the development of your Access projects. We will look at each of these, a Calender, a Scroll Bar and an Outline control, in more detail, after a closer look at capabilities.

OLE Custom Control Capabilities

OLE custom controls are accessed in your application by first adding them to a given form, then referring to properties and methods relating to the controls. For example, suppose you had a directory browser OCX. Some of the properties would include Path, Drive and perhaps an AllowDriveChange parameter. Before activating a method on the OCX, you would establish the properties as appropriate and then ask it to perform the action you desired, specifically GetFile in this case.

> **Note that controls will have some properties that you change in Design mode, while others can only be modified at Run Time. Check with the documentation to see which category a specific property falls under.**

Our example is simple, but here's what some sample implementation code might look like:

```
Sub BrowseDir()
    ...'establish objects, references here

    '
    'set up the parameters as needed for C:\
    '
    DirBrowse.Path = "\"
    DirBrowse.Drive = "C:"

    '
    'Don't allow the user to change drives
    '
    DirBrowse.AllowDriveChange = False

    '
    'Go get the file selection
    '
    DirBrowse.GetFile

    '
    'Go see what file was selected.
    '
    OurFile = DirBrowse.FileName
End Sub
```

You can expect OLE custom controls for Tabbed dialogs, specific functional actions such as accounting functions and different types of data controls such as grids, just to name a few. You will probably find that keeping on top of the custom controls market will pay off significantly as it's generally much cheaper to purchase and implement an OCX than it is to develop, implement and maintain unique functionality yourself. In addition, you will be able to establish standards for the look and feel of all your applications, leaving you free to concentrate on the functionality.

Differences Between VBXs, OCXs and OLE Server Applications

As mentioned above, OCXs are really the successors to the VBX victories already in place within Visual Basic. Here are some important distinctions between VBXs, OCXs, OLE objects and OLE Servers:

VBX Created to add functionality to the Visual Basic environment only. Not compatible with Access or other development environments outside of VB. Generally tool extensions providing new controls, enhanced controls and control types to the VB development palette.

OCX General Windows development tools. Will be rolled into development capabilities within VBA, Visual Basic, Access, Visual C++, etc. Generally tool extensions providing new controls, enhanced controls and control types to the development environment.

OLE Objects OLE objects are embedded or linked information items that become a part of the information residing in your system. OLE objects retain information about what applications are used to maintain them and allow you to employ these applications to edit the information objects at a later date. Some OLE objects can be edited in place, some actually shell out to the parent application for editing, returning the updated object to your application.

OLE Servers These are functional Windows components that can provide added functionality to your application. In our examples, we have shown OLE Servers in using Word to print a paragraph after entering it into Access. OLE Servers are not a part of your application, nor are they saved with your application.

The Calendar Custom Control

One example of an OCX tool is the Calendar custom control, which is included in the Access Developer's Toolkit (ADT). The Microsoft Access Developer's Toolkit is a product available separately from Access and is full of additional Access programming language documentation and other information that you will find extremely helpful in your development efforts. The ADT provides a help file outlining each of the properties of the control and in addition, the methods and notes on the actual use of the control are included. The calendar control gives you a way of putting a standard wall calendar date selection tool into your applications. The tool looks like this when first placed on a form:

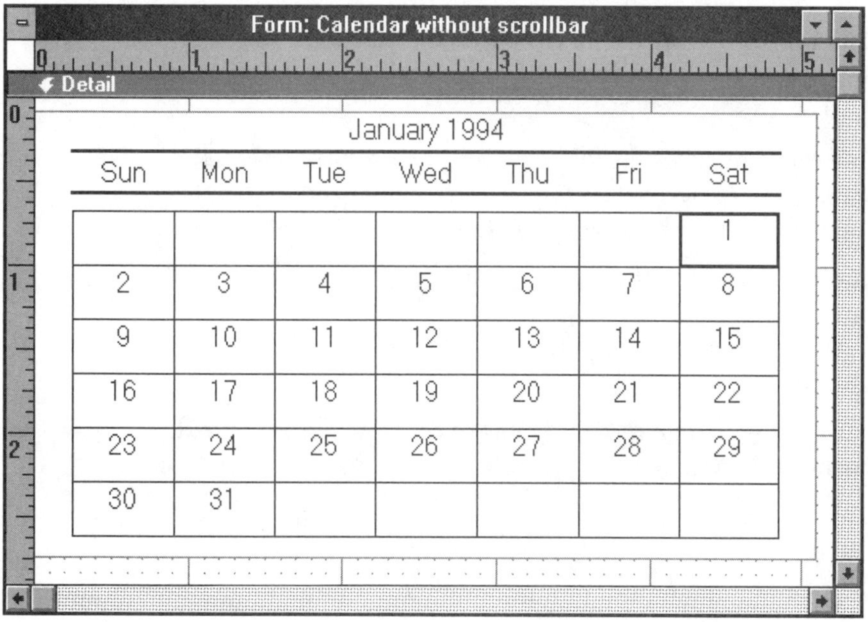

The calendar OCX provides you with the following different methods, all of which repaint the calendar:

NextDay — Increments the day and if it's the last day of the month, will reset the month

NextMonth — Increments the month and resets the year if necessary

NextYear — Increments the year

PreviousDay — Decrements the day and if it's the first day of the month, will reset the month

PreviousMonth — Decrements the month and resets the year if necessary

PreviousYear — Decrements the year

Refresh — Repaints the calendar

In addition, the following properties (and others) are supported by the control:

FirstDay — Set the first day of the calendar

Value — Get the selected date

You use these methods in the standard format 'Control.Method'. For example, if you want to retrieve the value of the date currently displayed by the control, you could use the following code:

```
DateNow = Calendar.Object.Value
```

This would, for example, return the value '01/01/95'.

Note that the actual format of the date is established in the control panel on your system. If you have established a different date format, that format will be used when the value is returned to your application.

Installing OCXs

Install the ADT from the diskettes as indicated in the instructions accompanying the Toolkit. By default, a new subdirectory, ADT, will be created under your Access subdirectory. The various ADT files and custom controls will be placed in this new subdirectory.

To add a custom control to a form you must first open the form in design view. The Forms Wizard will not place custom controls on your forms, so it's probably most beneficial, especially for our examples here, to simply open a new, blank form.

From the File menu select Insert Object... and you will see the screen below. Choose the Insert Control radio button and the display will show all known custom controls. You can add controls to your library of available controls by clicking on the Add Control button. This will bring up the standard file selection dialog box. From this dialog, you can select the custom control you wish to add. In this case, the control is **MSACAL20.OCX**, otherwise known as the Calendar Control.

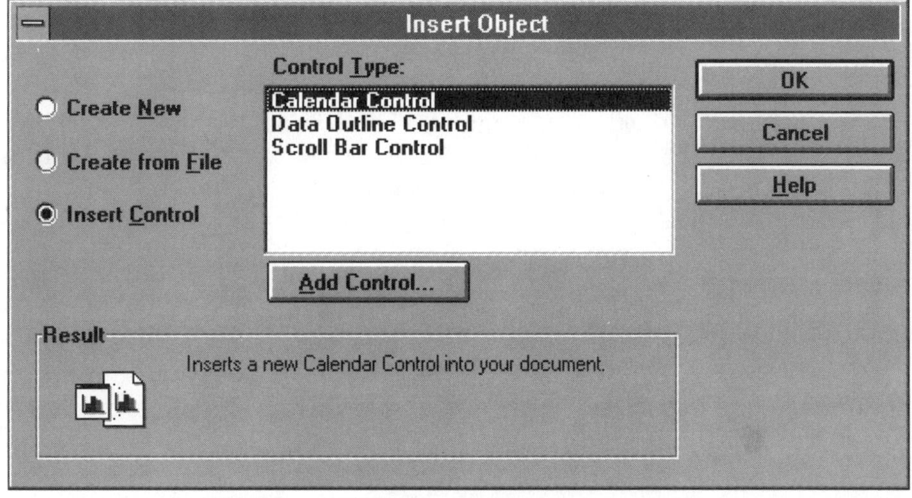

Selecting The Controls From Those Available

Once the control has been placed on your form, you can begin to work with the events and Access Basic code that you need to implement to control it. You can also set parameters by working directly with the control in design mode.

To call up this dialog box, right-click on the calendar control. Choose Calendar Object and then Properties. This allows you to configure specific characteristics of the control without having to programmatically set it up. It can be a real time-saver:

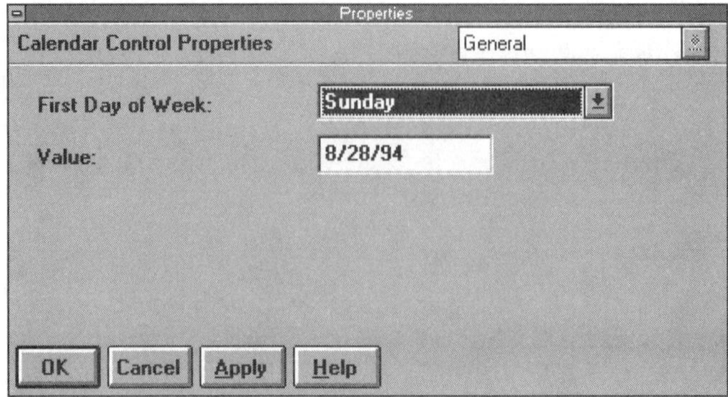

The Calendar Control Properties Box

Overview of Operation

OCX controls implement the same interface you are used to seeing with other controls within Access. They produce events that you can put code in and provide methods for causing different events to occur.

With the calendar OCX, you can manipulate the calendar as outlined above. In addition, you have the standard properties associated with an object; you can size the control, change colors, fonts, the look of the control, etc. By standardizing your selections in these areas, you can make the control look and operate in a way that is consistent with this and other applications.

Sample Implementation

For an example of using the calendar control, we will simply put up the control on a form and allow the user to double-click on a date and have our program return the date in a standard message box.

From your newly created form, call up the property sheet and go to the double-click event. Put the following code in the procedure:

```
Sub Embedded0_DblClick ()

    MsgBox embedded0.object.value

End Sub
```

> *As you enter the statement above that calls the MsgBox routine, be sure to include periods, not commas, in the call to the command.*

Now, close the code window and switch from Design mode to Run mode. When you double click on any date, you will get a message box showing a formatted date. You could, of course, use the Format$ function to change the look of the date. The calendar control simply returns the date as a variant, making it compatible with various manipulation and formatting functions available within the Access language.

You will notice, of course, that the default calendar doesn't provide a means of changing the month displayed. This is a feature that you must implement in the user interface. You can do this with Access Button Controls, showing perhaps a Next month and Prev month button, but the really elegant way of providing this functionality would be with a scroll bar.

The Scroll Bar Custom Control

The second custom control offered in the Access Developer's Toolkit is the scroll bar. This control, a natural companion to the calendar custom control, offers the capabilities of providing your users with the Windows style scrolling capabilities, whether it be to control the calendar, or browse through a list of records that you have retrieved.

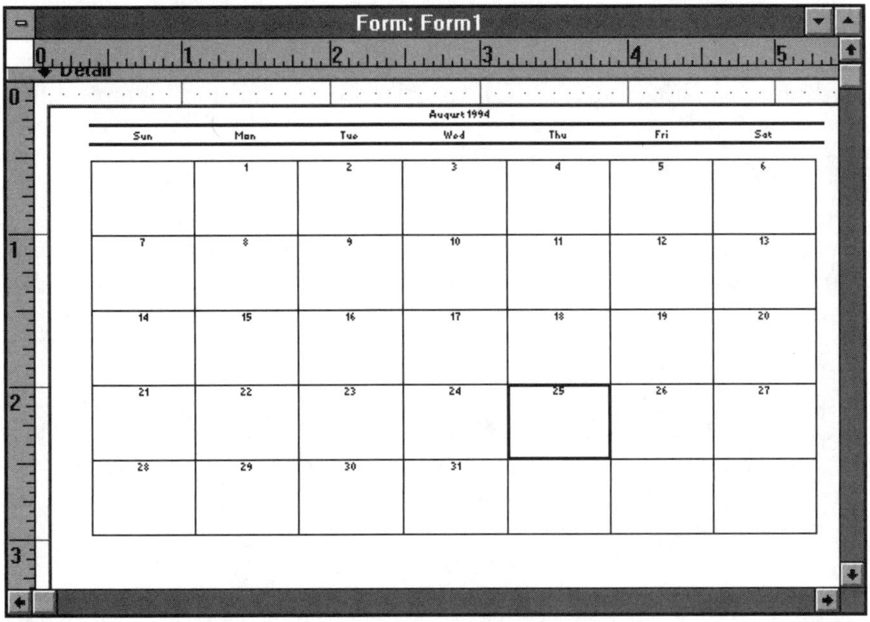

Using The Scroll Bar OCX With The Calendar OCX

Follow the same method as the calendar custom control to put the control on your form. That is, choose Edit, Insert Object. Next choose the Insert Control radio button and choose the scroll bar control. Once pasted on your form, you can re-size it as you desire.

Once again, after you have put the control on your form, right-click on the control, choose Scroll Bar Control Object and then Properties:

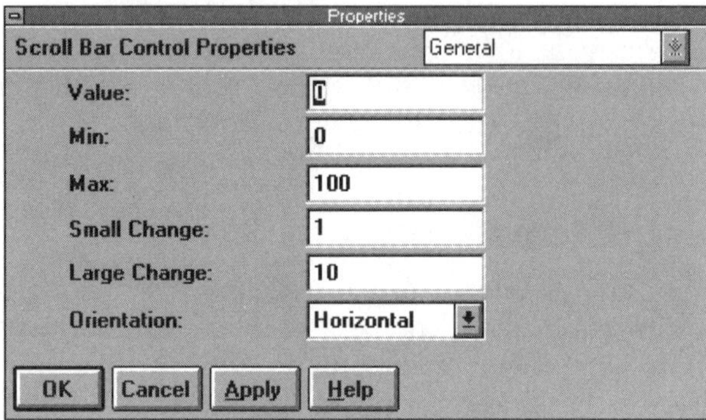

The Scroll Bar OCX Properties Box

Also notice that you can change the orientation of the scroll bar between vertical and horizontal. This allows you to associate it will all sorts of information, from lists and graphics to calendars, as in our example here.

Overview of Operation

The scroll bar setup will be very important to your application. Make sure you set the Value, Min and Max properties carefully. These properties, along with the standard Access-maintained values, will help you set up the control effectively.

> **In order to control the operation of the scroll-bar control, you must set the Value, Min and Max properties. If you don't set these properties, the OCX will default to values that may not make sense to the operation of the control within your application.**
>
> **As an example, if you are scrolling the months of the year, but don't set either Min or Max, you could end up scrolling to Month 15 or -3. Set the Min to 1 and the Max to 12 in this case. This will limit selection to the 12 months of the year, and will prevent the OCX from going past accurate values.**

Outlined below is a simple implementation of the scroll bar with a common use; controlling the calendar custom control. Review the help file, MSAB20.HLP for the details on additional properties.

Sample Implementation

The scroll bar introduces some unique events so that you can manage the movement of the information associated with the scroll bar. For example, if you want to have the calendar control increment the month depending on the users' manipulation of the scroll bar, the following event would apply.

Change When the user uses the arrow buttons on either end of the bar, this event is triggered. The event is triggered after the user has completed using the scroll bar.

In our sample, we want to catch this event and react accordingly. For our simple experimentation here, we will make some assumptions. First, set the following values in the scroll bar setup dialog:

Value 1
Min 1
Max 12

Next, change the name properties on the calendar and scroll bar to 'Calendar' and 'ScrollBar' respectively. To do this, click on the object and select Properties. These names will give more meaning to our demonstration.

On the calendar, change the setup by right-clicking the calendar control, then choosing Calendar Control Object and Properties. Set the Value to '1/1/94'.

Therefore, our assumptions for this example are that we are starting on month one on the calendar, and at position one on the scroll bar. The scroll bar will only recognize values in the range 1-12, so our month scrolling is able to be directly related to the current scroll bar setting.

Finally, in the Build Event code for the scroll bar, add the following line of code:

```
calendar.object.value = Str$(scrollbar.object.value) + "/1/94"
```

Note that you'll need to set up this value in line with your current date format in the control panel. For example, if the date format that you have implemented in the International portion of the control panel is for the United Kingdom, you should specify the following line:

```
calendar.object.value  =  "1/"+str$(scrollbar.object.value)+"/94"
```

In this case, if the month is December (12), then the date would be '1/12/94'.

This will change the calendar to show the month represented by the value of the scroll bar. The scroll bar will automatically manage its values to be between 1 and 12. These values are maintained in the 'Value' property of the control. If the scroll bar is changed, we take the new value, paste it into the date and set the calendar object to use that date for its display.

Very simple, but you can see the power that the scroll bar provides your application. Beyond the calendar, you can use it to scroll through items in a list. In cases where you can't use the standard Access list boxes, the scroll bar provides the added browse functionality you will need.

The Outline Custom Control

The final custom control shipped with the Access Developer's Toolkit is the Outline control. This control allows you to present the user with a more familiar, hierarchical representation of their data. The outline custom control is placed on your form using the same method as both the calendar and scroll bar custom controls, by choosing Edit, Insert Object and selecting the Data Outline Control.

When you select the Data Outline control, the Data Outline Control Wizard will step in and ask you to tell it how the control should display the information. See the following figure:

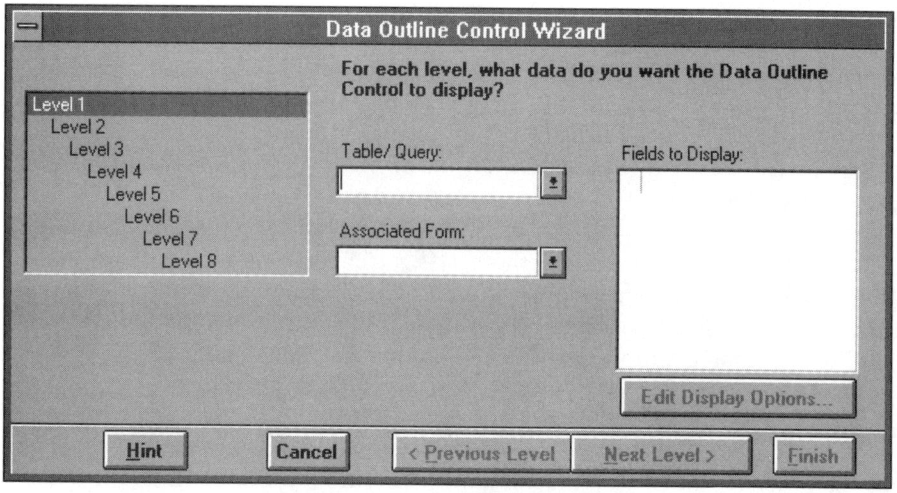

The Data Outline Control Wizard Steps In...

The Wizard prompts you for the tables, queries and associated forms that will be tied to each level displayed by the control. For each level you specify, the Wizard will require an existing query or relationship. If it doesn't find a relationship it can use, it will prompt you for one. The figure below shows the various features available when you set up the control. Take special note of the Form Name property; it is where you will indicate what form to load if the user double clicks on an item that is displayed at this level of the outline control.

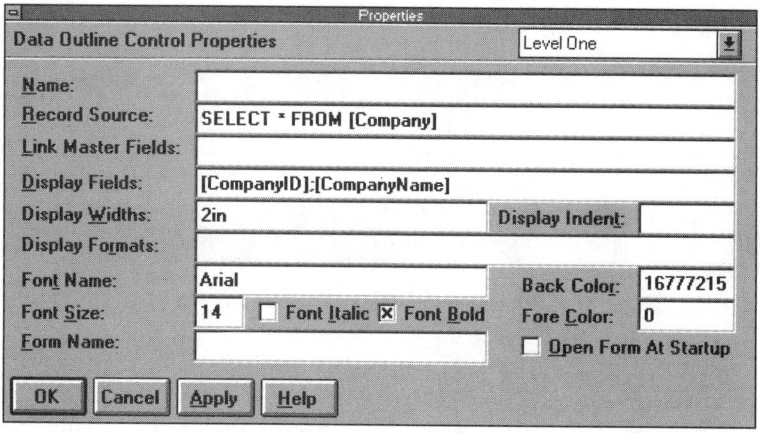

The Data Outline OCX Properties Box

Chapter 1

Overview of Operation

While there are several programmatic ways of controlling the outline control, in most cases setting different properties will allow you to implement just about whatever you need. Everything from font name, size and color to the form that is opened if the user double-clicks on an entry is available from within the property dialogs.

Once the outline control is active, there will be a plus sign, '+', before each line. If you click on the plus sign, the control will attempt to show detail for that line. If no detail is available, the plus sign will simply turn into a minus sign, indicating that no more levels exist under the line item.

Sample Implementation

For our sample, we have applied an outline control to the WROX PIM. We will use the outline control to show the relationship between companies and their associated contacts. To take this to the next logical step, we could show level three as the projects associated with a given contact.

Here's what our sample application looks like when using the outline control:

Form: Outline - Contact by Company
- 1 WROX Press Ltd (800) 814-3461
- 2 Marvelous Litera (602) 798-6268
  - 2 John Jones
  - 3 Julie Anne
  - 1 Create PIM Steve Wynkoop John Smith
  - 5 Brennan Jeffrey
  - 6 Caitlin Elizabeth
  - 8
- 3 Test Companies
  - 1 Sam Smith 6025551212 6025551210
  - 4 Stephen Wynkoop
- 4 Anom Guild
- 13 Test

Record: 1 of 1

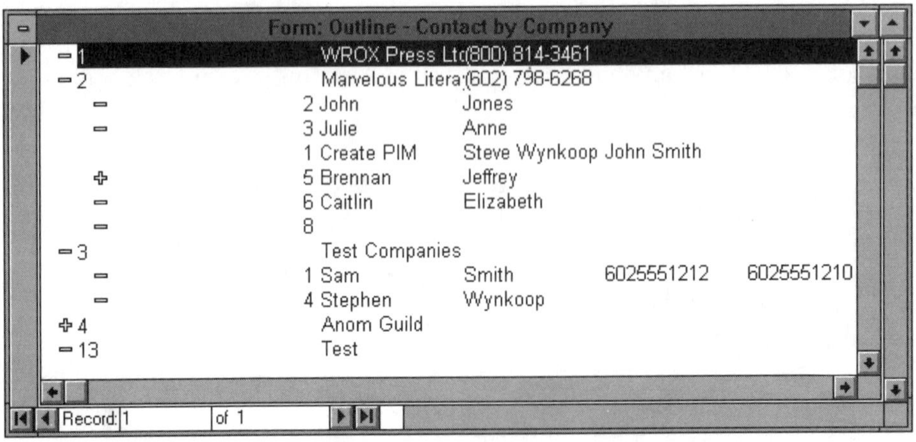

The Data Outline Control In Action

This shows that there is a relationship between the company record and the contact records. When the user is first presented with this screen, the outline is collapsed and only 'WROX...' shows. By clicking on the plus sign in front of the entry the user is shown the actual details behind each of the companies on file. Note too that by double-clicking on the contact row, the user is taken to the full screen edit form for the contact record. This is set up in the properties of the outline control:

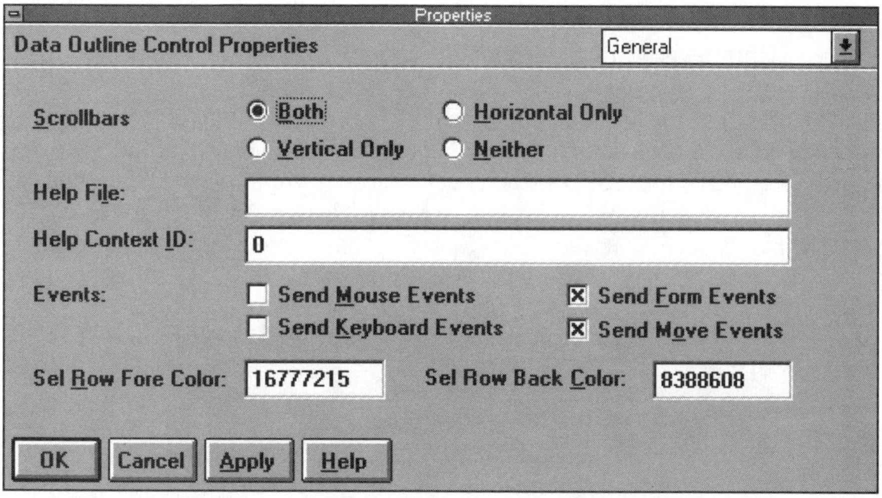

Properties
Data Outline Control Properties — General
Scrollbars: (•) Both ( ) Horizontal Only ( ) Vertical Only ( ) Neither
Help File:
Help Context ID: 0
Events: [ ] Send Mouse Events [X] Send Form Events [ ] Send Keyboard Events [X] Send Move Events
Sel Row Fore Color: 16777215 Sel Row Back Color: 8388608
OK Cancel Apply Help

These properties control exactly how the outline is displayed, the scroll bars that will be shown and so on. Also, in the top right corner, there is a list box that allows you to select the properties you wish to work with. In this case, the list box will offer you the capability of working with any of the different line definitions for the outline. Select the list box and choose Level One.

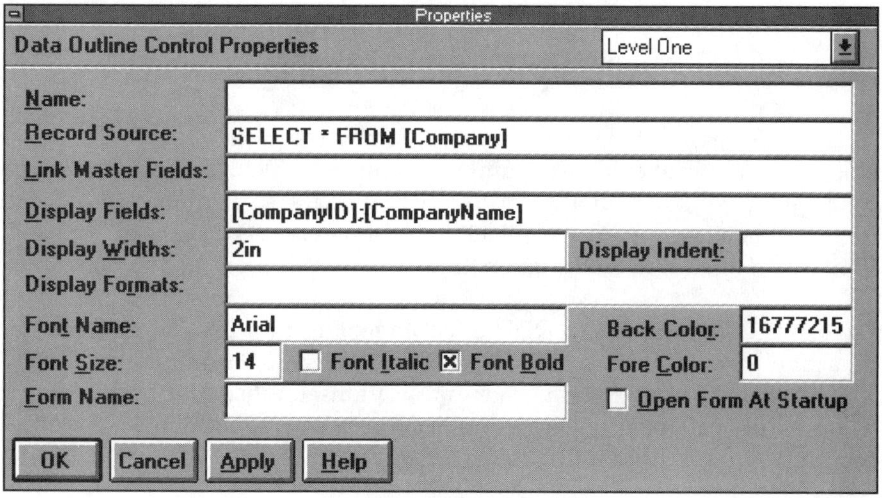

Properties
Data Outline Control Properties — Level One
Name:
Record Source: SELECT * FROM [Company]
Link Master Fields:
Display Fields: [CompanyID];[CompanyName]
Display Widths: 2in Display Indent:
Display Formats:
Font Name: Arial Back Color: 16777215
Font Size: 14 [ ] Font Italic [X] Font Bold Fore Color: 0
Form Name: [ ] Open Form At Startup
OK Cancel Apply Help

Check Out Level One

Notice on our outline that we have set up a bigger font (14 point) and have made this level bolded. This will help in picking out the company records in a fully populated outline control. In addition, notice the 'Form Name' field. This is where you indicate to the control what form to use if the user double clicks on an entry at this level of the outline.

As you develop your outline specifications for each level, you may receive an error message like the one shown next. This indicates that the value you've specified for the RecordSource for the level you're trying to open is incorrectly formatted or otherwise invalid. Check the RecordSource property for each level and carefully make sure that the fields listed, tables used, etc. are all valid:

A Review Of RecordSources Is In Order!

The outline control provides a powerful way of organizing your application and presenting it in a manner that is easy to use, easy to navigate and, with the use of the property sheets, easy to setup and maintain.

Dynamic Data Exchange and SendKeys

Dynamic Data Exchange (DDE) is a standard that was established as a means of allowing two applications to communicate directly. DDE doesn't allow you to call the functionality of another application directly so it differs significantly from the implementation of OLE and OLE Automation servers. DDE is used most as a way of sending information from one application to another.

One of the biggest caveats of a DDE environment is that both applications must be active in order to participate in the conversation to exchange data. There are no provisions for storing communications for use at a later date and if the remote application is not active, it is the calling application's responsibility to start it and re-try the conversation.

When to Use DDE

DDE is used to activate a remote application, begin a conversation with it and pass in certain information, formatted specific to the remote application. In many cases, the remote application is also asked to process the incoming information, while in some cases it is purely informational.

An example might be where you want to provide information from your application to a spreadsheet. Assume that your database has information about projects and specifically information relating to budgets. You may want to send this information to a spreadsheet.

DDE Conversations with Excel

To do this, you would establish a conversation with the host application, for instance Excel, and then send the information, formatted in a way that Excel will understand it, to the spreadsheet. You must specify where to put the information when it arrives (what cell and row combination) and you will have to specify each command that you want to take place against the information. For example, to select a series of values from a spreadsheet and create a graph, the command that you would send to Excel would be:

```
DDEExecute Channel, "[Select(""R1C1:R1C10"")][New(2,2)]"
```

This tells Access what conversation to use and passes the command to Excel. We will go over some specific implementations of DDE later in our sample application when we send information from our application to Word for use in a form letter. We will also be sending information from our project database to Excel for some possible reporting.

For now, it's important to understand that DDE is largely a means of pushing information from one program to another, usually one command at a time. DDE is really the outdated predecessor of today's more sophisticated OLE and OLE Automation capabilities.

NetDDE, explained later as and when it relates to our application, is a network implementation of DDE. With NetDDE, the same capabilities are available, but you are able to call and work with applications on systems located elsewhere on the network. The same rules apply relating to the other application being active.

Comparison of DDE and OLE

As mentioned above, DDE is really the ancestor to the OLE capabilities of newer applications. DDE is usually a link between specific pieces of information, between two applications. For DDE links to work, both applications must be active. The activation of a remote application for which you need services is the responsibility of your application.

With OLE, objects are 'intelligent' when they are placed in your form. Information is still shared between applications, but the whole piece of information, be it a spreadsheet, a single value, word, paragraph or drawing, is sent to the Server application. The Server application acts on the object, allowing the user to make changes. In addition, the Server application is responsible for the management of the information as the user works with it. When the changes are complete, the completed package is given back to the Container application.

DDE could be used to accomplish some of this type of work, but it would involve packaging up the information, sending it to the remote application, telling the remote application what to do with the information and then retrieving the updated object.

Comparison of SendKeys and OLE

SendKeys was around even before DDE. SendKeys is actually a way of sending keystrokes to another application. This is usually the fallback means of automating a process where the program required doesn't support either OLE or DDE. With SendKeys, you are working with the operating system in providing forced keystrokes to the required application. To the application, this looks exactly as if someone were sitting at the computer typing in the commands.

SendKeys is a one-way conversation. The only exception would be if you get fancy in cutting information to and from the clipboard. When you use SendKeys, there are several special character sequences that you use to specify backspace, control keys and so on. For more information, check the Access Help File for the topic SendKeys.

Note that a major drawback of SendKeys is that the application or object you want to send keystrokes to must have focus. The keystrokes are processed just as if you had typed them from the keyboard, so you must be able to put the receiving application in a known state prior to sending the keystrokes to process. If the application is not available, is at a different stage than you expect, etc., then the operation may perform in a way other than you expect.

Sendkeys is much less predictable and controllable than is DDE or OLE as a tool to your application. It is recommended that you not use SendKeys, except in the most controlled situations.

Comments and Suggestions

This chapter should have given you a good overview of the linking and embedding capabilities of Access. We've looked at the theory behind Object Linking and Embedding, OLE Automation and OLE Custom Controls. We've also looked in detail at the various OCXs that come with the Access Developer's Kit. We finished off the chapter with a look at other methods of connecting to applications, namely Dynamic Data Exchange and Sendkeys, and examined some of the differences between these methods and OLE.

In the next chapter, we'll begin to cover the specific aspects and methods that surround the implementation of OLE technologies in your applications. In addition, we'll begin to review sample source and implementations of these technologies that can help you along your way in your own development efforts.

CHAPTER 2

Object Linking and Embedding

OLE provides you with a powerful means to access the functionality encapsulated by other packages currently existing on your system. With OLE, you can implement rich text editing in your application, using an OLE Automation Server that provides your application with this added functionality, and rich text editing is only one of the advantages that this methodology opens up to you.

It should also be noted that OLE is also the chosen direction for future custom control development, as well as the future generic interface between applications.

What's Covered in this Chapter

In this chapter, we will cover the specifics pertaining to Object Linking and Embedding and it's use in your applications. The following concepts will be covered

- OLE future directions
- Using OLE Servers and methods from other applications
- Details on the Registration Database
- Creating objects for use in your Access Basic code

Each of these topics is designed to provide you with the information you'll need to make determinations regarding your use of OLE and OLE automation within your applications.

Chapter 2

How This Chapter Impacts Our Application

The WROX Personal Information Manager (PIM) makes use of embedded objects for maintaining information on contacts. Specifically, the PIM will send information to Word for printing and to Excel for working with project information in a spreadsheet environment.

This chapter will detail the implementation of these features and will cover how you can add this functionality to your programs.

In addition, this chapter will walk you through the creation of the opening forms for the application, including their associated code. We'll also cover how to implement OLE on your forms and how to use OLE Automation, providing specific examples for each.

The Future of OLE Integration

Microsoft Windows is undergoing a transformation into a programmable object environment. Right now Windows is a combination of executables, dynamic link libraries (DLLs), programmable objects and a whole flood of configuration files, collectively known as 'INI files'. With the impending release of Windows 95, also known as 'Chicago', Microsoft is moving aggressively toward a new architecture designed to support applications that are much more feature-rich.

Programmable objects are really OLE objects. These objects contain information on how to present themselves, what their user interface looks like and all the other attributes required to uniquely define the object. Some common capabilities of objects include:

- Printing
- Displaying information
- Saving
- Editing

When you work with these objects in your application, you are able to incorporate these capabilities without having to write the source code to accomplish the action. In the previous chapter, we discussed the use of OLE

Automation Servers and OLE custom controls. Both of these elements are examples of programmable objects that can be included in your application.

Microsoft is using OLE objects as one of the cornerstone of their new operating environment for a number of reasons, one of which is their ability to be shared across development platforms. Put simply this means that you can develop an application using programmable objects created by any combination of Visual Basic, Visual Basic for Applications or Access Basic. This allows you to really optimize your time and efforts. At the same time, you'll be presenting the user with a common look, feel and operation of the components you include in the complete application.

OLE objects obtain and present the details of their use in the **Registration Database**, or **Registry**. The Registry contains information on the configuration, capabilities and interfaces to all the programmable objects that are available in your system. Included in Chicago and the Windows NT environments, the security around the Registry allows you more control of the use of objects. With NT, you can restrict exactly what processes and users can have access to the objects on your system. The Registry is explained in more detail at the end of this chapter.

With the new Windows environments, NT, NT Server and Windows 95, you'll find that more and more functionality will be implemented in the shape of OLE objects. They will be seen in the core components of the major applications, like Visual Basic for Applications and all of the application objects, as well as utility functions such as spell checkers. OLE objects will range from system configuration objects, as in the control panel, to everyday functionality, including mail forms and objects specifically designed to control the peripherals on your system.

Memory and Platform Considerations for OLE Objects

OLE objects are programs that know how to operate on structured information objects or streams of information. Since these objects are loaded into the operating environment when they are needed, you can quickly come to understand why they require additional system resources and memory to be available.

While the RAM requirements of a given object are important, you'll have to weigh these benefits with the capabilities afforded to your application in using the object. Keep in mind that future versions of Windows will require, or at least highly recommend, a minimal configuration of 8 MBs of RAM (Windows NT requires 12 MB and Microsoft recommends 16 MB).

OLE custom controls, or OCXs, have additional requirements. OCXs are controls that are available to you as a developer and are implemented as OLE Servers providing all their inherent functionality to your application. One such requirement is that many OCXs require a 32-bit environment in which to run, while current DLLs and VBXs are designed for the 16-bit environment. If you have a tool that you're especially fond of, but is implemented as an OCX, check with the tool vendor and see if a 16-bit DLL version is available for use with Windows 3.x

As you choose your development tools, be sure to consider the target platform and not just the development platform. You may not be able to use OCX and OLE automation technology if your users' systems are not at least a 386-class system.

If you are using major applications as components of your system, you may have to be careful with memory configurations. You may need to close down some applications to get the best performance from others.

Often, all these decisions are based upon how much memory you have in the target system. If you have limited memory and notice that the disk is on almost solid during the time that Access is trying to load the server application, chances are good that Windows is paging to disk. As an example, here are some memory requirements for different types of embedded objects:

- Microsoft Word 474k
- Microsoft Excel 537k
- Microsoft Paintbrush 119k
- Microsoft Word, Picture Editor 567k

Be sure to keep this in mind as you make different features available to your users. Another consideration is the load time required by the editor for any given object. As you'll notice from the examples in the Samples database, when you double-click on an item, the time to load the server application can be significant. If you double-click on an Excel object, you're likely to get a message box saying that the server application is not responding:

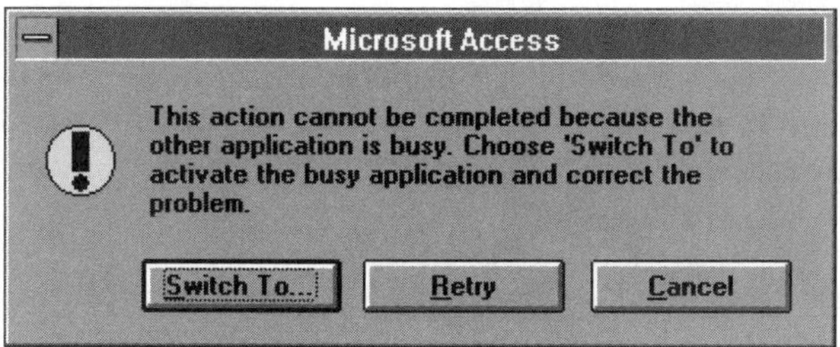

If The Application Is Busy, Retry, Retry Again

If this happens try selecting Retry. Often, this will give the server application more time to load. If this does not work, try switching to the other application using *Alt-Tab*. There may be some information that the other application requires before it can continue. This may prevent it from responding to OLE instructions being sent by Access.

Specifically with Excel, you can minimize load times by making sure you're not loading a bunch of Add-Ins each time it starts. When the server application is started, it still goes through its standard startup routines, so Add-Ins would be a part of this process even though they may not be useful to you in this context.

Of course, the time-out does depend on the server application you're trying to load. With OLE custom controls, you'll find that they are built to do one thing and do it well. Since their required capabilities are more focused, OLE custom controls will also require less in the way of resources on your system.

How to Use OLE Objects in Your Applications

In the first chapter, we investigated the basics of using OLE objects within your application. There are three different ways that OLE objects can come into play in your application:

1. You can use OCX's in your applications. These are the add-on tools that will provide you with custom controls and act in much the same way as the Visual Basic VBX's do. These are placed on your form, as outlined in

Chapter 1, and you then refer to properties, events and methods to work with these objects. This will probably be the most common way that you use OLE in the opening efforts within your projects.

We say that this is most common simply because custom controls are more likely to be used by your application on a regular basis than an embedded or linked object. The added functionality of embedded or linked objects is a specialized capability that is only likely to be implemented in certain situations.

2 You can use embedded or linked objects in your application. This is done by setting up the proper values in your database tables and then allowing the user to insert the objects as they require. Access can manage the insertion of objects or you can control this.

3 You can use OLE Automation (OA) to accomplish a specific task or function. This is the case with our example of sending text from a text box control to Word for printing.

We covered the OCX custom controls in detail in the first chapter. For more information, please refer to either the documentation accompanying the custom control or the help file. You may find it useful to remember that, in many cases, you can right-click on the control in design view and modify the properties with custom dialogs that are specifically tailored to the control.

For more information on custom controls and the types of tools available, refer to the appendices.

How to Configure Tables and Forms for OLE Objects

OLE objects can be included in your applications in several ways. The first way that we will cover is how you embed objects in your database.

How to Create Tables That Can Accommodate OLE Objects

To give users the ability to use embedded or linked objects in your application, you'll need to complete several steps. For an example of the process, open the **SAMPLES** database included on the disk supplied with this book. The tables, forms and procedures we're about to go through are included there. We would, however, recommend that you also follow along and walk through the steps to familiarize yourself with the process.

First, create the table. Open the **SAMPLES** database and create a New table. Don't use the Table Wizards at this point; choose New Table. The first screen you'll see is an empty table opened in design mode.

The figure below shows the completed database definition. The description is optional as it is just for your own information:

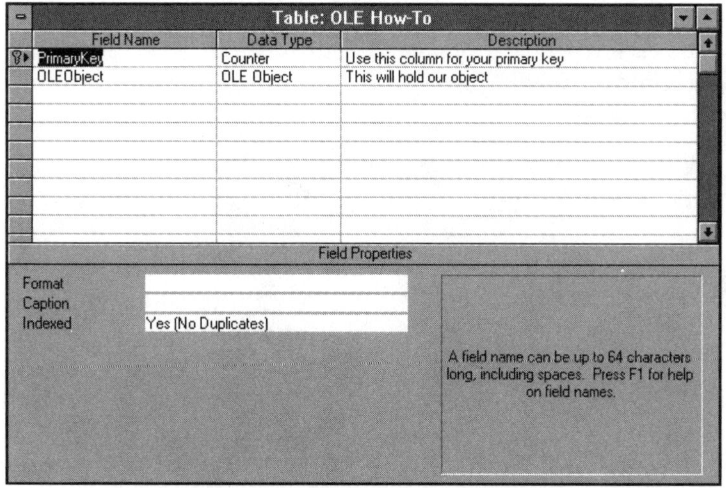

The OLE How-To Table Structure

Note that we've established a **Primary Key** for this table. To set up a primary key, click to the left of the field name for the item you want to be your key. Access will highlight the entire row that you selected. Next, from the Edit menu, select Set Primary Key. Access denotes the primary key column by placing a small key symbol next to the column definition when you view the table in design mode.

Primary keys provide a starting point for Access when it retrieves information from your database tables. The Primary Key must be unique and, if possible, it should be set up to be the most frequently used column referenced in lookups. You may often use Counters as a unique identifier with your databases. If you do, they are a good candidate for the Primary Key because of their guaranteed uniqueness within the table.

When you create a new table, if you don't define a primary key, Access will prompt you as to whether it should define one for you automatically. If you allow Access to create a primary key, it will insert a column at the top of your table definition, define it as a counter and set it to be the primary key.

From here, close the table and save it as 'OLE How-To'. Next, we will create a form on which the user can work with objects.

How to Create a Form to Support OLE Objects

The table that we've just created will be the basis for a new form designed to support OLE objects. Select the Forms tab, then select New. Enter the name of the table and choose Blank Form.

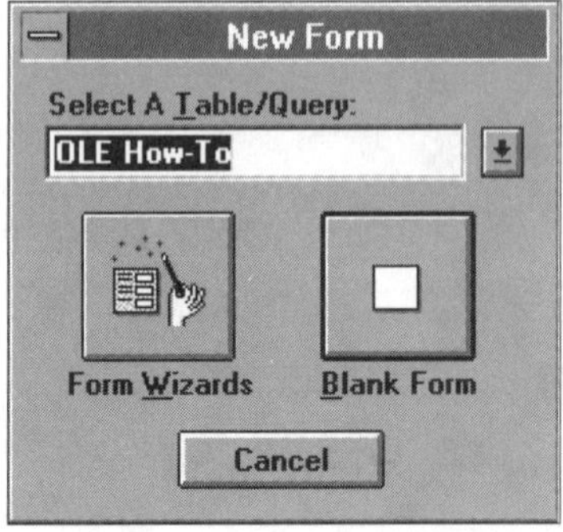

The final step is to paste the OLE Object Container onto the form by dragging the OLE Object field from the list of available fields and place it on your form. If the field list is not visible, click the Field List button on the toolbar to call up the dialog box.

Notice that when you paste it on the form, Access automatically makes it a large square field. This is because Access is guessing that you'll need a lot of room for the object to appear on the form. This is generally true and in fact, you'll probably want to make the control even bigger. Since the two most common things that will be pasted into the object are spreadsheets and documents, stretch the box across the page and down a bit. This will give you room to edit the contents of the box. Set the caption of the control to 'Object:' and place it in the upper left corner of the form.

The next figure shows what your form should look like at this point. It's not important to match this exactly as all we're trying to do is show the process of bringing an embedded object into your application:

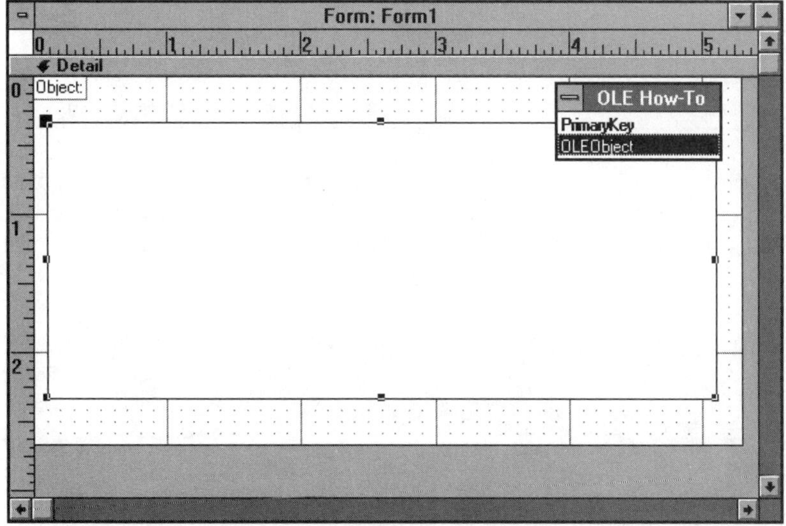

The Simplest Form You'll Ever Design

Close the form and save it as 'OLE How-To'. All that is left to do now is to Open the form and see how it works.

Chapter 2

How to Embed or Link Objects in Your Access Table

From the menu of forms, choose OLE How-To and select Open. The form should look like the screen below:

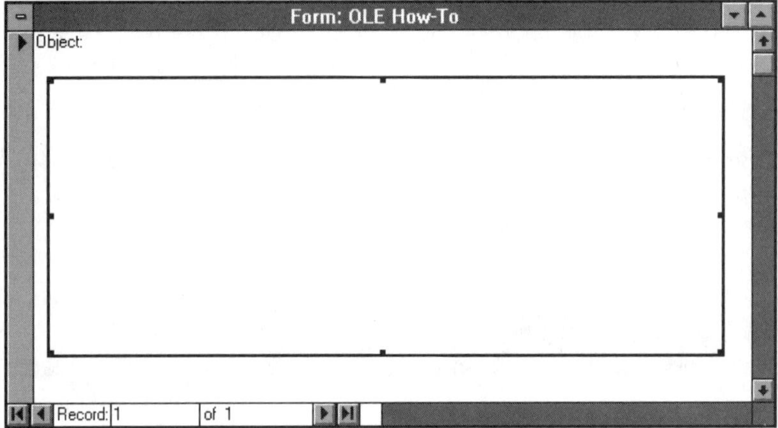

From this point, with a new record in the database, the user has to insert the object that they want to work with. To do this, choose Edit, then Insert Object from the Access menus. Next, choose the object to insert in the table. The Insert Object dialog box is shown next:

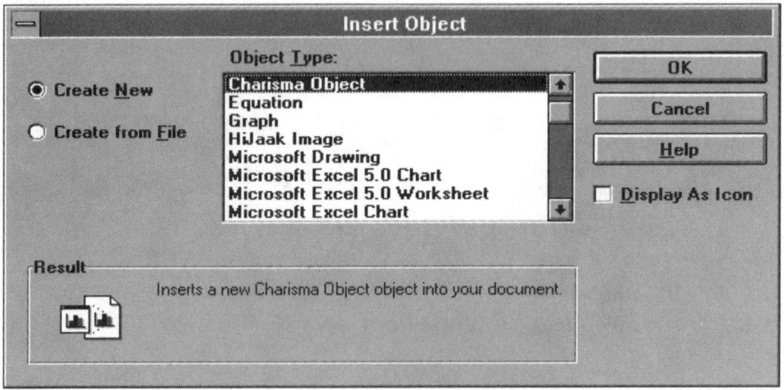

Select the object you want to insert into your database and select OK. For this example, choose Microsoft Word 6.0 Document. Next, you'll notice that the display will change, activating the object with the server application you've just requested.

Your form will be controlled by the server application as it relates to the editing and management of the object you've just inserted. You can see by the display that the object now has a hatched border, indicating that it's active. You can resize the object's editing area, and we recommend that you do so. The object 'remembers' your sizing settings, so size it to the underlying OLE Object control. The next time the object is edited, the server will know how to size the window correctly.

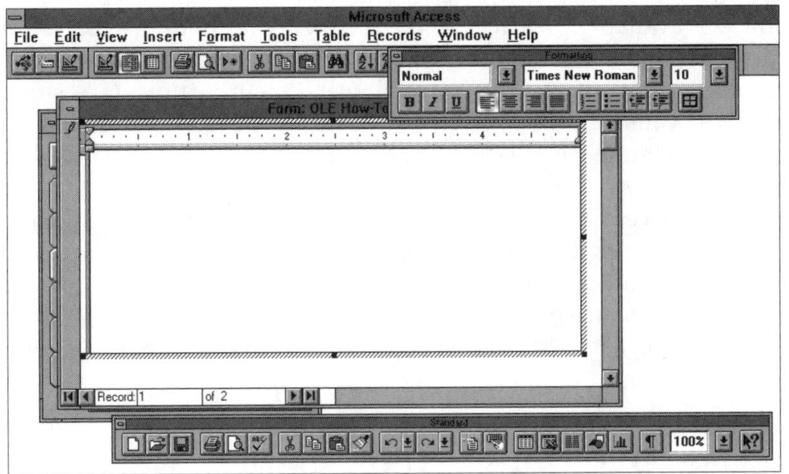

An OLE Object As It's Edited. Notice The Floating Menus

You may have also noticed that two new menus are now displayed: 'Standard' and 'Formatting'. These may differ on your system depending on your Word configuration, but they will be floating and are made available to you for the management of your OLE embedded object.

To exit the server application and return to your form, simply click anywhere else on the form, or choose the record positioning scroll bar on the bottom of the form. The server application will update the object in your tables and will exit.

> *If you are using a version of Word prior to version 6, Word will be loaded as if you had started it from the Program Manager. As mentioned earlier, in-place editing is not supported until version 6. To update the object in your database table, simply exit Word. The object will be updated automatically.*

Congratulations! You've just created your first embedded object. There are several different considerations that you need to be aware of before offering this functionality to your user base. Do you want to give them full access to determine what type of object to paste to the form, or do you want to control what is placed on the form? In most cases, you'll want to control this aspect of the user interface. We'll look into this in more detail in Chapter 3.

Next, be sure that the component objects that you want to allow users to paste onto the form are available on each of their systems individually or shared on a network that they have access to. Also remember that, if you insert an object whose server application resides on the network, response times are sure to be compromised. We would suggest that you move critical server components to the individual workstations if this becomes an issue.

When you provide access to OLE objects, be sure to present an easy to use interface in your program. In many cases, it will be easier to activate an object within your program rather than rely on the user to activate the object. Later, we'll discuss how you can control the insertion of objects into your Access tables, and how you can control the actions that are taken against a given object.

How to Use OLE Automation Server Objects

OLE Automation Servers are implemented as methods and properties to your application. When you decide to utilize OA, you have to know a great deal about the OA Server you plan to use.

In this section, we'll discuss the specifics of how you implement the example shown in Chapter 1. The sample shows a basic form, allows the user to type text in the text control and then sends this text to Word. The final steps include having Word print the text and then close the temporary document.

To create this sample form, first create a new blank form. You don't need to associate any database table with the form. In this sample, the form that you're creating will be a stand-alone demonstration.

On the form, create a text box and give it the name 'txtTextToSend'. When you create a text box Access will place a label beside it so change the caption property of this label to 'Text:'. Next, place a button on the form. Change the caption to 'GO' and change the name of the button to 'cmdSendInfoToWord'.

Aesthetically, you may want to change the background color of the form to Gray (12632256). For simplicity, you can put a text box at the top of the form to indicate what the user is to do when using the form. Here's what our sample form looks like at this point:

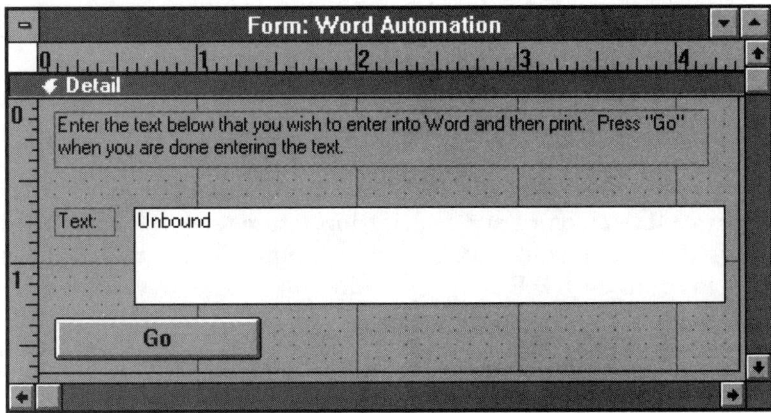

The Basic Design Of The Word Automation Form

Next, we'll have to add functionality to our example by adding code behind the 'Go' button that calls the Word Server application and tell it what to do. In this case, put the code shown below on the Click event:

```
Sub cmdSendInfoToWord_Click ()

    'this procedure will take the text entered into the box
    'and send it to Word, then asking it to print the text on
    'the default printer.

    'First, the declaration of Word as an Object,
    'specifically and OLE automation object for our uses
    'here.
    Dim Word As Object

    'next, set up word to accept our commands. We want
    'specifically to invoke the Word Basic capabilities.
    Set Word = CreateObject("Word.Basic")

    'let's start a new document, just to make sure we have a document,
    'and to keep from overwriting anything that may be currently loaded.
    Word.FileNew
```

```
    'next, let's send the text to the word document
    Word.Insert txtTextToSend

    'then print it.
    Word.FilePrint

    'exit the document - the "2" tells Word to close
    'without saving.
    Word.FileClose 2

End Sub
```

OLE Automation is a feature of OLE 2, so the automation code given above requires OLE 2 compliant applications. If you don't have Word 6, you can substitute commands above for an application that you have which does support the OLE 2 specification.

You may need to change the actions and properties that you are calling to the specific calls that are implemented in your specific OLE automation server, but the concepts will be identical.

Also remember that you will need to use the special `[.Quit]` commands with other automation servers.

Later, we'll implement this code in the Contact Database by automating the process of starting a form letter. The following sections discuss what is happening in this code sample.

How to Work With Objects From Your Programs

To control the behavior of an object from your program, you need to be able to create a reference to the object. Access allows you to do this with the Object type. The common ways of creating these references are the CreateObject and GetObject statements in the Access Basic language.

How to Use CreateObject to Work With OLE Objects

First, we have to create an object that we can refer to in the Access code. This is done with the new Access 2.0 'Object' type. The Object type allows you to reference OLE objects. With the Object type, you create a reference to the object, much the same as when using a Dynaset when working with records. Once DIM'd, the object variable can be assigned to the specific server you want to reference:

```
Dim Word As Object
Set Word = CreateObject("Word.Basic")
```

In our example, we create an object of type 'Word.Basic'. This gives us full access to the Word Basic commands and therefore the entire Word system, to all intents and purposes. This will allow us to use Word Basic commands to accomplish our goal of printing the text from the box, without leaving the realms of Access.

As from the release of version 6.0 of Word, the only object explicitly exposed by Word is the Word Basic object. You'll need to check with the appropriate vendors in determining what objects are exposed within any given server application.

The CreateObject call will also start the Word Basic Server if it is not already running. If it is running in the background, it will simply set up a reference to the object. You'll notice that if you run a process more than once, depending on your system configuration, there may be a dramatic difference in processing time between the first run and the subsequent runs. This is because the program will probably be cached and, in some cases, the program will still be running and not need to be re-loaded.

At this point, our object reference is set up, the server application is waiting on calls to its methods and we are ready to begin working with the server application.

How to Use GetObject to Work With OLE Objects

In our example above, we've created an explicit connection to the Word Basic Server and therefore the Word application. If you are working with objects, you may not always know which server application should be used on a given system to edit the object. Using an explicit connection insulates you from the user's system configuration by asking Windows to tell you the server application to use.

As an example, one user may use NotePad to edit his .INI files, but another user may use Windows Write. This is where file associations come in and they can allow your application to operate just as File Manager and other applications do, by recognizing which application is the preferred one for that type of file.

The GetObject command does the same thing as the CreateObject command with a notable exception in calling procedures. With GetObject, you pass in the name of the specific object you want to work with and allow the system to find out what server application to use. This information is determined from the Registry.

For example, if you have a file called '**TEST.DOC**' and want to allow the user to modify the file, he could be looking to use either Windows Write or Microsoft Word for the job. By using the GetObject command instead of directly specifying WordBasic in a CreateObject command, Windows will take care of resolving the association on that system, again based on the Registry. Here's what the new command would look like:

```
Set Word = GetObject("TEST.DOC")
```

There is an additional benefit to this approach. This call will not only initialize the server application, but also load the object into the server. In this case, the application associated with files on your system that have an extension of .DOC may not be Word at all. Whatever is registered on your system to work with files with this extension will automatically be loaded and will be passed the object to work with.

In short, CreateObject works with any objects related to a given server, while GetObject works with a given object and uses the Registration Database to locate the appropriate server.

As a quick check, you can go into File Manager and choose File, Associate. Next, type in DOC. The list box will automatically jump to whatever application is associated with that extension. This is the application that will be loaded with the GetObject call shown before.

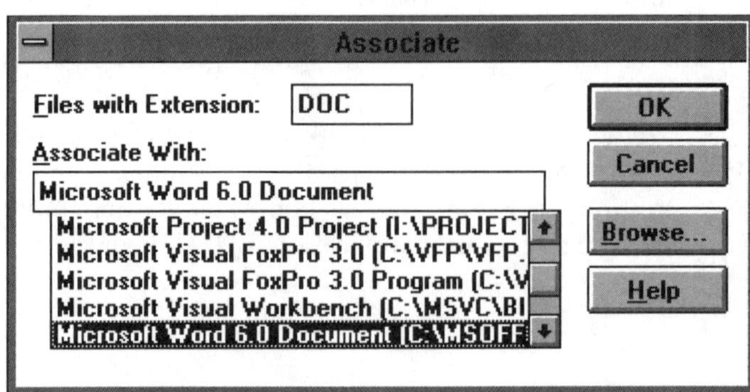

We are not using the GetObject method in our PIM application because we're not implementing a generic object editor. We're looking to use some of the capabilities of Word beyond just allowing the editing of an object in the system!

Working With OLE Automation Servers

OLE Automation Servers can become an integral part of your application, providing services that range from graphing to printing and spell checking. These services can be referenced in your Access Basic code and controlled from your program.

How to Pass Commands to an OLE Automation Server

When you use an Automation server, you establish a connection to the server with the GetObject or CreateObject commands as outlined before. Once the connection is established, you can issue commands, set properties and pass information between the server application and your application.

The next few commands are Word Basic commands that we are invoking as methods in our application:

```
...
Word.FileNew
Word.Insert txtTextToSend
Word.FilePrint
Word.FileClose 2
...
```

These commands, found in the Word Basic help files, tell Word to open a new document using the FileNew method. Next, the contents of txtTextToSend in our Access application is passed to the Insert method. This command simply takes the information we pass it and inserts it at the current location in the document.

The FilePrint command instructs Word to print the document to the current default printer, while the FileClose command tidies up the connection by closing the document. You should notice the parameter that is passed to the FileClose command; this informs Word that when the file is closed down, the document shouldn't be saved.

Try sizing your Access and Word windows accordingly so you can try to see the different commands executing in Word. Note that, in some cases, the commands may be processed before the display has time to update, giving the impression that nothing is happening. The commands will still be executing correctly in the background.

Special Actions and Commands

In many cases, the final statement is the `[.Quit]` action. When you work with OA, you need to make certain that you 'clean up' after you are done with an object. Server objects are notorious for not shutting themselves down, even if the object variable you declare goes out of scope when the function or the procedure is completed. Our example application, Word, does release its resources upon its completed execution, making the `[.Quit]` command unnecessary.

You should always issue the Quit command whenever you are unsure of the OA Server with which you are working. Note that not all servers support this command. In those cases, make sure you check with the vendor and see what command(s) should be issued to gracefully shut down the server application.

If you don't issue the Quit command, you can end up with a number of processes running on your system. This is a real resource drain and can end up causing 'Out of Memory' conditions in Access and other applications. The command will usually have the following syntax:

```
Application_Object.[Quit]
```

Notice that the Quit command is enclosed in brackets. If not, Access will attempt to interpret the command during the event compile. The compile will fail because Quit is a reserved word in Access Basic. In cases where a property, action, method or event conflicts with Access, but you are referring to it explicitly in code, enclose the item in brackets to get around the Access compiler.

Named Arguments

As you work with different automation servers, you'll most likely be using different properties, methods and actions with them. As you may have guessed, the industry is in flux right now as it tries to take advantage of the new OLE 2 standard.

In the past, with DDE and the original SendKeys implementations, far less flexibility was available relating to the passing of parameters. Prior to complete implementation of OLE 2 in applications, because of these restrictions, it may have been necessary to provide more information than is really required. This is due to the fact that **Named Arguments** are not supported on all platforms.

The industry direction is toward being able to specify only those parameters that apply to the work you're trying to do. For example, if you want to tell Word to center the page, you'll want to send the command '.FilePageSetup .VertAlign 1', compared to the standard VertAlign command which requires as many as 26 parameters.

Make sure you check with the documentation accompanying the object, the on-line help files and the vendor prior to working with automation objects. Named Arguments are specified as '.<parameter>' in the .HLP files associated with a control or server applications. In many cases, today's software will require that you send all parameters, not just the parameter you need to specify. In addition, this may vary drastically depending on the Container software you are using to call the OA Server. Visual Basic and Access Basic are examples of this discrepancy.

In the cases where Named Arguments are not supported, you'll have to pass the string with commas to maintain positioning, specifying your arguments as needed.

Registration Database

The Registration Database is the road map to the different OLE objects on your system. Both OLE and OLE Automation Servers are defined in the Registry. In addition, some of the DDE commands and topics are defined, making it easier for you to determine what interaction between your application and other applications is possible.

What is the Registration Database, or Registry?

The Registration Database is the replacement for today's .INI files. Each entry specifies the interface between the Windows operating environment and the application. A typical entry is shown on the following page:

```
├ CLSID = {000483F1-0000-0000-C000-000000000046}
├ protocol
│ └ StdFileEditing
│   ├ server = C:\HJPRO\HJPRO.EXE
│   ├ verb
│   │ └ 0 = Edit
│   ├ SetDataFormats = Native
│   └ RequestDataFormats = Native, CF_METAFILEPICT, CF_DIB, CF_BITMAP
└ shell
  ├ print
  │ └ command = C:\HJPRO\HJPRO.EXE %1 PRN
  └ open
    └ command = C:\HJPRO\HJPRO.EXE %1
```

When you activate an OLE object, or call an OLE Automation Server process, Windows looks up your request in the database first. With this information, Windows is able to execute the server application as needed and provide the functionality your application is requesting.

Use of Registration Database Editor

There is a Registration Database Editor (**REGEDIT.EXE**) included with your Windows system. This editor is not generally found in any of the standard program groups that Windows automatically installs on your system and with good reason. **REGEDIT.EXE** is one of the quickest ways to destroy the communications between your applications.

You can see that if Windows relies so heavily on the Registry for information on the inter-operability of programs, changing that database should only be done by planned processes or in a dire emergency. Nonetheless, it's very interesting just to look at the entries so that you understand what's really going on in your system as you implement these exciting capabilities.

Basic Usage

From the Windows Program Manager, select File, Run and enter REGEDIT.

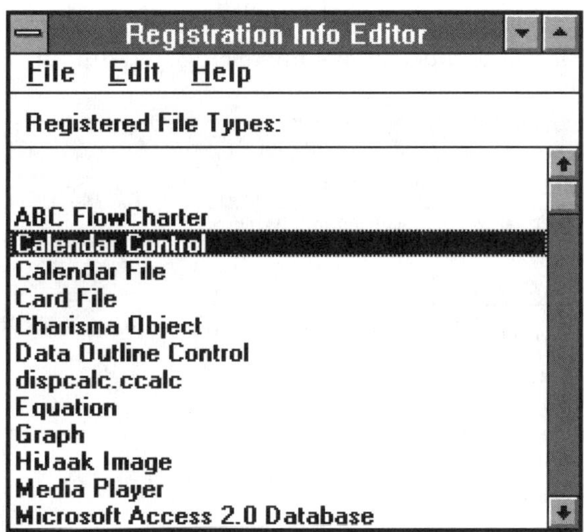

The listing shows the different objects that are known to your Windows operating system. There are quite a few different entries, many that may surprise you. Take special note that major applications like Excel have several different components displayed in the database because they can act as different types of servers, such as a chart or worksheet.

Accessing the systems in the Registry is more than just executing the program file. Looking back at our previous example, we sent text to Word using the Word Automation Object, 'Word.Basic'. If you scan down the list of topics in the database, you should come across 'Word Basic'. This is the item we were using. If you double click on the entry, you'll be shown a dialog box, most of which is not filled in. The only apparent capability of the object is that it can be opened. This will generally be the case with automation servers because they expose their methods directly to Container applications and don't rely on DDE conversations.

Choose Cancel and look for the entry for a Word 6.0 Document. Double click the entry and you'll see a much more interesting and useful dialog box.

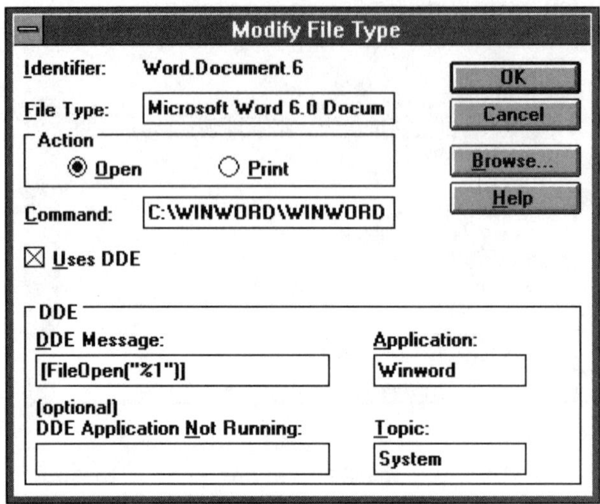

Application DDE and OLE Protocol Information

This screen shows information that we can really use. First, the OLE object can be opened, much the same as the Word Basic entry. In addition, the command line we use to open the object is provided. Notice that the 'Uses DDE' check box is checked. This means that, not only will the object support the use of OLE automation as we've seen, but it will also support DDE calls.

The DDE frame on the bottom of the dialog box shows information that we can use in dialog with the Word document object using DDE. The FileOpen command is shown, along with the parameter and formatting requirements. In addition, the Application and Topic are shown. All the information we'll need to access the DDE conversation with this object is shown.

Again, don't change anything unless you really know what is going on with the different parameters and other items listed. Choose Cancel and return to the listing. It's worth your time to see what capabilities are on your system that you may not have known about prior to this investigation.

Here are some other entries that you might like to review:

- Microsoft Excel 5.0 Worksheet
- Microsoft Excel 5.0 Chart
- Microsoft Word 6.0 Document

There will be others that you will need to review. Just browse through the list and see what's on your system.

Advanced Usage

Once you've mastered the basics of the OLE registration database editor, you can move on to the subject of what's behind the more user friendly dialog boxes we have just used above. Remember, there has to be enough information here for Windows to know how to execute these applications, pass information between them and so on.

Exit the Registration Database editor and go back to the Program Manager. Choose File, Run and enter 'REGEDIT /V'. This time, you'll get a much more programmatic view of the Registration Database:

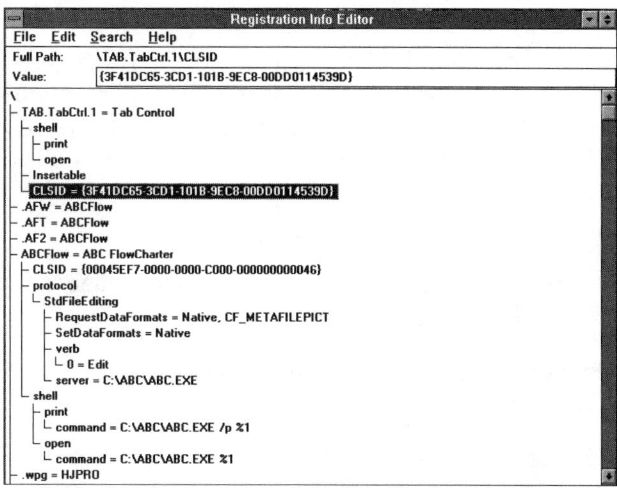

A Sample REGEDIT Output

Windows objects are separated into classes and the Microsoft standard is that all OLE objects belong to the same class. The tree displayed by the Registration Database Editor is much like a graphical display of your hard drive subdirectory structure.

There is a root entry that has sub-entries off it. Each entry is called a key and each object is stored under its key, which corresponds back to the object's class name.

The root key is 'HKEY_CLASSES_ROOT' and the full object class name will be the root key, followed by a backslash and the object class name. This can be seen if you choose File, then Save Registration File. The resulting text file shows each of the entries with their full key structure, a snippet of which is shown below:

```
HKEY_CLASSES_ROOT\TAB.TabCtrl.1  =  Tab  Control

HKEY_CLASSES_ROOT\TAB.TabCtrl.1\Insertable  =

HKEY_CLASSES_ROOT\TAB.TabCtrl.1\CLSID  =  {3F41DC65-3CD1-101B-9EC8  ↵
-00DD0114539D}
```

> *Note that editing the file may require the use of an editor other than the Windows NotePad. If the file is too large, try using Windows Write or your favorite DOS text editor.*

Following the class name is an equal sign, and an English description of the object. This is what you see when you use Insert Object from within an application. The CLSID (class ID) represents a unique identifier for the OLE object. The OLE CLSID for a given object is the same across all systems. A range of CLSIDs is assigned to vendors for their development efforts. The entries for MSGraph are shown below:

```
HKEY_CLASSES_ROOT\CLSID\{000208EC-0000-0000-C000-000000000046}  ↵
=  Microsoft  Graph  5.0  Application

HKEY_CLASSES_ROOT\CLSID\{000208EC-0000-0000-C000-000000000046}  ↵
\ProgID  =  MSGraph.Application.5

HKEY_CLASSES_ROOT\CLSID\{000208EC-0000-0000-C000-000000000046}  ↵
\VersionIndependentProgID  =  MSGraph.Application

HKEY_CLASSES_ROOT\CLSID\{000208EC-0000-0000-C000-000000000046}  ↵
\LocalServer  =  C:\WINDOWS\MSAPPS\MSGRAPH5\graph5.exe  /automation

HKEY_CLASSES_ROOT\CLSID\{000208EC-0000-0000-C000-000000000046}  ↵
\InprocHandler  =  Ole2.dll
```

> **Your entry may differ from this depending on which version of MSGraph you have loaded on your system. However, you should note that all the CLSIDs are the same for any one given application.**

Notice that some applications are defined several different times in the database. This provides the necessary backward compatibility. This is accomplished by mapping both MSGraph.Application and MSGraph.Application.5 to the same application. This way, if an application calls MSGraph.Application, it will run the most current version of the application.

The LocalServer entry tells Windows exactly where to find the server application. The full path and executable name are provided, as well as command line parameters that are used to start the application in the appropriate mode of operation.

You'll also notice entries of the format `HKEY_CLASSES_ROOT\.BMP` or `HKEY_CLASSES_ROOT\.TXT`. You may recognize these entries as the associations you've established in the File Manager. The associations are maintained in your `WIN.INI` file, and are also maintained in the Registration Database. This is how Windows knows how to load your favorite editor when you double-click on a .TXT text file.

How do Applications Get Entries into the Registration Database?

There are several different ways that an application can register itself with the system. First, when a software package is initially run, it will usually check to see that it is in the Registry with the correct information including version, location of files and so on. If the application is not correctly registered, it will register or update its entries at that time.

Alternatively, an application can manually register itself. This is the case with Word for Windows and Excel. Both of these application use a file, passed to the Registration Database editor, as the means of registering their objects with the system. The setup parameter for REGEDIT is used by these applications to accomplish these tasks.

The actual registration process is usually carried out in one of two different ways:

1 The Application explicitly registers itself. This means that the application makes the Windows calls directly to add or update the necessary entries in the Registry. This is probably less common due to complexity.

2 An application can pass the registration entries to the Registration Database Editor as a command line parameter. The command line:

```
REGEDIT  /s  <filename>
```

allows you to pass a file, usually with an '.REG' suffix, to the Registration Database Editor. This file has all of the necessary entries in it that need to be in your system. A sample **.REG** file is shown in the figure below. The example is for the Windows Setup program. These entries are created in the Registration Database when Setup is used to update your system. The /S parameter has the effect of suppressing the dialog boxes and user interface as the operation is completed.

The following listing is quite long. We've placed ellipses '...' to symbolize sections that have been removed for brevity. For a full listing of the different entries in the file, please examine the file on disk by searching for files with the extension of .REG. You can open these files with any standard text editor.

```
REGEDIT
(the above line used as a quick check that we are indeed a
registration script)

ALL LINES THAT DON'T START WITH 'HKEY_CLASSES_ROOT' ARE COMMENTS.

THIS FILE CONSISTS OF A LIST OF <key> <value> PAIRS. THE key AND
value SHOULD BE SEPARATED BY A " = " mark.

Some of these entries duplicate those found in win.ini, for example,
the file extension associations to executables. Shell.dll always
looks in the registration database before it looks in win.ini for
this information, so it is efficient to include it here.

ENTRIES FOR NotePad

HKEY_CLASSES_ROOT\.ini = txtfile
HKEY_CLASSES_ROOT\.txt = txtfile
HKEY_CLASSES_ROOT\txtfile = Text File
```

```
HKEY_CLASSES_ROOT\txtfile\shell\print\command = notepad.exe /p %1
HKEY_CLASSES_ROOT\txtfile\shell\open\command = notepad.exe %1

ENTRIES FOR Cardfile

HKEY_CLASSES_ROOT\.crd = crdfile
HKEY_CLASSES_ROOT\crdfile = Card File
HKEY_CLASSES_ROOT\crdfile\shell\print\command = cardfile.exe /p %1
HKEY_CLASSES_ROOT\crdfile\shell\open\command = cardfile.exe %1

ENTRIES FOR Terminal

HKEY_CLASSES_ROOT\.trm = trmfile
HKEY_CLASSES_ROOT\trmfile = Terminal Settings
HKEY_CLASSES_ROOT\trmfile\shell\open\command = terminal.exe %1

ENTRIES FOR Macro Recorder

HKEY_CLASSES_ROOT\.rec = recfile
HKEY_CLASSES_ROOT\recfile = Recorder Macro
HKEY_CLASSES_ROOT\recfile\shell\open\command = recorder.exe %1

ENTRIES FOR Microsoft Mail

HKEY_CLASSES_ROOT\.mmf = MicrosoftMail
HKEY_CLASSES_ROOT\MicrosoftMail = Microsoft Mail
HKEY_CLASSES_ROOT\MicrosoftMail\shell\open\command = msmail.exe /f %1

ENTRIES FOR Write

HKEY_CLASSES_ROOT\.wri = wrifile
HKEY_CLASSES_ROOT\wrifile = Write Document
HKEY_CLASSES_ROOT\wrifile\shell\print\command = write.exe /p %1
HKEY_CLASSES_ROOT\wrifile\shell\open\command = write.exe %1

ENTRIES FOR Regedit

HKEY_CLASSES_ROOT\.reg = regedit
HKEY_CLASSES_ROOT\regedit = Registration Entries
HKEY_CLASSES_ROOT\regedit\shell\open\command = regedit.exe %1

...
```

From here, you're ready to really start using OLE in your applications. In the coming chapters, you'll learn how to use not only the OLE capabilities of your system, but also DDE, NetDDE and messaging.

Chapter 2

Completing the Initial Set Up for the PIM

This section details how to set up the tables and initial forms for the Personal Information Manger included with this book. The files are installed on your system when you run the setup program. By default, these files are located in `C:\WROX` subdirectory. The name of the database is `CONTACTS.MDB`.

Setting Up the Tables

At this point we are ready to define the tables for the PIM that we're working with in this book. Go into Access and start a new database or, if you're following along with the system provided on disk, open the `CONTACTS.MDB` database.

The first thing you're going to do is create the three basic tables that will be the backbone of the system. These tables are the Contacts table, the Companies table and the Projects table. The next three figures show the database table definitions that you should now set up. First, the Company table:

Field Name	DataType	Size
CompanyID	Counter	-
CompanyName	Text	50
CompanyAddress1	Text	50
CompanyAddress2	Text	50
Company City	Text	50
CompanyState	Text	2
CompanyZIP	Text	10
CompanyCountry	Text	50
CompanyPhone	Text	50
CompanyFax	Text	50
CompanyNotes	OLE Object	-

Set the primary key on the Company table to the CompanyID column and set the Indexed property for the CompanyName column to Yes (Duplicates OK). Next, the Contacts table:

Field Name	Data Type	Size
Contact ID	Counter	-
Company ID	Number	Double
Prefix	Text	10
FirstName	Text	50
LastName	Text	50
Suffix	Text	10
Address	Text	50
City	Text	50
State	Text	50
ZipCode	Text	50
Country	Text	50
WorkPhone	Text	30
HomePhone	Text	30
FaxNumber	Text	30
ReferredBy	Text	50
Note	OLE Object	-

Set the primary key to the ContactID. Add two more indices, one to the LastName column and one to the ZipCode column. The remaining table, the Projects table, is outlined below:

Field Name	Data Type	Size
ProjectID	Counter	-
ContactID	Number	Double
ProjectDescription	Text	50
FirstContact	Date/Time	-
ProjectBudget	Number	Double
ProjectHours	Number	Double

Continued

Field Name	Data Type	Size
ProjectNotes	Memo	-
AccountManager	Text	50
ProjectManager	Text	50

On this table, set the primary key to the ProjectID, ascending.

After you have completed these steps, you have started work on your own Personal Information Manager. Refer to the PIM Usage Appendix for an idea of how the system will operate and what features will be used. As we work through the different areas of the book from this point on, we'll build on the tables you have defined here and you will soon have the system fully functional. Of course the application is also on the accompanying disk, feel free to follow along there as we go through these examples.

The two core tables, Contact and Company, both have provisions for the OLE embedded objects. This will allow us to work with new technology and therefore show exactly what you need to do to implement it.

How to Set up the Forms for the PIM

The next step will be to set up the basic forms for the PIM and put the Access Basic code behind a few of the buttons to show how you implement the OA features we're demonstrating. The three forms will match the three database tables we just set up. One will be for the Company information, one for Contacts and the last one is for data related to Projects. In addition, there are some supporting forms that we'll set up.

The Company Details Form

The form for the Company information is shown next. Either open the form in the **CONTACTS.MDB** database, or create a new form. We recommend that you use the Form Wizard as it's a quick and easy way to place the controls on the form. Select the Company table and let the Form Wizard go to work for you. Next, go into design view and move the fields and associated controls around on the screen until it resembles the screen shown on the next page:

> Note that the Company Notes box has been changed to allow a more generous editing area. This will be important; remember that the users will be using an OLE embedded object here. In the case of a Word object, it will be easier for people using the application if they are given some space to work within.

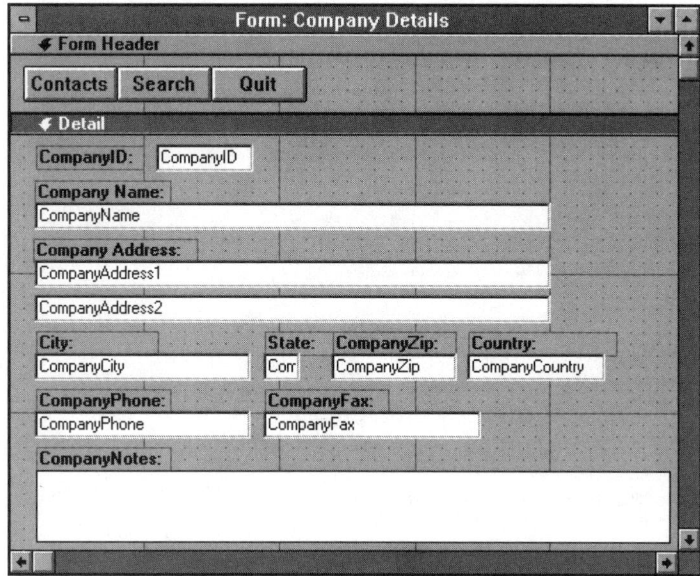

In the Form Header section place three buttons. The code behind the buttons allows us to go between the Contacts associated with the Company and allows us to return to our search screen, which we'll be discussing later.

Open the Properties window for each of the buttons and change the details as follows:

Button Caption	Button Name
Contacts	ContactDetails
Search	Search
Quit	Quit

Put the following code into the click event for the ContactDetails button:

```
Sub ContactDetails_Click ()
    '
    'This routine calls the contacts form for more
    'information on the contacts associated with this
    'company.
    '

    'set up the error handler
    On Error GoTo ContactDetailsErr

    'set up our variables
    Dim docname As String
    Dim LinkCriteria As String

    'set up the limitation on the contact details screen;
    'we only want records that have to do with the current
    'company.
    LinkCriteria = "[CompanyID]=" & forms![Company Details]![CompanyID]

    'the form name
    docname = "Contact Details"

    'go open the form, using the standard DoCmd command.
    DoCmd OpenForm docname, , , LinkCriteria

    ContactDetailsOkay:
    'everything's okay, get out of the routine.
    Exit Sub

ContactDetailsErr:
    'there was an error, show the message box, then exit.
    MsgBox Error$

    'note that you have to resume somewhere, so resume back
    'on the okay exit routine, effectively exiting the
    'procedure.
    Resume ContactDetailsOkay

End Sub
```

This code calls the contacts form, loading only those contacts that are related to the current company. If no contacts are found, then the Contact Details Form will be loaded and you will be ready to insert a new record.

Next, put the following code in the click event for the Search button:

```
Sub Search_Click ()
    '
    'Open or return to the search form, loaded in the
    'autoexec macro on entry into the system. Note that
    'if the form is already loaded, this simply returns
    'us to that form and closes the Company Details form.

    DoCmd Close
    DoCmd OpenForm "Find Form"

End Sub
```

These statements will close the form and load the search form, returning the user to the system starting point.

Finally, put the following code behind the Quit button's click event:

```
Sub Quit_Click ()
    '
    'close the form
    '
    DoCmd Close
End Sub
```

The purpose of this code is to simply close down the form. If other forms in the system were open, focus would return to them. If not, the user is returned to the standard Access tab dialog allowing access to the various forms, tables and other objects in the system.

The last step is to close the form, saving it as 'Company Details'.

The Contact Details Form

Next, set up the Contact Details Form. Again, the code and form sample is included on the accompanying disk. However, you may wish to go through the steps of creating the form to familiarize yourself with the process and the application.

The next screen shows the completed Contacts form:

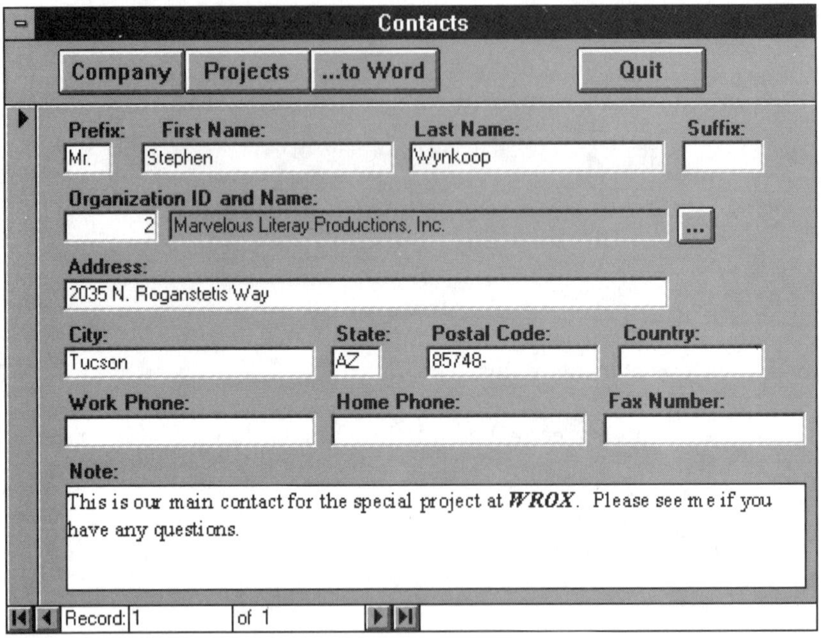

Note that if you use the Form Wizard to begin your form, the Company Name field will not be included. Since it is not part of the underlying Contacts table, you will have to manually add an unbound text box for the Company Name.

The same suggestion regarding the Company Contact Note field applies here. Make sure you allow a large editing area for the users of your program to use this field.

The buttons should be labeled and named as follows in the properties window.

Button Caption	Button Name
Company	Company
Projects	Projects
...to Word	Word
Quit	Quit
... (Ellipses)	LookupCompany

For the Company button click event, you should use the following code:

```
Sub Company_Click ()
    '
    'load the company details form for the company
    'associated with this contact.
    '
    DoCmd OpenForm "Company Details", , , "[CompanyID]=forms![Contact ⏎
        Details]![CompanyID]"
End Sub
```

This code opens the Company Details form and specifies that it should be opened for the companyID of the current Contact record. This allows the user of the system to swap back and forth between the Company and Contact Details.

The next thing that needs to be done is to set up the Projects button. Place the following code behind the click event for the button:

```
Sub Projects_Click ()
    '
    'open the project details form, limiting the display
    'to those items that relate to this contact.
    '

    DoCmd OpenForm "Project Detail", , , "[ContactID]=forms![Contact ⏎
        Details]![ContactID]"

End Sub
```

This code opens the Project Form, once again limiting what is displayed about the projects to the current contact. The project is keyed on the Contact ID.

The Word button is where the fun begins. We're going to put into practice some of the OA technologies that we've been working with. Once the contact name is displayed, we want to send the information to Word to automatically create the start of a form letter.

Here's the code to put behind the ... to Word command button's click event:

```
Sub Word_Click ()

    'Send the current record to Word, setting up
    'to write a letter. Include the date at the
    'top of the letter.

    'First, the declaration of Word as an Object,
    'an OLE automation object for our uses
    'here.
```

```
    Dim word As Object

    'next, set up word to accept our commands. We want
    'specifically to invoke the Word Basic capabilities.
    Set word = CreateObject("Word.Basic")

    'let's start a new document, just to make sure we have a document,
    'and to keep from overwriting anything that may be currently loaded.
    word.FileNew

    'next, let's send the information to the word document
    'setting up for a form letter.
    word.Insert Date$ & Chr$(13)
    word.Insert " " & Chr$(13)
    word.Insert " " & Chr$(13)
    word.Insert " " & Chr$(13)
    word.Insert " " & Chr$(13)
    word.Insert Prefix & " " & firstname & " " & LastName & " " & suffix & ↵
       Chr$(13)
    word.Insert OrganizationName & Chr$(13)
    word.Insert Address & Chr$(13)
    word.Insert City & ", " & State & " " & ZipCode & " " & Country & ↵
       Chr$(13)
    word.Insert " " & Chr$(13)
    word.Insert "Dear " & firstname & "," & Chr$(13)
    word.Insert " " & Chr$(13)
    DoEvents

End Sub
```

This routine uses the OLE automation capabilities of Word to send information to Word for the form letter. It sets up a new Word document and sends the information from the current form to the form letter. There are a couple of different things to note about the code.

First, we've placed **`Chr$(13)`** characters at the end of each line. This may seem strange, but this sends a carriage return to the Word system. Without these special characters, the string of information would all be placed on one line. In addition, we've built up strings of data items with spaces between the items. This allows us to create a single line of multiple items such as the full name for the contact (first name plus last name) and so on.

As you send information to other applications, you may want to use the `Trim$` functions within Access to be sure that no extra spaces are sent. If you enter spaces at the end of a name, for example, these spaces would be sent to Word. If you use the `Trim$` functions, the spaces will be trimmed off for you.

If you do use the `Trim$` function, be sure to `Trim$` the variables before you send them to the OA Server.

Lastly, you'll see the **`DoEvents`** special function. This is a call to the Windows operating system to go away and do any work that it may have pending. If you tile the Word and Access windows and then run this procedure, you may see that the Word document is not updated with our text until you click on the Word window. Without the **`DoEvents`** call, Windows may not have time to process the instructions sent from Access.

Here are the results when the procedure runs:

```
09-04-1994



Mr. Sam Smith
Test Companies 'R' Us
1234 S. Brennan Way
Tucson, AZ 85715 USA

Dear Sam,
```

This is a pretty good way to integrate your Access contact manager system with the automation capabilities of Word.

An additional function that you may wish to add is a text box that pops up and asks for the text of the letter. Your application sends this information to Word, formats and prints it and returns to the Access application, without the users' involvement in the creation of the letter. With the examples provided here, this modification is simple and straight-forward.

Add a new form for the text box. In the existing code under the Word button, add in your new text box after the 'Dear...' line. Using this technique you can use Access to compose the letter, then send it to Word for formatting and printing.

There's one more thing that you need to do to 'turn on' this form. You'll notice that the Company name field is Unbound. This field is manually added to the form and will show the company represented by the company ID. There is also an ellipses button, the one with the '...' caption.

Since we want to look up the company when the company ID changes, you'll want to create a new procedure. This procedure will look up the company based on the company ID. The results will be placed back on the form, showing what company is associated with the contact. As we mentioned earlier, you'll want to put this procedure in a module so you can call it from other places in your application. This is in case you update the Company ID programmatically; you'll want to also programmatically update the company name information.

Create the procedure by accessing the Modules tab and selecting the AB Code module. Create a new procedure named UpdateCompanyInfo. The following section details the code that you'll need to put into the procedure:

```
Sub UpdateCompanyInfo ()

    '
    'This routine will lookup the company ID from the
    'contact screen against the company database. It will
    'put the resulting company in the Company name field.
    '
    Dim sCompanyName

    'call the lookup function
    sCompanyName = DLookup("[Companyname]", "Company", "[CompanyID] = ↵
        Forms![Contact Details]![CompanyID]")

    'assign the return to the form.
    forms![contact details]![organizationname] = sCompanyName

End Sub
```

This procedure uses the DLookup function to lookup the value of the companyID against the Company Database. The results are placed on the Contact Details Form. We'll refer to this call whenever we need to update the Contact Details Form.

Place a call to this routine behind the change event for the Company ID field on the Contact Details Form:

```
Sub CompanyID_Change ()
    UpdateCompanyInfo
End Sub
```

The LookupCompany click event code is placed behind the ellipses button:

```
Sub LookupCompany_Click ()
    DoCmd OpenForm "Companies"
End Sub
```

This code will open the 'Companies' form, allowing the user to select a company with which to work. When the new company ID is written to the form, the Change event is initiated for the form. The `CompanyID_Change` routine above will then update the company name field, showing the company selected by the user from the list box.

The Project Details Form

The final core form for our system is the Project Detail Form. This form will hold all the nitty-gritty detail about a particular sales opportunity for a given client within a company. The Project Detail Form is shown in the next screen shot:

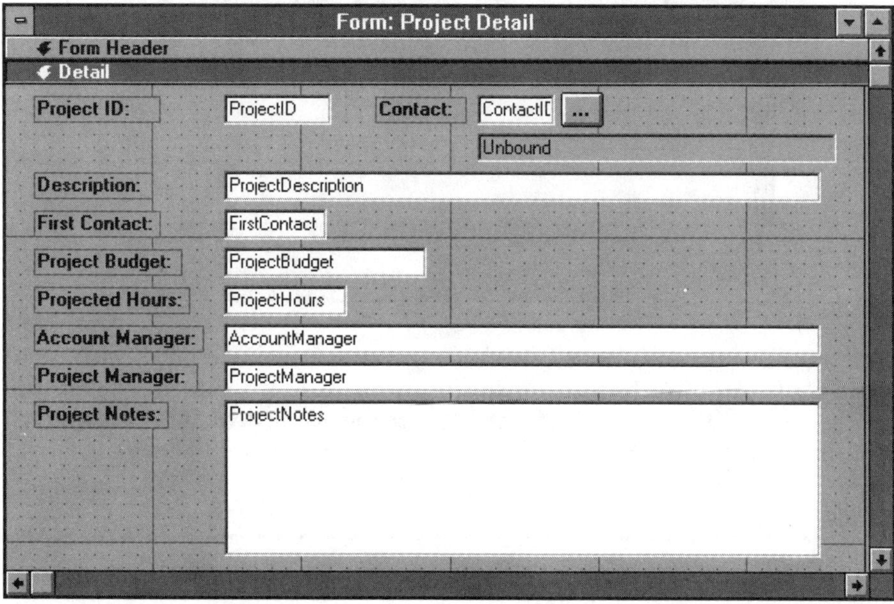

This form is implemented as a simple database editing tool, allowing you to add, change or delete records from the database using standard methods. When you load this form, the code to load it will limit its recordset to those records that relate to the contact record. If no records exist, you'll be able to add new records to the database. The standard database navigation controls are enabled.

Note that on this form the project notes are implemented as a Memo type field. This will give you some indication of the processing time and speed overhead of using the standard database editing tools versus using the OLE automation and OLE embedding tools that you're now learning about. As you use the system, compare and contrast what you like best about each of the implementations and keep this in mind as you design your own applications.

In our later chapters, we'll add functionality to this form, allowing it to send project information to Excel.

Company Lookup

The Company Lookup screen is used to select a different company when using the Contact Details form. The screen provides a simple list box from which the user can select the company they wish to associate with a given contact:

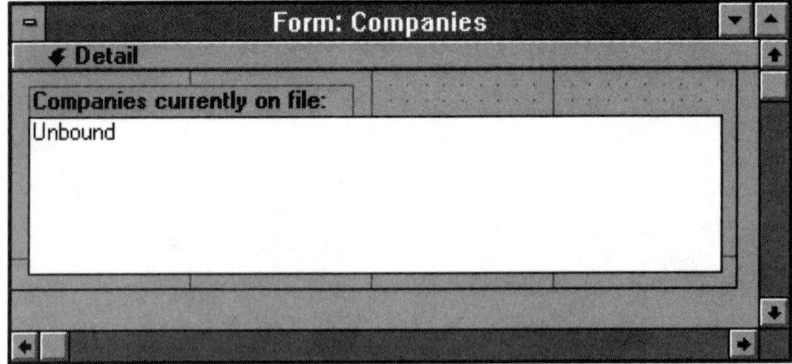

This form presents us with a list of companies currently on file. From the list, we can scroll and select the company we want inserted into the Contact Database record. Put a standard list box on the form, leaving it 'unbound'. In the property sheet for the list box, set the properties as shown in the following table:

Property	Value
Row Source Type	Table/Query
Row Source	Select [CompanyID], [CompanyName] from [Companies];
Column Count	2
Bound Column	1

Next, for the double-click event for the list box, put in the following code:

```
Sub lstCompany_DblClick (Cancel As Integer)
    [Forms]![contact details]![CompanyID] = [lstCompany]
    DoCmd Close
End Sub
```

This code will insert the default value of the list box, in this case column 1 of the selected row, into the Contact Details Form. When you set up the Bound property, you tell Access what information to associate with the Value of the control. You can then refer to the control without having to name the specific property that you want and retrieve its value by default.

Remove the Min, Max and Record Navigation features of the form. You could also set the form to AutoCenter on activation. Autocentering the form makes it easier for users to work with the form, as it's always in the same place and there is less need to Cascade or Tile the forms on the desktop to find it.

Save the form as 'Companies' and continue to the next form, Lookup Contact.

Lookup Contact

The Contact Lookup form provides us with a way to use a list box to review the Contacts Database. This is useful when setting up new projects in the system. By double-clicking on the list box, we return the contact ID to the Project Details Form:

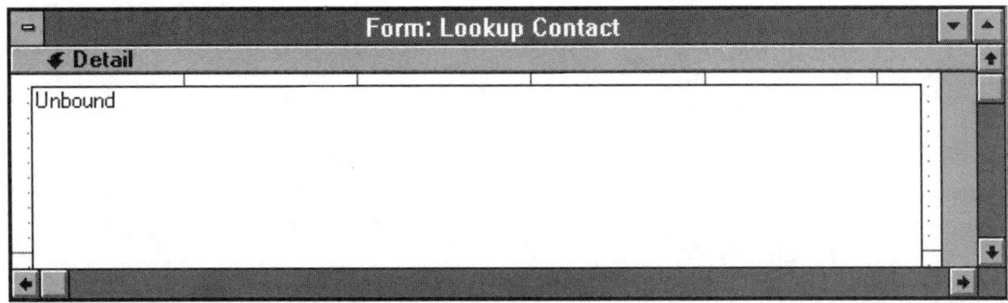

Add an Unbound list box to the form and set the following properties. These properties will set up the form to return the information we want:

Property	Value
Row Source Type	Table/Query
Row Source	Select [ContactID], [FirstName], [LastName] from [Contacts];
Column Count	3
Bound Column	1

Next, for the double-click event for the list box, enter the code shown below:

```
Sub lbContactList_DblClick (Cancel As Integer)
    '
    'when the user double-clicks on the selection, we want
    'to insert the record number in the Projects UI.
    '
    [forms]![Project detail]![ContactID] = [lbContactList]

    UpdateNewContact

    DoCmd Close

End Sub
```

The next step is to create a new subroutine for use in our application and we'll call the subroutine UpdateNewContact. This routine will be responsible for looking up the contact information and displaying the name at the top of the Project Details form. This routine is called whenever the Contact ID is changed, and we manually call it here to make sure our forms is updated correctly.

> *If you update a field using program code as we have here, the update or change events are not initiated for the control. In our example here, the code behind the contact ID field will call UpdateNewContact if the user manually enters or changes a contact ID.*
>
> *When you have a case where a certain process needs to be run within a change event, it's a good idea to put it out in a procedure so you can call it from within other procedure as we have here. This will prevent you from having to maintain several different copies of the same code.*

```
Sub UpdateNewContact ()

    Dim sContactInfo
    sContactInfo = DLookup("[Firstname]", "contacts", "[ContactID] = ↩
        Forms![Project Detail]![ContactID]")
    forms![project detail]![contactname] = sContactInfo

    sContactInfo = DLookup("[LastName]", "contacts", "[ContactID] = ↩
        Forms![Project Detail]![ContactID]")
    forms![project detail]![contactname] = forms![project ↩
        detail]![contactname] & " " & sContactInfo

End Sub
```

The code returns the value of column 1, the bound column, to the Project Details Form. In this case, the Project Details Form will be calling the Contact Lookup Form when projects are added or updated.

Remove the Min, Max and Record Navigation features of the form. You could also set the form to AutoCenter on activation.

Save the form as 'Lookup Contact' and continue to the next form.

Opening The Search Screen

When the PIM loads, it automatically loads the initial search screen. This is accomplished with a macro. The macro has been set up and named '**AUTOEXEC**' in the database. When Access loads a database, it automatically looks for an autoexec macro and, if it's found, executes it.

Choose the macro tab and create a new macro, naming it **AUTOEXEC**. The commands that you need to execute as part of the macro are shown on the next page.

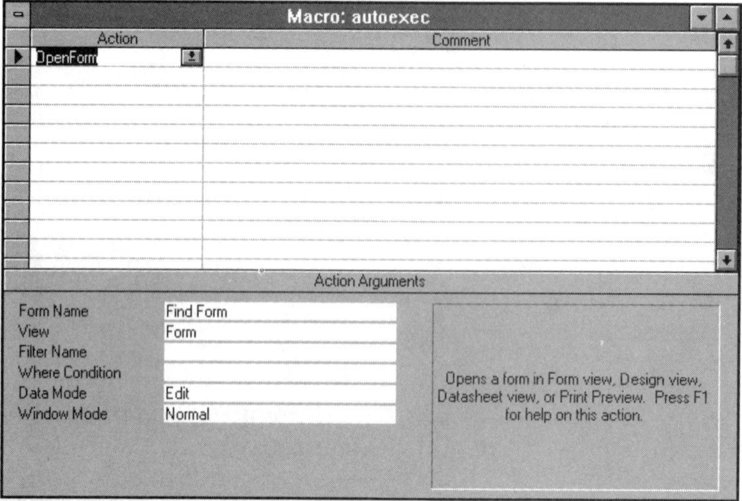

The macro simply loads the Find Form window. The form takes care of the rest, getting the user's input and so on. The Find Form is shown next:

To prevent Access from running an AUTOEXEC macro, press and hold down the Shift key while selecting a database to work with.

You may also want to do this during the time Access is loading if you've specified the database name on the command line from the Windows Program Manager.

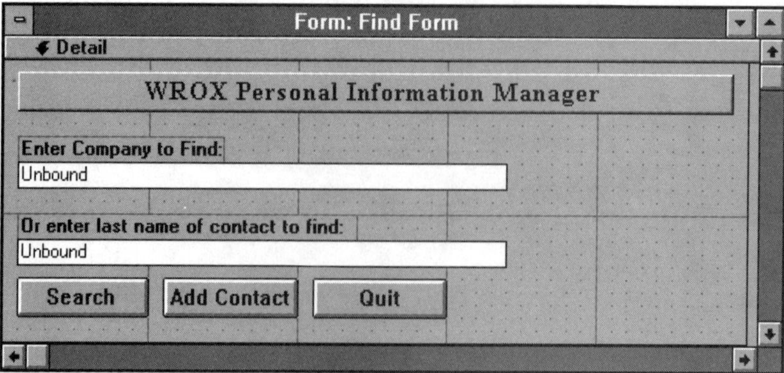

The form has two text fields and three buttons. Give yourself plenty of typing room in the text boxes. These text boxes will be where search parameters will be entered and you want to allow for easy searching of the database.

The buttons should be labeled and named as follows:

Caption	Name
Search	Search
Add Contact	AddContact
Quit	Quit

Now you can insert the following code behind the Search button's click event:

```
Sub Search_Click ()
    '
    'locate either the company or contact as requested.
    'if the company field is left blank, search on the
    'contact.
    '

    'set up our variable
    Dim findstring As String

    'get what the user entered.
    findstring = forms![find form]![company] & "%"


    'if it's blank, search on contact information
    If forms![find form]![company] <> "" Then
    DoCmd OpenForm "company details", , , "[CompanyName] like '" & ↵
        forms![find form]![company] & "*'"
    Else
    DoCmd OpenForm "contact details", , , "[lastname] like '" & ↵
        forms![find form]![name] & "*'"
    End If

End Sub
```

We've implemented the LIKE keyword on the lookups to find anything that comes close to matching what the user types in to find. Based on the user's input, we load either the Company Details Form or the Contact Details Form.

Next, update the code behind the Add Contact button. Here's the code that should be placed behind the button's click event:

```
Sub AddContact_Click ()
    '
    'load the contact form, blank, and allow
    'the user to add a new record.
    '
    DoCmd OpenForm "contact details", , , , Add

End Sub
```

This procedure simply opens the Contact Details form and gets it ready to add new records. The standard OpenForm command allows you to specify the mode for opening a form; in this case we've specified Add, preventing the user from accessing other information in the system.

Finally, you can enter the following code behind the click event for the Quit button's click event.

```
Sub Quit_Click ()
    '
    'exit and close the form.
    '
    DoCmd Close
End Sub
```

This routine closes the form and returns the user to the Access tabbed dialog box, allowing them to work directly with tables, forms and so on. In a production environment, you may want to make this command exit Access altogether, in which case the code would be:

```
Sub Quit_Click()
    '
    'exit Access saving any changes
    '
    application.Quit (a_save)
End Sub
```

Congratulations! You've set up the basics of the PIM application. We will now discuss how the automation features are accomplished and how to add additional advanced features to our software.

Comments and Suggestions

In this chapter, we have begun to look into how OLE can be used in your database applications, in the form of embedding OLE objects into your database tables and how OLE Automation can be used to integrate your Access applications with other OA Servers. We have built upon the foundations of the PIM and started to explore the functionality provided by OLE in a practical environment.

In the next chapter, we will continue to investigate the use of OLE in practical applications, as well as how to control object flexibility with Access Basic, a programmatic way of unearthing an object's verbs and actions, before moving onto an in-depth look at the Windows Object Packager.

CHAPTER 3

Implementing OLE in Your Applications

Learning about the theory behind a subject area is the most important aspect of learning for a student or a lecturer, but if you want to develop applications, both on a personal or professional level, then the knowledge that is gained by putting the theories into practice can be even more valuable. OLE can be a complex concept for the novice to grasp on a theoretical level, but when they finally take the plunge, everything can fall into place.

What's Covered in this Chapter

This chapter will explore using objects in your application by implementing them with Access Basic. In addition, we'll be covering the ways that you can automate the OLE Objects within the database; specifically, how to programmatically specify the types of objects that are placed on your forms. We will cover:

- Different types of OLE activation
- Compound documents
- Determining and using OLE verbs
- Using objects that support OLE as compared to OLE 2 objects
- Information contained in the Excel and Word developers kits that may be useful

Real-world implementation considerations for your systems will be the key in this chapter. We'll explore how you can make it easier for the users of your applications to insert OLE objects.

Chapter 3

How This Chapter Impacts Our Application

In this chapter, we'll automate the process of adding new contact and company records. We take a look at how to use Access Basic to control the various types of object and we'll also look into the different types of OLE objects in terms of how they relate to our application.

In addition, we'll discuss different alternatives that you can use when adding OLE functionality to your programs. Space and performance are two important considerations included in this discussion.

Using OLE to Its Fullest Extent

When you open your applications up to the capabilities of OLE, OLE automation and OLE custom controls, you are also presenting your users with more options. This is an advantageous feature, but may need to be limited from a programming standpoint.

For example, suppose that you place an OLE object in your database and tie it to a form, giving the user the ability to edit the object. You expect the object to be a Word object, so you've written some custom commands to work with the object and the Word Server. If the user tries to paste an Excel spreadsheet into the new OLE control, all of your handling of the object is going to be wrong.

The process of inserting and specifying the type of object can be automated and controlled by your application, a must if you are to provide consistent interface options to the users.

There is another challenge in implementing OLE in large installations. Large corporations often have a mixed bag of versions and types of programs on their systems. If you allow a user to paste any type of object he wishes onto a form, it may create a situation where it is impossible for other users to edit the object.

Because of all this reasoning, it's imperative that we control the use of objects for the user. We'll explain the types of automation controls you can provide in the following section.

Activating and Editing OLE Objects

When a user double-clicks on an OLE object, they **activate** the object. This means that they are telling Windows to call the OLE Server that is responsible for managing the object and pass the object's contents to it.

The expanded capabilities of OLE 2 include:

- **Drag-and-drop embedding**
- **In-place activation**
- **OLE automation capabilities**
- **OLE custom control capabilities**

Future versions of the OLE standard will begin to incorporate some exciting features. One of these new features could be 'Net-OLE'. These capabilities will be similar to NetDDE, as Net-OLE will allow you to use OLE Servers and object across systems in a workgroup environment using Remote Procedure Calls (RPC).

When an OLE object is activated, it makes a call to the OLE Server application. If the server is OLE 2 compliant and supports **in-place** activation, it steps in, taking over the display and editing of the object. In addition, it will often place a series of menus that pertain to the server application on the screen for the user. Examples of these are the Standard and Formatting menus from Word.

The actual menus that come up as floating menus will depend on your installation. For example, if you always show the drawing menu in Word, when you activate the OLE 2 object for Word, the Drawing menu, along with the other menus previously mentioned, will be displayed.

Linked objects can't utilize in-place activation. The object must be embedded for in-place activation to be available. You may recall that linked objects are really references to files stored externally to the container application. In these cases, the server application is shelled out and the reference to the external object is passed to the server.

When the server has finished working with the object, it updates the file on disk. Since the container application contains a reference to the file on disk, the object the container application refers to will always be current.

In our previous examples, this could be seen when you double-clicked on the object. You can see an example of this in the Company Details or Contact Details forms after you have inserted an object in the 'notes' field:

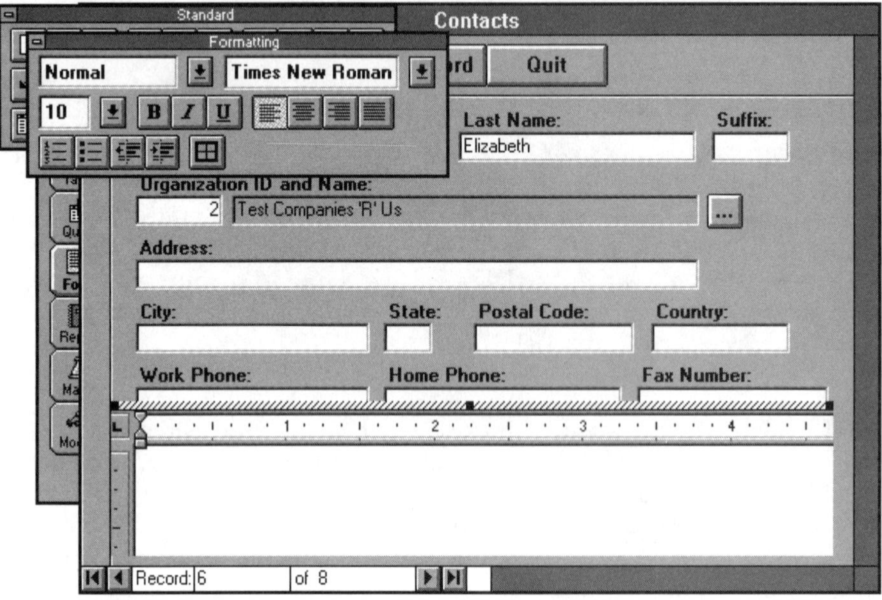

The in-place activation of the notes field. Notice the floating Word menus

Alternatively, if you embed an object that is not capable of in-place activation, or you use a link to the object, the server will be executing as a shelled out application. The object being edited is passed to the application and temporarily deactivated in your container application. This is illustrated by the gray hatched pattern surrounding the object container on your form during the time that you're editing the object.

The figure below shows an example of an embedded Paintbrush object being edited. However, Paintbrush is not OLE 2 compliant and so it is run as a separate, shelled application when the drawing is double-clicked:

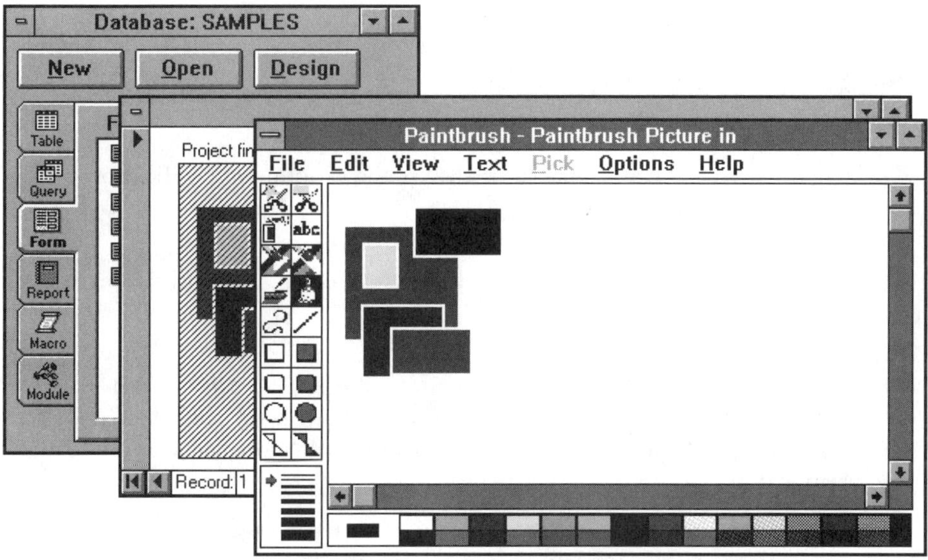

The title bar of the server application usually indicates that the object being worked with is an embedded object. Typically, it will say something like 'Paintbrush - Paintbrush Picture In...', although the specific text varies between applications. When you close the server application, it will usually ask if you want to update the object in the container application before continuing:

Note that if you are using a new form in Access, one without a defined caption, the OLE application may not be able to determine what application the object is being embedded into. In these cases, as shown next, the name of the application will not be shown in the Update dialog box.

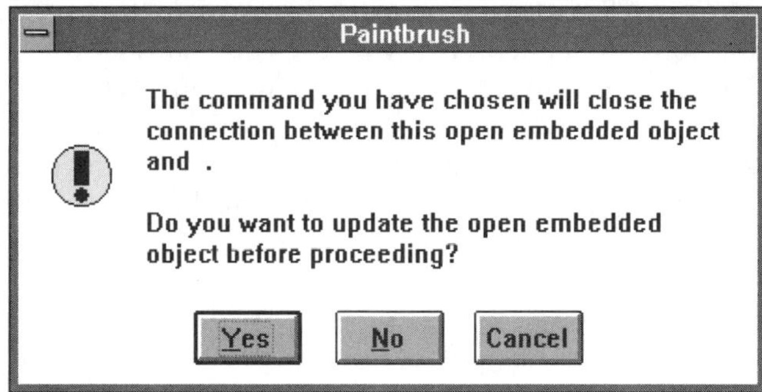

Note that if your application is using shelled server applications, there is the possibility that someone could do the following:

- Start the Container application.
- Double-click an object to edit it.
- Click back to Access and shut down the Container application while the server application is running.

If this happens one of three different things can occur, depending on the server application:

- First, with a well-behaved application, the server application will prompt you as to whether to save any changes to the object. Doing so will update the object in your form and will close down the server application.
- Second, the application may simply return the object to your Access application, either ignoring changes or automatically saving them, unprompted. In the case of Paintbrush, it returns the object to Access and updates it automatically. One thing to note about the Paintbrush demo is that the picture remains hatched and if you try *Alt-Tab* you'll notice that Paintbrush is still running - it only closes down when you close the form.
- Third, the server application may stay running and appear to be editing the object. In reality, it won't be possible to update the object because you have already shut down your container application. In these cases, users will lose the changes they have completed against the object.

Make sure your users know about these problems. Unfortunately, due to the number of server applications that are available, it's beyond the scope of this book to explore the idiosyncrasies of each. To test a specific server application, use the Embedded Object Experimentation form included in the **SAMPLES.MDB** database. Once the form is loaded, you can use Edit, Insert Object from the standard menu bar to insert any type of object on your system.

Assuming the server application is not OLE 2 compliant providing in-place editing, make some changes to the object. Once you have done this, either click on the Access application or use *Alt-Tab* to return to Access. Shut down the form and see what happens.

Since no comprehensive standards exist for OLE applications and the way that they handle their objects, you should check on each object you plan to work with in your application. For example, check to see if the server application will prompt the user to update the object when exiting. Also, see how it handles the display.

When you use a server application, check to see if it will update the title bar to indicate that it is working with an embedded object. It will be helpful for users of the system to understand that they are working with an embedded object. This is because the object isn't likely to be stored in the standard subdirectory structure, but rather as it relates to the container application.

The Various States of an Object or Object Frame

It's important to understand the different states of an object. When different states are active, different object capabilities are made available.

The different states for an object are:

- Inactive
- Selected
- Open

In addition, an OLE object control can be Locked or Enabled. Each of these different states comes into play in your application as explained below.

An object is **inactive** on your form when it is not selected and it is not being edited.

When you single-click on an object, its state will change to **selected**. This is much the same as when you click on a control on your form. You can tell when an object is selected because the drag points of the frame are activated. The drag points are the small black boxes on the frame of the object that are used to size an object.

An object is **open** when it is actively being edited by the server application. How you open an object depends on how you've defined the control in which the object lies. You can define one of three actions that can open an object.

If an OLE framed object is Locked, i.e. the Locked property is Yes, then certain limitations are enforced by Access when you work with the object. If you try to use actions that are not available in this state, Access will present a message box indicating that the action is invalid when used against a locked object. The following actions are the only ones available to a locked object:

- OLE_Copy
- OLE_Activate
- OLE_Close
- OLE_Fetch_Verbs

We will look in detail at all the actions available to an object later in the chapter.

The final state of an OLE framed object is Enabled. If an object has the Enabled property set to No, then the only action that is valid is OLE_Copy. This action causes Access to copy the contents of the object to the Windows clipboard. In essence, when an object is disabled it behaves like it is read-only.

There's a subtle but important thing to be gleaned from the list of actions available with a locked object. Notice that you can still activate it, copy it out and so on. If you have a system where the objects refer to protected data, you can provide the user with read-only access to the object by locking the OLE object control and setting the Enabled property to No, effectively disabling changes to the object.

If the user activates the object, or if you activate it programmatically, they can still view it with the server application, but they will not be able to update the database. This is an important capability in a shared information environment.

To implement some user control, you could modify the Locked and Enabled properties based on the current user and whether they are the creator of the specific object on the screen at the time. This way, a user has access to their own information, but can't modify other people's information, all of which are stored in a common database.

If you have a linked object that is referencing a read-only source, such as a CD ROM drive, you will get an error message if you attempt to edit it. Be sure to have a means of allowing the user, or your program, to be aware of objects like these. A simple dialog box indicating to the user that the object is read-only will provide a better degree of usability and will prevent a panic when they find out that changes are not possible.

Controlling When and How an OLE Framed Object is Activated

The AutoActivate property of the OLE control on your form allows you to specify Manual, Get Focus or Double-Click. If you use Manual activation, you elect to handle the activation of the object within your Access Basic code. To set the AutoActivate property of the OLE control, call up the properties for the control:

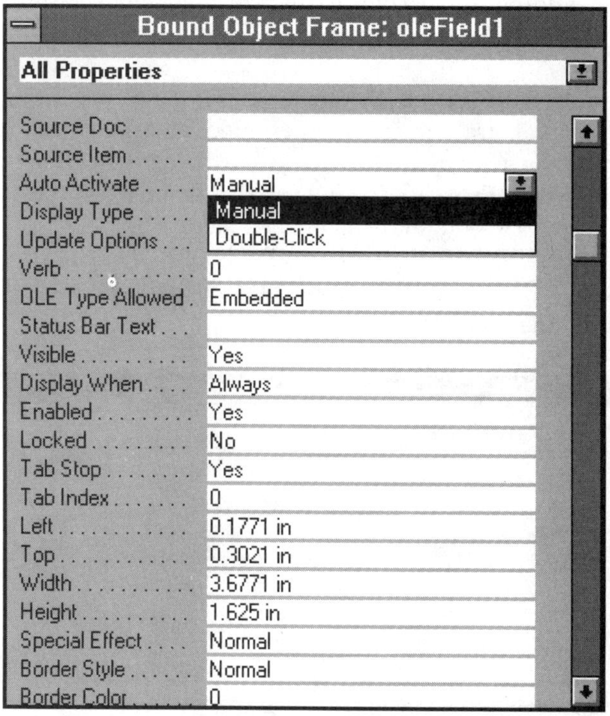

Bound Object Frame: oleField1

All Properties

Property	Value
Source Doc	
Source Item	
Auto Activate	Manual
Display Type	Manual
Update Options	Double-Click
Verb	0
OLE Type Allowed	Embedded
Status Bar Text	
Visible	Yes
Display When	Always
Enabled	Yes
Locked	No
Tab Stop	Yes
Tab Index	0
Left	0.1771 in
Top	0.3021 in
Width	3.6771 in
Height	1.625 in
Special Effect	Normal
Border Style	Normal
Border Color	0

You'll notice that the GetFocus AutoActivate event is not available on this form because the OLE object frame is bound, that is, tied to your database tables. The GetFocus option is only available for unbound object frames. With GetFocus as the event, whenever the user simply single-clicks, tabs to, or otherwise selects the OLE object frame, the object will be activated.

With the default setting, Double-Click, the activate action is kicked off when the user double-clicks the OLE object control. This is typical operation for an embedded object and is what many users will expect of the system.

Access Basic Control Over Inserting OLE Objects

As mentioned before, you can programmatically cause an object to be placed on your form. Without your program controlling the objects, the user must select the frame on your form, then select Edit, Insert Object. You can take control of the process by setting the AutoActivate property of the OLE control to Manual and then adding some code to the form to enable the process as you like.

When you are automating a process such as this and you need to present the user with options that are commonly presented in other applications, it's helpful to present the user with the common dialog box, if it exists, for the operation. In this case, there is a standard dialog box for the insertion of objects, so we'll cover using that dialog box here.

Open the Manual OLE form in the **SAMPLES.MDB** database and you'll be able to follow along with the examples:

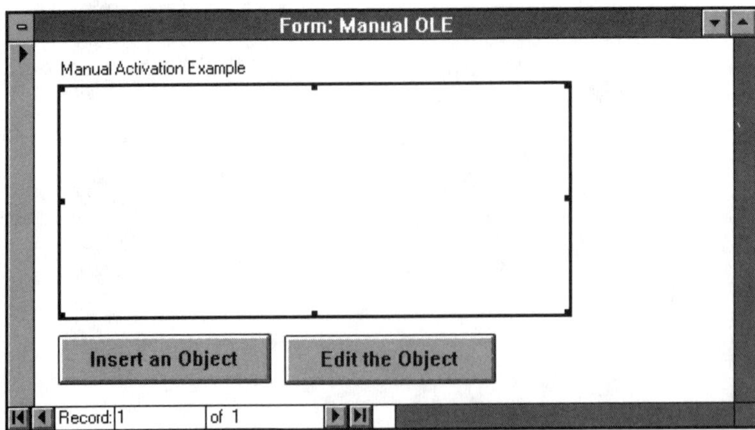

> *If you are manually entering the Access Basic code shown below and not using the **SAMPLES.MDB** database, you'll need to include the **CONSTANT.TXT** file in your modules.*
>
> *Create a new module and load the file called **CONSTANT.TXT** that you can find in **C:\WROX**. The constants discussed below are included in that file and will be required for these examples to work correctly.*

There is a small amount of code behind the two buttons. The most significant code is behind the Insert an Object button. The code is shown below:

```
Sub cmdInsertObject_Click ()
    '
    'allow the user to insert an object in the OLE control
    '
    On Error GoTo cmdInsertObjectERR

    oleField1.OLETypeAllowed = OLE_EMBEDDED
    oleField1.action = OLE_INSERT_OBJ_DLG

    GoTo cmdInsertObjectOKAY

cmdInsertObjectERR:
    MsgBox "OLE Object NOT inserted."
    Resume cmdInsertObjectOKAY

cmdInsertObjectOKAY:

End Sub
```

First, we establish an error handler so that if the user selects this button and then cancels the action, we can keep control in our routine. The routine handles the error by using the **MsgBox** function to inform the user that the routine has been abandoned and that an OLE object hasn't been inserted. The next step is to set up the type of object that can be inserted. The three different options are OLE_LINKED, OLE_EMBEDDED and OLE_EITHER, and are discussed in the table on the following page:

Type of Object	Value	Description
OLE_LINKED	0	Allows only linked objects to be inserted. Embedded objects will not be allowed.
OLE_EMBEDDED	1	Allows only an embedded object to be inserted. Linked objects will not be allowed.
OLE_EITHER	2	Allows both Linked and Embedded objects to be inserted. This is the most versatile method, but allows users to insert Linked objects that can't be edited in place. If this is a consideration, specify OLE_EMBEDDED.

These verbs are used with the Action property when you establish either a new OLE embedded object, or when you activate an existing object. These constants define the type of activation and type of object that will be initiated.

You can also set the property that determines whether the object is displayed as an icon or the picture representation of the object.

Set the DisplayType property of the object to OLE_DISPLAY_CONTENT to show the picture representation of the object and OLE_DISPLAY_ICON to show only the icon. Set this property prior to calling the OLE_INSERT_OBJ_DLG action. These constants can be found later in this chapter, along with a definition of what each of them does.

The next thing we do is to call the OLE handler and ask it to call up the Insert Object standard dialog box. This box is the same box used by other applications and Access itself when inserting linked or embedded objects, OCX's and so on.

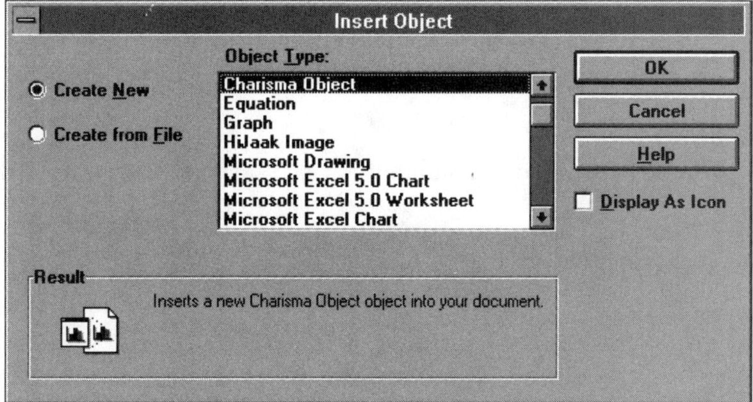

From this box, the user can select the type of object they need to work with in this frame. When the user selects the object, the appropriate server application will be called up to create the object.

When finished with the object, the server application will be shut down and the object will be updated or inserted into the frame control on the form. If the frame is bound to a database, the item is saved to the database.

If the user presses Cancel, or exits the server application without saving the updated object in the frame, the Access Basic error handler will be executed. The user will receive a simple dialog box indicating that an object was not inserted.

The code behind the Edit Object clicked event is shown below:

```
Sub cmdEditObject_Click ()
    '
    'activate the object that the user has inserted
    '

    oleField1.action = OLE_Activate
End Sub
```

Here we ask the object to activate itself and use the server application for the presentation of the user interface and other tools required to work with the object.

One final thing that we've done on the form is to initially disable the Edit Object button. This is because until an object is inserted, you can't edit it. So, in the property sheet for the Edit Object button, be sure to set the Enabled property to 'No'.

Next, set up the following code behind the Update event for the OLE frame:

```
Sub oleField1_Updated (Code As Integer)
    '
    'Turn on or off the edit button, depending on
    'whether there is an object in the control
    '
    If oleField1.OleType <> None Then
        cmdEditObject.enabled = True
    Else
        cmdEditObject.enabled = False
    End If
End Sub
```

You won't want to enable this button until there is a valid OLE object in the form's control. If you examine the OLEType property of the control, it will contain one of three numbers; 0, 1 or 3 corresponding to OLE_LINKED, OLE_EMBEDDED or OLE_NONE. By checking for OLE_NONE, we'll know whether to turn on the button. If the property is OLE_NONE, you should disable the button; otherwise, it should be enabled.

These properties relate back to the type of control that you previously have to appear on the form. If you recall, you can specify Linked, Embedded or Either. The values here pertain to the resulting object once it's been placed on the form.

> *This can be a bit confusing as there are 2 properties relating to the OLE type. The OLEType property can be LINK, EMBEDDED or NONE and determines how the OLE object is going to be used. The OLETypeAllowed property can be LINK, EMBEDDED or EITHER and is used when you first establish an OLE object to tell the system what types of action should be supported.*

Using Access Basic to Insert Specific Objects

You can imagine that, if you provide users with full capabilities to insert any type of object, you are giving them a double-edged sword. In some cases, this flexibility will be appreciated, while in other cases you will need to specify exactly what type of object will be inserted.

You may even want to use a file on disk as a template for the object about to be inserted. An example of this might be where you have a standard form for managing information about an account. You would want to make sure the users always use that same form when initiating a new account.

Next, we'll go through how to do this in a simple example and then we'll show how it's implemented in the PIM.

First, open the **SAMPLES.MDB** database and open the Automated OLE form. This form, similar to the form in the Manual OLE examples above, has two buttons, Insert New Object and Edit Object:

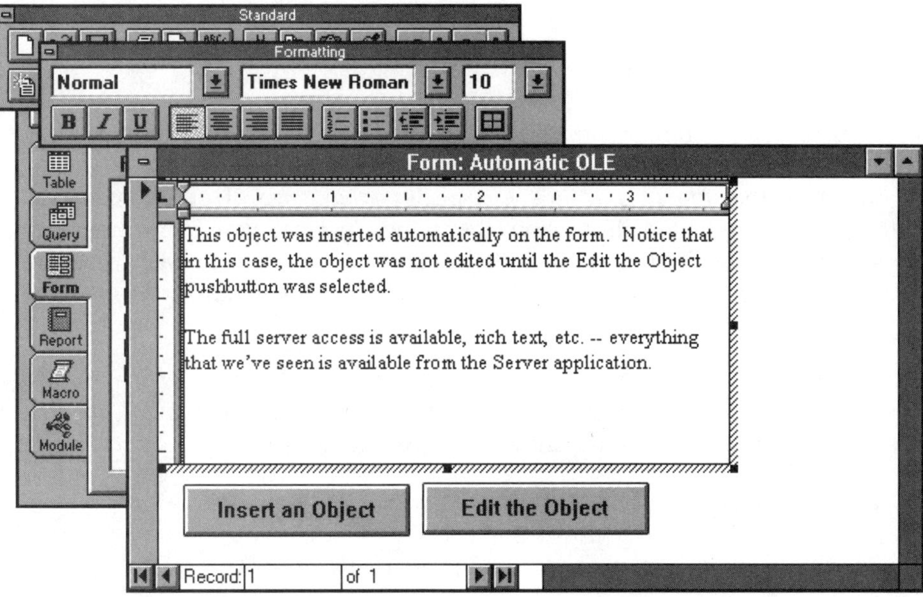

The only difference between this form and the Manual OLE form is behind the Insert an Object button. Instead of using the standard insert dialog box, we're specifying the type of object directly.

Here's the code that's behind the Insert an Object button:

```
Sub cmdInsertObject_Click ()
    '
    'Insert a new Word object on the form.
    '
    On Error GoTo cmdInsertObjectERR
```

```
    '
    'set up the object for the type of object we want
    '
    OLEField1.Class = "Word.Document.6"
    OLEField1.OLETypeAllowed = OLE_EMBEDDED
    OLEField1.SourceDoc = ""
    OLEField1.SourceItem = ""
    OLEField1.Action = OLE_CREATE_EMBED
    OLEField1.SizeMode = OLE_SIZE_ZOOM

    GoTo cmdInsertObjectOKAY

cmdInsertObjectERR:
    MsgBox Error$ & Chr$(13) & "OLE Object NOT inserted."
    Resume cmdInsertObjectOKAY

cmdInsertObjectOKAY:

End Sub
```

All of the necessary details about the object are provided in this code.

The first item, the **Class**, is where we specify what type of object we want to insert. Going back to the discussion about the Registry, you may remember that the class (NOT the CLSID) is the English text name given to each discrete entry in the Registry. This entry must tie back to one of those names.

To make your system truly generic, you should probably set the object class to a non-version specific entry. As an example, our entry specifies Word.Document.6, which potentially limits us to Word 6.

In a production ready database, you may want to simply specify Word.Document, allowing the Registry entry cross references to make the translation to the most current release on the system.

The OLETypeAllowed ties back to the OLE_EITHER, OLE_EMBEDDED or OLE_LINKED constants. These allow you to specify the type of link between your object and its source. This will be either the object itself in the case of an embedded object, or the file on disk in the case of a linked object.

If you specify embedded and provide a SourceDoc name, the file you specify will be used to create a 'template' for the object. The document will be called up as a starting point for the object, but when the object is saved, the document on disk will not be updated. Instead, the object will be saved back to your application's OLE object container.

`OLEField1.SourceDoc` represents the name of the document with which to link, or the name of the document to use as a template in the case of an embedded object. If you leave this blank, as an empty string, it will allow the user to start with a new document.

SourceItem will vary depending on the application that you use as your server. In Word, this entry can be left blank. In Excel, you can use it to specify a cell range.

> *Remember, if you are working with Excel, its native cell reference format is R1C1 type entries. Therefore, if you need the range A1..C10, you will specify R1C1:R10C3.*

Setting the Action property calls the OLE engine and tells it you want to embed an object (OLE_CREATE_EMBED). Alternatively, you could set the action to OLE_CREATE_LINKED and create a linked object. Since we've specified all the other values that the OLE engine needs, the object will be inserted without user intervention.

Here's a list of the options that can be used as the Action that is called when you work with the object:

Constant Name	Value	Description
OLE_CREATE_EMBED	0	Use to create an embedded object. Remember to first set the control's OLETypeAllowed and Class properties.
OLE_CREATE_LINK	1	Use to create a linked object. Remember you must first set the control's OLETypeAllowed and Class properties.
OLE_COPY	4	This action will copy the object onto the clipboard, placing all information about the object, it's related files (if any) and server information on the clipboard.

Continued

Constant Name	Value	Description
OLE_PASTE	5	Once an object is on the clipboard, this action will allow you to copy it into your application. As with the create operations, you need to first set the control's OLETypeAllowed and Class properties.
OLE_UPDATE	6	Useful for linked objects, this action will retrieve an updated image from the server application that supplied the object and displays that data as a graphic representing that data in the control.
OLE_ACTIVATE	7	Activate the object, invoking the server application. This is the same thing as a user double-clicking the object. Remember, if you programmatically insert an object for the user, you must activate it before they'll be able to use it.
OLE_CLOSE	9	Close the object and its connection to the server application.
OLE_DELETE	10	Delete the object from the OLE control. Until any underlying tables are updated, the object remains in the database table.
OLE_INSERT_OBJ_DLG	14	Calls up the standard Insert Object dialog box, allowing the user to specify what type of object is to be placed on the form.
OLE_PASTE_SPECIAL_DLG	15	This action requests the dialog box that is normally invoked when Paste Special... is selected from the Edit menu.
OLE_FETCH_VERBS	17	Queries the Registry for information about the verbs applicable to the object. Remember, the first verb, in location 0, is the default verb.

The final statement, setting SizeMode, determines how the item will be displayed in your OLE frame. This will depend largely on what type of data you are trying to display.

The types of SizeModes are:

SizeMode Setting	Notes
OLE_SIZE_ZOOM	This is useful if you need to see the entire contents of the object in the frame you've provided. An example of this is where you want to show a Word document. You would probably not want the text to scroll off the edge of the frame.
OLE_SIZE_CLIP	This will only show the portion of the object that will fit in your frame. If the object is larger than your frame, some of it will not be shown.
OLE_SIZE_STRETCH	The object will be sized to fit your frame, both in width and height. This would be appropriate for graphs or other primarily non-text types of information.

You'll notice one more difference between this method of inserting the object and the manual method. The difference is that, while the object is embedded in your container application, the server is not invoked. You will have to select the Edit Object button to activate the object and begin working with it. With the manual method, or in cases where the user is selecting Edit, Insert Object, the server is automatically activated at the time the object is inserted.

With this in mind, if you're going to automate the object insertion for your application, make sure you also activate it after you've inserted it. Otherwise the user won't think anything has happened because the server will not be invoked.

Implementation Details using OLE 2

The following sections will go into some detail about working with OLE 2 objects. Where possible, we'll contrast the OLE 2 implementation with its predecessor. These sections will cover some of the newer capabilities that may be useful in your applications.

OLE Compound Documents

With OLE, the concept of **Compound Documents** was born. Compound documents are those whose contents consist of one or more embedded objects. With Word, for example, you can embed an Excel spreadsheet and see the results right there on the Word document's screen:

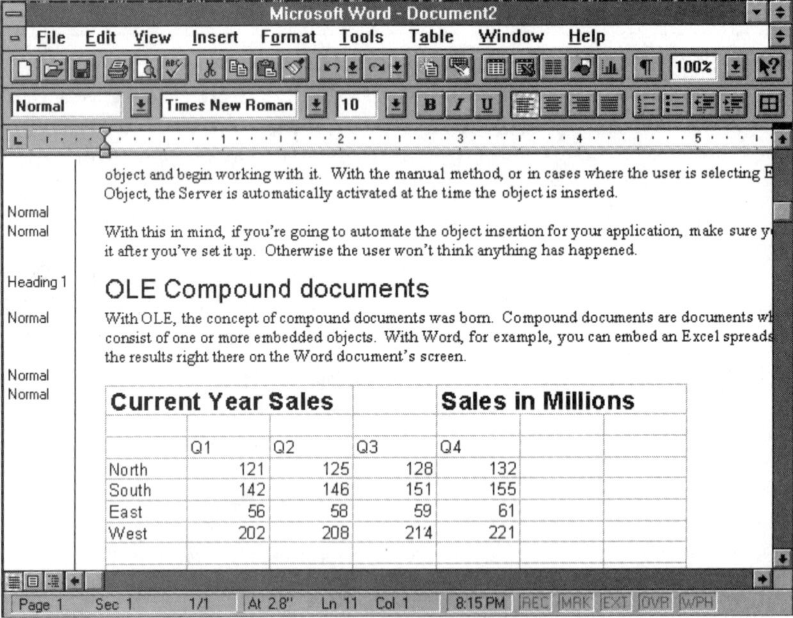

It's important to note that the term 'Compound Document' does not refer only to text-based documents. Microsoft's vision of the desktop is one of objects that are intelligent and which can be nested within each other. The starting point for this is the document. You'll increasingly be hearing spreadsheets called 'spreadsheet documents'.

The standard used for creating objects and controlling the communications between them is the OLE Component Object Model. It is in place to allow different components of applications the capability to maintain what they are good at, be it a spreadsheet, a text-based document or drawing object.

Considerations with Linked Objects

One of the possible challenges with an implementation of OLE involves the use of Linked objects. If the source file is moved, the process of updating the links to the new location of the object is manual at this point. In future versions of Windows, a start will be made to remedy this problem using a system of automated updates of this link information.

If you want to see how links are maintained in the application, try starting a new document in Word. Insert a picture into the document and select the linking option:

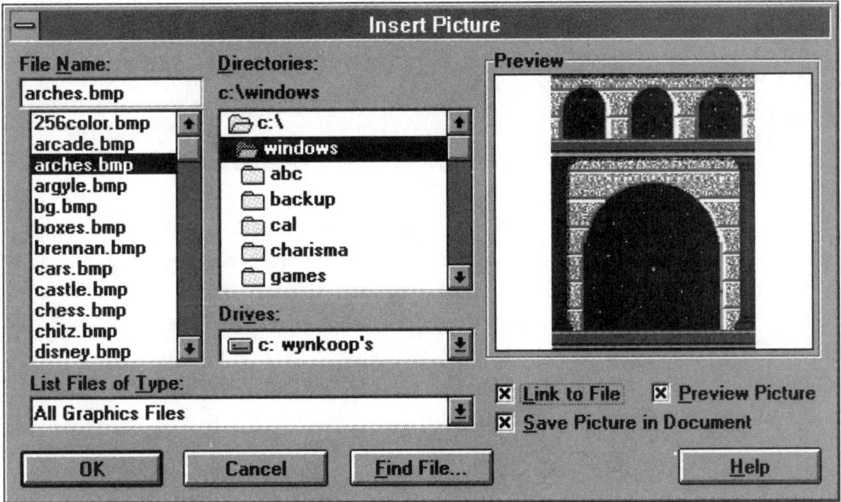

Once you have returned to the document, you'll see that the picture is properly inserted. Note that with compound documents, you can save enormous amounts of disk space by linking objects rather than embedding them. Linked objects are simply maintained by reference. Embedded objects are filed with a formatted data stream of the actual information needed to create the object. In an Access database, this can increase the size of your database and tables exponentially.

A good experiment to try with your application is to create one database with a linked object and one with an embedded object as columns. Set up the forms as we've done earlier and add some records to each table. Comparing the size of the tables, you'll see what a difference embedding an object can make in storage requirements.

Call up the link editor from the Edit menu and take a look at the links currently sent up in the document:

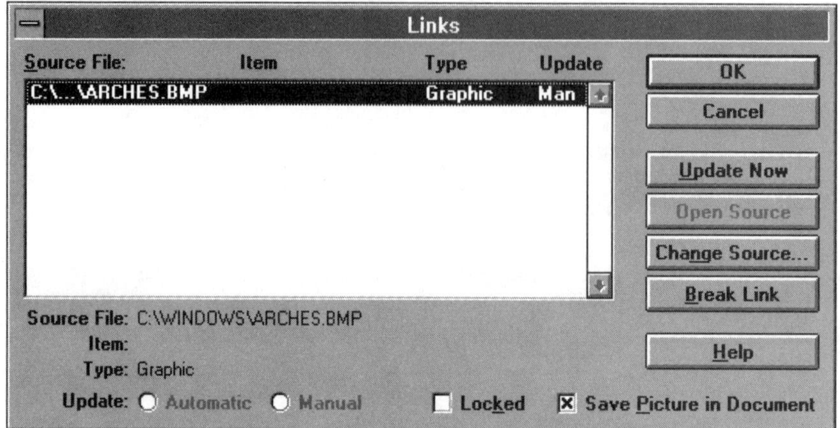

You can see that the source for the object is maintained with a full path specification. If you change the location of this file, you'll need to come into this dialog box and update the location with the Change Source option. In Access, the OLE Object field's Object property contains the object source. In the case of the Linked object, the property will contain the call to **GetObject("<<object>>")** with a full file and path specification. This is the item that will need to be updated if the source object's file is moved.

The OLE 2 standard now allows for the implementation of nested or 'Compound Documents'. The levels of nesting are not technically limited, but you may run into some practical limitations when working several layers deep in major applications like Word and Excel.

Some of the New Features of OLE 2

There are several new features included in the OLE 2 object model. Some of these capabilities are illustrated here.

Property Inheritance

Property inheritance is another new feature of OLE 2. Property inheritance refers to the capability of some OLE 2 objects to use the container application's environmental settings with their embedded objects. For example, if you are creating a document that contains worksheets and graphical information for a presentation, it may make the document more polished if the same font is used throughout. This font would be used for the spreadsheet, graph captions and so on.

Not all OLE objects support this capability, but you can expect this to become the standard as more of the capabilities of applications are pushed into OLE objects and inter-operability is emphasized.

Sub-Document Automation

A container application can now have visibility into all types of objects that are contained within it. For example, suppose you have an Excel spreadsheet with an embedded additional sheet. If you select the spell check option, or some other spreadsheet-wide type function, Excel will be able to apply the request to the sub-documents as well.

This is powerful when combined with the spell-checking, searching and formatting capabilities of the server application.

Object-Server Version Control

With OLE 2, the objects can now contain information about the version of the server application used to create it. This provides the key to the server being able to automatically prompt the user if the object should be converted to a newer release of the object.

There may be cases where an upgrade to a more recent version is not desirable. For example, if an organization is implementing the newest version of a word processor, it may be better to wait until everyone has received the upgrade to update the objects on the system. The new objects may not be compatible with the older release.

Determining Valid Actions and Verbs

When you work with automation objects, you'll constantly be searching for information about the actions and verbs that apply to the object server. The best place to look for this information is the documentation and on-line help files provided with the server application.

Your application can, however, determine what verbs are valid for most objects. Remember, the verbs are the actions that can be taken against the object, some of which include Open, Edit and so on.

The **SAMPLES.MDB** database contains an form, Determine Object Verbs, that will show exactly how this is carried out:

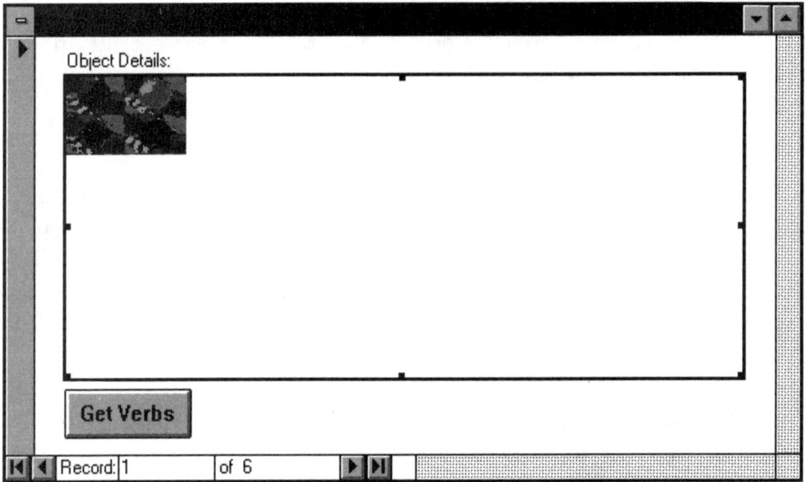

From this screen, use the record navigation keys to select the object you want to query, then select the Get Verbs button. Examples of objects to search for could be the Paintbrush demonstration and the Word document demonstration, both of which are included in the form. To see a new object, move to the end of the database, insert a new object, then choose the Get Verbs button:

The dialog boxes that return the information on the object show not only the number of verbs, but each of the verbs as well.

You'll notice that one more verb than the number indicated is actually returned. In other words, in our example above, 'Edit' would be shown twice. A property of an OLE object is its default verb. The default verb for an object is in location zero (0) of the list of verbs. For this reason, you'll always get the first verb twice when reviewing the verb results.

Open the form in design mode and you'll be able to see the following code behind the Get Verbs button:

```
Sub cmdGetVerbs_Click ()
    '
    'Routines to return the various verbs associated with the
    'object that is on the form.
    '

    On Error GoTo cmdGetVerbserr

    'set up the count and string to return the verb
    Dim I, VerbFound

    'call the object, asking what verbs are available
    OLE1Field.Action = OLE_FETCH_VERBS

    'tell everyone how many verbs we have
    MsgBox Str$(OLE1Field.ObjectVerbsCount - 1) & " verbs retrieved."

    'show off each of the verbs
    For I = 0 To OLE1Field.ObjectVerbsCount - 1
        VerbFound = OLE1Field.ObjectVerbs(I)
        MsgBox VerbFound
    Next I

    GoTo cmdGetVerbsokay

cmdGetVerbserr:
    'there was a problem, show the error message, get out
    MsgBox Error$
    Resume cmdGetVerbsokay

cmdGetVerbsokay:

End Sub
```

The first thing we do is to set up our variables and error handling. Next, we call the object, in this case **OLE1Field**, and select the **OLE_Fetch_Verbs** action. This action will query the Registry for the verbs that are registered for the given server application.

Next, we show the user how many verbs were returned and then put up a separate dialog box for each of the verbs that were returned. Remember, the first verb returned from position zero, is the default verb. The default verb is the one that is used if no specific verb is selected when the object is activated.

You can use this information when programmatically activating objects. In the above case, if you wanted to activate **OLE1Field** with a specific verb, you can set the verb to one of the values shown below:

Constant	Value	Description
VERB_PRIMARY	0	Select the default verb.
VERB_SHOW	-1	Edit the object.
VERB_OPEN	-2	Edit the object, use a separate server application window.
VERB_HIDE	-3	Only for embedded objects, this action will hide the server application that created the object when the object is activated. This can be useful if you want to embed a sound bite in your application. If you want to play it back for the user but don't want them to see the application playing the sound behind the scenes this verb will do the trick.
VERB_INPLACEUIACTIVATE	-4	For embedded object, this call will activate the object for editing, within the OLE control on the form if possible. Menus are included in the activation.
VERB_INPLACEACTIVATE	-5	For embedded object, this call will activate the object for editing, within the OLE control on the form if possible. Menus are **not** included in the activation.

When you call an OLE object and activate it, you must first specify the **.Verb** property. This indicates which of the above verbs you want to use. Finally, set the OLE controls **.Action** property to OLE_ACTIVATE.

Our Implementation in the PIM

For the PIM included with this book, we've implemented the OLE objects for the notes fields on the Contact Details and Company Details forms. We want to automate the insertion of the objects for the user when new records are created.

In addition, we want to incorporate the use of a template as a starting point when a new record is created. This template will prompt the user for basic information about the contact.

> *If you installed the sample databases and contact manager software to a directory other than* **`C:\WROX`**, *you'll have to change the path designation below as needed. Simply update the* SourceDoc *line, showing the new directory. The file* **`WROX.DOT`** *should be in the directory you specify.*

You may recall that to create an object based on a template on disk you must specify the SourceDoc when you set up the object for embedding. If you indicate a SourceDoc when you are creating a Linked object, the file will become the object that is referenced by OLE. In our case, we want to use **`WROX.DOT`**, located in **`C:\WROX`** as our template. Here is the Contacts Information Form:

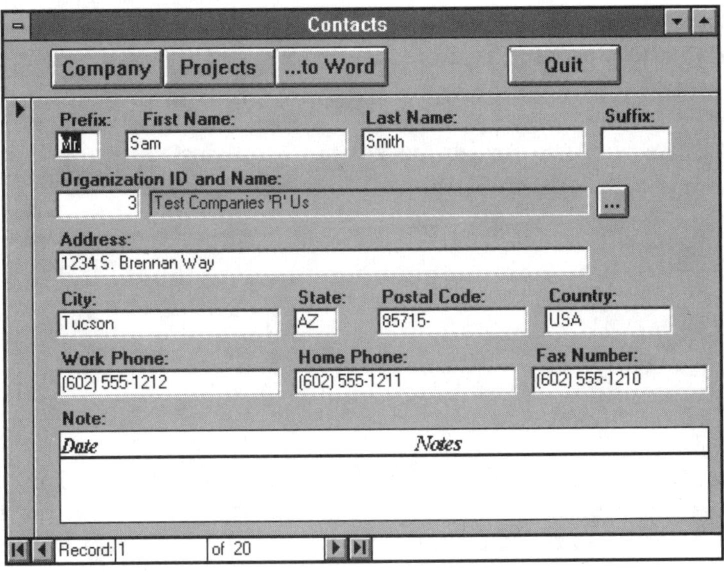

On this form, we've removed the Min and Max buttons and the scroll bars by changing the entries in the property sheet.

> *If you set the min/max buttons property to 'No' and then switch to run mode in the designer, the min/max buttons may still appear. Close the form, open it from the tab dialog and the buttons will be updated correctly. This is also true of the control box on some forms.*

Notice that the Note: box now contains both Date and Notes headings. This is because the object embedded in the OLE control was based on a Word template that allows us to start with this information already entered.

Here's a look at the **WROX.DOT** template:

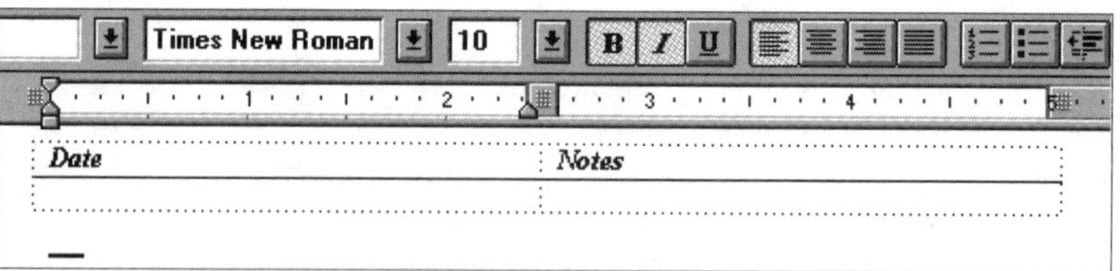

The template simply sets up a table with two columns and allows for the entry of dates and descriptive notes. In the PIM application, we've modified a few procedures to support the added automation of formatted data entry when adding new contacts to the system.

In the Find Form, the Add Contact button now contains the following code:

```
Sub AddContact_Click ()
    '
    'load the contact form, blank, and allow
    'the user to add a new record.
    '
    gAdding = True
    DoCmd OpenForm "contact details", , , , Add

End Sub
```

We've added a reference to the globally declared variable, **gAdding**. This variable is going to be a flag for the Contact Details form to tell the form when we're adding records from the initial search screen.

To implement the global flag, open the PIM's AB Module and add the following line to the General/Declarations section:

```
Global gAdding As Integer 'flag as to whether we're adding a new record
```

By declaring the variable in the module, it becomes global in scope and will be available between forms. Most importantly, the variable will remain in scope between the searching form and the Contact Details form.

> *There are three levels of scope that can be applied to a variable and it is this level that determines which procedures the variable is available to. If a variable is declared in a procedure then it is only available to that procedure. If it is declared in the declarations section of a module or form using the* **Dim** *statement then it is available to any procedures in that module or form. If it is declared in the declarations section of a module using the* **Global** *statement then it can be used by any form or module in the database.*

In the Contact Details form, for the Form Load event, add the following code:

```
Sub Form_Load ()
    '
    ' update the company name
    '

    If Not gAdding Then
        DoEvents
        UpdateCompanyInfo
    Else
        '
        'first, set back the global variable signifying that
        'we're adding.
        '
        gAdding = False
        '
        'Insert a new Word object on the form.
        '
        On Error GoTo FormLoadERR

        '
        'set up the object for the type of object we want
        '
        Note.Class = "Word.Document.6"
        Note.OLETypeAllowed = OLE_EMBEDDED
        Note.SourceDoc = "C:\WROX\WROX.DOT"    'set up the template
        Note.SourceItem = ""
```

```
        Note.Action = OLE_CREATE_EMBED
        Note.SizeMode = OLE_SIZE_CLIP

        MsgBox "You can now enter the new contact information.  You will ↵
            be using Word to edit the contents of the Notes field."

        GoTo FormLoadOKAY

FormLoadERR:
        MsgBox Error$ & Chr$(13) & "Could not set up Word object for the ↵
            new contact record."
        Resume FormLoadOKAY

FormLoadOKAY:

    End If
End Sub
```

This code is an enhancement to the code previously discussed. Before this point, the routine simply attempted to update the company information. We will still execute that same procedure if the **gAdding** flag is not set to 'True'. The check for the flag is the basis for the **If...then...else** construct of the routine.

In our case, if **gAdding** is 'True', we want to set up the form with blank fields. This is done by the calling routine specifying the **Add** parameter on the **DoCmd OpenForm** command. We've also decided that we want to establish the OLE control as a Word object, embedded in our database.

The first step is to set the **gAdding** flag back to 'False' so we can use it again in the future. Next, establish the error handler, just in case. This will be handy if you find you don't have Word loaded on the system after you execute this code.

> *As an important experiment to test your understanding, try changing the name of the object that you want to embed. If you change it to something that is not on your system, you'll get an idea of what to expect if a user tries the application with a server application that is not available.*

Next, we set up the class for the object. This is the Registration database entry that will be cross referenced to the object. Next come the specifics of the object. Setting OLETypeAllowed to OLE_EMBEDDED prevents a user from accidentally inserting a linked object.

The SourceDoc entry is where we're specifying the starting point for our object, which is a Word template, located in **C:\WROX** and entitled **WROX.DOT**. In the case of Word objects, SourceItem does not apply (by Microsoft's design), so you can leave it blank. You should, however, still specify that you want it blank, instead of ignoring the property. If garbage is in this property, you may receive an error from the OLE automation layer when it receives something it's not expecting.

The final step to creating the object is a call to the OLE engine to create and embed the object. We do this by setting the **Action** to OLE_CREATE_EMBED. The OLE engine will establish the new object, using the file as the template.

> **If you have not loaded in the** CONSTANT.TXT **file, you may receive a message that you can't embed an object in a field where Linking is specified. This is because the constants you're designating in the routine are undefined. If you get this message, File, Load Text the** CONSTANT.TXT **file into a new module and retry the operation.**

The last thing that we have to do is specify the sizing and viewing option for the object. This is something that takes some experimentation and you should try each of the different options to get a feel for what the results will be. The option is set by changing the SizeMode property of the OLE object:

Normal Picture

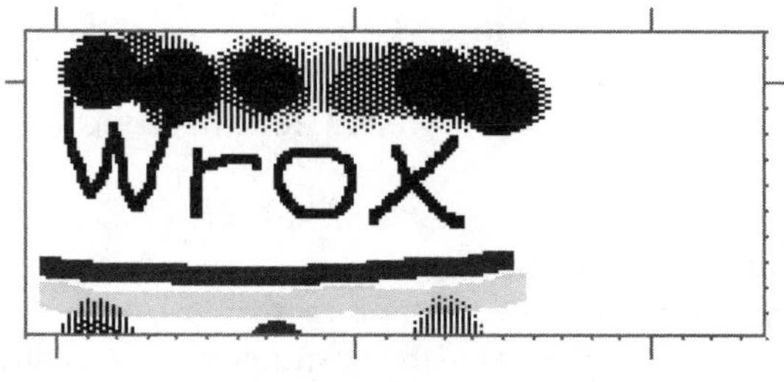

Clip

This is like a window onto the original picture - the clipped image will be the same size as the original and will show only what fits into the OLE frame that you've put on the form.

Stretch

The original image is stretched or compressed to fit the size of the OLE frame. In this case it has been stretched horizontally but compressed vertically.

Zoom

The original image is zoomed in or out to fit the OLE frame but note that the image is not stretched. The horizontal and vertical components have the same proportions as the original image.

We've added the call to the `MsgBox` routines so that we can notify the user that they are ready to go and that they'll be using Word to take notes on the account. Remember, if you don't activate the object, OLE will simply set up the references for the OLE control and then return you to your container application. If you want to automatically start the object when it's created, you'll also have to call the OLE_ACTIVATE action and specify verbs if necessary.

Using Notepad (OLE 1) to Edit Information

As an experiment, and to show the differences between the OLE 1 and OLE 2 implementations, this section will show how to modify the code given above to use the Windows Notepad for the editor rather than Microsoft Word.

In some cases, it may not be desirable to use a full-blown server application to edit an object because of memory constraints or processor speeds. In these instances, you may want to turn to a smaller application, like Notepad, to implement the same basic functionality, without the OLE 2 'glitz'.

From the code behind the Form Load event for the contact details screen, make the following changes:

```
...
'set up the object for the type of object we want
'
Note.Class = "txtfile"
Note.OLETypeAllowed = OLE_EMBEDDED
Note.SourceDoc = "" 'set up the template
Note.SourceItem = ""
Note.Action = OLE_CREATE_EMBED
Note.SizeMode = OLE_SIZE_CLIP

MsgBox "You can now enter the new contact information. You will be using ⏎
    Notepad to edit the contents of the Notes field."
...
```

Now, when this object is created, notepad will be called on to create or edit the object. In many cases, the user may have a favorite text editor. By using the `Note.Class` of `Txtfile`, you'll allow the Registry to be used to determine the editor that should be called on for this object.

Using the Object Packager to Create OLE Objects

Normally, you'll be inserting objects that are created with an OLE server. What do you do if you want to insert an object that is not associated with an OLE server? This might apply to a bit-mapped image, a sound bite or some other data, and so Microsoft's Object Packager was created with just this goal in mind.

The Object Packager is a way to create an OLE wrapper around an object. It provides the activation information necessary to work with the object in an OLE environment.

Another pertinent consideration is that of storage space. You can use the Object Packager to optimize storage space and scan times for the database as long as only the icon of the embedded or linked item is acceptable.

The storage space advantage comes from linking objects to files on disk; if they are not inserted in the database, they will only take up space on disk, not in the database. The scanning speeds are helped by the fact that the only thing that needs to be displayed for the object is its icon. Since the entire image of the object is not required, displaying only the icon can significantly decrease the wait times when scanning the database.

Embedded Objects Using the Object Packager

First, it's important to understand that there's no real difference between the use of a straight embedded object and an embedded object created with the Object Packager. The Object Packager will create the same relationship information to the object and the object will be stored in your database the same way. The one difference, and possible disadvantage, is that if you look at the database with the datasheet view, the OLE object column will read Package, rather than the name of the OLE Server application, as is normally the case.

On your form, inside the OLE control, you'll have the icon for the server application you set up for the object, but not the contents of the object as in our previous examples.

Using the Clipboard to Paste the Package Into the OLE Control

In this example, we'll use the Windows clipboard to paste the package into your OLE control. First, call up the **SAMPLES.MDB** database, then select the Embedded Object Experimentation form. Single-click on the OLE object and then press *ALT-TAB* until you have the Program Manager back on the screen.

Let's assume that you want to put a graphic, a .BMP file, in your OLE control. This section will explain how this is accomplished using the packager and Window's cut and paste technologies.

First, call up the Object Packager from your Program Manager. Once you've called up the Object Packager, you can use it to create the link and embedding information you need.

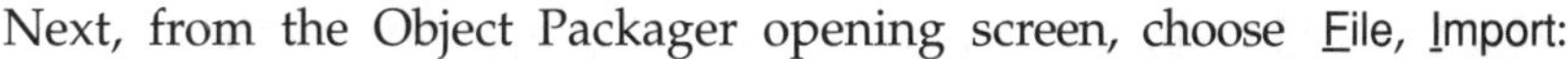

Next, from the Object Packager opening screen, choose File, Import:

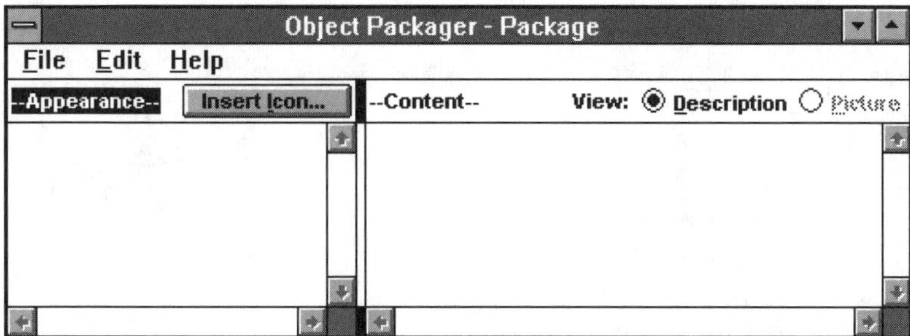

For our example, let's embed the **`ARCHES.BMP`** file from the Windows subdirectory. The file is a bitmap image of the arches provided as a Windows wallpaper alternative. After you've selected the file, the Object Packager will update the display to show the object and any associated applications, which in this case is Paintbrush:

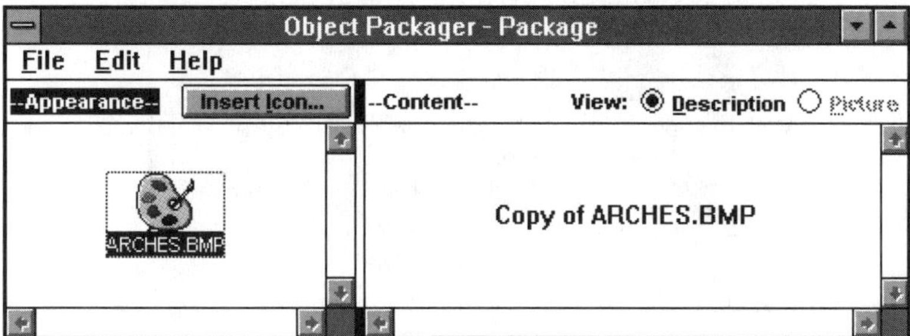

Next, choose Edit, Copy Package. This will copy the fully-formed package to the clipboard, ready for insertion into your Access database table.

Finally, *Alt-Tab* back to your Access application. Choose Edit, Paste Special to bring the object into your application. Access will prompt you as to the method of showing the object in your application. You'll have the option of displaying the item as an icon or a picture of the icon:

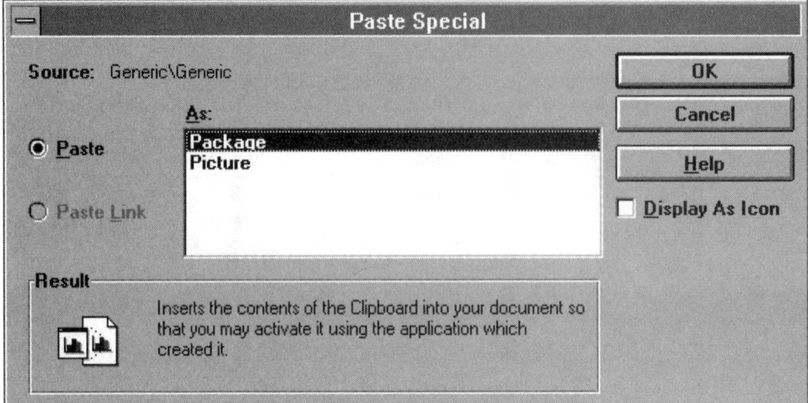

If you do choose to insert the object as a picture from the dialog, and then double click on it, you'll get a dialog box indicating that the operation is not valid for the object. This is because the object is not really an embedded object, but only a picture of the embedded object's icon:

The icon that will appear is that of the object that you imported into the Object Packager:

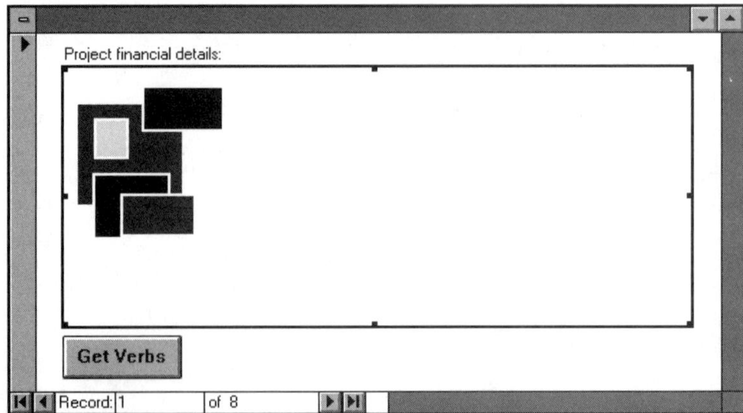

Directly Inserting Object Packager Objects into an OLE Control

In this section, we'll discuss using the Object Packager to provide the means of inserting an object into the OLE control much the same as we would any other object. With this use of the packager, very little differs in functionality from a standard embedded object; you can still edit the object by double-clicking, from program code and so on. The only difference is that it will be displayed as an icon as opposed to a picture of the objects contents.

The first step is to call up the Embedded Object Experimentation form in our **SAMPLES.MDB** database. Select a record in the table and then single-click the OLE control on the form. Next, choose Edit, Insert Object.

> *As is always the case with the OLE control, instead of choosing Edit, Insert Object, you can right-click the control and select Insert Object. The same operations will take place.*

The resulting dialog, as we've seen before, allows us to choose the type of object to insert. If you scroll down the list, you'll see an entry titled Package. Select this entry by double-clicking it:

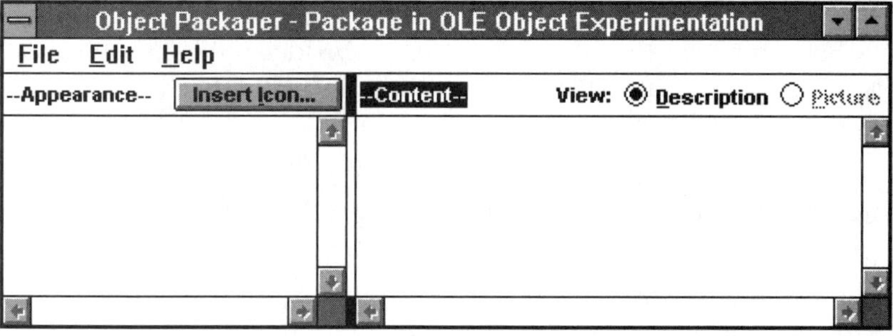

From here, as in our prior example, choose File, then Import. Select the file you want to reference in the package. For our example, again select the **ARCHES.BMP** file from your Windows subdirectory.

Finally, select the File menu. There is now a different option called Update. This option will save the contents of the object you've created back to the Access form.

One of the great features of OLE 2 is the ability to Drag and Drop OLE objects. We'll use this section to show off this feature. Find the ARCHES.BMP file and drag it to the Object Packager window.

Note that you'll have to put it into the right-hand pane, the content pane, of the Object Packager. You can easily tell where you can drop something simply by the shape of the icon that you are dragging. It will turn to a No sign (a circle with a line through it) whenever you are over a zone that does not support the release of the current object.

Once you drop the object on the contents pane, Object Packager will figure out that it's a Paintbrush object and get the icon for you. Finally, select the update or the exit option to save your object back to Access.

Drag and drop is one of the cornerstones of Windows '95, so you can begin to take advantage of this functionality in your applications today.

Whether you embedded objects by way of the clipboard or by the standard insert object means, if you double click the object, Paintbrush will be called up to edit the object. Notice in the caption of the Paintbrush window that the 'file' being edited will begin with a designation of '**~PKG**.' This is the temporary file where the object is saved so that it can be edited. This will be the case when you are editing any type of embedded object created with the Object Packager. This changes when the file is a linked file through the Object Packager, as discussed next.

Using the Object Packager to Insert Linked Objects

As we've seen above, you can use the Object Packager to provide the 'wrapper' functionality for a non-OLE-compliant object that you want to work with in your application. In some cases, you will want to use the Object Packager to create and maintain Linked objects.

First, call up the Embedded Object Experimentation form from the **SAMPLES.MDB** database if it is not already loaded. Once again, single-click the OLE control.

Select Edit, Insert Object as we did in our previous examples. However, this time minimize Access behind the Object Packager. This is not necessary, but it will make it easier to see what we're doing next. Start File Manager and select the Windows subdirectory.

Find the ARCHES.BMP file and select File, Copy then select the Copy to Clipboard option in the copy dialog box. This will copy the reference to the file onto the clipboard, thus beginning the linking process.

From the Object Packager, select Edit, Paste Link. You'll notice in the Object Packager that the contents pane will read 'Link to file...' indicating that only a link is established, not a copy of the file. As an experiment, try selecting Edit, Paste. Now the contents pane shows 'Copy of ...' and indicates that it contains an actual copy of the object, or in other words, it's embedded. Select Edit, then Paste Special to return to our linked object. Finally, choose File, Exit and answer 'Yes' when prompted as to whether to update the Access form.

These examples have shown how you can use the Object Packager to create OLE objects. This applies in cases where an object is not OLE compliant, or where you have a need to speed up processing of database scans by the user. Remember to use the Object Packager only in those situations where knowing or seeing the contents of the object is not important as only the icon will be shown.

For more information about OLE, be sure to check the appendices. In addition, the Microsoft Office Developer's kit, along with several third party references are available specific to the applications that you're using.

Comments and Suggestions

In this chapter, we've looked at the properties and actions available to OLE objects and shown how to reference these in your Access Basic code. We've shown you some more examples of how to implement OLE and developed our PIM application. We've also looked at some of the differences between OLE 1.0 and OLE 2.0 and looked in depth at the Windows Object Packager.

In the next chapter, we'll show you three specific examples of using OLE with other Microsoft packages: MSGraph, Word and Excel. This will emphasize one of the main goals of OLE; to use an application for its primary design function.

Practical OLE Implementations

With the appearance of Microsoft Office in shops around the world, the computer industry was given a glimpse into the future of application integration. Lotus and WordPerfect were quick to follow suit, thus putting more applications into the hands of end users, for a significant reduction in price. Now the users are beginning to demand the compound documents that the industry has been talking about for years. OLE is one possible answer, and a look at practical implementations of this technique will open up your developmental efforts.

What's Covered in This Chapter

This chapter has been created to provide you with three specific code samples that you can re-use in your applications. In addition, explanations of alternatives and suggestions for other uses of these routines are included.

The techniques we will examine are:

- Using Microsoft Graph to display information
- Using Word to spell check text in an Access form
- Using Excel to perform calculations on data in an Access table

Each of these sections is included with separate modules containing the code that makes them work. Each section will specify what modules, constants, files and other resources are required for its use.

Chapter 4

How This Chapter Impacts Our Application

This chapter is not directly tied to our PIM application. Portions of different functionality are implemented partially or completely in our application, but the overall goal of this chapter is to provide a set of stand-alone routines that you can re-use in your own applications.

Introduction

In the previous chapters, we've gone into detail on how to implement OLE in your applications. You'll recall that this can be done in two different ways. The first method enables you to link or embed objects directly into your database tables, while with the second method, you can use the features of OLE Automation together with those of OLE Automation Servers, thereby extending the functionality of your program by using that of other applications.

> **Before working with OLE Automation or OLE objects to any great extent, it's always a good idea to back up your registration database. The file REG.DAT is located in your `\WINDOWS` subdirectory by default and can be copied easily to a backup subdirectory or other location where it can be kept safely. While many OLE Automation components are quite safe, system configurations make it nearly impossible to predict the outcome of every operation on every users' system.**
>
> **When an OLE object 'breaks', it could corrupt your registration database. If you haven't taken precautions it can be a lengthy process re-installing your various software packages to rebuild the OLE registration entries required for them to run.**
>
> **As you work with and install different OLE objects, make periodic back ups of your registration database as a safety measure.**

When you are linking and embedding objects, you are creating database entries. This chapter will provide guidance and examples that will help when you need to incorporate OLE Automation in your application. Examples included here relate to Excel and Word, although these techniques will also apply to things like creating graphs, word art objects, as well as using other commercial packages that are OLE 2.0 compliant. All of these can be used with your forms, as editors with database values, interfaces with other applications and so on. Our goal in this chapter is to provide you with some samples that you will be able to put to use immediately.

These examples are all found in the **OLETOOLS** database, installed in your **C:\WROX** subdirectory. If you specified a different directory when you installed the accompanying disk, the database will be located in that directory.

> *In most cases, it's a good idea to automatically include* **CONSTANT.TXT** *in your application. This file, located in your Access subdirectory, provides system-level constants that are likely to come in handy as you develop your applications. If you don't include it, there may be cases when your application behaves unexpectedly when you specify an action or some other type of function based on these constants.*
>
> *To include this file, select the* Modules *tab in the Database window, then click* New. Select File, then Load Text. *From the resulting dialog box, select the* **CONSTANT.TXT** *file from the* **ACCESS** *directory and click the* Merge *button. This will copy the file into your new module. When you close the window, Access will prompt you for a name for the module.*

Using Microsoft Graph OLE Automation

The Microsoft Graph OLE Object provides a good demonstration and experimentation point between a simple embedded object and a fully-utilized OLE Automation Server. In this section, we'll investigate a few of the options you have available to you when working with the MSGraph server from your Access Basic program code.

To show how some of these options work, you'll need to work with the **SAMPLES.MDB** database. In addition, if you have the Access Developer's Toolkit or any other OLE object browser, it will come in handy when you investigate additional things you can do with the server objects.

Our example includes a graphic, based on a cross-tab query, and four buttons. There is also a text box control, allowing the user to modify the title of the graph. The text box is also used to show the ChartType ID when we use the Cycle Graphs button.

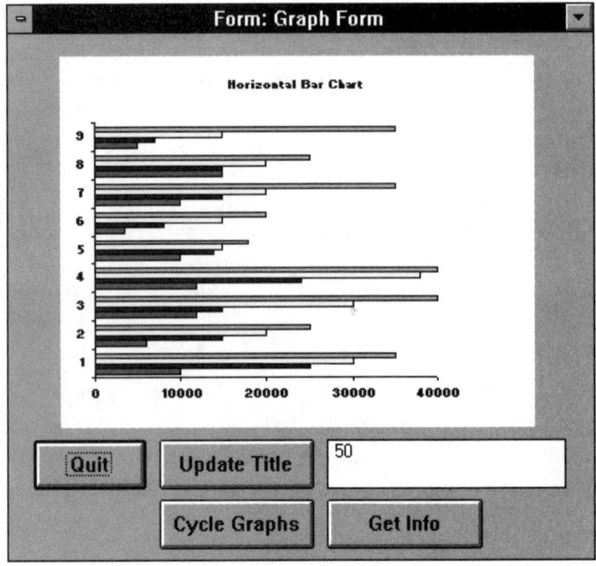

In the examples here, the values aren't particularly important. The point is to display the graph, show how to work with the server to determine characteristics of the graph and how to set new values for it.

When you work with an embedded OLE server, you will be referencing the object by starting with the object name on the form. To set up the examples, here's a look at the objects and their corresponding name property:

Object	Name
Quit button	cmdQuit
Update Title	cmdUpdateTitle
Get Info	cmdGetInfo
text box	txtNewTitle
Cycle Graphs	cmdCycleGraphs
graph	Embedded_Graph

The initial basic form was created using the Form Wizard's Graph form capabilities. When you start the Form Wizard, select Graph from the list of available form types:

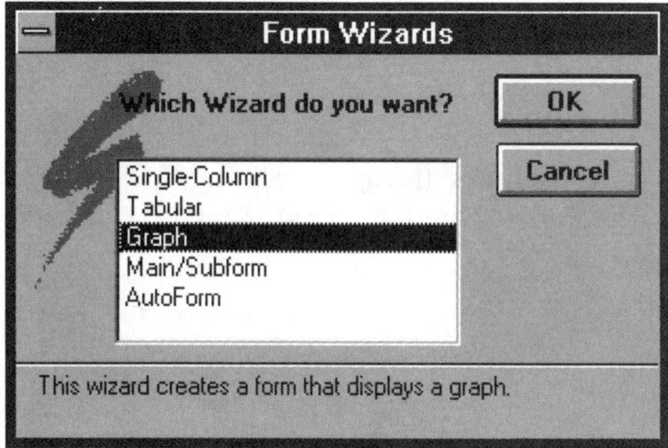

This will create a form that contains a single graphic, using the MSGraph OLE server. In our case, we specified the Sales Goals_Crosstab1 query as the source for our graph. The results of the query are shown below and provide a nice source of information for three-dimensional graphs.

Employee ID	1991	1992	1993	1994
1	10000	25000	30000	35000
2	6000	15000	20000	25000
3	12000	15000	30000	40000
4	12000	24000	38000	40000
5	10000	14000	15000	18000
6	3500	8000	15000	20000
7	10000	15000	20000	35000
8	15000	15000	20000	25000
9	5000	7000	15000	35000

Setting and Retrieving Chart Properties

Once the wizard has completed the form, you'll have to add the buttons and text box controls as outlined above. There are three functions implemented behind the form. The **Quit** functionality implements our standard close command by using the **DoCmd** command from Access Basic. This closes down the form and returns the user to the database dialog box:

```
Sub cmdQuit_Click ()
    'exit the form
    DoCmd Close
End Sub
```

Next, the Update Title button allows the user to enter text to change the title or caption of the graph. The code behind the **cmdUpdateTitle** button is as follows:

```
Sub cmdUpdateTitle_Click ()
    'This routine experiments with modifying the
    'graph's caption/title.  It uses OLE automation
    'to work with the OLE server providing the
    'graph capabilities for our form.

    'The txtNewTitle text box cannot be empty (Null)
    'or this routine will exit with a message box.
    If IsNull(txtNewTitle) Then
        MsgBox "You must supply a new title."
        Exit Sub
    End If

    'Check to see if the title is the same as the
    'new title, if so, let the user know and exit.
    If [Embedded_Graph].Object.Application.Chart.ChartTitle.Caption = ↵
            txtNewTitle Then
        MsgBox "New title is the same as the old title!"
        Exit Sub
    End If

    'Refer to the object by using the Embedded_Graph
    'control on the form, update the title.
    [Embedded_Graph].Object.Application.Chart.ChartTitle.Caption = ↵
        txtNewTitle
    MsgBox "Title updated."
End Sub
```

The first sections of the code checks whether or not there is actually any work to do. If the user has left the txtNewTitle text box blank, or if the new title matches the current title on the graphic, we indicate that there is no work to do and exit the routine. If these items are provided, we continue with the routine, calling the server object to update the title to the new value. When you set the caption, the OLE server will update the drawing on the form. You should be able to see the change to the graph title even before the message box is displayed indicating success.

Three MSGraph Properties

The next button on the form is the Get Info button. This provides some interesting functionality to demonstrate how to query the object. We inspect all of the 'Has...' properties of the MSGraph object to determine different information about the current graph. There are only three, but they are some of the most commonly referenced objects or properties. The three properties are:

- HasTitle
- HasLegend
- HasAxis

Inspecting these properties will tell you a bit more about the graph object and its current state. The code behind the **cmdGetInfo** button is shown next:

```
Sub cmdGetInfo_Click ()
    'This routine inquires into the status
    'of several elements of the Graph as it
    'is now displayed.  This information is
    'provided back to the user.

    Dim Graphic As Object
    Dim Results As String

    'Set up the reference to the embedded OLE server object
    Set Graphic = [Embedded_Graph].Object.Application.Chart

    'Retrieve the information
    Results = "Title? " & IIf(Graphic.HasTitle = True, "True", "False") ↵
        & Chr$(13)
    Results = Results & "Legend? " & IIf(Graphic.HasLegend = True,       ↵
        "True", "False") & Chr$(13)
    Results = Results & "Axis? " & IIf(Graphic.HasAxis = True, "True",   ↵
        "False")

    MsgBox Results
End Sub
```

In this routine, we establish a reference to the object by 'Dimming' a variable and setting its value to the **Embedded_Graph.Object.Application.Chart** object collection. Once we've done this, we can refer to the **Graphic** object rather than specifying the fully qualified reference to the object.

The only step left is to evaluate the different properties we're interested in. By using the IIF statement, we can accomplish both the testing of the value and the return of the results string, all in one step.

The format of the IIF statement is:

```
IIF(Test,<True Value>,<False Value>)
```

If 'Test' is true, then the function returns whatever is specified as <True Value>. In our case, this is the word 'True' since we're testing a Yes/No field. If the test fails, the value in <False Value> is returned. Again, since our case involves Yes/No type fields, we provide the word 'False' as the return value for this case.

The routine results in a message box indicating the values of the different properties:

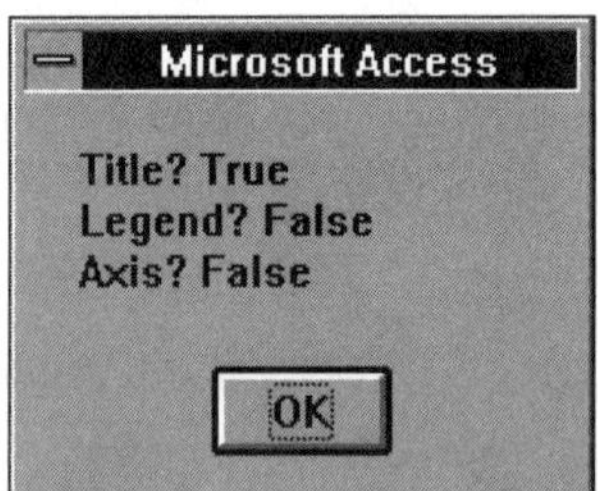

You can address any property or method related to OLE servers in this manner. The biggest challenge you face is in finding what the names of the methods and properties are and how to work with them. There are many different OLE browsers available; we reviewed one of them earlier when we looked into how you can review the objects that reside on your system. You may recall that they are really browsers on the Registration Database, and they allow you to see what capabilities and options exist for the servers and OLE objects on your system.

Browsing Chart Types

The demonstration form will also let you inquire into all available formats supported by the graph server. The Cycle Graphs button will allow you to incrementally go through all ChartTypes from 1 to 50. Initially, the Chart object will support 17 graphic types. The table on the next page shows the different types available, and their associated TypeID:

TypeID	Description
1	Layered Area Chart
2	Horizontal Bar Chart
3	Vertical Bar Chart
4	XY Chart
5	Pie Chart
6	Doughnut Chart
7	Radar Chart
8	XY Chart
9	3D XY Chart
10	3D Horizontal Bar Chart
11	3D Vertical Bar Chart
12	3D Horizontal Line Chart
13	3D Pie Chart
14	3D Surface Area Chart
15	Area Chart
16	Area Chart
17	Horizontal Bar Chart

When you run the **CycleCharts** process, the Access Basic code walks through the ChartTypes, displaying each as it goes. There is also a supporting table, Chart Types, that contains the TypeID and description (shown above) for each chart type supported by the graph object. If the type is found in this table, the caption is automatically set to the descriptive name of the chart. Here's a look at the code behind the **cmdCycleGraphs** button:

```
Sub cmdCycleGraphs_Click ()

    'This routine walks through the different graphs
    'supported by the Graph object.  If the graph ID is
    'found on file, the title of the chart is updated
    'with the description.  If the chart is not known, a
    'dialog box is displayed allowing the user to enter
    'a description of the chart type.
```

```
    Dim Graphic As Object
    Dim db As Database
    Dim tb As Table

    Set Graphic = [Embedded_Graph].Object.Application.Chart
    Set db = CurrentDB()
    Set tb = db.OpenTable("Graph Types")

    On Error GoTo ExitSub

    tb.index = "TypeID"

    For i = 1 To 50
        txtNewTitle = Str$(i)

        On Error GoTo clickerror
        DoEvents
        Graphic.type = i
        On Error GoTo ExitSub

        tb.Seek "=", i
        If Not tb.NoMatch Then
            Graphic.ChartTitle.Caption = tb("Description")
        Else
            DoCmd OpenForm "graphdetails", , , , , A_DIALOG
            tb.Seek "=", 1
            If Not tb.NoMatch Then
                Graphic.ChartTitle.Caption = tb("Description")
            Else
                Graphic.ChartTitle.Caption = "Unknown Graph Type"
            End If
        End If
        DoEvents

resumehere:
    Next i

AllDone:
    Exit Sub

clickerror:
    Resume resumehere

ExitSub:
    Resume AllDone

End Sub
```

There are several different things that are accomplished by this routine. Of primary importance is the ability to review the code used to set the type of graph that is shown. Since the OLE object will generate an error if a graph type is not supported, the **On Error** logic will simply allow the routine to continue looking for the next valid ID. We are not using **On Error Resume Next** because we want to skip over the statements that set the title for the chart.

If the chart type ID is valid, we look up the chart ID in the database. If found, the title of the chart is set to the description in the database. This will let us know which type of chart we're reviewing.

If the chart type is unknown, we prompt the user for the information about the chart. The GraphDetails dialog box prompts the user for the ID and description for the chart. This information is saved in the supporting Graph Types table for future reference:

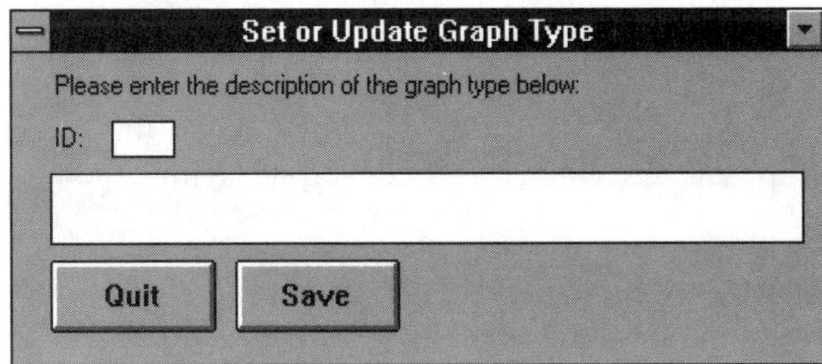

Using this code as a starting point, you can begin experimenting with these and other properties of the graph server. As a MSGraph developer, you'll need to become a lot more familiar with the different properties and methods available to you relative to the chart object. To find these out, use the object browser, described in the next section.

Additional Information about the Graph Object

The Office Developer's Kit includes an object browser that you can use to investigate the MSGraph object. This browser will show you the different things you can do, and it illustrates the **HasTitle**, **HasLegend** and **HasAxis** properties using it:

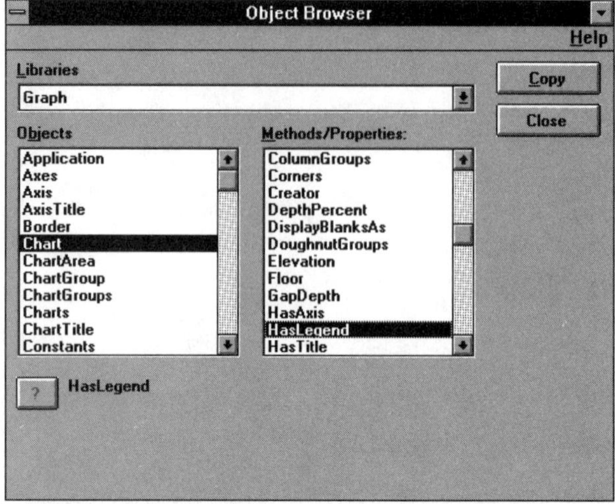

Sometimes, a help file is also available for OLE compliant applications. You can generally find these in the Windows directory, or in the directory established specifically for the application you're concerned with.

> **For the Windows applets like MSGraph, MSDraw and others, you should be able to find them in the `MSAPPS` directory under the `WINDOWS` subdirectory. Each applet is in its own directory in this area and help files are included in the directory. In some, but not all cases, you can find additional help about the object in these help files.**

Using OLE servers in this manner allows you to experiment a bit with a very visual object. Notice that you're working with an object embedded in a form. There really is no 'interface' to the object itself; it must be part of another application. In fact, if you try to start the **`MSGRAPH.EXE`** program, you'll receive a message that indicates that it may only be run from within another application.

The more complex and functional types of server stands alone and operates without the use of a user interface provided by your application. Word and Excel are examples of these types of applications and are explained next.

Using Word to Spell Check Text from a Text Box Control

One of the earliest benefits of computer based word processors was the capability to provide spell checking for documents. This was a real help to users and probably one of the key factors in persuading people to switch from typewriters to the predecessors of today's word processing systems.

In your applications, you'll often have the situation where you want to provide a text box for users to enter information into your system. The text box is useful because it uses the standard Windows navigation and editing capabilities and provides a good way to control how users will be presented with information.

This section will show how you can use the spell checker in Word to check the text that is displayed in an Access text box. We'll examine what happens on both the application and server side of the functions and how these suggestions might be best utilized in your applications.

> **Note that these examples were created with Word version 6 and will require modifications for versions prior to this.**

Overview

Since there are two main components to this functionality, Access and Word, you need to make sure that they can talk to each other. By this, we mean that the applications must be able to pass data back and forth and must be able to return error conditions if things go wrong. In Word, we can do this by creating **Document Variables** either from within Word itself, or with code in Access.

We will use Access Basic code to step through the contents of a text box and send each word individually to Word using the **`SetDocumentVar`** and **`GetDocumentVar`** commands. Word will then check the spelling and return an indication of whether it is spelt correctly and, if it is not, a list of suggestions.

To do this we need to provide a macro in Word to carry out the spelling check and return the results. We also need a series of functions and Access code to handle each word in turn. This code will be responsible for retrieving and displaying the results returned by Word.

The Word Macro

In the **C:\WROX** subdirectory, there is a text file called **DOSPELLC.TXT** that contains the macro code that you'll have to install. After the macro has been successfully executed, it will have checked the spelling of the word that is passed and, if it is misspelt, the macro will return a list of possible replacements.

This listing shows the macro code:

```
Sub MAIN
    'WROX Spell Checking Macro
    'Revolutionary Guide To Microsoft Access 2.0

    'First, create an array to put the words in that need to be
    'checked. Change the dimensioning of this array (currently 50
    'if you need to allow for more suggested replacement words

    Dim WordsList$(50)

    'In our Access code, we set the text to check to a variable for
    'WordBasic to work with. We tell WordBasic to retrieve this
    'variable and use it as the word to check.
    SpellCheckWords$ = GetDocumentVar$("txtProofingText")

    'Go out and check the spelling of the words; the number
    'of replacements for a possibly misspelled words is
    'returned by the ToolsGetSpelling function. If there
    'are no suggestions it returns -1
    PossibleMisSpelled = ToolsGetSpelling(WordsList$(), SpellCheckWords$)

    'Change the array back to a string, we need to store it for Access
    'to be able to retrieve it.
    SuggestionList$ = WordsList$(0)

    'Loop through and make our suggestion list if any misspelling
    'possibles were found.
    If PossibleMisSpelled > 0 Then
        For i = 1 To PossibleMisSpelled - 1
            SuggestionList$ = SuggestionList$ + Chr$(13) + WordsList$(i)
        Next i
    End If
```

```
    'Set up the return variables for Access to retrieve.
    SetDocumentVar "SpellSuggestions", SuggestionList$
    SetDocumentVar "NumSuggestions", Str$( PossibleMisSpelled)

    'Return to Access
End Sub
```

One important thing that you'll need to know when you're using these routines is that Access can't pass in a word to check directly. Apart from command properties, there is no concept of parameters. For example, you can't just say 'CheckIt ('terrific')' to have Word check the spelling of 'terrific'. For this reason, you must do several different things to first pass your word to the automation engine, and then reverse these steps to retrieve information from the engine.

Word's New Feature

A way around this is to use a new feature of Word that allows us to create variables within the document as mentioned earlier. These variables can be created by our calling routine and text can then be assigned to them. We then code the macro so that it knows the name of the variable and can retrieve the item we want to pass in to the process.

We'll put our word that we wish to be proofed into the Word variable **txtProofingText**. This will be established and initialized by the Access code shown later in this section. The first portions of our Word macro initialize the variables we'll need to hold the suggestions, and then retrieves the word to check from the Word variable.

Next, the ToolsGetSpelling macro is invoked, passing in the word to check and an array structure to hold the suggestions it returns. If you look in the Word Basic Help file, you'll see that other options exist that pertain specifically to the use of the user's custom dictionary, anagrams and so on, but they are outside the scope of our demonstration here. Should you need to modify the behavior of this macro, your changes may impact other properties and options associated with the ToolsGetSpelling command.

The final thing we do in our Word Basic macro is to loop through the possible replacement words (if any) and place them all in one string, because we can't return an array to Access using **SetDocumentVar**. The replacement words are separated by a return characters (**Chr$(13)**). Since we are using document variables to pass information between our applications, we'll take this string and associate it with a new Word variable, **SpellSuggestions**. Our Access Basic code will retrieve the results from this variable when processing returns to our Access procedures.

To create the macro, start Word and from the main document window, select Insert, File and then select the **C:\WROX\DOSPELLC.TXT** file. This will load the file into your current document. Next, copy the entire macro to the clipboard by selecting Edit, Select All, followed by Edit then Cut.

Creating Word Macros

The final step is to create the macro from the text you just brought in. Select Tools and then Macro. When prompted for a name, type DoSpellCheck and then select Create. Next, select Edit, Select All. Finally, select Edit, then Paste. This will paste the contents of the clipboard, the macro we imported earlier, into the macro window. Close the window and exit Word.

Your Word system has been updated with the DoSpellCheck macro and is now ready to work with Access in providing spell-checking services to your application.

> *To confirm that Word has loaded your macro, from within Word, go to the Tools menu and then select Macro. The resulting dialog box will show the macros currently on your system, including the DoSpellCheck macro you just installed.*

Setting up the Access Functions

From previous chapters, you're already familiar with creating controls on an Access form. For the first example, create a form with a text box and two buttons, as shown below:

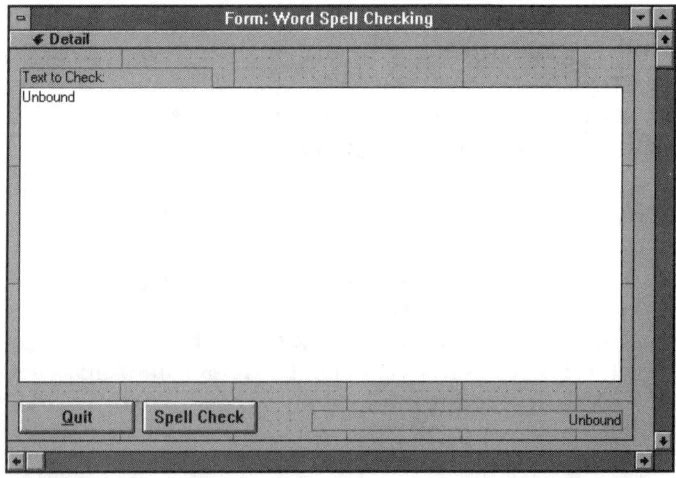

These examples are located in the **OLETOOLS** database, located in the **C:\WROX** subdirectory. Apply the following names to the different controls:

Control	Name
Large Text Box	txtProofingText
Quit Button	cmdQuit
Spell Check Button	cmdSpellCheck
Unbound text box, lower right corner	txtNumWords

Next, put our regular Quit button code in the **Click** event for the **cmdQuit** button:

```
Sub cmdQuit_Click ()
    'exit the form
    DoCmd Close
End Sub
```

This code simply closes the form and returns the user to the tabbed database window.

If you want to quit Access completely when Quit is selected from an application, substitute **DoCmd Quit** *for the* **DoCmd Close** *command above.*

Next, place the following code in the **Click** event for the **cmdSpellCheck** button:

```
Sub cmdSpellCheck_Click ()
    'Call our routine to check the spelling.

    'Set up the variables
    Dim sTemp As String
    Dim iStatus As Integer
    Dim iNumCorrected As Integer

    'To check the spelling in some other application, text box,
    'etc., copy this code to your application, along with the
    'module and replace "txtProofingText" below with your text
    'string that you want to check.  Be sure to update or remove
    'the references later to txtNumWords, or add a control to
    'your form to allow for these user informational messages.
```

```
    'Assign the text to check to our temporary variable sTemp.
    'To prevent an error when the text box is empty we check for
    'a NULL value first and exit if found.

    If IsNull(txtProofingText) Then Exit Sub
    sTemp = txtProofingText

    'Get the number of words that we'll be checking
    'and place it on the form to tell the user
    txtNumWords = Str$(NumWords(sTemp)) & " words."
    DoEvents

    'call the spell checking routine. This is an Access
    'function located in the database. It is described next.
    iNumCorrected = CheckSpelling(sTemp)

    'Trim off the period, add a comma, and let the user know
    'the number of possible mistakes.
    txtNumWords = Left$(txtNumWords, Len(txtNumWords) - 1)
    txtNumWords = txtNumWords & ", " & Str$(iNumCorrected) & " possible ⏎
        misspellings."

End Sub
```

As a courtesy to the user, this routine tells the user the number of words we're going to check. It then calls our **CheckSpelling** routine, passing in the string to check which is stored in the variable **sTemp**. To use this routine for your own software, simply change what's being assigned to the **sTemp** variable, which is the temporary variable that is used to hold the text to be checked.

CheckSpelling Returns

The **CheckSpelling** routine, located in the Do Spell Check module, will return the number of questionable words found in the document. It also displays a dialog box indicating when a word is possibly misspelt and showing the possible alternatives:

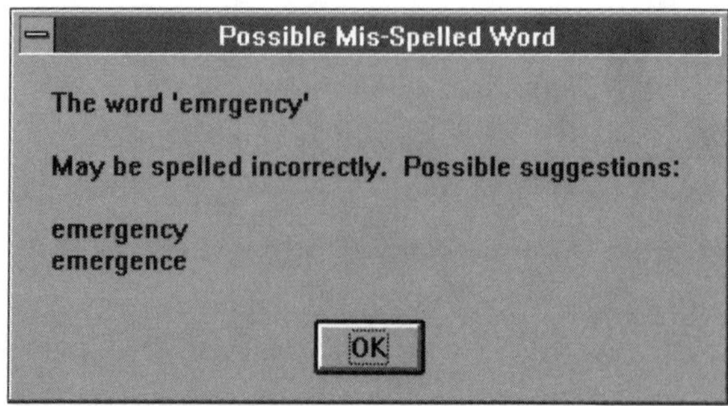

The code to accomplish the rest of the spell check relies on three routines. These functions, **CheckSpelling**, **NumWords** and **GetWord** are located in the Do Spell Check module in the Access database.

The following listing shows the code for the **CheckSpelling** function:

```
Function CheckSpelling (what As String) As Integer

    '- - - - - - - - - - - - - - - - - - - - - - - - - - - - - -
    'NOTE:  You MUST have installed the DoSpellCheck macro
    'in Word prior to running this procedure.
    '- - - - - - - - - - - - - - - - - - - - - - - - - - - - - -

    'Function to check the spelling of the string passed in
    'as the parameter 'what', and return the result to your
    'application in the form of a string.

    'set up a status flag and misspelled word counter.
    Dim Status As Integer
    Dim iBadWordCount As Integer
    Dim i As Integer

    'set up our 'working' and return strings
    Dim sWork As String         'Item to send to Word for checking
    Dim sReturned As String     'List of possible replacement words
    Dim sNumReturned As String 'No. of replacements sent from Word

    'Dim and set up the OLE object for Word
    Dim Word As Object
    Set Word = CreateObject("Word.Basic")

    On Error GoTo CheckSpellingErr

    'next, in order to pass the string to Word, we set up a
    'variable in a new document.  So first create a new document
    '(using File, New) and then create a variable and associate
    'the incoming string with it.
    Word.FileNew

    'You can only check a word at a time.  Loop through the words provided
    'in the text string, 'what', until done. Provide a dialog as necessary.

    'NumWords returns the number of words, based on the spaces in the
    'string. It is another Access function, and is described next.

    iBadWordCount = 0

    For i = 1 To NumWords(what)
        'Function returns the i'th word in the string passed in.
        sWork = GetWord(i, what)

        'send out the word to check.
        Status = Word.SetDocumentVar("txtProofingText", sWork)
```

```
        'check the word
        If Status = True Then
            'Call the Word macro, DoSpellCheck, to complete the
            'spell check.
            Status = Word.ToolsMacro("DoSpellCheck", 1)

            'The macro places the results of the spell check into
            'the Word variable named "SpellSuggestions" and the
            'number of suggestions into 'NumSuggestions'. If the
            'word is mis-spelled and there are no suggestions it
            'returns -1, or 0 if the word is correctly spelled.

            sReturned = Word.[GetDocumentVar$]("SpellSuggestions")
            sNumReturned = Word.[GetDocumentVar$]("NumSuggestions")
            If sNumReturned = "-1" Then sReturned = "No Suggestions"

            If Val(sNumReturned) > 0 Then
                iBadWordCount = iBadWordCount + 1
                MsgBox "The word '" & sWork & "'" & Chr$(13) & Chr$(13) ↵
                    & "May be spelled incorrectly.  Possible suggestions:↵
                    " & Chr$(13) & Chr$(13) & sReturned, , "Possible Mis-↵
                    Spelled Word"
            End If
        End If
    Next i

    'close down our temporary file.
    Word.FileClose 2

    CheckSpelling = iBadWordCount

    Exit Function

CheckSpellingErr:
    'Ignore a 'no data returned' error.
    If Err = 2779 Then Resume Next

    'otherwise, show the error and exit.
    MsgBox Str$(Err) & " " & Error$
    Exit Function

End Function
```

The routine requires one parameter, **`what`**, which is passed in as a string. This contains all the words that we want to check. The function returns an integer, indicating the number of possibly misspelt words that were found.

First, we set up our local variables and the reference to the Word.Basic automation object. In this example, we've used the **`CreateObject`** method, but you could also use the statement**`GetObject("","Word.Basic")`**. The results are identical; they establish a link between our application and the Word Basic automation engine.

Next, we'll create a new file to work within on the Word side using the **`Word.FileNew`** method. Remember, we'll have to put the word to be spell checked into a Word variable. To do so, we must have a document established even though we won't be directly using it. Our loop cycles through the words in the string, passing each to the engine and checking for returned suggestions.

Using NumWords and GetWord

We use the two functions **`NumWords`** and **`GetWord`**, both of which are explained later in this section, to give us a count of the total number of words in the text and to retrieve a specific word within it. The word that we are checking is placed into a Word variable called **`txtProofingText`** using the **`SetDocumentVar`** method of the Word object. The status returned from the call simply indicates success or failure, and serves as an indication that we can continue or not.

The call is then made to the Word object, specifying the **`Word.ToolsMacro("DoSpellCheck", 1)`** that we've previously installed in Word. The '1' parameter indicates that it's located in the **`NORMAL.DOT`** template.

> **Because of the way Access works, the call to the `ToolsMacro` is expected to return a value as it's referenced as a function. Since no value is actually returned, we've created an error handler that will ignore the 'No Data Returned' error, number 2779. All other errors will be passed through to the user interface with a dialog box.**
>
> **You'll notice that if you specify the call to `ToolsMacro` as the Word reference materials suggest, you'll get an 'end of statement expected' message from the compiler. This can be seen if you substitute**
>
> **`< Word.ToolsMacro "DoSpellCheck", 1 >`**
>
> **for the current**
>
> **`< Status=Word.ToolsMacro("DoSpellCheck",1) >`.**

Once the routine has completed, we retrieve the results from the document variables **`SpellSuggestions`** and **`NumSuggestions`**. If **`SpellSuggestions`** is not empty, we can use the returned list of possible replacement words directly.

However, if there are no suggested replacements, **SpellSuggestions** will be empty even though the word may be misspelt. In this case, the variable **NumSuggestions** returns '-1' so we can set the **SpellSuggestions** variable to the text 'No Suggestions'.

Finally we show a standard message box indicating a possible misspelling and the suggested replacement words. In addition, the incorrect word count is incremented.

To supplement the functionality of this routine, you could create a form that showed the selections available for the misspelt word. A suggestion would be to replace the **Chr$(13)** *in the Word macro with a semi-colon (';') when the string is created. If this is done, the string can be provided as the source for a list box from which a user can make a selection.*

Once the user has selected what he wants to do, such as Replace, *you can use the* **Instr** *function to locate that word and make the replacement in the original text.*

The last portion of the routine closes the Word document without saving it by specifying the '2' parameter to the **FileClose** method. The number of misspelt words is then returned to the calling routine.

The Error Handler

The error handler is provided, as mentioned above, to trap errors caused by Access, when you call the Word automation object. Typically, the only error that will be encountered will be the 'No Data Returned' error, which will simply result in the code resuming at the next line.

The two other functions, **GetWord** and **NumWords** support the spell check routine. You may remember from the macro overview that the macro checks only one word at a time. This means that, in our implementation, we need to make sure on the Access side that we only send over one word at a time.

Note that both of these routines will only work correctly with plain text. If you wish to use them with text containing formatting or other characters you will have to change them to allow for the additional characters.

The **NumWords** routine returns the number of words in the string. The implementation is crude, but it gets the job done quickly, and gives us the information we need in order to know when we're done checking the string.

Here's the listing for **NumWords**:

```
Function NumWords (what As String) As Integer

    'return the number of words in the string

    'set up our local variables
    Dim sWork As String      'our work string
    Dim iCount As Integer    'the counter
    Dim iLoc As Integer      'working location within the string

    iCount = 0
    iLoc = 0

    sWork = Trim$(what)

    'look for spaces in the string, use them as indicators of
    'breaks between words.
    iLoc = InStr(sWork, " ")
    Do While iLoc > 0

        iCount = iCount + 1

        'Get the next relevant portion of the string of words,
        'trimming it down in case our current break consisted
        'of more than one space.
        sWork = Trim$(Right$(sWork, Len(sWork) - iLoc))

        'any more spaces?
        iLoc = InStr(sWork, " ")
    Loop

    'add one to our count to account for the last word.
    NumWords = iCount + 1

    'return to the caller.
End Function
```

NumWords simply counts the number of words by locating spaces in the string and then adds one for the final word. Note that as each segment of the string is analyzed, it is **Trim$**'d. This prevents multiple spaces from causing a problem.

The final routine, **GetWord**, provides the access to specific words in the string. This is what is needed in order to walk down the string, passing individual words to the spell checking routine:

```
Function GetWord (iNum As Integer, what As String) As String
    'return the iNum'th word in the string.

    'set up our local variables
    Dim sWork As String      'our work string
    Dim iCount As Integer    'the counter
    Dim iLoc As Integer      'working location within the string

    iCount = 1
    iLoc = 0

    sWork = Trim$(what)

    'look for spaces
    iLoc = InStr(sWork, " ")
    Do While iCount < iNum
        If iLoc > 0 Then
            iCount = iCount + 1

            'always trim down our working string to catch
            'multi-space strings.
            sWork = Trim$(Right$(sWork, Len(sWork) - iLoc))
        End If
        iLoc = InStr(sWork, " ")
    Loop

    sWork = Trim$(sWork)

    'If we're not on the last word, we'll have to get rid
    'of everything to the right of this one.
    iLoc = InStr(sWork, " ")
    If iLoc > 0 Then sWork = Left$(sWork, iLoc - 1)

    'return the word to the calling routine.
    GetWord = sWork

End Function
```

This routine uses much of the same logic as the **NumWords** routine in determining where word breaks occur. It steps through the text counting words until it comes to the one specified by the calling routine, then removes this from the remaining text. It trims off any spaces and returns the requested word. This routine is crucial in working with our spell checking function which will only support one word passing between Word and Access at a time.

Possible Problems

This technique works well in many circumstances. There will be cases where you need to fine tune your routines. An example of this may be where punctuation marks appear in the text and you want code handles for them.

> **In Word, passing a '?' to the spell checker can be used to request a wildcard search but this is not supported by the macro calling convention used in the automation server.**
>
> **Be sure to check for punctuation in your words as you request spell checking.**

If you pass a question mark to Word, there is a bug that will often cause Word to fault and cause problems in your routines. After several attempts to access Word, you'll receive a message that the Registration for Word, (the Registration Database entries) is possibly corrupt. In fact, it is caused by Word not being able to operate correctly.

What is really happening is that Word is having problems because it was not allowed to gracefully shut down. You'll need to exit Windows to correct the problem. For this reason, you'll probably want to modify the **`GetWord`** function to trim out any punctuation marks for the words that are returned before they are sent to Word.

Using the Sample Application

When you use the application, you are first presented with the form that we've just designed. From here you can type in the text that you want to spell check and select the Spell Check button to start the process.

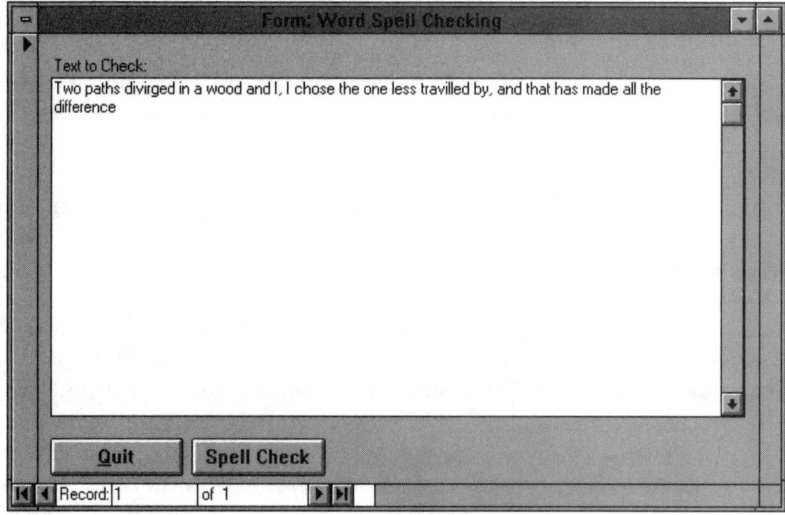

During the process Word will look at each word in your text and tell you if anything is spelt incorrectly and suggest alternatives:

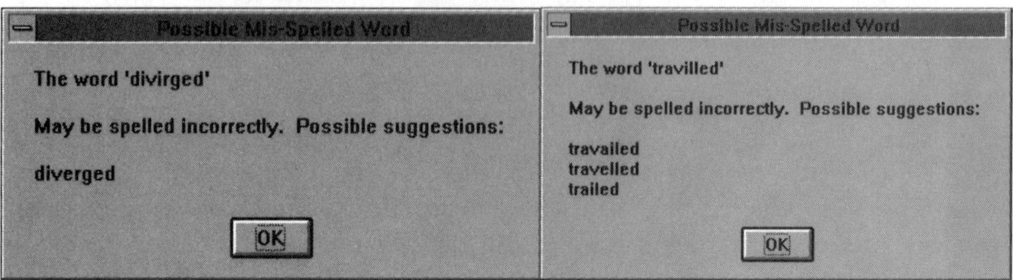

It will continue checking each word in your text until it comes to the end of the text when it will tell you how many words there were and how many possible mis-spellings:

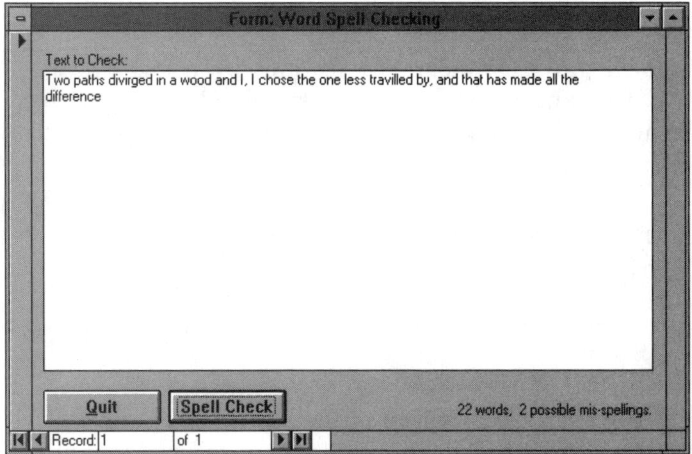

You can see that in our example there are 22 words and 2 possible mis-spellings.

Integrating Access with Microsoft Excel

Microsoft Excel is another application that supports the OLE automation environment and provides a rich set of functions to OLE clients. All of the functionality of Excel is available, ranging from simply placing numbers in a spreadsheet to sophisticated formatting, printing and saving of the information in the spreadsheet format.

In this section, we'll take the contents of an Access table, send them to Excel, add formulas to the Excel sheet to total the columns and then extract the resulting totals back to Access. The form that we'll create to accomplish this also has a status text box that will let you know what's happening every step of the way.

Special Set Up Requirements

You'll need to confirm that the **XLDEMO.XLS** spreadsheet is loaded on your system in the **C:\WROX** subdirectory. If you changed the subdirectory during the installation of the software, you'll need to modify the code behind the Excel button as outlined on the next page.

Setting Up Access

Excel's object model provides integration features by using a layered object model approach. This means that you must tell Excel what you need to work with by providing an object reference that includes a full 'path' to your required object or method.

For example, if you want to work with the spreadsheet values for a given cell, the following code would reference cell A1 (or R1C1):

```
Excel.Cells(1, 1).Value = 100
```

This indicates that we want to work with the object defined as 'Excel' and we need the **Cells Collection**. It also specifies that we want the cell at (1,1), and that the **`Value`** property should be set to 100.

A quick note needs to be made about Objects, Collections and MetaCollections. In the Microsoft Object Model, access to spreadsheets, databases, projects and other system objects is provided through Objects, Collections and MetaCollections. These objects are referenced by walking down a 'relational ladder' to get to the specific instance, item or method that you need to access.

In our example, the fully qualified 'path' to the **`Value`** property is really:

```
Excel.Application.Sheet.Cells(1,1).Value
```

This code provides a full reference to the **`Value`** property for the cell that we need. Typically, the model for object reference is:

```
Object.Collections.Collection.ObjectInstance. Method or
Property
```

The relationships between all of these can be shown as follows:

- Objects can reference multiple collections
- Collections can refer to multiple collection objects
- Collection objects contain references to multiple ObjectInstances, each having their own methods and properties

In Microsoft's specification, 'ObjectInstances' are simply objects. We've added the reference to 'Instances' to further clarify the reference chain.

This hierarchical model is also seen in the Data Access Objects that are implemented in Access. We'll go into more detail about that in a later chapter, but you'll see an example of Access's object model in this chapter when we look at how we read data from a table.

The Microsoft Office Developer's Kit CD contains a full listing of Objects, Collections, Methods and Properties for Microsoft Excel, Project and Access. This could prove to be one of your most valuable tool, if you are going to be developing solutions that heavily rely on these technologies. The combinations of these objects are seemingly endless and the reference materials provided on the CD could give you a tremendously useful helping hand in your development efforts.

You may remember from our previous discussion of OA Servers that you create a reference to the object using the **`GetObject`** or **`CreateObject`** Access methods. These are outlined in more detail below as we review the code in the Excel Experimentation form.

Sample Database Table Setup

Our example takes information from a checkbook transaction-type table and sends this information to Excel. Prior to working with these examples, you'll need to set up the table in Access. We'll be using the Access table Excel Demo to store the information to be sent to Excel. The structure of the table is shown below:

Field Name	Data Type	Description
RowID	Counter	Unique ID for the row
Date	Date/Time	Date the transaction took place
Description	Text	Description of the transaction
Type	Text	Type of transaction
Amount	Currency	Amount of the transaction

Next, enter some sample data into the table. For our simple example here, enter a transaction type of either 'W' for withdrawal or 'D' for deposit. This will be how we determine which column the amount of the transaction goes in when it's placed on the spreadsheet.

The following diagram shows what is in the sample table in the **`OLETOOLS.MDB`** database:

Table: Excel Demo

RowID	Date	Description	Type	Amount
1	10/1/94	Initial Balance	D	$100.00
2	10/1/94	Deposit	D	$1,103.45
3	10/2/94	Electric Company Pmt	W	$124.30
4	10/2/94	Water Company	W	$24.25
5	10/2/94	Car payment	W	$400.00
6	10/2/94	Groceries	W	$101.56
7	10/5/94	Dinner out	W	$10.50
8	10/6/94	Dues at club	W	$5.00
9	10/10/94	Babysitter	W	$20.00
10	10/11/94	Paying off Sam's bet	W	$10.00
11	10/15/94	Deposit; paycheck	D	$1,103.45
12	10/16/94	Night on the town	W	$45.00
(Counter)				$0.00

Record: 1 of 12

The routines will support any number of rows, so feel free to add additional information as you work with the sample. Once this table is established, you're ready to move to the next step, which is the implementation of the code to exchange the information with Excel.

Functions and Procedures to Exchange Information with Excel

This specific example is in the Excel Experimentation form. It provides the user with a simple form containing two buttons and three text boxes. If you open the form in design mode, you'll see the layout of the controls:

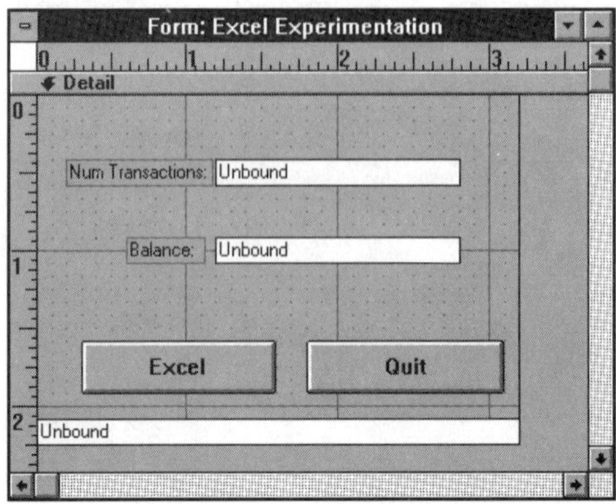

Apply the following names to the different controls on the newly created form with this layout:

Control	Name
NumTransactions text box	txtNumTransactions
Balance text box	txtTotal
Excel button	cmdExcel
Quit button	cmdQuit
'Select Excel to begin' text box	txtStatus

We've turned off the scroll bars, record navigation keys and max/min buttons to make it easier for the user to focus on the task at hand. In addition, we've changed the background color of the form to Gray.

There will not be much supplemental code in this example, but it provides you with enough information for you to start exchanging information with Excel.

The following shows the code in the **`Click`** event of the **`cmdQuit`** button:

```
Sub cmdQuit_Click ()
    DoCmd Close
End Sub
```

As is the standard in this book, this code simply closes the form and returns the user to the tabbed database window. This allows them to choose the next item they want to work with.

There are several supporting functions and subroutines that we should cover before seeing how this form actually works. They are:

- Global declarations
- StartExcel
- PutExcelValue
- GetExcelValue
- StopExcel

These are all located in the Excel OLE Automation module in the **OLETOOLS.MDB** database included with this book.

Global Declarations for Excel Automation

The declarations for this form are relatively simple. They set up a global object variable for us to refer to across the various routines. Also, a flag is declared that will help determine whether Excel is initiated before we start trying to work with the object. This will prevent someone from trying to put data into Excel prior to establishing a connection to the server.

Here are the declarations that are located in the Excel OLE Automation module:

```
'Use database order for string comparisons
Option Compare Database

'required for EXCEL OLE interface, OLE object
Global Excel As Object

'required for EXCEL OLE interface, active flag
Global ExcelStarted As Integer
```

The Excel object is established, as is the ExcelStarted flag. In the **Form_Load** event for the Excel Experimentation form, we establish the flag and provide the user with a basic prompt. Here's the code in the **Form_Load** event:

```
Sub Form_Load ()
    'put an introductory message on the status line, initialize
    'our variable(s)
    txtStatus = "Select Excel to begin."
    ExcelStarted = False
End Sub
```

If you have other variables that are global (either to the system or only this form), you should initialize them here. The next sections detail the utility functions that we use to implement the form and its link to Excel.

StartExcel() - Starting an Excel OLE Automation Session

In order to establish a connection to the Excel OLE Automation Server, you must specify the object to load, the server class and so on. This functionality will then be available to you with the call:

```
iStatus = StartExcel("<sheet name>")
```

If you leave out **"<sheet name>"**, an OLE object reference to Excel will be created but no spreadsheet will be loaded. You'll have to do that manually later in your program using other Access Basic or Visual Basic for Applications code. If you specify a spreadsheet name, the routine will start Excel and load the sheet automatically for you.

When Excel starts in OLE Automation mode, it starts invisibly. The routines involved in our demonstration only turn on the Excel user interface if the user wishes to review the spreadsheet. You don't have to make the application visible to be able to place values into it or take values out of it.

Here's the code in the **StartExcel()** function:

```
Function StartExcel (sFname As String) As Integer
    'Routine to start up a copy of Excel, loading the specified sheet if
    'needed.

    'Pass in the name of the sheet to open, if any, in sFname.
    'Returns the status, either 0 for success, or Err if a problem.

    On Error GoTo StartExcelErr

    'if a file name is passed, open the sheet with the file, otherwise,
    'just create a reference to the object.
    If Len(sFname) > 0 Then
        Set Excel = GetObject(sFname)
    Else
        Set Excel = CreateObject("Excel.Sheet")
    End If

    StartExcel = True            'pass back OK status
    ExcelStarted = True          'set global flag that we're started.

    Exit Function

StartExcelErr:
    'Return the error to the calling routine.
    MsgBox Error$ & " Attempting to unload Excel and return to calling ↵
        routine."
    StartExcel = Err
Exit Function

End Function
```

The first thing we do in this function is to establish an error handler, as we want to make sure we retain control of the program if there is a problem. If we encounter a problem, we put up a message box showing the error text (in **Error$**) and return the error number as the result for the function.

> **One of the most common problems you may encounter occurs when you are supplying an incorrect or incomplete file name. Be sure to specify a fully-qualified path and filename when you use this function.**
>
> **Alternatively, if you plan to use this with files that always reside in the same location, you could modify this routine to automatically add your path to the front of the file name passed in, for example,** `"C:\WROX\" & sFname`.

Recall from the previous chapter that there are two ways of establishing a link with an OLE Server. We can use **CreateObject** to directly specify the server that will be used, or **GetObject** to link to a server that is identified with the particular file type in Windows Registry.

In this example, if the filename is provided, that is, the length of the filename is not '0', we use the **GetObject** method to establish the connection to the server. Notice that if the calling routines were to supply a document here, such as **TEST.DOC**, and Word was set up as the server for that object, Word would be loaded and not Excel. If you want to force the object to be an Excel sheet, you can change the line that appears to the following:

```
Set Excel = GetObject(sFname)
```

to:

```
Set Excel = GetObject(sFname, "Excel.Sheet")
```

which will force the server to be Excel.

The last step in the function is to set up the global flags and return the status to the calling routine. If an error occurs the value in **Err** is returned, otherwise we return 'True' to the caller, which indicates success. We also set the **ExcelStarted** variable to 'True', indicating that we've established our connection to Excel and that other operations are now able to proceed.

The general calling convention for this routine is:

```
iStatus = StartExcel("spreadsheet")
```

where 'spreadsheet' is the name of the spreadsheet with which to establish the connection.

PutExcelValue() - Placing Values in Excel Using OLE Automation

Next, we need to be able to pass information into Excel. This is accomplished by referencing the 'Cells Collection' within the Excel object. To reference a cell, you specify the row and column for that cell. The **Value** property contains the information you wish to place there, whether it be a label (string), number or formula. The following **PutExcelValue** subroutine is found in the Excel OLE Automation module:

```
Sub PutExcelValue (what, X, Y)
    'this routine takes the value or string passed in (what) and
    'inserts it into the current spreadsheet reference using OLE automation
    If ExcelStarted Then
        Excel.Cells(X, Y).Value = what
    Else
        'there's no reference to the object set up yet.  Use
        ' StartExcel to establish the connection.
        MsgBox "Unable to put information into Excel before a reference ⇙
            is established.  Use StartExcel first."
    End If

End Sub
```

If you are putting a formula into a cell, it's probably easier to specify the formula using the R1C1 format; using this notation cell E7 would be cell R7C5. Using this technique, you can specify a formula relative to a given position on the sheet, making it easier to design dynamic links to the sheet.

This technique is explained in more detail later when we show the calling routines behind the `cmdExcel` **button.**

Notice that no explicit type-casting is done on the variable we're passing into this routine. This allows us to pass both strings or numbers with the same function. If you specifically type-cast the parameter, you would have to have a different function for each type of variable you wanted to send to Excel.

The next section of the code allows us to make sure the connection to Excel is already established and, if a problem occurs, it lets the user know of it and safely exit the routine.

If the connection is valid, we simply specify the cell that we want to work with, using the X and Y parameters to the subroutine call, and set the **Value** property. This will send the information to Excel and place it in the cell specified. This routine provides a very simple way to place text, formulas and numbers on the spreadsheet as needed.

General calling conventions are:

```
PutExcelValue "<text to place>", Row, Column
```

or

```
PutExcelValue <value to place>, Row, Column
```

where **<text|value to place>** is what you want to place into the cell located at Row, Column.

GetExcelValue() - Getting Values from Excel Using OLE Automation

Now that you can use OA tools to get information into the spreadsheet, by using **PutExcelValue**, you need a way to get information back from the server, and the **GetExcelValue** procedure performs that function. You pass in the variable to place information into, along with the appropriate cell coordinates and **GetExcelValue** retrieves the value.

The following listing shows the code for the **GetExcelValue()** procedure:

```
Sub GetExcelValue (what, X, Y)
    'This routine returns the value from Excel at the position indicated
    '(X,Y)
    'using OLE automation

    If ExcelStarted Then
        what = Excel.Cells(X, Y).Value
    Else
        'there's no reference to the object set up yet.  Use
        'StartExcel to establish the connection.
        MsgBox "Unable to get information from Excel before a reference ↵
            is established.  Use StartExcel first."
```

```
    End If

End Sub
```

The first thing we do is to make sure the Excel Server has been activated. This information is provided by the **ExcelStarted** variable. If the variable is not set to true (by the **StartExcel** function), then we exit after providing a message box for the user.

The actual process of retrieving the value is quite simple. The value is retrieved from the cell specified by the user's X and Y parameters for the procedure call. The value is placed in the parameter passed into the routine and the routine exits.

This will retrieve the value contained in the cell. Note that if the cell is a formula, this method will return the results of the calculation, and not the formula itself.

> *In your implementations on other systems, you can also specify a range of cells by providing the name of the range. For more information on this, check the Office Developer's Kit. Search on 'Cells', 'Excel' and 'OLE'. See the topic titled 'Assigning General and Specific Objects to Variables and Arguments'.*

The general calling conventions for this routine are:

```
GetExcelValue "<text to place>", Row, Column
```

or

```
GetExcelValue <value to place>, Row, Column
```

where **<text|value to place>** is what you want to retrieve from the Excel cell located at Row, Column.

StopExcel() - Stopping an Excel OLE Automation Server

The final thing that you need to do with the Excel Server is to clear the connection to it when you are finished. This is accomplished with the **StopExcel()** function, which is shown next:

```
Function StopExcel (what As String) As Integer

    On Error GoTo StopExcelErr

    'first, turn on the sheet to make it active so that we can
    'refer to the Activeworkbook object. It doesn't become
    'visible to the user as the Application is not visible.
    Excel.Application.Windows(what).Visible = True

    'First tell Excel that it's saved.  This prevents the
    '"Sheet has changed...do you want to save it?" prompt when we shut
    'everything down.
    Excel.Application.Activeworkbook.Saved = True

    'turn off Excel.
    Excel.Application.[Quit]

    StopExcel = True            'pass back OK
    ExcelStarted = False        'clear our global flag

Exit Function

StopExcelErr:
    'turn on the application so the user can see it.
    Excel.Application.Visible = True

    MsgBox Error$ & "  Unable to stop Excel."
    StopExcel = Err
    Exit Function

End Function
```

To begin with, we set up the error handler. As with the **StartExcel** function, if an error is encountered, the **Err** value is returned after a message box is displayed indicating the problem.

When you unload Excel, it automatically prompts you to save any changes that you've made. You'll notice that unless you tell Excel that all changes have been saved, it will not **Quit**. The symptom that you will encounter in your application will be an apparent 'hang' with Excel sitting in the background waiting on the user to save, abandon or abort the **Quit** action. To avoid this, we have to set the **Saved** property of the **ActiveWorkbook** to 'true'.

As mentioned earlier, when Excel is started as an OLE Server, it starts invisibly. This is also true of any sheets that you load into the server for OLE processing. Normally, from within Excel, you would select File, then Unhide to select the sheet to make visible. In our case, we need to be able to turn on the spreadsheet programmatically. To turn on the spreadsheet (or workbook), you need to set the **Visible** property of the window to 'true'. You can specify the window either by its numeric index relative to other open sheets, or with its file name.

In this implementation, we must provide the name of the sheet to close down as a parameter to the **StopExcel()** function. If there were other sheets open at the time that the Access application is run, the user will still be prompted to save these changes. In this case, the dialog box will be shown indicating that the Excel application has stopped responding:

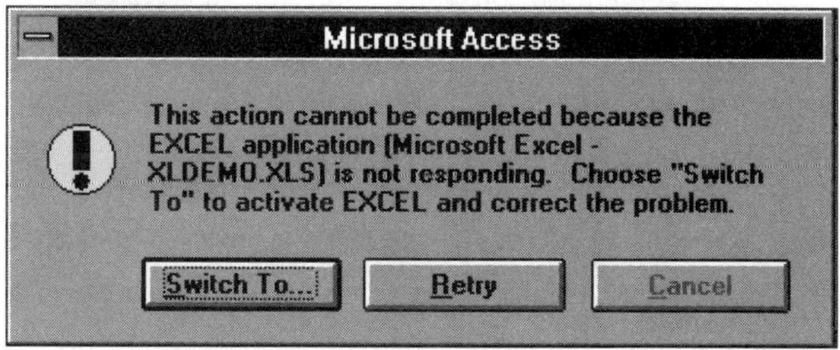

If this does happen, select Switch To and answer the save dialog presented by Excel. When you do, Access will resume its operations and complete the process of closing down the automation server and its object reference.

> *Remember, you must place square brackets around any parameters that Access will try to interpret as Access Basic commands. In our example, the* **Quit** *command must be enclosed in square brackets to force Access to pass the command through to the Excel Server application.*

The last thing we do is to clear the **ExcelStarted** flag and return status information to the calling routine. If an error was encountered, the **ExcelStarted** flag will remain as 'true', and the **Err** value will be returned. Otherwise, **ExcelStarted** is set to 'false', while **StopExcel()** returns 'true', indicating success in shutting down the server application.

The general calling convention for this routine is:

```
iStatus = StopExcel("spreadsheet")
```

where **"spreadsheet"** is the name of the spreadsheet whose connection should be terminated. Note that the name of the spreadsheet is no longer provided as a fully qualified path. You'll also notice that if you start Excel and open an existing spreadsheet, Excel will place only the actual file name on the caption of the window. This is also how you refer to the window you need to close.

Implementing StartExcel, PutExcelValues, GetExcelValues and StopExcel

Returning to our form, the implementation of automation behind the **cmdExcel** button is pretty straightforward:

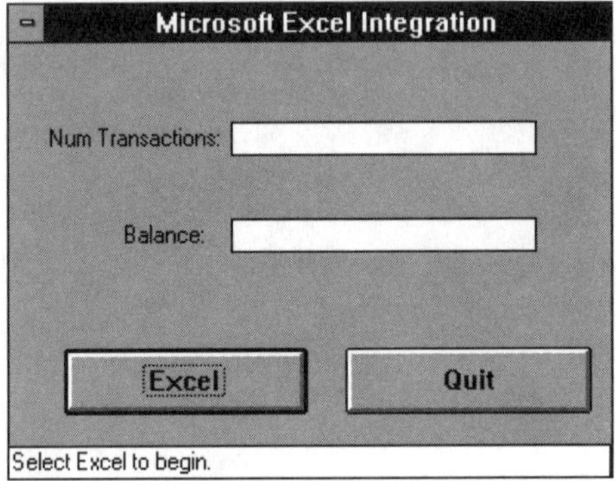

Place the following code in the **Click** event of the **cmdExcel** button:

We've broken up the listing of this routine to make it easier to follow along. When in Access, this routine should be entered as one continuous sub routine.

```
Sub cmdExcel_Click ()
    'call Excel, send it some values, retrieve values
    'from it and close it down.

    'first, set up our variables and initialize them if
    'necessary.

    Dim WS As WorkSpace
    Dim DB As Database
    Dim Rs As Recordset
    Dim tTotal As Currency , gTotal As Currency
    Dim iCounter As Integer
    Dim sText As String
```

```
txtNumTransactions = ""
txtTotal = ""

'first, let the user know what we're doing.
txtStatus = "Opening the Excel Demo table..."
DoEvents


'set up our database and table references.
Set WS = DBEngine.Workspaces(0)         'refers to the current workspace
Set DB = WS.Databases(0)                'refers to the current database
Set Rs = DB.OpenRecordset("Excel Demo") 'specify the Excel Demo Table

'go out and start up the OLE Server
txtStatus = "Starting OLE Server (Microsoft Excel)..."
DoEvents

'create the object reference

'---------------------------------------------------------------
'NOTE:  Change the file name/path below if you have moved the
'samples files to another subdirectory.
'---------------------------------------------------------------
If Not StartExcel("c:\wrox\xldemo.xls") Then Exit Sub
```

Starting from the beginning of the code, we set up the variables that we'll need in order to work with the database and the Excel object. We then initialize the status line to let the user know that we're opening the Excel demonstration table. In most cases, this message will go by very quickly as the application runs.

The next few steps set up our connection to the Excel Demo table. This shows how we refer to the various items in the layered object model mentioned earlier. We use our current **Workspace** and **Database**, and create a new recordset to access the table. This table contains the sample data that we'll be passing to Excel.

Using a Status Line

Once again, we need to update the status line for the user. This display is important as the next steps, which initiate our connection to the Excel Server, can require a little time to complete. The **StartExcel** command accomplishes this connection, specifying the demonstration spreadsheet as the sheet to load.

If you installed the sample files in a different subdirectory be sure to change the path to it in this command. If you don't, the error handler in the **StartExcel** function will trap the error and indicate that it was not able to find the file you've specified:

```
    txtStatus = "Setting up to send information..."""
    DoEvents

    'get the count of rows
    txtNumTransactions = Str$(Rs.RecordCount)

    txtStatus = "Sending information..."
    DoEvents

    'loop through the table, sending
    'each row out to Excel - start out 4 rows
    'from the top of the sheet.
    For iCounter = 1 To Rs.RecordCount
        'set up our row counter, leaving room for the
        'headings for the columns in Excel.
        row = iCounter + 3

        'send the date
        PutExcelValue Rs("Date"), row, 1

        'send the description
        PutExcelValue Rs("Description"), row, 2

        'get the type so we know where to put the value
        Select Case Rs("Type")
            Case "W"
                PutExcelValue Rs("Amount"), row, 3
            Case "D"
                PutExcelValue Rs("Amount"), row, 4
        End Select

        'move to the next row
        Rs.MoveNext
    Next iCounter
```

The first thing that this section of code deals with is how to figure out how many rows we're going to be sending. For this, we refer to the **RecordCount** property associated with recordsets.

Notice that the row that we start with on the Excel spreadsheet is actually row 4. This allows for the headers that we've placed in the spreadsheet. In our case the spreadsheet, before any information is place into it, is shown next:

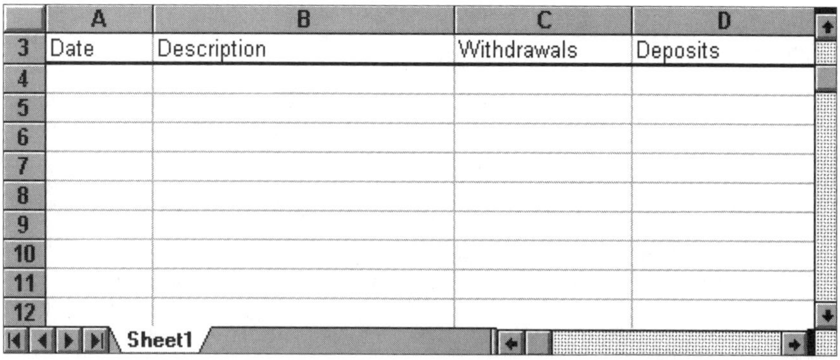

	A	B	C	D
3	Date	Description	Withdrawals	Deposits
4				
5				
6				
7				
8				
9				
10				
11				
12				

Sheet1

Note that in your application, the number of header lines and other formatting information will depend on the specific spreadsheet object you're working with.

It's set up as a basic ledger and shows the line item detail for transactions.

As we loop through records in the database table, we pull the various values out of the recordset and send them to Excel. For instance, the expression `Rs("Date")` refers to the Date field of the current record in the recordset Rs. Inside the loop, we examine the contents of the 'Type' field for that transaction and use it to determine whether the value for a transaction belongs in the 'Withdrawals' or 'Deposits' column.

Pulling Information Back

```
    'put the sum formulas in the appropriate columns and rows
    PutExcelValue "=SUM(R[-" & Trim$(Str$(Rs.REcordCount + 2)) & "]C:R[-
1]C)", Rs.REcordCount + 5, 3
    PutExcelValue "=SUM(R[-" & Trim$(Str$(Rs.REcordCount + 2)) & "]C:R[-
1]C)", Rs.REcordCount + 5, 4

    txtStatus = "Getting total information..."
    DoEvents

    'call Excel to get the values out of the two columns,
    'once we have the values, subtract the withdrawals from the
    'deposits to get a total.
    GetExcelValue tTotal, Rs.REcordCount + 5, 4
    GetExcelValue gTotal, Rs.REcordCount + 5, 3
    tTotal = tTotal - gTotal
```

```
    'show the total to the user
    txtTotal = Format$(tTotal, "$###,##0.00")

    'at this point, Excel is done.  Allow the user to switch to excel
    'to see the sheet if desired.  In a production environment, this
    'would not be an option.  It's provided here as a development
    'and understanding tool.
    If MsgBox("Do you want to switch to Excel to see the spreadsheet?", 35,
"Excel is Updated") = 6 Then
            'when you start excel as a server, it runs (by default)
            'invisibly.  Make it visible so the user can see it.

            sText = "When you have finished, DO NOT close Excel, simply Alt-
Tab back" & Chr$(13)
            sText = sText & "to Access and select OK from the 'Waiting...'
dialog."
            MsgBox sText

            Excel.Application.Visible = True
            Excel.Application.Windows("xldemo.xls").Visible = True

            MsgBox "Waiting for review of Excel sheet.  Press OK to
continue..."

End If
    'shut down...

    txtStatus = "Closing database connection..."
    DoEvents

    Rs.Close
    DB.Close
    WS.Close

    txtStatus = "Closing Excel..."
    DoEvents

    If Not StopExcel("xldemo.xls") Then  'must specify which window to break
connection with.
        MsgBox "Unable to unload excel.  Memory resources may still be in
use."
    End If

    txtStatus = "Done.  Select Excel to start."

End Sub
```

Once the transfer of records has finished, we put in formulas to calculate the sum for the 'Withdrawals' and 'Deposits' columns respectively. We reference the **RecordCount** again to decide where these formulas should be placed on the spreadsheet and which cells should be referenced.

With the sample data, the resulting formulas would be

```
=SUM(R[-14]C:R[-1]C)
=SUM(R[-14]C:R[-1]C)
```

This indicates the range from row 14 above ([-14]) down to the row directly above our current location ([-1]) in the current row, and in the current column (C).

Once we've told Excel to calculate these totals, the balance for the account is easy to determine. All we need to do is take the total for the deposits and subtract out the total for the withdrawals. The next lines do just that, and then update the user interface to show the balance on the account.

We then offer the user the chance to look at the resulting spreadsheet by displaying a standard Windows dialog box, by using the Access function, **`MsgBox`**. If this is desired, we must turn on the **`Visible`** property for the **`Excel.Application`** object. This brings forward the Excel Server and the user will be able to look at the resulting spreadsheet. Notice that not only do we change the Visible property for the Application object, but for the window as well. This brings both the application and the window into view.

Once we've exchanged all of our information with the server application, all that's left is to shut down our server application and close our connection to the database table. This is done in the remaining section of the code; the **`Rs.Close`**, **`Db.Close`** and **`Ws.Close`** commands will close the different connections to the Access database objects. We then use the **`StopExcel`** function to close our connection to the server application.

> **There is an excellent debugging tool that you may find helpful while sending information to and from a server application. If your sending and receiving routines are centralized, as they are in the** PutExcelValue **and** GetExcelValue **routines here, you can place a debug printing statement in the function which prints the current values in the 'Immediate' window.**
>
> **Using this technique will allow you to print out exactly what is being sent to the server. An added benefit is that when you run the program in 'production' mode, the statement will be ignored and the user will not see the output.**

Modify the PutExcelValue routine as follows:

```
...
Debug.Print  what
Excel.cells(X,  Y).value  =  what
...
```

To see the results while your program is executing, press *Ctrl-+ Break*. From the menu bar, select the Immediate Window icon.

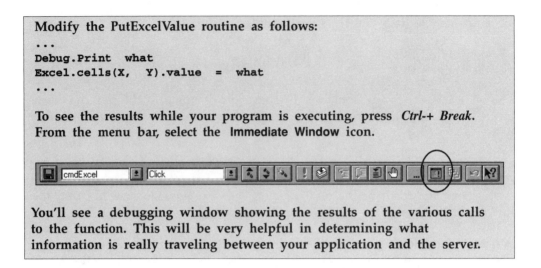

You'll see a debugging window showing the results of the various calls to the function. This will be very helpful in determining what information is really traveling between your application and the server.

Using the Sample Application

When you use the application, you are first presented with the dialog box that we've designed in this chapter. From this dialog, you select the Excel button to initiate the process of exchanging information with Excel.

During the process, the user interface is updated by changing the message on the status line:

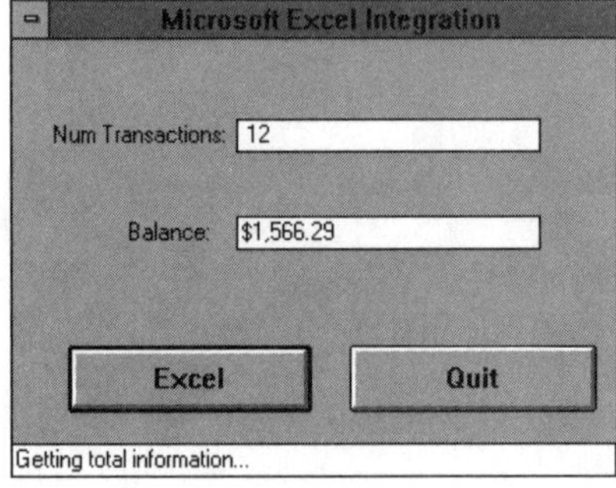

After the process of exchanging information is completed, the program prompts the user about whether they would like to see the resulting spreadsheet. This is done with the standard **MsgBox** call in Access Basic:

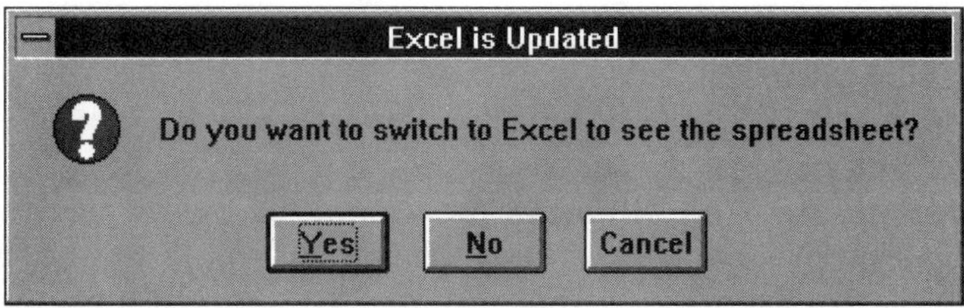

Depending on the user's selection, the routine will either unload Excel and return to the Access form, or will show the Excel server, with the newly built spreadsheet already loaded up. The spreadsheet contains all the values that are in the Access table and also indicates how the formulas were placed. The values on the spreadsheet will correspond directly with the values returned to the Access Basic routines and displayed on the form:

C2

	A	B	C	D
1				
2				
3	Date	Description	Withdrawals	Deposits
4	10/1/94	Initial Balance		$100.00
5	10/1/94	Deposit		$1,103.45
6	10/2/94	Electric Company Pmt	$124.30	
7	10/2/94	Water Company	$24.25	
8	10/2/94	Car payment	$400.00	
9	10/2/94	Groceries	$101.56	
10	10/5/94	Dinner out	$10.50	
11	10/6/94	Dues at club	$5.00	
12	10/10/94	Babysitter	$20.00	
13	10/11/94	Paying off Sam's bet	$10.00	
14	10/15/94	Deposit; paycheck		$1,103.45
15	10/16/94	Night on the town	$45.00	
16				
17			740.61	2306.9
18				

You can compare the values shown with those shown on the Access form. If you add new rows to the underlying sample table, those additional rows will be sent to Access and the formulas will automatically include them the next time you run the function.

Comments and Suggestions

The routines outlined here are ready-to-use in your applications. You can simply include the Excel OLE Automation module in your own applications and have ready access to the Excel Automation Server. While we're not doing anything in our example that you couldn't do just as simply by walking down through the database manually, the concepts and samples will provide a solid footing for your experimentation and development efforts.

As you gain more experience of using Excel in the Access environment, you'll want to become more familiar with the Excel's object model. You have access to charting, formulas and all of Excel's rich text formatting capabilities as well as all the other abilities that Excel users have at their beck and call. Also, remember that these capabilities are in addition to the option of simply embedding and linking objects in your database tables.

It is interesting to contrast the two different ways we have used OLE Automation in this chapter. While both use the functionality of another application to extend their abilities, they carry out the task from different standpoints.

In the spell-check example, we used Word to produce a single-purpose tightly integrated function. Access simply passed information in a particular format to Word using **Document Variables**. We then collected the result when Word had completed it's task. To achieve this, a Word macro, initiated by a call to Word's `ToolsMacro` method by Access, performed the operations and data conversions required. For this reason, each application had to understand the specific formats of data that was transferred and act in a planned and controlled manner.

In the second example, we use the exported object structure of Excel to allow Access to place and retrieve values directly in a spreadsheet object. This is a very loosely bound application where all control of the actions was carried out by Access. Excel simply responded as it would to a user typing at the keyboard by performing on-sheet calculations with the data it found in the cells. The result is a much more general approach, producing a series of routines and functions which are re-usable in many other circumstances.

These differences further emphasize the range of possibilities available from OLE Automation.

Summary of OLE and OLE Automation

In the past few chapters, we have gone from using simple embedded objects to full utilization of OLE Automation Servers. The power of the OLE environment will be far reaching and is sure to become pervasive in your programming efforts. The foundations provided in these chapters should help to prepare you for the coming technologies not only in Access, but also in Visual Basic 4.0 and other languages as they begin to convert to the OLE Automation model.

Future OLE implementations promise to be increasingly powerful, including everything from the utility functions we've discussed to full-feature sub-systems that you can incorporate in your applications.

In the coming chapters, we'll discuss the use of DDE and NetDDE, which are some of the other inter-application communication capabilities that Access has to offer. These technologies allow you to 'converse' with other applications. When combined with OLE, you'll find that your environment becomes more and more integrated and the lines between applications will become more blurred. After you've learned about the different inter-process communications capabilities, you'll be able to decide which method works best for your specific requirements.

CHAPTER 5

Dynamic Data Exchange

Following on from our discussion of OLE, Dynamic Data Exchange is another useful technique for sharing information between applications. One of its biggest advantages over OLE is its ability to share information across computers, using NetBIOS. Perhaps considered to be the poor relation of OLE, DDE still has a place in today's world of information sharing.

What's Covered in This Chapter

In this chapter, we'll be going into the implementation and use of Dynamic Data Exchange (DDE) in your applications. DDE is another method of Inter-Process Communications (IPC).

In this chapter, we cover the following:

- A look at the differences between DDE and OLE
- Using DDE with bound controls on your forms
- A discussion of where NetDDE fits into the picture
- How to initiate DDE and NetDDE conversations from your application

If you have a complete understanding of both OLE and DDE, you will be able to implement a truly information sharing application, using the most advantageous tool for the job.

Chapter 5

How This Chapter Impacts Our Application

By using DDE in our application, we provide the user with the capability to send contact information from Access to Word. This is implemented from within Word by providing a lookup option on the menu. This option uses DDE to communicate with our Access database and present information on the contact record in Word, as requested.

For more information on this additional functionality, please see the section relating to the PIM in Appendix 1. This section details other areas of interest that you can take advantage of when implementing DDE in the PIM.

Introduction

Over the past couple of years, the process-to-process communication model has matured into a useful development tool. It's moved from simple keystroke simulations using `SendKeys`, to more sophisticated conversations using Dynamic Data Exchange. The latest development in this area of inter-application communication is that of the Object Linking and Embedding concept, the ideas behind which we discussed in the first few chapters.

This chapter concentrates on the different aspects of the Dynamic Data Exchange model. Even though DDE is now looked upon by some developers as an outmoded technology, DDE is, in fact, an excellent conduit for the movement of information directly between applications. With DDE, you set up a communication link, or conversation, between the two applications, which enables you to quickly and easily pass information between them.

One of the major differences between DDE and OLE is that you don't use the concept of Objects, Methods and Properties when using DDE. The philosophy behind DDE is based more on the developer establishing a conversation between your application and the **destination software**.

When you do request that a function is executed, you work with the menu structure of the destination application, calling functions from the menus just as if the user had typed the commands manually. This is in contrast to our previous discussions of OLE objects where you use the exported Methods and Properties of the given object.

DDE employs much of the same theory as OLE. You still have the concept of a container, or **source application**, and a server, or destination application. When you set up a conversation between two applications, it is DDE that manages the movement of information between them. The actual mechanism used for the transition of information between source and destination is the clipboard. As the two applications 'converse', information is copied to and pasted from here.

The next stage on from DDE is NetDDE, the big brother of DDE that provides the functionality required to allow you to talk directly to an application on a remote system. This is extremely powerful and can be demonstrated, at least on a superficial level, in the 'Chat' program included with Windows for Workgroups.

In the examples throughout this chapter, you may experience a problem connecting to the server application. This could be because Excel is not included in the DOS path in your `AUTOEXEC.BAT` file. You will need to ensure that the following line is in your `AUTOEXEC.BAT`:

```
PATH  %PATH%;c:\msoffice\excel;
```

Of course, this path assumes that you have Microsoft Office and that Excel was installed to the Office directory.

If you still experience problems, try starting the server application first, and then re-trying the DDE operation that is causing a problem. This should clear up any difficulties you may be experiencing.

The Components of a DDE Conversation

When you start a conversation between applications, a **DDE Channel** is assigned to that conversation. You use this channel during the execution of your program as a way of directing your commands to the right application, as it acts as a unique identifier for any current DDE conversations. **Topics** represent the portions of the server application that can be talked to with DDE. Once you've established your connection to the application, you can change the topic and related **Items** within the context of the conversation. You won't need to re-establish the channel at any point, because it remains open until one or the other of the applications involved is closed down, or you specifically close it down yourself.

A conversation between applications has several different component parts. These parts are explained here:

Channel	The channel is a unique integer variable assigned to the communications pipeline established between the applications in the DDE conversations.
Application Name (or Service Name)	This represents the server application. This usually is the actual executable name, without the '.EXE' extension. For example, to use Excel, you would specify 'EXCEL', and not '**EXCEL.EXE**'
Topic Name	This determines the context of your conversation. For example, in Excel, this might be the spreadsheet you wish to work with, while in Word it would be the document that is under discussion. In addition, an application that supports DDE must provide a special topic called 'System' which is explained later in this chapter.
Item	The specific item, whether it be a bookmark, cell or any other positional marker, that you need to communicate with.

You should be aware that DDE doesn't start the destination, or server, application when it applies for a channel and the server isn't running: this will be up to your application to organize. The error produced when the other application isn't open, can be trapped by the **On Error...** process. Once trapped, you can either notify the user, offering an option to start the other application, or you can automatically start it from within your program.

If you need to start the server application, you can use Access' **Shell** *command in the error handler. Start the application and then* **Resume** *your code execution. We'll see how this is used later in the chapter.*

Two Types of DDE Implementation - Bound Cells, Program Control

In Access, there are two different options available to you when implementing DDE. You can have Access manage the connection for you, or you can control it yourself. You can imagine that the implementation allowing Access to maintain the connection has its limitations, but it is simple to implement. On the other hand, the programmatic model will allow for more flexibility, but forces much of the administrative overhead back onto you as the programmer.

Creating DDE Bound Controls

The simplest form of a DDE implementation involves the use of the Access **DDE()** function. This function allows you to assign a DDE conversation and specific topic/item to an otherwise unbound text control.

In the **SAMPLES.MDB** database, there is a DDE Bound Control Sample form that illustrates this point. This sample form shows how you can link your application to values in an Excel spreadsheet:

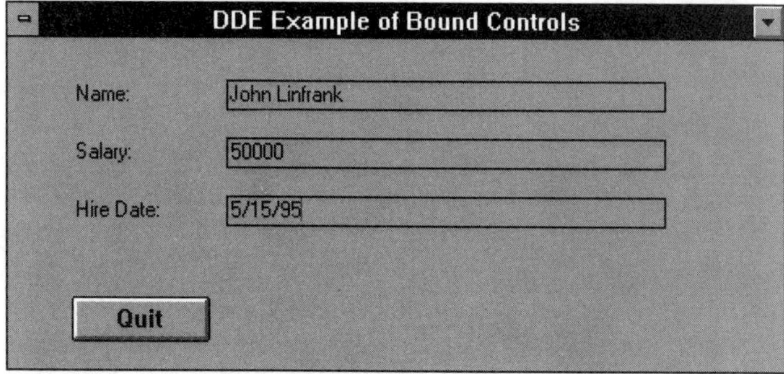

In this form, we tie three different text boxes to the different columns in the **DDESMPL.XLS** spreadsheet. We're retrieving the name, salary and hire date information from the spreadsheet in Excel. The only code behind this form appears on the Quit button to close the form. The remaining functionality is set up in the form's properties and is maintained by Access.

Employee Name	Salary	Hire Date
Steve Jo Smith	25000	10/1/95
John Linfrank	50000	5/15/95
Gordon Sregorov	65000	11/1/95

Our table contains three rows containing the name, salary and hire date for each of the employees. Our form looks explicitly at the row containing 'John Linfrank' and retrieves the information from there.

As mentioned earlier, the formula used to return this information is the **`DDE()`** function. The **`DDE()`** function has the following format:

```
DDE("<Application>","<Topic>","<Item>")
```

You enter the formula in the Control Source property of an unbound text box:

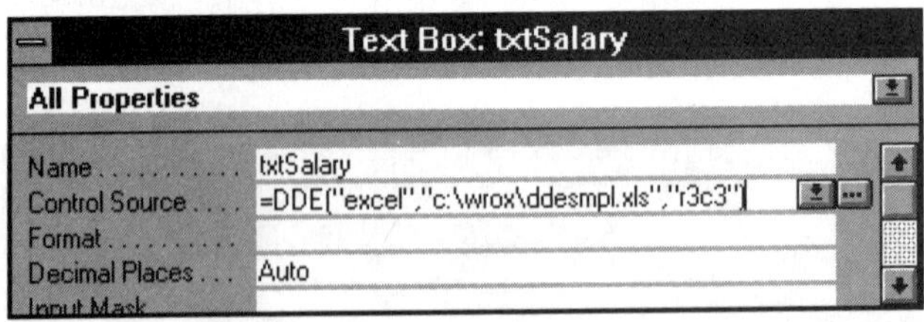

Make sure that the **`DDESMPL.XLS`** *file is located in the* **`C:\WROX`** *directory on your system. If it is in a different directory, then you will have to change the reference to it in the above example.*

In this case, the application is Microsoft Excel, and we are referring to a spreadsheet located in the **`C:\WROX`** subdirectory called **`DDESMPL.XLS`**. More specifically, we are referring to the cell at the intersection of the third row and third column, r3c3.

> **When you are using the `DDE()` function, you can also assign it to be the source for checkbox fields. A zero (0) value will leave the box unchecked, while any non-zero value will check the box. If the field contains text the checkbox is 'grayed'.**

If Access realizes that Excel is not yet started, and you load the form with the text boxes on it, Access will prompt you as to whether it should start the application.

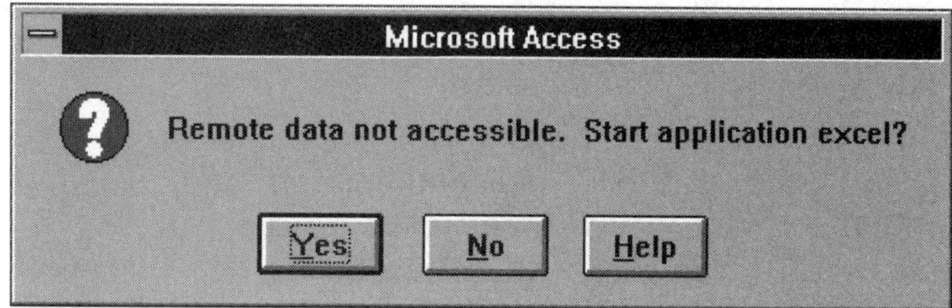

Remember, for a DDE conversation to be initiated, the remote application (the server) must be running. This is Access' way of telling you that it's not started and offering to load it for you. This is one of the benefits of using Bound Controls. Once started for the first bound field, Access will reference the same instance of the server application for other inquiries, such as those made by the other two fields.

> **Note that if Access is unable to begin a conversation with the server application for any reason, be it an incorrectly specified topic (incorrect file name) or the wrong format for the item, you will get a result of #Error in the text box. Examine the `DDE()` function call to make sure that the parameters are correctly specified and the server application is available.**

While this is DDE in its most basic form, it does provide some information exchange between the applications. Part of the challenge with DDE is knowing whether the target application supports DDE in the first place, and secondly, what the available topics are for the application.

If you use the Bound Control approach, remember that the controls are only refreshed when you manually indicate that they should be activated, except when you load a form, as the controls are automatically initialized at that point. If you need to re-query the data source to update the fields, consider using the **Refresh** method for the form. This will update the fields on your form that are bound to the data source.

Using DDE() to Determine Available Topics

This section describes how you can use the **DDE()** function to determine the status of the target application and, at the same time, it also allows you to discover how to retrieve the valid topics for that same application.

Using **DDE()**, you can determine this information by using a reasonably simple form that queries the source for you and then requests the information on that target application. To see which topics exist for a given server application's current state, create a text box with the following as the Control Source property:

```
=DDE("Excel","System","Topics")
```

All applications that support DDE have a special topic called 'System'. The System topic is the method by which you can establish communications with an unknown system and determine what other topics are available.

If you query the System topic of a DDE-aware application, you'll get back a list of valid topics as the response. The next example is based upon the DDE Server Inquiry form that can be found in the **SAMPLES.MDB** database.

> *If you wish to investigate the topics available for a particular spreadsheet, open Excel and load in the appropriate file before opening this form. Alternatively, you can add some code to the* **Form Open** *event that opens Excel, using the* **Shell** *command, and asks the user to specify the spreadsheet to examine.*

This sample application allows you to query any DDE-aware application. You can send and retrieve information, and you can inquire into the System topic to see what other topics are available. Using this tool, you'll be able to browse DDE applications and amass information about each that will allow you to set up applications of your own without as much hassle.

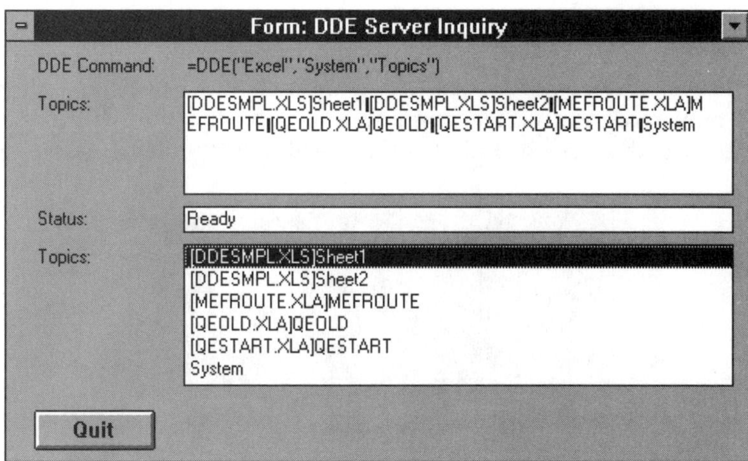

There are two topics controls on the form. One shows the 'raw' data coming back from the DDE call and the other shows a more formatted, easy to use version of the information after we've taken out the tab characters.

This form simply queries Excel for the list of available, valid topics. The DDE command specifies 'Excel' as the application, 'System' as the topic and 'Topics' as the item to query. The return result is a list, separated by the tab character (chr$(9)), of all of the various topics that are made available by Excel. The second topics list shows the same topics in a listbox format. The code that translates from the tab-delimited form of the list is in the Form Load event for the form.

Possible Problems with the DDE() Function

If Excel is not running when you open the DDE Server Inquiry, you will see the dialog box asking if you want to start the remote server:

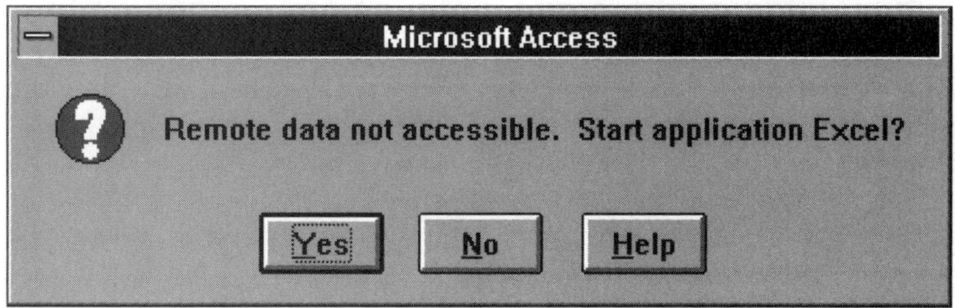

If you accept the offer, Access will execute Excel and attempt to open the file called **SYSTEM.XLS**. Excel will fail to do this, because this file doesn't exist. The reference in the DDE function call to System is a special parameter that Excel will only recognise if it is running when the function call is made. As Excel can't open this file, it will display the following dialog box:

However, Excel is minimized in the background, and you will therefore not be aware of the demand for user input from Excel. After a pre-defined period of time, the DDE command will be timed out and you will received the following error message:

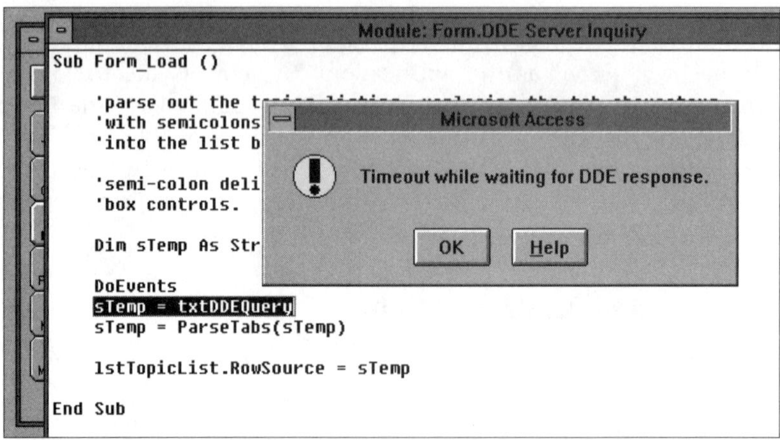

To get around this problem, when you select the Yes button, *Alt-Tab* to Excel and OK the 'Can't Find File' dialog box. Return to Access and the form should run correctly.

The length of time that you have available to switch to Excel and click the button is determined by the value that is set for the OLE/DDE Timeout (secs) *property. You can view this property in the general database options dialog box:*

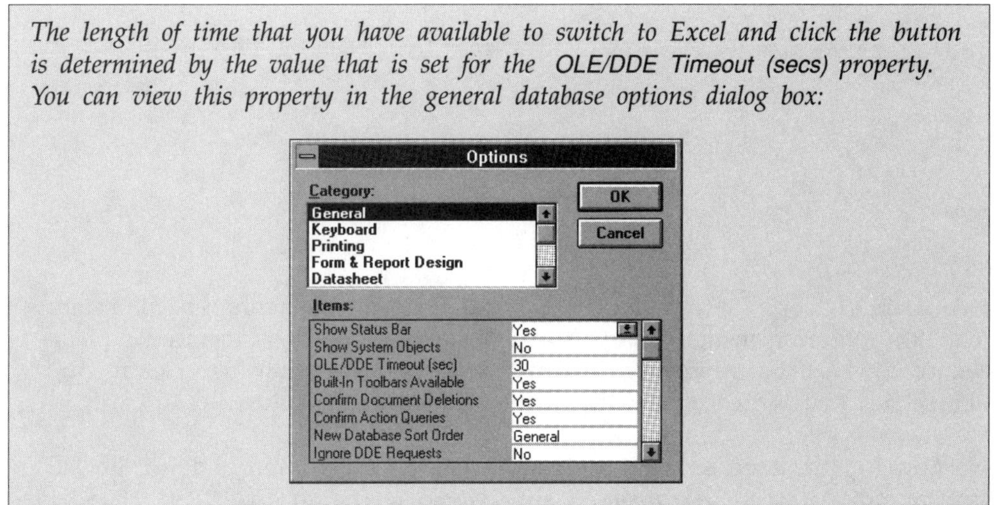

Character Delimited Text Formatting

The returned list is delimited with tab characters, but if you look at the contents of the second text box, you'll notice that these Tab characters are displayed as vertical bars. If your application will be using the information returned by DDE calls, it's important to remember that it will be furnished to your application in tab-delimited form. Your application will need to parse the returned strings to allow you to get at the information you require.

The first thing you will need to do is establish the supporting routine, **ParseTabs()**. This routine will take the information returned by a DDE call and change it to a predefined, more readable format:

```
Function ParseTabs (what) As String

    'parse out the string, replacing the tab characters
    'with semicolons.

    'semi-colon delimited lists are RowSource's for list
    'box controls.

    Dim sTemp As String
    Dim iTemp As Integer

    'loop through the string to parse out the tabs
    sTemp = what
    iTemp = InStr(sTemp, Chr$(9))
```

```
    Do While iTemp > 0
        sTemp = Left$(sTemp, iTemp - 1) & ";" & Right$(sTemp, Len(sTemp) -
iTemp)
        iTemp = InStr(sTemp, Chr$(9))
    Loop

    'return the updated string
    ParseTabs = sTemp

End Function
```

ParseTabs() loops through the string until there are no more tab characters (chr$(9)) appearing in the listing. As each tab is found, it is replaced with a semicolon. We'll be using results from this function to allow us to clean up any replies that we get from DDE conversations in the future.

Next, set up the code in the Form Load event. This code responds to the DDE results and cleans up the display, using **ParseTabs()**, to give a more readable form:

```
Sub Form_Load ()

    'parse out the topics listing, replacing the tab characters
    'with semicolons.  Then paste the newly formatted list
    'into the list box for easier viewing.

    'semi-colon delimited lists are RowSource's for list
    'box controls.

    Dim sTemp As String

    DoEvents
    sTemp = txtDDEQuery
    sTemp = ParseTabs(sTemp)

    lstTopicList.RowSource = sTemp

End Sub
```

The basics of this routine simply run through the string of values that results from the **DDE()** function call. It looks for the tab character and replaces it with the semicolon ';' character. The resulting string is then assigned to the RowSource for the list box, thus completing the clean up of the DDE conversation with the Excel System file. As you implement your applications, make sure you take into consideration the fact that you're going to have to parse the string to find the topic you require.

Using DDE in Your Access Basic Programs

The other method of using DDE is to use it in your program as part of the Access Basic program code. As we mentioned earlier, this requires some additional overhead on your part, but is well worth it because of the added functionality that you gain.

There is one very significant difference between DDE automation and its OLE counterpart. You'll recall that when you begin work with an OLE object, you establish a new object in your application and then refer to that object to exercise Methods, Properties and other characteristics associated with the object. If you wanted to change the reference to a different Method or Property, you didn't have to re-establish a new link to the object: all that is required is a change to the reference path. You basically set up a one-to-many reference to the object relative to the other components associated with it:

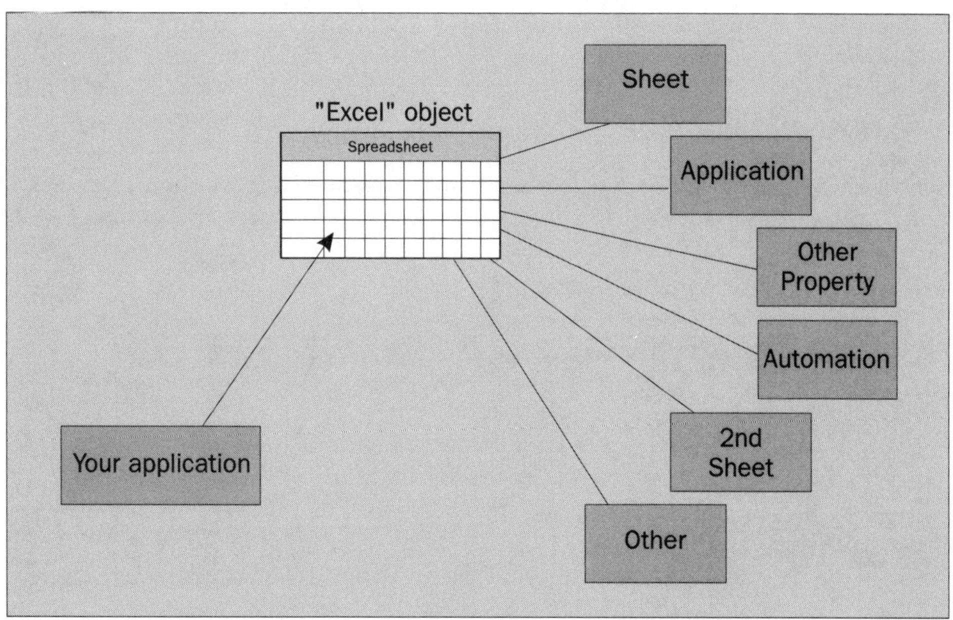

How OLE Automation Handles Requests for Items

When using OLE, you reference the items associated with the object through the object itself, so setting up an indirect link between the application and the required item, via the host object. This is not the case when using DDE, as now you make a connection directly with the item you need to work with.

For example, if you want to work with the **DDESMPL.XLS** spreadsheet, you'll specify Excel as the application and **DDESMPL.XLS** as the topic. Once the connection is established to the spreadsheet, if you needed to see what other spreadsheets were available with the System topic, you'd need to create a new connection to the System topic specifically for that purpose.

With DDE it's a one-to-one relationship between your application and the item that you wish to reference, while OLE sets up a one-to-many relationship with the object and lets the object sort out which item is required to satisfy any OLE requests.

Setting Up a DDE Conversation

The same basic components from the **DDE()** function apply to controlling a DDE conversation within your program code. You must still specify the application, topic and item that you wish to work with in your program. In addition, when you establish communications with a DDE compliant application, you set up a channel over which you will be communicating. All DDE methods rely on a channel designation, except for the **DDEInitiate** call, which returns the new channel assignment.

Each of these DDE functions is outlined in the sample application, DDE Basics, located in the **SAMPLES.MDB** database. This allows you to set the values for the various DDE function parameters and execute them individually. Open the DDE Basics form to see these methods in action:

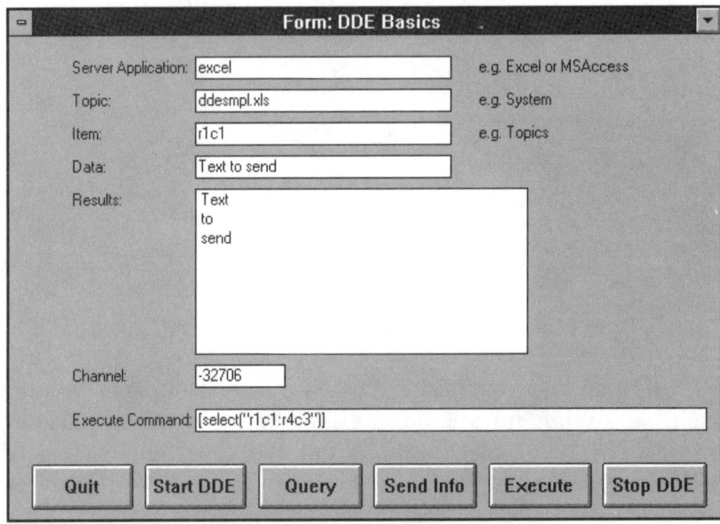

> **If you are going to be accessing your DDE Server application from different subroutines and/or functions, be sure to define your variable containing the channel as `Global`. It can be global to the form, or global to the database, but should be available across procedures.**
>
> **In our sample application, we've set up `iChannel` as the global channel variable. It's declared in the DDE Variables module as an `Integer` as show below:**
>
> ```
> Global iChannel As Integer          'DDE Channel to use
> ```

To send information to a cell in a spreadsheet, follow these steps:

1 Load Excel

2 Open `C:\WROX\DDESMPL.XLS`

3 Minimize Excel

4 Set the Server Application to Excel

5 Set the Topic to `DDESMPL.XLS`

6 Select Start DDE

7 Set the Item to R1C1

8 Set the Data to the text string you want to send

9 Select Send Info

10 Switch to Excel to see the results

This will send the information you specify to row 1, column 1 of the Excel spreadsheet. The different steps to carrying on a conversation using DDE are shown in the table on the next page.

Function	DDE Method	Command Button
Starting the conversation	DDEInitiate	Start DDE
Get information	DDERequest	Query
Sending information	DDEPoke	Send Info
Executing commands on the Server Application	DDEExecute	Execute
Ending the conversation	DDETerminate	Stop DDE

The DDE Basics form uses the various methods we're talking about to provide the different pieces of functionality you see in the user interface.

The Quit button has the standard **`Quit`** code that uses **`DoCmd Close`** to unload the current form. The table below shows the controls and their associated control names:

Control on Form	Control Name
Server Application text box	txtServerApplication
Topic text box	txtTopic
Item text box	txtItem
Data Text Box	txtData
Results list box	lstResults
Channel text box	txtChannel
Execute Command Box	txtCommand
Quit button	cmdQuit
Start DDE button	cmdStartDDE
Query button	cmdQuery
Send Info button	cmdSendInfo
Execute button	cmdExecute
Stop DDE button	cmdStopDDE

Now we have the basic structure for the form, let's discuss the different DDE functions that we have available to 'power up' the form.

Using DDEInitiate to Start a Conversation

When you start up a DDE conversation, you use the **DDEInitiate** function call. This function sets up the connection to the server application and assigns a unique channel number to the conversation.

The syntax for **DDEInitiate** is:

```
iChannel = DDEInitiate(sApplication, sTopic)
```

where:

iChannel	is the channel established by the call
sApplication	is the name of the application to start a DDE connection with
sTopic	is the topic with which to associate the conversation

> **Remember that sApplication should be supplied as the name of the service or server application that you want to use. This is generally the file name of the server application such as WINWORD, EXCEL and MSACCESS without the .EXE extension.**

In our example, the Start DDE button begins the connection to the server application. The following listing shows the Access Basic code associated with initiating a connection to a DDE server application:

```
Sub cmdStartDDE_Click ()

    'initiate the DDE conversation, set up the channel
    'for future use in other procedures.

    '(See note about Excel starting up and not
    'having the System topic available.)
```

```
    'first, set up the error handler.   This
    'will trap the error of the server app
    'not being already loaded.
    On Error GoTo cmdStartDDEErr

    'our variables
    Dim iStatus As Integer
    Dim iResult As Integer
    Dim sTemp As String
    Dim flag As String
    flag = "notset"
    'establish the connection to the server, get a
    'channel to use for further communications
    iChannel = DDEInitiate(txtServerApplication, txtTopic)

    'put the channel on the UI, just to confirm.
    txtChannel = Str$(iChannel)

    'all done.
    Exit Sub

cmdStartDDEErr:
    'error handler
    Select Case Err
        Case 282:
            If flag = "set" Then Resume
            'if err = 282 => other application not started.
            iResult = MsgBox("The Server Application is not started. Do ↵
                you want to start it?", 36, "Application Not Started")
            If iResult = 6 Then
                'Yes, start it, use Shell to start minimized,
                'without focus.
                iStatus = Shell(txtServerApplication & ".exe" & " " &    ↵
                    txtTopic, 6)
            Else
                Exit Sub
            End If
        Case Else
            'unknown error, let the user know about the problem.
            MsgBox Str$(Err) & " " & Error$, 16, "DDE Problem"
    End Select
    flag = "set"
    Resume

End Sub
```

If we do need to start the target application, we use the **Shell** command. When you specify the executable filename, don't forget to add the '.EXE' extension.

> *Remember that the entry for the DDE application is generally the EXE file name, **without** the .EXE extension.*

We start the application minimized, without focus, to keep it from coming up over our Access application, by using the following snippet of code:

```
iStatus = Shell(txtServerApplication & ".exe" & " " & txtTopic, 6)
```

Back in the procedure code, the call to start the conversation is quite simple. We initiate the conversation and a channel is allocated. We assign it to a global variable, **iChannel**, and update the user interface with the value. This is obviously not required, but in our example it helps to understand what's going on.

> *Channel numbers simply represent a handle that we can use to refer to the conversation between our Access application and the remote server. The channel can be a negative or positive number, either of which is valid. In our example above, it's negative.*

We set up our error handling code at the top so we can be sure to trap any errors while setting up the call to the server application. You should notice that in the error handler, we're doing something a little different, by reacting to a specific error condition and applying a tighter solution in an attempt to correct it. The error condition, error 282, signifies that the remote application is not responding or is not available. If we get this error, we'll let the user know and offer to start the application for them.

Once we're finished, we can continue on and use **DDERequest** to pull information from the server application.

Using DDERequest to Retrieve Information

When you need to retrieve information from the server application, you should use the **DDERequest** function.

The syntax for **DDERequest** is:

```
sResult = DDERequest(iChannel, sItem)
```

where:

sResult is a string or variant that will contain the results of the call

iChannel is the channel to use for the conversation which allows us to select the application we wish to communicate with

sItem is the item to request

The **DDERequest** function is used in the Query button of our DDE Basics form. The following listing shows how it is used in this context:

```
Sub cmdQuery_Click ()

    'using an already established DDE channel,
    'request information as specified in the UI
    'from the Server Application.

    'set up our variables
    Dim sTemp

    'set up the error handler
    On Error GoTo cmdQueryErr

    'if iChannel = 0, we don't have a channel established yet.
    'tell the user about it and exit.
    If iChannel = 0 Then
        MsgBox "DDE Conversation not started. Cannot request information. "
        Exit Sub
    End If

    'make the request.
    sTemp = DDERequest(iChannel, txtItem)

    'call ParseTabs to convert tab characters to
    'semicolons for our list box.  Assign the results
    'to the RowSource of the text box.
```

```
    lstResults.RowSource = ParseTabs(sTemp)

    Exit Sub

cmdQueryErr:
    'show the error number and message, then try to resume
    MsgBox Str$(Err) & " " & Error$, 16, "DDE Request Info Problem"
    Exit Sub

End Sub
```

There are two different things that we must do before actually attempting the call. First, we make sure that a valid DDE conversation has been established. This is done by checking the channel number and making sure it's not zero. If it's not zero, we can continue.

Second, we establish the error handler so we can keep control of the program if a problem occurs with the call. In this routine, any error that we get is a problem, so we display all errors and their associated text.

Error 285 can occur when you incorrectly specify the item you want to query. For example, if you request a bookmark from Word that doesn't exist, you'll get the 285 error indicating that the bookmark was not found. If you get a 285 error, check the syntax of your topic and try again. If the problem persists, check with the software manuals for the server application to make sure no other dependencies exist for making the call.

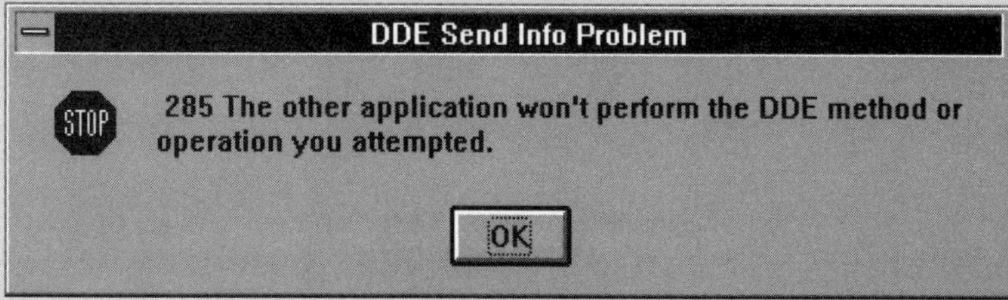

You may also get this message if you attempt to Poke (send) information to the System topic on the server application. Be sure you connect to a valid topic that accepts input.

You should also note that not all applications support DDE: if you continuously get errors, even when specifying 'Topics' as the item, check with the software vendor to make sure the package supports DDE.

We make the call to the server application based on the values in the user interface, assigning the result to **sTemp**. This gives us the ability to manipulate the results in our program environment.

You could somewhat simplify this routine by replacing the following lines:

```
...
sTemp = DDERequest(iChannel, txtItem)
...
lstResults.RowSource = ParseTabs(sTemp)
...
```

with

```
lstResults.RowSource = ParseTabs(DDERequest(iChannel, txtItem)).
```

We've placed the results into a temporary variable to make it easier to see interim results of the call by placing a `MsgBox sTemp` command immediately after the `DDERequest` call. This may help in debugging your application and its interaction with DDE.

Since we've implemented a list box to clean up the display of the resulting information, the last thing we do is to strip the tabs out of the string and replace them with semicolons. The **ParseTabs()** routine, located in the DDE Tools module and discussed earlier in this chapter, provides this functionality for us.

DDEPoke

When you need to send information from your Access Basic program to another application, you should use the **DDEPoke** method.

The syntax for **DDEPoke** is:

```
sResult = DDEPoke(iChannel, sItem)
```

where:

sResult	is a string or variant that will contain the results of the call
iChannel	is the channel to use for the conversation
sItem	is the item to request

The **DDEPoke** command is implemented behind the Send Info command button on our example form. To use the function, you must first establish a connection to the server application using Start DDE. Next, set the Item and Data fields as appropriate.

The following code listing, when executed, places the given information into the spreadsheet (or whatever other server application you have defined):

```
Sub cmdSendInfo_Click ()

    'using an already established DDE channel,
    'send information as specified in the UI
    'to the Server Application.

    'set up the error handler
    On Error GoTo cmdSendInfoErr

    'if iChannel = 0, we don't have a channel established yet.
    'tell the user about it and exit.
    If iChannel = 0 Then
        MsgBox "DDE Conversation not started.  Cannot send information. "
        Exit Sub
    End If

    'send the information
    DDEPoke iChannel, txtItem, txtdata

    Exit Sub

cmdSendInfoErr:
    'show the error number and message, then try to resume
    MsgBox Str$(Err) & " " & Error$, 16, "DDE Send Info Problem"
    Exit Sub

End Sub
```

The error handler and channel verification are the same in this routine as the others that we've shown previously. The only difference in this procedure is the use of the **DDEPoke** command. We pass out the channel, the target item and the data to put into or against the item. If this call fails, it may be because the topic or item you've selected doesn't support input.

If you Start DDE against the System topic, for example, and then Send Info to it, you'll get an error message. The error message, shown above in the **DDERequest** section, is just an indication that you've specified the wrong destination for your information. If you get a **DDEPoke** error message, then you know that the topic that you are trying to write to doesn't allow alterations.

You can use **DDEPoke** to send any type of information to the server application, from text to numbers to formulas. **DDEPoke** is the primary method of sending information from your Access system to a server application.

Using DDEExecute to Automate the Server Application

Once you've sent information to the server application, you'll often need to tell the server to do something with the information. You can execute menu commands, macros or keystrokes that a user may use in day-to-day use of the server application, with the **DDEExecute** command. The actual capabilities that you can use will vary from server to server.

The syntax for **DDEExecute** is:

```
DDEExecute iChannel, sCommand
```

where:

iChannel is the channel to use for the conversation

sCommand is the command to execute

In our example, we have implemented the option of entering a command and then using the **DDEExecute** command to run it against the server. However, there are a couple of key points about commands that you pass to servers that you should be made aware of. Again, these are general rules and you'll need to check with your specific server vendor to see how their automation capabilities are implemented:

- Each command must be enclosed in square brackets.
- Multiple commands can often be sent at once but make sure that each command is enclosed in the square brackets, and not the entire command line.
- If you are programmatically setting the string to execute, rather than letting a user type it into a field, you may have to use embedded quotation marks. This is the case with Excel, where you must have double quotes around cell references. You can do this by appending Chr$(168) at the correct position, or by specifying the quotes as you build your string. An example of this technique might be ""String to Build"" which creates "String to Build" in the variable to which it's assigned.

If you specify a command without providing the square brackets around it, your server application will generally treat the command as incoming text and it will place the text at the current cursor location in the application's workspace. If you notice that the command you're trying to execute ends up just being 'typed in' to the server, check your square brackets.

In our example, the **DDEExecute** code is behind the Execute button. Type the following line into the Execute Command text box and click on the Execute button:

```
[Select("r1c2:r5c5")][New(2,2)]
```

The Select command simply selects the specified cells in our **DDESMPL.XLS** spreadsheet and the New command opens a new file and charts the selected cells.

If you switch to Excel using the *Alt-Tab* keys, you'll see the chart shown on the next page.

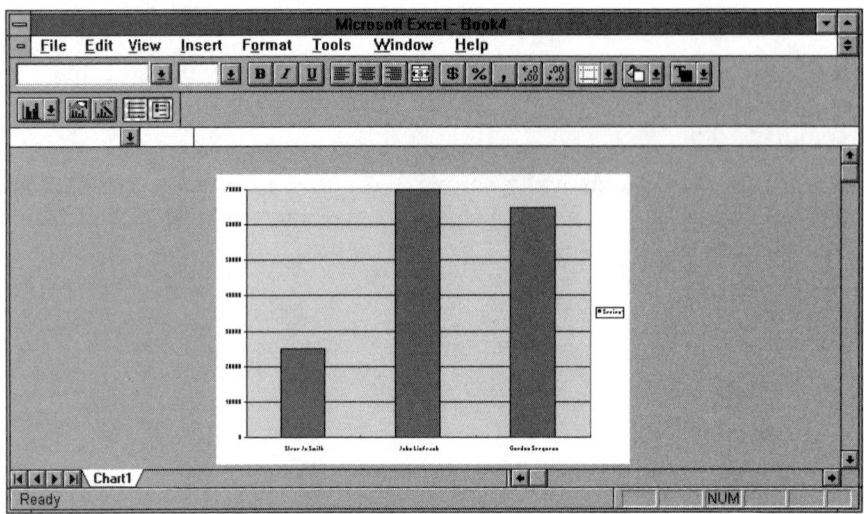

Here's the code behind the Execute button:

```
Sub cmdExecute_Click ()

    'using an already established DDE channel,
    'execute command as specified on the form
    'against the Server Application.

    'set up the error handler
    On Error GoTo cmdExecuteErr

    'if iChannel = 0, we don't have a channel established yet.
    'tell the user about it and exit.
    If iChannel = 0 Then
        MsgBox "DDE Conversation not started.  Cannot send information. "
        Exit Sub
    End If

    'execute the command(s)
    DDEExecute iChannel, txtCommand

    Exit Sub

cmdExecuteErr:
    'show the error number and message, then try to resume
    MsgBox Str$(Err) & " " & Error$, 16, "DDE Execute Problem"
    Exit Sub

End Sub
```

Once again, we verify that the channel has been correctly established and that we have an error handler in place. Next, we issue the command specified by the user in the Execute Command text box. The command is passed through to the server application without modification by specifying the channel and command as parameters to the **`DDEExecute`** command.

In order for the display of the server application to be updated, you may have to give it the focus. For example, if the command you send is to select a range of cells, the actual highlighting will probably not take place until Excel gets focus. This doesn't mean that the cells are not selected, only that the display has not yet been updated.

If you are experiencing server application timeouts on your DDE calls, you can adjust the timeout value that Access uses. From the View menu, choose Options...:

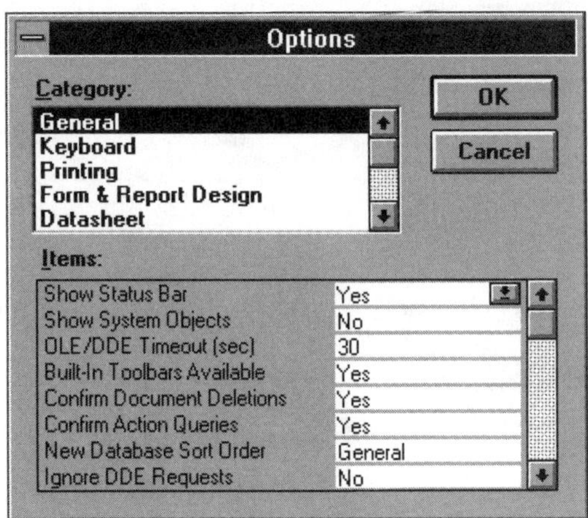

Set the OLE/DDE Timeout (sec) value to a longer time period. It may take some experimentation to determine what the best value is for this option depending upon the system the application is working upon.

If you execute a command against a server application and you notice that either the title-bar of the application or the icon for the application are blinking, it means that the application requires user input to continue. Switch to the application and answer any prompts that may be required to continue. Once the server application is able to continue, your Access application will move on as well. If you're running Access full-screen and notice that the call to another application is taking an excessively long time, try task-switching to it to see if it requires input. You may not be able to see it requesting input if Access is taking up your entire screen.

While you experiment with the applications in these examples, it's helpful to size both the Access and the server application windows so you can see them both at once. This will give you a feel for response times and will also verify that the server application is responding as you expected.

Using DDETerminate and DDETerminateAll

Once you have completed your conversation with the server application, you should terminate the connection to the application. This is done with the **DDETerminate** or **DDETerminateAll** function calls.

The syntax for **DDETerminate** is:

```
DDETerminate iChannel
```

where:

iChannel is the channel to use for the conversation

For **DDETerminateAll**, the syntax is:

```
DDETerminateAll
```

With **DDETerminateAll**, you don't have to specify a channel as you have asked to close them all. In our example, we update our internal variables to indicate that the connection is no longer open. Here's the code listing that appears behind the Stop DDE button on the DDE Basics form:

```
Sub cmdStopDDE_Click ()

    On Error GoTo cmdStopDDEErr

    If iChannel = 0 Then
        MsgBox "DDE conversation not yet started.  Unable to stop."
        Exit Sub
    End If
```

```
    'shut down the channel
    DDETerminate iChannel

    'Note:  can also use DDETerminateAll, without a channel.

    txtChannel = ""
    iChannel = 0

    Exit Sub

cmdStopDDEErr:
    MsgBox Str$(Err) & " " & Error$, 16, "DDE Shutdown Problem"
    Exit Sub

End Sub
```

As usual, the first thing we have to do is set up the error handler and then make sure that a valid channel exists.

> *In our examples, we're only supporting the use of one channel. You may find that you want to have connections to more than one DDE Server application. If this is the case, you can open multiple channels at the same time, one to each server application. If you're using more than one channel, you'll need to update the channel checking logic to check a specific channel for a valid value.*

If the channel exists, we terminate the connection over that channel. The last thing we need to do is clean up the **iChannel** variable, and the user interface, which means the **txtChannel** variable. If we do receive an error, we display the error box and return to the form for other operations.

If you have multiple channels open and are exiting, you may want to use the **DDETerminateAll** function. This function closes all open DDE channels. A good example of how this function can be put to use might be in the Form Unload event:

```
Sub Form_Unload (Cancel As Integer)
    'close down any open DDE channels

    'set the error handler to ignore errors returned.
    On Error Resume Next

    'close the channels.
    DDETerminateAll
End Sub
```

With this code in the Unload event, you'll be assured of closing all pertinent connections when the form is unloaded. We simply set the error handler to ignore errors by continuing with the next line after the error. Finally, in our DDE tidy up function, we issue the **DDETerminateAll** command, and so close all the connections the user may have opened during the session.

> **An important item to note about both of the terminate commands is that they don't close down the server application. You can shut down the server application manually by using the Windows task switcher to change to it and then closing the application.**

Access DDE Server Capabilities

Microsoft have enabled Access with the capability of serving other applications as a DDE Server application, as well as being a client, which means that you can set up your database to exchange information between users, using the concept of DDE.

When you use Access as the server, the DDE conversation is initiated by another application, making Access into the server and then the foreign application can reference the database and its component parts as and when it needs to.

When you use Access as a DDE server, you initiate the conversation using exactly the same syntax as in our prior examples:

```
iChannel = DDEInitiate("MSACCESS","C:\ACCESS\SAMPLES.MDB")
```

This sets the system up to query any of the components associated with the **SAMPLES.MDB** database. When you specify the database name, you can specify it with or without the extension, and you may also be able to specify it without the full path. If the database file doesn't reside in the applications default subdirectory, you'll need to provide the path specification.

Once the connection is established, you have a number of options available to you. For example, if you establish a connection to the database topic as in our example, the items given on the next page are available:

- TableList
- QueryList
- FormList
- ReportList
- MacroList
- ModuleList

Each of these will return a list of the available topics in the database. To see these topics in action, follow the steps given below:

1 Open another instance of Access and open the **CONTACTS.MDB**.

2 On the DDE Basics form, enter MSAccess as the server application and enter **C:\WROX\CONTACTS.MDB** as the Topic.

3 Enter FormList as the Item and click on the StartDDE button.

4 Now click on the Query button and you'll see the Results box fill up with the names of the forms in the **CONTACTS.MDB**:

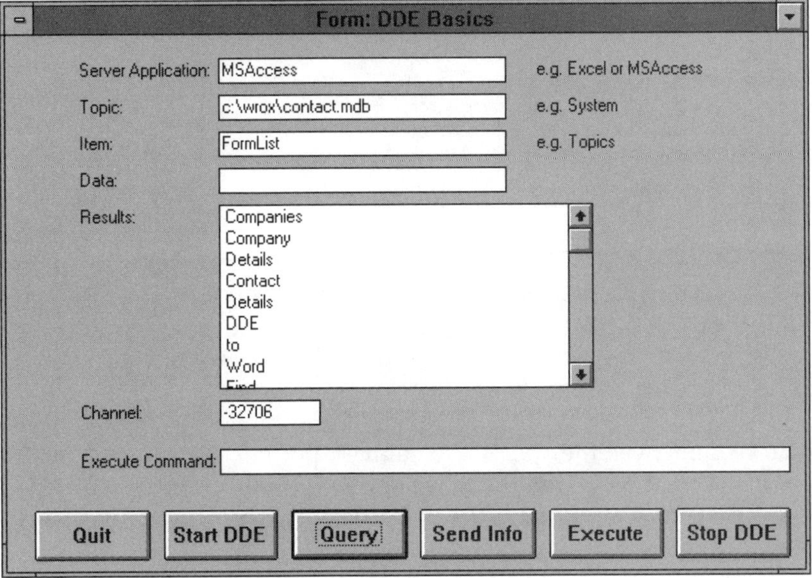

You can see that our **ParseTabs** procedure has split up the form names and put each word on a separate line. You could easily stop this happening by changing the string handling commands in the **ParseTabs** procedure.

In addition, if you know the item that you want to work with, you can specify a table, query or SQL string that you need to communicate with. If you do use one of these topics, the following syntax structure must be followed when you establish your link to the topic:

```
iChannel = DDEInitiate("MSACCESS","SAMPLES;<Type>")
```

where **<Type>** is either **TABLE**, **QUERY** or **SQL**. For example, to create a connection that allows you to do a query on the fly using SQL, you would specify:

```
iChannel = DDEInitiate("MSACCESS","SAMPLES;SQL")
```

Then, using the **iChannel** returned by **DDEInitiate**, you can send the information for your **SELECT** statement. The listing given below shows an example implementation that will return the information in the DDESample table:

```
...
dim sSQLText as string

iChannel = DDEInitiate("MSACCESS","SAMPLES;SQL")

sSQLText = ""
sSQLText = sSQLText & "Select * from DDESample"
DDEPoke iChannel "SQLText",  sSQLText
DDERequest iChannel, "NextRow"

DDETerminate
...
```

This set of statements establishes a connection to Access and the SQL query topic. We then build up a string to pass in with the SQL command we want to use. Using **DDEPoke**, we send the information to Access, specifying that it should be placed in the **SQLText** item.

After we've sent over the query, we request the next row based on that query. When the information is returned, we terminate our DDE connection and return to the user. This routine could be easily reconfigured to allow for retrieving all of the data, if that was what you needed to do. The example we have shown here should give you the information you need to begin using DDE functionality in your applications.

For more information on other DDE Topics that are available to your application, please see Appendix 2.

Some Examples of Using DDE with Access Tables

This section discusses two macros that can automate Word's interaction with Access. We'll look into how we can push information into Word, as well as how we can pull information out of it. We'll use the PIM **CONTACTS.MDB** database for the source of the information in each of these examples.

> **It's important to understand that there are many, many different ways to do a specific task. In a previous chapter, we've shown how to use OLE automation to send information to Word, but in these sections, we're looking at how to use DDE to do the same task. In addition, there is a Mail-Merge Wizard that will automate the task of sharing information between Word and Access.**
>
> **We provide these examples as a means of seeing the real-world implementations of these technologies, but you should investigate the way that makes the most sense for you. Your considerations will be system resources on the client computers, applications that are available and versions of software installed.**
>
> **DDE is much more forgiving in the way it handles older software. That fact alone may make it desirable to fully investigate DDE for your information exchange needs.**

Using Word to Extract Information from Access

Often you'll want to use information from your database system as a starting point for information in a document in Word. This section reviews a couple of different options for moving information between Word and Access.

The example we are going to use is an implementation that, from within Word, prompts you for a last name, retrieves the information from the Access database, and puts it into the document you are editing:

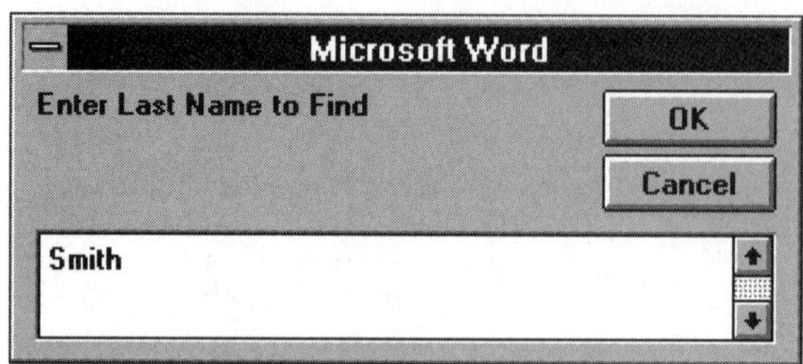

Our goal is to present a simple interface to the user that allows them to type in a last name of the contact that they wish to locate in the database. We then take this information and use it to search the **CONTACTS.MDB** database.

Once we've found the contact record that was requested, we'll use the **Word Insert** method to place the information in the current document, at the current cursor position. The Word macro to accomplish this is outlined below:

```
Sub MAIN
    'establish a connection to the database, prompt for and
    'retrieve a name, then close our connection to the
    'database.

    On Error Resume Next

    Dim iChannel, sSearchText
    Dim sResults

    'opens Access and returns to Word

    Shell "msaccess"
    AppActivate "Microsoft Word", 1

    'establish our connection to Access.  Start out with the System
    'topic so we can get the database opened up with the
    'OpenDatabase method. Sendkeys is used to get passed the opening
    'application screen.

    iChannel = DDEInitiate("MSACCESS", "SYSTEM")
    SendKeys "{enter}"
    DDEExecute iChannel, "[OpenDatabase c:\wrox\contacts.mdb]"
    AppActivate "Microsoft Word", 1
```

```
    'We've now got the database as a topic; shut down
    'this connection to re-establish a connection to the
    'specific database (CONTACTS.MDB)
    DDETerminate iChannel

    'Connect to the database
    iChannel = DDEInitiate("MSACCESS", "CONTACTs;SQL")

    'Find out what to search for
    sSearchText$ = InputBox$("Enter Last Name to Find")

    'Build the string on the DDE Server
    DDEPoke iChannel, "SQLText", "Select [FirstName], [LastName], "
    DDEPoke iChannel, "SQLText", "[Address] "
    DDEPoke iChannel, "SQLText", "from [Contacts] "
    DDEPoke iChannel, "SQLText", "where [LastName] = '" + sSearchText$ ↵
        + "';"

    'get the results row, NextRow returns the first row on its
    'first use
    sResults$ = DDERequest$(iChannel, "NextRow")

    'print it out for the user
    Insert sResults$ + Chr$(13)

    'shut down our connection
    DDETerminate iChannel

End Sub
```

You may need to change the paths to Access and the database specified above to point to the correct location for those files.

Each of the steps in the macro are reasonably straightforward. First, we run Access using the Word **Shell** command and return to Word. Next, we attach to the server application and ask it to open the database. This ensures that we can then attach to the specific table that we want access to. After the table is open, we shut down that connection and re-attach to the server and, more specifically, the table that we need to work with.

Once we're connected, we prompt the user for what name to search for and then use that name in building the SQL **SELECT** statement. The **SELECT** statement will query the Contacts table and return the row that matches the one requested by the user.

In our example, we're assuming that only one row is returned by the query. It's obviously possible that more than one match could be returned. In this case, in a production environment, you may want to first query on the last name and first name. If more than one is returned, you'll want to allow the user to select the one to work with and then go back after the remaining information, such as address, city and so on.

After we get the information back from Access, we insert the results at the current position in the document and close our connection to the server.

If you decide to integrate this functionality into Word, you can add the macro to a menu, providing quicker access to the features for you or your users.

Some obvious improvements to this procedure would be:

- Format the contact information appropriately for a form letter
- Check for duplicates, prompt for a selection
- Error handling for a record that was not found

This should provide you with a good basis for your Word and Access integration work. The next section shows how to send information to Word proactively rather than having Word extract the necessary information.

Using Access to Send Information to Word

We've just seen how to 'pull' information out of Access into a Word document. This section shows how you can 'push' information from Access into your Word document. This would also work for any other application's workspace that supports DDE:

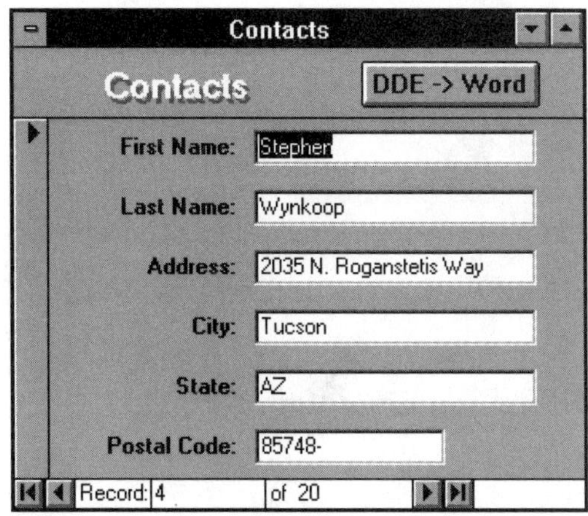

We've used the Contacts table as the basis for this new form. The easiest way to create this form is to use the Columnar Form Wizard, asking for the six fields that you can see on the form above.

Rename the text box controls and labels in the properties as follows:

Label Caption	Text Box Name
First Name	txtFirstName
Last Name	txtLastName
Address	txtAddress
City	txtCity
State	txtState
Postal Code	txtZip

Next, add a new button to the header, giving it a caption of DDE -> Word and naming it **cmdDDE2Word**. This is the button behind which we'll be adding the code to send the information to Word.

The following listing shows the code that we'll need to place behind the button, if we are to 'power up' this form:

```
Sub cmdDDE2Word_Click ()

    'send the current contact information from Access to
    'Word

    Dim iChannel As Integer

    'go out, attach to the System topic and open the
    'file we need
    iChannel = DDEInitiate("WINWORD", "SYSTEM")

    '
    'NOTE:  if you changed the installation directory for the samples,
    '       you'll need to change the file name shown below.
    '
    DDEExecute iChannel, "[FileOpen .Name=""c:\wrox\ddedoc.doc""]"
    DDETerminate iChannel

    'now that the file is open in Word, create a connection to it
    iChannel = DDEInitiate("WINWORD", "c:\wrox\ddedoc.doc")

    'send the information from our form to Word.  We put the information
    'into bookmarks ("BM_*"), predefined in Word.
    DDEPoke iChannel, "BM_Name", txtFirstName & " " & txtLastName
    DDEPoke iChannel, "BM_Address", txtAddress & " "
    DDEPoke iChannel, "BM_City", txtCity & " "
    DDEPoke iChannel, "BM_State", txtState & " "
    DDEPoke iChannel, "BM_Zip", txtZip & " "

    'all set, close the connection
    DDETerminate iChannel

End Sub
```

As in our Word macro listing, we first have to make sure the correct Word file is open. We do this by hooking up with the System topic for the server application. Once the connection is made, we can send the appropriate commands to the server to open the file we need.

Word Basic, which is what we're calling upon to do the work of opening the file, uses named arguments. If you search Word's help system for WordBasic, then `FileOpen`, you'll get a complete listing of the arguments available for the function.

> **Notice that `FileOpen` is specific to the server application. This means that the implementation of `FileOpen` in Access is different from that in Word. Be sure to check your respective vendor's documentation for details on what functions are supported and the exact syntax of working with those functions.**

Once the file is open, we close the System topic channel and open a channel to the actual document topic. Our document consists of nothing more than the following basic items:

- A date field, allowing the date to be updated automatically
- Bookmarks defined (Edit, Bookmark..., Add from within Word) in appropriate locations

From this, all we need to do is reference the bookmark as the item we need to send information to. In our example here, the bookmarks all start with **`BM_`** and have names that tie back to the fields that we place in them from the database.

After we've sent the information to Word, we can close down the channel and exit the routine. Try this out and then switch to Word to see the results:

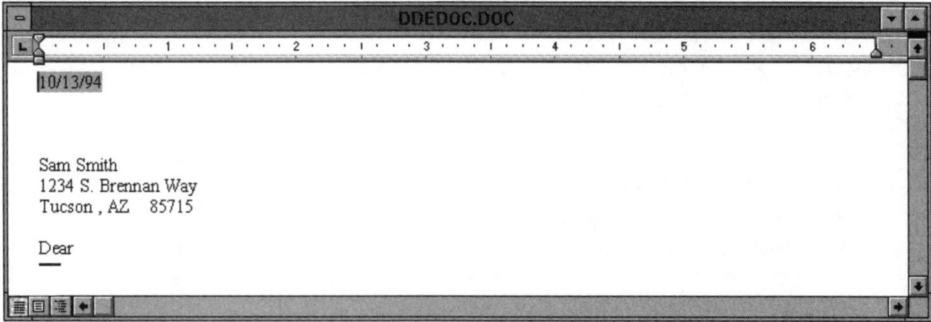

With these routines, you've seen how to send and retrieve information between Access and other applications. Remember that many applications have adhered to the DDE standard and support these functions or different implementations of them.

If you have computer systems on a network and need to be able to exchange information between them, NetDDE may be just the answer. The following sections describe how NetDDE works and the benefits and pitfalls that you may encounter in using it.

Using Network Dynamic Data Exchange - NetDDE

As we've seen with DDE, you can use the DDE toolset to send information between applications on your own personal system. This is a powerful capability, and one that is being implemented in more and more systems today.

As you can imagine, DDE is a popular method of data storage in systems that hold information for reference by other systems. Examples of these might be calendaring systems, personal information managers and other EIS systems. All of these, as well as many others are moving toward offering the capabilities of interfacing with DDE and, in the near future, OLE automation options.

You've probably experienced times when you'd like to share some information on your system with a colleague using another system on your local area network. If you are using a network that supports the NetBIOS protocol, you may want to investigate using NetDDE as a possibility.

NetDDE allows you to establish a DDE conversation between two systems on a NetBIOS-based network. Once established, the conversation between these two systems is identical to your DDE conversations that we've established previously, i.e. you can send and retrieve information, as well as being able to execute commands on the remote system.

> *Error handling for NetDDE calls is handled exactly the same way as in standard local system calls. You should always implement an error handler that uses the* `On Error Goto` *construct to control program execution in the case of a problem.*

Capabilities and Limitations

`NETDDE.EXE` runs as a background task under Windows. When Windows loads, it attempts to load NetDDE. In order for NetDDE to work on your system, you must have the NetBIOS protocol active on your system.

If you are running a Novell Netware system, prior to entering Windows, make sure you run `NETBIOS.EXE` from the DOS command prompt. This loads a compatibility layer that will make the NetBIOS protocol available to your Windows environment.

Windows for Workgroups is required for NetDDE. It is the first operating system to support the protocol.

One of the most simple examples of NetDDE in action is the 'Chat' program, provided with Windows. Chat allows you to literally call another computer and begin a conversation. The words you type on your system appear in the remote user's system and vice versa: it's a rudimentary version of electronic discussions.

You'll recall from our discussion of DDE that the server application must be running in order for your application to initiate a conversation with it. When the application resides on your local system, you can start the application with the Access Basic's **`Shell`** command. In the situation where you're trying to communicate with a remote system, you don't have this capability.

There are two different ways that you can handle the case of a remote server application not being active at the time you call it. First, if the link to the remote application is maintained by the Clipbook or DDEShare, explained later in this section, these applications can be told to automatically start the application when the shared link is accessed.

Second, if you're attaching to an application on the remote system, as our examples here show, your routines will need to make sure the remote application is up and running. If not, you'll have to handle the error condition in your software and retry the operation later.

Next, we'll cover the specifics of working with a remote application to send and receive data from the application. Note that NetDDE is no different from DDE once the application communications' channel has been established, i.e. once you've established communications with the remote system, you can use the same **`DDEPoke`**, **`DDERequest`** and **`DDEExecute`** commands that we've previously outlined in this chapter.

Using the Universal Naming Convention

NetDDE requires the use of the Universal Naming Convention (UNC) that Microsoft has put into place. The UNC is a way of identifying a computer name in relationship to the information or resources available on the system.

To establish a UNC name for a NetDDE share, you'll need to know the network computer name of the remote system. You can determine this from the control panel, under the network setup icon.

Once you've established the computer name, the UNC name for the computer is created by placing a double backslash before the name. For example, if the remote computer's name is 'MIKEB_COMP', then the UNC name would be '\\MIKEB_COMP'.

You use the UNC name of the remote system when you are establishing the initial connection the system. Instead of specifying only the application name for the system you want to access, you also specify the UNC name and then '\NDDE$', for example, '\\MIKEB_COMP\NDDE$'.

Calling Another System

Once you've established the UNC name for the remote computer, you establish a connection to the system by using the `DDEInitiate` just as when you call an application residing on your local system. The change comes in what you specify as a topic name on the initial share.

When you are calling another system, you actually connect to `NETDDE.EXE` running on the remote system. NetDDE then looks up your request and figures out what application it refers to. For that reason, you need to set up the share cross reference on the remote system prior to calling the remote application.

On the WINAPB forum on Compuserve there is a utility available from Wonderware that makes it simple and straightforward to create shares on your system. This is the DDE Share utility:

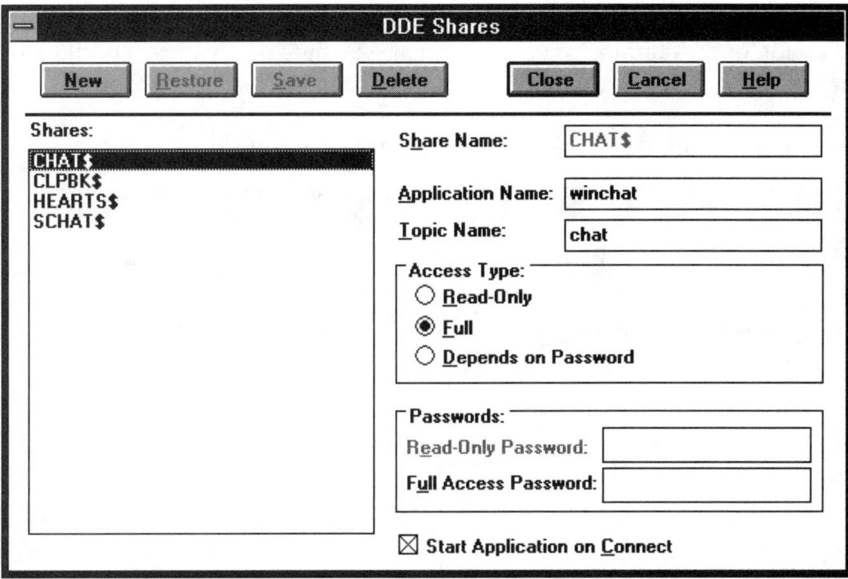

When you first run **DDESHARE.EXE**, you get the display shown in this diagram. The form shows what shares you have defined and the different attributes about them that pertain to your system.

> *The initial shares that are automatically set up on your system provide access to your clipbook (CLPBK$), the chat utility (CHAT$ and SCHAT$) mentioned earlier and the hearts (HEARTS$) game included with Windows.*

To set up a new share, select New, and then enter a new Share Name, Application Name and Topic. These are what will be accessed when you initiate a conversation with this remote system.

The remaining options on the form relating to Access Type and Password are straightforward. Notice that **DDESHARE.EXE** also provides you with the capability to designate an application as one that should be started when the DDE conversation is established.

You need to establish a share to whatever it is that you want to 'talk' with later. So, for our example here, we'll create a share to Access, specifically to the Access System topic, and then to the Access Contacts;SQL topic.

Here are the examples, created in the **DDESHARE** interface:

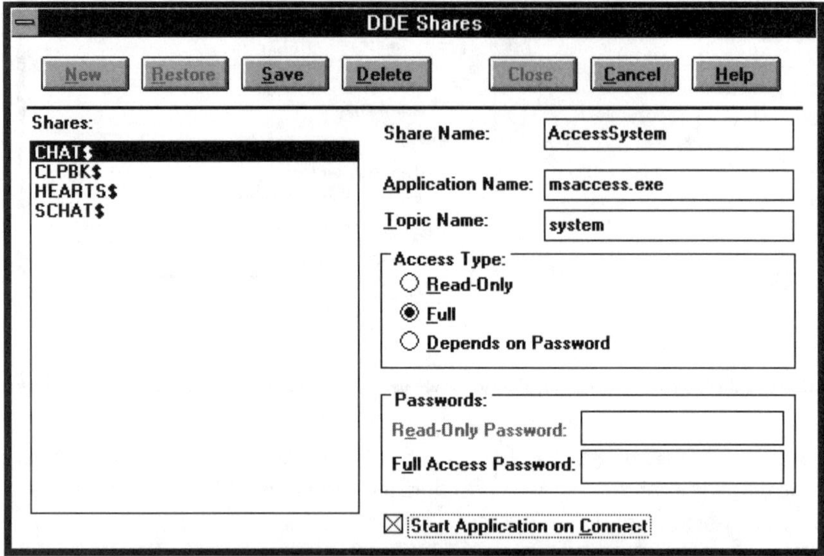

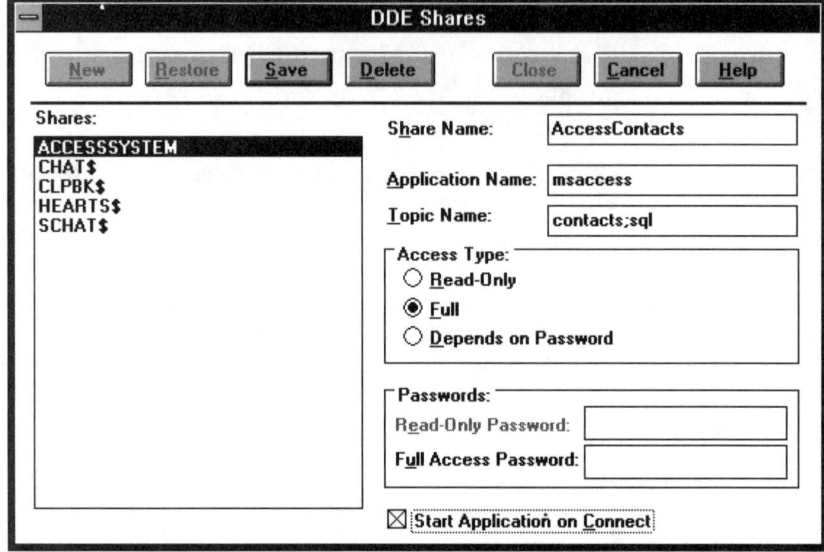

The definitions for shares are stored in the **SYSTEM.INI** file. The entries are under the **[DDEShares]** heading and will look like the following list. In addition, there will be any additional shares you may have defined:

```
[DDEShares]
CHAT$=winchat,chat,,31,,0,,0,0,0
SCHAT$=winchat,chat,,31,,0,,0,0,0
CLPBK$=clipsrv,system,,31,,0,,0,0,0
HEARTS$=mshearts,hearts,,15,,0,,0,0,0
ACCESSSYSTEM=msaccess.exe,system,,31,,16,,0,0,0
ACCESSCONTACTS=msaccess,contacts;sql,,31,,16,,0,0,0
```

While it's beyond the scope of this book to discuss all of the parameters in each line, it's important to know that you can investigate the active shares on a system by examining the **SYSTEM.INI** file. The share name that you specify in your **DDEInitiate** call is the Share Name in our setup program, and the first parameter on the line in your **SYSTEM.INI** file.

You may need to increase the DDE timeout value in your Access options screen. This value determines the time that Access will wait before no longer waiting on results from a DDE or OLE call. Since the DDE call may result in a remote application starting, you may want to increase the value for the timeout from 30 (the default) to 180 seconds. Remember, you must account for other activities that may be operating on the remote system, including printing, other applications running, and so on. These all have an impact on your application's load time.

Also, remember that the reverse is true. As you are making requests of the remote system, if there is a user on the system at the time, you may impact the performance of the remote system for that user. Be sure to coordinate with them on best times to 'use' their system.

The syntax for the NetDDE version of **DDEInitiate** call is as follows:

```
iChannel = DEInitiate("\\<ComputerName>\NDDE$","<ShareName>")
```

where

iChannel is the variable that will give us our unique conversation ID

ComputerName is the name of the remote computer ('MIKEB_COMP')

ShareName is the share on the remote system ('ACCESSSYSTEM')

This will establish communications with the remote system, starting the application, if we've checked the **DDESHARE** box, so asking NetDDE to do so. Here's the completed line:

```
iChannel = DDEInitiate("\\MIKEB_COMP\NDDE$","ACCESSSYSTEM")
```

and

```
iChannel = DDEInitiate("\\MIKEB_COMP\NDDE$","ACCESSCONTACTS")
```

These calls would establish a connection to the remote system's System and Contacts;SQL topics respectively. This would allow you to pass commands, run SQL queries against the database and all the other options offered by normal DDE conversations.

Note that in our sample DDE Basics form, you can experiment with NetDDE connections by specifying the fully qualified '\\computername\NDDE$' and sharename on the form. The remaining functions will continue to operate correctly, so producing the same effects as normal DDE.

Comments and Suggestions

If your application is going to be used as a database store for other applications, or if your application will be receiving data from other applications, you will want to seriously consider using DDE or NetDDE in your application. DDE provides a method of communication between applications that is more widely implemented in today's marketplace than OLE or OLE automation. While this will probably change in the future, if your requirements are immediate and OLE carries too much resource overhead for your system, DDE may be just the ticket.

It's also possible that you will have a mixed environment and will be using DDE for remote communications and OLE for localized management of objects. This may be the balance between interoperability and functionality that you will see implemented more and more in the future.

In the next chapter, we'll look into optimizing your applications and how you can use the transaction processing capabilities of Access. Combining these techniques together with the inter-process communication capabilities that you've worked with so far, will add a new level of functionality to your systems.

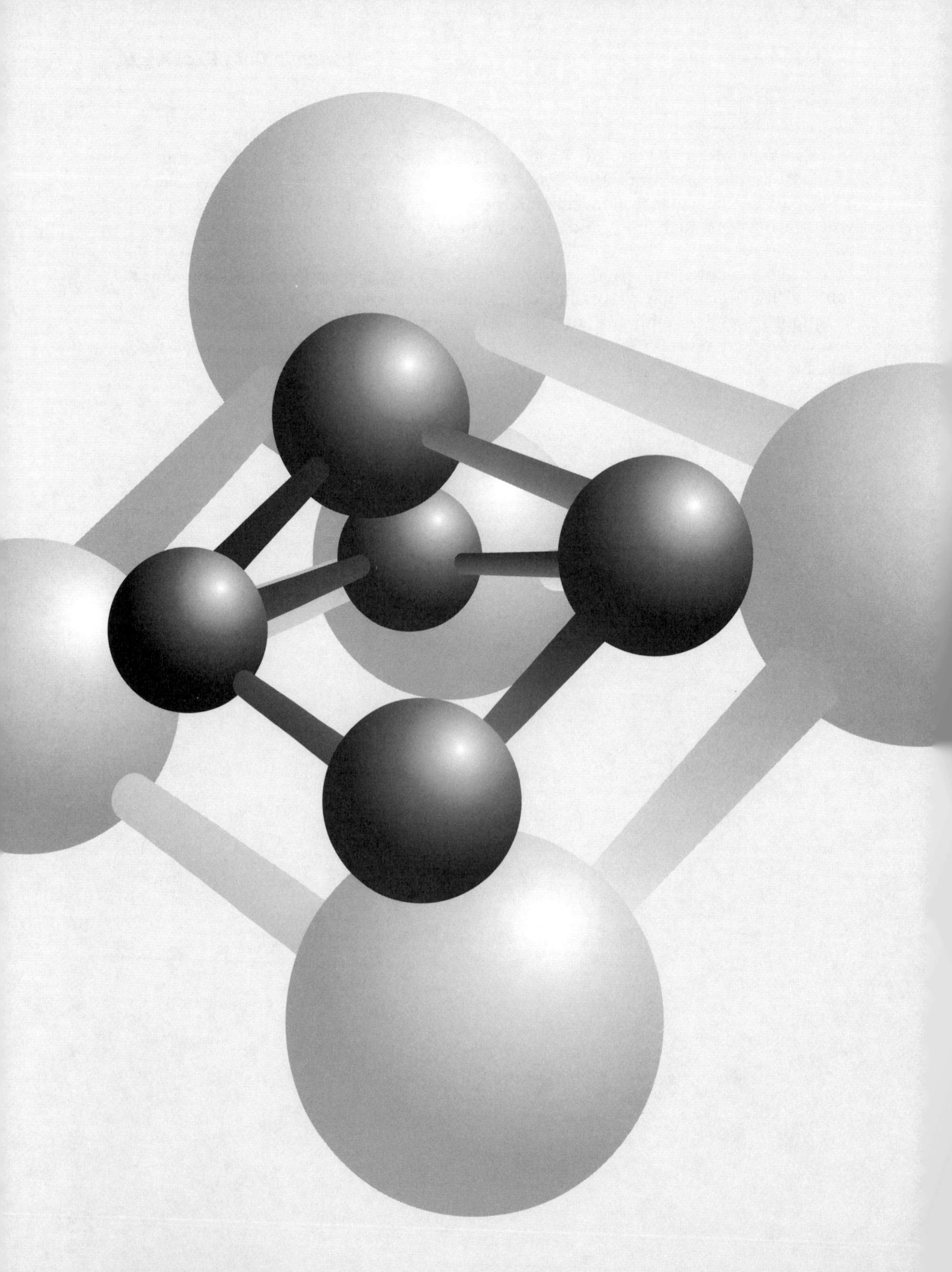

CHAPTER

Optimization Using Transactions and Referential Integrity

Computers are wonderful inventions but they are not superhuman. We have become accustomed to having information at our fingertips and expect computers to provide us with it in a fraction of a second. Sometimes, it's not the computer's fault if it can't perform at superhuman speed. There are many ways that we, as developers, can optimize our databases; transaction processing and referential integrity are just two of them.

What's Covered in This Chapter

This chapter introduces some different ways that you can optimize the performance of your applications. In particular we'll discuss the use of transaction processing and how to maintain referential integrity in your database tables.

The topics and techniques include:

- Working with transaction processing applications
- Performing Mass Updates
- Maintaining information integrity
- Normalization

The implementation of these techniques, both on a theoretical and practical level, is covered in this chapter, using the PIM as a source document.

Chapter 6

How This Chapter Affects Our Application

In our application, we have a data-dependency between the Company, Contacts and Projects tables. This dependency means that for every Project we need a valid Contact and for each Contact we need a valid Company. We will look specifically at multi-tier cascading deletes which is implemented in our application to maintain the integrity of our PIM database tables.

Introduction

When you begin to create larger, more complicated and comprehensive applications in the Access development environment, you'll need to start implementing more controls over the information that you're managing.

There are several different things to keep in mind when developing your applications for distribution. Some of these things include:

- Making sure that all aspects of a transaction occur correctly and completely
- Giving users a chance to change their minds on a series of database updates
- Providing for referential control and integrity in your information
- Forms design considerations

In this chapter, we'll be showing how to use **transactions** in your programs to accomplish several different things. First, we'll show how to use transactions as a tool for controlling updates to your system. This will make sure that all aspects of a group of related actions happen together.

Second, we'll show how you can use transactions to do mass updates to your database. Transactions can significantly reduce the amount of time it will take to complete large-scale updates, providing a very useful, real-time advantage for your system.

In addition, the user interface design chapter provides more in-depth information about considerations for form and application designs, including the different things you can do to control program flow, placement and sizing of controls and so on.

Other areas that will be covered include working with **On-Line Transaction Processing (OLTP)** systems, batch systems and table locking considerations.

Transaction Processing in Access

Using the concept of transaction processing in Access can provide three different levels of functionality in your programs:

- Group activities
- Enhance performance
- Offer users a way of canceling updates

Using Transactions to Group Activities

The first use of transactions that's under review is the capability to group logical functions together, requiring that all or none of the items are completed at one time. The best example, and the one that you'll see most often, is of financial transactions.

Imagine that last week you asked Fred for $5. You gave him an IOU to the value of $5 when he gave you the money. This week, as it's time for you to repay Fred, you want to exchange the money for the IOU, so you can destroy it.

If you hand Fred the $5, but he doesn't give you back the IOU, you'll want to get your $5 back. Also, if you don't give Fred the money, he'll not want to give you the IOU back. In this example, a transaction could be wrapped around the events that would require that both parts are completed successfully before the transaction is pronounced complete.

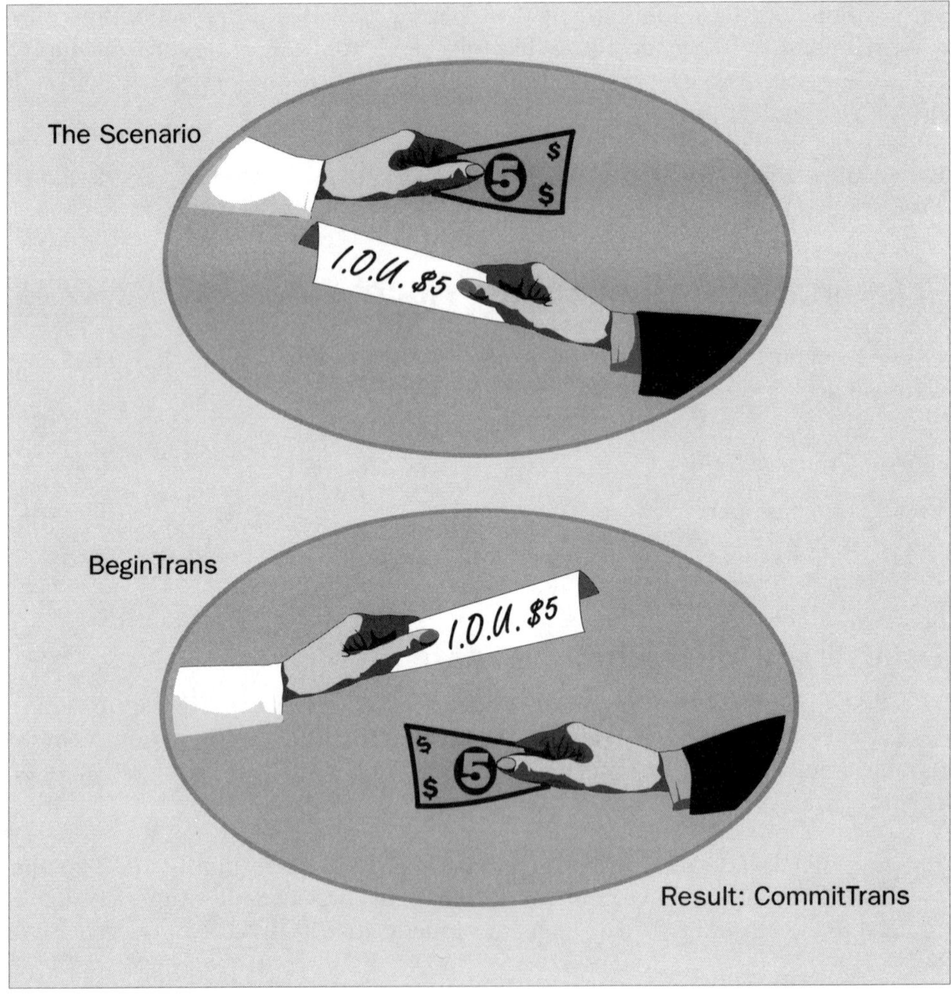

Actions that take place within transactions are bracketed by the BeginTrans and CommitTrans methods that apply to the Access Workspace. An example of our scenario, described in pseudo-code, would be:

```
WorkSpace.BeginTrans
    Credit money to Fred
....Get back IOU from Fred
WorkSpace.CommitTrans
```

An example of the error processing would be the wrong IOU or the money not being to the correct amount. The pseudo-code for this transaction would look something like this:

```
WorkSpace.BeginTrans
    Credit money to Fred
    Get back IOU from Fred
    If Money <> $5 then RollBackTrans
    If IOU is not mine then RollBackTrans
WorkSpace.CommitTrans
```

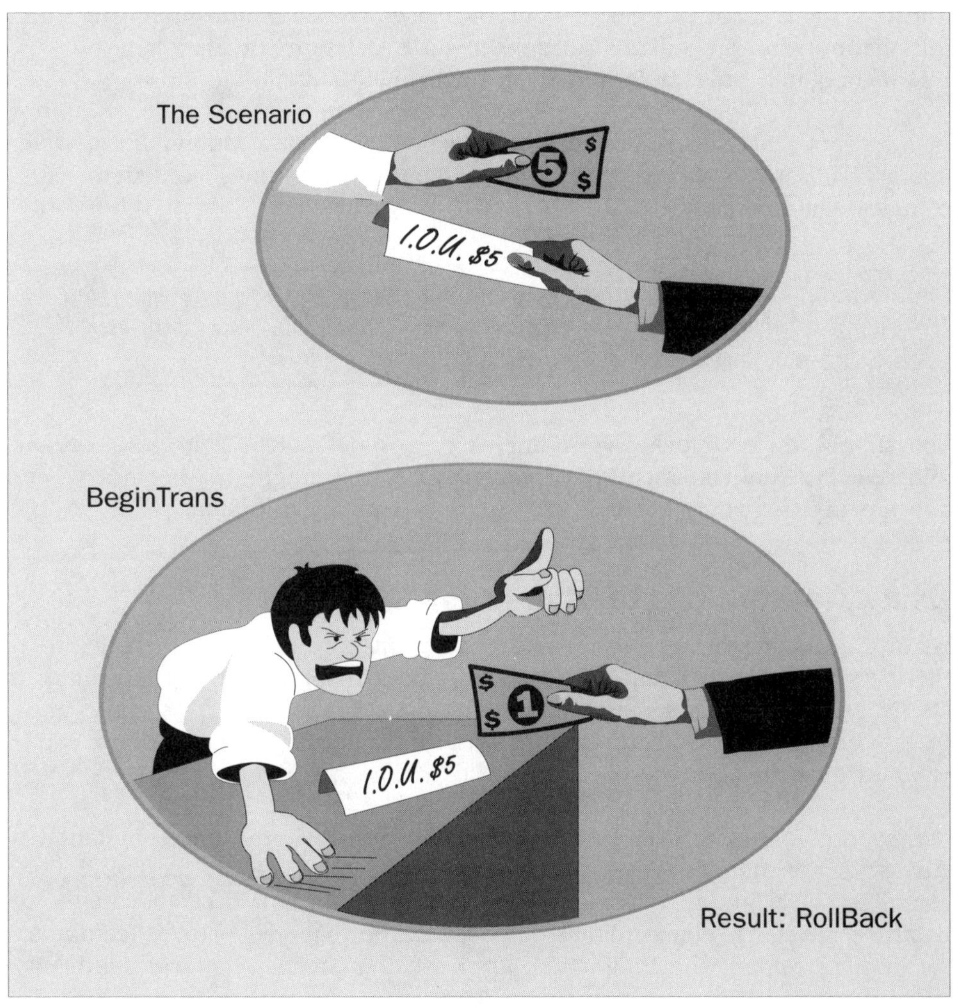

In this case, the money is incorrect. Fred obviously won't accept one dollar for a $5 IOU, so the transaction is rollbacked. While this example is very simple, you can see how transaction processing is used to make sure that all actions happen, or the whole ball game is called off.

Using Transactions to Enhance Performance on Mass Updates

There are many different operations that you may need to perform that will impact upon a large portion of your database. These include importing information from an outside datasource, mass deletions or insertions of information into your table and other such operations.

In these cases, if you make use of transaction processing around the update operations, you will see a drastic improvement in the times needed to complete the operations.

> *In one case, a database table import containing some 100,000 rows took more than 14 hours to complete without using transaction processing. When transaction processing was enabled, the operation took only 20 minutes!*

You should always bracket your import or update routines with **`BeginTrans`** and **`CommitTrans`** statements. The exception to this might be the case where you are updating only a single row or record in a single table.

Using Transactions to Offer Users 'A Way Out'

As an added benefit, when you use transactions you'll have the chance to tell the user the impact of the operation, providing them with the opportunity to stop the operation before you commit the data to the table. This could apply to cases where you're about to do a wide-scale update to a table and you want to give the user the opportunity to change his mind.

An example of transaction processing in this respect is the implementation of Access' Action queries. When you perform an action query, Access will complete the action and then tell you what the impact will be to your database table(s) if you continue. If you indicate that you want to continue, Access will commit the transaction, applying the changes, updates or deletions as you've requested:

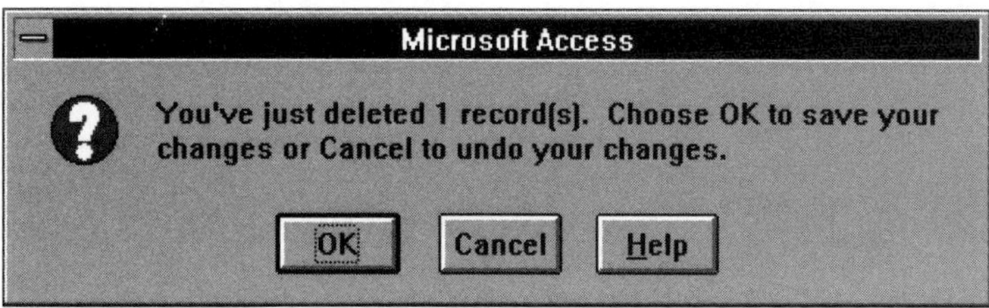

This is also true of deletions that you make while in the datasheet view. Access will prompt you for verification before it commits the transaction to delete the record(s) as you've requested.

You can do this in your own applications if you bracket operations within transactions and then prompt users for confirmation just before you commit the transaction. If the user indicates that he doesn't want to continue, you can simply rollback the transaction and he will be back where he started.

A Sample Application - a Transaction Processor

In the **SAMPLES.MDB** database, there are several items associated with this demonstration, the first of which is the Access form called Transaction Demonstration:

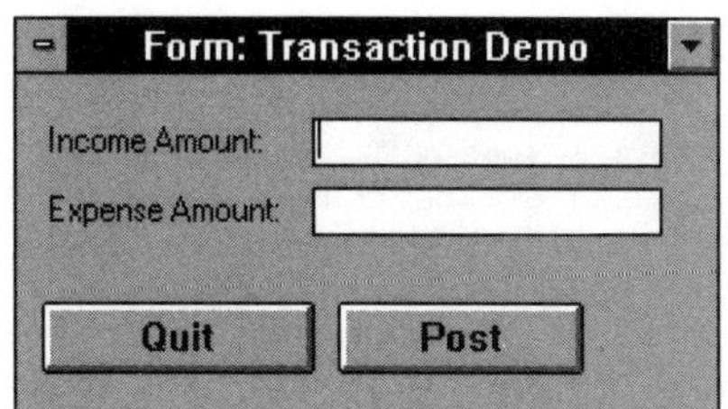

This user interface is quite simple. It asks for either an income or expense amount and presents the option of posting it to the database or quitting the application.

The Quit button, named **cmdQuit**, has the standard **DoCmd Close** code behind it. It unloads the form and returns the user to the tabbed dialog in Access.

The **cmdPost** button, the real worker of the demonstration, contains the demonstration code for our discussion. The following is the listing of code from behind the **Click** event for the button:

```
Sub cmdPost_Click ()
    'the cmdPost button determines which way the
    'transaction is going, then applies the update
    'to the database.  Transactions are used
    'to make sure the funds are available, etc.

    'set up our variables
    Dim WS As WorkSpace
    Dim DB As Database
    Dim rsIncome As Recordset
    Dim rsExpense As Recordset
    Dim rsTotal As Recordset

    Dim cIncome As Currency
    Dim cExpense As Currency
    Dim cTotal As Currency

    'first, set up our references into the environment, databases,
    'tables, etc.
    Set WS = DBEngine.WorkSpaces(0)
    Set DB = CurrentDB()
    Set rsIncome = DB.OpenRecordset("Income")
    Set rsExpense = DB.OpenRecordset("Expenses")

    'next start the transaction
    WS.BeginTrans

        'Hint: you can easily test the val of a text
        'field by appending a space. If it is non-null
        'it returns zero, and can be tested
        'in this statement.  If the field has a
        'value, the space will
        'not affect it.
        If (Val(txtIncome & " ") > 0) Then
            'we readily accept deposits
            'add the row to the table.

            'Create a new record in the table
            rsIncome.AddNew
            rsIncome!TransactionDate = Now
            rsIncome!transactionAmount = Val(txtIncome)
            rsIncome!TransactionDescription = "Demonstration income ↵
                transaction"

            'save the changes
            rsIncome.Update

        End If
```

```
        If Val(txtExpense & " ") > 0 Then

            'Create a new record in the expense table
            rsExpense.AddNew
            rsExpense!TransactionDate = Now
            rsExpense!transactionAmount = Val(txtExpense)
            rsExpense!TransactionDescription = "Demonstration expense ↵
                transaction"

            'save the changes
            rsExpense.Update

            'next, we have to determine if there's enough
            'money in the account to process the charge.  We've
            'saved the expense transaction at this point, but
            'we can roll it back if there's not enough money.

            'set our total, using the two
            'queries, "IncomeTotal" and "ExpenseTotal" as the
            'foundation for the total calculations.
            cTotal = 0
            Set rsTotal = DB.OpenRecordset("IncomeTotal")
            cTotal = rsTotal!IncomeTotal
            rsTotal.Close
            Set rsTotal = DB.OpenRecordset("ExpenseTotal")
            cTotal = cTotal - rsTotal!ExpenseTotal
            rsTotal.Close

            'as of this point, cTotal contains the net total of the
            'accounts from the two tables.

             If cTotal < 0 Then
                'the amount of the expense exceeds the total we have
                'available on account.  Let the user know that the
                'transaction is denied.
                MsgBox "Unable to complete the transaction. You don't ↵
                    have enough money.  Make a deposit first. "

                'reverse the transaction, removing the row from the
                'expenses table
                WS.Rollback
                Exit Sub
            End If

        End If

    'everything is okay; save the changes permanently and let the user know
    WS.CommitTrans
    MsgBox "Transaction applied, balances have been updated. "

End Sub
```

This code is examined in the next few sections, each describing how transactions are handled in the example.

Using Access' BeginTrans Command

When you work with transactions, there are three distinct coding parts to the transaction concept. The first, **BeginTrans**, is outlined here:

```
...
'next start the transaction
WS.BeginTrans
...
```

The first thing to notice is that the transaction commands are relative to the **Workspace**, not to any particular table or recordset that you have open or plan to open during the procedure. This allows your transaction to span several different tables, each of which would be affected by the transaction's operations.

You create a workspace object by using the statement **Dim WS As WorkSpace**, and use **Set WS = DBEngine.Workspaces(0)** to set up the reference to the current workspace maintained by Access.

> *It will help your code maintenance efforts if you indent the code between the* **BeginTrans** *and* **CommitTrans** *statements. Treating them like an* **If...EndIf** *statement will increase the readability of your code now, as well as increasing your understanding of the code at a later date.*

Once you've established the beginning of your transaction with the **BeginTrans** command, all database updates until the **CommitTrans** command will be considered as part of the 'package'. That is, all of the things that you do between the two commands must succeed before the transaction can be committed, or completed. If a problem is found with the transaction, you simply rollback the transaction and the database tables will return to the state they were in when the **BeginTrans** command was issued.

> *Note that during the time you are processing information in the transaction, the table rows that you are working with are locked. Be sure that you don't issue the* **BeginTrans** *when any items that will require user intervention and therefore possibly delay processing are still to be obtained. Get all information you need and then, when you're ready to do the actual data manipulation, start the transaction at that point.*

Using Access' CommitTrans Command

In our example, we commit the transaction as a default action as if nothing went wrong with the process:

```
...
WS.CommitTrans
MsgBox "Transaction applied, balances have been updated. "
...
```

When the `CommitTrans` method is used, the database updates are written to the tables. In our example, the income or expense row is written to the appropriately named table. In either case, we know the transaction was valid. In the case of the expense, the balance on the income account supported the cost of the expense. If there had been a problem, the `CommitTrans` command would not have been executed.

The `CommitTrans` also releases any locks that are held on the tables involved in the transaction, allowing updates from other users or processes to gain access to the table(s).

After the `CommitTrans` action is processed, we notify the user that we've finished with the processing and return control to the user.

Using Access' Rollback Transaction Command

In our sample application, the transaction can't fail on an income entry. The only time we will fail a transaction will be on an expense where not enough money exists in the account to cover the transaction.

The balance of the account is determined by the two queries, IncomeTotal and ExpenseTotal. These queries simply provide the totals for the two tables, Income and Expenses. The totals from the queries are assigned to the value in `cTotal` as a temporary total that indicates the balance available to spend:

```
...
'set our total, using the two
'queries, "IncomeTotal" and "ExpenseTotal" as the
'foundation for the total calculations.
cTotal = 0
Set rsTotal = DB.OpenRecordset("IncomeTotal")
```

```
cTotal = rsTotal!IncomeTotal
rsTotal.Close
Set rsTotal = DB.OpenRecordset("ExpenseTotal")
cTotal = cTotal - rsTotal!ExpenseTotal
rsTotal.Close
...
```

The next step compares the total in the expense field with the total available balance. If the total is insufficient, we notify the user that there are insufficient funds. We then rollback the transaction and exit the subroutine, presumably allowing the user to make a deposit.

```
...
If cTotal < 0 Then
    'the amount of the expense exceeds the total we have
    'available on account.  Let the user know that the
    'transaction is denied.
    MsgBox "Unable to complete the transaction.  You don't have enough ↵
        money.  Make a deposit first. "

    'reverse the transaction, removing the row from the
    'expenses table
    WS.Rollback
    Exit Sub
End If
...
```

You should also remember that the **Rollback** command is used against the workspace. When the **Rollback** command is issued, the row(s) that you previously inserted into tables are not written to the tables and the transaction is aborted.

In your application, if you determine that a lengthy transaction is about to be rolled back, you may want to consider providing the user with a dialog box or further directions. You can allow them to correct the problem and continue, rather than simply throwing away the items that made up the failed transaction.

Using Transaction Management with a Remote Server

Access transactions control updates to native tables within the Access environment. You will run into a challenge when you need to implement transactions that encompass updates to attached tables.

For example, suppose your process includes updates to two native Access tables and to two different Microsoft SQL Server tables. The updates to the Access tables would be contained within a specific procedure or function and bracketed by a transaction. The problem arises when you need to make sure that all the updates are possible, including those on the SQL Server tables. Access has no way of controlling the impact on the remote server, so it is impossible for Access to rollback the transaction to reverse the action on the remote server.

Depending on the type of database you are accessing, you may be able to implement transactions that include remote database table updates. The secret to this capability is that the database server must be able to accomplish the following tasks:

- It should be an intelligent server; or more specifically, the server must be processing your requests for data and it must be able to act independently on the request. This is commonly referred to as Stored Procedure capabilities.
- The server must support transactions.
- The server must be able to return a status to your application.

If you don't have any intelligence in the back-end (for example with dBase or FoxPro) then you may not be able to get transaction processing, especially across database types. If you have SQL Server, you can use stored procedures, or native transaction processing to get the control you need.

If a dynaset or table is based entirely on Microsoft Jet database engine tables, the Transactions property is 'true' and you can use transactions. Dynasets and tables based on tables created in other database products may not support transactions. For example, you can't use transactions in a dynaset based on a Paradox table.

The pseudo-code for your Access Basic code would be:

```
Start AB transaction
    Update first Access table
    Update second Access table
    Call stored procedure with parameters to update SQL tables
    If SQL update failed
        rollback SQL transaction within the stored procedure
        rollback the AB transaction
        exit sub
Commit AB transaction
```

The key to this organization is that committing the Access transaction depends on the successful completion of the SQL transaction. You should also note that you should have no processing that takes place on the Access side of the procedure after the SQL process has run. If the SQL process fails, you can roll back the SQL transaction within the stored procedure and return a status indicating the failure.

When the Access routine sees that the stored procedure failed, it will rollback the Access transaction. The database tables, both internal and those located in the SQL database, will be in the same state as they were when the process started.

If the SQL procedure succeeds, then the Access transaction is committed and you're able to make certain that both sides of the transaction were successful.

Considerations when Using Transactions

There are some interesting and important things happening behind the scenes when you use Access for transaction processing. First, to make sure that data will not change during the processing of a transaction, Access locks the records that need to be updated.

Generally, Access employs a page locking algorithm. This means that not only the record you need, but also the records logically surrounding the record are locked.

If your routines call for user input during the processing of the transaction, it can prevent other users from accessing the system until the user has completed the operation. For this reason, we strongly recommend that you limit or avoid user intervention in your program during the processing of a transaction.

For example, if a user decides to go for lunch halfway through a transaction where they are required to input something, the system would be locked up until they got back. Obviously, this isn't the ideal situation!

You should gather up the information you need to accomplish the operations included in the transaction prior to initiating the **`BeginTrans`** command. This includes database calls that are not updates, but provide background information for the processing of the transaction. If you put as little processing as possible within the transaction, performance will increase and database locking will be decreased. Try to structure your transactions with a 'get in, do it quickly and get out' philosophy.

Another thing that you may want to consider doing with transactions and user confirmation of saved changes is the management of a batch processing system. Your application can allow the users to enter their information into a temporary table. From this table, the information can be verified and then posted against the production database within a transaction to ensure that all changes and updates will be saved. This prevents the tables being locked on a regularly repeated basis during normal operation time.

An additional point about transactions is that they are created and maintained on a procedure or function level scope. Consider the following pseudo-code listing:

```
...
WS.BeginTrans
    Do_something
    Do_something_else
    Do_subroutine_call
    Do_the_final-something
WS.CommitTrans
...
```

You would assume that the code between the **BeginTrans** and **CommitTrans** statements would presumably be controlled by the transaction. However, when you are using Access, the transaction processing will go out of scope when you step into the **Do_subroutine_call** statement. When you return, the remaining statements will still be controlled by the transaction. You'll need to move the code that is to be executed within the transaction inside the procedure containing the transaction control statements.

The transactions that your system commits to the tables must adhere to any rules of relational integrity that have been defined for your database. Now that we've seen how to use transactions to control updates and enhance the performance of your system, we'll look at how to protect the integrity of the data.

Chapter 6

Maintaining Integrity in Your Database Tables

When you develop systems that contain multiple related tables, you'll need to ensure that those tables remain synchronized with each other. Often, you'll have a master table with one or more supporting 'sub-tables' linked to it. In these cases, you'll want to look into different ways to maintain referential integrity in your system. When you establish a main table that references a child table, if a record is removed from the main table, it may produce orphan records in the child table. Referential integrity checks will prevent this from happening.

This section goes over some of the considerations that can lead to better integrity of your information when designing and implementing your systems.

Normalization of Database Tables

When you design a system's database and table structure, it's important that you normalize the database to the largest extent possible. In a nutshell, database normalization is accomplished by limiting or removing redundant information in any given table.

For example, consider our PIM application. We have a table of contacts, a table for companies and a table of projects. All of the contacts can have a company and all of the contacts can have projects associated with them. You should also note that more than one contact can refer to the same company.

One way to implement this would be to prompt for and save the company information (company name, address and phone number) with the contact record. This would allow you to enter the contact and company name information, just as you can in our implementation.

One-To-Many Relations

The challenge with this scenario comes when you have multiple contacts at the same company. While you can certainly enter multiple records, you end up having to re-enter all of the company information into each contact's record. Also, if the company name should change, you'd either have to change each record that referred to the company, or write an action query that updated all of the different records in the database.

There is a better way to accomplish all of this. What you should do is normalize the databases in our scenario. This means you should pull out the redundant information and place it in its own table. In our example, this would amount to putting the company information into a 'Company' table and create a reference between the contact and company tables.

Unique ID Fields

This is often done by assigning a Counter type ID field as the key in the Company table, and then using a numeric field in the Contacts table to link each record to one in the Company table. Every time you enter a contact name, you wouldn't enter the company. You would simply enter the ID of the company they work for. You can then retrieve the company record for that contact by referencing the CompanyID field.

You might think that this provides for a more difficult interface for the user to follow. Most, if not all, of the management of the relationships and the coherent display of the information in the tables can be made in code, with forms designed to present the information exactly as the user needs to see it. In many cases, a normalized database will result in increased speed for the user application as well.

Advantages Of Normalization

By normalizing these two tables, we can provide several different things. First, we eliminate typing mistakes on the company information. If each contact had to have company information entered for it, you can imagine the possibilities for data entry errors are exponentially increased as the number of records entered increases.

Second, we provide a common company record for changes. If the company address were to change, you would simply have to update the company table. The changes to the company information would be shown for every contact that referred to it.

Third, as a rule, normalization tends to increase performance. The tables you are creating are usually smaller, which provides for better utilization of the Windows cache. Also, since the records are smaller, the network traffic is reduced if you are working over a network.

Note that normalization doesn't always increase performance. Increasing the complexity of the processing required to build a dynaset you work with regularly may negatively impact performance. Depending on the things you may have to do to retrieve some data elements, it may make sense to de-normalize some information. If you are required to do several joins across tables to retrieve information, investigate the database design and see if it would make sense to break the normalization rule in favor of better performance.

Fourth, normalized database tables tend to take up less room on your system. This is because you're not duplicating information for each record. Instead, you are simply creating a reference to existing information on the system. This alone can be a huge plus in favor of normalization of your system tables.

You should consider diagramming your tables prior to implementing your database design. Determine which tables have a one-to-many relationship (as in the Company to Contacts relationship) and which are one-to-one. As a minimum requirement, the tables that have a one-to-many relationship should be linked by a common field, usually a numeric ID, to reduce redundant information in your system.

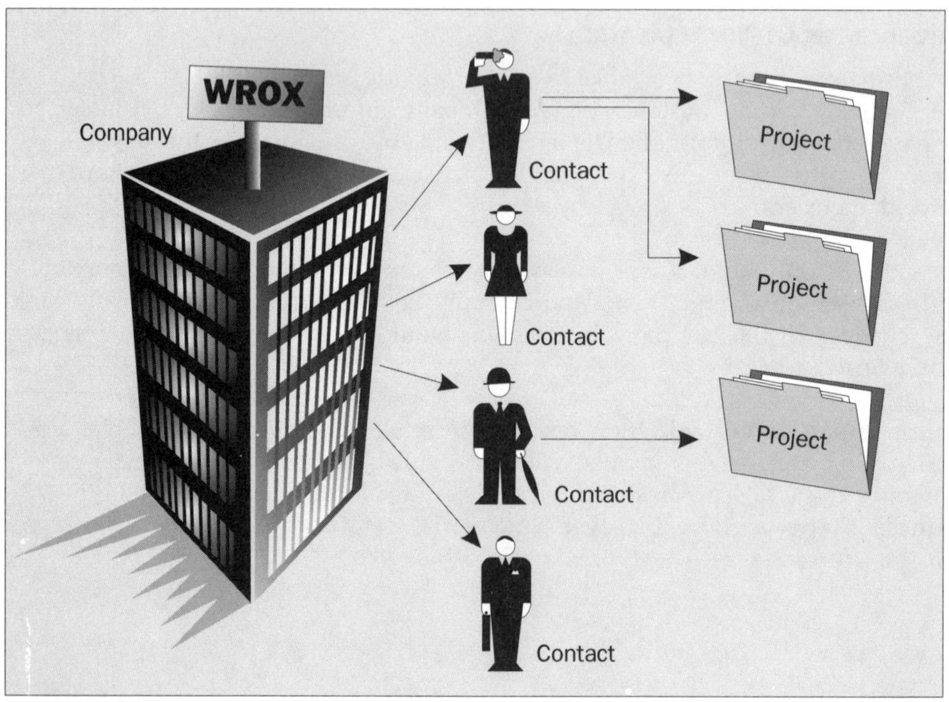

Wherever you may have information being duplicated over several records, consider placing that information into a separate table and creating links between the tables as needed.

If you find it time-consuming to be constantly including full path references on your blank form to fields from different tables, you might want to create a query that creates the view of the tables that you need, as the basis for your form. On many other database systems, what Access refers to as queries are called **Views** for just this reason. By creating this multi-table query, you're really creating a view of the data that includes the resolved references between tables. You can use queries the data source for forms, reports as well as other queries. In Access, a query is logically equivalent to a table in these respects.

Note that using a query in place of a table can be slower. Access will be processing the query to prepare the information for your use whenever you reference it, rather than just opening a table.

The next section explains how you can establish logical relationships between tables, normalized or not, and have Access maintain the relationships for you. In addition, information on maintaining these references in your programs is covered.

Implementing Referential Integrity between Database Tables

Referential integrity refers to the maintenance of logical links between different pieces of physical information. As an example, if you have a customer record, there may be several orders associated with the customer. Referential integrity would ensure that the orders which have the customer numbers assigned to them are valid and that no customer could be removed from the system until the orders were purged from the Orders table.

In our examples above, we worked with a contact and company table set. Our examples here will explain how you can implement the automatic Access functionality, or implement it yourself in code, to ensure that changes are managed by using a Contacts table - Orders table relationship.

Once you have the two tables defined in your system, you can establish a relationship between them by using the Relationships... command on the Edit menu.

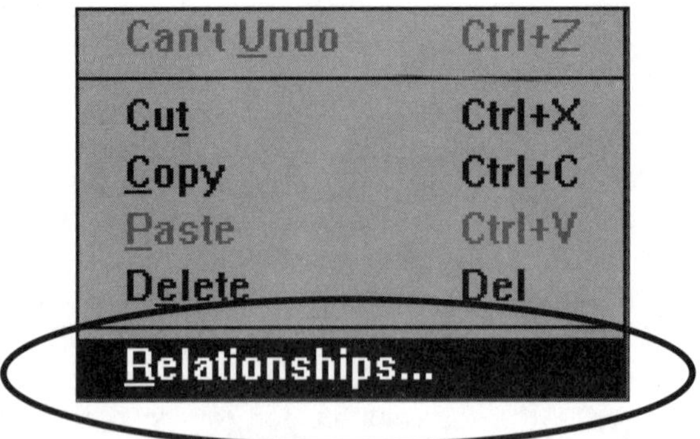

The Relationships... menu option allows you to define which field in a given table is to be used as a link to other tables. In this example, both tables have been set up to contain a 'Contact ID' column. In the Contacts table, this column serves as the primary key for the table. It is defined to be unique and is implemented as a counter data type. In the Orders table, the field is a long integer and therefore is compatible with the counter data type.

When you first select the relationships options, you'll be presented with a dialog box asking what tables and queries you need to work with. In the **SAMPLES.MDB**, a relationship has already been set up between the Contacts and Orders tables, so you'll see this relationship already defined:

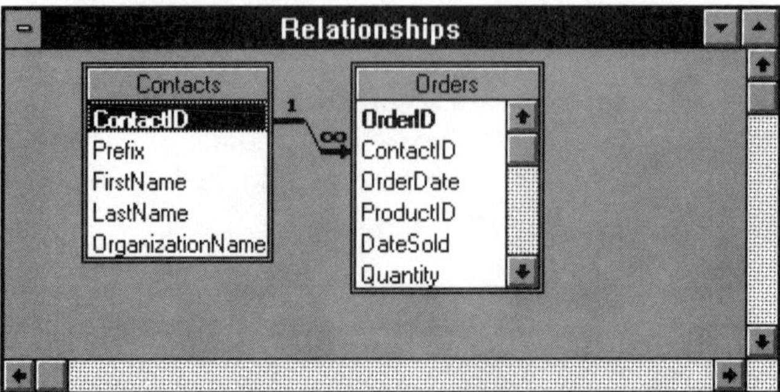

Once you've started the Relationship Manager, you'll be presented with a screen that allows you to add tables to the relationship environment. If you have existing relationships defined, you'll need to use the toolbar option to add new tables to the Relationship Manager and Access will automatically insert the relationships diagrammically into the picture:

Select the add table button to add new tables to the Relationship Manager's control.

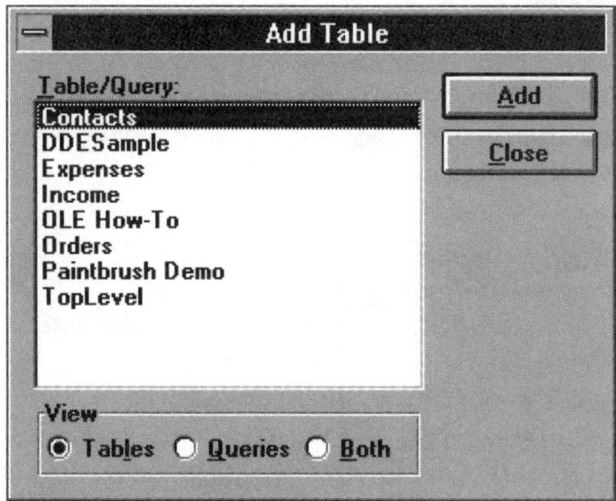

Select the tables and/or queries that you want to work with, pressing the Add button after each one. When you've selected the appropriate tables, you're presented with a form similar to the Query builder's graphical display of the tables and their relationships.

To establish a new relationship, you designate what columns correspond to each other between the tables. Click upon and drag a column name from the first table's field listing to its counterpart in the second table's field listing. In our example, you'll want to select the ContactID in the Contacts field listing and relate it to the ContactID in the Orders field listing.

When you 'drop' the column on the second table's list box, a new dialog box will come up, allowing you to create the relationship:

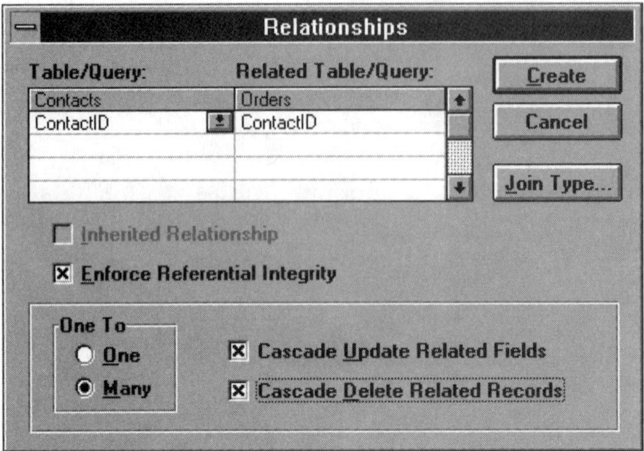

> *If you want to edit an existing relationship, double-click on the line joining the tables. This will bring up the dialog box shown above. To delete an existing relationship, click on the joining line and hit the* Delete *key.*

The left column of the dialog box shows the originating table or query and its key field(s). The right column is the related table and linked fields(s). These have been filled in automatically by Access when you dragged the field from one table to the other to create the link.

In our example, the Table/Query side of the relationship is the source table, Contacts. The dialog lists this table and the field that we've chosen for the relationship, ContactID. The Related Table/Query side of the relationship is the Orders table.

Enforcing Referential Integrity

Initially, the Enforce Referential Integrity check box is not selected. Until it is selected, the One To... and Cascading options are disabled. Select the Enforce Referential Integrity check box.

To enforce referential integrity (and maintain cascading deletes), Access needs to know which is the **main** table (at the **one** end of the relationship) and which is the **sub** table (at the **many** end). This is because you can delete linked records from a sub-table with no ramifications. Doing so in a main table without deleting linked records in **all** sub-tables leaves 'orphan' records, or in other words, records which run the risk of having no means of reference.

Next, you select whether Cascading Updates and Cascading Deletes should be implemented. Simply put, this means that if you update the field or fields that represent the relationship between these tables on one side of the equation, Access will automatically update the other side. This keeps your tables synchronized and will maintain the referential integrity between the tables without any modifications in your code.

For example, if you have a phone number duplicated in two tables, you can have Access update the second table if the phone number in the first is changed. This update takes place regardless of how the tables are accessed, be it from a user interface that includes forms, or from a Visual Basic program that is using the database you've set up.

We will be using a **One-to-Many** relationship between the Contacts table and the Orders table. We can have many orders associated with a given contact, but only one contact can be associated with a given order. Since this is the case, select the Many option in the One to... frame.

The Type of Join

The final step is to inspect the join that will be created to support this relationship. Select the Join Type... button on the Relationships dialog box to open the Join Properties dialog:

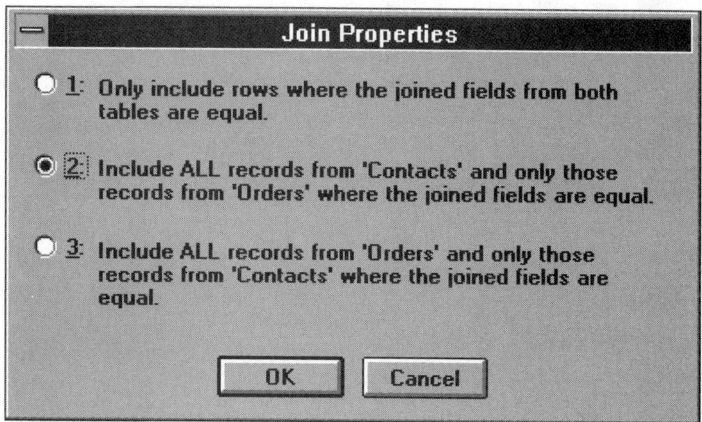

There are three different options available on the Join Properties dialog box:

1. Option one has the effect of excluding records that did not have ContactIDs in both tables from the join, omitting orphan records. This is also known as an **Inner Join**.

2. If you select option two, the effect will be to only work with records from the Orders table that relate to the current ContactID. This is the option we want to enable for our sample. This is also known as an **Outer Join**.

3. Selecting option three has the opposite effect of option two. That is, all records from the order database will be active, but only those contacts records that had orders records would be impacted by changes. In our table, since all orders must theoretically have customers first, this would not be an applicable option.

Select option 2 for our sample tables. When you select Create from the Relationships dialog box, the relationship will be created and you'll be returned to the workspace that shows your two tables. There would be more tables shown if more relationships were set up. Notice that Access has diagrammatically represented the relationship for you:

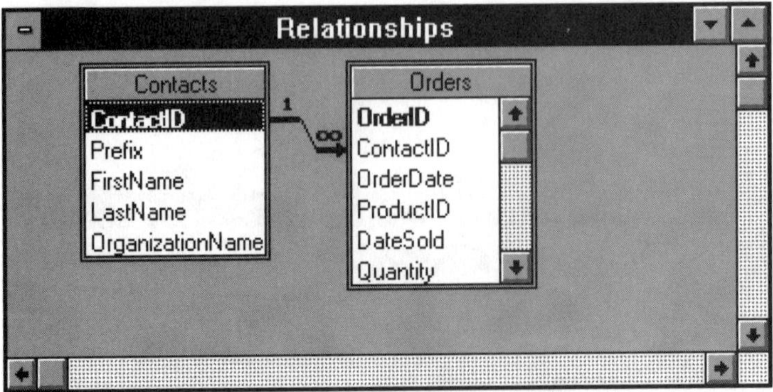

The diagram also illustrates the one-to-many relationship by including a 1 and an infinity (∞) character. This shows that one contact record can have one or more order records linked to it.

This is the correct relationship for our demonstration. To test the relationship, open the Contact Orders form. This form allows you to enter a contact and then add order information for them. The form was created with the Form Wizard, using the Contacts table as the top portion of the form and the Orders table as the bottom portion:

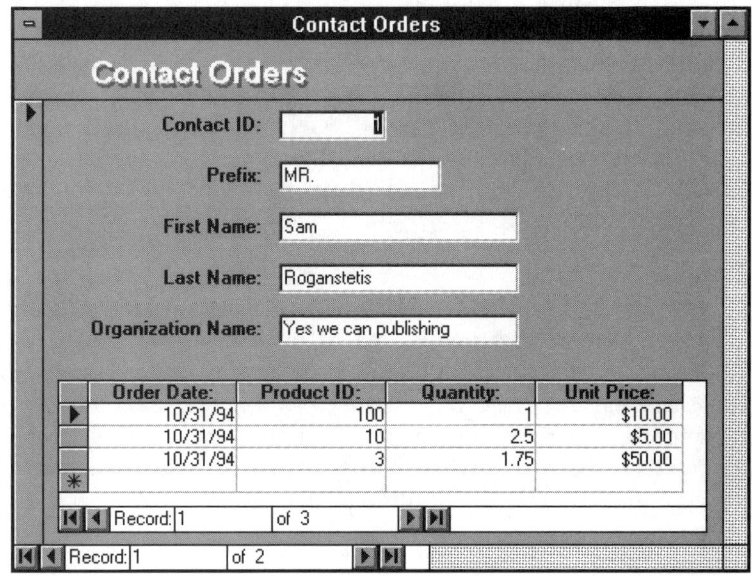

Enter a new contact record, then add several line items as orders. The formatting of the order line fields is shown in the diagram. Once you've added a few lines, close the form and look at the contents of the Contacts and Orders tables.

Verify that not only the contact you've entered is listed, but also the order line(s) you entered. Close the tables and re-open the Contact Orders form and go to the record you just entered. Delete the contact record by choosing Select Record from the Edit menu and hitting the *Delete* key. The record and associated order rows are deleted. You should verify this by returning to the datasheet view for both of the tables.

What's happening here is that Access is managing the 'Cascading Deletes'. When you delete the contacts record, Access recognizes that it's related to the orders record. You've instructed Access to update or delete rows from the Orders table as rows in the Contacts table change or are deleted. When you deleted the contacts record, Access automatically removed all associated records from the orders table.

One thing that you may need to consider when determining how to set up your relationships is whether or not the operation should always **be carried out. In other words, if you delete the contact record, do you want to delete the orders record(s) on each and every occasion? Are there any exceptions at all? If there are exceptions to the rule, don't set up a cascading update or delete, whichever the case may be. For more information on this, see the next section for information on implementing cascading actions in code.**

Creating relationships like this is a great way to make sure that any application that may access your application 'keeps to the rules' in working with your tables. Remember, as databases and the interfaces to them become more and more open, such as when the ODBC specification becomes the industry's accepted standard of database connectivity, it becomes more likely that your application will not be the only one accessing your database tables. You need to provide as much control as possible when different users access your tables.

Creating Program-Maintained Cascading Updates

There are cases where you'll want to programmatically control relational updates between the tables in your system. These cases call for more control over the process than can be afforded by the automated relational 'triggers' introduced in the last section. Some of these types of situations might include:

- When you may not always want to update or delete a related table's contents
- When you don't want to delete the contents, but instead want to copy the record to another table. This might be the case where you are establishing a past history for the table. If this was the case, you would need to remove the row from the original table and insert it into a history table

In these, as well as other cases, you'll likely find that the automated relational controls afforded by Access will simply not handle the task. You need to be able to put hooks into the update process at specific points throughout the action. Access provides a set of **Events** that we can work with which help to do just this.

Using Forms-Level Capabilities for Cascading Actions

At the form level, you have two properties available that are applicable only to the form. These are the BeforeInsert and AfterInsert properties. For each of these, you can set up a macro, expression, function or procedure.

The BeforeInsert event is initiated by Access after the information that has been entered is saved to the database table. This offers you the capability to update an alternate table with information, before the new information is entered into the initial table.

The AfterInsert event is triggered by Access after information entered into the control has been saved to the underlying table. This is a good way to update information after the user has entered and accepted it.

There are other events that you can use, such as OnDelete and OnCurrent, that can provide even more control for your application.

To access the properties sheet for the entire form, you can use the short cut of double-clicking the white box in the upper left corner of the form.

This will automatically call up the properties box for the form.

One of the more common uses for a form-level control of inserts is where you need to set up records in one table, when a new record is created in a master table. For example, if your company employed part-time workers and had a master employee table and a part-time employee table, you could enter a new employee's details in the master table and use the **`AfterInsert`** event to create a new record in the part-time employee table.

Using Field or Control-Level Capabilities for Cascading Actions

In addition to controlling the Insert properties for the whole form, you can control the interaction with the database as it relates to specific controls on your form. As you make changes to the form, if a control that is bound to the database is updated, the changes are written to a copy of the record in the edit buffer. The underlying table is then updated with this new information when the record is explicitly saved, or when the user moves to a different record.

It's likely that you'll more commonly need to control updates to a table at the control or field level, rather than the form level. This is because you will usually only need to manage changes to certain controls on a form or to certain fields in a table.

There are many different events that relate to the operation of any given form. Each has its own property on the Properties sheet, but it is three of these that are of the most interest:

- OnChange
- BeforeUpdate
- AfterUpdate

Using the OnChange Property of a Control

The **`OnChange`** property for a control is initiated by Access whenever a change is made, either by the user or by an Access Basic program, to a control, so triggering the **`OnChange`** event. An example of this might be when a user enters a new Company ID.

Note that the **`OnChange`** event is initiated for each change to a control. If a user is going to enter a six digit ID code, this event will be initiated six times or the number of digits in the ID. For obvious reasons, the ID would not be valid until after the sixth digit had been entered.

Using the Before Update Property of a Control

As mentioned earlier, Access stages changes in an edit table, updating the 'real' table only when the record is actually saved. Prior to writing the information to the edit table, Access initiates the **BeforeUpdate** event. You can place code in the **BeforeUpdate** property of the control that will manage how the information will be handled. As an example, we've put the following code in the **BeforeUpdate** event of the Prefix text box on the Contact Orders form in the **SAMPLES.MDB**.

```
Sub Prefix_BeforeUpdate (Cancel As Integer)
    'see if the new field value makes sense; it must be
    'mr, mrs, miss or ms

    'set up our variables
    Dim sTemp As String

    'do the test
    If Prefix <> "mr" And Prefix <> "mrs" And Prefix <> "miss" And ⮠
            Prefix <> "ms" Then
        'invalid value, set back to the prior value
        Cancel = True

        'let the user know
        sTemp = "The Prefix is not valid - sorry no Doctors "
        sTemp = sTemp & "or Professors allowed! Please re-enter."
        MsgBox sTemp
    Else
        'valid input
        Cancel = False
    End If
End Sub
```

The code tests the value of the Prefix and, if it isn't valid, changes the **Cancel** parameter to **True** and displays a message box telling the user and asking them to re-enter the Prefix:

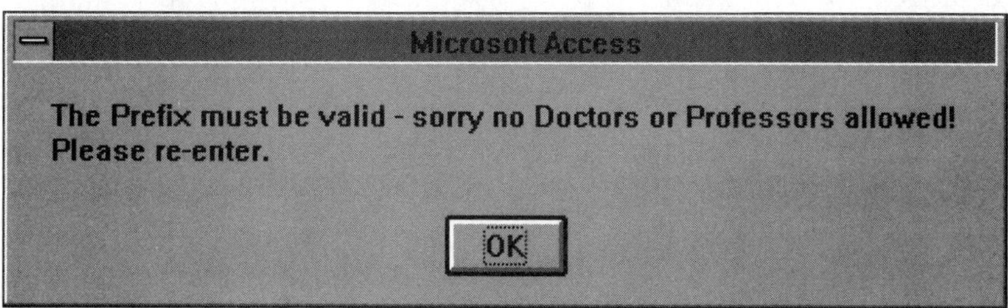

The only option you have is to click the OK button and re-enter a valid Prefix. The code won't let you move off the text box control until you enter a valid Prefix.

If you try to close the form the message box will be displayed again and when you click the OK button you'll get a standard Access dialog box telling you that you can't save the current record:

Using the AfterUpdate Property of a Control

The **`AfterUpdate`** property and associated event don't support the **`Cancel`** parameter because they occur after the control has been updated. However, they do offer you the opportunity to take the newly updated information and save it to another file. You can place code in the event that will take the new value and update another table.

> *Notice that in the* **`BeforeUpdate`** *event, the change is not yet made in the value for the table. In the* **`After Update`** *event, the value has been changed and saved to the table.*

There is a special property that will more than likely come in handy for these types of operations. The **`OldValue`** property of the control will contain the value of the control prior to the last update to the field. This value is not persistent, which means that the value will not be maintained, but is available until the current record is saved.

What follows is an example of some code that will roll-back changes to a table if the user changes their mind. We've put this code behind the LastName text box on the Contact Orders form.

```
Sub LastName_AfterUpdate ()
    'confirm that the user wants to make the
    'requested changes.

    'set up our variables.
    Dim iAnswer As Integer
    Dim sTemp As String
    Const IDYES = 6, IDNO = 7

    'create the message string
    sTemp = ""
    sTemp = sTemp & "Are you sure you want to save "
    sTemp = sTemp & "your changes to the Last Name field?"

    'get the user's answer
    iAnswer = MsgBox(sTemp, MB_YESNO, "Confirm Changes to Field")

    'parse the answer
    If iAnswer = IDNO Then
        'Don't want to save, cancel the operation
        LastName = LastName.OldValue
    Else
        'save the changes.

    End If

End Sub
```

The first thing we do is display a dialog box asking the user if they are sure they want to make the changes to the LastName field:

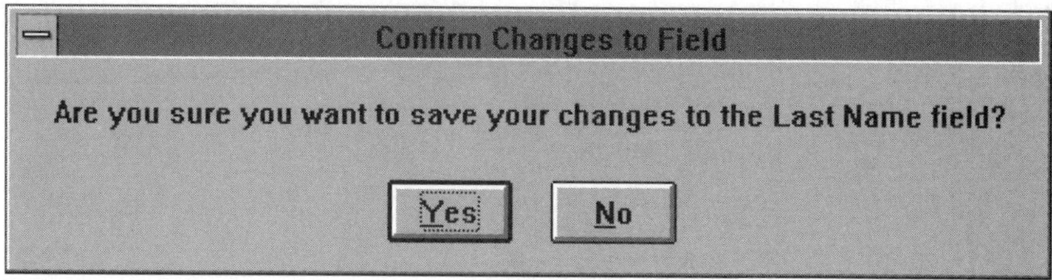

Then we check which button the user clicks on and if it is the No button we use the **OldValue** property to change the LastName back to the previous value. If the user clicks on the Yes button we do nothing and let the changes take place.

The **OldValue** property also provides an excellent way of updating fields that relate to other tables. For example, suppose you're changing a reference to a related table. Both tables A and B refer to table C, with a one-to-one relationship:

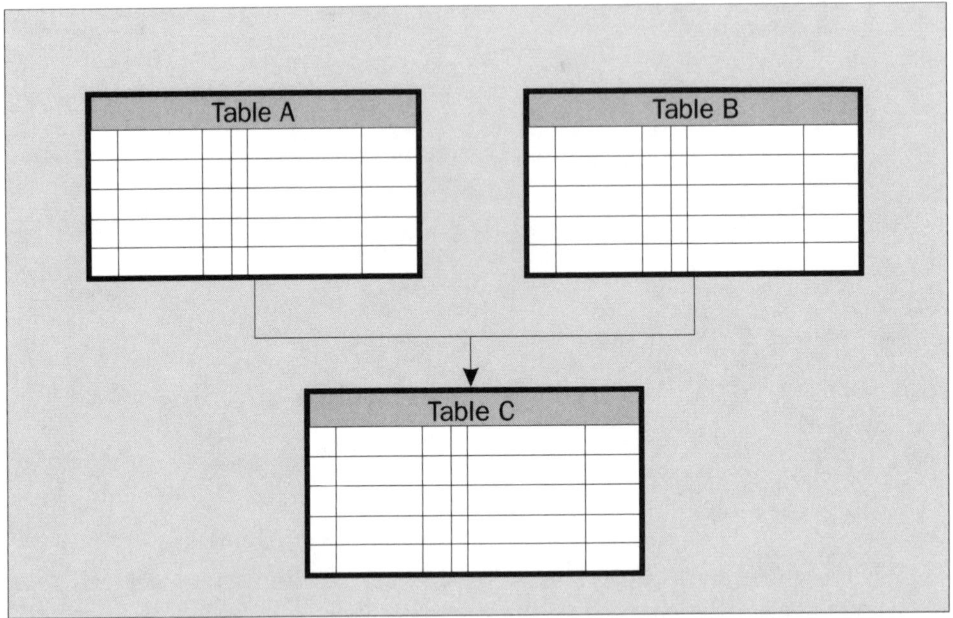

Suppose your user interface allows you to update the reference in table A to point to a new record in table C. Since table A and B must point to the same record in table C, you also need to update table B with the new record ID.

You could accomplish this as follows:

1. Look up the value from Table A in Table B using Table A's OldValue property
2. Change it to the new value using the current value from Table A
3. Save the changes

Remember, you'll have to perform a lookup against the other table using the **OldValue** first, before you can update the value(s) as needed.

> There is one very important thing you should know about the **`BeforeUpdate`** and **`AfterUpdate`** events. They are not initiated if your Access Basic code changes the contents of the fields on a form, a limit imposed by Access itself. If you change values from your Access Basic code, you should be sure to either call the update routine yourself, or add a global function or procedure to validate the information as needed.

Creating Program-Maintained Cascading Deletes

When you work with your tables in Access Basic, you may also find that you need to manage the **`Delete`** event as it relates to the table. To accomplish this, as in the update and insert situations, there are several form and control-level events and properties, each available to you as a database developer.

At the form level of your application, you have three different property and event combinations that you can use to control the deletion of information. For each of the following events, you can assign a Macro, Access Basic code or expression to control the operation:

- OnDelete
- BeforeDelConfirm
- AfterDelConfirm

Using the OnDelete Property of the Form

Initiated by the **`Delete`** event, you can use this procedure as a way to cancel a delete attempt, provide more information about a delete operation due to take place and so on. Typically, this might be used where you have certain master records in the system that can't be deleted if the system is to function correctly. You can put a small procedure in this event code that will check to make sure the requested deletion doesn't impact any of those master records.

In the context of maintaining referential integrity in the database, you can also use the **`OnDelete`** event to see if records exist in other related tables. At this point, the user has not confirmed that they wish to delete this record, but you can gather information on the number of records that may be impacted by the removal of this one.

Storing this information in a variable that can be accessed by the other deletion routines allows you more flexibility for the user interface. When the user goes to confirm the removal of the record, the dialog box can present more meaningful information by showing the total number of records that would be impacted by the removal of the current one.

> *The* **OnDelete** *property and associated event are not available at a field or control level.*

Using the BeforeDelConfirm Property of a Form

When a user chooses to remove a record from a table, he is first asked to confirm the removal of the information. Just before this confirmation is presented to the user, the **BeforeDelConfirm** event is triggered. If there is an action to be performed, described in the **Before Del Confirm** property of the form, the code, expression or macro is run before the confirmation dialog box is presented to the user.

In our example in the previous **OnDelete** section, we mentioned that it might be helpful to present more information to the user as they decide whether to confirm the deletion request. To accomplish this we would use code something like the following:

```
Sub Form_BeforeDelConfirm (Cancel As Integer, Response As Integer)
    'provide the user with an enhanced confirmation dialog box.

    'set up our variables
    Dim iResponse As Integer
    Dim sTemp As String
    Dim CRLF As String
     Const IDYES = 6, IDNO = 7

    CRLF = Chr$(13) & Chr$(13)

    'note:  iNumTotalRecs would be defined as a global variable
    '       that will contain the total number of records that would
    '       be impacted by the delete request.

    'first, turn off the standard dialog box.
    Response = DATA_ERRCONTINUE

    'next, build a meaningful message to indicate the
    'impact of the delete request
```

```
        sTemp = "If you remove this record, you will be " & CRLF
        sTemp = sTemp & "impacting " & Str$(iNumTotalRecs) & "." & CRLF
        sTemp = sTemp & "Are you sure you want to continue?"

        iResponse = MsgBox(sTemp, MB_YESNO, "Confirmation of Delete Request")
        If iResponse = IDNO Then Cancel = True

    End Sub
```

The first thing this does is to turn off the default confirmation dialog box by modifying the value of the **Response** parameter. Setting it to **DATA_ERRCONTINUE**, causes Access to avoid the use of the standard dialog box and display the custom dialog box.

We then check the response to our custom dialog box and if it is 'No' we set the **Cancel** parameter to **True.** Access will abort the delete request just as if the user had selected 'No' to the Access delete confirmation dialog box.

The **BeforeDelConfirm** is a powerful way to enhance the information presented to users when it is time for them to decide whether or not to remove a record from the system.

Using the AfterDelConfirm Property of a Form

If a record deletion request is approved by the user, Access removes the record from the underlying database table. After the removal has been completed, the **AfterDelConfirm** event is triggered and the **After Del Confirm** property for the form is inspected. If you have designated an expression, macro or some Access Basic code to this property, it is executed.

The **AfterDelConfirm** capability is helpful where you want your program to confirm the status of a delete request, or in cases where you want to provide the user with additional options after the request is completed.

The **AfterDelConfirm** event provides a status parameter. The parameter can have a value of **DELETE_OK**, **DELETE_CANCEL** or **DELETE_USER_CANCEL**.

If the event returns a value of **DELETE_OK**, the operation has succeeded. This is the time to remove other records from related tables, update references between tables and so on. It may also be the time to update records in a transaction log or any tables that refer to the one from which we have just removed a record.

If the **DELETE_USER_CANCEL** value is returned, Access has prompted the user with the standard dialog box and the user decided not to continue with the operation. As mentioned for **DELETE_CANCEL**, your Access Basic code should inspect the status parameter carefully to make sure the user went through with the delete operation. Otherwise, unneeded or unwanted deletions against the tables may result.

If the event returns the value of **DELETE_CANCEL**, Access Basic was used to stop the delete operation. In our example in the previous section, if the user chooses 'No' to the continuation prompt, the **DELETE_CANCEL** parameter is returned by the event. Be sure to inspect for this value; or you could end up removing records from other tables prematurely if you don't realize that a delete request was canceled.

The AfterDelConfirm code is executed regardless of whether the user opted to continue with the delete or not. Be sure to check the status parameter for details on what actually happened with the request.

How Relational Integrity is Enforced in our PIM Application

In the sample PIM application, there are two scenarios that are automated using the 'Access Relationship Manager'. The first scenario occurs if a company is deleted, as all associated contacts and projects must also be deleted. This is enforced at the database level by setting up the appropriate cascading deletes for the Company table - Contacts table and Contacts table - Projects table relationships.

The second scenario occurs if a contact is deleted, because we want to remove the related project information. Again, this is implemented with the 'Access Cascading Delete' capability. Each of these scenarios is outlined below.

Sample Application: Implementing Cascading Deletes Based on Company

Our goal is to provide functionality, at the database level, that will enforce the rule that a contact must have a company related to it, and that a project must be assigned to a contact. With this in mind, our goal is to have Access remove all associated contact and project records if a company is deleted.

The first step is to add each of the tables to your relationships workspace. From the Edit menu, select the Relationships... option. When you are presented with the relationships workspace, add each of the tables, Company, Contacts and Projects:

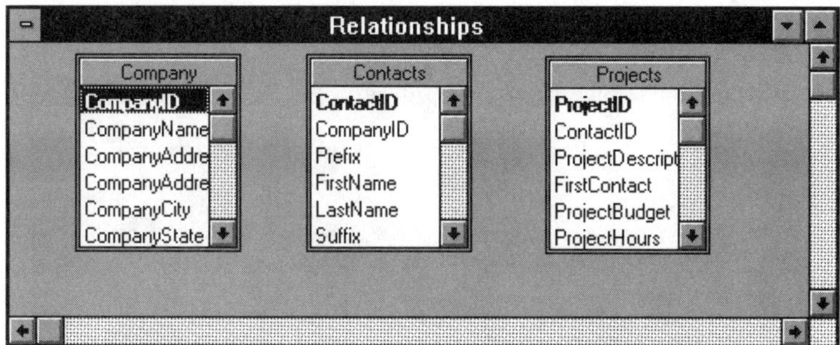

Next, establish the relationship between the Company and Contacts tables by dragging the CompanyID in the Company field listing to the CompanyID in the Contacts field listing. This will have Access display the Relationships dialog box, allowing you to determine how you want to set up the relationship:

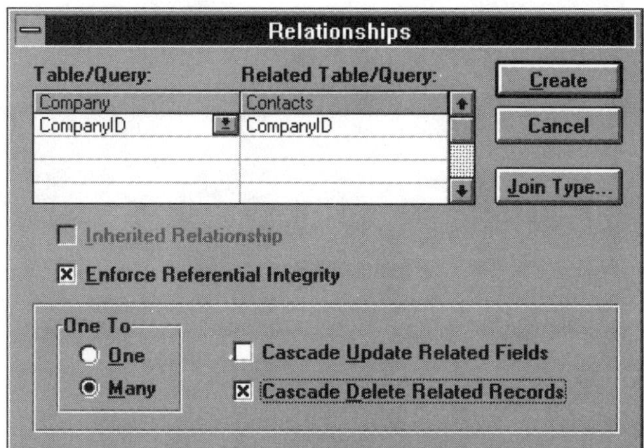

Check the Enforce Referential Integrity option and turn on Cascade Delete option. Since we can have many contacts for a given company record, select the One To Many radio button.

The relationship we're establishing doesn't have to be concerned with updating fields, only record deletions. The final step is to review the Join Type that will be created. You should accept the first option, allowing Access to work with only the records that appear in both the Company and the Contacts tables that have a common CompanyID:

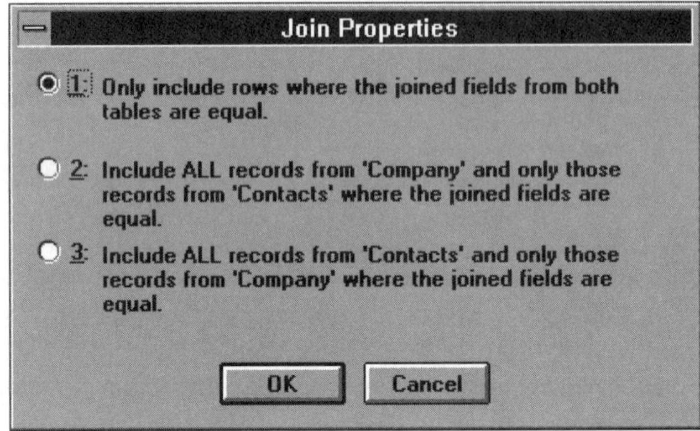

Repeat this process for the relationship between the Contacts and Projects tables. The next figure shows what your relationship workspace should now look like:

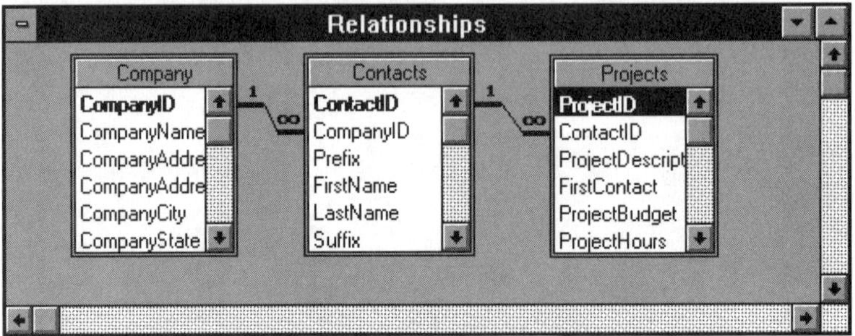

The diagram indicates our one-to-many relationships between the tables. In addition, since we've established the relationships as being relational, if you delete a record from a table in the chain, updates will cascade down through child tables. In other words, our relationships provide for protection in the case of a company being deleted, but also in the case of a contact being deleted.

If a company is deleted, the contacts and projects will be deleted, just as we'd planned. Since we've established a connection between Contacts and Projects, it's also true in our scenario that if you delete a contact, all associated projects will be removed.

If you are relating fields based on a Counter field type in the originating table, you have to use a compatible field type in the second table. Number fields, with their Field Size set to Long Integer are the only types compatible with the Counter type. You will need to use this type of field when relating tables based on Counter types.

From this point on, we can be assured that Access will take care of any deletions from our tables. This includes when outside sources like Visual Basic or other ODBC tools are involved. If an application or user removes a record, we have now provided the assurance that it will not create an orphan record in our system.

You should test the relationship between your tables so you understand what's happening. The easiest way to do this is to experiment with your tables in datasheet view.

To set up the experiment, add a record to the Company table, noting the CompanyID that is assigned. Next, add a record to the Contacts table. Make sure you provide the CompanyID you just created in the appropriate field. Take note of the ContactID that you're adding.

Finally, add a new Project record. Enter the ContactID you just created and other appropriate information. Since this is only a test, you need not worry about the contents of the records, only that they exist in each of the tables.

Close the Contacts and Projects tables and return to the Company table. Select the row containing your newly added test record and delete it.

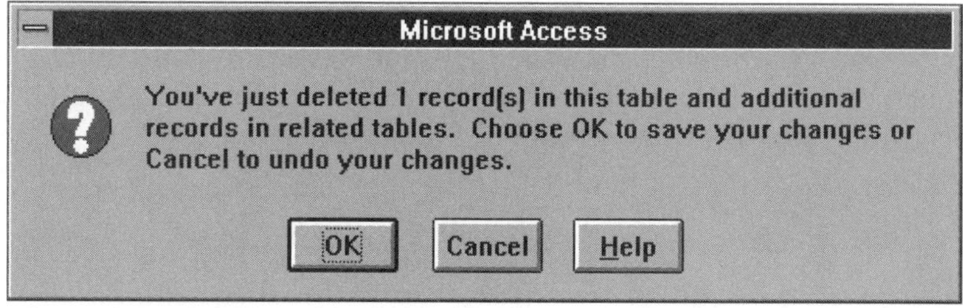

Access will give you the delete confirmation box, but this time there is a difference. Notice that Access is also warning you that records in related tables will also be removed. Select OK and the records you just entered, in all three tables, will be deleted.

> *Note that you will only see this dialog box if the* Confirm Record Changes *option is set to* Yes.

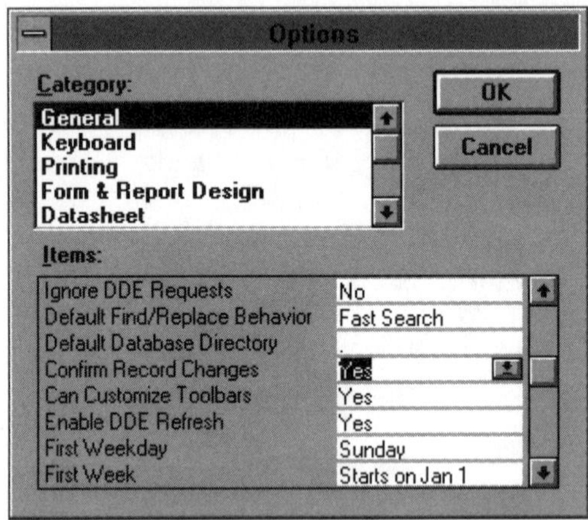

What's happened is just what we wanted. You deleted the company record, but Access also stepped in and removed the contact record associated with the company. Before Access could remove the contact information, the Projects table was updated and the related project was removed. You've deleted records from all related tables in one command, letting Access do all of the related record deletion work.

Comments and Suggestions

Now that you can ensure that database table updates are made throughout your systems, you can provide an added comfort level for your users. As you develop your systems, always take a 'worst case scenario' and assume that things will go horribly, horribly wrong:

- Put transactions around any operation that requires multiple tables to be updated
- Use cascading actions wherever possible when you have tables dependent on each other for information
- Use the **`Insert`**, **`Update`** and **`Delete`** events you have available to your Access Basic environment where cascading actions and transactions are not viable

In the next chapter we'll look at designing the user interface and see how you can optimize the screen real estate in your applications. We'll show you various methods to improve the useability of your forms with custom menus and toolbars.

User Interface Design

No matter how smooth data transfers between client and server, with super fast queries, taking full advantage of Rushmore Technology, network traffic to a minimum and all costs under control, if the user of your application can't work out the interface that you present to him, the whole system is a failure. The more polished and user friendly that you can make the user interface, the greater the benefits to the system.

What's Covered in This Chapter

In this chapter, we'll be going over several different aspects regarding the design and implementation of the user interface. There are many different options available as you develop systems and it's important to have a consistent, easy to use and functional interface to present to users. Some of the topics we'll be covering include:

- Creating and using custom menu systems
- Creating and using custom toolbars
- Ways to optimize screen real estate

Learn how to put together a user interface, taking into consideration the needs of the database and the user as well as the physical page size constraints that the interface designer must tackle every time a new interface is required.

How This Chapter Impacts Our Application

While not all areas of this chapter directly impact our sample application, they do show some of the thought that goes into the creation of an application such as the PIM. To that end, many of the user interface concepts, including custom menus and forms design, are incorporated in the sample application. This chapter will help explain some of the different considerations that came into the design of forms and other components of the system.

Introduction

When you create applications, you must pay attention not only to your application, but also to other applications with which the user is familiar. This is where Microsoft's Common User Access (CUA) specification is useful. The idea behind the specification is to provide a way that developers can create applications more readily understood by their users. This is accomplished by such general things as a common look and feel to the menu system and windows that make up the environment, layout and contents of the menus and the look and feel of the screens or forms that comprise the system.

The biggest benefit of using the CUA specification as a guideline is that you will see results faster from your users, because they won't have to re-learn the interface to your application. Except for any custom options that you've enabled, the user will already know what items to expect on the File menu, how the help screen works, and so on. The savings in training and support times can be substantial.

The user interface that you create is one of the artistic parts of developing software. It will reflect your biases in the software development process and will show off your vision for the project. Keep in mind that we'll try to present some standards, some experience and some suggestions. Each of these is certainly subject to your own interpretation, implementation and individual taste. None of these is set in stone: you should implement what is right for you, your application and your user base.

Probably one of the hardest things to do is to look at all forms, reports and other user interface-oriented items objectively. It's hard to consider that there may be a better way than the form you've been working on for over a month.

As a software developer, it's your responsibility to continually look for a better way to increase the functionality of your software, increase the usability of the functions and to polish the presentation of the information in your system. It's a bold statement, but it's a fact: software that stagnates will soon be lost, as will old methods of information presentation.

Microsoft, and many other vendors, are famous for their usability labs. In these labs, people are brought in, placed in front of a computer and asked to basically just 'get to work'. Cameras, software and people watch intently to see where the person goes to find options, complete tasks, and so on. Mouse movements, menu selections, both correct and incorrect, are tracked. All of this information is combined with the results from other participants and the net result is a better feel for how people want to use systems, not how systems should change the way people work.

When you design your systems, be sure to review the current process that encompasses what you're trying to automate. If there are paper forms, pay careful attention to the layout of the forms, and where the user's eye travels when trying to complete his task. Who sees the information? Do they see all of the details, or only summary information? In what order are people used to seeing the information?

Most importantly, **Why?**

The biggest question you can ask as you work through the design process is 'Why?' From this, you'll begin to understand why the process exists in the first place. In addition, you'll be able to re-engineer portions of the process simply due to the benefits provided by the computer software you're implementing.

Your user interface, its functionality, the overall look and feel of the design and so on, will all go towards determining the success of your software as much as the functions performed by the software.

General Guidelines

There are a few things that you should keep in mind to help you create a user interface. The user interface should make sense, be easy to use and take into account the different systems that your application may be running on. Also, when forms are called up, they should be laid out logically relating to the application.

In many cases, you can obtain forms that were used to complete the work before automation. These forms, combined with any other available systems, can provide you valuable information about how information flows into and out of the system.

Use of Colors on Forms

Generally speaking, you shouldn't use colors on your forms beyond the standard grays, blacks and whites. Exceptions to this rule will come up, especially in cases where you want to highlight a field or information item for the user.

You can create a standard for each control that you use on your forms. Once you do, Access will apply the standard to any control you designate. This will help immensely when you train new users of your systems: the look and feel of the different controls will be the same across forms.

To set the default for a given control, you will first set up the control as you want it to appear. Using a command button, for example, you should set the color, sizing, font information, etc., so that it appears as you want all buttons to appear. From the Format menu, available in Form Design Mode, select Change Default. This will save the different attributes of the control.

To apply a set of defaults to a control, simply highlight the control on the form. Select the Format menu and choose Apply Default. Access will modify the control's appearance to match the standard for that control.

Design Your Forms from Left to Right, Top to Bottom

Keep in mind that the Windows environment allows users to size windows. This being the case, you should remember that windows are sized from the lower right corner up to the upper left corner. This means that when you size a window, the portion of the window that is clipped or exposed comes from the right side, lower corner of the window.

When you design your forms, be sure that necessary command buttons, scrollbars and other controls and information on the form take the sizing situation into account. This will keep you from creating a situation where, after sizing a window, the user is unable to exit the system or otherwise use your form.

Set Proper Tab Orders on Your Forms

If you right click in the white box situated in the upper left corner of a form in design mode, you'll be presented with a menu allowing you to select the Tab Order for the form. This option is also available with the tab button on the button bar and from the Edit menu.

Setting the Tab Order is probably going to be the last thing you do with your forms. This is because you'll constantly be adding and removing controls from your forms during development. Each time you add a control, it goes to the bottom of the tab order and will be accessed last.

You can set the Tab Order in the Properties box for each control, or you can use the Tab Order dialog box to set the order of the fields:

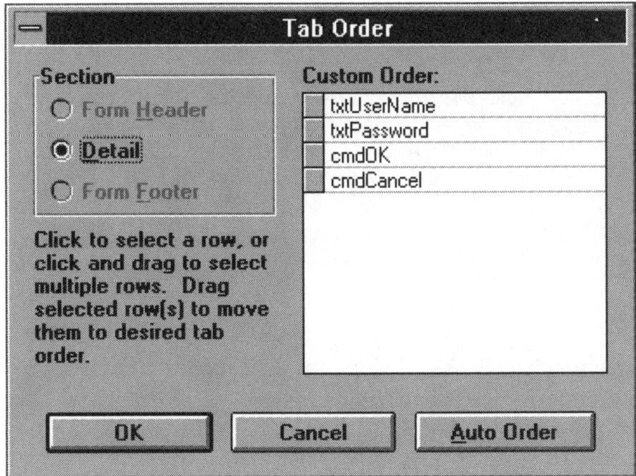

The easiest way to set the tabs is to select the Auto Order button. The tabs will be set from top to bottom, left to right on your form. The control's property sheets will be updated for you automatically.

If you want to set the Tab Order manually using this dialog box, you can do so by clicking and dragging items around on the listing to get them where you want them to be.

Using the Palette Toolbar

The Palette Toolbar offers many different options that help in standardizing your interface. The toolbar is activated by selecting Palette from the View menu or clicking on the Palette button.

Line widths - You can set the border style for the selected controls with these buttons. It's generally not a good idea to have borders around fixed text. If you can use borders around informational items only, it can make the form easier to read.

3-D effect - These options allow you to control and set, or reset, the 3-D effect for a control or set of controls. The options are No Effect, Raised and Sunken.

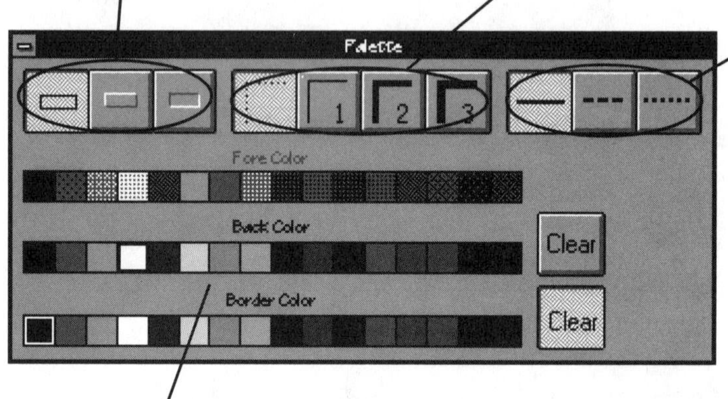

Line styles - If you want to change the style of line that will be used for the currently selected control, you can use this option. Options include solid, large-dashed and small-dashed.

Coloring - This option provides you with a visual palette that you can use to set the various color properties for the highlighted control or controls. It's very important to have consistent coloring. A suggestion in this area is to make the data on the form stand out with a good set of contrasting colors, e.g., black lettering with a white background. For labels, it's a good idea to make them stand out a bit less to avoid visual confusion when using the form. Good guidelines are black lettering on a background that matches the coloring for the form.

> **You can apply these options to multiple controls by selecting the first control and then selecting all remaining controls while holding down the control key. This will allow you to alter one specific property for a series of controls all at the same time.**

As you create forms, you'll undoubtedly change your mind several times on the placement and appearance of controls. If you place the controls roughly where you need them and then implement colors and the other properties accessed with the Palette toolbar, you'll have an easier time making sure all the controls appear in the same format.

Techniques for Maximizing Screen Real Estate

In many cases, if you're automating a paper-based process, you'll find that more information was presented on the paper form than will fit on a reasonable computer screen. In those cases, you'll have to organize the information into sections and find a way to present the information so the user can find what he needs quickly and easily.

While you can create 'pages' of fields and allow a user to scroll around a form that is larger than the physical screen, it's generally not a good idea to implement forms in this manner. This is because of many factors, but of primary concern is that users will often not understand that additional information is present on the 'bottom' portion of the form: they don't get to that area of the form to enter or update information. If you enforce the review of the data, the user can become annoyed with being constantly bounced to the off-screen portion of the form.

What's the answer? There are several different ways that you can bring more screen 'real estate' to your application. We'll outline a few ideas here.

Tab Control

With Microsoft's Word 6.x and Excel 5.x products, Microsoft introduced a relatively new concept to mainstream software development. The tab method of paging informational forms was implemented to better organize large displays of information. An example of this is the Word 6.x Tools, Options... dialog box shown on the next page.

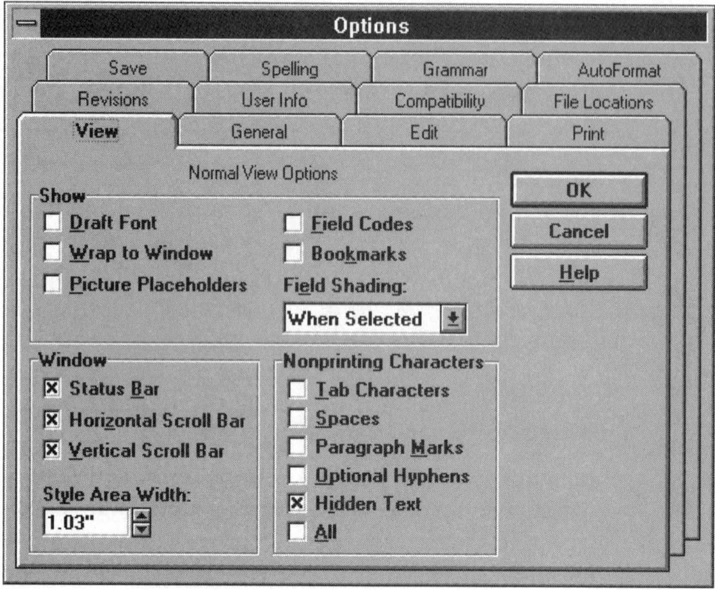

You can see that, while only one 'screen' of information is currently shown, it's very apparent that 12 screens of information are really represented in this one dialog box. You select the different informational topics by selecting the appropriate folder tab.

As can be seen from many sources, including books published by Microsoft, the tab control will be prevalent in Microsoft's new operating system, Windows '95. This includes the various accessory software tools provided with the operating system. It's an accepted and strategic option for working with large amounts of information.

You can implement the same type of tab control in Access. Microsoft has introduced a Tab OCX, mentioned in the first chapters of this book. This custom control allows you to introduce the tab idea to your applications written in Access.

The popularity of the tab control has allowed it to become a very mainstream, almost expected control, available in many development environments. You can expect to see the control available, either shipping with the product, or as a third party add-on, in many upcoming products. The next release of Visual Basic and the C are among some examples of this.

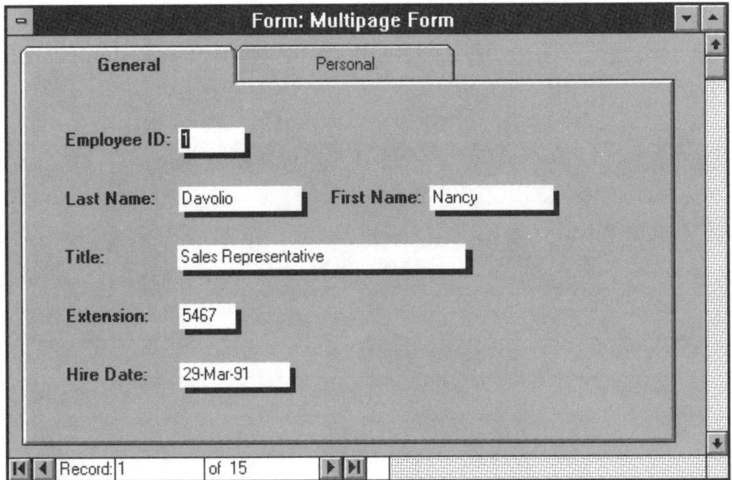

The way the tab-type controls work is quite clever. They are implemented as a logical set of frames, each frame being associated with a specific button, which looks like a folder tab, instead of a button. When one of these buttons is pushed, the frame that corresponds to it is made visible, while all others are made invisible.

Using Frame Management to Enhance Screen Possibilities

Since the frame also manages the display of controls that are contained within it, this effectively turns on and off the display of the controls based on what tab they are associated with. You can see a demonstration of this using the Tab Fake demonstration form, located in the **SAMPLES.MDB** database:

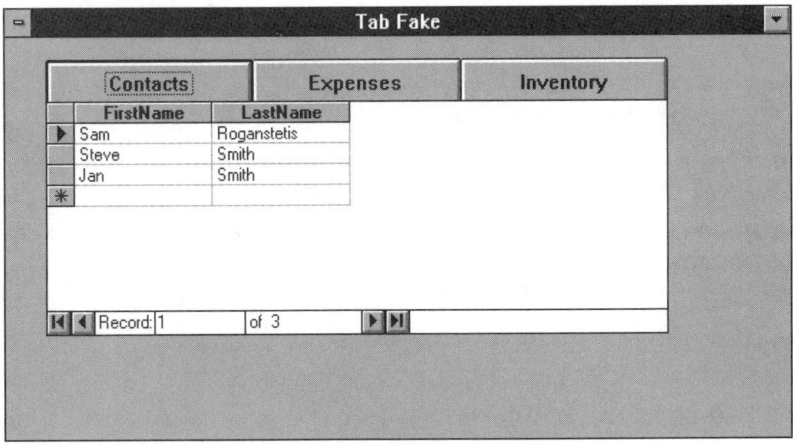

This form, in design mode, looks quite different. It's really a form with three buttons and three sub-form frames. The buttons control the display of the frames:

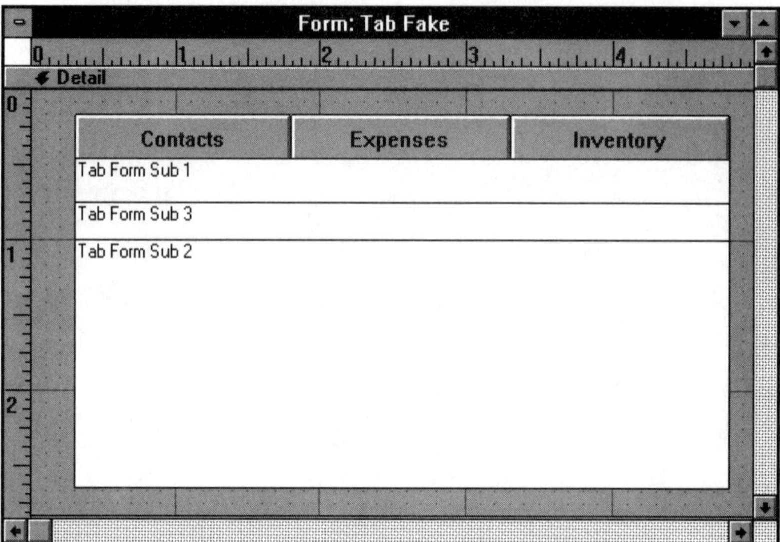

The Tab Form Sub 1, 2 and 3 are simple datasheet forms that serve as the source for the frames. The code behind the Expenses and Inventory buttons is almost identical. The statements set the position of the frame, turn it on and turn off any other frames that may be active:

```
Sub cmdInventory_Click ()

    'move the frame to the correct location on the
    'form
    fraInventory.Top = fraContacts.Top
    fraInventory.Left = fraContacts.Left

    'Turn on this form
    fraInventory.visible = True

    'turn off all others
    fraContacts.visible = False
    fraExpenses.visible = False

End Sub
```

If you work with different controls on top of each other, you can save yourself a great deal of grief if you slightly offset the controls from each other. At run time, you can adjust the location of the controls so they are positioned correctly, but during design time it can be difficult to determine what control you're working with.

On the click event for the button, we first position the frame according to the position of our 'anchor' frame, the fraContacts frame. We refer to this as the anchor frame only because we've ensured that it is in the correct position and we then use its positioning information to determine where to put the other frames. Assuming that the frames are all identical in size, if you set the Top and Left properties of the frames to be the same as the anchor frame, you can be assured that they will be placed at the exact coordinates of the anchor frame.

Next, turn on the visible property for the frame that we're concerned with. This will bring it into view for the user. The last step is to turn off the visible property of the other frames on the form. This will ensure that no other information is shown while the current frame is 'on top' and visible to the user.

> **Note that in the Tab Fake form, we don't have any forms visible when the form is loaded. This is only for demonstration purposes. You would need to have a default choice already visible when the user is first presented with the form.**

Using Radio Buttons to Manage Frames

In some cases, using the above button method, it can be difficult to tell which frame is currently visible. If the button loses the focus, it will lose the indication that it was selected. An alternative is to use a more visually persistent method of selecting the appropriate frame.

While the basic logic behind the functions is nearly the same, if you use radio buttons to select the type of information you need to view, you'll provide a better visual indicator of the information being shown.

In the **SAMPLES.MDB** database, open the Radio Frames form to see an example of this technique:

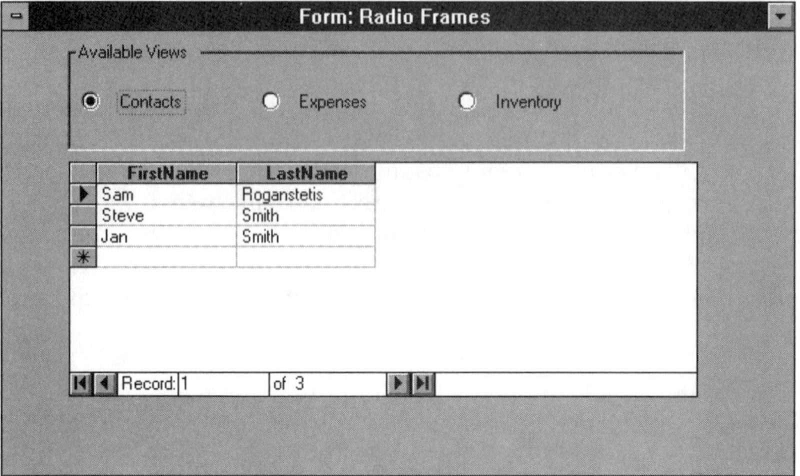

The same frames are implemented here in exactly the same way as in the Tab Fake demonstration. Each frame is a sub-form, showing the datasheet view of a particular table. In our example, the tables we use are called Contacts, Expenses and Inventory.

Once loaded, we monitor the **Click** event associated with the radio buttons for each type of information. As the user selects a specific radio button, we determine which button was selected and make the appropriate form visible, position it on the screen and make the other forms invisible.

The following subroutine shows how you can test the value of the user's choice and use that test to determine which frame should be shown.

```
Sub optViews_Click ()
    'process the user's choice of information
    'to view.

    Select Case optViews.value

        Case 1:         'contacts
                'make this frame visible
                fraContacts.visible = True
```

```
            'turn off other frames
            fraExpenses.visible = False
            fraInventory.visible = False

    Case 2:         'expenses
            'move the frame to the correct location on the
            'form
            fraExpenses.Top = fraContacts.Top
            fraExpenses.Left = fraContacts.Left

            'Turn on this form
            fraExpenses.visible = True

            'turn off all others
            fraContacts.visible = False
            fraInventory.visible = False

    Case 3:         'inventory
            'move the frame to the correct location on the
            'form
            fraInventory.Top = fraContacts.Top
            fraInventory.Left = fraContacts.Left

            'Turn on this form
            fraInventory.visible = True

            'turn off all others
            fraContacts.visible = False
            fraExpenses.visible = False
  End Select

End Sub
```

When you use a control array, by which we mean a set of controls bound by a control frame, you are able to handle all the controls in one Access Basic routine. Access will assign a value to each option and will set the .Value property of the option frame to that value when the user selects the given control. In the case of our example, the control array returns a value ranging from 1 to 3, depending on whether the user needs to see the Contacts (1) information, Expenses (2) information or the Inventory (3) information.

Based on the .Value property, we set up the form as desired and allow the user to continue. Notice that, even when the user leaves the radio button to enter information into the tables, the radio button still shows the active view, which was our goal.

As in the Tab Fake routines outlined earlier, we control our positioning based on the location of the Contacts frame, which we position in exactly the right spot during the design of the form. Since we set the Left and Top properties when the frame is requested, we can be assured of its proper position on the form.

You can accomplish the same goal with push-buttons on the form. You can use the same Radio button code with little or no change if you put the push-buttons inside a control frame and set the values returned by them accordingly. The push-buttons also provide a good visual cue as to the currently active window.

We've shown some different ways to add virtual forms to your application. Keep in mind that when you're presenting information, if the frames appear similar you may need to take additional steps to make sure the user is aware of what information is currently displayed. You could, for example, have a form with four windows, each showing a different year's financial information. If this is the case, be sure to use a method of displaying your information that gives a persistent indication of the information shown.

In cases where it will be obvious just by looking at your form which set of information is shown, consider using the Tab control, or create your own by using the multiple button approach. The most important thing is to make it very obvious to the user exactly what information is shown on screen at any one moment.

Laying Out the Screen

As we've seen so far, there are many different tools and techniques available to you for developing the user's environment. From Tabs to radio buttons, you can exercise a great deal of creativity in creating forms. There are many cases that fall outside the ideas presented so far, and in this section we will cover as many as is possible.

General Field Placement Options

Placement of controls on forms is defined as much by personal taste as it is by any industry standards. While a look and feel in popular software packages is emerging, it's far from standardized. In this section, we'll be showing several different ways of presenting your information on forms. It's best to select a single display method and use it throughout the application. If you can incorporate the style in all, or most, of your applications, your users will thank you as they will quickly get used to working with the information presented in a consistent manner.

There are several different ways you can present labels and fields on a form. These include:

- Vertical placement
- With or without leaders
- Left or right justified (labels)
- Above or next to the field

Vertical Control Placement

The following screen shows an example of vertical field placement with labels left justified:

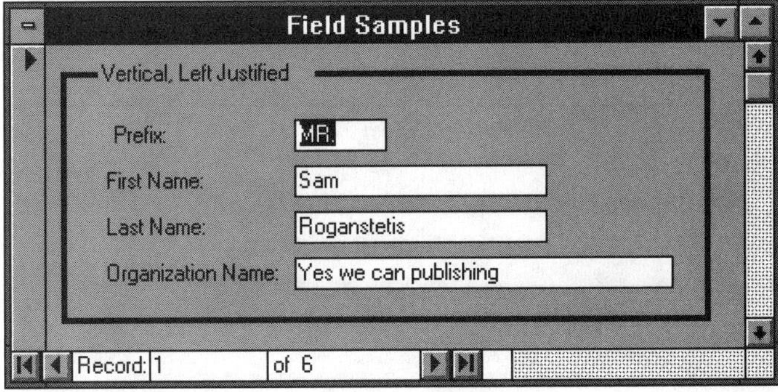

There are several different things to note on this form that may be helpful to consider for your own application development:

Field labels are left-justified This makes the labels easy to read, providing a 'margin' of sorts for the user to follow as he scans the screen looking for the necessary information. This can also help keep the screen clean and 'block' oriented, somewhat like a paragraph on a written page.

Field labels are to the left of the field they are related to

While this may be more what people are used to as far as historical systems development goes, it is also costly in terms of screen real estate. When you have large quantities of data on the screen, consider using the label-above method of showing the information.

The frame around the controls

Even in cases where you are not implementing a control array (see Radio Frames above), it can be visually helpful to the user if you place a frame around logically related items on the form. It can make it simpler to read the form, while at the same time you can provide emphasis for important groups of items.

Using Left or Right Justified Labels

In the example above, we used left-justified labels. There are many people that prefer to have the fields right justified with the block effect being on the side of the field to which they are related.

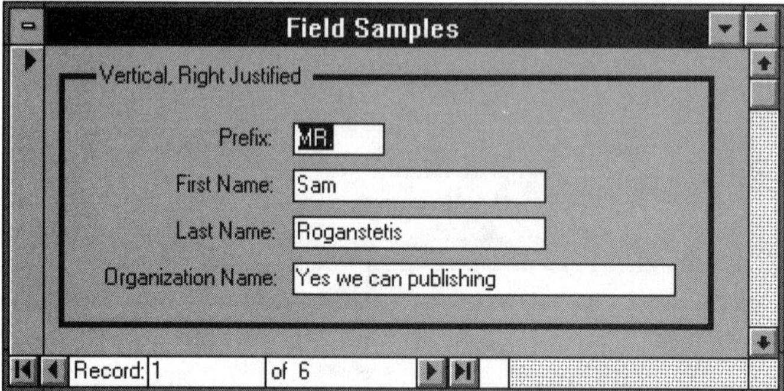

One of the factors to consider when you think about right or left-aligned fields is how the form will be viewed. If the same people will be using the same form over and over, your emphasis will be on the data on the form, as the users will have learned where the information is presented. In these cases, you may want to consider using the right-aligned labels.

If, on the other hand, the system is not used repetitively by the same users, you should consider the left-justified labels. This is because the user of the system will want to be able to quickly read the screen to find the location of the information they need. It's generally easier to follow the format of left-aligned labels.

Placing Labels above the Field

You can somewhat optimize a display by placing labels above the controls they are linked to. In this scenario, you can sometimes combine logically linked fields under one label. Doing so can make the screen much easier to read and understand:

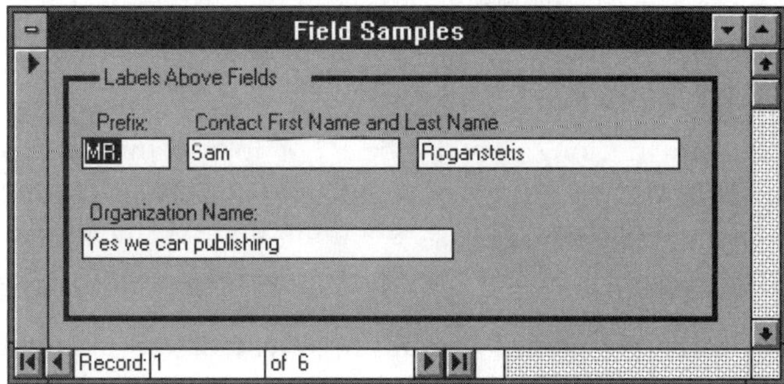

In our simple example, we're showing the use of a contact information screen. Since names are generally known to contain a first and last name, you can combine the labels for the FirstName and LastName fields and move the label above the controls for the information. We're effectively using up only about half the screen real estate that we were using before.

In addition, this format is very easy to read. If you set the tab stops from left to right, you will create a form that reads and operates in a mode that most people are used to with operations moving from side to side, top to bottom.

Using Labels with Dot Leaders

Many systems have been implemented using dot leaders between the label and the control that it is linked to. This can help tie the two controls together, as it forms a line between them.

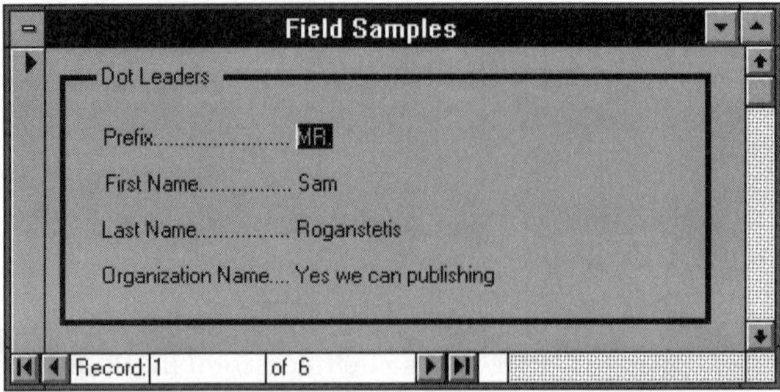

If your form has a limited number of fields and assorted controls on it, this may be an option for you. In addition, if you're converting from a system that had screens implemented with this technique, it can be helpful to continue in those traditions. It can ease the pain of transition for users of the software.

You may find that in the long run it's best not to use this technique. More complex screens can get a cluttered feel about them, and you can end up confusing the issue of related fields, even though the original idea was to provide clarification in that area.

If you are given carte blanche in the development of the interface, it's recommended that you avoid dot leaders, but, as mentioned above, legacy systems may impact upon your decision. If you are faced with this type of constraint, consider implementing them in the first release and then moving away from them in subsequent releases.

Automating the Movement between Forms

Often you'll be working with one form and need to move to another form, either to finish the current operation or simply to use a function that is available on the other form. In these cases, you may wish to put a button on the form that takes the user directly to the other form.

In many cases, you'll want to take the user to a supporting form, one that relies on the current form to determine what information to show. In the sample PIM application, you can see this in the main contacts form as it offers the ability to call up the projects form, listing only those projects relating to the displayed contact.

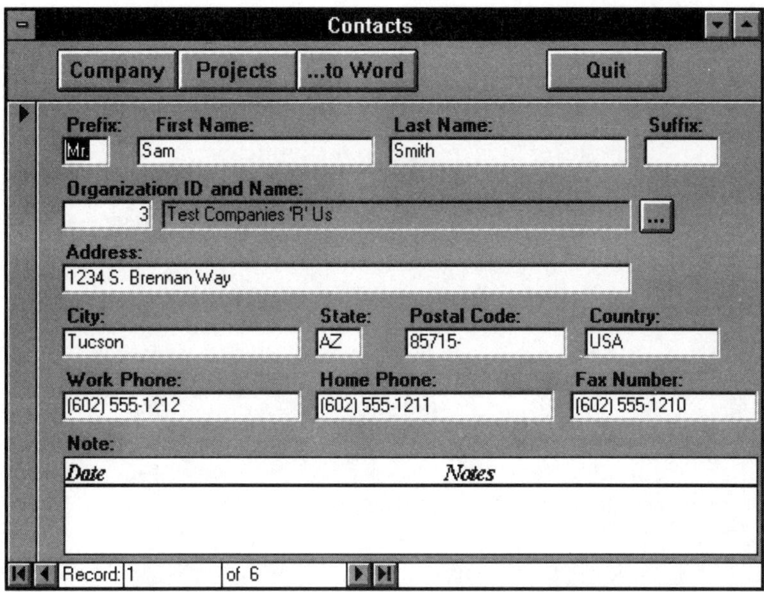

When the Projects button is pressed, we want to call up the Project Detail form, but limit its scope to the ContactID's that match the Contact Details form. You can use the **DoCmd** statement to accomplish just this. Here's a look at the code behind the **cmdProjects Click** event:

```
Sub cmdProjects_Click ()
    '
    'load the project details form for the contact
    'currently shown
    '
    DoCmd OpenForm "project detail", , , "[ContactID]=forms!
[contact details]![ContactID]"

End Sub
```

When you use the **OpenForm** action with **DoCmd**, you can specify an opening 'where' clause as the fourth parameter. This is the equivalent of a SQL **WHERE** clause, without the keyword 'where'. When the form is loaded, it will check to retrieve only those records with a **ContactID** equal to the **ContactID** on the calling form.

This is a good way to chain together logical collections of forms, providing a consistent flow of information throughout the system without having to search the database again to find a specific bit of information.

You can see an example of this in the main launcher form of the PIM as well. It serves the dual function of starting the application and initiating the search request, calling the form after the search has been defined by providing either a name or company name.

Creating a Control Panel

Now that you've seen how to call forms from within Access Basic, creating a Control Panel type application to start one of several forms for the user is pretty simple. As an example, you can review the Northwind Traders launcher, or the PIM's opening screen, allowing for the search on the provided name. The opening screen to the PIM is shown below:

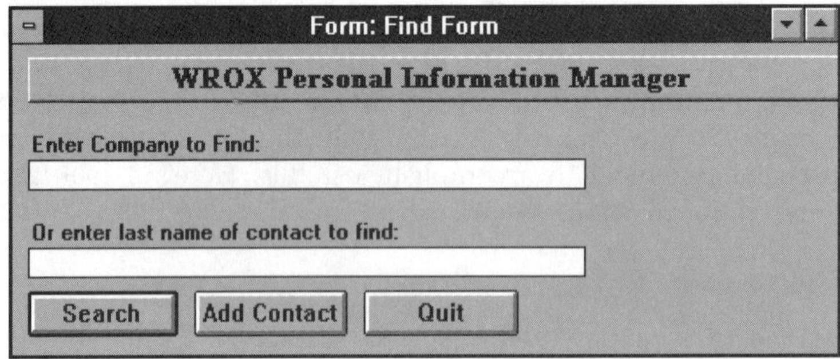

The search button, as we've seen in an earlier section, loads the appropriate form, either the company or the contact, based on what information is provided as search criteria.

If the user wants to simply add a new contact, the Contact Details form is loaded, but instead of standard browse mode, we load the form in **Add** mode, making it easier for the user to actually add information to the system. To load a form for data entry, you can again use the **DoCmd OpenForm** command:

```
DoCmd OpenForm "contact details", , , , A_Add
```

Other options you have when opening a form are:

A_EDIT This option allows full access to the underlying table, subject to the `WHERE` clause that may have been passed in by the `OpenForm` statement. The user can add, change and delete entries in the database table.

A_READONLY The user can review the information in the table, but can't make changes.

With the use of these options, combined with the `WHERE` clause capabilities mentioned earlier, you can completely control and automate the movement around the different forms that make up your system.

If you want to turn off the database tabbed dialog box that is shown in the Access workspace, you can use a macro to do so. Create and run a macro that uses the `DoMenuItem` action. Set the Menu Bar to Database, the Menu Name to Window and the Command to Hide. This will remove the database window from the desktop, a bonus for confused users who aren't familiar with our application or Access:

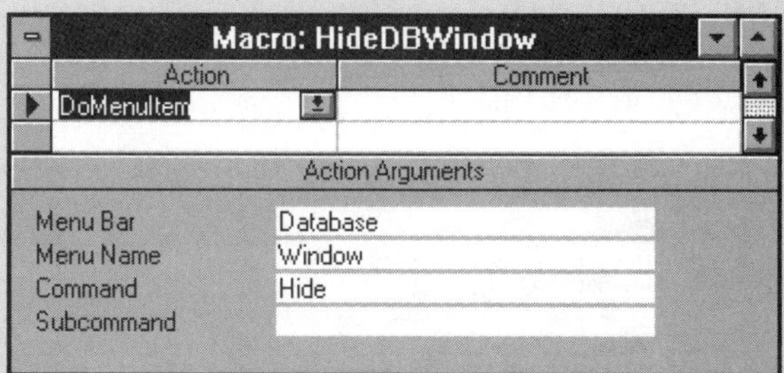

If you do hide the database window, make sure you unhide it prior to allowing the user to exit your application without exiting Access. To unhide the database window, create and run a macro exactly as above, but specify Unhide as the Command.

Using the Header on Forms

You can use the header and footer options on forms if you need to implement a form-specific button bar or if you have some information that changes in the body of the form, and some that should remain constant at the top. Examples of this include:

- Keeping the contact's name on the title bar and browsing through different pieces of information about the contact in the body of the form. Recall the Radio Frames and Tab Fake examples that allow you to show several different subforms on a master form. In these cases, you'll want to keep some information constant, so as not to confuse the users when they need to remember what master record they are working with.
- Creating a form-specific button bar, an example of which can be seen in the PIM, on the Contact and Company Details forms. These forms implement a button bar that pertains only to that form, allowing access to other forms in the system. It's possible to implement this as a custom toolbar, but since the toolbar is physically removed from the form, it may cause confusion.
- Providing a utility bar, such as adding a search capability. In the **SAMPLES.MDB** database, there is an example of this type of functionality in the HeaderExample form:

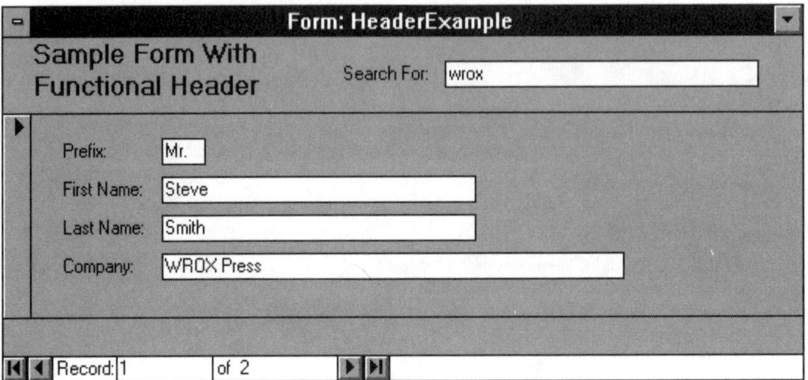

The form implements the header as a search designator for the form. While it's possible to implement the search capability in the body of the form, removing it to the header bar creates a logical break between the search criteria and the form showing the data.

In the sample, you can type in any portion of the `Company Name` you want to find. Pressing Enter activates the search. Once searched, the form will only display companies whose `Company Name` contains the search criteria.

Now that you've seen more information about screen design, button bars and so on, we'll investigate how you implement custom menus for your application. In addition, later sections will provide information on how to implement custom toolbars. Combined, these tools provide some powerful capabilities to manage the interface that you present to your users.

Using the Menu Builder

As you develop your applications, you'll find that you'll want to gain more and more control over the operating environment. One of the things you'll want to start doing is limiting a user's access to the full-blown Access environment. This is usually because you don't want the user to be modifying tables directly without the control of your program or because information in the tables is confidential.

Menu Guidelines

In this section we'll show what a typical Microsoft menu includes. Wherever possible, you should implement your functions with the same conventions.

Some of the common menus that are implemented in Window's user interface compliant systems are shown on the next page. You can use these examples as a starting point in designing your own menu systems.

File
New...
Open...
Close

Save
Save As...
Save All

Print Preview
Print...

Exit

Edit
Cut
Copy
Paste
Paste Special...
Clear
Select All

Find...
Replace...

Insert
Object...

Tools
Options...

Window
New Window
Arrange All
Tile
Cascade

<Window List>

Help
Contents
Search for Help on...
Index

About...

Of course, there will be exceptions and additions to the menu items shown. You'll need to add items, for example, to the Tools menu that allow you to manage options specific to your application. The Options... menu choice is becoming a standard way of managing preferences, so with this in mind, perhaps other hardware or software options could be configured with the menu choices.

Working with Custom Menus

When you create custom menus in Access, there are three distinct steps to setting up the options for your application. These are:

1 Create the macros or functions that you will use in the menu.

2 Create the menu and incorporate the macros and functions from step 1.

3 Implement the menus in your application.

In the **SAMPLES.MDB** database, open the Menu Demo form. This form will load a very simple Demos custom menu:

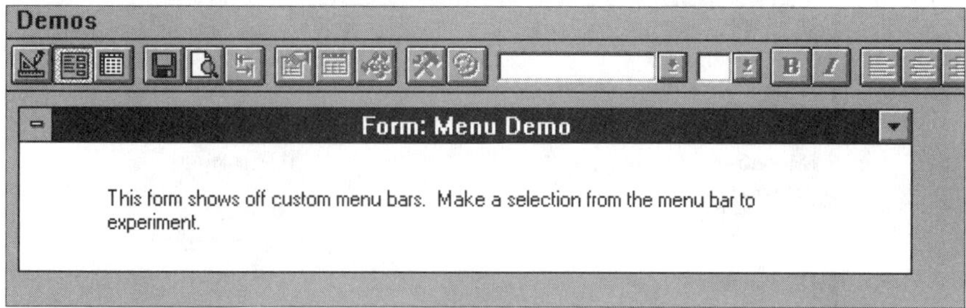

You'll also notice a little floating toolbar appears when you open the form. This is a custom toolbar that we've created and we'll go into how you create toolbars later in the chapter.

From the Demos menu, you can select any of the three different demos. These represent the three different ways to create menu options. They are macros, functions and subroutines called by functions. In addition, the menu offers the choice of exiting the form and returning to the database tabbed dialog box.

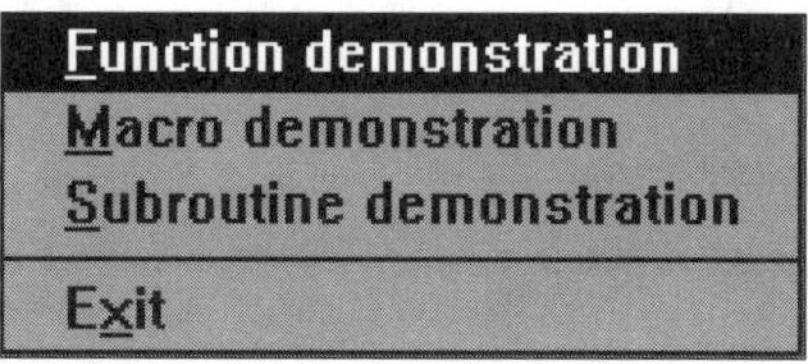

Each of these different options is discussed in the sections following the menu builder overview.

Menu Builder Overview

The Menu Builder will allow you to create custom menus that are presented to users as they navigate the system. To access the Menu Builder, select Add-ins from the File menu. The Menu Builder option will display a list of custom menu bars that have been created. In the **SAMPLES.MDB** you'll see the list shown on the next page.

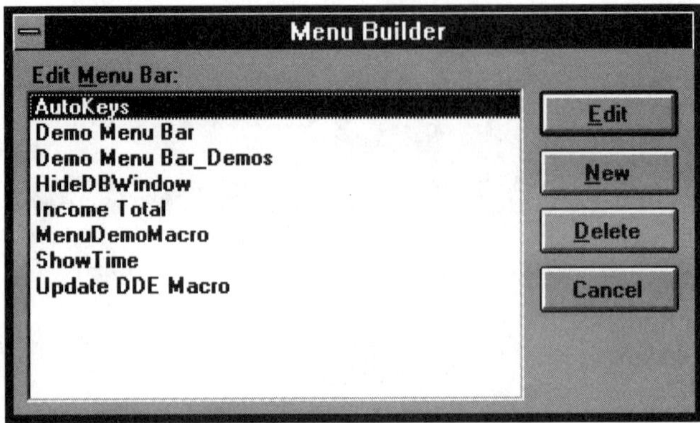

You can choose to edit an existing custom menu bar or create a new one. If you want to edit an existing one, select the appropriate one and then Edit. Otherwise, select New, which allows you to select an existing Access menu bar as the template for your custom menu bar. The next dialog box allows you to define your own menu system including the standard separator bars, secondary menus, and so on. For an example of an existing menu, select the Form menu:

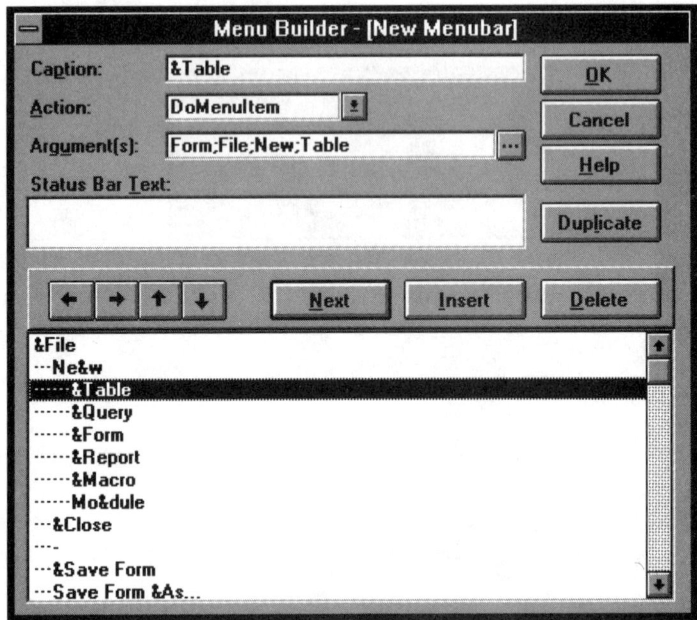

Windows conventions dictate that you use the ampersand character, '&', just prior to the character that you want to be underlined. If a character is underlined, it has been set up as the accelerator for that function. An accelerator allows the user to press Alt and the underlined character to activate the item. This is also true for other controls like the command buttons and text boxes.

For text boxes, set the underline character in the caption or label for the text box. When the user uses the accelerator, Access will automatically bounce the focus to the text box.

Notice the indented structure of the menu. The navigation keys allow you to move an entry around on the menu structure. The left and right facing buttons will indent and outdent the highlighted item. If an item is indented under another, the item will be part of a secondary menu, one that 'pops out' when the user selects the parent item. For example, in the above listing, if the user selected New, then a secondary menu offering the Table, Query, Form, Report, Macro and Module options would be displayed.

It's generally good practice to put ellipses at the end of any item that results in another dialog box or menu being displayed. In the example above, notice that the Save Form As option is using this method. When the user selects the option, a secondary menu will be shown, allowing the user to select from that menu.

To put a separator bar on a menu, specify a dash for the caption and indent the dash at the same level as the other items at that point in the menu definition.

After you create menus, you'll see that new macros have been added to the database. These macros represent the functionality of the menu and are what is executed when you 'run' the menu from your application. For our Demo Menu Bar, the Demo Menu Bar and Demo Menu Bar_Demos macros are created to support the menu commands offered.

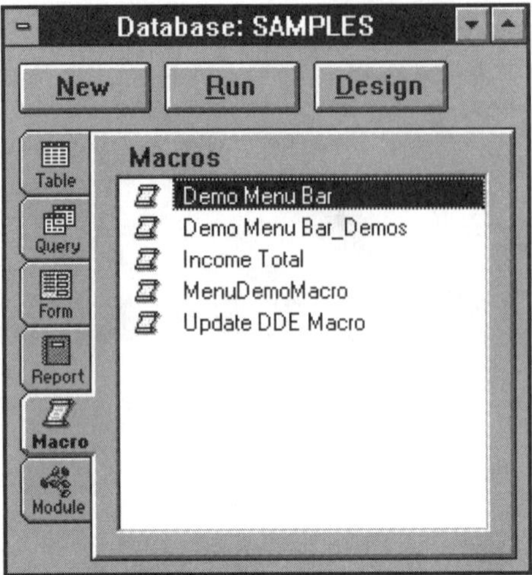

The Demo Menu Bar macro creates the menu using the AddMenu action. This macro defines the top level menu choice, under which the other items will reside:

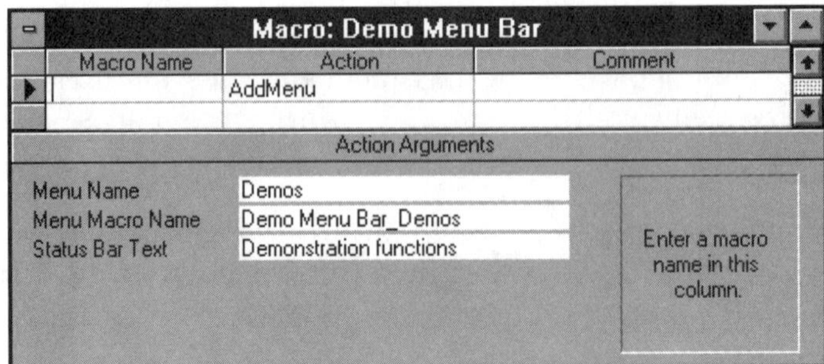

Notice that Demo Menu Bar_Demos is specified as the macro that will be run for this menu item. If you review the macro for the submenu items, you'll see exactly what you've defined for the menu.

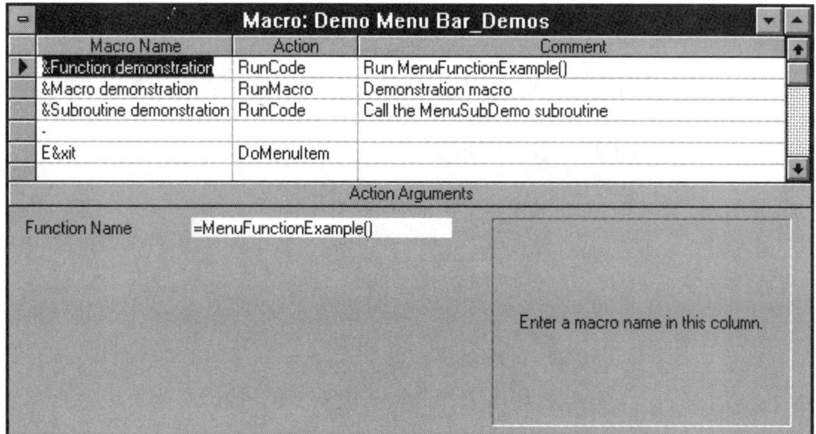

In a more complex system, you can investigate each of the macros with either the macro editor or the Menu Builder. Both modify the underlying macro sheets that drive the functionality behind the menu choices.

Creating Macros for Use in Menus

Once you've determined that you are going to use a custom menu, you need to have the operations that will be performed by the menu set up in either a function or a macro. You create the function or macro the same way as you would for any other. When you want to add a macro to a custom menu, go back into the Menu Builder add-in:

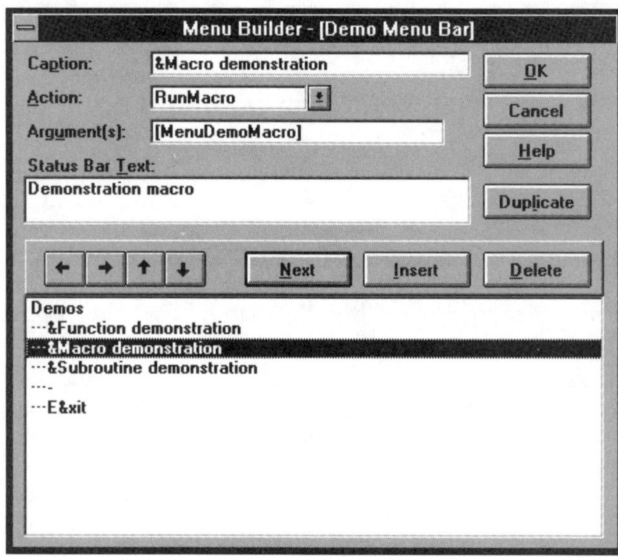

When you set up the menu option, you specify RunMacro as the option for the Action field and in the Argument(s) you specify the name of the macro you want to run. You can also specify what text you want to appear in the Status Bar.

Creating Functions for Use in Menus

If you want to call a function from the menu, you specify RunCode as the Action and in the Argument(s) you specify the function you want to run in the format:

```
=functionname()
```

For example, in the **SAMPLES.MDB** database, the Function Demonstration item is defined as shown in the next screenshot:

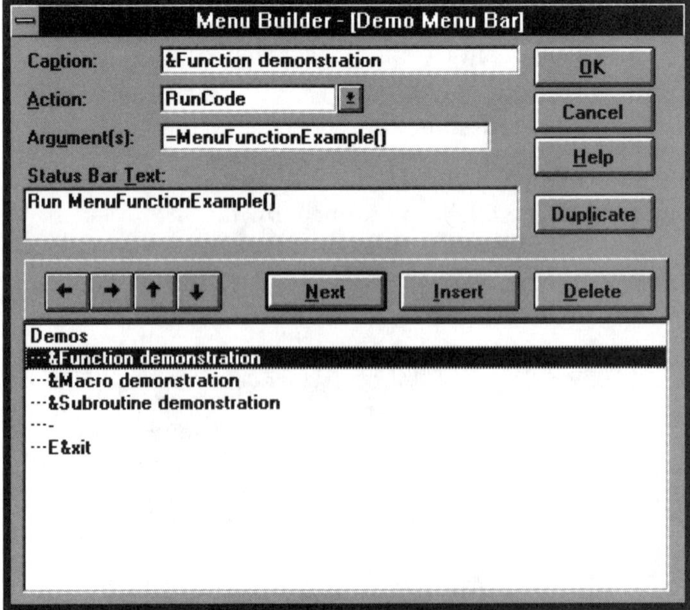

You can specify any arguments within the parenthesis that are required to run the function. Standard function calling rules prevail when you use this method. The important thing to remember is that the '=' is required and you must specify the parenthesis with the command even if you'll not be using any parameters.

In our function example, the code is quite simple as it shows a dialog box indicating a successful use of the function:

```
Function MenuFunctionExample ()
    'Sample function called by a menu
    Dim tString As String

    tString = "This calls a function (MenuFunctionExample) "
    tString = tString & "which does a deed and then returns..."
    MsgBox tString
End Function
```

This function, and the function and subroutine in the next section, are in the Menu Demo module of the **SAMPLES.MDB** database.

Creating Subroutines for Use in Menus

You'll recall from earlier discussions that you can't directly call subroutines from a menu option, but you can call a subroutine from a function. So, if you need to call a subroutine, you should create a 'shell' function that will in turn call the subroutine that you require.

First, establish the shell function that will call your subroutine. In our samples database, the shell is the **CallSub** function:

```
Function CallSub ()
    'Routine to call the subroutine
    'This is required because you can't call
    'a subroutine directly from a menu option.

    MenuSubDemo

End Function
```

The MenuSubDemo subroutine displays a message box and exits, indicating success in calling the subroutine.

```
Sub MenuSubDemo ()
    'This subroutine is called by the CallSub
    'function to demonstrate procedure "chaining"
    'from a custom menu.

    MsgBox "This message generated from the MenuSubDemo subroutine."

End Sub
```

You can see the calling procedure is quite straightforward. The most important point to remember is to use the function to provide access to subroutines only when you need them.

Implementing Custom Menus for Forms

Once you've created the menu, you need to tell Access where the menu should be implemented, i.e. you need to set up the form that will be active at the time when you want your new menu to be displayed. Open your form in design mode and select the Properties sheet for the entire form:

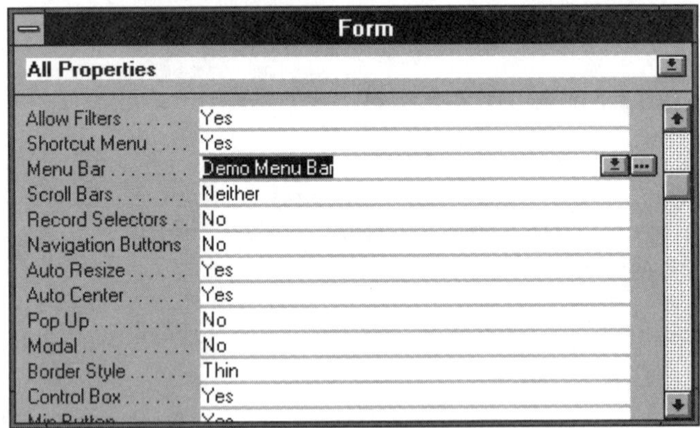

In the Menu Bar property, specify the menu that you want to be used with this form. From this point on, whenever this form is loaded, the default menu will be replaced by your new menu. If you select the ellipses button from the Menu Bar property, you'll be taken directly into the Menu Builder. It doesn't matter whether you load the builder from the property sheet or the Add-in Manager, the results are the same.

Creating Custom Toolbars

Along the same lines as the custom menu is the ability to add a custom toolbar to your application. This offers the same graphical, button oriented interface that is seen in the native Access toolbars, while at the same time allowing you to control the functions that are available to the user from a given toolbar.

You can create custom toolbars in two different ways. You can use the View, Toolbars..., Customize... options to add or change existing toolbars and you can also use the New... option to create a new toolbar:

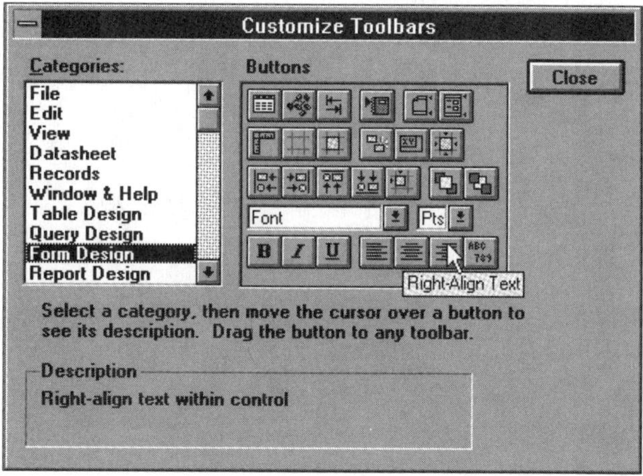

When you are in customization mode, you can click on a button on any toolbar shown, both in the editor dialog box and on the Access workspace screen, and drag the button to another menu.

To remove an existing button, you can drag the button to the workspace. You'll notice that it is placed on its own toolbar, complete with a title bar. If you close the window in which it resides, you'll remove the button from your environment.

If you want to add a new option to a menu, you'll notice that Access allows you to add not only items that relate to procedures, functions and so on, but also reports, queries, forms and tables. This can be a great way to provide access to different parts of your system, all from a custom toolbar.

Modifying Toolbar Items

To add any of these items, macros included, to a toolbar, first create a new blank toolbar. You do this by selecting the New button on the toolbar selector screen. You'll be asked for a name for the new toolbar first. Next, Access will display a blank toolbar on the desktop, or workspace area of the Access environment.

Select the macro or other function that you require and drag it to the new toolbar. If you're adding a macro, the scroll icon will be shown by default:

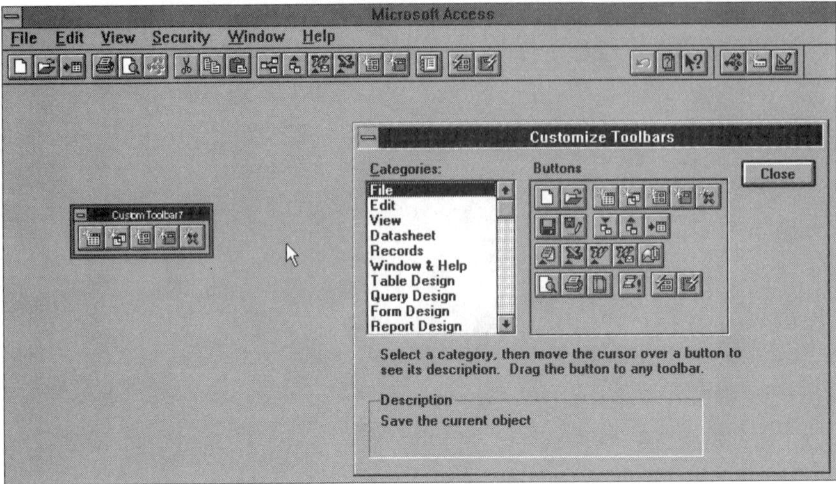

Changing Toolbar Icons

If you want to change the icon order on the toolbar, you can click and drag the buttons to different positions. To change the icon shown on a button, while you're customizing the toolbar, right-click on the button. You'll be given the choice of selecting a new icon face for the button:

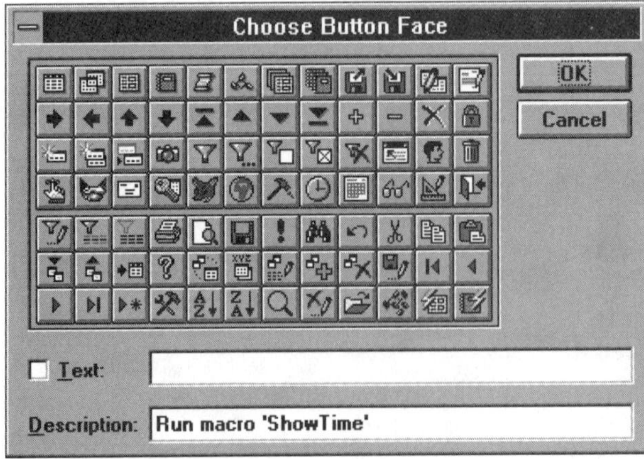

If you select the Text: check box, you can provide a caption for the button that will appear instead of an icon. To reset to an icon view, clear the checkbox and re-select an icon that you want to use. The information that you enter for Description will be used for Tooltips, if enabled, and will be shown in the status line of the Access environment whenever the mouse moves over the button.

We've created a toolbar as shown below which includes 6 options:

- Create a new report
- Create a new form
- Create a new query
- Create a new table
- Create a new module
- Run a macro which displays the current date and time

Using Access Basic behind the Toolbar

The show time button calls the Show Time macro. This macro's sole purpose is to call the **Show Time** function, which is responsible for displaying the current date and time:

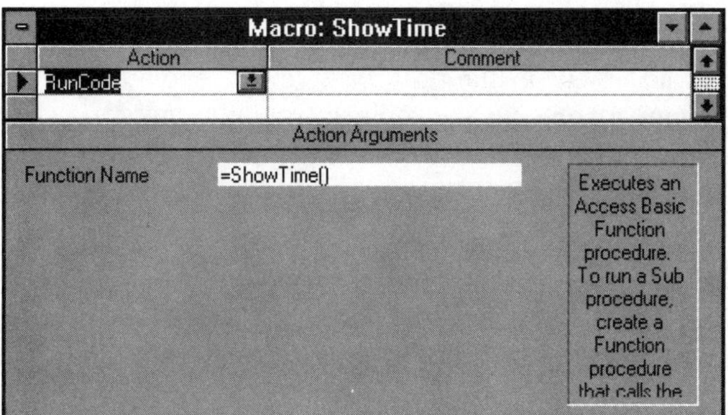

The function, shown below, is also simple:

```
Function ShowTime ()
    'Show the time and date
    MsgBox "Time is " & Time$ & " on " & Date$
End Function
```

If you click on the button you'll get a display of the current date and time:

As you can see, you can easily add new toolbars, and new functionality to your systems. Use the toolbars to provide ready access to often-used functions or procedures. Use the menu options to provide a logical, concise way to gain access to other portions of the system that may not be in as high-demand.

Managing the Display of Toolbars from Access Basic

Using Access Basic, you can control the display of toolbars from within your program modules. You can use the DoCmd ShowToolbar statement to request that a toolbar be displayed or hidden. The format of the statement is:

```
DoCmd ShowToolbar "ToolBarName" [, show]
```

You can put this statement in the OnActivate event of your form to enable the toolbar. If you want to remove the toolbar from the environment when the form is unloaded, you can also add this statement to the form's DeActivate event, turning it off at that point.

The options for the `[,show]` parameter are outlined next:

A_TOOLBAR_YES	This will cause the toolbar to be shown at all times until it is turned off using A_TOOLBAR_NO.

A_TOOLBAR_WHERE_APPROP	This will show the toolbar only where appropriate, i.e., where its functions are able to be performed. With native Access toolbars, Access will know where a toolbar is appropriate and where it is not. It will use this information to determine whether to display the toolbar requested. With custom toolbars, this has the effect of telling Access to only display the toolbar when a window is open. If no windows are open, the toolbar will not be displayed.
A_TOOLBAR_NO	This option, the default, removes the toolbar from view.

We've implemented this code in the OnActivate and DeActivate events of the Menu Demo form. You may have noticed the toolbar appear earlier when you opened this form.

Comments and Suggestions

We've reviewed some interface design guidelines and different techniques for controlling the user's interaction with the application. Access provides some good functionality here with standard control appearances, the ability to update the default look and feel for a control, and so on.

As in most cases that relate to design standards, these areas are subject to exceptions and change in your applications design efforts. The biggest thing you can do to help in your development of applications is to create your own standards. Once established, your standards will undoubtedly evolve, but at least you've taken the first, and most painful, step toward a standard look and feel to your applications.

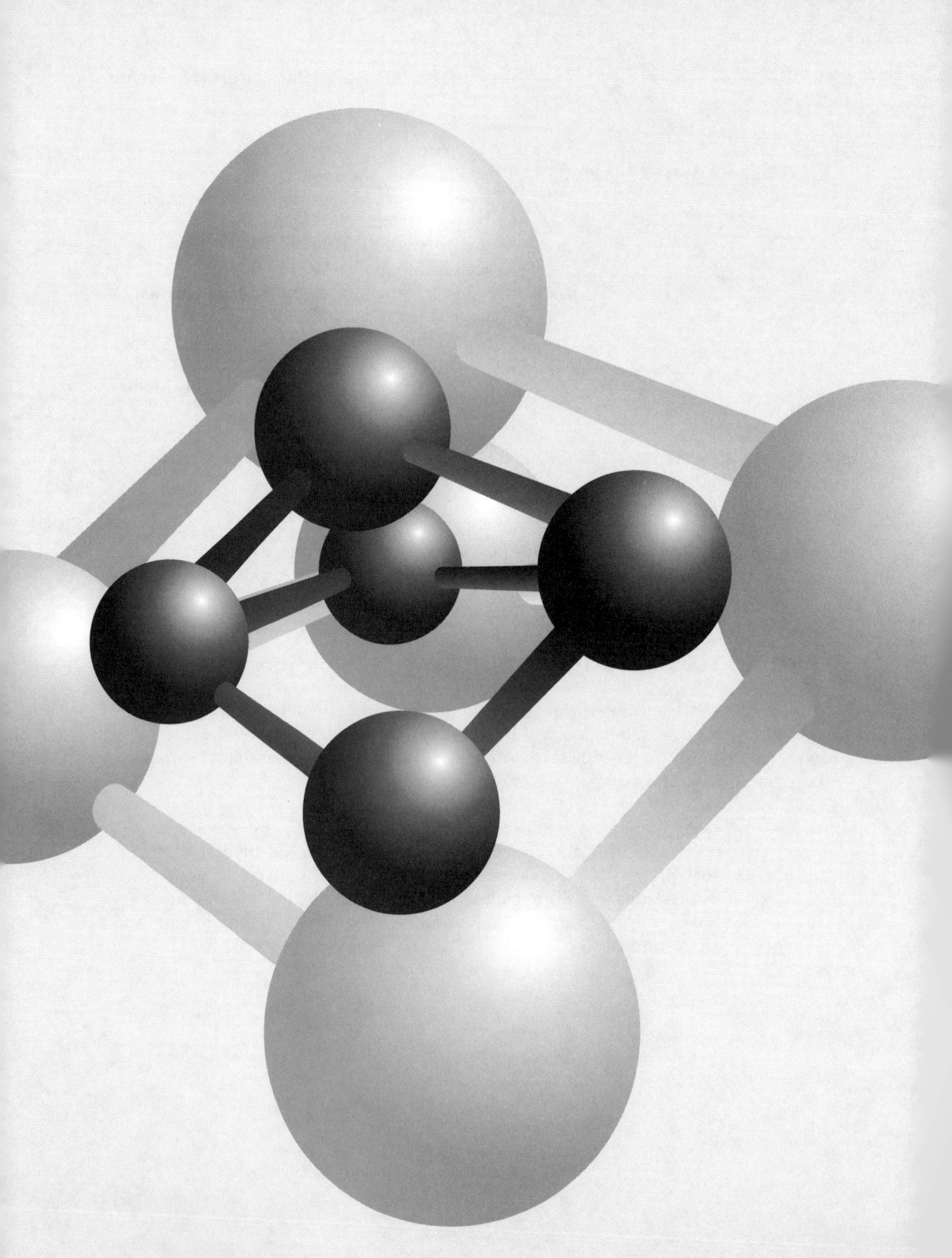

Advanced Access Wizards

With the inclusion of its Wizard Technology, Microsoft have made Access into the perfect learning environment for the novice database developer. Wizards are looked upon by developers as 'interesting toys' and nothing more. However, with a little investigation and a bit of inspiration, developers can get as much use out of the technology as the novice.

What's Covered in This Chapter

In this chapter, we'll investigate the various aspects of the different wizards and Add-Ins included with Access. We'll cover how to use these tools, but perhaps more importantly, we'll discuss how to customize them for your system's environment and personal preferences. In addition, we'll examine how to extend the wizards, if it's at all possible to do so.

The following topics are included in this chapter:

- Using Access Wizards in your application development efforts
- Extending and customizing the wizards
- Using the Database Documentor Add-In

This chapter will inspire you to delve into the subject of wizard creation and modification, an interesting topic for the both beginners and experienced developers.

Chapter 8

How This Chapter Impacts Our Application

This chapter doesn't directly affect our application, but it does show the different tools that you have available to use as a developer creating an application such as the PIM. The development techniques outlined in this chapter should be valuable to your own development projects.

Introduction

Microsoft has introduced some powerful new tools in their whole range of applications. For most operations requiring one or more steps, Microsoft have provided new **Wizards** to guide both the new user and experienced developer, through the creation of a wide variety of product related objects. These wizards guide you through the operation, step by step, prompting you for the information necessary to complete the task at hand.

Wizards are becoming more and more prevalent in applications. You can now see the wizard technology in Microsoft's Word, Excel, Powerpoint, Project and Access products, just to name a few. Other software manufacturers have also developed their own versions of Microsoft's wizards, such as Borland's Experts and Lotus' SmartMasters. Access takes the wizard capability one step further by allowing you to create your own wizards, as well as the ability to customize and modify the existing wizards shipped with Access.

To begin with, we'll investigate how the wizards work and how you can make changes to them to allow them to work in a more compatible way with your environment.

Using Wizards to Aid in Your Development Efforts

Wizards can become one of the most useful tools that are available to a database developer throughout the different aspects of the development cycle. First, you can use wizards to teach you how different operations are performed, by allowing the wizard to walk you through the steps to create the item you're working on. These items can range from the facets of table design all the way through to the dynamics of option group definition. The wizard's results can then be reviewed and modified if you go into design mode for the feature you just created.

Secondly, wizards can be used to speed up application development by providing a starting point based on 'best guesses'. Access wizards can, for example, be used to quickly create a basic form layout for you based on an underlying table. The form will include the fields you designate and will be formatted in a way that a user can manipulate the information on the form. At that stage, all that's left for you to do is to add your own custom features and application personality to the form.

This can be accomplished by adding a menu bar, additional fields as well as other form design related extras. You may also want to change the overall appearance of the form, but one of the great advantages of using wizards comes into play if you want a quick and dirty object. Whether you want this object for database testing or basic application development, because the results that the wizards create are fully functional and require no extra developmental work, you have a great lever for the development time and costs of an application in the shape of Microsoft's wizard technology.

In the following sections, the various Access wizards are covered, along with the uses that they can be put to. This coven includes:

- Form Wizards
- Report Wizards
- Table Wizards
- Query Wizards
- Other Wizards

Using the Form Wizards

The Access Form Wizards gives you a simple way to create template forms based on your database tables and queries within Access.

Overview

The Form Wizards will only create forms that contain fields defined in your database tables or queries, but it will allow you to create several basic types of forms. These types are the Single-Column, Tabular, Graph, Main/Subform and AutoForm options:

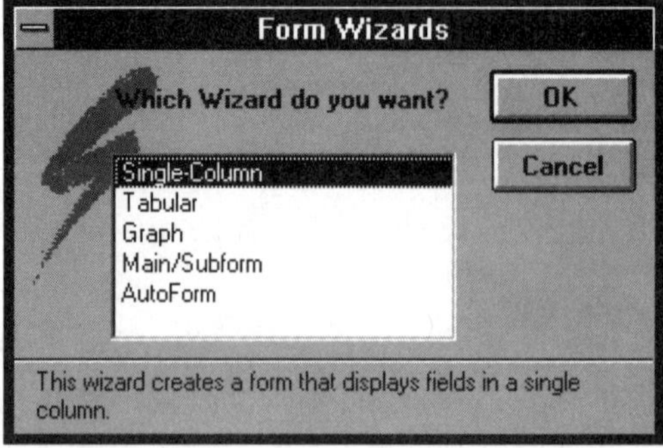

The Single-Column Form Wizard

The Single-Column Form Wizard will produce a form with the fields you select presented vertically on the form. The tab orders will be set so that the top field is first and the bottom field is last:

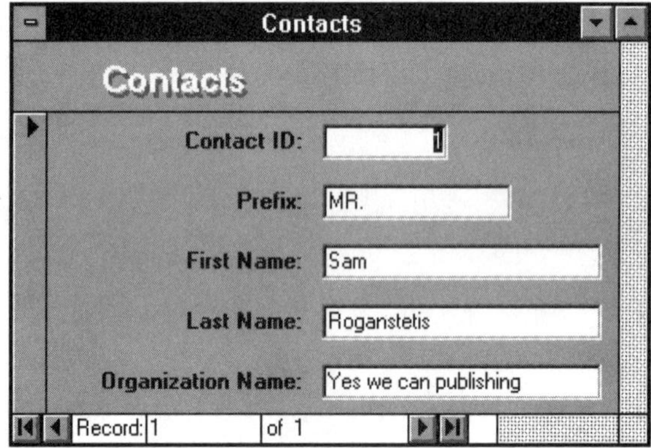

The Tabular Form Wizard

The tabular format is similar to the format of a table's datasheet view. The fields are presented across the screen, with the tab order being set from left to right across a row, representing a single record in the table. The difference between this format and that presented by the datasheet is that you can use the special effects available including the embossed text boxes, different coloring and code to jump forward a screenful of records at the click of a button upon an Access form:

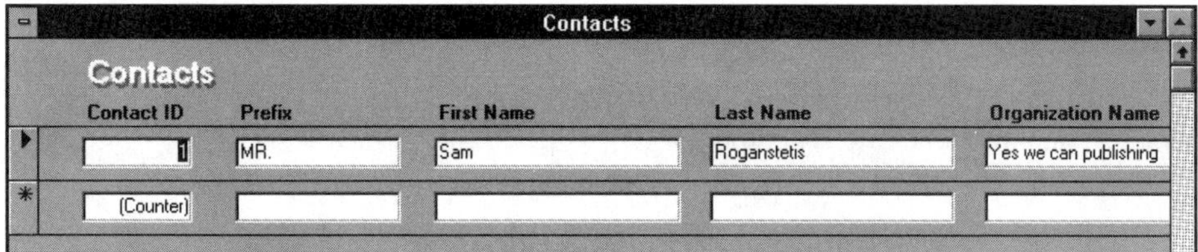

The Graph Form Wizard

The Graph Form Wizard will create a form showing your numeric data as a graph, with each record presented with its own graph. This format may be helpful to you if you have records containing historic summary data that you wish to graph. For example, if each record contained a year's worth of electric bills, you could have Access present the graph on a year-by-year basis, in order to represent your annual power consumption:

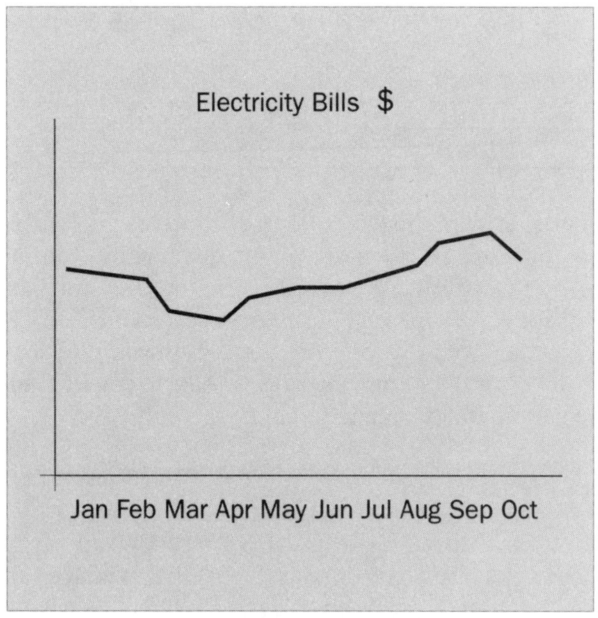

The Main/Subform Wizard

Perhaps the most helpful wizard available to help you with your development efforts is the Main/Subform Wizard:

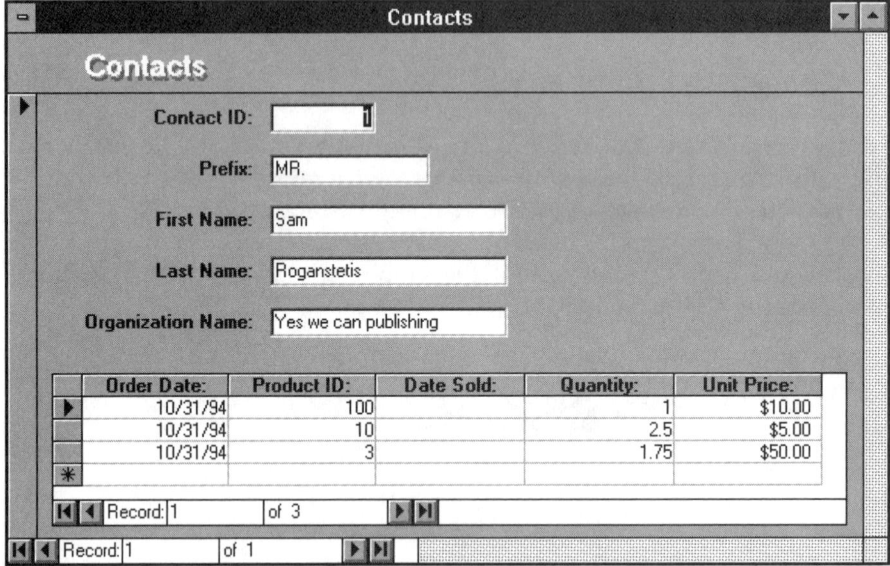

This wizard creates a form that shows the contents of two related tables or queries, related together by a one-to-many relationship, although the relationship needn't be formally set up in the Access database system. In the example shown above, there are multiple order records for each contact record. Access will place the single record on the top portion of the form and will create a sub-form on the bottom portion of the form, in datasheet format, to show the information in the related table.

The Autoform Option

Autoform will create a form for you without asking all of the intrusive questions the other wizards are obsessed with. It produces a form of either the single column or tabular type, with a preset style. The resulting form will include all fields from the table you designate as the source of the form. It is possible to alter the type of form and the style used to display the information on your form, as we will continue to discuss in the next section.

Customizing the Form Wizard

If you find yourself using one of the Form Wizards to create a base form and then changing certain aspects of it over and over again, you may want to make a permanent change to the wizard. Microsoft has provided you with the ability to modify certain aspects of the forms created by the wizard.

From the File menu of Access, select Add-Ins. The next menu will offer you a choice of options and you should select Add-in Manager:

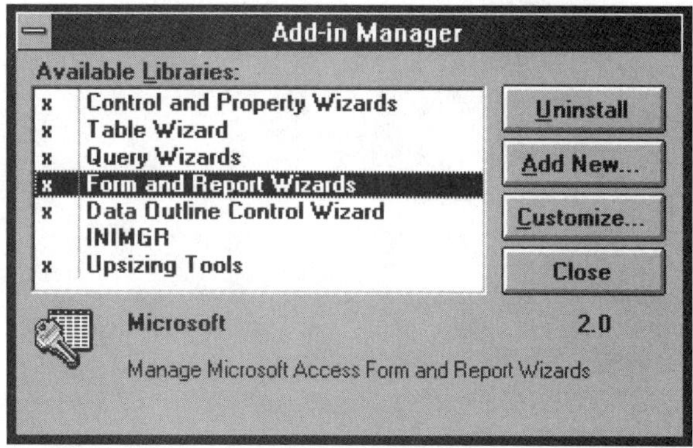

The Add-In Manager allows you to modify and update several of the different Add-Ins offered within the Access environment. Select the Form and Report Wizards option, then select Customize:

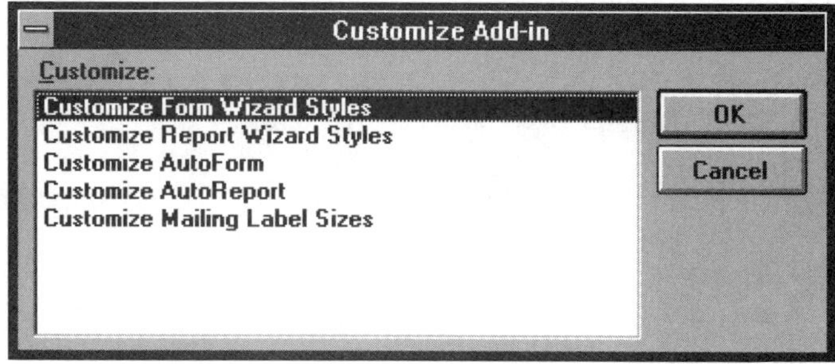

Using Customize Form Wizard Options

Select the Customize Form Wizard Styles. This will allow you to change the options that control the wizard as it creates your forms. The resulting dialog box will allow you to change different properties for the form's labels and text boxes, establish a default background color, as well as any other properties of the basic template that the wizard will use to create the form.

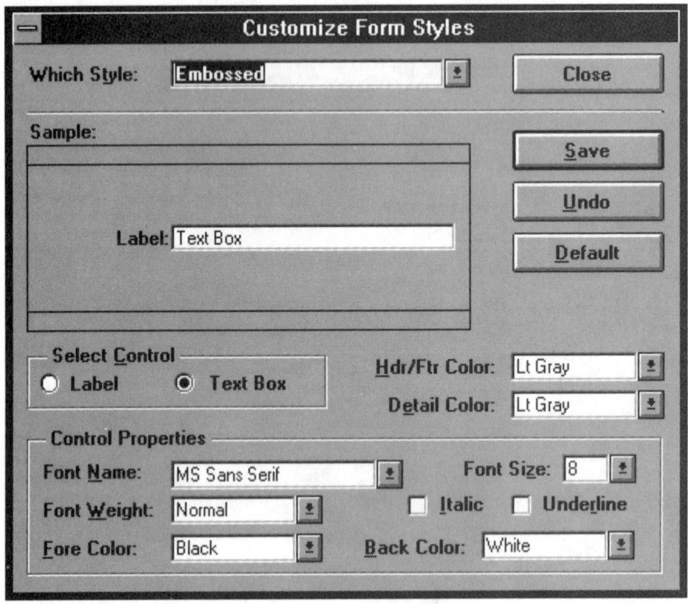

Make sure you select the correct control style to set up. The top list box in the dialog box allows you to select the style that you will be modifying. The effects available with the standard Access installation are:

- Standard
- Chiseled
- Shadowed
- Boxed
- Embossed

You can select each of these and modify the various properties that are associated with them. Once you do, the next time you use the Form Wizards, the new properties you established here, will be put into effect.

> *Note that the* Select Control *frame dictates which items you are working with as you designate changes. Be sure to select the type of control you want to work - either* Label *or* Text Box, *prior to making changes.*

Apart from the general options relating to the color of the header, footer and detail, the remaining items relate to either the labels or text boxes that will be created.

> **One of the best things you can do to familiarize yourself with the capabilities and meanings within this dialog box is to run the Form Wizard appropriate to each of the form types. Note the look and feel for each of the types and think about the options offered. The options in this dialog box will make more sense in the context of each of the forms once you've seen them in action.**

Using the Customize AutoForm Option

You can also change the behavior of the AutoForm option within the Form Wizard. Select the Customize AutoForm item from the Add-Ins Manager list box to make modifications to the wizard.

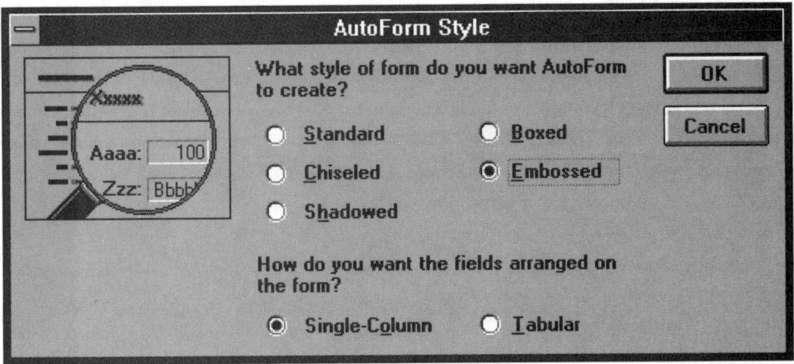

You can change the style of the forms that will result from the AutoForm Wizard. In addition, you can choose between having the forms produced as either Single-Column or Tabular.

Since AutoForms don't prompt the user for more information after they are selected, there is no capability for subforms or graphics; these types of forms must be created by the user manually or with the appropriate wizard.

Extending the Form Wizard Results

As we've shown in the previous sections, you can change the behavior of the Form Wizard in several different ways. Beyond these options, you can also use the Form Wizard as a starting point and customize the form beyond that as required.

As an example, consider the Contacts form from the PIM:

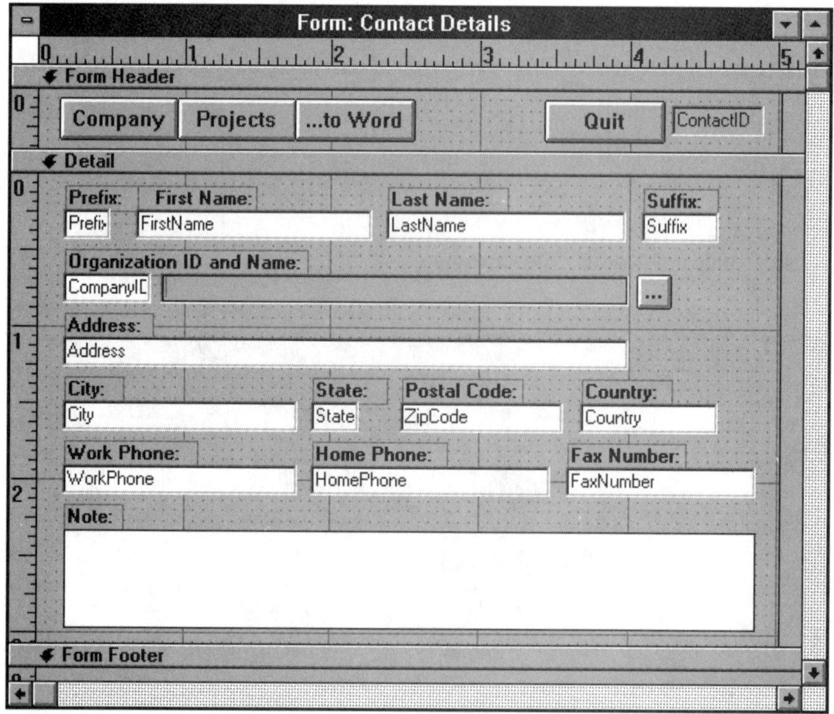

The form was initially created using the Form Wizard to create a single-column form. That form was then reshaped to display the information in a way that made more sense. A specific example of a change that was needed is that the form created by the Single-Column Form Wizard was longer than a single screen.

It's generally not a good idea to force a user to scroll the screen unless you have a specific feature or requirement that forces the issue. Instead, consider creating a more compact screen, or using separate dialog boxes to present any extra information.

You can usually find logical breaks in the information, so providing the opportunity to create the additional dialog boxes. At first, this may seem as if it will slow down the user's interaction within the system, but as long as you are careful about laying out your screen in a manner that makes sense to the user, you should avoid any usability problems by using the dialog box method of optimizing your screen real-estate.

Combo boxes, radio buttons and check boxes can also be helpful in keeping the amount of information on a given form to a manageable level. In Chapter 7, we'll go into some of the philosophy behind form design in more detail.

In the Contact Details screen, we've also added buttons to the header portion of the screen and added an unbound field showing the company information. In addition, the ellipses button to the right of the company field is a new feature.

Typically, you'll want the Form Wizard to create a starting point form for you. From there you'll modify menus, button bars, header and footer information, sizing of fields, location of fields and so on, as it makes sense for your system.

If, after you've established a form, you need to add new fields from the same table that you originally requested, you can use the Field List menu button.

This will give you a dialog box containing a list of table or query fields and you can drag a field from the table list onto your form. If you need to add a field from another table to your form, you can select the field you want to associate with the other table, then open the properties box. In the `Control Source` property, you can name the table and field that you want it to represent.

As an example, on the Contact Details form, if you want the Organization field to contain the name of the company, and don't want to programmatically maintain the values in the field, you can enter the expression:

```
=[Company]![CompanyName]
```

resulting in the company name being displayed in the field on your form.

> **You must specify the table name as `[Company]` in this case because the field is in a different table from the one that is the record source for the form.**

In our PIM example, we use the company name field to exhibit several different features of Access so we've opted to implement this field in the Access Basic code instead.

Further Modifying the Form Wizard

If you need to further dissect the Form Wizard, you can review and make changes to the actual code behind the wizard itself. To do this, you will need to 'turn off' the wizard in your Access environment, review the code and make any desired changes, and turn the wizard back on.

> **Making changes to the wizard is not something to be taken lightly. Unless you have a burning desire to modify the wizard, consider making changes to the results from the wizard rather than the operational behavior of the wizard.**

First, call up the Add-In Manager dialog and select the Form and Report Wizards as before. Next, select Uninstall. This will simply remove the 'x' from the left hand column of the display. You'll also notice that the Uninstall button changes to Install.

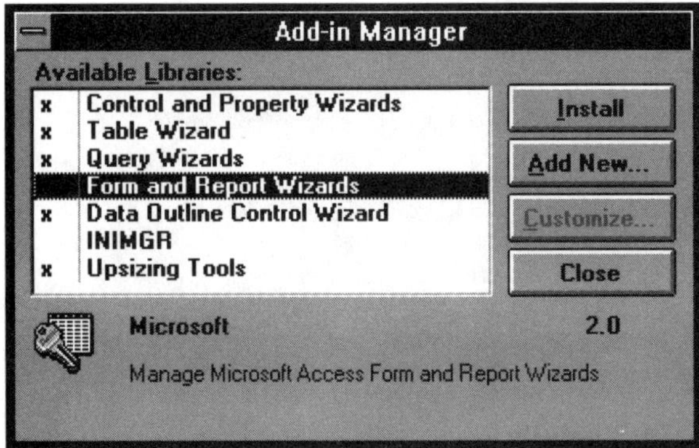

You'll need to close the Add-in Manager, then exit Access. When you return to Access, the Form and Report Wizards will not be loaded.

You need to uninstall the wizards and re-start Access because if you try to work with them while they are installed, Access will give you an error message indicating that the wizard database file is already open.

Now, look for and open the file called **WZFRMRPT.MDA**, which is typically located in your Access subdirectory. If this is your first review of this or any other wizard, it's a good idea to select the Read Only check box in the Open Database dialog box. This will prevent any accidental mishaps by not allowing changes.

Once opened, you'll notice that several tables and forms are in the database. Each table represents a parameter or other bits of information that are used by the Wizard as it does its magic.

If you have the Access Developer's Toolkit, you have access to annotated versions of the modules. Open the .MDA file from the ADT subdirectory rather than from your standard Access subdirectory. You will still need to uninstall the wizard that you want to review prior to opening it.

If you select the Tables tab, you'll see the different tables that support the functionality of the wizard. Remember that the database **WZFRMRPT.MDA** contains both the form and report wizards, so you'll see references to both within the database:

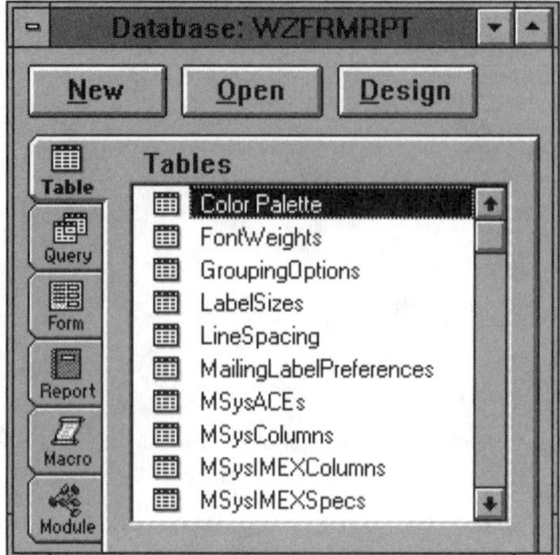

Browse through the tables and you'll quickly find that most potentially variable portions of the wizards have been moved to the tables. The function of the tables range from controlling the colors for controls and backgrounds to the actual messages and application states that are in effect as the wizard executes.

When you select the Form tab, you'll notice that the different screens you see when you use the wizards are all defined there:

If you call up a form in design mode, the QuickFormStyle for example, you'll notice that the graphic in the upper left corner will go through several changes as the form is painted. When the wizard runs, it simply 'turns on' the graphic applicable to the specific function being carried out. This way, a single form can serve as the interface for many different functions or phases. If you want to make changes to the wizard's screens, this is where you'll want to do it.

The Modules tab shows you how the wizard is called from Access:

In the **MSACC20.INI** file, located in your Windows subdirectory, Access is told exactly what the entry points are to the wizard. The following listing shows a sample of what is in this .INI file:

```
[Form Wizards]
Single-Column=zwForm,1,{This wizard creates a form that
displays fields in a single column.}
Tabular=zwForm,2,{This wizard creates a form that displays
each record as a row of fields.}
Graph=zwGraph,,{This wizard creates a form that displays
a graph.}
Main/SubForm=zwMainSub,,{This wizard creates a form that
contains another form.}
AutoForm=zwAutoForm,,{AutoForm automatically creates a
simple form based on the selected table or query.}
```

Access adds and removes these lines as you install and uninstall the Wizards. You can of course place a semi-colon at the start of a line in the .INI file to disable them completely

The first field, to the left of the equal sign, contains the name of the wizard. The next field in the line contains a module function name that ties back to the wizard's modules. This is the function or procedure that is called to start the wizard. You can see this by comparing the lines in the .INI file with the module procedure and function names.

After you've made your changes or finished reviewing the wizard, don't forget to exit the database. Return to the Add-ins Manager and Install the Form Wizard. If you don't, the wizard won't be active the next time you start Access.

Using the Report Wizard

The Report Wizard provides an automated jump start that will satisfy many of your reporting requirements. There are several different formats and types of reports available, many that may suit your needs immediately without any alterations. With some changes, you can quickly implement personalized reports into your applications.

Overview

The Report Wizard creates several different report formats and can create sophisticated reports. These reports can be based on tables or queries and can be readily incorporated in your application.

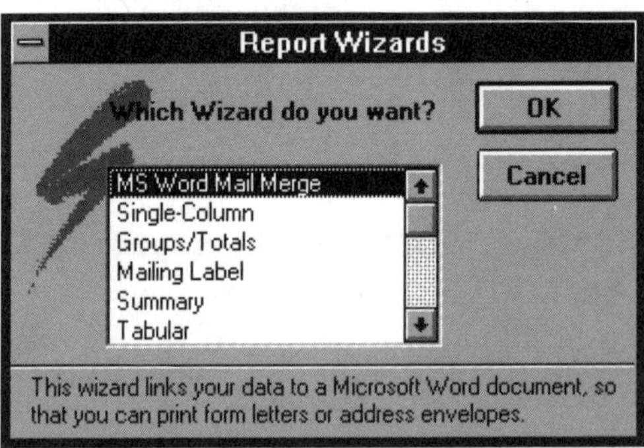

An overview of each of these options is presented in the next sections.

The MS Word Mail Merge "Report"

If you have created a database containing names and addresses, as in our PIM, you may want to create a mass mailing for those names. You can automate the process quickly and easily between Word and Access by using the Mail Merge Wizard:

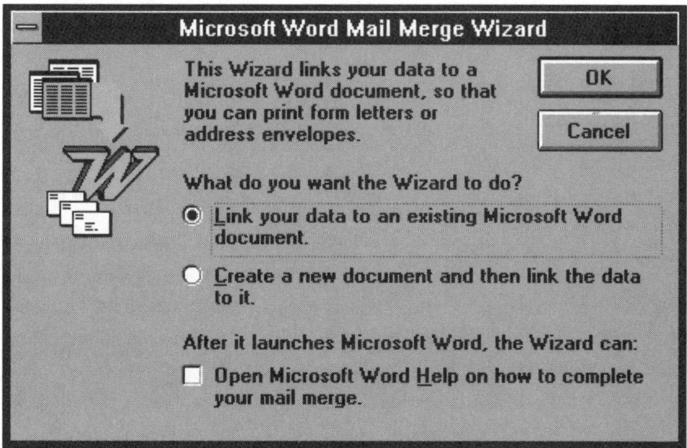

The Wizard allows you to insert your database information into an existing document, or to create a completely new one. If you choose to initiate a new document, Word can walk you through the steps necessary to create a document that will merge with your database.

Of course, as with other Access tools, you can base your mail merge on either a database table or a query. With this in mind, you can imagine how straight-forward it is to create a mail merge to a specific group of contacts. You would simply create a query that returns the selected contacts and reference that query in your mail merge set up. This will limit the mailing to only those records that you dictate.

Once in Word, a new menu, the Merge Fields menu, will be shown. This menu allows you to select from the fields available in the database table:

For more information on the Word merge menu, look up "Merging" in Word's on-line help.

Mailing Label Reports

The Mailing Label Wizard lets you create labels using the name and address fields in your database. You can establish parameters in the Add-In Manager that will be applied when you use the wizard to create labels.

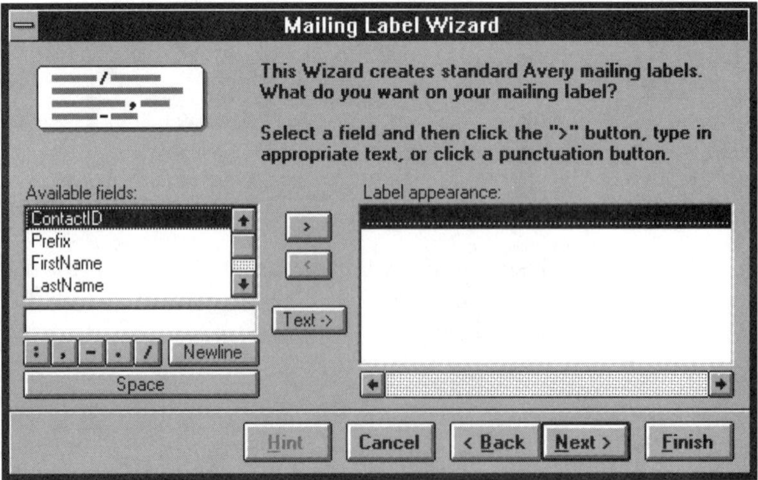

You can set up many different types of labels. Once you've selected the fields that you want on your labels and specified the order you want them sorted by, you'll be prompted to select a label format when you start the Mailing Label Wizard. First, you'll be presented with the built-in formats:

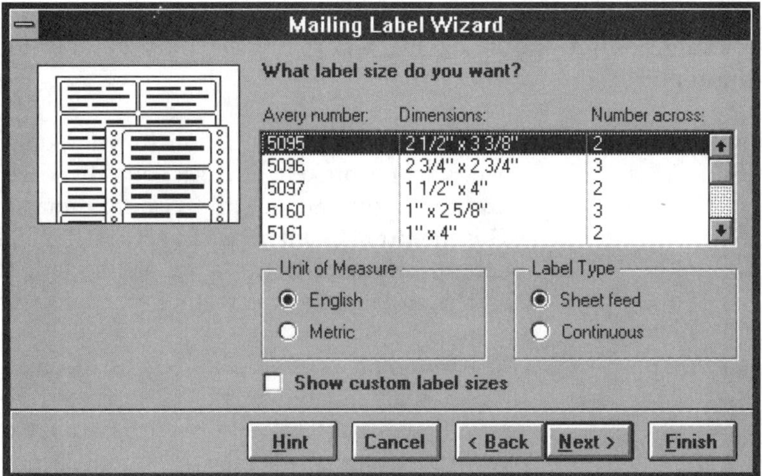

Note that if you don't have any custom mailing label sizes defined, you won't see the Show Custom Label Sizes *checkbox.*

If you want to work with your own custom formats, simply check the Show custom label sizes check box. The list of labels will change to show any custom labels that you have defined in the Add-In Manager. For details of how to create custom label sizes, see the section 'Modifying Mailing Label Sizes'.

As with the other report wizards, once you finish the specification of the labels, you'll be able to review the labels in preview mode to make sure they are correctly formatted.

Other Report Wizards Available

There are several other formats available within the Report Wizard. The other standard wizard formats are outlined below:

The Single-Column Report The Single-Column report is commonly referred to as a standard data processing report. The report, presenting data in a single column, is quite basic. As a default, it presents one record per page of the report.

When you start the wizard, you'll be prompted for the fields to include along with the sort value. After specifying the report name, you'll be able to see the results of the report.

The Groups/Totals Report When you have information in your database that needs to be broken into sections, by date for example, you can use the Groups/Totals report. This report will take the query or database table you specify and create a report, sorted, grouped and subtotaled in the manner that you specify.

The Summary Report The Summary option allows you to create a report that, much like the Groups and Totals report, will subtotal and total based on criteria you specify. In this case, the intent is not to show the detail records, only the subtotals and totals.

The Tabular Report The Tabular report is much the same as the Single-Column report, with the exception that the information is presented horizontally across the page. Each row is representative of one record in the database table. This format is similar to viewing a table or query in datasheet view.

The AutoReport Option The AutoReport option will use either the Single Column or Tabular formats to automatically create a report for you. The style, page orientation and field layout of the report created will depend on the settings in the AutoReport Style dialog in the Add-In Manager. This is similar to the AutoForm dialog discussed earlier.

You can see that there are several different options available to you when you use the Report Wizard. As is the case with the Form Wizard, you can customize the output of the wizard to closely match your own personal requirements.

Once the wizard has generated the report you've requested, select exit to return to design mode. After you've completed any changes, Access will prompt you for a name for the report, saving it in the database file.

Customizing the Report Wizard

You can change several aspects of the Report Wizard. These range from the way the actual reports are formatted to the report type that is generated when you select the AutoReport option.

Go back into the Add-In Manager and select the Form and Report Wizards, then Customize:

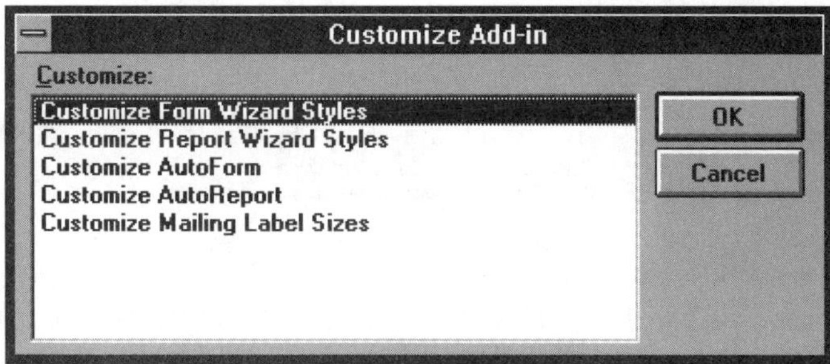

You'll notice three different options that apply to the Report Wizard. The Styles, AutoReport and Mailing Label Sizes options all provide you with the mechanism to customize the behavior of the wizard.

Modifying Report Wizard Styles

If you want to change the fonts that are used upon, the look and feel of or any other aspects from the results generated by the wizard, select Customize Report Wizard Styles from the list:

You'll be able to modify just about every aspect of the built-in effects. Note that you will need to use the Which Style list box and Select Control option to select the item that you are working with as each style and control type maintains its own list of option settings.

Modifying the AutoReport Settings

The AutoReport setting controls some basic information about reports that are created with the AutoReport function. First, the type of report is established as either a Tabular or Single-Column report. Second, the look and feel of the report is defined:

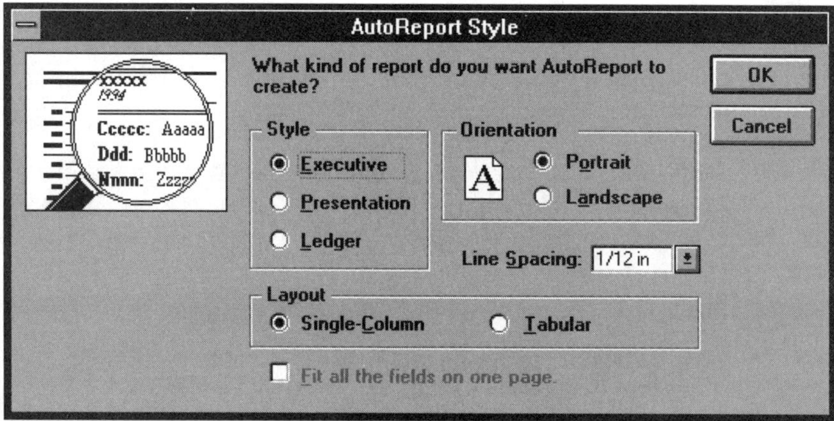

It's important to keep in mind the preferences that your users place upon the facets of the user interface when you make changes here. In many cases, it will be helpful to make permanent changes to the AutoReport settings to make the reports act more like the end-user expects.

> The **Line Spacing**, initially set at 1/12 in, can cause quite a bit of white space on the report. The vertical space between the lines is controlled by this value. To compress a report and perhaps reduce the amount of white, or blank, space on a report, set this value to zero (0) when using a Tabular layout.
>
> In addition, consider checking the **Fit all the fields on one page** check box. This will tell Access to attempt to fit all possible information on a single page. Without this option, if there are more fields than will fit horizontally on a page, Access will create a second page horizontally for each page of the report. This is much like a 'fit to page' option, which can come in quite handy for the developer who needs to create a simple report as quickly as possible.

Modifying Mailing Label Sizes

Setting up the mailing label sizes in the Access Wizard is much easier if you have a ruler and the actual label stock before you start.

From the Add-In Manager, select Customize Form and Report Wizards and then Customize Mailing Label Sizes. This dialog displays a list of custom (user defined) label sizes if any have been defined. Select New... (if there are no custom sizes) or Duplicate... to create a new label size.

> *Note that 107 different label formats ship with Access. Make sure the label you are creating doesn't already exist in the system. Most of the labels are referred to by part number and size for easy reference to the label stock you are attempting to print on.*

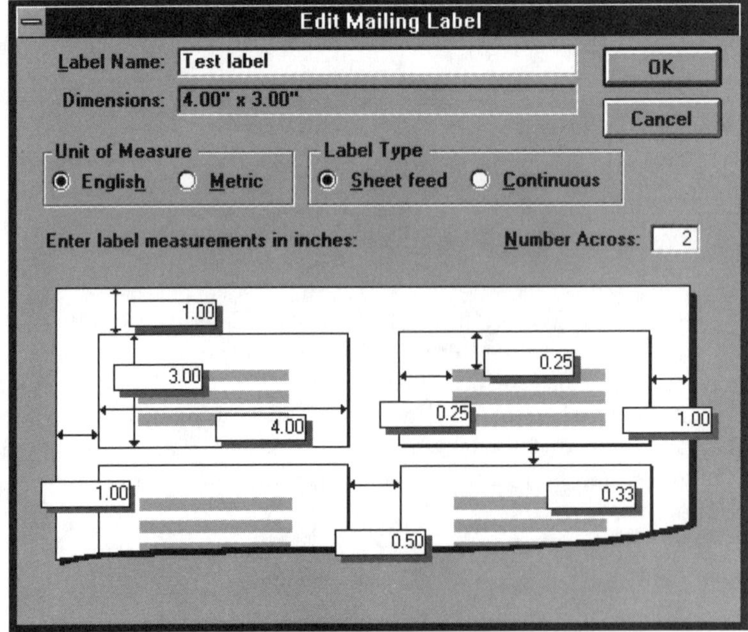

You create the format for the label by selecting the Unit of Measure and the type of stock (continuous or single-sheet). You enter the specific dimensions of the label on a graphical display. This information is saved in the wizard's database and is made available to you during your use of the wizard. The name you give the label format becomes the name listed in the custom label list when you call upon the Mailing Label Wizard.

Further Modifying the Report Wizard

If you need to make additional changes to the Report Wizard, you can do so by working with the actual wizard database, **WZFRMRPT.MDA**. The file, located in your Access subdirectory, is where all of the different setting are maintained for report formats, fonts, look and feel for the reports and so on.

> **You must uninstall the Form and Report Wizard from within the Add-In Manager and re-start Access prior to opening** `WZFRMRPT.MDA`**. If you don't, Access will not allow you to open it. Access opens the database when it loads and will not allow another instance of it to be opened.**

In addition, the actual forms and module code are maintained in the database.

The database shares some information between the Form Wizard and the Report Wizard, but it's reasonably apparent when you review the forms, tables and modules which ones belong to the Report Wizard.

As an example, look at the LabelSizes table:

Table: LabelSizes

Hardcopy	LabelList	ItemsAcross	ID	fMetric	dxLabel
4143	15/16" x 4"	2	1	0	5760
4144	15/16" x 2 1/2"	3	2	0	3600
4145	15/16" x 3 1/2"	1	3	0	5040
4146	1 7/16" x 4"	1	4	0	5760
4160	2 7/16" x 3 1/2"	1	5	0	5040
4161	2 15/16" x 4"	1	6	0	5760
4162	15/16" x 3 1/2"	1	7	0	5040
4163	15/16" x 3 1/2"	1	8	0	5040
4166	3" x 5"	1	9	0	7200
4167	3 1/2" x 6"	1	10	0	8640
4168	2 1/6" x 4"	1	11	0	5760
4169	3" x 5"	1	12	0	7200
4240	1 1/4" x 4 3/4"	1	13	0	6840
4241	2 3/4" x 2 3/4"	1	14	0	3960
4249	15/16" x 3 1/2"	1	15	0	5040

Record: 1 of 107

Each row in the table represents the available label sizes and their associated properties. You'll recognize the column names pretty quickly as the actual coordinates and parameters that you enter when defining a label. The LabelSizes table is the table that ships with Access' Report Wizard; these are the 'built-in' label formats provided with Access, so there's no interface to it from the Add-In Manager.

The custom label formats that you can maintain from within Access reside in the User Sizes table. If you open the table, you'll see any custom label formats that you've defined. The table format is identical to the LabelSizes table.

The WizStyleLib table contains information on the different styles that you've seen offered during the use of the wizard:

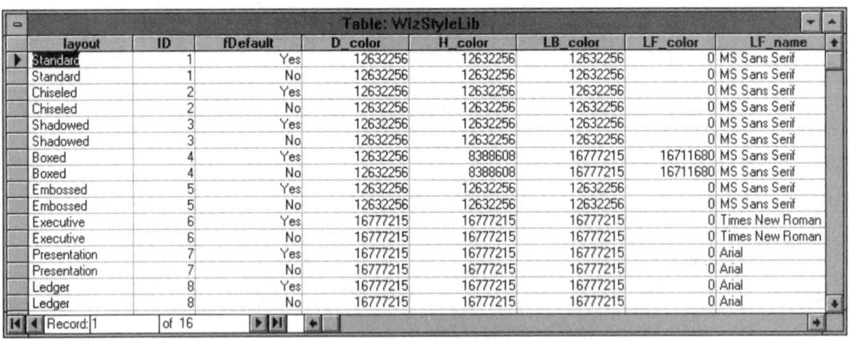
Table: WizStyleLib

layout	ID	fDefault	D_color	H_color	LB_color	LF_color	LF_name
Standard	1	Yes	12632256	12632256	12632256	0	MS Sans Serif
Standard	1	No	12632256	12632256	12632256	0	MS Sans Serif
Chiseled	2	Yes	12632256	12632256	12632256	0	MS Sans Serif
Chiseled	2	No	12632256	12632256	12632256	0	MS Sans Serif
Shadowed	3	Yes	12632256	12632256	12632256	0	MS Sans Serif
Shadowed	3	No	12632256	12632256	12632256	0	MS Sans Serif
Boxed	4	Yes	12632256	8388608	16777215	16711680	MS Sans Serif
Boxed	4	No	12632256	8388608	16777215	16711680	MS Sans Serif
Embossed	5	Yes	12632256	12632256	12632256	0	MS Sans Serif
Embossed	5	No	12632256	12632256	12632256	0	MS Sans Serif
Executive	6	Yes	16777215	16777215	16777215	0	Times New Roman
Executive	6	No	16777215	16777215	16777215	0	Times New Roman
Presentation	7	Yes	16777215	16777215	16777215	0	Arial
Presentation	7	No	16777215	16777215	16777215	0	Arial
Ledger	8	Yes	16777215	16777215	16777215	0	Arial
Ledger	8	No	16777215	16777215	16777215	0	Arial

Record: 1 of 16

You'll notice styles that include Embossed, Standard, Executive and so on. Each style has its properties defined so when the wizard runs, it will know exactly how it is to be used.

As with the Form Wizard, the modules provide the entry points into the Wizard from Access.

The **MSACC20.INI** file, located in the Windows subdirectory, provides Access with the information on what module procedure or function to call to start a given wizard. Once installed, the lines shown next are placed in **MSACC20.INI** to support the Report Wizards.

```
[Report Wizards]
MS Word Mail Merge=PM_Entry,, {This wizard links your
data to a Microsoft Word document, so that you can
print form letters or address envelopes.}
Single-Column=zwReport,3,{This wizard creates a report that
displays fields in a single column.}
Groups/Totals=zwReport,4,{This wizard creates a report that
groups together and displays totals for each group.}
Mailing Label=zwMailingLabel,,{This wizard creates standard
Avery mailing labels.}
Summary=zwReport,12,{This wizard creates a report that
displays totals for groups of records.}
Tabular=zwReport,11,{This wizard creates a report that
displays each record as a row of fields.}
AutoReport=zwAutoReport,,{AutoReport automatically creates a
simple report based on the selected table or query.}
```

The first item in the line shows the name of the wizard, followed by the procedure that will be called to start the specific wizard.

When you have finished working with the wizard, be sure to Install it from within the Add-In Manager. If you don't, it won't be available to you the next time you want to use it in the creation of a report.

Using the Table Wizard

The Table Wizard provides you with many different layouts that you can use in the creation of your tables. You can select the table you wish to use as a template and then make changes to the table layout as you desire.

Overview

The Table Wizard first presents you with a list of the different tables that it knows how to build. Each table is defined down to the field and field formatting level:

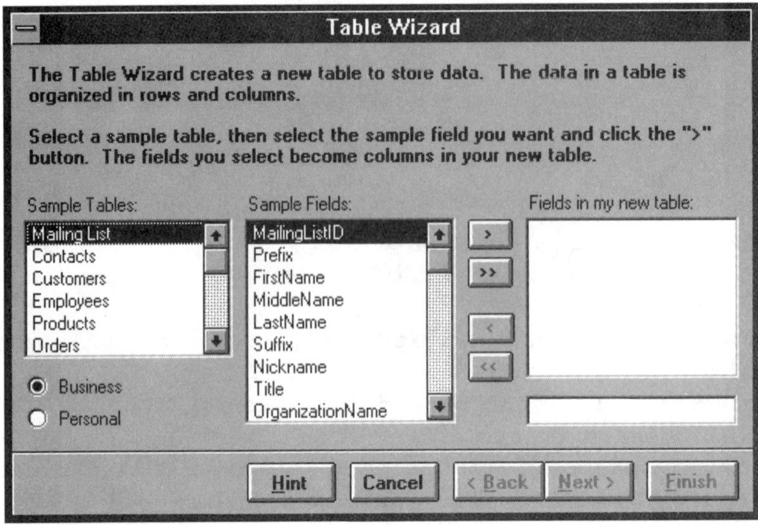

The tables are grouped by their expected use, either Business or Personal. Note that you can select fields in the Sample Fields list box from multiple template tables. You can mix and match the fields you need until you get exactly the type of information you require for your new table.

Refer to the appendices for complete information about the various tables that are included with the Table Wizard. The following information shows some of the tables and their related fields:

Table	Related Fields
Contacts	FirstName, LastName, Address, City, State, Country, WorkPhone, FaxNumber, LastMeetingDate, PostalCode, ContactID, OrganizationName, Birthdate, Note, EmailName, Region, Suffix, Photograph, Prefix, ReferredBy, MobilePhone, ActionItems, HomePhone, ContactType
Diet Log	WhichMeal, DietLogID, Note, Vitamins, DietType, TotalCalories, GramsFat, GramsCarbohydrates, GramsProtein, MilligramsSodium, PersonID, DateAcquired

Continued

Table	Related Fields
Friends	AlternativePhone, SpouseName, Address, LastName, FirstName, Photograph, Region, Nickname, EmailAddress, Note, Birthdate, FriendID, FaxNumber, WorkPhone, Country, MobilePhone, City, Hobbies, DateLastTalkedTo, ChildrenNames, HomePhone, CompuServeID, DateUpdated, PostalCode, HealthProblems, State
Investments	AccountID, InvestmentID, Note, Clear, Action, SecuritySymbol, SecurityName, Type, SecurityType, SharesOwned
Music Collection	NumberofTracks, Note, YearReleased, Format, DatePurchased, RecordingLabel, Title, Photograph, MusicCollectionID, PurchasePrice, GroupName, SampleSoundClip, ArtistID
Wine List	ServingInstructions, Color, Vineyard, WineListID, PercentAlcohol, SweetOrDry, WineName, OstetatiousProse, CountryofOrigin, Vintage, Region, Note, Variety, WineType

To browse the table definitions, open the **SAMPLES.MDB** database. If you open the Table Wizard Inquiry Tool form, you'll be able to browse the tables and their associated fields.

The form depends on the use of attached tables, located by default in your Access subdirectory. If your .MDT files are located in a different subdirectory, as they would be if, for example, you installed Access with MSOffice Pro the directory would be MSOFFICE\ACCESS, you'll have to update the links to the file. Select Add-ins from the File menu and then Attachment Manager to display the dialog box that allows you to update links.

Table Wizard Inquiry Tool

Table Wizard Inquiry Tool

TableName: Accounts

Fields in Table	Field Type:
AccountType	Text 50
AccountName	Indexed Text 50
AccountID	ID Field
AccountNumber	Text 50
Description	Memo
Note	Memo

Record: 1 of 43

As you browse through the tables, the bottom subform will be updated to reflect the fields for the given table. A complete listing of the various fields that are available from the Table Wizard is included in Appendix 3. These fields, when used from within the wizard, include formatting, length restrictions and so on. They can help you control the user input functions that relate to the table definitions you establish, which can be a great aid in your applications' development cycle.

Customizing the Table Wizard

The Table Wizard is contained in the **WZTABLE.MDA** file, located in your Access subdirectory. If you have the Access Developer's Toolkit, the annotated version of the wizard is located in the ADT subdirectory under the same file name.

> **You have two different options for exploring the Table Wizard. First, if you own the Access Developer's Toolkit, you can open the .MDT version of the wizard. If you open the .MDT file while the Table Wizard is installed, you'll receive a message about several duplicate definitions, but you can acknowledge these warnings and continue and Access will still be able to open the database. You won't be able to view some of the Module files, but you will be able to review the Forms and Tables.**

> **If you don't have the developer's toolkit, you'll need to first uninstall the wizard using the Add-in Manager. Next, exit and re-start Access and you'll then be able to open and review the .MDA file.**

Once you have loaded the database, you'll notice there are several different tables that the wizard uses to accomplish its functionality:

Here's a summary of some of the tables and what they are used for:

tblField This table contains the different fields that are available during the building of a table from within the wizard. In addition, the captions that can be used with the fields are defined in this table.

tblFieldType The different field types are defined in this table. These types range from Text to different Date types. There is a numeric identifier associated with each field type. This identifier is used in the Field definitions to indicate the type of control that the field should be associated with.

tblInputMask
tblInputMaskType

These tables control the different input masks that are available. The InputMaskType table identifies the different types of masks available, while the InputMask table dictates where these formats are applied.

tblTable

This table contains the various tables that are defined and available to the Table Wizard. If you want to add a new table, this is the starting point for that operation. You'll first insert the table name and reference information. Next, you'll specify the table fields that are available.

tblTableField

This table provides the link between the tblTable and tblField tables. The references in this table associate the fields with the various tables in which they are implemented.

> **Note that with the exception of tblInputMaskType, the tables are not stored in the wizard itself, but are attached to it. They reside in another database, `WZTBLDAT.MDT`**

You will recall that the wizards are referenced in the **`MSACC20.INI`** file located in your Windows subdirectory. This .INI file tells Access which routine should be called to initiate a given wizard. In addition, the mode that the wizard is opened in is determined there. Wizard databases can be opened in RO (Read-Only) or RW (Read/Write) mode. The default is Read/Write and the wizards are installed with this option each time you use Add-Ins Manager to install them. For normal, everyday use, it's recommended that you use the RO mode. In this mode, there is slightly less overhead required of Access, which can in turn help speed response times.

The following listing shows the entries in your **`MSACC20.INI`** as they relate to loaded wizard add-ins:

```
[Libraries]
wzlib.mda=rw
wzTable.mda=rw
wzQuery.mda=rw
```

```
wzbldr.mda=rw
wzoutl.mda=rw
wzfrmrpt.mda=rw
```

Adding or Modifying Field Types

You can change many of the parameters for the wizard field types by selecting Customize for the Table Wizard in the Add-Ins Manager. If you decide that you want or need to modify these settings, it will be helpful to understand the relationships between the tables. You'll need to follow the same methodologies when adding tables or fields to these tables as Microsoft used in the creation of the wizard:

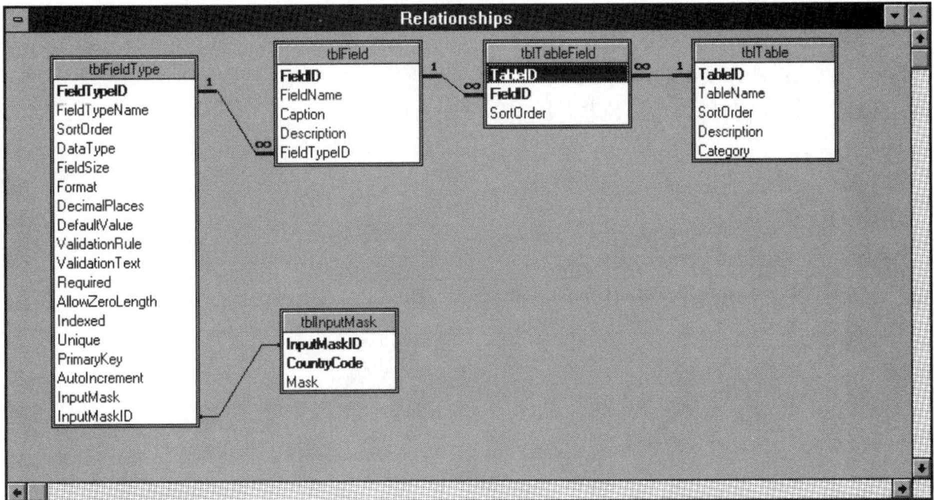

The tables that support the wizard are normalized and, as such, most references are relational in nature. Take, for example, the relationship between the tblTable and its associated fields. The defined relationships serve as the key to the types of fields and their associated input masks.

Using this methodology, you can have a field definition shared by multiple table definitions. In addition, you can define new types of fields and make them instantly available to other tables without duplicating the definition.

If you decide to make modifications to the Table Wizard, you'll need to first uninstall it. Use the Add-in Manager to uninstall the wizard, and then restart Access.

You can make the changes direct in **WZTABLE.MDA**, or directly on the tables in **WZTBLDAT.MDT**. If you modify the MDT file, you'll be able to work with the tables while the wizard is installed.

Here are the lines from your **MSACC20.INI** file that are used by the Table Wizard:

```
[Table Wizards]
Table=TW_Entry,,{This wizard creates a new table to store
data.}

[Table Wizard Data Files]
wztbldat.mdt=Standard MS Sample Fields
```

You can open this file by specifying it in the Access Open Database dialog box:

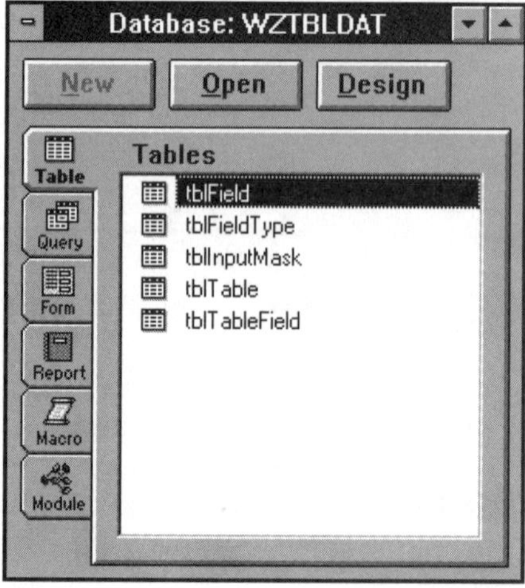

The five tables listed here are the tables that are referenced by the wizard. They are maintained here for several different reasons. First, since the tables are external to the wizard, they can be maintained, updated and generally developed as needed without having to modify the wizard itself. This is extremely advantageous and can prevent accidents from occurring in the wizard's code modules or tables.

Second, the tables are accessible to other programs in this mode. Since the tables are outside the wizard and are not 'unpublished' or otherwise locked down, other applications can access them. The maintenance routines provided as queries give you the tools that you'll need to purge unnecessary field definitions and the like.

If you are merely adding tables or fields to the wizard, you will be better off making those changes to the tables in **WZTBLDAT.MDT**. The additional benefit is that if you are going to add tables, fields and so on, you won't have to uninstall the wizard before accessing the database. You can edit the database while the wizard is active without causing problems.

If you do make changes to the wizard, be sure to reinstall the wizard when you are finished. If you don't, you won't be able to use the wizard.

Using the Query Wizard

Some of the core components of Access are its query capabilities. The ability to base forms, reports and many other functional aspects of your applications on tables and queries greatly enhances the types of applications you can develop.

Overview

When you begin building an application, you'll generally set up the database tables first. One of the things that you'll come up against immediately is the need to extract different views of the information in the underlying tables. You create these views using queries.

When you first begin to create a query, you'll be prompted to create either a new query from scratch or use the Query Wizards:

If you select Query Wizards, you can choose from one of the four different Query Wizards available with the default installation of Access:

Each of the Query Wizards works in a similar way; you'll be taken step by step through the creation of the query prompted for the information necessary at each stage. The last step offers you the option of running the query, modifying the design or opening the Cue Cards to help you work with the query.

In the **SAMPLES.MDB**, we've put together example queries using each of these wizards. We'll look at each of the examples in turn to give you an idea of how the wizards work and what is possible with each of them.

Crosstab Query

Crosstab queries allow you to summarize information in tables or other queries in a tabular format. A common use of these types of queries is the summary of sales information across regions for various products or when you want to look at your company sales history information month by month over a given period.

The example query that we'll be looking at is the Sales_Goals_Crosstab1. When you run this query you'll get the following:

Crosstab Query: Sales Goals_Crosstab1

Employee ID	1991	1992	1993	1994
1	10000	25000	30000	35000
2	6000	15000	20000	25000
3	12000	15000	30000	40000
4	12000	24000	38000	40000
5	10000	14000	15000	18000
6	3500	8000	15000	20000
7	10000	15000	20000	35000
8	15000	15000	20000	25000
9	5000	7000	15000	35000

Record: 1 of 9

In the sample database, the values represent nine different employees' sales goals over the span of four years. You should put the least occurring information, in this case the year, along the top and put frequent or variable information down the side in the form of rows.

In our example, we've used an interval of 'Year' since each employee's bonus goals are on a yearly basis but we could have specified any other interval.

Looking at the design of this query, we can see what the wizard has done:

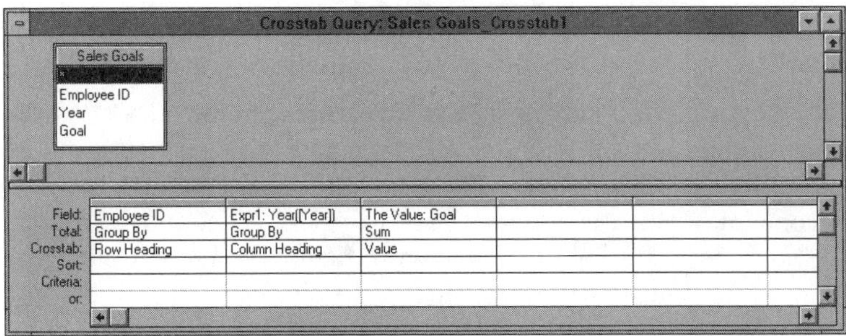

The Crosstab row in the QBE grid is the important part. This tells us which fields have been specified for the row and column headings and which field we want to look at for the 'table' information. We could have set up this query manually using the Crosstab Query button:

However the wizard can do all the work for you and is a good starting point if you want to further modify the results. Crosstab queries make excellent data sources for graphs, based in Excel or with an embedded graph, such as those created by the Graph Wizard.

Find Duplicates Query

There are many cases when you need to be able to determine what duplication has occurred in your system. A typical example of this may be a table of contact names where you need to find any records that have been entered for the same company and contact.

The example query that we'll be looking at is the Find duplicates for Contacts query. If you run this query, you'll get the following:

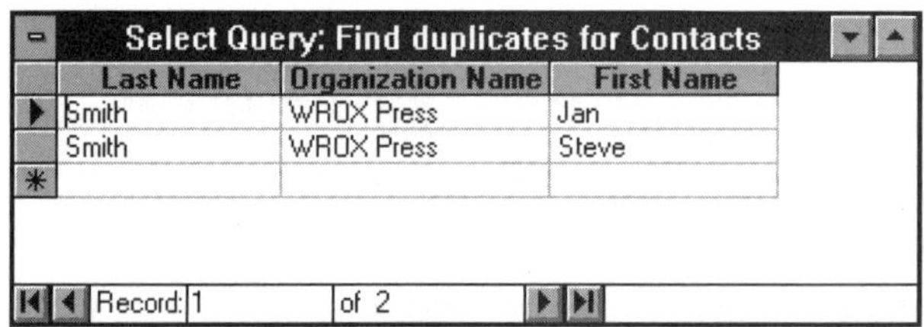

We've specified that we want to check for duplicates in the Last Name and Organization Name fields. Be sure to use a reasonable qualifier for this selection. Selecting a zip code, for instance, may not be the best way to find duplicates. However, zip code may not be a good item to select in combination with something else such as a last name. This would allow for multiple 'Smith' records in the table as long as they don't live in the same zip code. If they do, they will be included in the results set of the query, but they may not be the same person!!

Note that the query won't remove anything from the database table. It's used to produce an informational data set only. If you want to delete records based on the information provided, you'll have to take additional steps, either from the datasheet view or by programmatically using the results set to work with the database tables.

Looking at the design view of this query shows us how complex the query actually is:

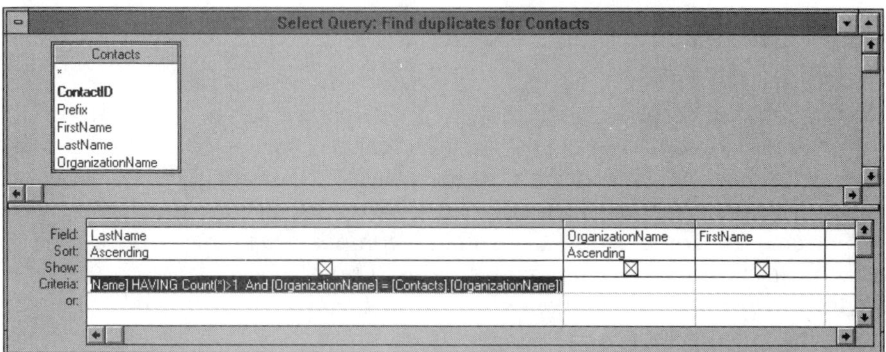

We've expanded the LastName column in the QBE grid to show the highlighted Criteria entry for this column. The full entry reads:

```
In (SELECT [LastName] FROM [Contacts] As Tmp GROUP BY
[LastName],[OrganizationName] HAVING Count(*)>1 And [OrganizationName] =
[Contacts].[OrganizationName])
```

Again, we could have defined this query manually but unless you're an SQL guru it makes more sense to let the wizard do the work for you.

> *In a later chapter, we'll look at using SQL in Access so maybe, after reading this chapter, you'll prefer to manually enter the SQL code in the* Criteria *row!!*

Find Unmatched Query

The Find Unmatched Query Wizard will allow you to find records that have been orphaned in a table processing operation. For example, in our case we want to know what records have been successfully archived into the client archive table. The Contacts Without Matching Contacts Archive query determines what records need to be archived:

Select Query: Contacts Without Matching Contacts Archive

Contact ID	Prefix	First Name	Last Name	Organization Name
3	Ms.	Jan	Smith	WROX Press
(Counter)				

Record: 1 of 1

We selected the source of the information, the Contacts table, the name of the table we wanted to compare against it, the Contacts Archive and which fields we wanted to check for, in our case, the ContactID. This final point is important as it means you can check information in two tables that have completely different structures. For example, you could compare customer names in a Customers table against customer names in an Orders table to determine which of your customers haven't placed an order in a given time period or to determine the customers who have placed an order, but haven't been set up on your system in the Customers table.

Again, looking at the design of this query will show us what the wizard has done:

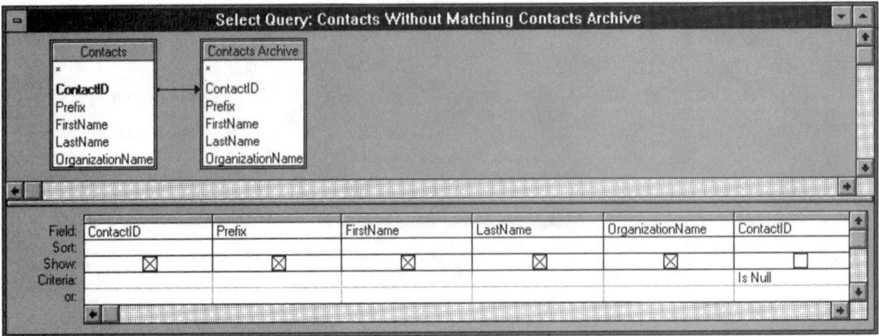

You can see that the wizard has simply created a relationship between the two tables and set an 'Is Null' criteria in the ContactID field at the right-hand side. If you double-click on the relationship line you'll see what type of relationship has been defined:

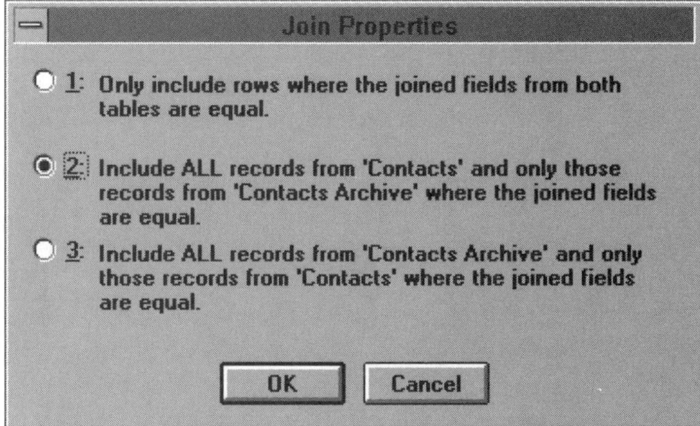

Again, we could create this query manually now that we know exactly what the wizard does but we may as well make use of the facilities Microsoft has provided for us and spend our own time working on things that the wizards can't do!

Archive Query Wizard

The Archive Query is used to copy or move information from one table to another. This is useful when backing up information on the system, providing a working table of information and so on. Our example is the Append to Contacts Archive query. If you run this query, you won't see much happening because everything is going on behind the scenes. What we've told the wizard to do is take every record in the Contacts table and archive it to the Contacts Archive table. If you look at the query in design view, you'll see that it is simply an append query:

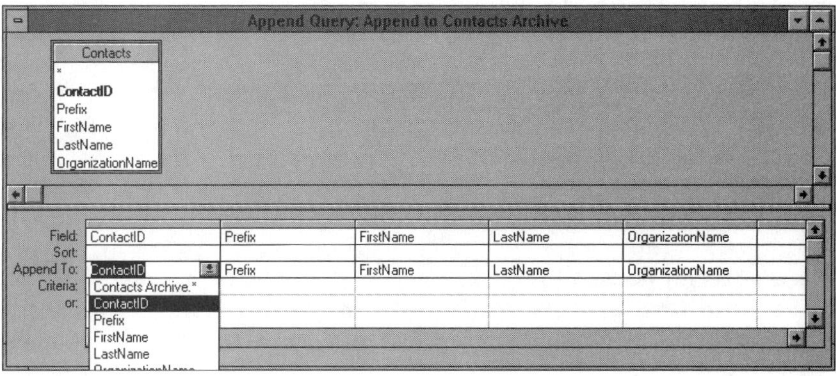

We've specified the Contacts table as the source, the Contacts Archive table as the destination and told the wizard to move all the records in the source table without deleting the archived records from the source table. We could have specified some criteria, for example, archive only the records with a LastName of 'Smith' or with an OrganizationName of 'Wrox Press' and we could have told the wizard to delete the archived records from the source table.

If you look at the queries in the **SAMPLES.MDB** you'll see a second archive query called Append to Contacts Archive 2 and a corresponding delete query called Delete from Contacts2.

We created a second archive query choosing Contacts2 as the source table, but this time we told the wizard to delete records from the source table. The Wizard has done all the work creating the append query as before, but also creating a delete query which will delete the records that we have successfully archived.

> *Note that in a production environment you would have to specifically run these two queries to archive and delete the source records. Running the archive query doesn't automatically run the delete query.*

The archive query is a useful tool for several different operations that occur on a daily basis. The first, as we've explained here, is to backup information from a production table to a backup table, possibly located in a different database, on a different server.

The second use of the archive query is to remove 'old' information from the system. In some transaction processing systems, such as a point of sale system, you'll often have a requirement to keep information on-line for a specific amount of time, such as 13 months (just enough time for the annual company reports to be compiled).

After this period, you'll want to move the information off the production system and into an archive. You don't want to simply delete the information in case you have a query that concerns it at a later date. Using the archive query, together with the delete option, will accomplish exactly this task. The information will be backed up to the alternate table and then deleted from the production database tables when you run the corresponding delete query. Less records in the production systems 'active' tables provide faster querying of the records and so provide for the 'real-time' operation of the system.

Customizing the Query Wizards

You can't customize the Query Wizards from within Access as you can with the other wizards. You'll notice that if you highlight the Query Wizards in the Add-in Manager, the Customize button will be grayed out:

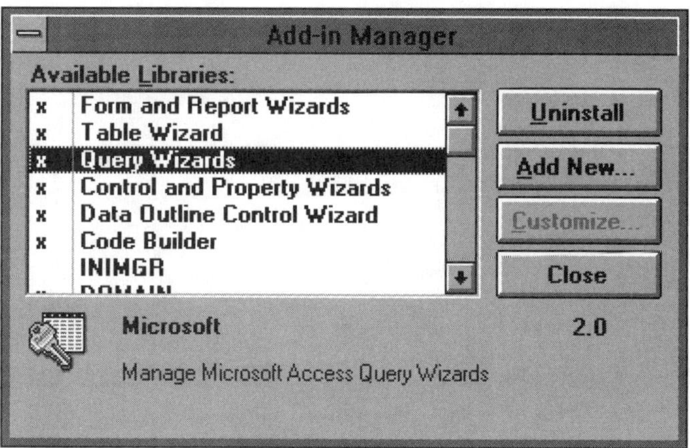

However, you can modify the wizards in the system file, **WZQUERY.MDA**. As before, you will have to uninstall the Query Wizard from the Add-In Manager and close down Access before opening this file, available to you from your Access subdirectory.

If you look at the forms, tables and modules, you'll get a good idea of how the wizards work, but we can't think of a good reason why you would want to modify anything. However, you could design your own query wizard. For example, if you have a specific type of complex query that you use a lot, you may want to design a query wizard that will automatically create the query for you, using all your own pre-defined parameters.

If you open the USysAddIns table you'll see that this is where the list of Query Wizards is kept:

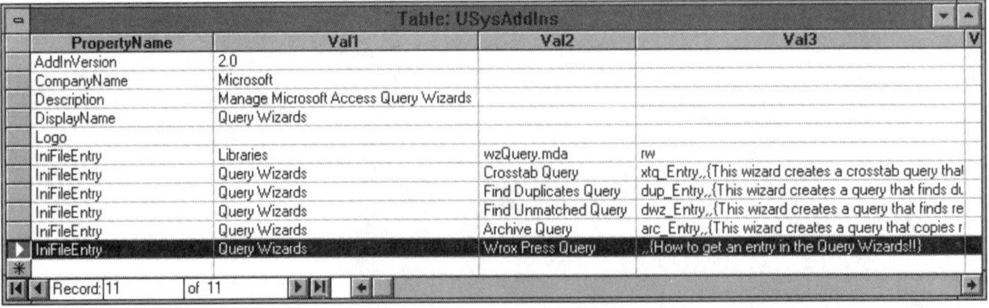

Table: USysAddIns

PropertyName	Val1	Val2	Val3
AddInVersion	2.0		
CompanyName	Microsoft		
Description	Manage Microsoft Access Query Wizards		
DisplayName	Query Wizards		
Logo			
IniFileEntry	Libraries	wzQuery.mda	rw
IniFileEntry	Query Wizards	Crosstab Query	xtq_Entry,,{This wizard creates a crosstab query that
IniFileEntry	Query Wizards	Find Duplicates Query	dup_Entry,,{This wizard creates a query that finds du
IniFileEntry	Query Wizards	Find Unmatched Query	dwz_Entry,,{This wizard creates a query that finds re
IniFileEntry	Query Wizards	Archive Query	arc_Entry,,{This wizard creates a query that copies r
IniFileEntry	Query Wizards	Wrox Press Query	,,{How to get an entry in the Query Wizards!!}

Record: 11 of 11

We've added an extra entry that won't be in your table - the Wrox Press Query. Add this into your table exactly as shown and then close the WZQUERY.MDA. Re-install the Query Wizards and take a look at the wizards that are now on offer:

You can see that our new Query Wizard has been added to the list along with the micro help text that we entered. Of course, if you select the Wrox Press Query and click the OK button, you'll get an error because we haven't put any code relating to this option in the **WZQUERY.MDA** file. This was merely intended to show you how you would go about it. As we said before, we can't think of a good reason for wanting to do this so we'll leave the actual coding to you!

Other Types of Wizards Available with Access

Access provides the wizard functionality on many different fronts. Wizards can help you in many different areas and are generally called up when you begin work in a certain area, function or portion of the Access environment:

Combo Box Wizard — When you add a combo box to a form, this wizard can help in setting it up and outlining how the information will be displayed.

Command Button Wizard — When you work with command buttons, this wizard will walk you through the assignment of icons, captions and actions as necessary. You can change the list of icons available, and create new ones, by selecting Customize... from the Add-ins Manager for Control Wizards.

Graph Wizard

The Graph Wizard helps you set up graphs on your forms, allowing you to provide input for the graph from a table or query. The graph is created using the **MSGRAPH OLE** utility included with Access.

Input Mask Wizard

Input masks allow you to specify the format of the data that the user wishes to enter. For example, you can create an input mask that will only allow a valid, formatted phone number or Zip Code. You can change the format of available input masks and create new ones by selecting Customize... from the Add-Ins Manager for Control Wizards.

List Box Wizard

As with the Combo Box Wizard, this wizard will be called when you add a list box to a form. The wizard helps you set up data sources for a list box control.

Option Group Wizard

When you create a new option group, used in the creation of a logical grouping of radio button controls, this wizard can help set up the different properties for the options in the grouping.

Wizards are available in many different locations and operational areas of the Access environment. This list is not exhaustive, but you can see that the wizards can be helpful by jumping in and helping whenever possible.

You should consider turning off any wizards that you are no longer using by de-installing them. For each wizard you have installed, the load time for Access is increased. You can save some load time by only loading the wizards that are important to your development efforts.

Using Other Microsoft Access Add-ins

In the previous sections, we've been reviewing the use and modifications of some of the wizards available within Access. To do this, we've been using an Add-In, specifically the Add-in Manager.

Access Add-Ins are tools that developers can use to extend the functionality of their system, by producing modules or functions that become a part of the Access environment. The Add-Ins that are currently available are very diverse, ranging from the automatic analysis of your database structure to new security subsystems.

The Access Developer's Toolkit provides you with the information and tools you need to develop Add-Ins for your use. We'll go into this in more detail in a later chapter, but for the rest of this chapter, we'll review the database documentor as an example application.

Using the Database Documentor

The database documentor provides you with a tool that will use Access to analyze and report on the structure, security rights and other information that pertains to your database systems:

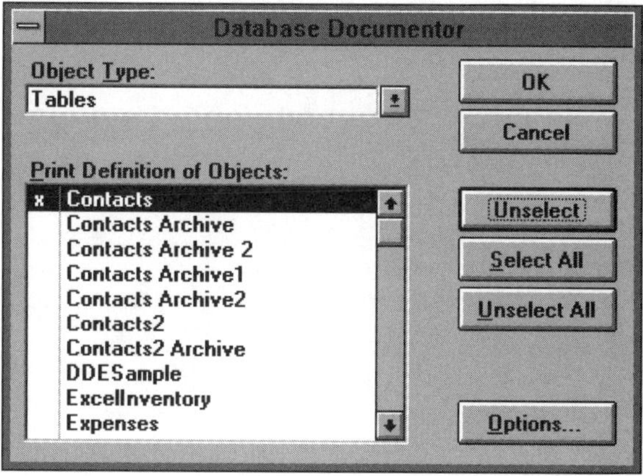

You can document any or all of the different objects within your database. In addition, you can specify exactly what aspects should be examined for the item(s) you have selected by clicking on the Options... button:

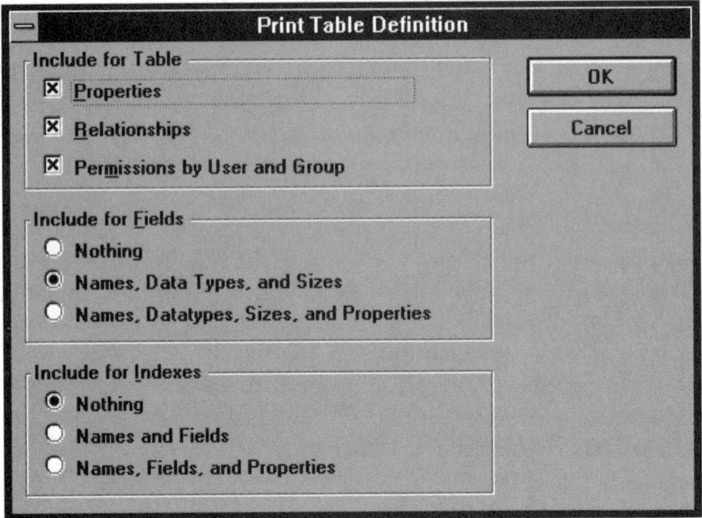

The output created by the Add-In is limited to a report that may be printed, or you can tell the documentor to place the results of the examination in a database table. An example of this, taken from our **SAMPLES.MDB** database, showing the definition of the Contacts table is provided next:

G:\GRAHAMM\TESTMDB\SAMPTEST.MDB
Table: Contacts

Saturday, February 04, 1995
Page: 1

Properties

Date Created:	10/19/94 8:26:58 PM	Def. Updatable:	Yes
Last Updated:	2/4/95 11:14:53 AM	Record Count:	3

Columns

Name	Type	Size
ContactID	Number (Long)	4
Prefix	Text	20
FirstName	Text	50
LastName	Text	50
OrganizationName	Text	50

Relationships

Reference

Contacts		Orders
ContactID	1 — ∞	ContactID

Attributes: One to Many, Enforced, Cascade Updates, Cascade Deletes, Left Join

User Permissions

admin	Delete, Read Permissions, Set Permissions, Change Owner
guest	

Group Permissions

Admins	
Guests	
Users	Delete, Read Permissions, Set Permissions, Change Owner

You can save the results to a table by choosing Save as Table from the File menu. The resulting table from our example is the Object Definition 1 table and looks like this:

Table: Object Definition1

ID	ParentID	Object Type	Name	Extra1	Extra2	Extra3
1	0	Table	Contacts			
2	1	Property	Def. Updatable:	Yes		
3	1	Property	Date Created:	10/19/94 8:26:58 F		
4	1	Property	Last Updated:	2/4/95 11:14:53 AI		
5	1	Property	Record Count:	3		
6	1	Column	ContactID		Number (Long)	4
7	1	Column	Prefix		Text	20
8	1	Column	FirstName		Text	50
9	1	Column	LastName		Text	50
10	1	Column	OrganizationName		Text	50
11	1	Relationships	Reference	-1		
13	11	Property	Attributes:	One to Many, Enfoi		
14	1	User Permissions	admin	Delete, Read Perm		
15	1	User Permissions	guest			
16	1	Group Permissions	Admins			
17	1	Group Permissions	Guests			
18	1	Group Permissions	Users	Delete, Read Perm		

Record: 1 of 17

It's a good idea to run the database documentor against all production database systems that you are working with. This will provide some useful documentation that you can use when training new support staff. It can also be used in a disaster-recovery type of operation. Everything from permissions to structure is reported and can be printed for future reference.

A useful option when using the documentor with your queries is to include the SQL statements in the print-out:

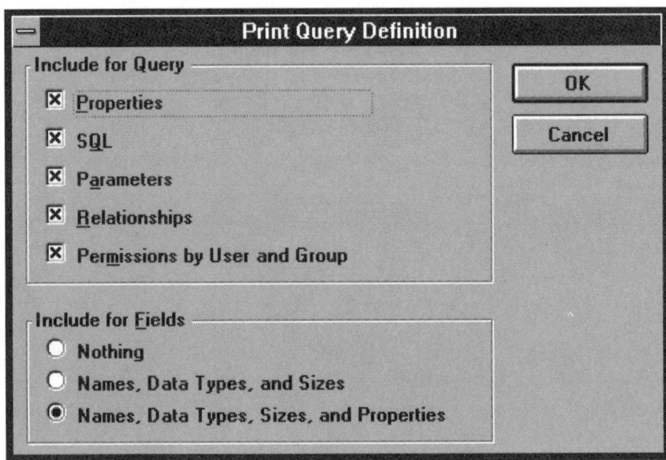

Selecting all options in the Include for Query frame will provide excellent reference and learning information as you begin working directly with the SQL statements that are used to generate the queries on your system. We'll give you a grounding in using SQL directly with an Access database in a later chapter.

Comments and Suggestions

Access Wizards and Add-Ins offer some greatly enhanced features for your development environment. As you work on your projects, if you have access to the Internet or other on-line services, you may want to periodically review their libraries to see what other tools become available. In addition, you can be assured that different software publishers will be providing tools for use in this environment as well.

After you've used these tools, you'll find that small changes make a big difference. Try to keep track of those things that you are constantly changing after the wizards have done their work. After you've narrowed it down, consider making some changes to the wizard to make it perform more to your taste.

In the coming chapters, we'll go into more detail on how you can create your own Add-ins. In addition, we'll work on creating a setup program that will prevent you from having to carry out a custom installation for every user of your system.

Developing Production-Ready Applications

One of the key requirements that a developer must include in any production-ready application is a comprehensive, idiot-proof installation routine. Microsoft have addressed this problem with the introduction of the Setup Wizard and this, together with a well implemented series of error handlers and a selection of your own add-ins, allows you to produce a well polished and professional application.

What's Covered in This Chapter

In this chapter, we'll be covering several different aspects of creating production-ready applications. We'll be reviewing the Access Developer's Toolkit and taking an in-depth look at the different components that come with it. It's important to understand that, while the Access Developer's Toolkit is important to this chapter, many of the concepts, ideas and other points outside the scope of the Toolkit are relevant to your application development.

In particular, this chapter deals with the following:

- Installing the Wrox .INI Manager Add-In
- Building and optimizing your own add-ins
- Error handling techniques
- Creating distribution diskettes and using the Setup Wizard

Although this chapter doesn't cover any details that are inherently necessary for a functioning database, if you want to produce applications that have a professional appeal and are 'user proof', then you'll find the information in this chapter invaluable.

Chapter 9

How This Chapter Impacts Our Application

Our application uses the Access Developer's Toolkit to create the setup files that install the Personal Information Manager on an end-user's system. In addition, many of the concepts we cover here including error handling, optimization techniques and so on are constituent parts of the PIM application.

Introduction

The Access Developer's Toolkit (ADT) includes many different items that are helpful in the creation of your applications. Some of these items are toolsets that will help the developer in the actual process of creating application but the ADT is also a useful informational resource, containing scripts on many features that have so far remained undocumented.

Also included in the toolkit are the Microsoft Access Run-Time executables, which allow you to design applications that are able to run independently of a full-blown Access environment. As we saw in Chapter 1, several new custom controls are also available to the developer, resulting in reductions in development time, as well as effort and cost.

Microsoft have made several expanded help files available to the developer through the ADT, specifically covering much needed information on the Windows API, Wizards and their creation and a complete reference guide to the Microsoft Access Basic language.

In this chapter, we'll be focusing on the different things that you can implement to get your applications ready for distribution to a large user base. You'll have to take into consideration the need for a more robust error handling environment as well as a method of installing the application on the users' systems. This is almost a necessity unless you intend to go to each system and install the software personally.

Once you've created an application, you should be thinking of reviewing several aspects of it. A minimum list of considerations is investigated below. There will also be other elements such as the look and feel of your application, possibly due to your computing culture or environment, that you are sure to encounter. If your environment requires the use of custom toolbars, common interface designs and so on, then making use of add-ins can be a great time-saver for you.

Building Add-Ins for Use in Access

In previous chapters, we've investigated the use of and how to customize the Access wizards. You've seen how some of the systems are implemented through the use of custom forms, database tables and Access Basic code.

You may be able to think of cases where you'll want to provide much of the same functionality to users. In these areas, you may want to consider creating your own add-in. Before we look at the techniques behind developing your own add-in, a closer look at those already present in the RDBMS may provide fortuitous.

Microsoft Add-Ins come in three different implementations although all are similar in their behind-the-scenes operation:

Access Wizards — The wizards are implemented as a series of dialog boxes that guide the user through an often complex series of operations to implement or control an Access function. Examples of wizards include the Form and Report Wizards reviewed in the last chapter.

Access Builders — The builders are generally based on a single form that the user works with when trying to create a predefined and desired result. Examples of builders include the Macro Creator and the Expression Builder, which are illustrated on the next page. Generally, a builder provides an interface used to create a command or statement that may require or allow for several different components. This is the case with most macros and expressions as they often require parameters.

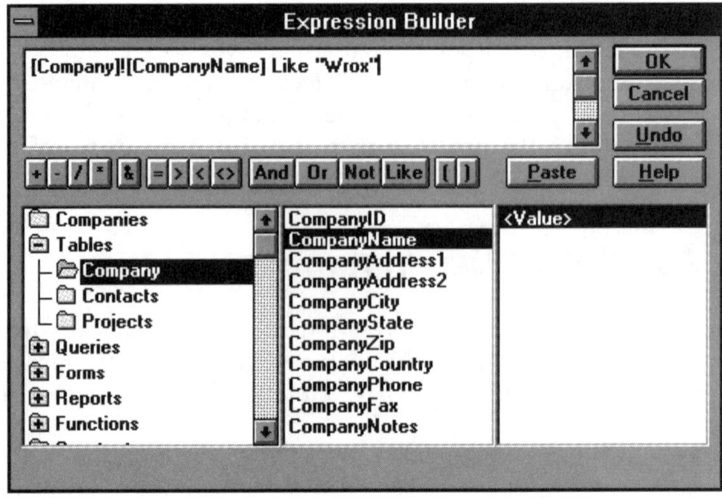

Access Add-Ins

Add-ins allow you to do just about anything to help the user in his use of your system. If you need a tool that doesn't fall into the category of wizard or builder, you'll most likely be creating an add-in. Examples of Access' add-ins include the Database Documentor, used to give a definitive printout of your database plan and the Menu Builder, which is designed to allow you to quickly construct menus for your application.

One important difference between wizards, builders and add-ins is the fact that once a database is loaded the add-in becomes available. Wizards and builders can only be called up from a situation in which you'll be using them. For example, you only see an Expression Builder when you're ready to create an expression.

Add-ins are much more general in nature. If the user selects Add-ins from the File menu he will have access to any installed add-in, regardless of the current operation. For this reason, they should be implemented as ways of controlling the user's system or environment and shouldn't be specific to any given operating context.

> *If your system is requiring large amounts of time to start Access, it would be worth investigating which add-ins you use and which you don't. If you remove the unnecessary add-ins from the startup process, you can greatly reduce the amount of time required on load up.*

Creating Access Libraries

Add-ins, wizards and builders are generally created in Access Libraries. If you recall from the last chapter, the wizards we reviewed were contained in external files, usually with a file name extension of **.MDA**. These add-in databases are really standard Access .MDB files, which have been re-named with the MDA extension for clarification.

The `MSACC20.INI` file, located in your Windows subdirectory, contains the listing of all libraries that are loaded when Access is loaded:

```
[Libraries]
wzlib.mda=ro
wzTable.mda=ro
wzQuery.mda=ro
wzbldr.mda=ro
wzoutl.mda=ro
wzfrmrpt.mda=ro
```

Your entries may have an 'rw' specified after the equal sign, since this is the default. This indicates that the libraries are opened with Read/Write access.

You can speed the load process somewhat for Access if you set the flag to RO, or Read Only. This reduces the overhead required by Access when it loads the databases, thus allowing slightly more memory to be allocated to more active requirements such as your application and development environment.

Each table is loaded when Access is started, so making the different modules, Access Basic routines, forms, macros and tables that are contained in each database available. In addition, if externally attached databases are referenced, these external references become part of the environment.

Note that when a library is loaded, due to its design, it is able to support a multi-user environment. However, it is important that if you are establishing temporary files, updating tables within your add-in or any other such function, that you make sure you track which tables and/or files may encounter errors and handle them accordingly.

All add-in supporting databases must be listed in this entry in the .INI file. Once these databases are loaded, the routines become available to the environment, making other entries in the .INI file valid. For example, also in the **MSACC20.INI** file, you'll notice information pertaining to the Menu Add-Ins. The following listing, an excerpt from the **MSACC20.INI** file, shows the Menu Add-Ins that may be defined on your system. The resulting menu is also shown for reference:

```
[Menu Add-Ins]
&Add-in Manager==Wm_Entry()
&Database Documentor==Doc_PrintDataBase()
A&ttachment Manager==Am_Entry()
Im&port Database...==Doc_ImportDatabase()
&Menu Builder==CustomMenuBuilder()
```

For each add-in that is supported, an 'entry point' is defined. This entry point is a function or subroutine that should be called when the add-in is initiated. In our example entries, you can see that the Import Database... Add-In will be started by calling the **Doc_ImportDatabase()** function.

The WROX .INI File Manager Add-In

The software accompanying this book includes a custom add-in that you can install on your system. The .INI File Manager resides in the **INIMGR.MDA** database. You should make entries in the **MSACC20.INI** file, found in your Windows directory to enable this add-in. When you next reload Access, this custom add-in will be loaded in addition to the others and will be ready for action.

The following listing shows the two entries that you'll need to make in the **MSACC20.INI** file, along with their associated section headings:

```
[Menu Add-Ins]
...
INI Fi&le Manager==ini_EntryPoint()

[Libraries]
...
inimgr.mda=ro
```

> **If the .INI Manager was not installed to your Access directory, you'll need to preceed the line above with the full path to the MDA file. For example, if the add-in resides in `C:\ADDINS`, the entry should read as follows:**

```
[Libraries]
...
c:\addins\inimgr.mda=ro
```

> **This will tell Access explicitly where to find the add-in database.**

These entries will activate the Add-In. This new Add-In will provide a tool that you can use to retrieve values from and write values to any .INI file on your system.

Using the .INI File Manager

When you start Access and open a database, the Add-in Manager menu option is enabled. After you've made the new entries to the **`MSACC20.INI`** file, you'll notice a new option on the menu. This option provides you with the ability to call the .INI File Manager at any time while you're in the Access environment:

When you start the new add-in, you are presented with the form below. You can use the ellipses button to select an .INI file using the standard Windows dialog box or you can manually type the file name into the form's fields:

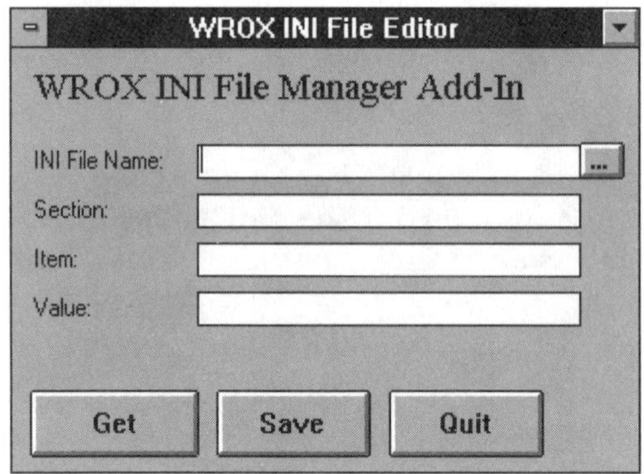

If you specify an .INI file name without a full path specification, Windows will automatically look in the `\WINDOWS` subdirectory, or wherever you are currently running the Windows environment from. For example, if you specify only `MSACC20.INI` and your Windows subdirectory is '`C:\WINDOWS`', the call will look for the file '`C:\WINDOWS\MSACC20.INI`'.

Reading .INI File Entries with the .INI File Manager

Once you've selected the file to work with, enter the section and item name that you want to read. Sections are the items in the .INI file surrounded by square brackets. These are actually referred to as 'Applications' in some materials. This is largely a throw-back to pre-OLE days when the .INI file format was used to control all applications. The more common term for the heading in today's implementation is 'Section'.

The Item that you specify is found within the section and is followed by an equal sign and a value. The value to the right of the equal sign is what will be returned and placed in the **`txtValue`** control when you press the Get command button.

Writing .INI File Entries with the .INI File Manager

Using the Save command button is almost identical to the Get button. You must specify the name of the .INI file. Next, indicate the section and item that you want to update or establish in the file. Finally, specify the value that you want to save for the item.

> **If you specify a section and/or item that doesn't already exist in the .INI file, it will be created for you automatically. If a new section is being added, it is placed at the bottom of the file. If a new item is being inserted, it is placed at the bottom of the section to which it relates.**

For example, if we wanted to check for an entry of 'blahdeblah' in the Menu Add-Ins section of the **MSACC20.INI**, then we'd type in the file name, section and item and select the Get button.

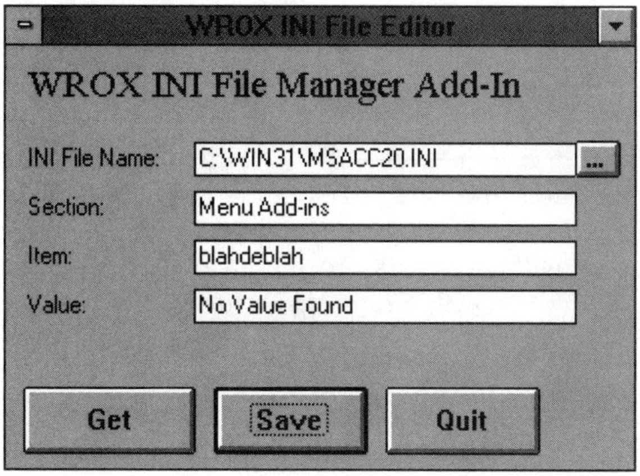

The value comes back as No Value Found, so we know that there isn't an entry for the 'blahdeblah' item. To put an entry in there we could select the Save button and if we look in the Menu Add-Ins section of the **MSACC20.INI** we'll find the new entry:

```
[Menu Add-Ins]
&Add-in Manager==Wm_Entry()
&Database Documentor==Doc_PrintDataBase()
A&ttachment Manager==Am_Entry()
Im&port Database...==Doc_ImportDatabase()
&Domain Function Wizard==StartDomainWizard()
&Menu Builder==CustomMenuBuilder()
INI Fi&le Manager==ini_EntryPoint()
blahdeblah=No Value Found
```

Adding to or deleting from your .INI files can have a profound effect on your system. It is suggested that you use a dummy INI file for your experimentations, until you get use to the workings of the add-in.

Creating the .INI File Manager

There are several different elements implemented in the .INI File Manager that you might find interesting. To begin with, the actual process of managing the .INI file entries by using the Windows API is detailed. This includes calls to the Windows functions 'GetPrivateProfileString' and 'WritePrivateProfileString'. Both of these functions require you to pass in a section name, topic name and file name. The routines then query the .INI file for the value corresponding to the item you requested and return two different pieces of information.

The first thing you will receive is the length of the resulting string. In other words, if the value 'C:\ACCESS20' were returned, the call to the `GetPrivateProfileString` would return a value of 11, the length of the string. In addition to this information, the actual string itself is also returned as a parameter to the call.

There is also a function called 'GetProfileString' which is available in the Windows API. This function assumes that you are referring to the `WIN.INI` file and therefore doesn't require you to pass in the file name. It's highly recommended that you use the `GetPrivateProfileString` for all accesses to .INI files, regardless of whether it's `WIN.INI` or other files. This is an attempt to promote common coding and will help you in the future maintenance of your systems.

In order to create the .INI File Manager, the first thing that you need to do is remove the two references to the add-in in the **[Menu Add-Ins]** and **[Libraries]** sections of your **MSACC20.INI** file.

> **Illustrating how useful the add-in can be, you could use the .INI File Manager to do this. Remember that the add-in information in your MSACC20.INI file is only used when Access is loaded up, so you will suffer no penalty until you reload and lose the use of the add-in.**

You could also do this by editing the file with your NotePad editor, removing the references by commenting them out with a semi-colon and saving the changes to the file. Exit and re-start Access for the changes to take effect.

Open the **INIMGR.MDA** file to review the implementation of the add-in.

> **If you are creating a new add-in, you will first create it in a standard access database file, usually with an MDB extension. Change the extension to MDA, to be consistent with other add-ins, when you are ready to actually implement the add-in.**

In the modules section, open the API Declarations module. This module creates the interface between your application and the Windows environment. This includes establishing the Windows API calls, any variable type declarations that are required and laying out the constants that may come into play as you implement the different options.

The following list is the declarations that allow us to read and write to the .INI files:

```
'The following declarations set up the calls to the Window's libraries
'to manage the .INI file

Declare Function GetPrivateProfileString Lib "Kernel" (ByVal ⏎
lpApplicationName As String, ByVal lpKeyName As String, ByVal ⏎
lpDefault As String, ByVal lpReturnedString As String, ByVal ⏎
nSize As Integer, ByVal lpFileName As String) As Integer

Declare Function WritePrivateProfileString Lib "Kernel" (ByVal ⏎
lpApplicationName As String, ByVal lpKeyName As String, ByVal ⏎
lpString As String, ByVal lplFileName As String) As Integer
```

Information about these functions is available in the Windows API help files included with the ADT, but please note that there is a modification that should be made to the declaration for the `GetPrivateProfileString`.

You'll notice in this listing that the `lpKeyName` argument is specified as `ByVal lpKeyName As String`. In the API help files, the definition is described as `lpKeyName as Any`. This latter definition will cause your routines to fail. There will be no error returned, but the routines will always return the value you define as the default value.

The next set of declarations defines a structure that is passed to the common dialog routines to allow the user to select an .INI file from the standard Windows dialog box to open a file.

```
Type dlgFileName
    lStructSize As Long
    hwndOwner As Integer
    hInstance As Integer
    lpstrFilter As Long
    lpstrCustomFilter As Long
    nMaxCustFilter As Long
    nFilterIndex As Long
    lpstrFile As Long
    nMaxFile As Long
    lpstrFileTitle As Long
    nMaxFileTitle As Long
    lpstrInitialDir As Long
    lpstrTitle As Long
    Flags As Long
    nFileOffset As Integer
    nFileExtension As Integer
    lpstrDefExt As Long
    lCustData As Long
    lpfnHook As Long
    lpTemplateName As Long
End Type
```

Next, the functions that are used to call the Windows common dialog routines are established. Notice that we're declaring an arbitrary variable name, **`dlgParms`**, in the function definition. This establishes our structure with the same type as that of the variable that will be passed in from the call.

```
Declare Function GetOpenFileName Lib "COMMDLG.DLL" (dlgParms As
dlgFileName) As Integer

Declare Function GetSaveFileName Lib "COMMDLG.DLL" (dlgParms As
dlgFileName) As Integer

Declare Function lstrcpy& Lib "Kernel" (ByVal lpDestString As Any,
ByVal lpSourceString As Any)
```

The last thing to be established in this module's declaration section is the constants used to control the operation and presentation of information in the common dialog box. While not all of these constants are implemented in our sample application, you may need them in your system depending on the type of environment and the type of access you want to grant users:

```
Global Const OFN_READONLY = &H1
Global Const OFN_OVERWRITEPROMPT = &H2
Global Const OFN_HIDEREADONLY = &H4
Global Const OFN_NOCHANGEDIR = &H8
Global Const OFN_SHOWHELP = &H10
Global Const OFN_ENABLEHOOK = &H20
Global Const OFN_ENABLETEMPLATE = &H40
Global Const OFN_ENABLETEMPLATEHANDLE = &H80
Global Const OFN_NOVALIDATE = &H100
Global Const OFN_ALLOWMULTISELECT = &H200
Global Const OFN_EXTENSIONDIFFERENT = &H400
Global Const OFN_PATHMUSTEXIST = &H800
Global Const OFN_FILEMUSTEXIST = &H1000
Global Const OFN_CREATEPROMPT = &H2000
Global Const OFN_SHAREAWARE = &H4000
Global Const OFN_NOREADONLYRETURN = &H8000
Global Const OFN_NOTESTFILECREATE = &H10000
Global Const OFN_SHAREFALLTHROUGH = 2
Global Const OFN_SHARENOWARN = 1
Global Const OFN_SHAREWARN = 0
```

Now we need to create an entry point routine for your application. Remember that you define the entry point in the **MSACC20.INI** file. In the modules for the **INIMGR.MDA** add-in file, there is a function called **ini_EntryPoint**. This function is defined in the Access .INI file as the function to be called to start the add-in:

```
Function ini_EntryPoint ()
    'This is the function that is defined in
    'MSACC20.INI; this is how Access will start
    'the .INI File Manager Add-In.
```

```
    'Open our interface form
    DoCmd OpenForm "INISearch", A_Normal

End Function
```

The only thing this function does is to open our form in 'Normal' mode. This initiates the user interface and allows the user to get started working with their .INI file. Your function shouldn't return values as Access will not be returning values to the user. The function simply serves as a starting point and a handle to your routines. If you need to return feedback to the user on the operations you are performing, be sure to take care of it inside your application before exiting.

Calling the Windows Common Dialog Box

The actual call to initiate and manage the common dialog is contained in the **OpenCommDlg** function. This is stored in the Common Dialog Module in our **INIMGR.MDA** database. This function is called from the main .INI File Manager form whenever the user selects the '...' button. The code sets up the parameters needed to call the dialog box and then returns the results to the calling procedure or function.

> *Note that, in the section defining the* **tdlgFileName** *structure, ellipses have been inserted for brevity. A full listing can be found in the* **INIMGR.MDA** *file.*

```
Function OpenCommDlg () As String

    Dim tdlgFileName As dlgFileName
    Dim sMessage As String
    Dim sFilter As String
    Dim sFileName As String
    Dim sFileTitle As String
    Dim sDefExt As String
    Dim sTitle As String
    Dim sMsg As String
    Dim szCurDir As String
    Dim iResults As Integer

    'First, set up Access to only review .INI files by establishing
    'the filter for the dialog box.
    sFilter = "INI Files(*.INI)" & Chr$(0) & "*.INI" & Chr$(0) & Chr$(0)
```

The **sFilter** variable contains the different types of files that will be shown to the user. In our case, we limit the selection to files with an extension of .INI. Note that the format of the line is:

```
<Display Name>NULL<Filename Pattern>NULL
```

In addition, a terminating **NULL** is placed at the end of all items. If you want to have multiple file types available to the user, you can add more types following the format above.

In the section of code that follows, note that you must create the space allocated to the strings. You can't simply pass a string variable and allow the DLL to place the value in the string. In this section of code, we also set up the caption for the dialog box that is shown. The default extension of .INI is specified, allowing the user to type a filename in without an extension and still get an .INI file as a result:

```
'Allocate string space in strings to pass to the DLL routines
sFileName = Chr$(0) & Space$(255) & Chr$(0)
sFileTitle = Chr$(0) & Space$(255) & Chr$(0)

'Set the caption for the window
sTitle = "Select INI File" & Chr$(0)

'Set the default extension to INI
sDefExt = "INI" & Chr$(0)
```

This section, somewhat abbreviated, sets up the structure that is passed to the common dialog. This structure defines the operation and presentation of the dialog box. The next thing to do is to set the current directory. Note that you may want to set this to the user's Windows subdirectory, but in this example, we simply use the current default directory:

```
'Set up the default directory
szCurDir$ = CurDir$ & Chr$(0)

'The following structure will be passed to the common
'dialog box.  The different options are used in displaying
'the information to the user.

tdlgFileName.lStructSize = Len(tdlgFileName)
tdlgFileName.hWndOwner = Screen.ActiveForm.hWnd
```

```
    tdlgFileName.lpstrFilter = lstrcpy(sFilter, sFilter)
    tdlgFileName.NFilterIndex = 1
    tdlgFileName.lpstrFile = lstrcpy(sFileName, sFileName)
...
    tdlgFileName.lpstrDefExt = lstrcpy(sDefExt, sDefExt)
...
    tdlgFileName.lpstrInitialDir = lstrcpy(szCurDir, szCurDir)
    tdlgFileName.nFileOffset = 0
    tdlgFileName.nFileExtension = 0
...
```

Finally, we make the call to the DLL routine, passing in our **`tdlgFileName`** structure. The Windows API will prompt the user for the file, allowing the user the ability to traverse the directory structure in search of the file.

In the routines, there are several lines commented out. These indicate how you can use the routines to provide additional information ranging from the path of the selected file to the extension of the file selected:

```
    iResults = GetOpenFileName(tdlgFileName)

    If iResults <> 0 Then
        sFileName = Left$(sFileName, InStr(sFileName, Chr$(0)) - 1)

        'selection returned in sFileName,
        'Path is in Left$(sFileName, tdlgFileName.nFileOffset)
        'Filename (w/o extension) is in
        '    Right$(sFileName, Len(sFileName) - tdlgFileName.nFileOffset)
        'File extension (should be INI) is in
        '    Right$(sFileName, Len(sFileName) - ↵
        '        tdlgFileName.nFileExtension)

    End If

    'return the filename to the calling routine
    OpenCommDlg = sFileName

End Function
```

When working with this many API functions, a Pointer to a string is required as the parameter, not the actual string. To create a pointer to a string, use the `lstrcpy` Window function. The function returns the address of a string that is the destination for a copy procedure.

> **If you use the function to copy a string to itself, the result will be the desired pointer to the string. Pass this value to the DLL and it will be able to access the value at the address you specify.**
>
> **You can see this demonstrated at several places in the previous code listing where different values are being placed into the `tdlgFileName` structure.**

The call to this function is handled in the **`Click`** event for the **`cmdFileLookup`** button on the .INI Manager user interface:

```
Sub cmdFileLookup_Click ()
    'use the Windows common dialog box
    'to prompt for and return a file
    'name to work with
    txtFileName = OpenCommDlg()
End Sub
```

When we are ready to search the requested .INI file, we use the Get command button. The button packages up the **`txtSection`**, **`txtItem`** and **`txtFileName`** values and passes them to the **`GetIni`** routines:

```
Sub cmdGetValue_Click ()
    'Using the values in the user interface,
    'search the requested file, section and item,
    'returning the value or default value and
    'placing it in the txtValue control.
    Dim iResults As Integer

    txtValue = "Searching . . ."

    Dim x As Integer
    GotInfo = GetIni(txtSection, txtItem, txtFileName)

    txtValue = GotInfo

End Sub
```

The **`GetIni`** routine takes the values passed to it and asks the Windows API call to read a string from the .INI file. The **`GetPrivateProfileString`** call returns the value associated with the section and item we specify. We have implemented this as a separate function to show how you can declare the parameters to the call:

```
Function GetIni (lpSection, lpEntry, lpFileName) As String

    'take the section, item and file name passed in and
    'query the ini file for the information requested.
```

```
    'return the trim'd string.  If a value is not found,
    'return "No Value Found"

    Const BUFSIZE = 255
    Dim lpDefault As String, GotInfo As String
    Dim lpReturnVal As String * 255
    Dim iResults As Integer

    lpDefault = "No Value Found"

    iResults = GetPrivateProfileString(lpSection, ByVal lpEntry, ↵
        lpDefault, lpReturnVal, BUFSIZE, lpFileName)

    GetIni = Left$(lpReturnVal, iResults)

End Function
```

Alternatively, if the Save command button is selected, we can show how you can call the function directly from within the **Click** event:

```
Sub cmdSave_Click ()
    'save the item in the txtValue field to the .INI file
    'as requested.

    Dim iResults As Integer

    iResults = WritePrivateProfileString(txtSection, txtItem, txtValue, ↵
        txtFileName)

End Sub
```

When you call the function, you pass in the contents of the **txtValue** control. The value in this field is saved to the file that you indicate in the interface. Remember that whether you are updating an existing item or creating a new one, you will use the same API call. Windows will update an item if it already exists, or will create a new item that you specify, using the section and item you provided as parameters to the call.

The final piece of code that is implemented on the form is the Quit button. The **cmdQuit Click** event simply calls our standard **DoCmd Close**, unloading the form and returning the user to the Access environment.

Naming Considerations

When you create a library function and it loads on startup, the names of all tables, macros, forms, procedures and functions are loaded into the common name space for Access. This means that it is extremely important that you pick names that are going to be unique to your application and not cause conflicts with another application on the users' systems.

You should consider implementing a prefix, followed by an underscore character for your add-in's objects. For example, as we're writing an add-in to automate the management of .INI file, we are using a prefix of 'INI_' followed by the actual name of the object throughout the design. Remember that variable names, unless they are declared as global, are only in scope within their respective forms, modules and so on, and therefore don't pose such a hazard to your implementation. However, you should pay special attention to form, table, procedure and function names.

As you find yourself using different Windows API calls, you may want to consider creating a library that contains the calls that you refer to most frequently. This will save your having to re-declare the calls each time you want to use one of your API calls. For example, if you commonly use custom .INI files in your application, it may be helpful to simply create a library that contains the reference to the API calls to update the .INI file. This will make the calls available to your application, whenever needed without further declare statements.

Special Behavior in Library Implementations

As you might guess, there are some functional portions of your programs that may behave slightly differently if implemented in an Access Library. The biggest considerations concern the range and scope of operations; that is, what do different operations performed by the add-in affect? The following sections outline some general guidelines to be considered when you create your add-in.

Behavior of Forms and Reports within a Library

Forms and reports run relative to the library database. When the form is loaded, the underlying table(s) or queries must be found in the library database. This facilitates the use of temporary tables within your library that will hold interim data that you collect from the user.

Consider the Form Wizard. As you progress through the wizard's various screens, there are several places where the information can be stored to use in future operations of the wizard. This is the case in the configuration of the wizard's operation. The tables controlling the look and feel of the wizard's forms are private to the wizard's corresponding library file.

Since the libraries are private, if you use tables to store temporary information, your application will also need to make sure that these temporary work tables are cleared out before operations begin. If lookup information is required, your application should ensure that the information exists in the correct form in the

Library databases and that the content and format are what your application is expecting. In addition, if you are not shipping this data with your application, don't forget to create an installation and maintenance program that will give users access to the libraries, databases and tables as needed.

Behavior of Macros, Custom Toolbars within a Library

When your library uses Macros and Custom Toolbars, the actions that are executed are always parsed by first searching the library database, then the current database in the Access environment to find the corresponding macro, function, table or other components needed to function.

You should avoid using Macros in your add-ins due to the limitations placed on them when it comes to debugging and error handling, especially when most macro operations can be coded in an Access Basic module. Error handling (even if rudimentary) must be implemented, potentially saving the users of your software many aggravating and possibly cryptic Access error messages.

The exception to this rule is the implementation of custom menu options. Since you can't refer to Access Basic within the menu options, you will have to use Macros. You can still control execution and provide error handling if you utilize the `RunCode` macro action to call an Access Basic function:

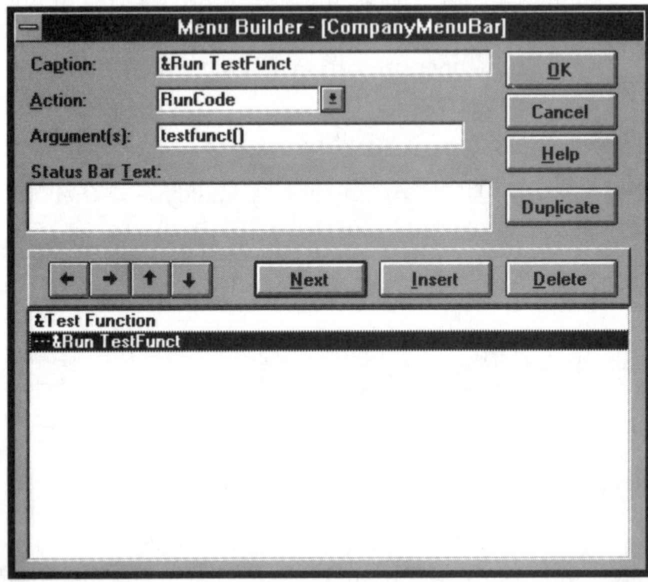

When you create each menu item, you should first create an Access Basic function that can be activated by a **RunCode** macro action on a menu choice. In the function, complete the operation that you need to carry out, including the error handling code. If you need to call a procedure, you should create an Access Basic function that will call your procedure itself. This is because you can't specify a procedure as the Argument to a menu option.

To declare your menu choice, go into the Menu Builder and create the menu. When you highlight the item you want to set up, enter **RunCode** in the Action text box. In the Arguments box, enter the name of your function, followed by parenthesis and any arguments that you want to pass in. When the item is selected from the menu, the function will be executed, running your code.

The only thing not covered by this technique, at least as far as error handling goes, is the actual transition from the menu to the underlying function. For example, if the underlying function doesn't exist, the user will get a standard Access error message and will have to respond appropriately. If you make sure the function is available, this error message will never appear:

Followed by the macro Action Failed error message:

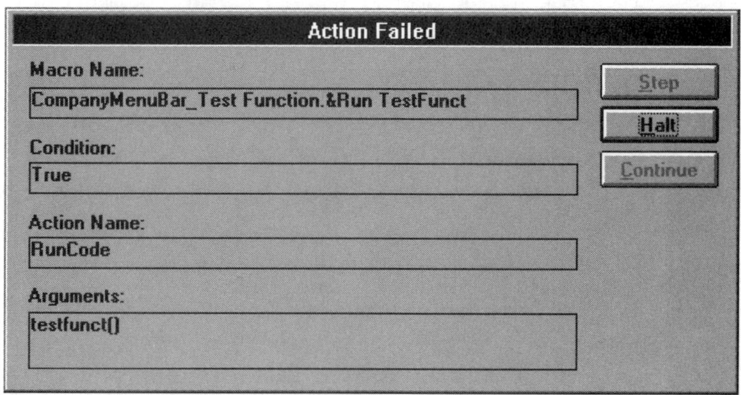

Steps to Creating an Add-In

Once you've decided what type of add-in you'd like to create, you can begin implementing the code, menus, forms and other facets of the add-in.

First, create your forms and other objects that you will be referencing in your code. Test each of these objects thoroughly before moving on to the next. When you have created the different pieces of your system, test all of the pieces jointly. Be sure you have the error handling code in place and that you test the results when an error is encountered. Later in this chapter we'll investigate different ways of implementing error handling.

Next, you'll have to convert the add-in to a library. You should rename the file with an MDA extension. For example, if your add-in is called **INIMGR.MDB** in the development mode, make a copy of it and name the copy **INIMGR.MDA**. The final step is to implement the add-in in your system for testing.

You'll have to make the appropriate entries in your **MSACC20.INI** file, or you can use the Add-In Manager to install the new module for you. When the .INI file is updated, you will have to update more than one section. First, update the **[Libraries]** section, entering the name of your new .MDA file:

```
[Libraries]
...
inimgr.mda=rw
...
```

The next step is to add a corresponding entry that will tell Access how to start your new add-in. When you created the add-in, you made a function that was to be used as the entry point. This function must be referenced in the .INI file so that Access is able to start the add-in when it's called upon to do so.

INI File Entry for a Table or Query Wizard

If you are creating a Table or Query Wizard, you'll need to add a new entry under either the **[Table Wizards]** section or the **[Query Wizards]** section of the .INI file. Locate the corresponding section and make your entry using the following syntax:

```
Add-in_Name=EntryPoint,,Status_Line_Text
```

For example:

```
INI Manager=ini_EntryPoint,,Add or change INI file entries
```

INI File Entry for a Form or Report Wizard

If you are creating a Form or Report Wizard, the process is very similar. The sections are named `[Form Wizards]` and `[Report Wizards]` respectively and you'll have to make the entry in the format:

```
Add-in_Name=EntryPoint, Wizard_ID, Status_Line_Text
```

For example:

```
My Report Wiz=mrz_EntryPoint, 3, Run my fancy reports
```

INI File Entry for a Menu Add-In

The entries for a menu-based add-in are simpler than those of the other add-ins. The menu entries, placed under the `[Menu Add-Ins]` section of the .INI file, are formatted as follows:

```
Add-In_Name==EntryPoint()
```

For example:

```
&INI Manager==ini_EntryPoint()
```

You can use the ampersand character '&' to create an accelerator key for the option. Place the ampersand just before the character that you want to be used as the accelerator. When the menu is displayed, the option will be underlined, indicating to the user that they can select the item by simply pressing the corresponding key.

If you need to use the actual ampersand character, simply place two ampersands in sequence, e.g. '&&'.

Optimizing before Distribution

Once you've created and tested your add-in, there are a few things that you should consider before you distribute your application. Some of these items impact upon the performance of your code when running in the add-in environment.

On a general level, remove any and all debugging procedures, forms, tables, functions and so on that you have defined, but are not using in the production system. This is also true of any type definitions, constants or other variables that are established in your system.

Also, consider removing comments from the code you have developed. This should be done as a last step, and you should first make a copy of the database file with the comments still in it for future reference. Make any further changes to the code in the commented file, and then update the production system as appropriate.

Two options that can help decrease the size of your database are the Repair and Compact commands. You should run these against your add-in database just prior to sending it out. These options will make a final verification check of the integrity of your system, and will compress the tables and other structures to their smallest possible size.

Always re-test your code after each optimization step. Never wait until all steps are completed before testing your evolving application. If you wait until all steps have been completed and encounter a problem, it will be more difficult to narrow down the cause of the problem.

Of course you should run your routines through a final test as well, just before and just after you implement the code as an add-in in your own system.

Setting Your Add-In to be Read-Only

If at all possible, you should implement your add-in as a read-only utility. The way that add-ins are loaded during Access' startup process is defined in the `MSACC20.INI` file. As we discussed early in this chapter, for each line in the `[Libraries]` section, you can specify either Read-Only or Read-Write access.

If you will want to be able to open the wizard in the standard Access environment while it is loaded as a Wizard, you can set the flag to RW. When the add-in is loaded manually by opening the MDA file, you may receive error messages about duplicate definitions.

If you didn't comment out the references to the **INIMGR.MDA** *in the* **MSACC20.INI** *before looking at the* **INIMGR.MDA** *file earlier, you will have received these error messages.*

Generally these settings shouldn't cause any problems. However, if you are going to be making changes to the add-in, you should uninstall it, make the changes and then reinstall it.

Your ability to set this flag will depend on your implementation. If you are saving information into tables for later use, it may not be possible to set the read-only flag. However, you can consider using externally attached tables, explained later in this chapter.

Turning on Code Debugging for Your Add-in

By default, you can't trace calls into an add-in. If you want to have this capability, first set your add-in load state to RW to allow edits. Next you enable the debugging option in the **[Options]** section of **MSACC20.INI**. Make a new entry as follows:

```
DebugLibraries=True
```

This will allow Access to step through the code in the wizard or other add-in and let you see what's happening.

Remember that if you have the Access Developer's Toolkit, you can change to the 'annotated' versions of the wizards by changing the references in the MSACC20.INI file to point to the MDA files provided with the ADT. Also remember to set the mode flag to RW so you can review and make changes to the add-ins.

Using Externally Attached Database Tables within an Add-In

If you have tables within your add-in, you should consider establishing them as external database files attached to and referenced by your add-in's database. Using native tables presents no real challenges relating to your program's use of the tables, but there are advantages to using attached tables instead of them.

One such advantage is that the tables can be maintained while your add-in is loaded and active in the Access environment. You'll recall from our earlier discussions that you must unload the add-in, exit and re-start Access before you can edit, or even review, the native tables associated with an add-in. By using the concept of attached tables, you can get around this limitation.

If the tables are attached, they are not opened until the user is actually using the add-in and has actually loaded the tables into memory. You or your users can create a reference to the tables from within another database that will allow them to add, change or delete records in the tables without having access to your add-in. This gives you the added security of knowing that you don't have to open up your software code to non-development end-users.

Another advantage is security itself. You can establish open security on the add-in database while locking down the security on the tables, or vice-versa. For more information on establishing security, refer to your Access manuals and in particular, Chapter 14 on 'Building Applications'. One use of Access' object level security can be seen if we look at form design.

When you design your add-in, you'll need to determine how much of an open interface you are going to implement. Earlier in the chapter, we've attached some tables from the wizards to our Samples database. If you don't want to give this level of access to your supporting tables, you can set up the accounts on the tables database to prevent it.

Error Handling Concepts

Since you'll be implementing routines that are running as processes within Access, it is very important that you implement comprehensive error handling in those routines. Error handling should be designed to ensure that Access doesn't encounter an untrapped error which causes it to halt execution. You must anticipate all sources of error and trap them yourself; allowing a graceful exit or another attempt at the operation.

There are two common ways that you can implement error handling in your programs, both of which are outlined briefly below.

Form Level Error Handling

At the form level, you can enable error handling that will cover all actions and interactions that pertain to a given form. Form-level handling is established in the On Error property of a form. When an error is encountered, it initiates a call to the form error handler, which in turn can call a custom designed expression, macro or Access Basic code.

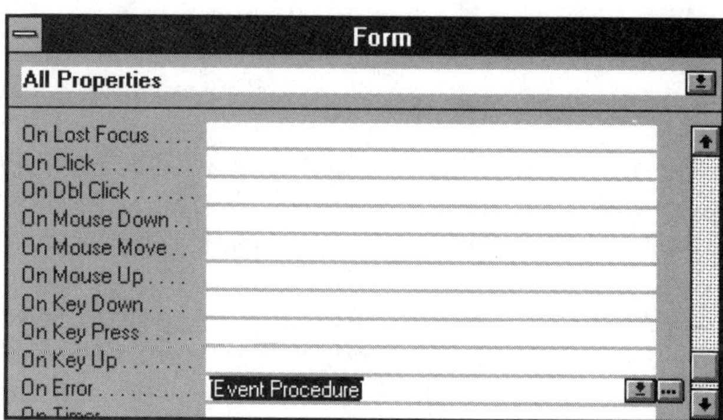

In its simplest implementation, you can display a standard **MsgBox** and let the user know about the problem. Remember to display the contents of Error$ and the value of Err in your message box to let your users know which error has occurred:

```
...
Dim sMessage as String

sMessage = "A problem was encountered." & Chr$(13) & Chr$(13)
sMessage = sMessage & "Error:  " & str$(Err) & " " & Error$
MsgBox sMessage, MB_ICONSTOP, "Error Encountered"
...
```

The **MB_ICONSTOP** *constant allows you to specify that you want the familiar Stop Sign icon displayed in the dialog box presented to the user.*

A more sophisticated implementation uses the same error handling code as in an Access Basic error handler. You can control the system's response to the error and attempt to re-try the operation, or exit out of the add-in altogether. This is shown in the **Select Case...** code blocks show in the next section.

Chapter 9

Access Basic Error Handling

As we've seen in some of the sample code listings that we've reviewed both in this chapter and others, the method of establishing an error handler in Access Basic code requires two distinct steps to complete the implementation.

First, you should set up the error handler in each procedure individually. You establish the error handler by using the **`On Error Goto...`** construct. Note that you must establish an error handler in all procedures and functions for which you want to retain control in the event of a problem. Consider the sequence of events where a procedure calls other procedures or events.

You can't establish a single, global error handler that will encompass all of the functions, procedures and form level operations. There are some advantages to this restriction, though it seems limiting at first glance.

The biggest advantage provided by this restriction is control. If you limit your functions and procedures to a single operation and wrap the operation with an error handler, you'll know exactly where to look when it comes time to correct a problem that's been encountered. Be sure that your error handling routines display a module name and the Error$ and Err as mentioned above. This information will prove extremely useful in your debugging efforts.

The following example code listing will prove helpful in your development considerations:

```
Function DemoError()
 ...
 Dim MyModule as String
 MyModule = "Demo Procedure - Error Handling"
 On Error Goto MyErrorHandler
 ...
 'Do statement here
 ...
 DemoError = Status
 Exit Function

MyErrorHandler:

    sMessage = "An error was encountered.  "
    sMessage = sMessage & " Module: " & MyModule & ", Message: "
    sMessage = sMessage & str$(Err) & " " & Error$ & "Continue?"

    sTitle = "System Problem"
```

```
    Select Case MsgBox(sMessage, MB_ICONSTOP + MB_YESNO, sTitle)
        Case IDYES
            Resume
        Case IDNO
            Exit Function
    End Select

End Function
```

This function will test the return value after the user has been prompted with a message box indicating the problem. This has the added advantage of allowing the user to retry the operation by selecting Yes from the dialog box. We use the **Resume** command to begin again with the line causing the error and re-try the operation.

Using the Setup Wizard

The Microsoft Access Developer's Toolkit provides you with a Setup Wizard that you can use to create the distribution files for your application. The Setup Wizard is installed in your Program Manager program group associated with the ADT.

Before You Start

You can use the Setup Wizard to create setup discs for either a full run-time installation of your application (one that doesn't require a copy of the Access program on the user's machine), or just to install one or more database files for use with an existing copy of Access.

There are some key pieces of information that you'll need to know before you start the setup process. First, you'll need to have a good working knowledge of the target system for your software. Specifically, here are some questions to consider:

- Are all of your target machines the same or will different physical system components need to be taken into consideration?
- Are network installations a possibility?
- Are subdirectory structures consistent across systems, or will they vary from user to user?

You'll need to know this information before you'll be able to complete the setup process. Find out the answers to these questions, along with any other details that you may know about the user who will be installing your software. Do they want OCXs installed in their **WINDOWS\SYSTEM** subdirectory, or is there a common, specific subdirectory where all utility functions should be destined? Garnering as much information as you can about the target installation will enable you to tailor your use of the Setup Wizard and therefore the resulting setup disks.

You will need an .INI file for your application if you are distributing it as a run-time program, but one is not required if you are merely distributing the MDB and allowing people access to it. When **MSARN200.EXE** runs, it looks for an .INI file that will lay out the different database interfaces that are used by your application.

Are there procedures, programs, or other functions that need to be run immediately after the Setup program has successfully installed the system on the target system? For example, if you are requiring OLE Registration Database entries, you'll want to include a program that can install or update the necessary entries in the target system's Registration Database.

Creating the Distribution Disk Set

When you run the Access Setup Wizard, you have the ability to create one of several different setup installations.

These installations will provide you with the capability to provide your software, in a self-installing format, for a network installation, on a 3.5" diskette (1.44M) format, or a 5.25" diskette (1.2M) format. These options allow you to distribute your application in all of the popular formats demanded by today's systems.

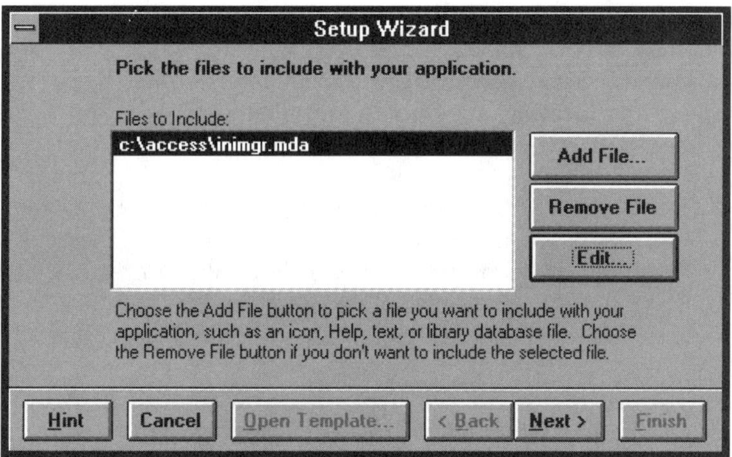

You start the Setup Wizard either from the icon created when you installed the Access Developers Toolkit, or by loading the file **SETUPWIZ.MDB** into Access directly. The first step to creating your distribution disks is to provide information about the files you need to include on the distribution set. The Setup Wizard will automatically include the runtime Access program files. Select the Add File button to specify what files to add to the distribution definition.

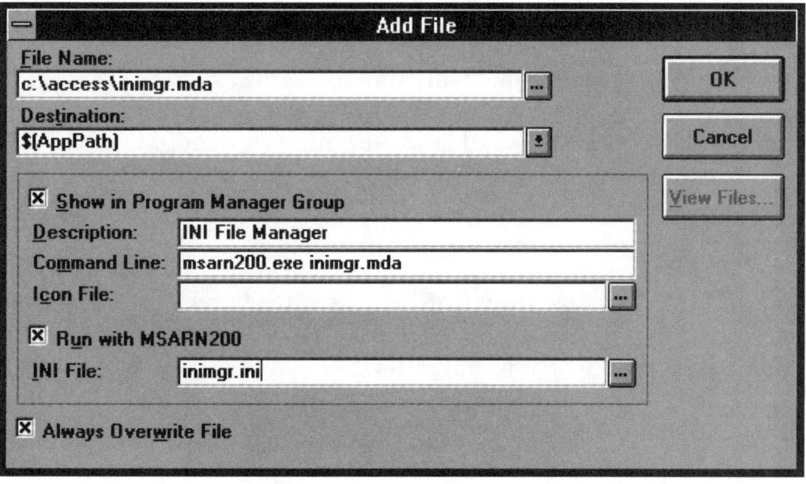

Remember that if you have custom add-ins, these must also be included, along with any attached supporting databases or .INI files. When you specify the files to add, you can also specify a destination for the file. You can type in an absolute path to the location in which to install the file, or you can select any one of the three built in options, AppPath, WinPath or WinSysPath:

AppPath Files will be installed in the same directory as the main application. When the user is running the Setup program, they are prompted for the destination directory for the installation process. This directory becomes the AppPath and will be the location for your files if you select this option.

WinPath This specifies the user's Windows directory. A common location for this will be **C:\WINDOWS**, but it may vary on some systems.

WinSysPath This is the path to the **WINDOWS\SYSTEM** directory on the user's system. It is determined by adding '\system' to the WinPath. If you have custom controls, for example, you may want to install them in this directory.

The Show In Program Manager Group option will tell the setup program to create a new icon for the software in the Program Manager. The user will be prompted to select a program group where the software should be installed. In addition, if you select this option, you can elect to run the software with the Access Run-Time modules. The Access Run-time modules, with **MSARN200.EXE** at the core as the execution engine, allow you to provide software that doesn't require the full Access environment to run.

Setting this option automatically adds all the files required for a run-time installation. If you do specify the Run-time option, you are required to provide an .INI file that is used in the startup and management of the software you're installing.

The next step is to select the types of databases that you'll be supporting with your application. These include, for example, the Microsoft SQL Server engine and the Paradox engine to name but a few:

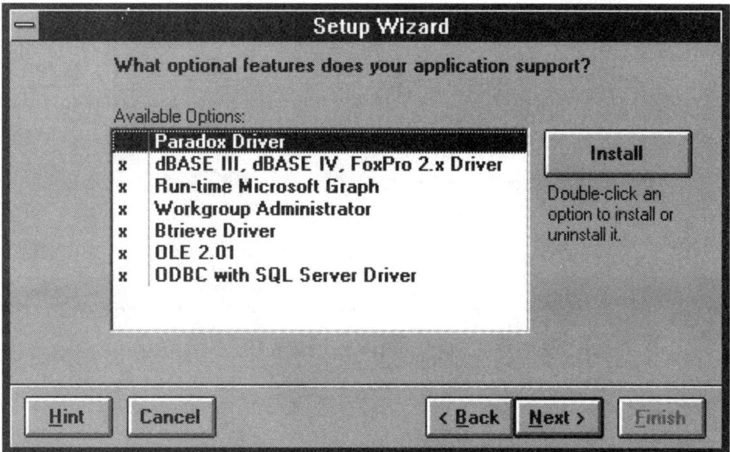

Select each function that your application depends on. When you do, the Setup Wizard will know all of the different supporting files that must be included in the distribution files. In many cases, this will include different files, DLLs and other supporting options.

> **The Setup Wizard maintains this information in internal tables. If you open the wizard, you can review these tables and get a better feel for how the wizard is implemented. Remember to hold down the shift key when you open the `SETUPWIZ.MDB` database. This will keep it from running the AutoExec macro which starts the wizard under normal circumstances.**

For each of these supporting files, specific sections from the **`MSACC20.INI`** file should be included in your application's specific .INI file. You can copy these from the Access .INI file for ease of installation. For a complete listing, including which sections and topics from the Access .INI file pertain to the different options, see your ADT Advanced Topics manual. See Chapter 2, Part 1 for details on the items that you will need to include.

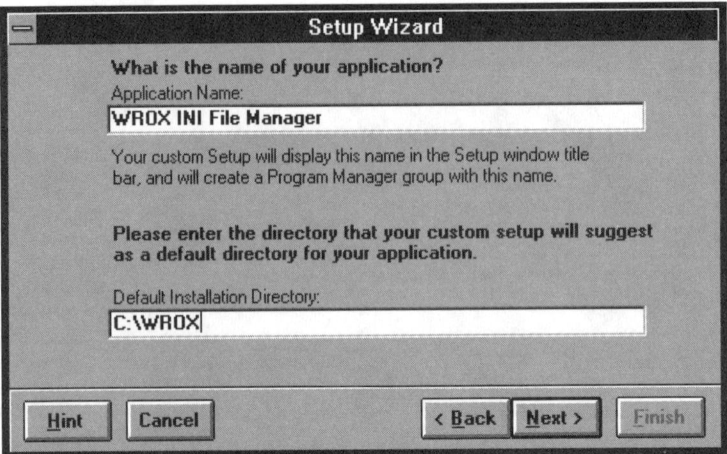

The next step in the process is to specify the name of your application and the directory that will be displayed as the default destination when the user runs the setup. The user will be able to change the setting for the directory during the setup process; this only provides a default starting point. As with the standard Setup programs, if the directory you specify doesn't exist, the user will be prompted as to whether it should be created.

Next, the Setup Wizard will ask for the name of any program that you want to run after the files have been successfully installed on the target system. If you have any of the following considerations, you should begin to think about using this option:

- OLE Custom Controls that need to be registered on the target system
- Special initialization routines that need to be run to further set up your software
- A software registration procedure
- Updates to existing databases, .INI files and so on

This function will provide you with the mechanism to implement the software for these requirements. You can run the **REGEDIT.EXE** program with a file as a parameter to update the registry, or call a completely separate program that may update several different things on the target system.

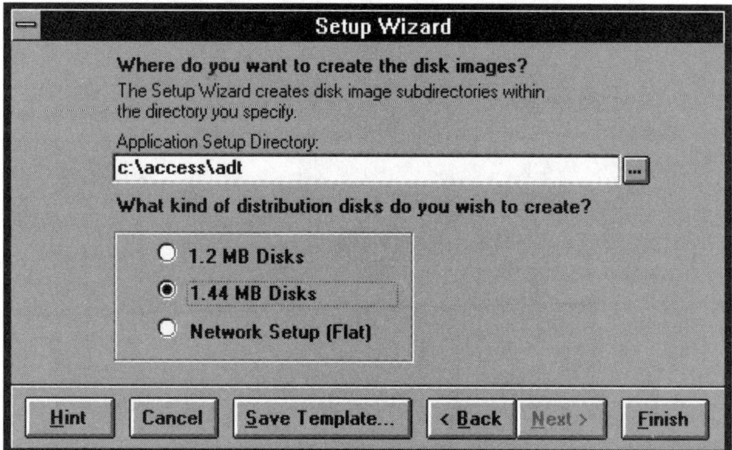

The last step is to select where you want the disk images created. It is highly recommended that you don't build the distribution set directly to a floppy diskette drive. You should specify a subdirectory where you can create the set and then copy that information down to the floppy disk as needed.

The Setup Wizard will create a subdirectory for each diskette that will be required, based on the type of distribution diskette you want to create. These types are 1.2M, 1.44M or a Network setup. Note that if you're installing to another type of high-capacity device, such as a CD-ROM, use the Network setup option and then copy the contents of the resulting Disk1 subdirectory to the device.

Images will be created in subdirectories named DISK1, DISK2 and so on as required until all files are allocated to a diskette. The Setup Wizard also compresses all files during the creation of the distribution set. The actual compression process will take a few minutes and you should keep this in mind when you are ready to go through the creation process.

If you select the Network installation, all files are installed into a single subdirectory. Placing all files from this subdirectory onto a network shared drive allows users to go to the directory and run the Setup program to install the software on their local systems.

Finally, when the Setup program runs, you get the benefit of Microsoft's legal department. The standard copyright notice is presented and the ever-familiar Setup Process begins:

After pressing OK, the user is prompted to accept the destination directory that you specified from within the Setup Wizard. If the directory is not acceptable, a new selection can be made and the installation will be directed to the new directory.

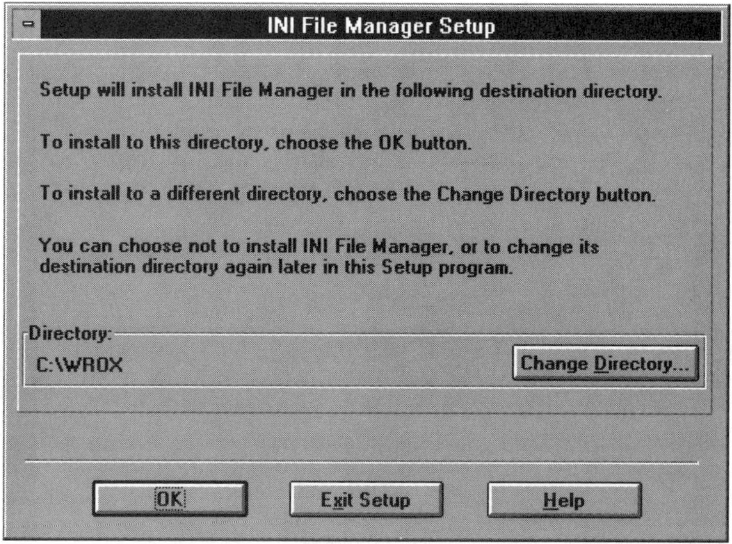

Once the destination directory is selected, the process of installation can begin. The user is prompted to select the installation button to begin:

One of the nice features of the Setup program is that it will not update files on the target system if they are equal to, or more recent than, the versions provided by the installation program set. This means that you can safely specify all components required, but the user's system will only be updated with latest needed component parts.

What is Created?

When you run the Setup Wizard, several different actions are completed for you. Of major significance is that the Setup Wizard knows about many of the 'behind the scenes' files required to run your software. These include the DLLs and other supporting files that may be needed like the ODBC installation program.

Here's a listing of the files created with a barebones installation:

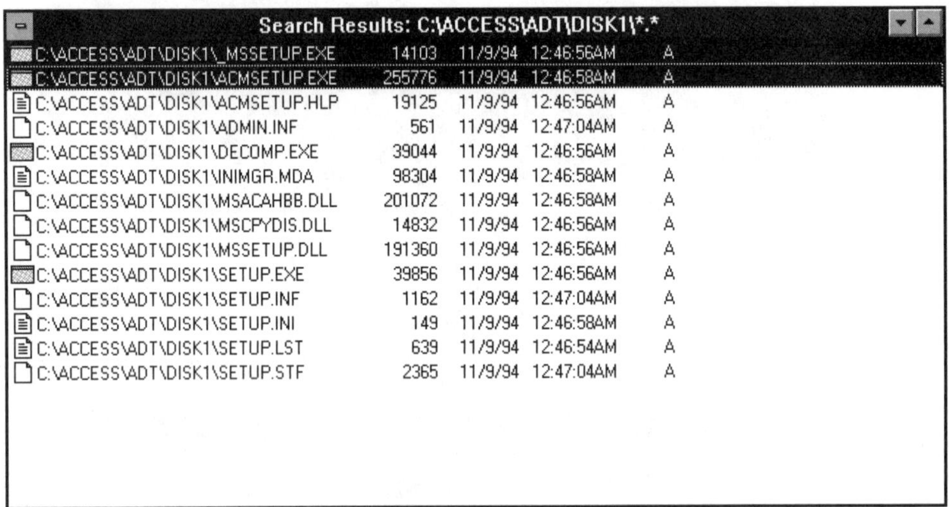

Search Results: C:\ACCESS\ADT\DISK1*.*

File	Size	Date	Time	Attr
C:\ACCESS\ADT\DISK1_MSSETUP.EXE	14103	11/9/94	12:46:56AM	A
C:\ACCESS\ADT\DISK1\ACMSETUP.EXE	255776	11/9/94	12:46:58AM	A
C:\ACCESS\ADT\DISK1\ACMSETUP.HLP	19125	11/9/94	12:46:56AM	A
C:\ACCESS\ADT\DISK1\ADMIN.INF	561	11/9/94	12:47:04AM	A
C:\ACCESS\ADT\DISK1\DECOMP.EXE	39044	11/9/94	12:46:56AM	A
C:\ACCESS\ADT\DISK1\INIMGR.MDA	98304	11/9/94	12:46:58AM	A
C:\ACCESS\ADT\DISK1\MSACAHBB.DLL	201072	11/9/94	12:46:58AM	A
C:\ACCESS\ADT\DISK1\MSCPYDIS.DLL	14832	11/9/94	12:46:56AM	A
C:\ACCESS\ADT\DISK1\MSSETUP.DLL	191360	11/9/94	12:46:56AM	A
C:\ACCESS\ADT\DISK1\SETUP.EXE	39856	11/9/94	12:46:56AM	A
C:\ACCESS\ADT\DISK1\SETUP.INF	1162	11/9/94	12:47:04AM	A
C:\ACCESS\ADT\DISK1\SETUP.INI	149	11/9/94	12:46:58AM	A
C:\ACCESS\ADT\DISK1\SETUP.LST	639	11/9/94	12:46:54AM	A
C:\ACCESS\ADT\DISK1\SETUP.STF	2365	11/9/94	12:47:04AM	A

Some of these files support the setup process itself. These include the **SETUP.*** files, **DECOMP.EXE** and many of the .INF files. In addition, these files will contain information about OLE registration entries, operations that should be performed on the target system and other such necessities for a successful installation.

The remaining files will be pertinent to the operation of your software on the target system. If you specify ODBC data sources, you'll also notice **ODBCINST.DLL** and other software that supports the ODBC standard. In addition, attached databases, OCXs and so on will all be placed into the appropriate subdirectory for you.

The following table provides background information on some of the files that are created by the setup process:

File Name	Description
ACMSETUP.EXE	Microsoft Setup executable file
ACMSETUP.HLP	Microsoft Setup Help file
ADMIN.INF	Setup information file created by the Setup Wizard
DECOMP.EXE	Decompression executable file
MSACAHBB.DLL	Microsoft Setup dynamic-link library
MSCPYDIS.DLL	Microsoft copy disincentive dynamic-link library
MSSETUP.DLL	Microsoft Setup dynamic-link library
SETUP.EXE	Microsoft Setup executable file
SETUP.INF	Setup information file created by the Setup Wizard
SETUP.INI	Setup initialization file
SETUP.LST	Microsoft Setup file list
SETUP.STF	Microsoft Setup program file
_MSSETUP.EXE	Microsoft Setup executable file

When setup runs, it relies on the INF, LST and .INI files for the information about files to copy, destination directories and all the other relevant and required information.

Advanced Setup Considerations

Under certain circumstances, you'll have additional things that you'll need to take into account when you create the setup program for your software. Some of these items are outlined below.

Workgroup Installation

When you install in a workgroup situation, you have a choice to make regarding how your application will be made available to the users. With an administrative setup, the system administrator installs the contents of the distribution disks to the network. When users install the software to their workstation, setup will, by default, make a backup copy of their **SYSTEM.MDA** file and create a new one. This will result in the loss of any custom settings and configuration options that they may have stored in the previous system configuration database.

If you want to prevent this from happening, Microsoft recommends making a change to the **SETUP.INF** file which controls some of the installation process carried out by the setup wizard. This file, located in the installation subdirectory, should be backed up prior to making these changes.

The **SETUP.STF** file is ASCII delimited text, and therefore will need an editor that is able to work with this type of file. Excel will serve as a great editor for this task if you have it available, but if not, you'll need to find an editor that will support the format.

In order to customize this file, follow the instructions given below:

1 Open **SETUP.STF**.

2 Scroll down to the row that contains ObjID in the first column.

3 Go to the third column (Title) and find the row for the object whose title is 'Create SYSTEM.MDA'. Write down the Object ID (ObjID) for that object.

4 Find the row for the object whose title is '---- User Non File Work ----'. In the Object Data column for that object, remove the Object ID you wrote down above.

5 Find the row for the object whose title is '&Complete'. In the Object Data Column, add the Object ID that you wrote down in earlier.

6 Save the file.

This process prevents the setup program from overwriting the system database and allows you to keep the existing preferences and configuration options.

Software Dependencies

In many cases, your software functions may be based on other toolsets or complete programs that must be present on the user's system. In these scenarios, you will want to tell the Setup Wizard exactly what components 'must' be included when the Setup Wizard creates the distribution disk set.

In your Windows subdirectory, there is a file called **SWDEPEND.INI** which contains all of the software dependencies for Access. This file is how Access knows that, for the installation of an OCX, you must also include the **OC1016.DLL** file to support the OLE custom control.

```
[oc1016.dll]
Dest=$(WinSysPath)

[outl1016.ocx]
Uses1=oc1016.dll
Dest=$(AppPath)

[msasb20.ocx]
Uses1=oc1016.dll
Dest=$(AppPath)

[msacal20.ocx]
Uses1=oc1016.dll
Dest=$(AppPath)
```

When you add an item that requires that something else is installed, the Setup Wizard will tell you that other items are required. You'll be able to review a list of items that Access recommended that you should install and it allows you to accept or reject this list. Once you have accepted this list, the wizard will place the files in the list of files to include with the installation. If you want to remove a file, select it and choose the Remove File button from the 'Pick the files...' dialog box:

You can also create your own dependency relationships in the **SWDEPEND.INI** file. To do so, you create a section with the name of the file for which you want to create the relationship and list the items that are required. For example, if the **INIMGR.MDA** depended on the above **OUTL1016.OCX** control, you would make the entries shown next in the .INI file:

```
[INIMGR.MDA]
Dest=$(WinSysPath)
Uses1=OUTL1016.OCX
```

You can also specify where the files should be placed on the destination system. This is helpful if you are installing custom controls that should be placed in the user's **WINDOWS\SYSTEM** subdirectory. The same key indicators are available for designating the destination as for the standard Setup Wizard add file dialog box; $(AppPath), $(WinPath) and $(WinSysPath). When the setup process runs, the Setup Wizard will update the files necessary to make sure the files are placed where you need them.

If you wished to, you can append a subdirectory name to the key indicators, in order to further refine the locating of the files. For example, if your application resides in a directory called **C:\MYAPP** and all OCX tools reside in a **TOOLS** subdirectory under the **MYAPP** directory, you can specify this as follows:

```
[INIMGR.MDA]
Dest=$(AppPath)\TOOLS
Uses1=OUTL1016.OCX
```

When you next add in the INIMGR to create a setup program, you'll be prompted to include not only the outline OCX, but also the support files required for it to function, in this case, **OUTL1016.OCX**. This is a very powerful way of ensuring that all the information is transferred to the user's system and that the tools that they'll require are included.

Note that this option is especially effective if you use the Always Overwrite File option with the 'No' option selected. In this case, you'll be including all the necessary tools on the distribution disk set, but only the outdated versions of files will actually be copied to the destination system.

Comments and Suggestions

You can see that there are a number of tools, considerations and options when you are dealing with a more wide-spread distribution of your software. Error handling, optimization of your software and the setup program are important aspects of providing a quality product to the users of your software.

In this chapter, we've covered these topics with an eye toward providing you with the information you need to make decisions in these areas. Consider breaking your application into component parts that allow for the use of libraries, wizards and add-ins. You can use these technologies to provide a layer of insulation between the user and the program code that is providing the functionality required to work with their database, independent of the programs you create.

Finally, break your system apart at the database table layer as well. Consider the technique of using 'code' databases that reference attached tables. You can then apply security to prevent unwanted access to your system tables.

In the next chapter, we will take a look at the Structured Query Language (SQL) in preparation for the later chapters on ODBC, using SQL Server and the new wizard from Microsoft, the Upsizer.

CHAPTER 10

Using SQL in Microsoft Access

The Structured Query Language (SQL) is the international standard database query language used in almost every database package on the market today. Whilst Microsoft have created the idea of the Query By Example grid for novices to construct SQL statements through a graphical interface, the full power of SQL can only be drawn upon when you talk to the SQL engine in it's native language. By learning SQL, you will add further functionality to your applications with this impressive addition to your arsenal of database design tools

What's Covered in This Chapter

In this chapter, we'll be reviewing some techniques that you can use to quickly get started into the SQL world. While it's beyond the scope of this book to investigate all aspects of the SQL language, there are some core components that you should understand, each of which will lay the foundation for your increasingly complex efforts.

Some of the topics we'll cover include:

- The **`SELECT`** statement
- SQL joins
- The Data Definition Language
- Creating tables and indexes

We won't look at all the available SQL commands as that is a book in itself, but we will give you a taster of how easy SQL can be and show you how you can learn the language by looking at existing queries.

Chapter 10

How This Chapter Impacts Our Application

As Access uses SQL at the core of the RDBMS's querying ability, this chapter impacts throughout the PIM. However, this chapter is designed to give you a good, general overview of the language and it's practical applications.

What this means is that this chapter doesn't directly affect any one specific part of the PIM, but a general understanding of SQL will aid your investigation of the queries and Access Basic code that are part of the foundation that the PIM is built upon.

What is SQL?

When you use Access, you may not realize it right away, but you're also using the Structured Query Language, or SQL. SQL provides a way to manipulate information with English-like commands and this is put to good use in Access, where all the actions that impact the database tables are built from SQL statements.

Of course, you're not necessarily entering these actions as SQL statements directly into the RDBMS. By using the QBE grid, you are getting Access to step in behind the scenes, and translate your request into the appropriate statements. However, the QBE grid does place some restrictions upon the SQL that can be generated. Therefore it is important that you are comfortable with the basics of how to use SQL to produce queries directly, thus allowing you to apply a much more powerful approach to your system's queries.

Where to Start

Access works with SQL statements most predominantly created from your QBE grid definitions. If you want to get started with SQL and find following examples a good way to learn, this is the place to begin your investigation. You can use the translation ability that is innate with Access, to look at the SQL statements generated by certain QBE grids and indeed the QBE grids generated by given SQL statements.

As you work through the SQL statements in this chapter, let Access do the grunt work for you. After you've entered an SQL statement, press the Design button to see how Access would represent the query graphically. On the other hand, if you just aren't sure how to enter an SQL statement, you can probably take a very good stab at it using the QBE grid. After that, select the SQL button and begin working with the SQL statement created by Access:

You should also remember that it is possible to experiment with the SQL statements, whether they be in the form of the grid or an SQL statement, by using the Run button:

This will run the query, check the syntax and then display the results in a datasheet. This allows you to check whether a QBE grid is producing the correct results before you review the generated SQL statements or it means that you can get Access to check the syntax and the generated recordset from your SQL statement before you commit it to your application.

We'll be focusing on the statement that will serve quite a few of your needs, both in basic and more advanced systems, the **SELECT** statement. Other statements are available that allow you to add indexes to tables, delete existing tables as well as other database creation and maintenance functions. In the second part of this chapter, we'll look into some of these Data Definition Language (DDL) statements that are available in Access.

The Foundation of SQL: the SELECT Statement

For these examples, we'll be using the **NWIND.MDB** sample database included with Access. This database is a great resource, as it covers all the major query constructs that you are ever likely to require.

> **Remember, to avoid loading the automatic startup macro in the NWIND.MDB database, you can press and hold down the shift key when loading the database. Instead of running the AutoExec macro, you'll be taken to the database tabbed dialog box.**

Take a look at the Categories table in design view. As you'll to see, this table provides the information on the different food categories used by the system. The format of the table includes four different fields, or columns as shown in the following diagram:

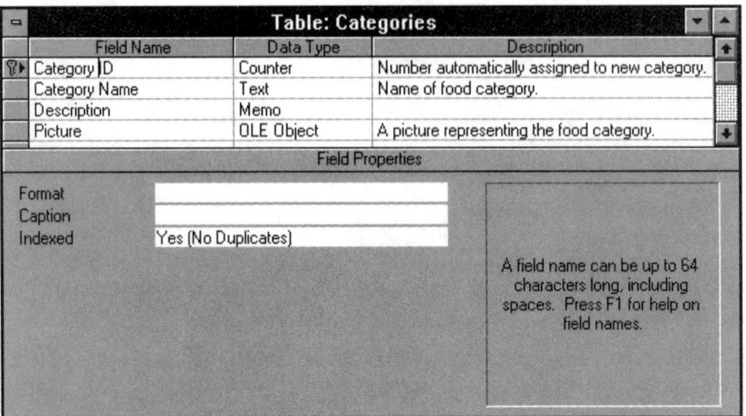

In the first example query that we'll be looking at, all we need to do is return all records from the table, sorted by CategoryName. We only care about the Name and Category ID fields as we'll be using the results of this query as the source of data for lookups. Here's a look at the query, as defined in the QBE grid:

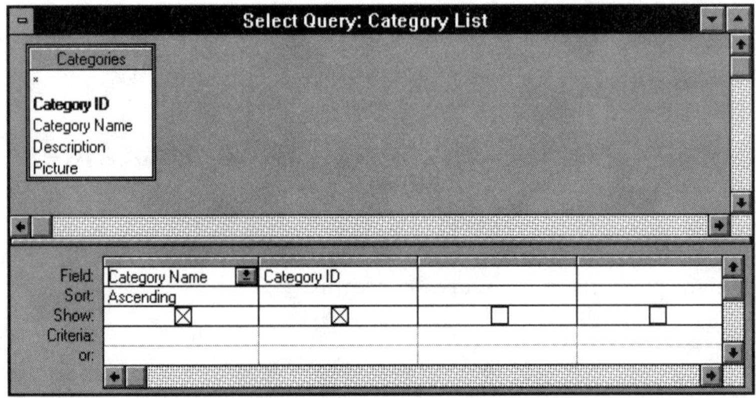

If you hit the SQL button, Access will translate this QBE grid into the following SQL statement:

```
SELECT DISTINCTROW Categories.[Category Name], Categories.[Category ID]
FROM Categories
ORDER BY Categories.[Category Name];
```

The basic format for a **SELECT** statement is:

```
SELECT <what>
FROM <source>
[WHERE <criteria> ]
[ORDER BY <sort order> ]
```

where:

<what> Required.

Represents the field, or list of fields separated by commas, that you want to have returned as the results for the statement.

There is a special case that applies to the '<what>' portion of this statement. If you want to return all fields in the underlying table, you don't have to specify each field name. By using the special asterisk (*) character, the SQL engine will return all the information held in every field for each record that satisfies your criteria.

<source> Required.

The name of the table or query that is the source of the data for your statement.

<criteria> Optional.

You can specify a filter for the information that will be returned such as only the records whose entry in the name field is 'Wrox'

<sort order> Optional.

With this parameter you can define the order that you wish the information to be returned. You can base the order on any field that appears in the current database and the appropriate SQL engine will return the records as you request.

A **SELECT** statement, in its most simple form, would be:

```
SELECT * FROM MyTable
```

This most basic use of the **SELECT** statement will result in the creation of a recordset comprised of every record with every field from the MyTable table, in the order that the records appear in the table.

Access also provides an extension to the standardized SQL language options. This is the 'DistinctRow' option that you can specify as part of your **SELECT** statement. **SELECT DISTINCTROW** will tell the Access engine that you want all records included in the specified table, as long as they are unique. If any duplicates exist in the table, only the first instance will make it into the generated recordset.

Note that the 'DistinctRow' option looks for uniqueness based upon all the fields that make up the suspect records, no matter what fields you have requested for your recordset.

Access inserts the **SELECT DISTINCTROW** statement as the first statement to any SQL statement that you may be creating from the QBE grid. If you don't want this option, you'll have to remove it in the SQL code before you run your statement.

Note that **SELECT DISTINCTROW** is specific to Microsoft Access. The command is not available when you are developing server-specific statements. For example, Microsoft's SQL Server doesn't support this method of information retrieval.

Reviewing SQL Statements Found in NWIND.MDB

In this section, we'll review some example SQL statements that may help in the preparation of your own SQL queries. There are many different ways that you can use a SQL type query, and we'll cover the general ones here.

Defining a Sort Order

In the **NWIND.MDB** database, select the Category List query and look at it in design view:

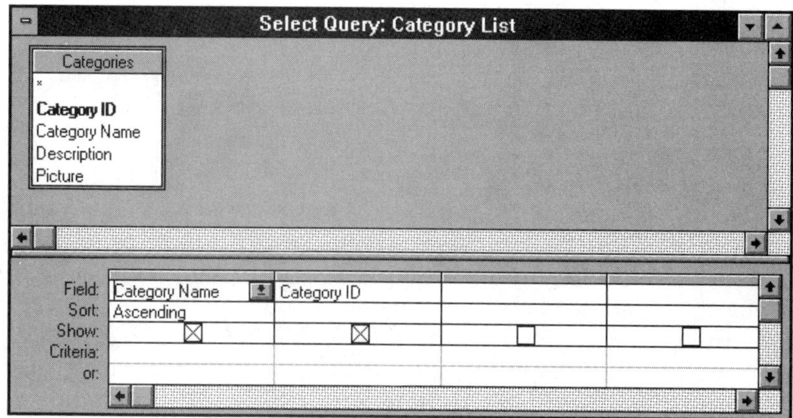

If you click on the SQL button, you'll see the SQL equivalent:

```
SELECT DISTINCTROW Categories.[Category Name], Categories.[Category ID]
FROM Categories
ORDER BY Categories.[Category Name];
```

This query returns all category names and IDs from the underlying Categories table. To see the results of the query, select the run button from the toolbar:

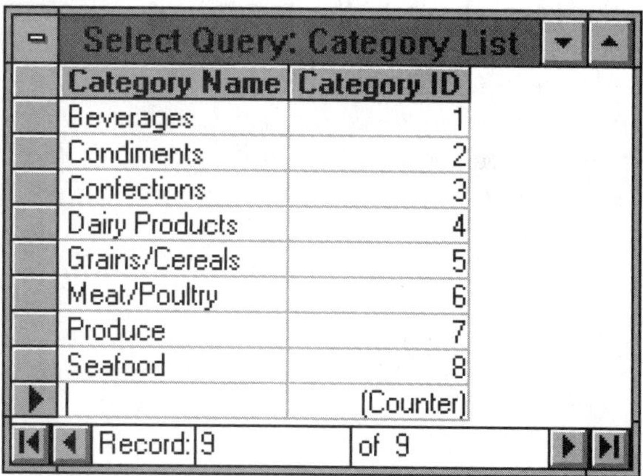

Select Query: Category List
Category Name
Category ID
Beverages
1
Condiments
2
Confections
3
Dairy Products
4
Grains/Cereals
5
Meat/Poultry
6
Produce
7
Seafood
8
(Counter)
Record: 9
of 9

One of the things that you'll notice about the SQL statement is that we're specifying a sort order by using the **ORDER BY** clause. Using this clause, you can specify any type of sort you need, including sorts that include multiple fields. If you need to sort first by **State** and then by **City**, the query might look like the following example:

```
SELECT * FROM Locations
ORDER BY State, City
```

This will extract all information from the Locations table and sort it as you need.

If you're creating queries as information sources for reports, you will force Access to perform double work if you specify a sort order in both the SQL statement and report definition. To avoid this, you can simply issue a `SELECT * FROM ...` type statement and omit the `ORDER BY ...` clause, although you should still specify all the other items that will limit the scope of your resulting recordset as needed. You should just try to avoid using two different requests to sort the data if possible.

As another example, suppose you have an employee database, as in the **NWIND.MDB** system. If you wanted to search by Last Name, a comma, and the First Name, such as 'Smith, John', you could use the following query:

```
SELECT DISTINCTROW [Last Name] & ", " & [First Name] AS [Employee Name],
Employees.[Employee ID]
FROM Employees
ORDER BY [Last Name] & ", " & [First Name];
```

This is the Employee List query from the **NWIND.MDB** sample database and shows several different things. In the first part of the statement, you'll notice that we're concatenating two different fields that will be displayed as one in the results set. More information on aliasing, which is the creation of 'virtual' fields, is provided in a later section, but this method of 'adding' the contents of the two fields together is a useful way of returning formatted sets of results to your application. Running this query produces the following results:

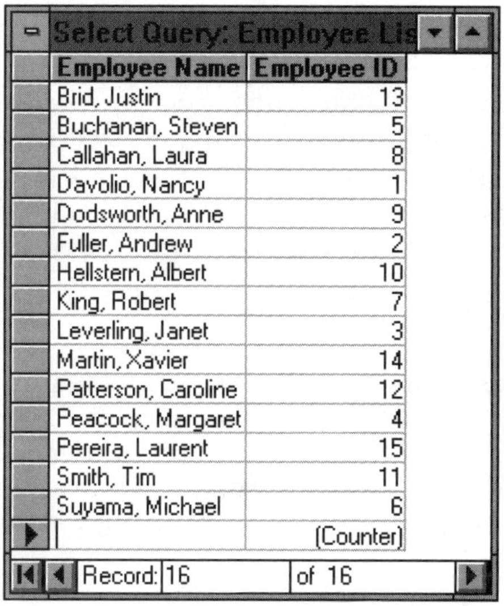

Select Query: Employee Lis

Employee Name	Employee ID
Brid, Justin	13
Buchanan, Steven	5
Callahan, Laura	8
Davolio, Nancy	1
Dodsworth, Anne	9
Fuller, Andrew	2
Hellstern, Albert	10
King, Robert	7
Leverling, Janet	3
Martin, Xavier	14
Patterson, Caroline	12
Peacock, Margaret	4
Pereira, Laurent	15
Smith, Tim	11
Suyama, Michael	6
	(Counter)

Record: 16 of 16

The names are stored in the database table as separate first and last names. With the query, we're creating a 'virtual' field, which not only contains the data from the fields, but also an added fixed constant, the new **", "** that provides the comma and the space between the two names.

You should also notice that you can sort using the same type of logic as with the concatenation of the names in the **SELECT** portion of the statement. In this case, we're telling Access that it should use the value of the fields, formatted as we need, as the sorting information. This allows Access to sort on the same **Employee Name** that we'll be using from the results set.

You could accomplish the same type of sort by changing the SQL as indicated below:

```
SELECT DISTINCTROW [Last Name] & ", " & [First Name] AS [Employee Name], ↵
    Employees.[Employee ID]
FROM Employees
ORDER BY [Last Name], [First Name];
```

> **Remember, when you're specifying column names, you should get in the habit of delimiting the name with square brackets. If you don't, Access will become confused if the column names include spaces or reserved words. You should also use the brackets whenever there's a question about the origin of the field. In addition, you should specify the tablename.[fieldname] construct whenever there are ambiguous names. This can often be the case as you start developing SQL statements that use multiple tables.**

The advantage of using this method of field concatenation is that you are specifying the sort information in the same way that you're specifying the select data set. This can enhance the readability of the query when you need to perform maintenance on the query at a later date. However, until that point, you'll be able to readily see what you intended to use as the sort order.

Defining a Grouping or Sub-Total

There are many times where you need to extract the information from the underlying table, subtotaling the information based on a certain field. You can do this by using the **GROUP BY** clause, a clause that allows you to specify what column to 'watch', so determining when to stop totaling up the results set. For example, in the SQL statement for the Daily Order Totals query, you can see that the grouping is done on Order Date:

```
SELECT DISTINCTROW Orders.[Order Date], Count(Orders.[Order ID]) AS ↵
    [CountOfOrder ID], Sum([Order Subtotals].Subtotal) AS ↵
    SumOfSubtotal
FROM Orders INNER JOIN [Order Subtotals]
ON Orders.[Order ID] = [Order Subtotals].[Order ID]
GROUP BY Orders.[Order Date];
```

> *We'll cover more information on the* ***INNER JOIN*** *and the* ***ON*** *clause in the Creating Joins section, later in this chapter.*

When the database engine parses the command, it will continue summing up the values in the **Count(Order.OrderID)** and **Order Subtotals.Subtotal** fields until the **Orders.Order Date** changes. The result is a summarized results set, showing only one row for each Order Date

Here's a sample of the data that is returned by the statement:

Select Query: Daily Order Totals

Order Date	CountOfOrder ID	SumOfSubtotal
23-Mar-94	3	2741
24-Mar-94	4	2525.35
25-Mar-94	3	5448.57
28-Mar-94	3	2473.93
29-Mar-94	4	7632.47
30-Mar-94	4	2778.65

Record: 1 of 720

In this example, eleven different orders are covered by the last three lines of these results, thus making this type of query ideal for summary type applications. For this reason, these types of SQL queries are often created for reports.

Creating 'Aliases' in SQL Statements

There are many times when you may want to create 'virtual' fields within your SQL statement. For example, if you need to add the contents of two other fields and present them as a new field, you could use the statement:

```
SELECT Value1, Value2, (Value1 + Value2) AS [Value Total]
FROM MyTable
```

This SQL statement is in the **SAMPLES.MDB** database called MyQuery and summarizes the table with the following recordset being returned:

Select Query: MyQuery

Value1	Value2	Value Total
1	2	3
1	3	4
1	2	3
7	6	13
5	2	7
8	7	15
8	2	10
0	2	2
9	2	11
0	2	2
6	1	7
5	5	10
5	4	9
4	3	7
0	2	2
3	1	4
6	3	9
7	2	9
0	0	

Record: 1 of 18

To any process using the query, the Value Total column will represent a normal field, but you can't update the field directly as it's a derived value. To update it, you would have to update the values that it is based upon and re-run the SQL statement.

Another example of using a derived or **Aliased** field can be seen in the Category Sales for 1993 query in the **NWIND.MDB** sample database:

```
SELECT DISTINCTROW [Sales for 1993].[Category Name], Sum([Sales for ⇙
    1993].[Product Sales]) AS [Category Sales]
FROM [Sales for 1993]
GROUP BY [Sales for 1993].[Category Name];
```

This query assigns a value from the Sales totals to a new field called Category Sales. Remember from the Grouping Order section, the **GROUP BY** clause will subtotal the values based on the Category Name. This query will return only two fields, the category name and total sales for that category.

Creating Joins

As you work through the SQL statements that form the core of your applications, you'll probably come across situations where you want records from one table, supplemented by information from a second or third table. When you design highly normalized database systems, this will be the rule rather than the exception.

Consider the structure of the following tables:

MyNames

NameID	Unique ID for the name
Last Name	Last name of the person
First Name	First Name of the person

MyAddresses

AddressID	UniqueID for the address
NameID	Reference to the name that 'owns' this address
Address1	Street address

Continued

City	City where address is located
State	State where address is located
ZipCode	ZipCode for the address

MyPhones

PhoneID	Unique ID for the phone number
NameID	Name that 'owns' the phone number
PhoneNum	Phone number
PhoneType	Phone number type

Suppose you wanted to present the user with the name, address and phone number information for a given person in the database. How would you accomplish this? Since there may be one MyNames record with one associated MyAddresses record and different numbers of MyPhones record, what would the SQL statement be to retrieve this information, given that we already know the NameID?

```
SELECT MyNames.[Last Name], MyNames.[First Name],
MyAddresses.[Address1], MyAddresses.[City], MyAddresses.[State],
MyAddresses.[ZipCode], MyPhones.[PhoneNum], MyPhones.[PhoneType]
FROM MyNames, MyAddresses, MyPhones
WHERE ((MyNames.[NameID]=MyAddresses.[NameID] AND
MyNames.[NameID]=MyPhones.[NameID]));
```

This SQL statement will pull the various records from each of the tables, keying on the NameID. Notice that while we don't bring back the NameID, or the unique IDs associated with each table, we are still using them to create the commonality, or Join, between the tables. This is the MyJoinQuery2 query in the **SAMPLES.MDB**.

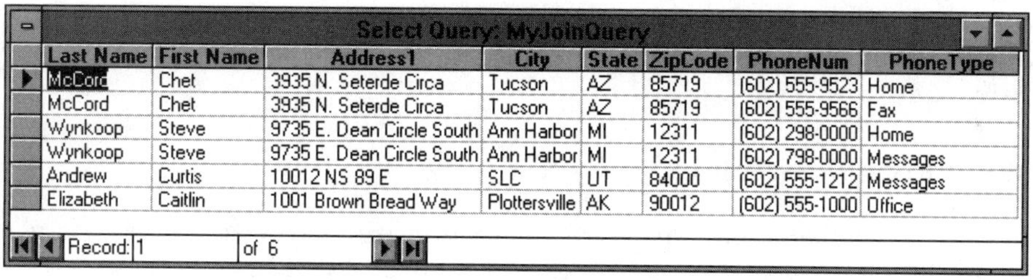

Select Query: MyJoinQuery

Last Name	First Name	Address1	City	State	ZipCode	PhoneNum	PhoneType
McCord	Chet	3935 N. Seterde Circa	Tucson	AZ	85719	(602) 555-9523	Home
McCord	Chet	3935 N. Seterde Circa	Tucson	AZ	85719	(602) 555-9566	Fax
Wynkoop	Steve	9735 E. Dean Circle South	Ann Harbor	MI	12311	(602) 298-0000	Home
Wynkoop	Steve	9735 E. Dean Circle South	Ann Harbor	MI	12311	(602) 798-0000	Messages
Andrew	Curtis	10012 NS 89 E	SLC	UT	84000	(602) 555-1212	Messages
Elizabeth	Caitlin	1001 Brown Bread Way	Plottersville	AK	90012	(602) 555-1000	Office

Record: 1 of 6

The result is a listing for each record in the MyNames table that has a corresponding value in both the MyAddresses and MyPhones tables. In cases where multiple entries exist in the MyPhones table, one row is returned for each phone number found. You can see this if you look at the information returned for both 'Chet McCord' and 'Steve Wynkoop'. In the case of the Andrew and Elizabeth entries, only one phone number is on file, so only one results set was returned.

Inner Joins

The first thing you'll notice is that our results set doesn't include names that don't have phone numbers on file. This can be an advantages, or it could remove some entries from your results set that you expected to be there. In most cases, as with an example like ours, we'd still like to see the information that is on file, even if we don't have a phone number or address for the person.

When you join tables using SQL, you use a concept of equations, indicating that one side of the equation must equal the other. For example, we indicate that we need to have the NameID field of the MyNames table equal the NameID field of the MyAddresses table before the records are included in the recordset as occurred in our previous example.

This query could have been written another way using the **INNER JOIN** statement. The query MyJoinQuery in the **SAMPLES.MDB** uses this syntax:

```
SELECT MyNames.[Last Name], MyNames.[First Name], MyAddresses.[Address1],
MyAddresses.[City], MyAddresses.[State], MyAddresses.[ZipCode],
MyPhones.[PhoneNum], MyPhones.[PhoneType]
FROM (MyNames INNER JOIN MyAddresses ON MyNames.[NameID] =
MyAddresses.[NameID]) INNER JOIN MyPhones ON MyNames.[NameID] =
MyPhones.[NameID];
```

If you try running this query you will get exactly the same results. The **INNER JOIN** tells Access that you want the information from one side of the **JOIN** statement that has a corresponding value on the other side of the **JOIN** statement.

Left and Right Outer Joins

There are two other modifiers you can place on the **JOIN** equations when you wish to link tables at execution time. **LEFT JOIN** and **RIGHT JOIN** allow you to specify that you want to include only those records where the fields are equal, but allow all records from either the left or right side of the equation.

For example, a **LEFT JOIN** between MyNames and MyAddresses would include all records from the MyNames table (the left side) in the output regardless of whether an address exists. If address or phone number information is found that matches, or equals, the ID in the MyNames table, then it is included in the recordset as well, but if not, the entries should be left blank. This SQL statement would probably be more along the lines of a general reporting or extract SQL request, when we usually need to see all information, not just all 'completed' records.

Here's a look at the SQL that will accomplish this request:

```
SELECT MyNames.[Last Name], MyNames.[First Name], MyAddresses.[Address1],
MyAddresses.[City], MyAddresses.[State], MyAddresses.[ZipCode],
MyPhones.[PhoneNum], MyPhones.[PhoneType]
FROM (MyNames LEFT JOIN MyAddresses ON MyNames.[NameID] =
MyAddresses.[NameID]) LEFT JOIN MyPhones ON MyNames.[NameID] =
MyPhones.[NameID];
```

Before you panic about how complex things just became, break it down. First, you know you can, for the purposes of understanding the statement, ignore the portion of the **SELECT** statement that immediately follows the **SELECT** keyword. These parameters represent the information to return and are quite easy to understand.

Next, we specify the tables that we need to include in the search and indicate that we're looking for a **LEFT JOIN**, one that will always return the records from the MyNames table, regardless of whether information is found for addresses and phone numbers. Before we investigate this further, take a look at the results that are produced. This is the MyJoinQuery (All) query in the **SAMPLES.MDB**:

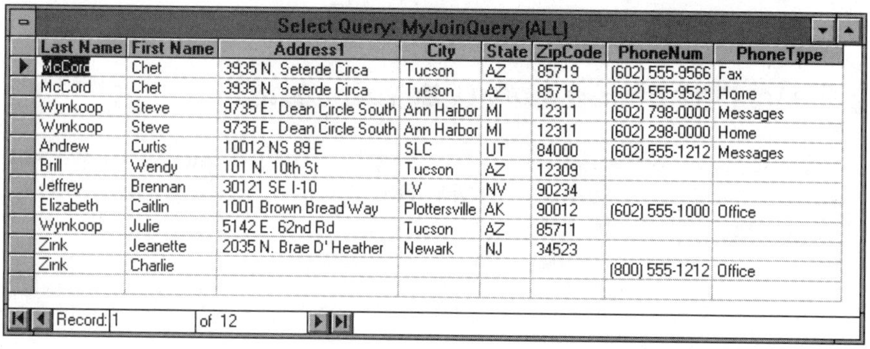

Select Query: MyJoinQuery (ALL)

Last Name	First Name	Address1	City	State	ZipCode	PhoneNum	PhoneType
McCord	Chet	3935 N. Seterde Circa	Tucson	AZ	85719	(602) 555-9566	Fax
McCord	Chet	3935 N. Seterde Circa	Tucson	AZ	85719	(602) 555-9523	Home
Wynkoop	Steve	9735 E. Dean Circle South	Ann Harbor	MI	12311	(602) 798-0000	Messages
Wynkoop	Steve	9735 E. Dean Circle South	Ann Harbor	MI	12311	(602) 298-0000	Home
Andrew	Curtis	10012 NS 89 E	SLC	UT	84000	(602) 555-1212	Messages
Brill	Wendy	101 N. 10th St	Tucson	AZ	12309		
Jeffrey	Brennan	30121 SE I-10	LV	NV	90234		
Elizabeth	Caitlin	1001 Brown Bread Way	Plottersville	AK	90012	(602) 555-1000	Office
Wynkoop	Julie	5142 E. 62nd Rd	Tucson	AZ	85711		
Zink	Jeanette	2035 N. Brae D' Heather	Newark	NJ	34523		
Zink	Charlie					(800) 555-1212	Office

Record: 1 of 12

What we've done, in essence, is to specify that names are our most important data element in the SQL statement and, if other information is available, present it. Notice for the last two 'Zink' names, one has an address and no phone number, while the other is just the opposite. Both records are still presented even though some of the tables don't have related records, which therefore translates to missing information.

When you're determining how the join should be structured, you'll need to know where your core information resides. Once you've determined that bit of information, you'll be able to create simple queries, join-type queries and much, much more to drive the functionality of your system.

Additional Resources - General SQL Assistance

You can search Access' on-line help for general information on specific SQL statements, but you should also review the documentation associated with the database server you're using.

For example, SQL Server includes a Transact-SQL Reference manual that reviews the complete syntax of SQL and its application to the database engine. You may have to experiment with cross-platform issues in SQL, until you come to grips with the different flavors. If you find yourself fighting with Access to send a specific command to your underlying database engine, you can turn to the Pass-through mode and work directly with the server, without translation from the Access database engine.

> *If you're new to SQL and are looking for a fast introduction to the language, syntax and capabilities look out for the forthcoming title "Instant SQL" from Wrox Press, written by Joe Celko and coming to a store near you soon!*

SQL Data Definition Language Queries

In Access, you can use Data Definition Language (DDL) queries to work with your database tables and indexes. DDL allows you to accomplish several things with your system. These include:

- Creating new tables
- Changing existing tables

- Deleting tables
- Creating indexes
- Deleting indexes

You can also modify indexes, column definitions and other attributes of the tables in your system by working directly with the objects in the system. For more information on this, inspect Access' on-line help topics as they relate to Indexes and Fields.

In the next section, we'll review each of these and how to use them. Each of the DDL queries is run by either creating a temporary `QueryDef`, or by running the query from the SQL editor.

Running DDL Queries from the SQL Editor

When you run DDL queries, you'll be running them as SQL-specific queries. They are not interpreted as other types of queries because they don't return any information and are used in a different way, to alter the database tables and indexes in your system.

To create and run a DDL query, create a query as normal, but don't add any tables to the QBE Grid. From the Query menu, select SQL Specific, and then Data Definition.

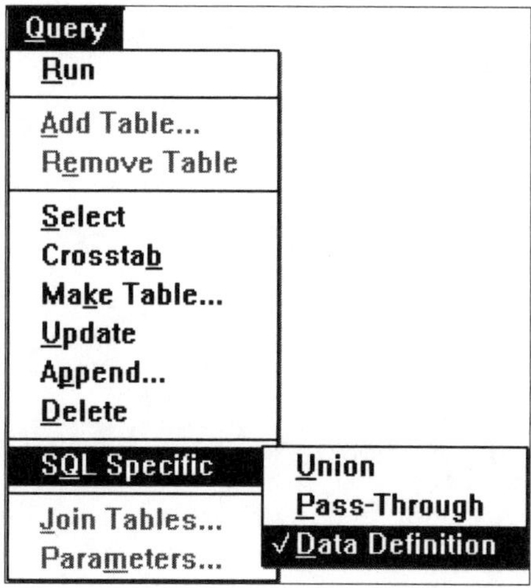

This will bring up the standard SQL statement editing window, but will omit the standard Access **SELECT DISTINCTROW** that is usually added for you. From here, you can enter the statement as you need.

As you read through the commands and their uses given below, the SQL statements can be entered and executed from this SQL editing window, or can be entered as temporary **QueryDef**s as outlined next.

Running DDL Queries from Access Basic

You can also run DDL queries from within your Access Basic routines. Since these creations are generally only run once, you'll probably be running them as temporary queries. You can create temporary **QueryDef**s by not specifying a name for the query when you create it. With this in mind, you can create temporary queries that you can use to perform DDL tasks. Here's an Access Basic example, taken from the **SAMPLES.MDB** in the DDL Samples module:

```
Sub CreateIndexProc ()
    'This procedure creates an index on the table
    '"MyTable" on the Field1 field.  If successful,
    'a message indicating success is printed to the
    'debug (immediate) window.  If not, the error
    'message is printed to the window.

    On Error GoTo CreateIndexProcErr

    Dim MyDB As Database
    Dim MyQuery As QueryDef
    Set MyDB = CurrentDB()
    Set MyQuery = MyDB.CreateQueryDef("")
    MyQuery.SQL = "Create Index Test on MyTable(Field1)"
    MyQuery.Execute (MDB_SQLPASSTHROUGH)
    Debug.Print "Index created on MyTable.Field1"

ExitSub:
    Exit Sub

CreateIndexProcErr:
    Debug.Print Error$
    Resume ExitSub

End Sub
```

To see this running, open the immediate window and type in createindexproc:

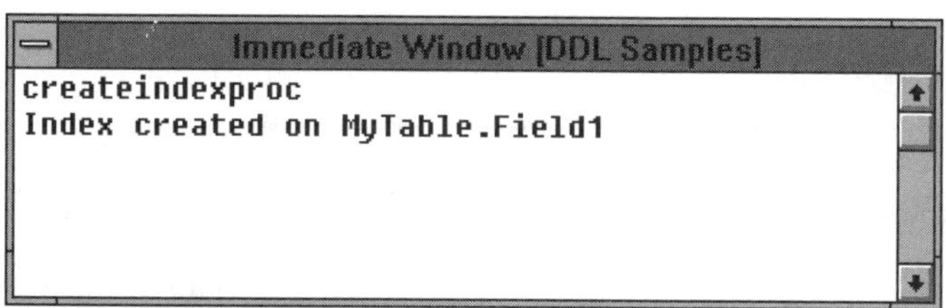

You can check that the procedure has done its work by looking at the MyTable table in design view, and more specifically the indexes created upon that table:

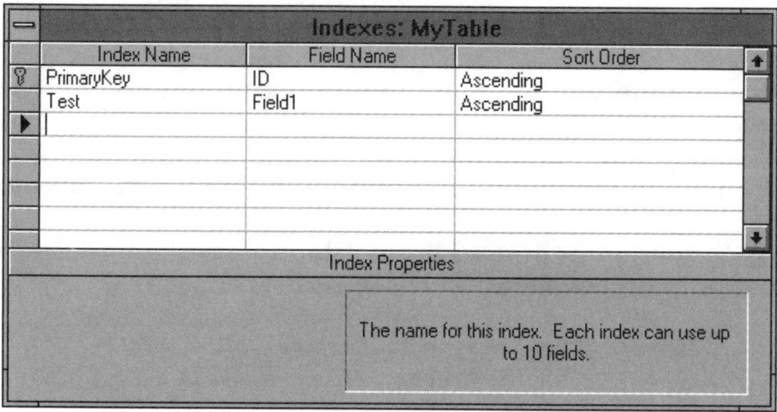

As you can see, Field0 is now listed as one of the indexes. The next sections outline the different DDL statements available and how to use them.

Creating New Tables with DDL

The Access DDL language statements support the creation of tables with the use of the **CREATE TABLE** statement. This statement allows you to specify the name of the table and the fields that we make up the table. Once created with initial fields, you can use the **ALTER TABLE** statement to modify the structure of the table.

The syntax for the **CREATE TABLE** statement is:

```
CREATE TABLE tablename ([Field1] Type (Size), [Field2]
Type (Size), .....)
```

For example, suppose you want to create the following table:

Field	Type	Size	Description
Name	Text	50	Name of the individual
Phone	Text	20	Phone number for the person

To create that table using DDL, you would use the following statement:

```
CREATE TABLE MyDemo ([Name] TEXT (50) , [Phone] TEXT (20))
```

If we wanted to add an index to the Name field we would use the **CONSTRAINT** clause on the end of the **CREATE TABLE** statement. The syntax for the **CONSTRAINT** clause is:

```
CONSTRAINT ConstraintName ConstraintType ([FieldName])
```

Therefore, the complete SQL statement to take full advantage of the DDL statements we have covered would be:

```
CREATE TABLE MyDemo ([Name] TEXT (50) , [Phone] TEXT (20),
CONSTRAINT MyConstraint UNIQUE ([Name]))
```

This code is in the CreateTable query in the **SAMPLES.MDB**. If you run the query and switch to the Tables tab, you'll see that a new table called MyDemo has been created and if you open it in design view, you'll see the two fields defined, with a unique key applied to the Name field.

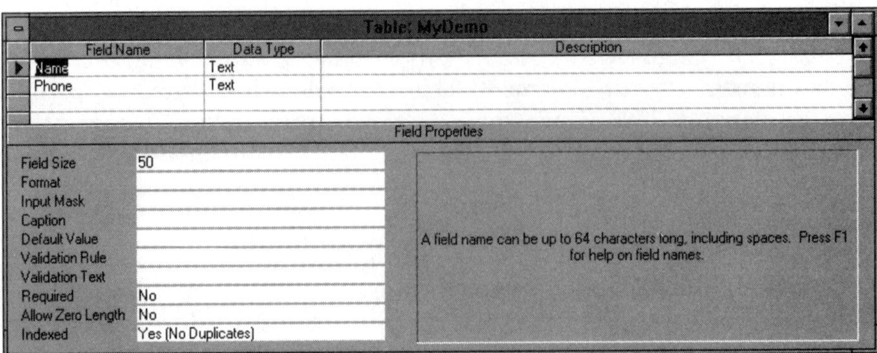

The **CONSTRAINT** statement has many forms, the simplest of which is shown here. The different types of constraint available are:

UNIQUE	All values entered in the specified field must be unique. If it is not, Access will fail updates to the database, returning an error message or number to the requesting application.
PRIMARY KEY	This is the same as setting the primary key in the design view of a table. This indicates that this key is the first and most commonly used method of accessing the information in the table. Often this is a record counter and, by definition, the primary key must also be a unique key.
FOREIGN KEY	If you specify a foreign key, you can use fields in the current table to reference another table. These are often used to maintain relational integrity.

If there is already a table defined with the name you specify, you'll receive an error message, and this is also true for the indexes. In addition, if you specify that you want to create an index as a Primary Key and a primary key already exists, you'll also receive an error message. For example, if you try running the CreateTable query again, you'll get this error message:

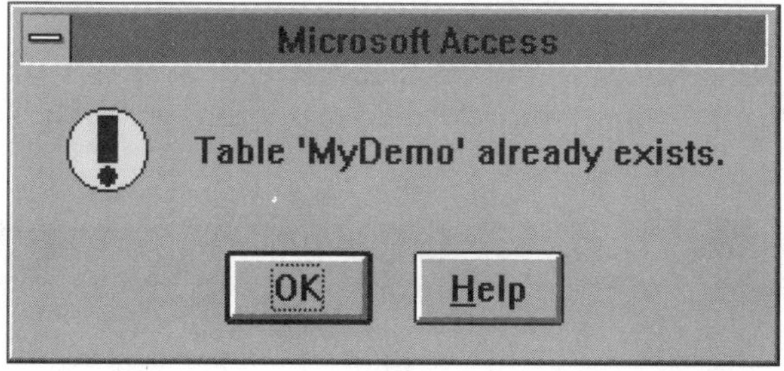

As we indicated above, you can execute the **CREATE TABLE** command either from the SQL editor or from Access Basic. Once you've created a table, you can use the **ALTER TABLE** and **DROP TABLE** statements to further refine its structure.

Changing Existing Tables with DDL

Often you'll need to add fields to an existing table after it's in production. This may be the case in a system upgrade, or it could come into play in the daily operation of a system when you realize that an additional field would be helpful. You can change the database from the design mode, but you can retain more control over the update process if you implement the changes from within your program. From within an Access Basic program, you'll be able to ensure that the changes are made and are successful, which is helpful as you won't be relying on the user to make the changes for you.

When you need to change an existing table, you should use the **ALTER TABLE** statement. The syntax is almost the same as for the **CREATE TABLE** command with the addition of two keywords, **ADD** and **DROP**.

> *For information on adding and deleting indexes, see the Creating and Deleting Index section that follow.*

```
ALTER TABLE tablename ADD [NewFieldName] Type (Size)
```

or

```
ALTER TABLE tablename DROP [ExistingFieldName] Type (Size)
```

For example, to add a field to our example table, the statement would be:

```
ALTER TABLE MyDemo ADD [NewField] TEXT (50)
```

This is the AlterTable query in the **SAMPLES.MDB**. If you run this and review the table, you'll notice that the NewField field has been added to the top of the table definition:

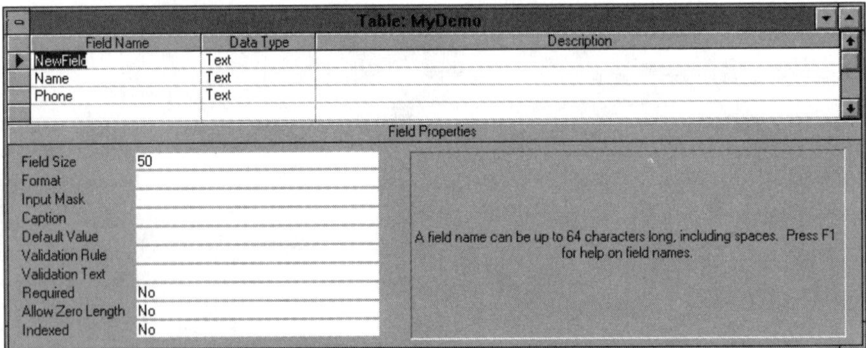

This won't impact your use of the table, except in extreme situations. For example, if you have routines that take the fields in order without regard to their name and type, you would have to alter your routines to recognize the field names.

Using DDL, you can create and manage temporary tables as needed for your applications. As we've seen, you can create tables and modify their structure, but if you are working with temporary tables, you'll also need to know how to delete them from the database. The next topic, about dropping database tables, will explain exactly how you can do this using DDL.

Deleting Tables with DDL

Deleting, or dropping, tables is one of the easiest things you can do with DDL. This fact warrants an informational warning, as there is no run-time warning or option of canceling this action. Make sure you've backed up all information that you don't care to lose prior to removing a table.

The DDL statement to drop a table is:

```
DROP TABLE tablename
```

For example, to drop the MyDemo table we would use the command:

```
DROP TABLE MyDemo
```

If the database table doesn't exist, you'll receive an error message indicating the problem, otherwise the table will be removed from the database immediately. After you remove a table, it's probably a good idea to 'compact' the database. This will free up the space in the database no longer used by the table and help to keep your database optimized.

Note that you can't compact a database when it is open and that you must have enough memory on your hard drive for the old database and the compacted one.

Creating Indexes with DDL

As explained under the **CREATE TABLE** options above, you can create indexes when you create the table. However, after you have created the table you may need to add an index to it, often to enhance the overall performance of the system. Once you've determined which field or fields you want to include in the index, you can add new indexes, or modify existing ones, using the DDL statements outlined here.

To create a new index, you use the **CREATE INDEX** statement. The syntax is:

```
CREATE INDEX indexname ON tablename ([fieldname])
WITH PRIMARY
```

or

```
CREATE INDEX indexname ON tablename ([fieldname])
WITH DISALLOW NULL
```

or

```
CREATE INDEX indexname ON tablename ([fieldname])
WITH IGNORE NULL
```

The **WITH** clause allows you to specify three different options:

PRIMARY Create the index as the primary key. If there is already an index defined as the primary key, you'll receive an error message indicating the problem.

DISALLOW NULL Don't allow Null entries in this index fields. If the user enters a null value in this column, they will receive an error message indicating that nulls are not allowed.

IGNORE NULL Nulls will be allowed in this column, but they will not be used as index values. In essence, rows that have null entries in the column will be ignored if the data access path is using this index.

The CreateIndex query in the **SAMPLES.MDB** creates an index on the Phone field of the MyDemo table called phonenum with the disallows nulls option:

```
CREATE INDEX phonenum ON MyDemo ([Phone])
WITH DISALLOW NULL
```

If you run the query and look at the MyDemo table definition, you'll see that the index has been added to the Phone field:

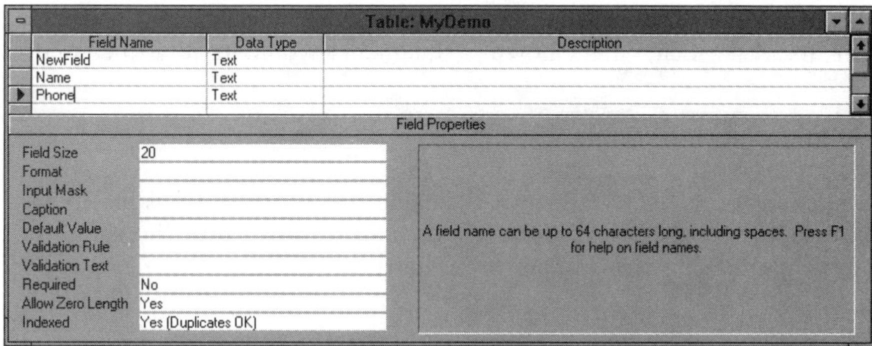

Once the index has been created, you can reference it by the name you assigned to it. So, in our example we would refer to the index using the name phonenum.

Deleting Indexes with DDL

As with tables, removing indexes is quite straightforward. Unlike the operation with tables, no information is removed from the system, other than the pointer information maintained within the index and no data is lost.

To remove an index, you use the **DROP** statement, as outlined below:

```
DROP INDEX indexname ON tablename
```

So for our example above, we would remove the index on the Phone field using the following statement:

```
DROP INDEX phonenum ON MyDemo
```

This will remove the index from the database. Since you generally reference indexes by name from within Access Basic code, you'll need to update the module code to use a different index if you have routines that refer to the index you have just removed.

Changing Indexes with DDL

There is no direct way to change an existing index on an Access table. The only way to modify the index and its associated settings is to issue two commands. The first command will drop the index, while the second will recreate it to match your changed definition.

For example, if we wanted to change the phonenum index created above to index on the Name field, the following statements would need to be used:

```
DROP INDEX phonenum on MyDemo
CREATE INDEX newindex on MyDemo([Name])
```

This would create the new index on the table and make it available to the application. This would also be true if you needed to modify the status of the index, perhaps making it a unique or primary index.

> *Note that if the name of the new index is the same as the old one, then any code that used the old index will automatically make use of the 'modified' addition to the table.*

Additional Uses

You can use the DDL and SQL commands in your applications in many ways. The first and most obvious place that you'll use these commands is within your application itself. However, you should keep in mind that these commands may come in handy if you are faced with any of the following situations:

Performing a system upgrade — In this case, you can use the DDL commands to insert new tables from within the Setup program. You can specify the program to run after the setup process has completed. You use the Setup Wizard to create the installation program and the script that will run the additional application after the installation process has been completed.

Making changes to existing production databases — If you are faced with a requirement to update production databases, you can use the DDL functions to add indexes, columns and modify definitions included within the database tables. All of this can be accomplished while operating with live data in the system.

You should always backup any system before performing this type of operation, or any other upgrade or installation operation.

Tuning the system

As you and your users implement a system, you can begin to watch for usage patterns and other workflow issues. These items will help you determine whether additional indexes are in order. It may be a good idea to add a derived column and create an index on it. This can greatly enhance performance on the system.

As you can see, the DDL and SQL commands are very powerful. Be sure to use the QBE's SQL statement building capabilities as you learn more about creating statements for your systems. Additional assistance can be found by searching Access' on-line help system for the specific method or property you need to work with.

Comments and Suggestions

This chapter has been a gentle introduction to SQL but we hope that we've shown you how powerful it can be. We've looked at the most commonly used SQL statement, the SELECT statement and seen how you can use the DDL commands in your Access Basic code to create and define tables. If you want to learn more about SQL try searching in Access's on-line help or look in the Language Reference Manual.

CHAPTER 11

Using ODBC or Jet Data Sources

Due to its inherent design features, Access is a very flexible data exchange tool. Microsoft have implemented as much functionality as they could into the product, supporting it with ODBC and supplying a whole range of ODBC drivers for other systems. This makes Access into a 'gateway' for Legacy to Client/Server transfers.

What's Covered in This Chapter

This chapter shows how you can use Access in a slightly different manner than you may expect. In several examples, we show how you can use Access to filter data from an external source, such as a mainframe download, and then how to import this information into Access. We'll also show how you can then send this information from your Access tables to a back-end server, such as SQL Server.

In this chapter, we'll cover the following different areas:

- How to install and set up ODBC drivers
- How to attach tables to your Access database
- How to convert information from a text file
- How to use Access to channel information from an external, non-database file to an ODBC database, converting data types along the way
- How to create a system in Access, then convert it to an intelligent back-end server, such as Microsoft SQL Server

Using Access can save you many hours of time when working with unknown or foreign database export file formats, externally attached database tables and other data sources. This chapter will explain all of these details and more.

Chapter 11

How This Chapter Impacts Our Application

While not impacting the design and implementation of our PIM directly, this chapter can be used as a starting point for importing data from an existing system into the PIM application. In addition, this chapter shows how you can send the information from your PIM database table structure to external database systems, providing an 'up-sizing' capability for the PIM application.

Introduction

Access employs many different tools designed for developing and maintaining Access-based systems. These tools can prove to be extremely helpful if you are involved in a lot of conversion or test projects. Once information is under the control of Access, you can modify the database table formats, create relationships and otherwise clean up the information before moving it to its final destination.

Our sample scenarios guide you through the process of importing a file of text values, cleaning up the file for use in another system and exporting the file to the other database structure. Access provides the data modeling and structure tools that you will need to accomplish this.

Since Access is so visual in its presentation of information, it provides some added benefits over more traditional data manipulation techniques. Specifically, you can see the structure and modify how the import process will run as well as many other useful functions, all from within the user interface.

When you're working with systems that are moving over from legacy systems, it's usually easier to allow Access to do the table creation against the other servers, control the import and all the other processes involved. Access makes the conversions much faster and much easier. Many times when people are cutting over from legacy systems, the conversion process can be largely automated using Access' built-in intelligence.

What are Open DataBase Connectivity Data Sources?

The Microsoft Open DataBase Connectivity (ODBC) specification was created with the hope of making it easier for a developer to write to different database back-end providers. The goal is to allow creation of programs that can talk to multiple back-end data servers without modification. You could create a program that used an Access database and associated tables today, and you could take this same program and use it against an SQL Server, dBase or Btrieve back-end tomorrow.

This would all be possible without changes to the actual program code because it would be the layer of drivers situated between the Access application and the back-end database that needed to be altered.

ODBC is shipped with many different packages. Some specific packages are Microsoft's Office automation suite, Access and Visual Basic. You can also find the full ODBC API and reference materials on Microsoft's suite of technical reference CDs. Version 2.0 of ODBC is due to be released shortly and should be available by the time this book goes to press. While functionality will be increased and some setup options may be added, the information that is important to us here will not change.

If you are creating a system to replace an existing setup, you should check with the database vendor for your existing system to see if an ODBC driver is available. There are drivers now on the market for everything from Mainframe systems to dBase, Btrieve and other ISAM systems. There is a good possibility that a driver is available and this can greatly ease the conversion of your existing databases to your new system.

A Transition Layer

ODBC serves as a translation layer between your application and the underlying database system. When you make a call to the database system, ODBC will determine whether Access can work with the database natively, with the Jet Engine, or whether it will need to translate the instructions traveling between the processes. Functionally, your application won't be able to tell the difference as the database access is implemented 'under the covers'. More information on the Jet Engine is provided in the next section:

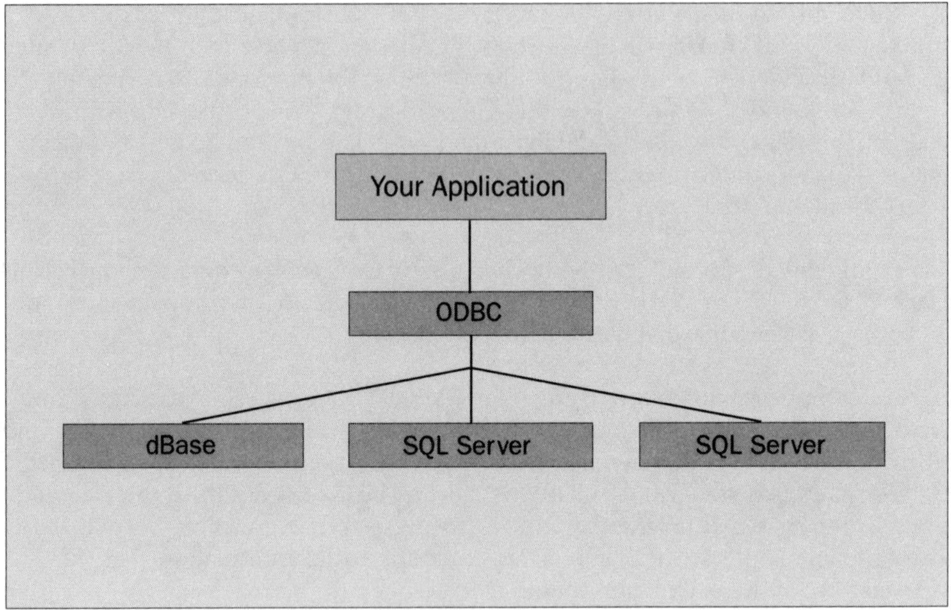

When your application makes a request of the database, whether it's a **SELECT** type statement or a complete table query, the ODBC layer will be called in to translate the call. The ODBC DLLs know how to translate your request into the language understood by the underlying system. In addition, the ODBC layer will manage the return of information to your application in a manner that Access will understand.

The Consequences of Using ODBC

You can imagine that this functionality doesn't come without consequences. There are a few things that you'll need to consider when using an ODBC data source in your applications.

First, by definition, ODBC must use a least common denominator approach to working with the database it supports. This means that the functionality and the calls supported by the driver must be limited to the abilities of the least capable system. Since ODBC must allow you to make the same call to any supported subsystem, the call must be supported by all subsystems. This can come into play in how you work with intelligent back-ends like those from Microsoft, Sybase and Oracle. Each of these server products have different features. It may be that your purchase decision for your database server was made based on a specific feature or capability. Check with your vendor for an ODBC driver and documentation for a complete listing of features that are, and are not, implemented in the ODBC driver.

Second, ODBC is not highly optimized for all sources. While it does a great job managing the information, again it must be able to talk with database back-ends in a standard way, not a different way for every server. The overhead associated with ODBC can be substantial and shows in the performance of your system.

There are places you can help in the optimization of different queries and other operations and some of these will be outlined in both this chapter and the next.

Third, be sure you understand the data type mapping between your specific server and your Access application. In many cases, the data types don't map in a one-to-one fashion. A good example of this one-to-many mapping are dates, which require either coding or database structure modifications on one side of the equation. Specific data type representations for many servers are included in the next chapter; you should also check with your ODBC driver documentation for any other type mappings.

In the examples in this chapter, we're using several different database table formats. It's important to understand that the rules and observations that apply to these database types may apply to multiple formats, not just the specific formats listed. The table on the next page indicates similar file types as they relate to these discussions.

Database Type	Related Providers
xBase Type Files	dBase, Foxpro
Client server information providers	Microsoft SQL Server, Sybase SQL Server, Oracle Server. There may be some differences in specific instructions you pass to the server, especially in the case of creating pass-through queries.

When we mention these data source types in the discussions, we'll be using them interchangeably. The one important database that is not covered by these global formats is that of Btrieve. Since this is such a different format, the specific implementation steps to using a Btrieve file have been discussed separately.

ODBC Maintenance

ODBC data sources are maintained in the **ODBC.INI** file, located in your **WINDOWS** subdirectory. The entries in this file are used when you select the type of database to access from within Access or other services that use ODBC. They are also used by the name you specify as the Data Source Name during setup. The **ODBC.INI** file is broken into two basic sections; one showing the different sources available and one showing specific configuration information for each of these sources:

```
[ODBC Data Sources]
MS Access Databases=Access Data (*.mdb)
FoxPro Files=FoxPro Files (*.dbf)
dBase Files=dBase Files (*.dbf)
Paradox Files=Paradox Files (*.db )
NWind=dBase Files (*.dbf)
MS Access 2.0 Databases=Access 2.0 for MS Office (*.mdb)
```

This header portion shows each of the different ODBC sources that are installed, along with the plain English description of the source and its file specification. You may recall from our use of the .INI File Manager add-in that you use this information to operate the Windows Common Dialog box for file selection. This is the information that Access will use to open databases when the user requests it to do so.

A typical set of ODBC entries is shown next:

```
[FoxPro Files]
Driver=C:\WINDOWS\SYSTEM\simba.dll
FileType=FoxPro 2.5
SingleUser=False
```

The driver's DLL file that should be used, along with other information, is provided under this entry. When a file of this type is accessed, the ODBC layer will then know what other software needs to be loaded to help in the translation process.

You shouldn't make changes to this file directly; instead, use the ODBC Manager from the control panel to maintain these data sources. The ODBC Manager is configured to provide information specific to the driver you are setting up and will ensure that all the required information is provided in the .INI file's settings. More information on using the ODBC Manager is provided in the next section.

Installing ODBC on Your System

The first step is to install the ODBC access files that are required for the data source. Typically, the database that you need to access will provide these for you. The ODBC installation process follows the same steps as typical Windows installations, prompting you for subdirectories and other information required to initialize the drivers. Several DLLs are copied to your system, generally into the **WINDOWS** and **WINDOWS\SYSTEM** directories.

The setup process will also prompt you for the types of ODBC access that you need to install:

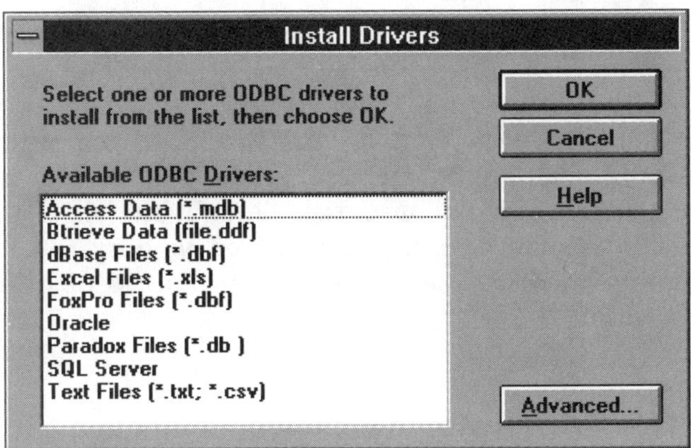

Select the driver and press OK. You'll be prompted for any additional information that may be needed to complete the installation. This information will vary depending on the type of driver you are installing.

After the files are copied into your Windows installation, you can configure the ODBC driver so that it points directly to the data source you need. For example, you can establish an ODBC data source that specifies the .MDB file as its target. Then, when you reference that ODBC setup, you will not need to select a specific database as it will already be specified.

Using the Control Panel to Set Up Data Sources

Before you can begin using ODBC data sources in your application, you must first set them up. This is done with the ODBC Manager that is started from the Control Panel. The ODBC icon will not appear in the Control Panel until after you've installed an ODBC-aware application. These applications include Microsoft Office, Access and Visual Basic:

When you start the ODBC Manager, you are first presented with a list of drivers indicating the interface or database option you want to set up. This information is determined by the **ODBC.INI** file and lists all of the different ODBC data sources that are currently installed on your system. For each existing data source, you have the option of setting it up or deleting it, as well as adding a new driver:

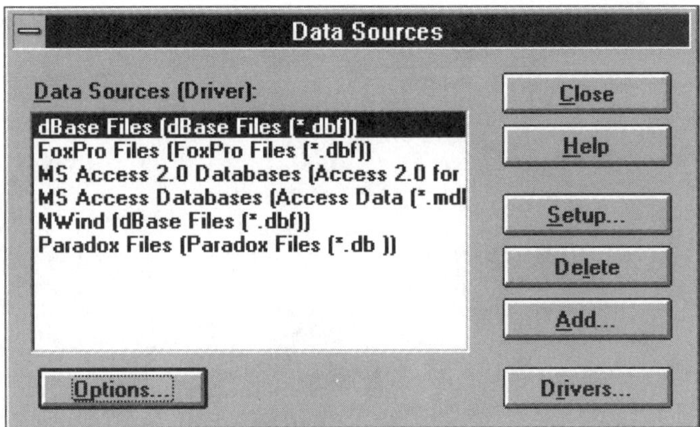

The ODBC setup dialog box allows you to establish exactly how the driver should function, including what database to attach to, what language translation layer to use and so on. Note that the actual configuration options available to you for any given ODBC setup will vary. This is because the information required to attach to the database will vary depending on the back-end.

The following two screens show the setup screens, after the Setup... button was selected, for both Access and SQL Server ODBC database setup:

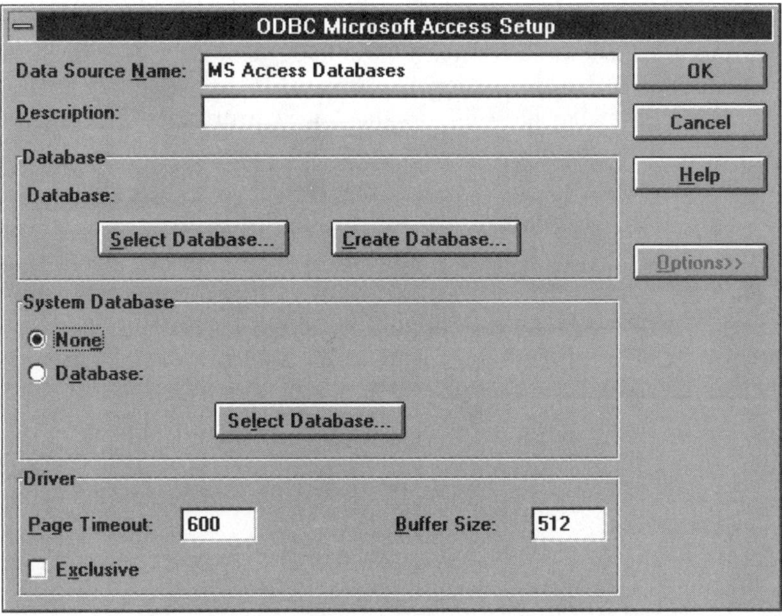

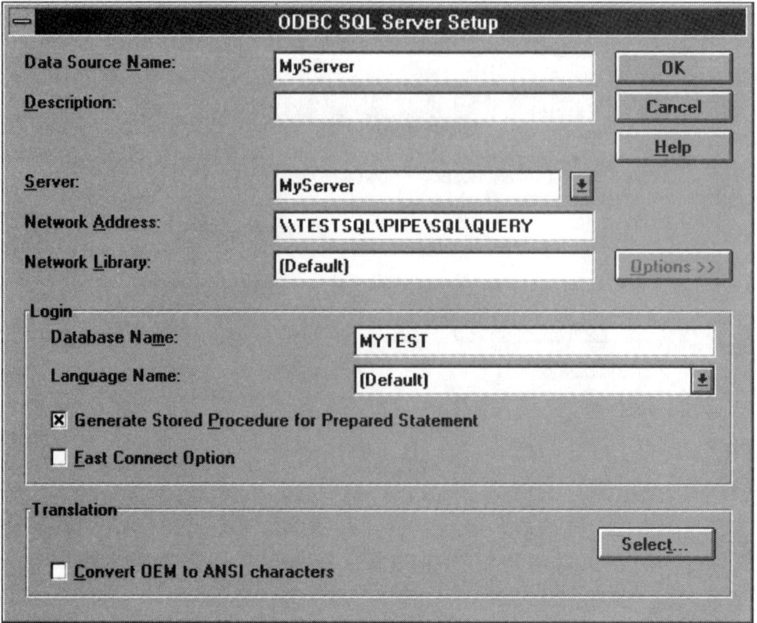

From this dialog box, you can select an existing database or create a new one that will be referenced by ODBC when you use this configuration option.

You use the name you provide as the Data Source Name in your connect string from within Access Basic code or with the ODBC Connection String Builder. To access the builder, create a new query in Access. From the Query menu, select SQL Specific, then Pass-Through. Call up the query properties from the View menu to set the ODBC Connect string.

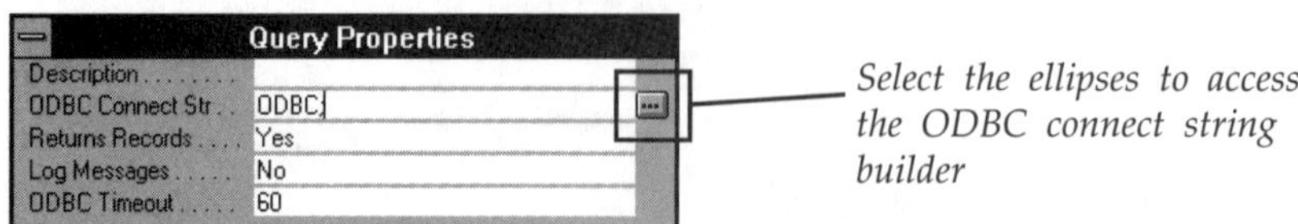

Select the ellipses to access the ODBC connect string builder

The connect string is used by ODBC to determine what type of data source you need to access. Note that if you specify only 'ODBC;', you will be prompted for the ODBC data source to connect to. The list that will be shown is the list of installed ODBC drivers that you've set up with the Windows control panel:

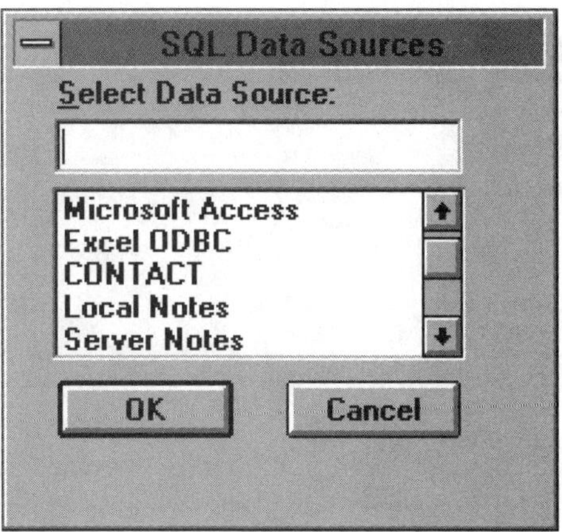

You should keep the name of your Data Source to a reasonable length. There is a bug in the ODBC handler that may require you to re-enter your user ID and password to the data source if the data source name is too long.

This problem appears by forcing you to use the login screen and specifying the data source name, your user ID and password. The first portion of the data source name is shown in the top portion of the dialog box correctly, but you'll notice it's truncated.

While the bug is intermittent, you can see if this is the culprit by shortening the name to under 15 characters and retrying the operation. If you no longer get the login prompt, you should use the shorter **Data Source Name** in your application.

Tracing ODBC Calls

On the ODBC setup dialog box, the Options button will allow you to establish tracing on all calls that are made to the ODBC API layer. This can be helpful in debugging situations where the server may not be responding exactly as you'd expect:

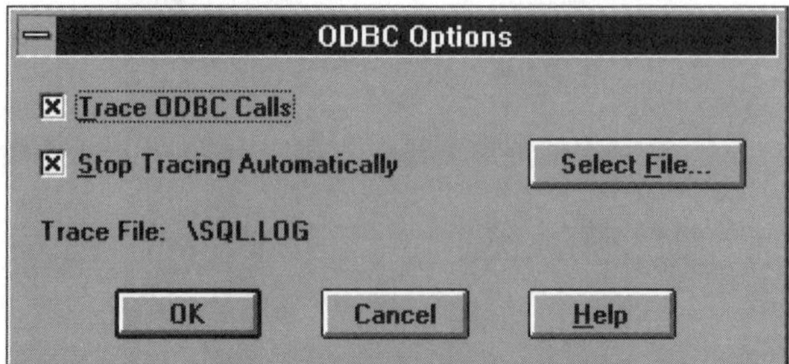

You should be aware, however, that the dump file can become quite large very quickly. In the case of SQL Server, you'll be tracing all calls made to the server engine along with supporting calls to the library layers in between ODBC and the server engine:

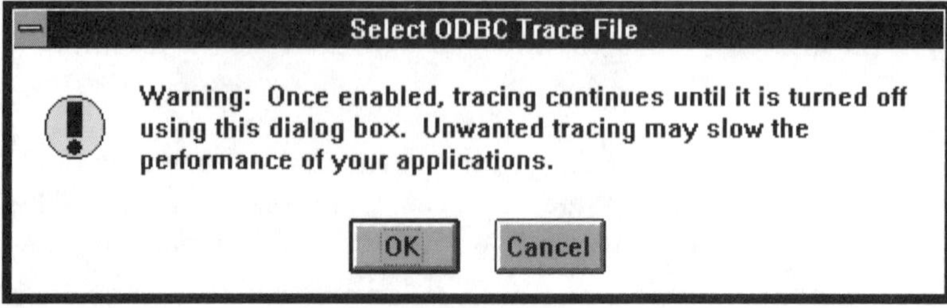

The option to Stop Tracing Automatically will trace the calls for the next session and will stop the tracing function when the session is completed. It's highly recommended that you use this option, both for file size considerations and for readability. If you know that the information in the file pertains only to a specific area of functionality that you're testing, this option will make the file contents much easier to understand.

An ODBC session runs from the time the connection to the database table is initiated to the time it is closed. You can make several queries, updates and other table operations during a single ODBC session.

The next listing shows a portion of a log file. This section attempts to connect to the SQL Server, before disconnecting immediately. Typically, your trace files will include additional items, such as querying, opening tables and so on:.

```
SQLAllocEnv(phenv782F0000);
SQLAllocConnect(henv782F0000, phdbc64670000);
SQLSetConnectOption(hdbc64670000, 103, 00000014);
SQLDriverConnect(hdbc64670000, hwnd3668, "(null)", -3,
szConnStrOut, 255, pcbConnStrOut, 1);
SQLFreeConnect(hdbc64670000);
```

What Are Jet Data Sources?

The database engine based at the heart of Access, allowing entrance to your database tables as well as other data sources is called the Jet Engine. Jet was developed as a high-performance database access layer to get at the proprietary level of several database formats, namely dBase and Paradox files. Jet provides access to defined data sources, whereas ODBC provides a driver-level interface. ODBC is more versatile as it can be modified by simply inserting a new library function to support new, updated database back-ends. The Jet Engine is optimized to work with the selected databases and therefore may be incompatible with some more obscure systems.

If you plan to use Visual Basic 3 Jet Engine with your Access databases, you may need to install the Compatibility layer. This layer updates the interface between VB and the Jet Engine to work with the new Access 2.0 formats. Be sure to run the compatibility layer in a test environment prior to installing it on a large number of systems. Since the Jet Engine impacts more than just the Access databases, you should confirm that no other adverse effects are apparent with your other data sources prior to introducing it to a production environment.

Jet is somewhat like ODBC in that it provides the access to the underlying database tables. The differences are that it is aimed at providing an interface to more specific database types, like Access, xBase and Paradox. ODBC was developed as a more open standard in an attempt to avoid limiting its focus and capabilities. Jet's capabilities include attaching external files to the current database definition and the provision of access to more than one .MDB at a time.

The Jet Engine can become a resident on your system when you install many different products, including Access, Visual Basic and Microsoft Office. Configuration options within Access are maintained in the `MSACC20.INI` file; for Visual Basic, the `VB.INI` file is used. The ISAM section contains two settings that allow you to tune your installation:

MaxBufferSize This option's default value is 512, but can range from 18 to 4096. Each step is one 2,048 byte (2K) page of data that Access will read in.

Note that, on systems with smaller amounts of installed memory, decreasing this value will allow other Access functions more memory and may increase performance. Before you change this option, determine whether your system is disk bound.

If you notice that there is a large amount of disk access time, increasing this value may improve performance. The setting will vary from system to system as installed options, like add-ins, active Windows applications and so on, will have an impact upon the best setting for this option. The only way to determine the best setting for your system is by experimenting.

ReadAheadPages This option configures the number of 2,048 byte pages of memory to optimize disk access. As Access retrieves information from disk, it is read in pages. Increasing this value from its default setting of 16 may increase performance on your system. It will also detract from the amount of memory available to other Access processes, so experiment with this option as well. This can be set to any value from 0 to 31. Setting this option to 0 will disable the read-ahead option altogether.

In Access, the section name is **`[ISAM]`**. *In other systems, the section name may change. For example, in Visual Basic, the section name is* **`[Installable ISAMs]`**. *You'll have to review your .INI file for the specific section name used. In addition, your application may have a custom .INI file that specifies the database interface options available. In this case, be sure to contact the vendor if you have any questions and before you make changes to their system settings.*

In addition, the Jet engine implements the Data Access Objects Model when working with your databases. While Dynaset and Snapshot type objects are still valid and available with the new Data Access Objects, additional objects and collections are also available to you. The following figure shows an abbreviated listing of the various objects and collections available:

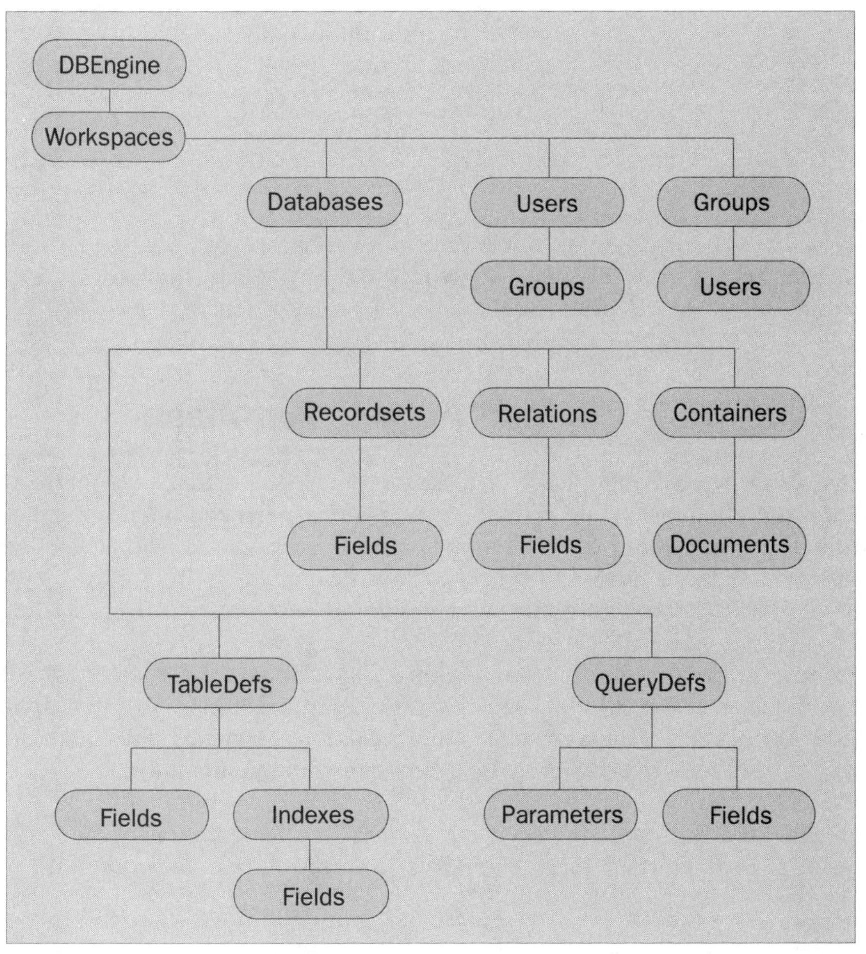

Jet Object/Collection	Description
Database(s)	Open database/collection of open databases
DBEngine	The reference to the Jet database engine
Field(s)	Field in a table, query, recordset, index, or relation/collection of fields in a table, query, recordset, index or relation
Index(es)	Table index/collection of table indexes
Parameter(s)	Query parameter/collection of query parameters
QueryDef(s)	Saved query in a database/collection of saved queries in a database
Recordset(s)	Set of records defined by a table or query/ collection of recordsets
TableDef(s)	Saved table in a database/collection of saved tables in a database

Objects are singular, while collections of objects are plural. For example, the Database object refers to a specific database, while the Databases collection refers to all of the databases currently open.

Attaching Tables to Your Access Database

When you first started working with Access, chances are that you worked with native Access databases. This is how most people learn the environment and how to create the custom forms, reports, queries and macros. However, one of the most prized facets of Microsoft's PC based database is its ability to use database tables that are not of its own native format.

For example, suppose you have an existing name and address database from which you'd like to be able to keep the existing information. You can **attach** this database to your Access system. Once you have attached the database, you can use the different tools offered by Access to manipulate the data.

Attaching databases is accomplished by Access' implementation of two different standards. The simplest of these standards used by Access to work with various databases is the Jet database engine. This engine provides access to many different database formats and is optimized to enhance performance for those systems.

Microsoft's ODBC interface standard provides access to an ever-increasing array of varied database systems. Everything from Microsoft's SQL Server to proprietary database systems is supported by this standard, with more support announced on a regular basis.

How to Attach Files to an Access Database

Attaching files is a simple and straight-forward process when working within Access. From the File menu, select Attach Table... You will be presented with a dialog box prompting for the type of file to attach:

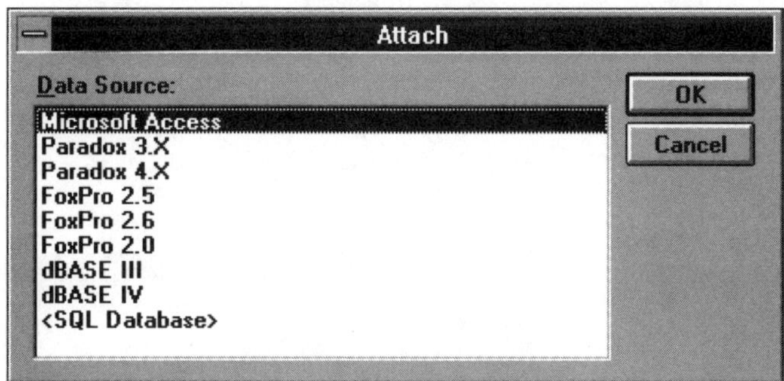

After you've selected the database type, the process of choosing the exact table to attach will vary slightly from type to type. For example, if you select <SQL Database>, you be prompted for the data source, followed by the UserID and password for the data source. Access will attempt to sign-on to the SQL database and will then present you with a list of available tables.

Tables in a SQL Server type environment have an 'owner', usually specified in Access by showing a table name with a prefix of DBO. When the table is attached, the DBO is changed to a prefix of 'dbo_' and becomes part of the table name as a default. You can rename the table as you wish.

If you select another type of Jet or other ISAM-type database to attach, you will be allowed to select the file that contains the database. The Select File dialog box is used to allow you to select the file:

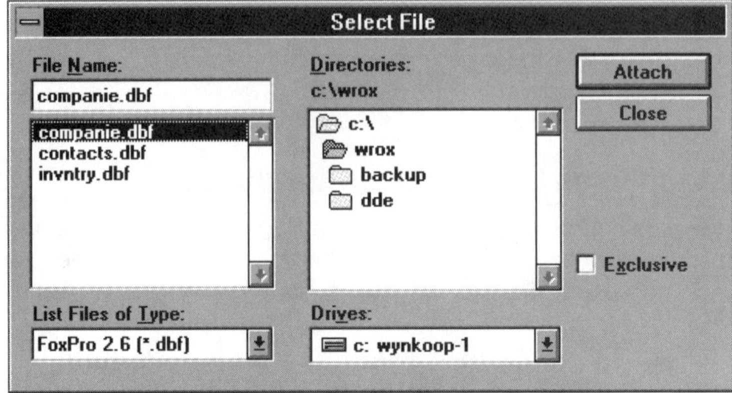

Once you select the file, you may be prompted to indicate any externally maintained indexes that should be used with the attached file:

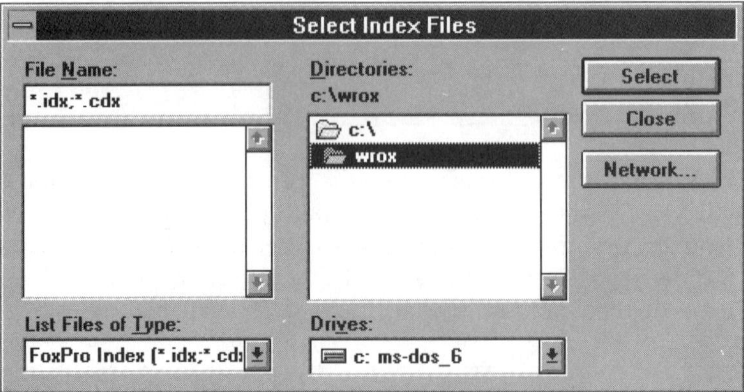

If there is an index, specify it and click the Select button. Once completed, Access will insert the file in the database tabbed dialog and place a custom icon next to it indicating that the listed table represents an attached table.

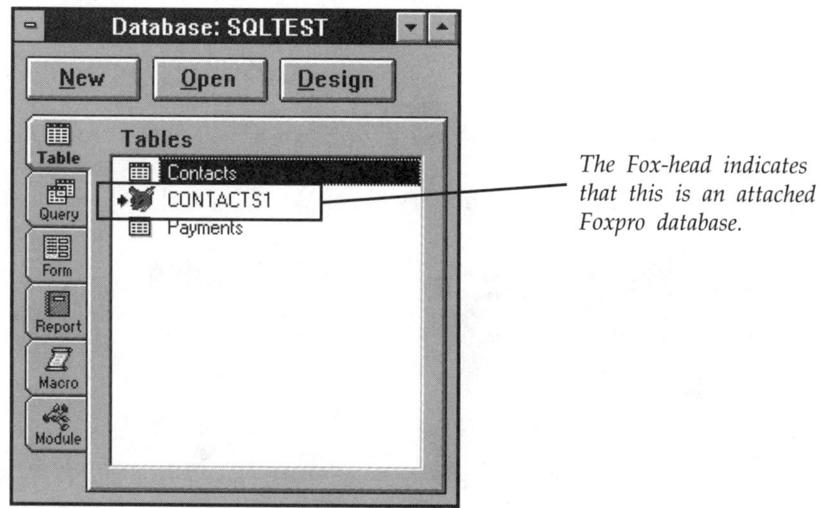

As you attach a table, and a table of the same name already exists, Access will add a number to the end of the new table's name, thus making the name unique.

If you attach a .DBF file and associate an index (.IDX, .CDX, .NDX or .MDX) file for the attached table, Access will need the index file you specify to open the attached table in the future. The location of the index file is maintained in an information file with an .INF extension. If you delete or move index files or the created information (.INF) file, you won't be able to open the attached table.

You may want to keep all .INF files created for your system in a common location, or you may be using a source drive that doesn't allow you to write to it. In these cases, you can modify the **[dBASE ISAMs]** section of your **MSACC20.INI** file.

If you want to place the .INF file in the **C:\ACCESS** directory, you would add the following line:

```
INFPath=C:\ACCESS
```

All .INF files would then be stored on your C: drive, in the **ACCESS** directory.

Designing Attached Tables

There may be some operations that you can't complete against the external database that you've attached. As a reminder of this fact, when you go into design view for an attached table, Access will warn you that certain facets can't be changed. These unchangeable items include database table structure and field attributes, but you can modify the field names, if you require:

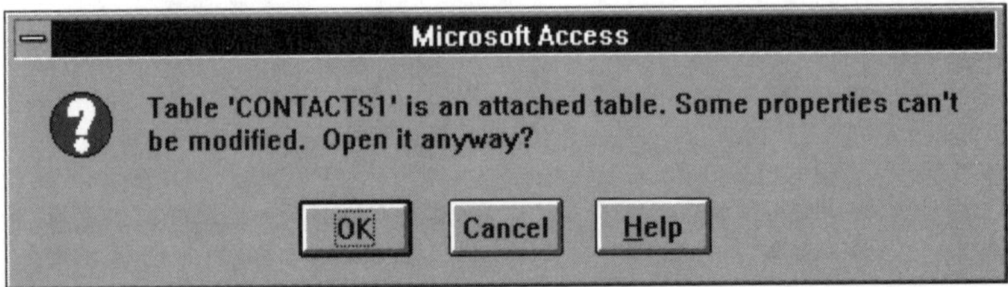

Pros and Cons of Having a Mixed Database Environment

It may have occurred to you that if you use a mixed environment in your application, several things may become considerations. Of primary concern is performance. With attached tables, complex operations can be a real performance detriment. When you create a relationship across attached tables, Access must manually maintain this relationship, while translating commands to the languages and protocols understood by the underlying database system at the same time. The rule to remember here is to avoid creating joins between tables of different types.

If you have a varied database environment, it's generally a good idea to convert to either a native Access format or intelligent server back-end product rather than maintain a system of attached flat-file or ISAM-type databases. The capability to use sophisticated processing across technically unrelated, foreign database types is better used as a conversion and upsizing tool, rather than a long-term strategy.

Transaction Considerations

From our discussions in earlier chapters, you may recall that using transactions in a mixed environment can be very difficult. One of the reasons for this is that you often can't `RollBack` an action made on an attached table. However, you may write calls within an Access transaction that watch the status of operations and manually cause the Access transaction to roll-back in an error condition.

There are some database back-ends that will support 'integrated' transaction processing. These databases, generally supported by the Jet database engine, are able to support transactions across databases. For information on which databases support this capability, check with either the database vendor or the Microsoft Office Developer's Kit.

Working with Btrieve Data Files

If you are going to be working with Btrieve data files, you'll need to take a few additional steps before you can begin working with them. Of primary importance is that Btrieve data access requires a Novell-specific function library, **WBTRCALL.DLL**, not included with Access. You'll need to obtain this from either Novell or a software vendor that is using the Btrieve function libraries. In any case, you will not be able to access Btrieve files without this library.

General Information

The following list is a compilation of interesting items about the use of Btrieve files in an Access system. If you encounter problems when working with this file format, it will probably be due to one of these situations. Some relate to your options and configurations, while others will define whether or not the system will actually work at all:

- Access will not recognize indexes created with alternate collating sequences. The most common of these is UPPER, forcing the index to ignore the case of the index contents. You can determine if you're using the UPPER alternate collating sequence by reviewing the file structure. Btrieve will indicate whether an alternate collating sequence is in use.
- Access can't work with manual, external or null indexes.
- If you have indices defined by segmenting partial fields together to form the index, Access will not be able to use the index.
- Other indices will be used by Access automatically.

Data Definition Files

If you've worked with Btrieve files in the past, you'll know that Btrieve works with the files without regard to the concept of fields or columns of information. Btrieve works with a buffer of data, indexing on specific sections of the data, specified by indicating a start and stop location in the buffer.

Access is a field-driven system and maintains the names of the information, the type of underlying data and so on, in the database file. Because of this, you must define the layout of the file to Access before it is able to work with it.

The files created to provide this information to non-Btrieve systems are called DDF, or Data Definition Files. These files contain various information items about the Btrieve database and allow Access to work directly with the file. Once the DDF file is created, you'll not need to export the information from the Btrieve file to Access to begin working with it.

DDF files are created in a number of different ways. There are many shareware and publicly available DDF file builders available. CompuServe Access and Visual Basic forums are good starting points for these tools. You can also use Xtrieve, a reporting and querying tool from Novell. Xtrieve allows you to define these data dictionaries for your databases.

One final way that you can create the DDF file is from within Access. If you create a macro to reference the **TransferDatabase** command and have installed the Btrieve drivers, Access will allow you to export the database. When Access completes the process, it will have created a DDF file referencing the fields as they were defined in Access.

Settings Maintained in WIN.INI

If you're currently using Btrieve in an existing system and are trying to configure Access to read the data files from that system, you'll probably need to find out what command-line switches are used when the existing application loads. In Access, you specify startup parameters in either **WIN.INI**, for Btrieve versions before version 6.x, or **NOVDB.INI**, for versions from 6.x onwards, depending on the version of Btrieve you use. There will be a **[btrieve]** section in the file where you can place command line parameters for the initialization of the Btrieve engine:

```
[btrieve]
Options=/m:64 /p:4096 /b:16 /f:20 /l:40 /n:12 /
t:C:\ACCESS\BTRIEVE.TRN
```

As mentioned earlier, the command line switches represent the options defined by Btrieve for operations with your data files. You should carefully consider your settings for a few of these options.

Setting the Compression Buffer

One of the specific options to carefully consider is the option of setting the compression buffer. The /u switch allows you to set the compression buffer for all Btrieve database access. This parameter, specified in 1024 bytes of space, must be larger than your largest uncompressed record.

Setting the Page Size

You may be accustomed to determining the page size and setting it on the command line. In Windows, the command line must specify 4096 for the page size. This will accommodate the page size options that you may have selected when creating the database files you'll be using. The page size must be equal to or larger than the largest page size of the databases you'll be using.

Establishing the Location of the Multi-User Transaction File

If you're using a multi-user implementation of a Btrieve database, you're going to be setting up the Btrieve driver to use the Transaction file, located in a shared directory. This file enables Btrieve to determine whether a record is locked when it is requested by a system. The /t parameter specifies this option and should point to the same file on each system where it is required.

Setting Other Options

Other options are available that can be established when Btrieve starts up. These include number of open files, locks, files in a transaction and so on that are supported. Be sure to search the Access Help files for Btrieve for more information. In addition, you can find more assistance with the Microsoft ODBC Desktop Driver set. This set includes additional help files and drivers that allow you to access many different ODBC-compliant databases interfaces.

Settings Maintained in MSACC20.INI

Most of the work in using Btrieve with Access comes in making sure that the settings are defined correctly in the Access .INI file. There are several options available, ranging from command line parameters to data file configuration information. These settings are maintained in the Btrieve ISAM section of the `MSACC20.INI` configuration file:

```
[Btrieve ISAM]
DataCodePage=OEM
```

This information is taken from the Setting Microsoft Access Options for Btrieve help topic in Microsoft Access Readme Help file:

Option	Description	Example
DataCodePage	Determines the code page used for reading and writing text data. Possible values are 'OEM' and 'ANSI'. The default is 'OEM'.	DataCodePage=ANSI
OpenAccelerated	Determines whether Microsoft Access uses Btrieve accelerated access. If you set this to 'On', all other applications sharing the same tables must also use accelerated access. The default is 'Off'.	OpenAccelerated=On
NetworkAccess	Determines whether Microsoft Access uses file locking. If set to 'Off', Btrieve tables are opened exclusively regardless of how you specify options when opening the table. The default is 'On'.	NetworkAccess=Off
PageTimeout	The length of time between when data is placed in an internal cache and when it's marked to be refreshed. The settings are expressed in 100 millisecond units. The default is 600 (60 seconds).	PageTimeout=50
DDFPassword	The owner name used when opening `FILE.DDF`. You must set this option when Xtrieve-style security is enabled for your DDF file.	DDFPassword=myname

Continued

Option	Description	Example
IndexDDF	Determines whether Microsoft Access creates and maintains the **INDEX.DDF** file. Use the Maintain setting if you want Microsoft Access to update **INDEX.DDF** when it exists. Use the Require setting to always create or maintain an **INDEX.DDF** file. The default setting is Ignore, with which an **INDEX.DDF** file is never created or maintained.	IndexDDF=Maintain
XTRPATH	The list of file paths that Microsoft Access searches when trying to open Btrieve data files.	XTRPATH= c:\data;m:\data
XTRENV	The location and file name of an Xtrieve-style environment (.ENV) file that includes an XTRPATH setting.	XTRENV= c:\windows\myown.env
XTRPINDX	A number indicating which of the directories specified in the XTRPATH variable that Microsoft Access should use for newly created Btrieve data files. For example, a value of '2' indicates the second directory listed in the XTRPATH variable.	XTRPINDX=2

Once you've established the configuration options that pertain to your Btrieve database tables, you'll be able to attach, import and export Btrieve tables easily.

Chapter 11

Using Access as a Migration Tool

ODBC provides an important tool for the use of different data sources cohabiting on your system. In many cases, as you move from one type of database to a newer implementation in Access or other ODBC databases, you'll be faced with the challenge of converting the data from one type of database to another.

Using Access as the mediator, you can create a connection to each of the data sources and have Access bring in the data. It can then make any necessary modifications, and write the information to the new database format:

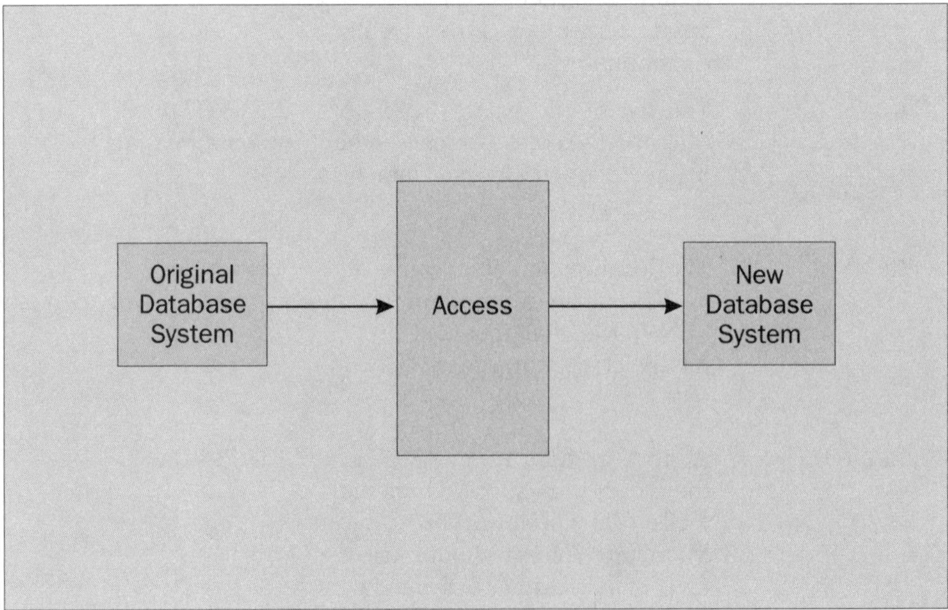

Importing Information from Other Data Sources

You can work with information between data sources in a one-, two- or three-step process, using Access to:

1 Move information directly from one system to another

2 Import the information into an Access table

3 Import the information, make changes to it, before putting the information back into the other database format

Some of the powerful facilities that Access has to offer are some good import utilities. You can import files from many database or spreadsheet formats and you can also import ASCII formatted files, either specifying the layout of the file manually or by allowing Access to make a best guess where possible:

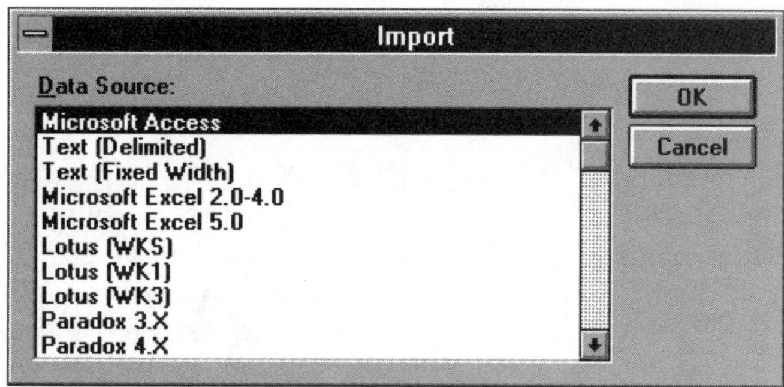

After you select the type of originating database type, you will be able to either directly import the file or specify further information so that Access will know how to work with the database file.

An important, and often overlooked feature of Access, is its ability to import spreadsheet databases. A very common use of spreadsheets is the stockpiling of information on contacts, stock quotes, portfolios and other such financial data. You will probably find as you implement office automation systems that there are many spreadsheets that are candidates for being converted to an Access-based system. You won't lose any capabilities in these situations because many spreadsheets can read an Access (or other ODBC-type) database, or at least an export created from Access, and present the information in the same fashion that the user is use to.

Working with Undelimited, Fixed Width Source Files

If you select Text (Fixed Width), you will be able to specify how information is laid out in the source file. This is extremely helpful if you're importing from a Host-based system that uses fixed length records and is able to create a text file for your use:

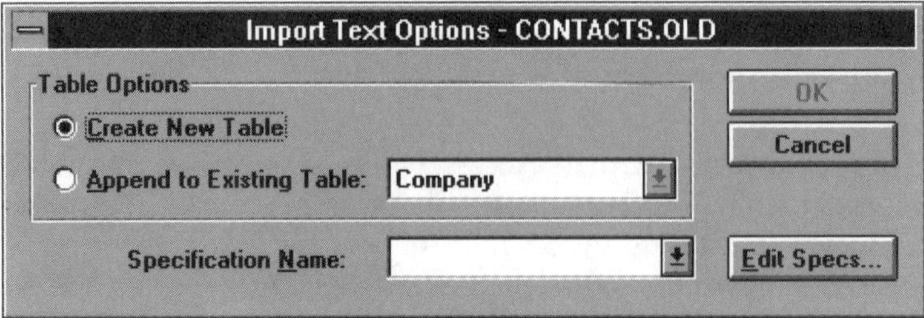

You have the option of appending the incoming information to an existing table or you can have Access create a new table for you.

> **It's highly recommended that you import to a new table if possible. This allows you to make sure the process succeeds before changes are committed to a production system. You may want to import to a temporary table and then use a query to place the information into the production table after you've verified the contents. This provides a layer of insulation against any data problems that you may encounter in the source file.**

You should be aware that you can also use a saved specification. The specification will tell Access where each of the fields is located in the import file. Specifications can be established by selecting the Edit Specs... button:

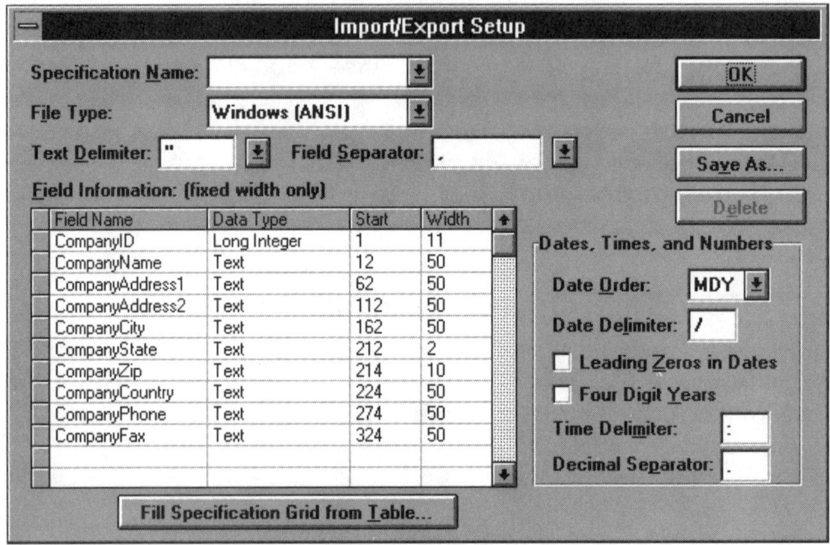

You'll need to know the definitions for both the incoming and the destination file if you are appending to an existing file. If you are appending, you should use field names in your specification that match field names in the existing file.

There are a few key items in the dialog box that are very helpful when importing text based information. The option to select the Text Deliminator allows you to use something other than quotation marks to indicate a character string field where the host system is not able to place quotes around strings, but is able to work with other deliminators.

The Field Separator text box allows you to indicate what character will signify the break between fields. For example, on some host systems, a tab character is issued between fields. Use this field to indicate a character other than the standard comma.

One of the really nice abilities of the import routine is the capability to base the definition on an existing Access table structure using the Fill Specification Grid from Table... button. If your import file structure provides fields in the same order and the same length as your table, this option will save you a great deal of time defining the layout of the file.

If you have a field in the incoming file that represents what will be a Counter type in Access, select Long Integer as the Data Type in the import definition. This will correctly map the field to the Counter in your existing system. If you define this field as another data type, Access may truncate the number or cause an error condition.

As you create your definition, make sure you account for commas in the source data file when you are determining the field widths and that you pass over any unneeded fields in your character count. Also, you don't have to take the fields in order from the source file. If it's easier to take the fields in the order of your Access table instead, you can pull the fields you need from the source file in the order you need them.

When you create the export file on the source system, be sure to place quotation marks around strings. This is especially important if you are going to be using the 'Comma Delimited' import utility, because there can be real confusion caused by string fields. The quotation marks allow Access to easily determine where a field starts and finishes.

The Text (Fixed Width) import process depends on the concept of a line of data per record, with each field always occurring in the same location on the line. You won't use this method for anything other than a fixed field width ASCII text file.

Working With Delimited Source Files

If you are using a file that is delimited, that is one that has proper field and record identifying characters, Access will be able to read the file with less effort. Creating the definition for the import process requires a few less steps, merely because you won't be counting field widths.

To start the import, select File, Import... from the Access menus. You'll be asked to select an import type, just as in the previous section. This time, select Text (Delimited) from the list of options. Next, select the source file you want to work with. The final definition step is to describe the file, as we did in the prior section. This time, however, you'll be selecting some slightly different information:

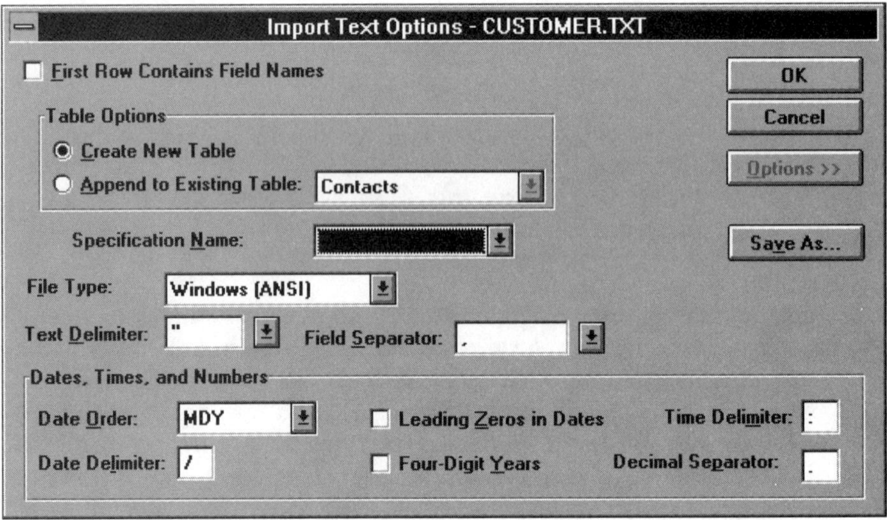

In this scenario, you'll be defining the text delimiter and field separator. Access will use this information to determine where different fields are in the source text file. Once you've provided this information, Access will import the file and tell you how many records have been processed.

If any errors occur in the import process Access will create an error table and tell you how many errors have occurred:

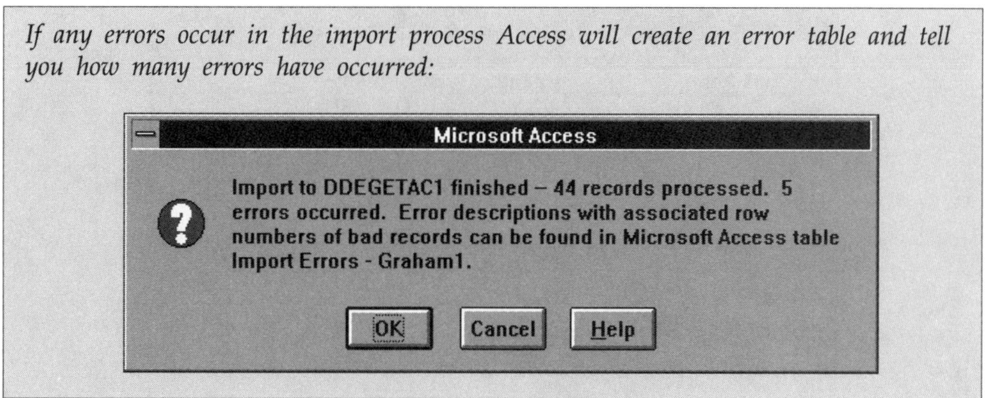

Using Access as a 'Gate Keeper' to Other Sources

Even if you're forced to maintain information in non-Access databases, you can still use the interface of Access as a front-end to the information. Attaching a file to an Access database is easy to do and can provide a new interface to the other database format.

Using this as a springboard into the new environment can be a great help. Software users are often hesitant to convert to a new system. If you can show them that their old information is still intact and available to them, you can ease the pain of transition greatly.

After the users of your software have become used to the new interface, you can convert the system to a full Access implementation, or even move to the client server world. A phased transition will generally be an easier sell than a complete cold change to a new system, and if your environment affords you this alternative, you should consider it carefully.

An Example of Converting Two Foreign Databases

As an example, we're going to convert a table from Excel to Foxpro. The file we require to accomplish this is included on the CD provided with this book. The Excel spreadsheet in question is called `INVNTRY.XLS` and contains inventory and pricing information:

INVNTRY.XLS

	A	B	C	D	E
1	Book Name	Quantity	Price	Sale	Cost
2	All Too Human	1.00	8.00	20.00	7.00
3	Don Quixote	8.00	10.00	0.00	3.50
4	Hamlet	3.00	3.50	10.00	15.50
5	Histories	1.00	5.95	0.00	4.90
6	Kidnapped	3.00	23.45	0.00	17.23
7	Madame Bovary	9.00	20.48	35.00	9.76
8	Moby Dick	2.00	10.35	5.00	14.54
9	Paradise Lost	3.00	17.50	10.00	12.95
10	Principia Mathematica	3.00	4.73	0.00	2.98
11	Spring Snow	11.00	22.73	40.00	4.97
12	The Brothers Karamazov	5.00	8.10	25.00	17.41
13	The Joy of Cooking	4.00	10.95	5.00	7.35
14	The Odyssey	4.00	6.98	0.00	11.67
15	The Prince	1.00	2.70	10.00	13.58
16	The Republic	3.00	1.25	5.00	1.06
17	The Tempest	8.00	12.60	0.00	12.62
18	The Time Machine	7.00	11.48	20.00	4.02
19	Thus Spoke Zarathustra	5.00	9.23	0.00	8.80
20	Zorba the Greek	1.00	10.99	5.00	7.86

Inventory

The first step is to import the existing file to a temporary Access table. This will allow us to work with the data, make any necessary format changes and then export it as a Foxpro 2.6 database.

Importing the Excel Spreadsheet

From the File menu, select Import.... Select the Microsoft Excel 5.0 format and bring up the following dialog box:

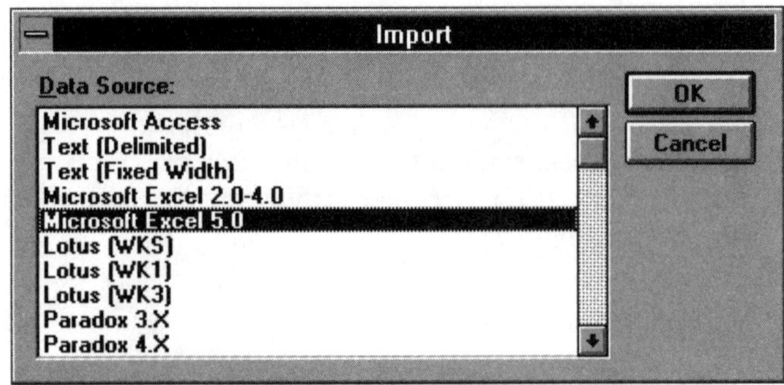

From the file selection dialog box that follows, select **INVNTRY.XLS** and select Import. Next, the dialog box shown will prompt for the other information that is required to complete the import process:

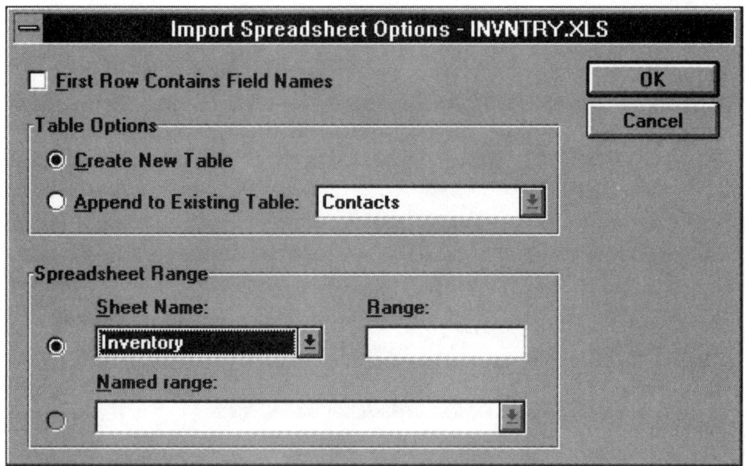

Be sure to check the first option, because our spreadsheet already contains the field names. This will allow Access to set up the underlying table for you using the column names in Excel as field names for the table in Access. If you don't specify this option, or the spreadsheet doesn't contain field names, Access will create sequential numeric field names for you. You'll then have to go back and assign meaningful field names at a later date.

In the lower pane of the dialog box you'll be able to select from the list box the name of the sheet to import. Once the process has been completed, Access will display a message indicating how many rows were imported, along with the status of the import process. As before, if any errors were detected, Access will create a new table to document them and indicate where you can find more information about those errors so that you can re-try the operation or make updates right in the database as needed:

After the process, you'll have a new database table, INVNTRY, that contains the 19 rows we just imported. This is our temporary table, which is the one that will be used to store the information to be sent to the FoxPro database.

Exporting the Data as a Foxpro File

You can have Access create a new database file in the format you need and export the records to that file, all in one step. Select File, Export from the menus. Select the destination file format, which in our case is FoxPro 2.6 and select OK.:

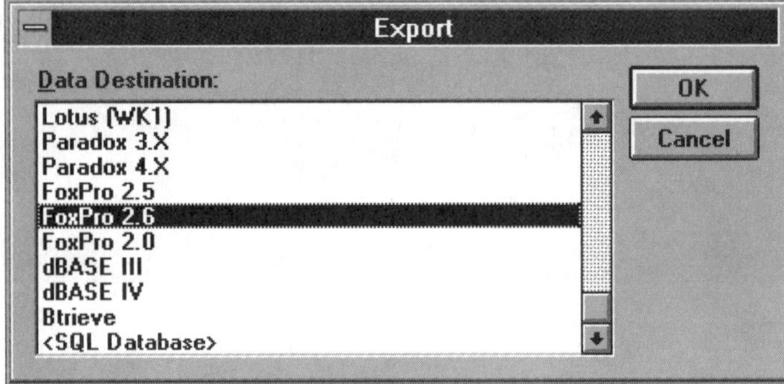

You'll be prompted to select the object to export. In our example, select the INVNTRY table and select OK. Note that you can export queries in the same way. This is another occasion where Access treats queries like tables:

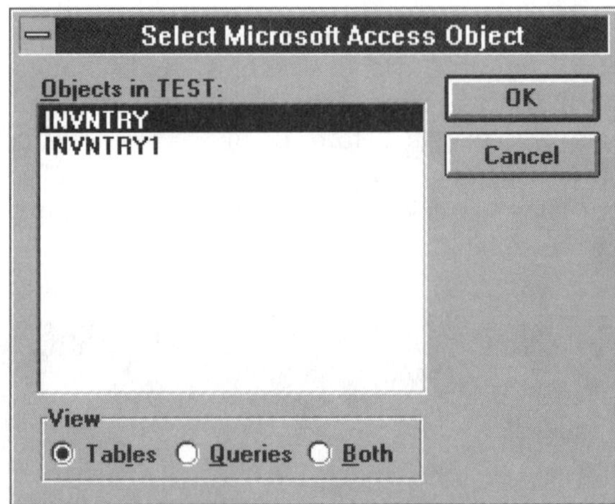

The final step is to give Access a file name for the export process. Once the export process has been completed, you will be returned to the database tabbed dialog box.

If you specify a file that already exists for this process, the information you are exporting will overwrite the existing file.

You can now open the new file in your other database package and view the data:

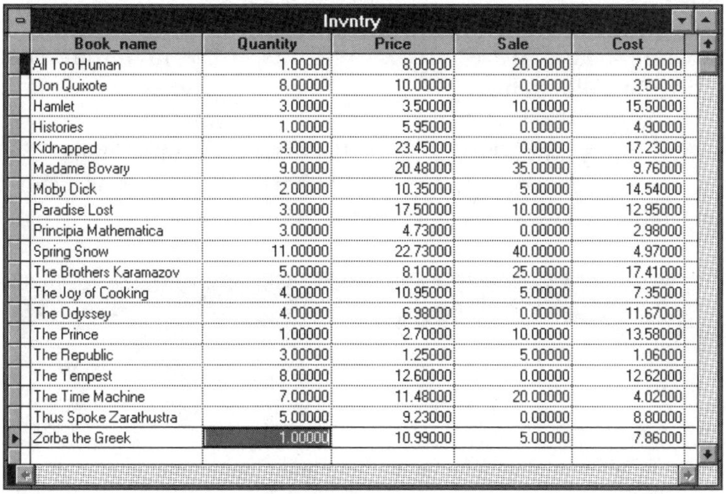

Invntry

Book_name	Quantity	Price	Sale	Cost
All Too Human	1.00000	8.00000	20.00000	7.00000
Don Quixote	8.00000	10.00000	0.00000	3.50000
Hamlet	3.00000	3.50000	10.00000	15.50000
Histories	1.00000	5.95000	0.00000	4.90000
Kidnapped	3.00000	23.45000	0.00000	17.23000
Madame Bovary	9.00000	20.48000	35.00000	9.76000
Moby Dick	2.00000	10.35000	5.00000	14.54000
Paradise Lost	3.00000	17.50000	10.00000	12.95000
Principia Mathematica	3.00000	4.73000	0.00000	2.98000
Spring Snow	11.00000	22.73000	40.00000	4.97000
The Brothers Karamazov	5.00000	8.10000	25.00000	17.41000
The Joy of Cooking	4.00000	10.95000	5.00000	7.35000
The Odyssey	4.00000	6.98000	0.00000	11.67000
The Prince	1.00000	2.70000	10.00000	13.58000
The Republic	3.00000	1.25000	5.00000	1.06000
The Tempest	8.00000	12.60000	0.00000	12.62000
The Time Machine	7.00000	11.48000	20.00000	4.02000
Thus Spoke Zarathustra	5.00000	9.23000	0.00000	8.80000
Zorba the Greek	1.00000	10.99000	5.00000	7.86000

Appending Information to an Existing Table

If you want to add new information to an existing file, rather than creating a new one, you can use an archive query but both the existing file and the file that contains the new information must be attached or imported to your current database. In our example, we're going to import information from an Excel spreadsheet and append it to an attached FoxPro file.

In our **SAMPLES.MDB** database, we've created a query called Append Query, that will show how you accomplish this task. There are two database tables, ExcelInventory, which has been imported from the **INVNTRY.XLS** spreadsheet and FoxProInventory, which is an attached FoxPro table which points to the **INVNTRY.DBF** file in the **C:\WROX** directory.

If you need to change the location of the external file, you can use the Attachment Manager, *located on the* File *menu's* Add-ins *option.*

The query pulls the information from the ExcelInventory table and inserts it into the FoxPro file. The SQL code for the query looks like this:

```
INSERT INTO FoxProInventory ( BOOK_NAME, QUANTITY, PRICE, SALE, COST )
SELECT DISTINCTROW [BOOK NAME], QUANTITY, PRICE, SALE, COST
FROM ExcelInventory;
```

Notice that the Book Name field has an underline character substituted for the space. This is because FoxPro doesn't support spaces in field names. If you export a table as a FoxPro file, Access will insert the underline character for any spaces in the field names.

If you run this query and then look at the **INVNTRY.DBF**, or the FoxProInventory table if you don't have FoxPro, you'll see that all the records from the ExcelInventory table have been appended:

Invntry

Book_name	Quantity	Price	Sale	Cost
All Too Human	1.00000	8.00000	20.00000	7.00000
Don Quixote	8.00000	10.00000	0.00000	3.50000
Hamlet	3.00000	3.50000	10.00000	15.50000
Histories	1.00000	5.95000	0.00000	4.90000
Kidnapped	3.00000	23.45000	0.00000	17.23000
Madame Bovary	9.00000	20.48000	35.00000	9.76000
Moby Dick	2.00000	10.35000	5.00000	14.54000
Paradise Lost	3.00000	17.50000	10.00000	12.95000
Principia Mathematica	3.00000	4.73000	0.00000	2.98000
Spring Snow	11.00000	22.73000	40.00000	4.97000
The Brothers Karamazov	5.00000	8.10000	25.00000	17.41000
The Joy of Cooking	4.00000	10.95000	5.00000	7.35000
The Odyssey	4.00000	6.98000	0.00000	11.67000
The Prince	1.00000	2.70000	10.00000	13.58000
The Republic	3.00000	1.25000	5.00000	1.06000
The Tempest	8.00000	12.60000	0.00000	12.62000
The Time Machine	7.00000	11.48000	20.00000	4.02000
Thus Spoke Zarathustra	5.00000	9.23000	0.00000	8.80000
Zorba the Greek	1.00000	10.99000	5.00000	7.86000
All Too Human	1.00000	8.00000	20.00000	7.00000
Don Quixote	8.00000	10.00000	0.00000	3.50000
Hamlet	3.00000	3.50000	10.00000	15.50000
Histories	1.00000	5.95000	0.00000	4.90000
Kidnapped	3.00000	23.45000	0.00000	17.23000
Madame Bovary	9.00000	20.48000	35.00000	9.76000
Moby Dick	2.00000	10.35000	5.00000	14.54000
Paradise Lost	3.00000	17.50000	10.00000	12.95000
Principia Mathematica	3.00000	4.73000	0.00000	2.98000

If you are bringing information in from a Microsoft SQL Server, you may notice that table names are specified as <DBO | *username*>_FieldName. SQL Server stores table names as DBO.FieldName, but Access doesn't support a period in table names. The table name conversion process will change this for you as appropriate.

If you are the owner of the table, the prefix will be 'DBO', otherwise the username will be added to the table as the new prefix.

You can also set up the query to move the rows to the FoxPro table. This process will allow Access to not only copy the information to the FoxPro table, but also delete it from the Access Table. Until you are sure of your process, it is best to make the removal of information from the intermediary file a manual process. This will allow you time to make sure the data transfer was successful.

Using Access as a Test Environment for Client/Server Development

In most cases, as you develop Client/Server systems to be used with an intelligent back-end server, you'll want the capability to develop in a separate environment from the target production system. As an example, consider development of a Microsoft SQL Server system. Within Access, you can create the database tables and compile the queries and reports. After you've had time to test them and make sure that all the functions are operating correctly, you can convert the tables to attached SQL Server tables. In addition, you can convert queries, relationships and other objects in the Access system to objects that your back-end server can work with.

We've created a simple example database that you can use to walk through the conversion process. The database, **SQLTEST.MDB**, is installed with the samples accompanying this book. Open the database and review the tables that are provided. The database is a two-table system that contains contact information and a related table of payment history.

These sample tables were created by selecting fields from the Table Wizard's Friend database and by adding a few other fields manually. The relationship was defined by the Table Wizard when the Payment *table was created.*

The following figure shows the tables and the relationship established between them based on FriendID:

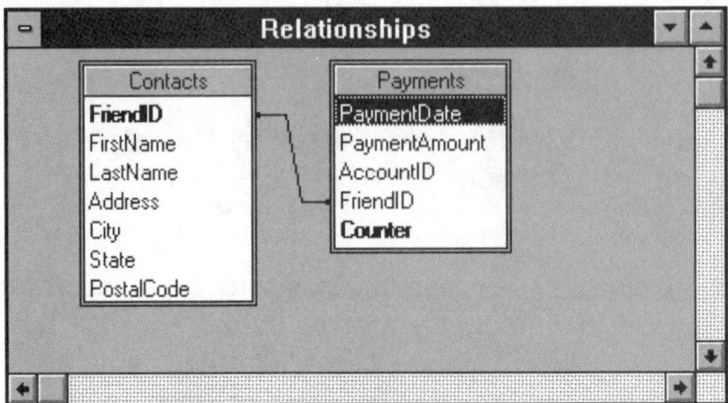

In addition, a simple form has been created to show the tables in a main/subform implementation. This is typical of a system that could be developed and then converted to a more comprehensive back-end environment:

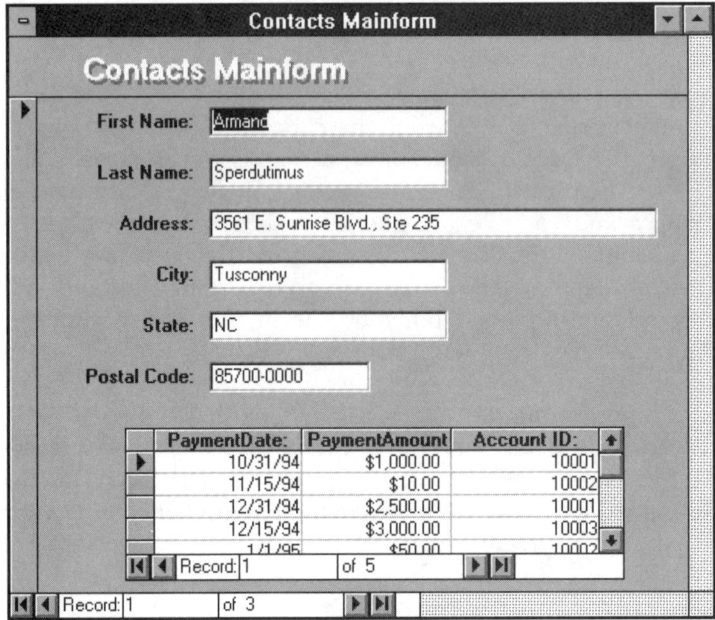

The final two pieces of the application are used to query and report on the database tables. These consist of a query, Payment Query, and a report, Payment Report. The next figures show the definitions of these two items:

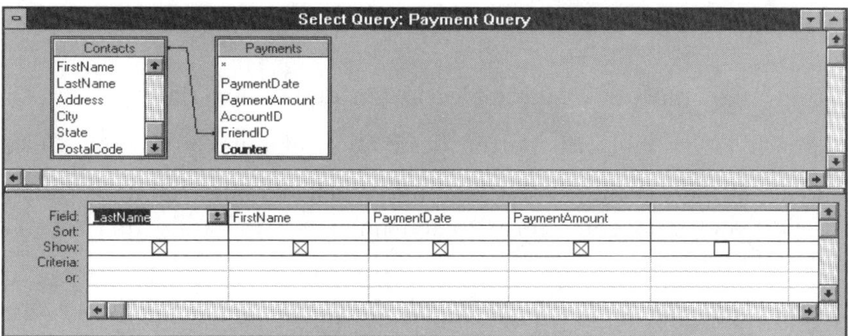

The query selects the LastName and FirstName from the Contacts table and the matching PaymentDate and PaymentAmount from the Payments table.

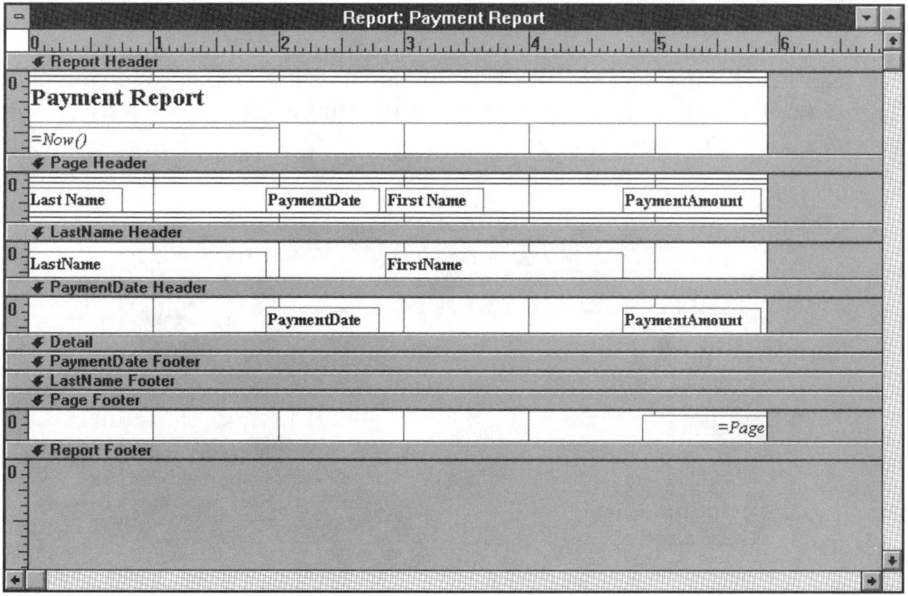

In the report, we have compressed the details section and put the relevant controls in the LastName and PaymentDate header sections. This gives us a well spaced out report.

Now that we've established a working system using these tables, we will go through the process of establishing these tables and relationships in another back-end data source.

There will be several steps to this process:

- Copy the contents of the tables to the destination files
- Attach tables that will be the destination of our conversion efforts
- Rename the existing tables and the attached tables, allowing our query, report and data entry form to remain intact and fully functional without modification
- Consider what would be required to convert the query to a stored procedure in an intelligent server environment

Now, using the information we presented earlier in this chapter, we can export the two tables to the SQL Server system. Select File, Export... from the menu and specify <SQL Database> as the file type:

> **You can select an alternate file type if you are not using SQL Server. The examples will still function correctly as long as you select a supported ODBC data source.**

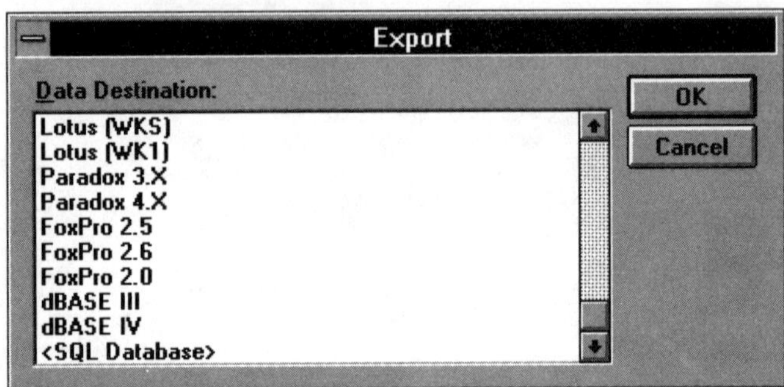

Once you've selected the export type, you'll be prompted for the object that you want to export. Select the Contacts table first and then export the Payment table. If you are exporting to a data source that supports multiple tables per database, as is the case with SQL Server, you'll be prompted for the table name to create:

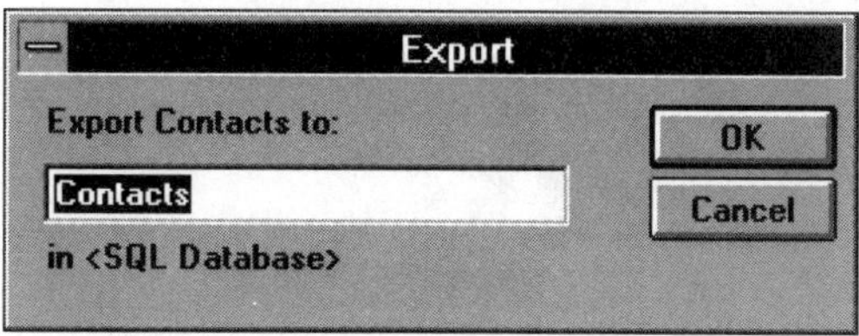

If the data source supports only one table per database file, you will be prompted for the database file name that should be created:

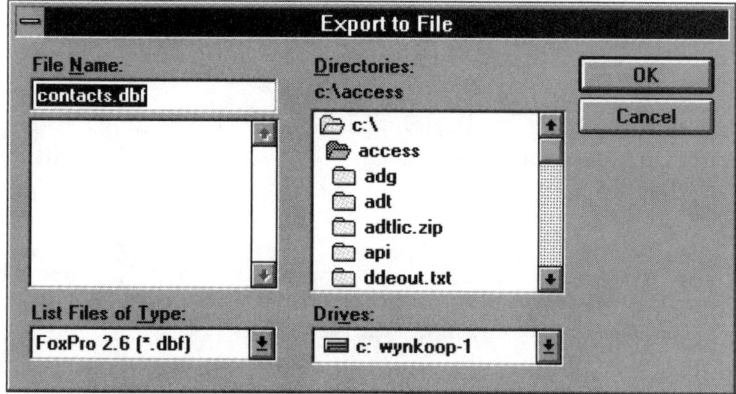

Once you have exported the files, attach the two newly created files to the **SQLTEST.MDB** database, in the same way as you would attach a non-SQL file described earlier, with one notable exception. With SQL-type databases, you must specify the Data Source Name first, and then select the table you want to attach.

Attach the tables to your database. Once attached, you should have four database tables available, as shown below:

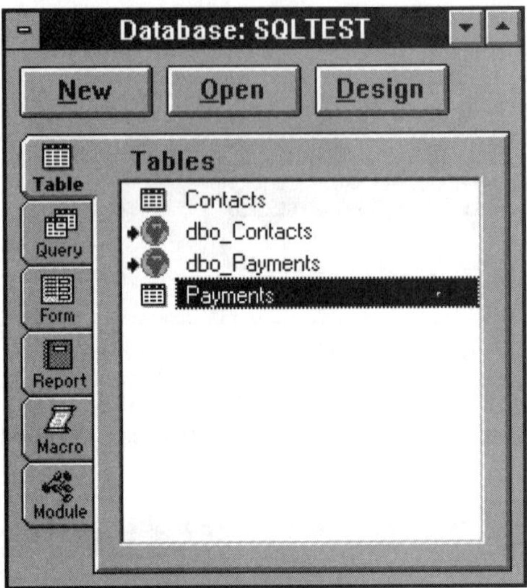

The next step is to rename your original tables. This will allow us to then rename the new, attached tables so the query and report will be using those new tables as data sources.

> **Note that the field name requirements for the underlying database engine are still in force. If the engine only allows 10 character field names, as in FoxPro, the field names will be truncated during the export process. This will cause an #Error message on the subform. If this is the case, consider using a different data source, or rename the fields in the table to use shorter names.**
>
> **If you decide to rename the fields, don't forget to regenerate the editing form and query. Both are simple implementations and therefore you can use the appropriate wizards for their creation.**

To rename the table, simply right-click on the table and select Rename... from the pop-up menu. Rename the Contacts table to OldContacts and the Payments table to OldPayments.

Finally, rename the dbo_Contacts table to Contacts and the dbo_Payments table to Payments. You've completed step one and your database tables are now linked between your Access system and your SQL Server.

This is a significant step. You've just taken tables created and tested in Access and moved them to a possible production environment. Without modifying your form code, report code or query code, you're able to begin using the new database system's architecture while drastically reducing your time to move from a development system to a production environment.

Post Transfer Testing

At this point, you should test all the forms, queries, modules and so on, that refer to the database tables. Make sure that the procedures still function as you'd expect and no problems are apparent. Remember that there are some concerns that may come into play at this point.

Of primary concern will be field naming requirements for the underlying system and any data type conversions that will have taken place. More information on data type conversions is presented in the next chapter.

A side effect of this is that while you are developing your database system, you won't be impacting your production environment. One of the biggest benefits of this is that, if your program should have any unforeseen bugs, it will not harm production databases. Second, you'll be reducing network tension upon the server that provides the functionality for the data source. These are significant benefits that warrant careful consideration in your development environment.

An additional item that you'll need to be planning for is the addition of Unique indexes to the SQL tables. The process of adding indexes is straight-forward, but requires the use of a SQL query. Create a new query and select the SQL button. You create the index with the statement (removing the **SELECT DISTINCTROW;** provided by Access):

```
CREATE UNIQUE INDEX <IndexName> ON
<TableName>(FieldName1[,FieldName2...) WITH PRIMARY
```

for example,

```
CREATE INDEX test ON contacts(FriendID) WITH PRIMARY
```

This creates an index that is independent of the server, but allows Access to work with the table. The keyword **PRIMARY** indicates that this is the default index, just as in the table design for a native Access table.

A interesting effect of attaching and renaming tables in this manner is that the relationships are maintained against the attached tables. As long as you name the tables the same name as their Access counterparts, and the Access counterparts had relationships defined, Access will manage those relationships for you. The downside to this is that Access is doing all the work, not the database provider. We'll go into more details on the rules and triggers that can be moved into the database provider system a little later in this chapter and also in the next, where we cover the Upsizing Wizard.

A Quick Primer to Converting Queries to Stored Procedures

It is well beyond the scope of this book to teach all of the ins and outs of stored procedures, views and the like. However, it is worth reviewing some basic information about stored procedures that can help get you going in your development efforts.

What Is a Stored Procedure?

If you use queries extensively and are referring to the queries in your Access Basic code, you'll want to consider moving them to the server as stored procedures. Stored procedures are routines that reside on the server, are compiled and executed by the server, and are called simply by an **Execute** statement.

Stored procedures offer many benefits over queries, especially when used against an external database such as SQL Server or Oracle. When you call a stored procedure, you simply provide the procedure name and any relevant parameters. This is identical to the calling procedure for a standard function or subroutine. The difference is that you specify a stored procedure as a source of information rather than a processing function. Some of the benefits of stored procedures are illustrated below:

Decreased network traffic — When you are using a typical Access implementation on a network, the entire table is passed back and forth over the network. This is because all of the processing is being done on the client system. The added traffic can be an obvious strain on a network and can cause application delays, not only on the Access software system, but on other applications that are running and dependent on the network. A implementation stored procedure is activated by passing only an `Execute` command to the server, and operates entirely on the server. Only the results are then passed back over the network.

Enhanced performance

Since you're only passing the procedure name and its associated parameters across the network, network traffic is significantly decreased. The only information traveling across the network is the request to run the procedure and the actual results set, if any. This can be a significant savings in network traffic over slower, possibly remote network connections.

Another real benefit is that the processes are executed at the server's clock and disk speed. A typical installation places performance emphasis on the server and typically less horsepower is focused on the client workstations. In these cases, the difference in processing time can be significant as the query will be processed at a much faster speed than the workstation can provide.

Easier system maintenance

Stored procedures reside in the database itself and are not part of the Access Basic system. If changes are needed to a stored procedure, you can make the changes on the server and they will affect everyone that uses the procedure from that time on.

Enhanced security

In many cases, you can implement security on stored procedures that allow them to be run to obtain specific information, but prevent the users from directly accessing the underlying data. This can be a good way to keep information private and confidential, or simply to protect the integrity of the information in a database.

How Do You Convert Queries to Stored Procedures?

Our query from the last few sections is a simple extract query that provides the information from the Contacts and Payments tables. The tables are joined by the FriendID field. A join is created when relationships are defined between tables.

The Query Builder offers a tool that can get us well on our way to creating stored procedures beginning with a query. The SQL button on the toolbar will take the query, defined in the QBE grid, and convert it to a relevant SQL statement that produces the results we've requested. In reality, when we create the query on the grid, Access is writing the underlying SQL statements for us; SQL is the language used to query the database and return the information requested:

In our example query, the SQL code is as follows:

```
SELECT
    Contacts.LastName,
    Contacts.FirstName,
    Payments.PaymentDate,
    Payments.PaymentAmount

FROM
    Contacts, Payments

WHERE
    Contacts.FriendID = Payments.FriendID
```

This has some pretty typical SQL **SELECT** statements included, with a twist when it comes to joining the two tables together. Remember, our tables employ a one-to-many relationship between the contacts and their related payment history. To accomplish this, an **Inner Join** is created. The results of this join are that a payment is retrieved, followed by the corresponding contact:

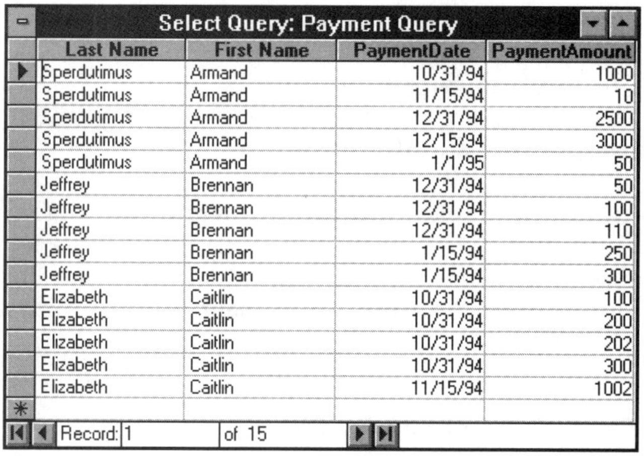

Last Name	First Name	PaymentDate	PaymentAmount
Sperdutimus	Armand	10/31/94	1000
Sperdutimus	Armand	11/15/94	10
Sperdutimus	Armand	12/31/94	2500
Sperdutimus	Armand	12/15/94	3000
Sperdutimus	Armand	1/1/95	50
Jeffrey	Brennan	12/31/94	50
Jeffrey	Brennan	12/31/94	100
Jeffrey	Brennan	12/31/94	110
Jeffrey	Brennan	1/15/94	250
Jeffrey	Brennan	1/15/94	300
Elizabeth	Caitlin	10/31/94	100
Elizabeth	Caitlin	10/31/94	200
Elizabeth	Caitlin	10/31/94	202
Elizabeth	Caitlin	10/31/94	300
Elizabeth	Caitlin	11/15/94	1002

Select Query: Payment Query — Record: 1 of 15

To convert this query to a stored procedure, you generally add a simple prefix to it, specifically **`Create Procedure PaymentQuery as`** followed by the text of your query.

For example, here's what the query would look like as a stored procedure declaration for Microsoft's SQL Server:

```
Create Procedure PaymentQuery as
    /* Query the database returning the contact and */
    /* their associated payment history            */
SELECT
    Contacts.LastName.
    Contacts.FirstName,
    Payments.PaymentDate,
    Payments.PaymentAmount
FROM
    Contacts, Payments
WHERE
    Contacts.FriendID = Payments.FriendID
```

To create this query, you can use Access' SQL-specific, SQL-pass-through options. Alternatively, you can use ISQL, the inquiry tool provided with SQL Server. There are many different ways to send this information to the server. The point of this discussion is to show the types of things that can be created, the tools you use to create them. Whether you, as a user, can create them, due to position with permissions is best determined by your SQL support staff.

Then, when you want to call the **PaymentQuery** stored procedure, you would simply specify it as a recordsource for a control. To do this, you'll need to create a query that calls the stored procedure using SQL Pass-through. Refer to this query in the recordsource for the control, and you'll be able to reference the return values from the stored procedure.

Note that this specific procedure will actually return four different columns of information, the LastName, FirstName, PaymentDate and PaymentAmount. Depending on where you are using this query, and for what type of control or report, you'll want to limit the **SELECT** statement to return only the specific field you want to display.

Special Stored Procedures - Triggers

If you set up relationships as we've been discussing in this and previous chapters, you'll often have a complex relationship between the tables in your system. This is to say that if you delete a record from one table, you'll want certain checks or other deletions to occur. This is where **Triggers** come into play.

A Trigger is a stored procedure; that is, it is initiated at the time a specific class of action is started against a table. For example, if you say that 'any time a row is deleted from this table, make a copy of it in another table before actually deleting it', you can put a **Delete** trigger on the table to make sure this happens:

```
/* This trigger will make a copy of the record in a backup */
/* database table before allowing SQL to delete the record */
Create Trigger DeleteTrigger on Contacts
for Delete as
Insert Into ContactsBackup
    (FriendID, FirstName, LastName, Address, City,
    State, PostalCode)
SELECT
    FriendID, FirstName, LastName, Address, City,
    State, PostalCode
FROM
    Contacts, Deleted
WHERE
    Contacts.FriendID = deleted.FriendID
```

The reference to the Deleted table is a reference to a virtual table created by SQL when a row is deleted from the table. The row is copied to the deleted table temporarily. You can reference this row until the transaction is committed.

By referencing this special table, you can allow SQL to 'remove' the contents of the row from the original table, but you'll still be able to get a copy of the row (or rows if you're backing up multiple rows) before it is permanently removed.

This stored procedure is automatically called whenever a `Delete` request is received for Contacts. To the user, regardless of the front-end application he is using, he simply makes a request to delete a record. This has the benefit of enforcing the data integrity on the back-end. You can do additional processing within Triggers, such as sending Email notifications to system administrators, updating other tables with information about the deleted record and so on. Triggers are powerful automation tools that can help place the functionality of managing the database in the hands of the database engine rather than the application.

Comments and Suggestions

Access is a powerful companion product for the process of converting systems to a new architecture. Even in those cases where Access is not the final destination, the import, export and definition utilities provided by Access can be very helpful when working with diverse data providers.

Working with other tools such as Excel and Microsoft Query, you have a powerful suite of data conversion and modeling tools. In addition, if you are working with a SQL Server, you can use Access to create the tables for you and manage the objects in the SQL environment.

In the next chapter, we'll go into more detail about how specific data formats convert to Access-usable information. We'll be presenting information on data type conversions, as well as the restrictions and requirements for each of the data sources. In addition, we'll review the Microsoft Access Upsizing Wizard, a tool for automating the process of upsizing your applications to work with SQL Server.

Using the Microsoft Upsizing Tools

Access is a very flexible database development tool, but if you are looking for power processing, then why not look to the SQL Server as the answer to your problems. Following this line of thought, Microsoft have worked towards making the Access/SQL Server team work well together, until the crowning glory, their upsizing tools, was released, making it a reality. The bridge between platforms had arrived!

What's Covered in This Chapter

In this chapter, we cover some final topics that relate to using Access within a non-Access database environment. We'll cover some of the big names in database standards and include information on how to work their database files within Access.

In this chapter, we will cover:

- Microsoft's new Upsizing Wizard
- The SQL Server Browser
- General hints and tips on upsizing your applications

By 'upsizing' your application, you are moving it from the client-only environment of Access to the Client/Server, high-performance environment of SQL Server.

Chapter 12

How This Chapter Impacts Our Application

We'll be upsizing our application to the SQL Server environment following the major concepts behind this chapter. We'll show how different aspects of the application can be converted and what the consequences may be for your application.

In addition, we'll be reviewing what exactly is accomplished when you upsize your application. This includes changes that are made on the server and what information can stay local to your Access application.

Introduction

In the previous chapter, we reviewed several ways to use Access with other data sources. Server products like Microsoft's SQL Server can make your application more suited for a larger scale implementation. In addition, you'll often find that other legacy systems, by which we mean those systems already in place that will require ever increasing support far into the future, often come in many different formats.

We've covered how to connect to some basic ODBC sources. Here, we'll be investigating the Upsizing Wizard and what it can do to help in your efforts to move up to the SQL Server environment. We'll also cover different considerations when you're working with dBase-formatted information and Btrieve databases.

Currently, there are two versions of SQL Server in the market, one from Microsoft and the other from Sybase. The products were, until only recently, built and maintained in a joint venture between the two companies, but they have now decided to pursue the SQL Server platform independently.

For the purposes of this chapter, when we refer to SQL Server, we are referring to either implementation, as both products are still inherently the same.

In some of the examples in this chapter, we'll be referring to the Pubs database on SQL Server. The database is installed on the server by selecting the option during the installation process. It can also be installed afterwards by running the installation process again and selecting the option.

If you are unsure or unfamiliar with the installation process for SQL Server, it's highly recommended that you seek assistance from someone who has been through the installation process and can provide guidance in that area.

Using the Microsoft Upsizing Tools

In December 1994, Microsoft released the Microsoft Access Upsizing Tools. This software is provided to give access to SQL Server using the Access environment as the starting point. As you've seen, Access is a good environment for developing database-centric applications. The Access Basic language provides an excellent way of automating processes and controlling the interface presented to the user.

The database design tools offered by Access can also be readily applied to other data sources. There are two distinct parts to the Upsizing Toolkit:

The Upsizing Wizard

The Upsizing Wizard gives you the ability to take an existing application and upgrade it to work with SQL Server. This includes the export of tables, queries and other aspects of your application environment.

The SQL Server Browser

This application brings much of the capability of the typical ISQL for Windows and DOS, SQL Object Manager and SQL Administrator. These applications allow you to define objects in the SQL environment. The Browser provides this functionality at the Access level, using tools and a method of presentation of the information that you'll already be familiar and comfortable with.

An Overview of SQL Server Objects

Before we get into the actual manipulation of SQL Server objects, it's important to understand exactly what different objects are. Also, you need to understand how they relate, if at all, back to Access Objects. In most cases, there is a close correlation between an object on SQL Server and an object in Access.

There are five basic objects that are exposed to you by the Browser application. These objects are tables, views, defaults, rules and stored procedures. The Browser utility included with the Upsizing Tools not only allows you to view the current objects, but it also gives you the ability to create new objects in the system.

For each of these objects we'll be explaining the following items:

- An explanation of what the object is
- An explanation of how to add, change or delete objects of that type
- Functional notes about the Browser relative to the object

Using the SQL Server Browser

The Browser provides you with the familiar Access tabbed dialog as a means of working with the server objects.

When you install the Upsizing Tools, two new options are added to the Add-in menu. These options, Upsizing Wizard and SQL Server Browser, provide you with the capabilities we're covering here:

When you start the Browser, you're prompted to select the SQL Server you want to work with. If you specify a non-SQL Server database, you'll receive the following error message:

Once you've selected a valid SQL Server, you'll be prompted for user ID and login information. The information for the server selections is retrieved from the ODBC setup, completed in the ODBC Administrator. You can access the administrator from the Control Panel. See the chapter on working with ODBC data sources for more information.

Exploring an SQL Server Database with the Object Browser

> **In your system, the MSysConf table may not be present. There is a section later in this chapter that explains this table, how to create it and what purpose it serves.**

From this dialog box, you can select the various objects that you want to work with. In addition, if you need to send SQL commands directly to the Server, you can do so with the View, Ad Hoc SQL command from the menu. We'll cover each of these options next.

Working with Tables in the Object Browser

As shown in the last section, when you start the Browser, the first options shown are the various tables in the database you've selected.

> **Default databases are established when users are set up in SQL Server. If you sign in as SA, or System Administrator, your default database will be Master. You should avoid making modifications to this table if you're not absolutely sure what you are doing and how to do it. You can impact all users of the SQL Server if incorrect changes are made to the Master database.**

What Are Tables?

Tables in SQL Server are exactly the same as they are in Access. Tables are generally application specific and contain the information in the database. Each record in the database is referred to as a row, while each field is a column. In many cases, these terms will be used to refer to Access objects, largely due to their similarity in architecture and functionality to the SQL environment.

The difference in overall architecture is seen at a slightly higher level. In Access, you define a database first, with tables and associated objects residing within that database. With SQL Server, while it's also true that you define a database that contains these objects, there is also another piece to the puzzle, the device.

SQL Server devices contain a database or databases. Here's a diagram of a typical SQL Server system:

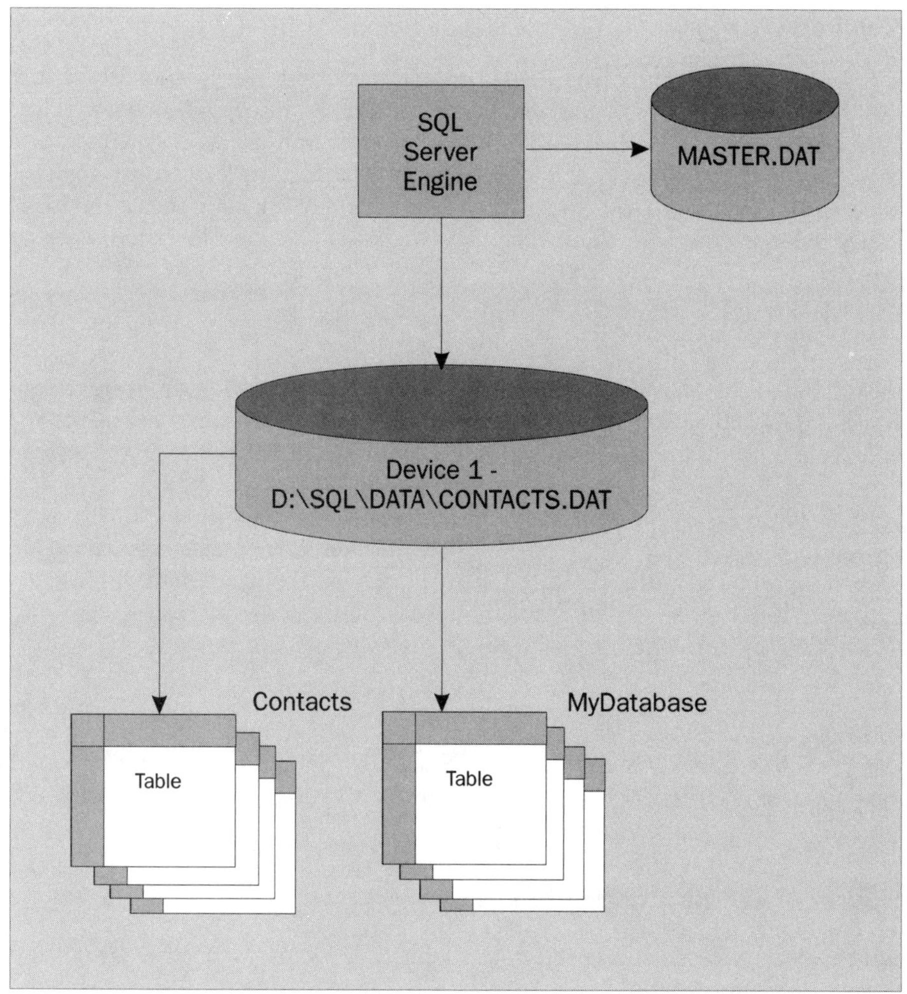

A device corresponds to a physical file on disk that contains one or more databases. Device sizes are defined at the time the device is created and don't change. Each database will contain the objects that pertain to that database. In addition, a database can span multiple devices. In situations where you need to enlarge a database, it's common to establish a new device and use the **ALTER DATABASE SQL** command to expand the database to include a part, if not all of a new device.

Transaction Logs

With SQL Server, a **Transaction Log** is maintained that tracks each change to the system. This transaction log maintains a copy of information both before and after it has changed. In the event of a system failure, you can restore the database as of the last backup and then restore consecutive transaction log backups until all transaction logs have been restored. Since transaction logs are generally smaller than the databases they document, it's easier and faster to do incremental backups of the transaction log on a regular basis rather than several backups of the entire database.

One of the most common occurrences with new SQL Server systems is that the transaction log will quickly fill up. When it does, your system will come to a halt until the log is cleared.

You'll need to keep an eye on the transaction log and dump it frequently. It's beyond the scope of this section to explain the various options that you should consider. If you review the documentation accompanying the server product, you should be able to find more information on the options available.

In addition, SQL Server uses a central system management database, the Master database (MASTER.DAT in the figure), to maintain information on the various objects, security options, users, groups and logging information in the system.

Viewing or Modifying Existing Tables

As with native Access tables, select the table you want to browse by clicking on it and choosing Design:

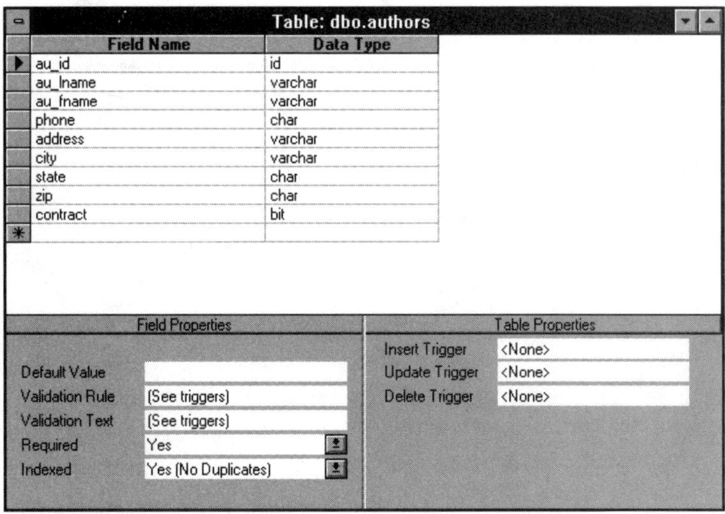

While this form is designed to be much like the Access form for designing tables, there are a couple of items that are different. The first thing you'll notice is that the data types are not the same as Access' field types: SQL Server supports different data types to those defined in Access. When you connect to a SQL database, the ODBC driver and/or Jet engine translate between data types for you.

As you work with SQL tables in their native environment on the server, they are presented as they are defined. The table below shows the data type mappings that relate to SQL Server and Access:

SQL Server Data Type	Access Data Type
Binary(n)	Binary(n)
Bit	Yes/No
Char(n)	Text(n)
Datetime	Date/Time
Float	Number, Double
Image	OLE Object
Int	Number, Long Integer/Counter

Continued

SQL Server Data Type	Access Data Type
Money	Currency
Real	Number, Single
SmallDateTime	Date/Time
SmallInt	Number, Integer
SmallMoney	Currency
Text	Memo
TinyInt	Number, Integer
VarBinary(n)	Binary(n)
VarChar(n)	Text(n)

In addition to different data types, the Field Properties and Table Properties portions of the form have been added. These areas allow you to define properties and attributes, as they relate to the columns individually and to the table as a whole. The Required and Indexed fields are identical to those found when defining Access tables.

Triggers are used by SQL Server to maintain referential integrity between tables. In Access, you defined 'triggers' by using the Relationship option. You set up a defined relationship where Access could manage record deletions and modifications based on a set of rules you provided. In SQL, you attach a stored procedure to Insert, Update and Delete operations that occur against a table:

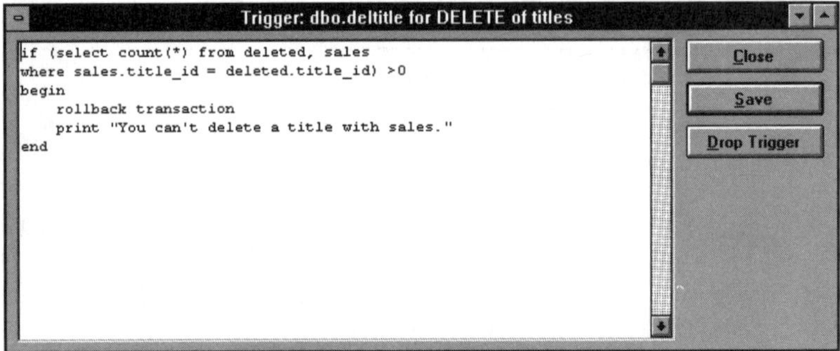

When a row is deleted from a table, you can still refer to it within the trigger by preceding the column name with 'Deleted'. Using this method, you can reference the information in the row in your trigger definition. In the example above, we use the deleted row's `title_ID` to see if sales exist for it.

In the **PUBS** database, there is a trigger on the Titles table that prevents an item in the table from being deleted if sales have been entered against it. On the table design form, if you select the Delete Trigger option, the ellipses will appear next to the field. If you click that button, it will call up the trigger modification dialog box shown above. As indicated by the buttons, you can save updates to the trigger, as well as dropping, or deleting, the trigger altogether.

Creating New Tables

As with the standard Access environment, you can create new tables in the databases on SQL Server. When you select New from the table dialog, you'll be prompted for a table name.

You must have created privileges on the server, in the database that you are working, to be able to create new objects. If you receive an error message when creating a new table, check with your system administrator to verify your user rights in the database.

When you create a new table, a form that is nearly identical to the Design Table form is displayed. As you enter new column names, the Data Type column will show the various SQL Server data types available.

In SQL Server, you can define your own data types. If you have user defined types, they will also show up in the list.

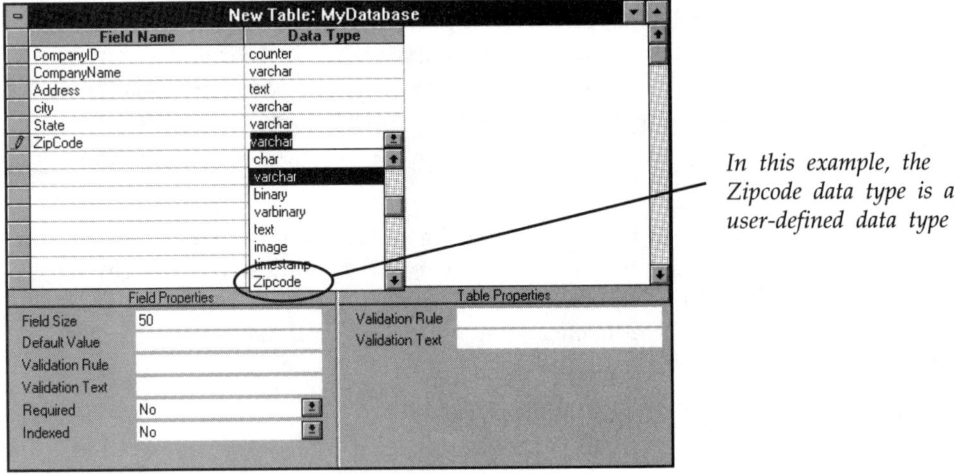

In this example, the Zipcode data type is a user-defined data type

Enter the information just as you would when defining an Access database table. When you close the form, the table will be created on the server.

Counter Types

Counter types are not directly supported on SQL Server. If you select a counter type for a field, the Object Browser will automatically create an insert trigger for you. This trigger will calculate the next value to use for the counter field, effectively emulating the functionality of the counter field. Here's a look at the trigger created by the Object Browser for the table that was just created:

```
DECLARE @maxc int, @newc int   /* FOR COUNTER-EMULATION CODE */
/*
 * COUNTER-EMULATION CODE FOR FIELD 'CompanyID'
 */
SELECT @maxc = (SELECT Max(CompanyID) FROM MyDatabase)
SELECT @newc = (SELECT CompanyID FROM inserted)
IF @newc = 0 OR @maxc <> @newc SELECT @maxc = @maxc + 1
UPDATE MyDatabase SET CompanyID = @maxc WHERE CompanyID = @newc
```

You'll notice that, in the Table Properties, the Insert Trigger is now completed for you, specifying the **`MyDatabase_ITrig`**. As with the Delete Trigger reviewed earlier, there is a special value associated with insert triggers. The reference to Inserted allows you to retrieve fields just placed in the database table. Using this information, we can update the counter with the next unique value.

Once the table has been created, you'll be prompted as to whether you want to attach the table to your open database in Access:

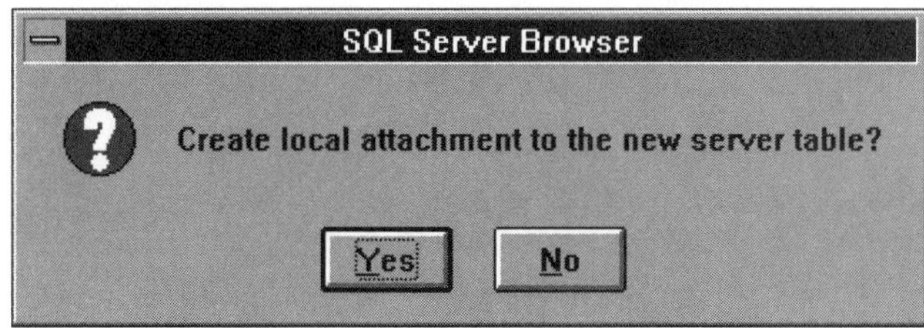

If you select Yes, you'll be able to refer to the table from your local .MDB, using it like any other attached table. Just prior to attaching the table, the Browser will ask what to name the attached table and whether to store the password for the table. If you allow Access to store the table's password, you will not be prompted for this information when you use the table at a later date:

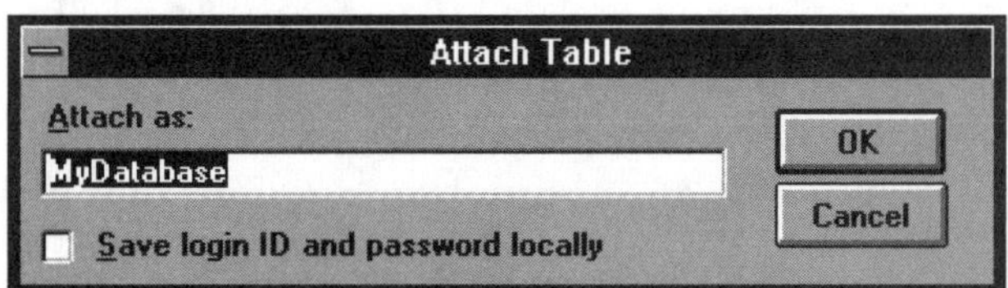

If your system is a secure system requiring a password, leave the check box blank. Your users will be prompted to login to the server prior to accessing the database table.

Configuring the Jet Database Engine

There are several options available that pertain to how the Jet database engine retrieves information from the server. Some of the key options are explained in this section.

Settings Maintained in MSACC20.INI

The **`MSACC20.INI`** file that configures Access contains several items that can impact the performance of Access and the various data sources that it supports. These can be found in the **`[ODBC]`** section of **`MSACC20.INI`**. While not all options will be outlined here, you can find more information on these by searching Access' on-line help:

Item	Type of Parameter	Description
LoginTimeout	Numeric	Changes the amount of time that can pass without canceling a login. If you are experiencing delays in logging on to the server, either due to heavy traffic or a remote connection, you can increase this number The default is 20 seconds.
QueryTimeout	Numeric	As with the LoginTimeout, if you are experiencing delays and are receiving query timeout messages, you can increase this value to allow more time. The default value is 60 seconds. You should also note that you can set this value in the Options dialog in Access. The ODBC Timeout in the Multiuser/ODBC section allows you to bypass this .INI file setting.
ConnectionTimeout	Numeric	This is the amount of time that an idle connection is kept open to the host. Inactive connections are automatically re-attached when a request is made of them. The option may become an issue if you have remote users. Remote connections may require more time than usual to reconnect to the data source.
TryJetAuth	Numeric	If you are not using local Access security, you can tell Jet not to worry about user security. Security will be maintained at the server level. Setting this value to true, a value of 1, will tell the Jet database engine to try local authorization first before prompting for the user's ID and password. If you set this option to false, a value of 0, the user will always be prompted for the user ID and password.

Setting Up the MSysConf Table

In Access, a configuration table can be used to control certain options about database access. The MSysConf table is such a configuration table, which Access will search for when attaching to a database. If the table is found, it is searched for options that relate to how information is retrieved from the database and whether passwords should be stored to provide access to the database in the future.

The table structure is outlined below and is followed by an example of a working MSysConf:

Column	Data Type	Description
Config	SmallInt	Configuration option represented in the record. This column has a unique index on it and is not required. (By definition, there can only be one blank with the unique index.)
chValue	VarChar	This field, 255 characters long, is where text-based options are specified. This field is required.
nValue	Int	This required field is where numeric options are specified.
Comment	VarChar	This 255 character field contains a text-based description of the option.

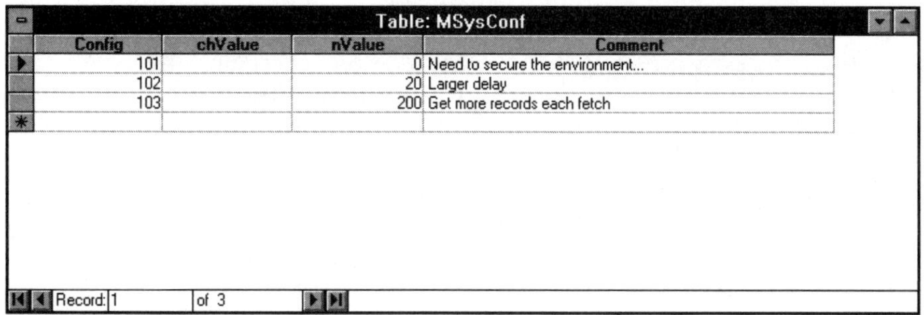

Table: MSysConf

Config	chValue	nValue	Comment
101		0	Need to secure the environment...
102		20	Larger delay
103		200	Get more records each fetch

Record: 1 of 3

When you first establish a connection to an external database, you should create this table. It will provide Access, and the Jet Database Engine, with the information necessary to manage the capabilities of the database. One of the applications of this table that you may find useful is the ability to prevent Jet from 'remembering' passwords to the tables. If your environment requires that people provide a password each time they re-start their application, you can set this value so that Access 'forgets' the password after authentication.

There are several different values that are maintained in the MSysConf table.

Config	nValue	Description
101	0	Don't allow the user ID to be stored for accessing attachments. This provides a more secure database access environment.
101	1	Allow passwords to be stored for accessing attachments. This is the default.
102	Secs	The number of seconds to wait between background retrieval of database rows chunks. The default is 10 seconds.
103	Rows	The number of rows to retrieve on each background retrieval of database information. The default is 100.

You can improve performance by experimenting with options 102 and 103. Using a higher setting for rows on option 103 will provide more information with each retrieval. This can improve performance if small to medium size databases are being used. If large databases are in use, be sure to take into account that, while records are being retrieved, the user may see some degradation in performance while records are being retrieved.

Option 102 allows you to specify the number of seconds between background retrieval passes. You may want to consider making this number in option 103 smaller. If you have more passes, but fewer records are returned, the performance on the client system will seem to be operating faster for the user. Remember, though, that the user will be waiting on the information to be returned. If the number of rows retrieved is substantial, this option can severely impact performance. Also, in the case of large tables, there may be many retrieval passes required, interrupting the user application far too often.

Working with Views in the Object Browser

The next objects exposed by the Object Browser are Views. Views can provide a new way of presenting the information in your database system, as outlined next.

What Are Views?

In Access, you can create a query that extracts information from one or more tables and presents it simply by calling the query. You have the option of requiring parameters, and you can limit how a query can be accessed by imposing security on the query objects.

In SQL Server, a view equates to the Access query. You create a view by using a standard SQL **SELECT** clause. For example, consider the two tables shown next.

Customer Table

Column Name	Description
CustID	Customer ID
Company	Company Name
Address	Address of the company
City	City of the company
State	State for the company
Zip	ZipCode for the company

Services Table

Column Name	Description
CustID	Customer ID
ServiceName	Name of service purchased
AmountPaid	Dollar amount collected

If you wanted to retrieve information from the tables and have each record contain all information about a company and its selected services, you could use the following SQL statement:

```
SELECT * FROM Customer, Services WHERE Customer.CustID = Services.CustID
```

This would retrieve all customer records from the system that have a corresponding services record, based on CustID. Those company records without a corresponding services record wouldn't be returned. If you were to use the information returned by this query in a recordset, the recordset would be as follows:

Customer Table

Column Name	Description
CustID	Customer ID
Company	Company Name
Address	Address of the company
City	City of the company
State	State for the company
Zip	ZipCode for the company
CustID	Customer Id (from Services table)
ServiceName	Name of service purchased
AmountPaid	Dollar amount collected

For each record returned, you'd have access to the ServiceName and AmountPaid fields. This view is updatable; SQL Server will manage to place new values in the correct tables, based on the **SELECT** statement used to create the view. However, in many cases, you'll want to create read-only views of information to allow your user base to create reports and perform other queries against the information in your system.

For more information on security assignment in your server product, be sure to review the system administrator's guide for the server engine.

Browsing Views

When you work with views, you are working with SQL **SELECT** statements. The dialog box for the viewer is a simple text box, allowing you to enter the **SELECT** statement that will produce the results you desire:

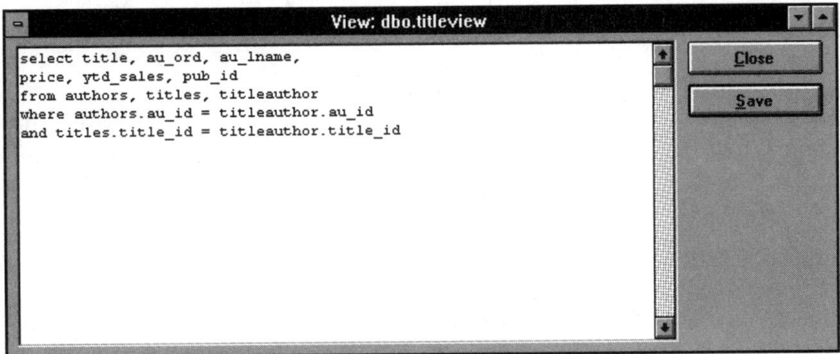

You enter views in this window and select Save to make changes or insert a new view. Remember that in the Access environment, a view is very similar to a query. If you've read the SQL chapter you shouldn't have too much trouble creating the SQL statements, but remember that you can always create the query in the Access QBE grid and then select the SQL button to display the SQL code. You can then cut and paste the query into the View text box as a starting point. Remember, however, that there may be some SQL statements in Access that are not supported on your SQL Server, for example the **DISTINCTROW** clause.

> **You'll have to use the keyboard shortcuts to Copy (Ctrl-C) and Paste (Ctrl-V) the information from Access into the Browser since no Edit, Paste function exists for the Browser.**

Working with Defaults in the Object Browser

SQL Server also supports server-enforced defaults. These can be established by the Object Browser from within Access.

What Are Defaults?

Defaults in SQL Server are almost identical to the DefaultValue property in Access. You establish defaults as a way for the server application to insert information into a table for you.

SQL Server defaults are defined by SQL functions with calls to stored procedures that return values, or by values that are 'hard-coded'. When you create a table, you assign a default to specific columns of the table by using the Default property in table design mode.

When the table is accessed and a new row is added, the specified column will contain the value you have just establish. Be sure that your default value satisfies any rules that you may have established that relate to the values in the column.

Browsing Defaults

Defaults are referenced in the Table Design form. Defaults determine starting values for a given column and can be defined using the defaults tab of the Object Browser dialog box.

When you Design a default, you're presented with the now-standard SQL statement editing form. With this form, you specify the statement or statements that will provide the information for which you are creating the default:

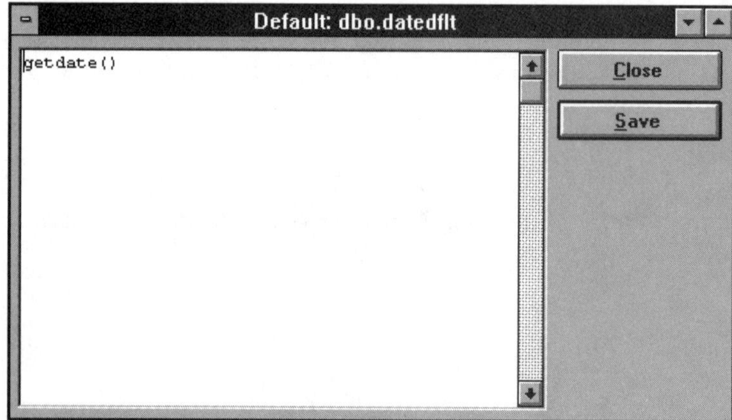

In the example shown above, the SQL getdate() function is used to return the current date. When you refer to the DateDflt default in your column definition, it will always retrieve the current date as a starting point for the column.

> **If it's important to have a valid date in the column, you'll want to consider putting a rule on the column that won't allow it to be inserted if the date is invalid. This is because defaults can be over-ridden by the user of the system.**

Working with Rules in the Object Browser

Intelligent server processing includes the ability to enforce conditions on the information stored in the database. These conditions are known as **Rules**.

What Are Rules?

One of the biggest benefits of an intelligent server is that it is able to process information and manage your database for you. Your application doesn't have to manage all of the business rules and conditions that control the data in the system. You can tell the server the condition that you expect the information to appear in the database by imposing rules and defaults.

The defaults help users understand what is expected in a field and they allow you to provide information in critical fields that may otherwise be missed. Rules provide SQL Server with a means of testing the information provided when a record is added or updated. Generally, a rule is a SQL expression, which must return a 'true' or 'false' condition. Additionally, the rule must also specify the name of the column to which it is bound. You'll see later when we work with the SQL Object Browser that you establish rules on the server in the Table Design dialog box.

An example of a simple rule for our table shown in the earlier section would require that the Services.AmountPaid field be greater than $0.00. The rule to enforce this would be:

```
@AmountPaid > 0
```

If the rule fails during an insert or update operation, an error message is returned to the calling application and the operation is aborted. Rules must be passed in order to update the database.

Remember, other applications are likely to be accessing your database. The times of closed, completely controlled systems have come to an end. They are being replaced by an open architecture allowing a myriad of applications to access your database files. However, rules can allow you to prevent someone in another application from updating the database with information that you don't necessarily want in it.

Browsing Rules

Rules are referenced in the table definitions and are defined by providing the condition against which the value of a column must be tested. The rule editing form is identical to the views editor.

Whatever the format of the rule, it should produce a 'true' or 'false' condition. You should be able to say to yourself, 'If this is not true then fail, otherwise succeed'.

For example, to make sure that all digits of a zip code are numeric, you can use the example provided with the **PUBS** database:

```
@zip like "[0-9][0-9][0-9][0-9][0-9]"
```

This will compare all five characters of the zip code and make sure that all are numeric. If the characters don't pass the test, a message is issued to the calling application and the update is not allowed to complete.

You can also have much more complex rules. Another example from the **PUBS** sample database provides a means of checking to make sure a Pub_ID is valid within a certain range. The first test would see if the ID is in the 5 values specified. If it's not, it must be formatted as four numeric digits and the first two must be '99'.

```
@pub_id in ("1389", "0736", "0877", "1622", "1756")
or @pub_id like "99[0-9][0-9]"
```

You should take note that it is possible to perform the check with a sub-**SELECT** statement instead of the hard-coded listing of valid IDs. If, for example, you're inserting authors and need to make sure that the specified **Pub_ID** is valid and on file, you could modify the statement above to read as follows:

```
@pub_id in (SELECT Pub_ID FROM Publishers)
```

This could prevent an author from being inserted without a corresponding publisher in the system.

Working with Stored Procedure in the Object Browser

SQL Server's programmable engine uses the SQL language to control operations. You establish routines, much the same as you do in Access, that control the functionality of the server. These routines are called **Stored Procedures**.

What Are Stored Procedures?

We've talked a little about stored procedures in other chapters, as we discussed different ways to manually export your application to the SQL Server environment. Stored procedures are program routines that run on the server as a server process. They are run, acted upon and interpreted by the SQL Server.

When you call a stored procedure from a typical application, you use the **`Execute`** command, specify the name of the stored procedure and pass in any applicable parameters.

```
...
Dim MyQuery As QueryDef
Dim MyData As RecordSet
...
'This sample runs the stored procedure
'sp_GetMyRecords, returning the results to
'your program.

Set MyQuery = db.CreateQuerydef("")
MyQuery.Connect = "ODBC;"
MyQuery.SQL = "sp_GetMyRecords @CustID = 0002"
Set MyData = MyQuery.OpenRecordSet(DB_OPEN_SNAPSHOT)
```

The results from the query are what comprises the resulting **`MyData`** recordset. Stored procedures, at the simplest level, are merely SQL **`SELECT`** statements. Here's an example of a simple stored procedure taken from the **`PUBS`** database on SQL Server:

```
SELECT au_id FROM titleauthor
WHERE titleauthor.royaltyper = @percentage
```

This stored procedure has one parameter, **`percentage`**. The **`@percentage`** reference allows the stored procedure to refer to the parameter and retrieve the information required.

A more common use for stored procedures is to use them to automate a process on the server. For example, if you have a procedure that returns a row from several different tables, computes some information and trims the name field down to the first 15 characters, the following stored procedure could be called:

```
SELECT type, pub_id, titles.title_id, au_ord,
 Name = substring (au_lname, 1,15),
 ytd_sales
FROM titles, authors, titleauthor
WHERE titles.title_id = titleauthor.title_id
AND authors.au_id = titleauthor.au_id
AND pub_id is not null
ORDER BY pub_id, type
COMPUTE avg(ytd_sales) by pub_id, type
COMPUTE avg(ytd_sales) by pub_id
```

This stored procedure is creating a join between the titles, authors and titleauthor tables, based on title_id and au_id. Within stored procedures, standard SQL functions, results of other stored procedures and **SELECT** statements are used to provide a comprehensive data manipulation environment.

Browsing Stored Procedures

When you work with stored procedures in the Object Browser, you use the standard browser form. When you use the Browser to work with your stored procedures, you have an added option, Parameters.... With stored procedures, parameters that are passed in to the routine are referenced in the routine by the at sign, '@'.

When the browser works with SQL Server, it forms the **SQL CREATE PROCEDURE** statement header and inserts the information specified behind the Parameters... button to the declaration of the stored procedure:

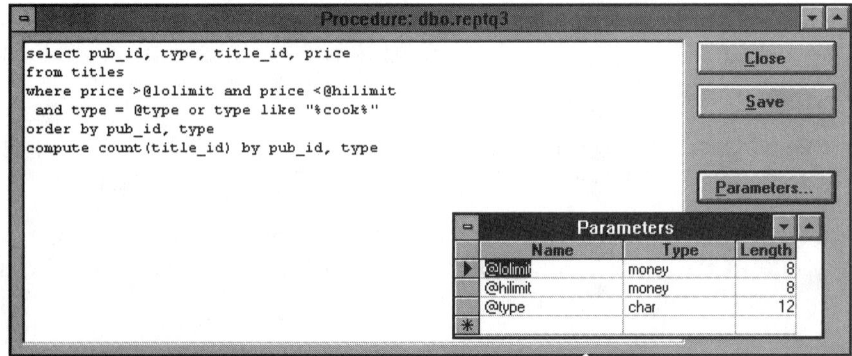

When you establish a new stored procedure, you first provide a name, then you'll be presented with the editing form. Enter the SQL statements that you want to execute in the form. If you have parameters that are required for the procedure, select the Parameters... button. From the resulting dialog box, you can specify what parameters will be required, as well as the Type and Length of the parameter.

If a system tries to use the stored procedure without first specifying the parameters, the call will fail and the user will receive a message indicating that an expected parameter was not provided.

When you call a stored procedure, there are two different ways to specify parameters. First, you can simply provide the information parameters in the order in which they are specified. In our example, the calling convention would be:

```
ReptQ3 100, 10000, "TranType"
```

Alternatively, and preferably, you can specify the parameters by name. By doing so, you eliminate any possible future incompatibility with the stored procedure, should the definition change. The following listing shows what the calling convention would be in this case:

```
ReptQ3 @LoLimit = 100, @HiLimit = 10000, @Type = "TranType"
```

In our sample implementation, both statements are equal. The difference comes in future portability of the code. For this reason, it's highly recommended that you use the second option of naming the parameters. This allows you to specify parameters without regard for order.

You can attach stored procedures from SQL Server as tables with an Access database, but not by using the standard Access **Attach** command. You'll need to use the File, Attach command from the Browser menu. Just as with tables, you'll be prompted for a table name to use with the local system. You'll also be prompted about whether to save the user ID and password. When you use this option Access will create a stored pass-through query that runs the stored procedure and returns the results to Access. This process of creating the pass-through query is transparent to you when you attach the stored procedure.

Once completed, you'll be able to access the stored procedure as a query in your system.

Since the query is based on a stored procedure and not an underlying table or tables, the query is read-only. You can't add or change information presented by an attached query.

Using the Upsizing Wizard

The Upsizing Wizard will help you automate the process of implementing many of the different things we've covered in the chapters on Client/Server implementations. To illustrate the wizard's capabilities, we'll walk through one use of the Upsizing Wizard and review what options are available, what they do when they are run and how they work with the server application.

The first thing that you'll want to do is to make a copy of your database. You should not work with the original in case you encounter problems during the upsizing process. Most conceivable problems have been accounted for, but you should always work from a backup when you are making wholesale changes to your system.

The ultimate goal of the wizard is to move your tables and objects to SQL Server, changing the references to them in Access so that attached tables and queries are used, rather than local copies. As we've shown in previous sections about this topic, this can increase your application's execution speed and produce a decrease in network traffic.

Before you begin, you should review your system to determine some base information. Here's an overview of the information that you'll need prior to continuing:

- Will you be creating a new database or using an existing one? If you're creating a new database, you'll also need to know the size and device for the database and log.
- What tables do you want to upsize to SQL Server, and what objects will remain in the local database?
- What other objects do you want to upsize to SQL Server, and what objects will remain locally implemented?

Creating a New Database and Log for Your Application

When you run the wizard, the first thing you'll be prompted for is whether you want to use a new or existing database for your upsized system. Generally, you'll want to use a new database because this will give your application more of a separate and distinct environment to run in for your testing:

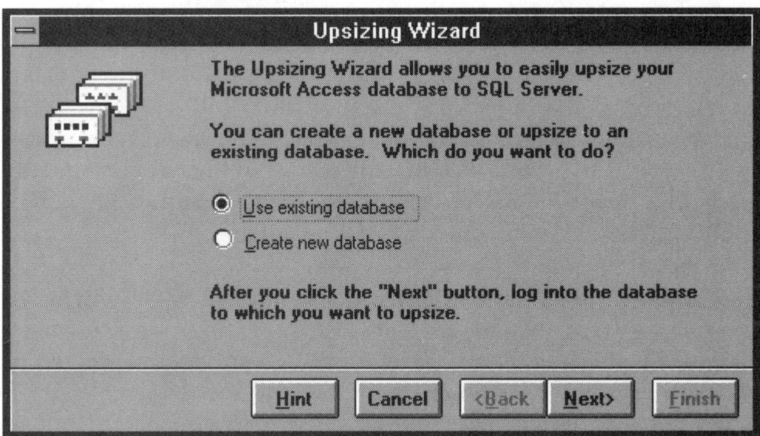

If you select Use existing database, you'll be asked to provide the name of the database to use. If you select Create new database, you'll need to provide some additional information. In addition, if you're creating a new database on the system, you'll need to have appropriate access rights. After you select the source for the upsizing effort, the wizard will begin the process of converting your system:

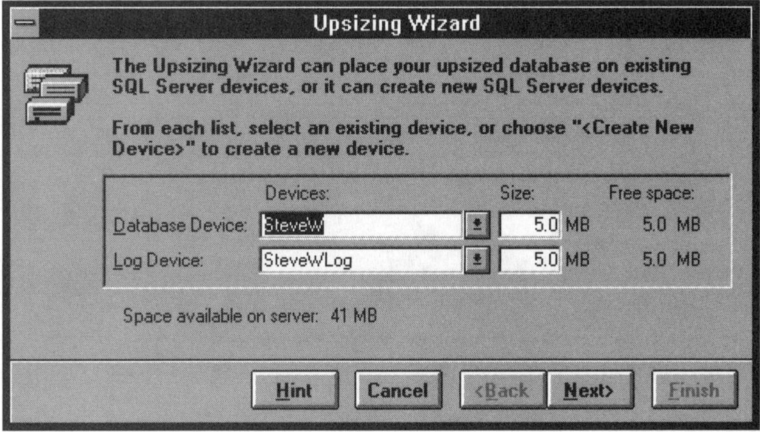

When you create a database, you'll need to provide information about both the database and the log device.

Log databases are used by SQL Server to manage transactions. As changes are written to the database tables, a snapshot of the changing row, both before and after the update, is copied to the log. This will allow it to be updated in a recovery mode if the need arises.

For each of these devices, the drop down list box will provide you with a list of all available choices. In addition, you can select <Create new device> from the list. If you do, you'll be prompted for the name of the device and the amount of disk space to allocate to the device. In the screen shown on the previous page, you also need to define the size of the device.

If you select a device that already exists, the Free space column will show you how much space is available on that device. Remember, devices are fixed sizes and you define databases that reside within a given device. Therefore, the free space is an indication of how much room on the device is not currently being used by database and/or log objects.

Once you select a device, you'll be prompted to provide information about the database. In the case of using an existing database, you'll simply select the database name from the list box. If you are creating a new database, you'll need to tell SQL Server how big to make the database. The size will be constrained by the free space on the device you've designated for the database:

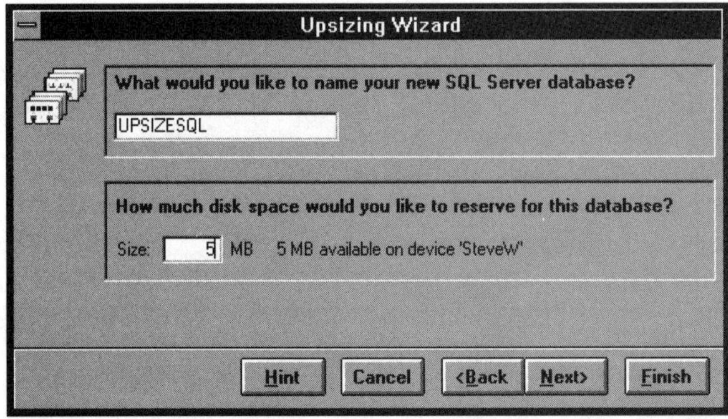

> **Note that the process of creating a device and database is not carried out immediately. Instead, the commands are accumulated and held to the end of the upsizing process so that all server processing can occur uninterrupted.**

Once you've specified all of the different options relating to the database, you'll be able to move on to the creation of the tables and other items that are included in the upsizing effort.

Steps to Upsize Your System

When started, the Upsizing Wizard allows you to export many of the different objects in the Access environment to SQL Server. The first thing you'll be prompted for is the list of tables that will be sent to SQL Server.

There are a few rules of thumb when selecting tables:

Table Use	Local/SQL Server Candidate
Work table	Local
Static Information	Local
Frequently Updated Information	SQL Server
Shared Information	SQL Server

For example, in our sample application, you wouldn't want to send the messages table to the server. If you did, as users access their inbox, they would see messages to other users since the inbox would have the same name between applications:

You can experiment with the results of the Upsizing Wizard by selecting the various tables that appear to fit the model of Client/Server systems. If you find that you want to move a table back to the local system at a later time, you can. See the section on 'Undoing' the Upsizing Wizard for more information.

Next, you'll be prompted to select the types of objects you want to convert to the SQL environment:

There are two options of note that are not checked by default when you start the wizard. The Structure only, no data option allows you to tell the wizard to build the table on the server, along with its associated indexes and so on, but not to export the information currently in the system to the new table.

Selecting this option will often be the correct choice. For example, if you're converting a system from development to production, this will allow you to discard any test data and start fresh with empty database tables.

The other deselected option is to Save password and user ID with attached tables. If you are signed in as the System Administrator (SA), you should leave this option blank. Otherwise, other users of the system will be using the database tables at the SA access level.

When the wizard has finished, the new SQL Server tables will be attached to the Access database.

The final step is to decide whether you want the wizard to produce an upsizing report. It is highly recommended that you request the report. It is the only record that you will have that relates to what was done between the two systems:

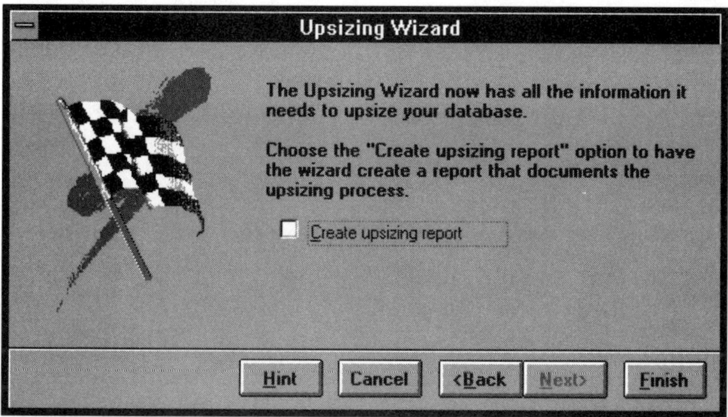

The final phase of the wizard is automatic. The wizard will create the objects required on the server. These include the device, database, tables, rules, triggers and defaults.

The Results from Running the Upsizing Wizard

When the wizard has completed its tasks, you'll notice that the tables that are in your database tables window have changed slightly. They now indicate that the Company, Contacts and Projects tables are externally attached tables:

In addition, your old tables are still listed, but have been renamed to show that they are local and not the production database tables. By adding '_local' to the name of each table, you retain the table for recovery purposes, but also allow the wizard to attach the references to the SQL Server tables.

You may recall, from our prior work with moving an Access application to SQL Server, that we went through the process of exporting the table to SQL Server, renaming the tables locally and then attaching to the SQL Server tables. This is exactly what's happening here, although the wizard accomplishes this for you automatically.

You should run your application to make sure that it functions exactly as it did before the upsizing process was undertaken. If you have any problems, see the section on undoing the Upsizing Wizard. The tables, rules, defaults and triggers have been defined and now reside on the SQL Server. If you use the object browser, you can see the following objects have been created:

Tables	Views	Defaults	Rules	Stored Procedures
Company		UW_ZeroDefault		
Contacts				
Projects				

Also, since we've defined relationships between the tables on the Access side, the wizard has created the rules necessary to uphold those relationships. If you open the table in design mode, you'll see the triggers defined in the Table Properties portion of the window:

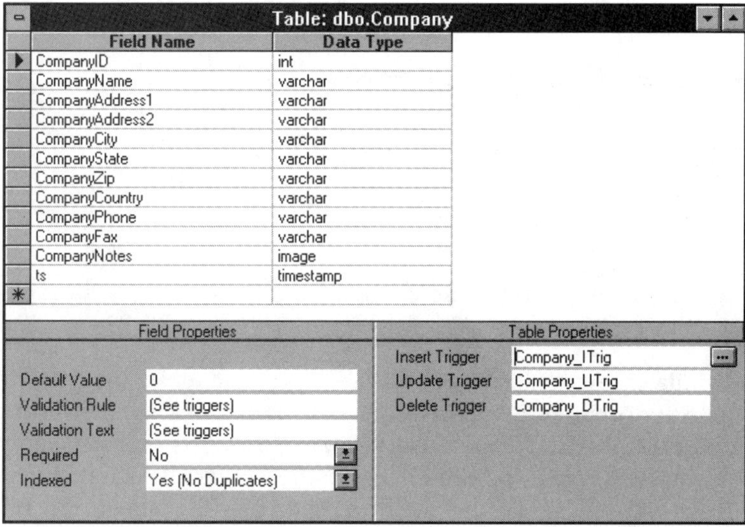

You'll also notice that the wizard inserts a new column in each table that it creates. This field, defined as a timestamp, is used to determine a unique record. It's used by the database engine to know if a record has been updated since it was retrieved.

In a typical update operation, the database layer issues a general command as follows (MyTable contains a ts column):

```
SELECT * FROM MyTable
...    DO UPDATES
UPDATE MyTable SET Value=NewValue WHERE ts = OrigTS
```

This will only succeed if a record is found with a timestamp identical to the original. Timestamps are maintained by the server and represent the last time the record was inserted or updated. If the record is found with the original timestamp we can be confident that the record has not been changed by another user or process.

Let's now take a closer look at the various triggers created for the Company table by the wizard.

The Insert Trigger

The code for the Insert Trigger is as follows:

```
DECLARE @maxc int, @newc int    /* FOR COUNTER-EMULATION CODE */
/*
 * COUNTER-EMULATION CODE FOR FIELD 'CompanyID'
 */
SELECT @maxc = (SELECT Max(CompanyID) FROM Company)
SELECT @newc = (SELECT CompanyID FROM inserted)
IF @newc = 0 OR @maxc <> @newc SELECT @maxc = @maxc + 1
UPDATE Company SET CompanyID = @maxc WHERE CompanyID = @newc
```

This trigger emulates Access' counter variable type. It looks up the current maximum value for **CompanyID**, adds one to it and saves the new ID as the current **CompanyID**. The real benefit here is that this process will happen regardless of how the record is submitted to the server. It is not up to the application to assign an ID, as the database server will manage the process.

The Update Trigger

The code for the Update Trigger is:

```
/*
 * PREVENT UPDATES IF DEPENDENT RECORDS IN 'Contacts'
 */
IF UPDATE(CompanyID)
    BEGIN
        IF (SELECT COUNT(*) FROM deleted, Contacts WHERE (deleted.CompanyID =
Contacts.CompanyID)) > 0
            BEGIN
                RAISERROR 44446 "Cannot delete or change record.  Since
related records exist in table 'Contacts', referential integrity rules would
be violated."
                ROLLBACK TRANSACTION
            END
    END
```

Since the company is related to contacts, we have to be careful when updating it. This is one case where we've said that there exists a one-to-many relationship with the Contacts table and that we need to enforce referential integrity. Since the contact record must have a company, deleting a company would cause an orphan contact record. The default trigger, shown here, would simply fail the update request. If you wanted to allow updates to the CompanyID, you could add the logic inside the loop to update dependent contacts records instead of failing the request.

The Delete Trigger

The code for the Delete Trigger is:

```
/*
 * CASCADE DELETES TO 'Contacts'
 */
DELETE Contacts FROM deleted, Contacts WHERE deleted.CompanyID =
Contacts.CompanyID
```

Since we're deleting the company, we also need to delete all associated contacts records. This will make sure we don't end up with orphaned records in the system.

If you review the other tables, you'll notice that similar triggers have been created for you. You can edit these triggers, adding functionality or additional tests to their processing if needed. The triggers presented by the Upsizing Wizard represent a good starting point and give you a strong head start into the process that, in most cases, will be perfectly suited to the need for database control.

Undoing the Upsizing Wizard

If the need arises, you can reverse the processes accomplished by the Upsizing Wizard. This occurs with one preliminary consideration. Specifically, if you have upsized the system and then added any information that you want to keep, or if you have since removed the _local versions of the Access tables, you'll need to take additional steps to back the information out of the SQL Server tables.

Nuances of Adding Information to the Server Or Deleting Local Tables

In either of these cases, you'll have to first import the information from the server into tables on your local system. Call up your **CONTACTS.MDB** database and select Import... from the File menu. You'll be prompted through a series of steps in which you can attach to the SQL Server. Once you have, you can select the tables you want to import:

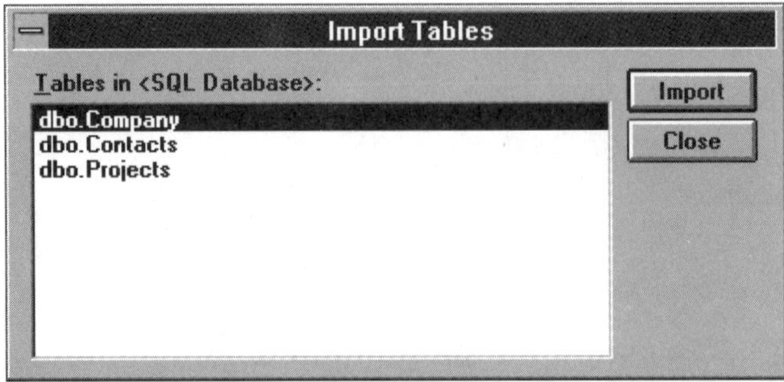

You'll recall from our earlier discussions on attaching or importing files that, since SQL Server has a concept of an owner assigned to each table, the dbo. is automatically placed before each table name. When imported into Access, the period is changed to an underscore. Your table listing in the **UPSIZE** database would look like the following:

Next, rename the tables that represent the production tables. In our example, these would be Company, Contacts and Projects. Rename them, rather than delete them, as a safety measure. You can delete them later after the downsize operation has successfully concluded. Rename each table with an extension of '_SQL'.

Finally, rename the tables we just imported, dbo_Company, dbo_Contacts and dbo_Projects, to their original names, without the dbo_ prefix. Redefine the relationships between the tables and run your application. Verify that all the components work correctly and that the information is correctly transferred between the SQL Server system and Access.

After you're comfortable that the information is being transferred correctly, you can remove the references to tables that are not used. In the example shown previously, you should remove the references to the _local files and _SQL files. You can remove the tables and defaults from the SQL Server using the Object Browser. If you added other items, such as stored procedures or rules, you can remove those as well. Contact your SQL administrator for assistance with the necessary commands to drop the database, log and device if desired.

A word of warning: Don't forget that other databases may be sharing the device you set up. If so, and you delete the device, you'll render those other systems inoperable. Be sure to check database allocation assignments to ensure that no conflicts exist.

Comments And Suggestions

With the Upsizing Tools from Microsoft, we've come full circle in how to use Access in a Client/Server environment. In the prior chapters, we detailed how to move much of your application to the SQL environment. Combining those other techniques with the upsizing options outlined here, means that you will be able to ensure that the two environments work well together.

In the next chapter, we'll be working in more detail about how to design client server systems and how to consider dividing up existing and new applications between the client and server components.

CHAPTER 13

Designing Client/Server Systems

If you combine the regular cost reductions that hardware companies are making on their products, with an increasing user-based demand for software that perform more tasks and shares more information on an enterprise-wide basis, you have the foundation for a shift in computing focus. Mainframe systems provide very good computing power, and it is this power that is being used as a basis for far-reaching database, transaction processing and global information system-type development. When used in conjunction with powerful desktop systems, users can begin to realize a significant boost in the capabilities of their software.

What's Covered in This Chapter

In this chapter, we'll look at the various areas that can be influenced in a Client/Server system based in Access. In many cases, there are pros and cons to all the different flavors, each of which you should consider as you design, develop and implement your system. We'll cover many different things, including:

- A look at different types of network structure
- Setting up a basic definition of Client/Server computing
- Showing ways that Local Area Network (LAN) servers can be used to implement Client/Server systems
- Showing ways that Mainframe-based systems can be used in Client/Server situations
- Using Microsoft SQL Server

This chapter also explains some caveats and suggestions to keep in mind as you design your systems, based around Microsoft's SQL Server as an example back-end database server.

Chapter 13

How This Chapter Impacts Our Application

At different points during the chapter, we'll show how you can take some of the features and functions of the PIM and implement them in a Client/Server environment. Since the servers that are used in today's workplace vary so widely, we've not actually implemented these suggestions on the accompanying disk. Where possible, we've included the code samples on disk so you can easily apply the concepts and ideas presented here, not only to the PIM application, but also to your own applications.

Introduction

This chapter is a bit different in comparison to other chapters. It's important to understand the forces behind the Client/Server emphasis in today's software, and so in this chapter, we are going to explain quite a bit of the theory behind the applications created for this environment.

Client/Server technology is the hot topic in today's computer circles. The phrase 'Client/Server' is a descriptive term referring to the division of computing responsibility between two components of a system. Consider the following examples:

- A workstation on a LAN is a Client to the Fileserver on the LAN
- Access can be a Client to SQL Server
- Access can be a Client to Word's OLE Automation Object (the Server)

The tools you use to implement this architecture vary based upon the platform, development environment and application requirements in demand. The goals of a Client/Server implementation allow for the optimization of your target computing environment, using technologies that have evolved in the recent past.

In general, computer systems and associated software have undergone a major transition over the past decade. These changes are not only in the area of physical hardware capabilities, but also in the architecture and software advances that are being applied to the systems being built today. Over this period, several schools of thought have developed.

In this section, the term 'Host' refers to a mainframe or minicomputer system. A 'Server' is part of a system where that computer is shared on a local area network, and a 'Workstation' is an intelligent terminal. As an example, a workstation could be a personal computer attached to a local area network, or used as a terminal to a host. A server can also be a workstation on a network, depending on the network operating system that is installed, or it may be a dedicated system providing shared file and print services.

To begin our review of the Client/Server alternatives that are available, a little history and explanation of the various architectures and systems is in order.

Host-Based Systems

Host systems provided the processing power and expansion capabilities needed by business and industry. These systems ran entire businesses and used a series of fixed-function terminals, also known as 'dumb-terminals', to provide the input capabilities to the user base. The systems required a staff of support personnel, ranging in expertise from database specialists to systems maintenance.

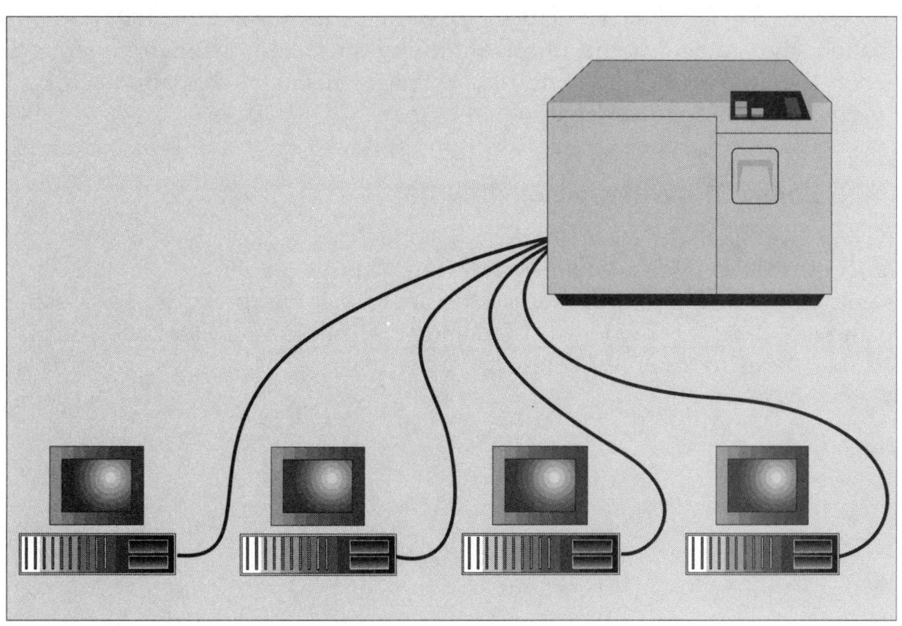

Hosts generally operate in 'burst' mode. They process information in packets, returning results in a similar format back to the terminals connected to them. For example, if you consider an input screen presented to a user of the system, the screen is sent, along with formatting information about the fields, the locations of the fields and so on, all in a batch to the terminal. Once the screen has been sent, the host is free to go on about its work with other sessions.

The terminal takes this information and displays the screen. As the user moves around the screen, there is no interaction with the host. During this time, the host is polling each of the attached terminals to see if any work is needed. The host timeslices its resources according to the number of active sessions currently initiated.

Once the operator has completed his work with the screen, he submits the screen to the host. At that point, the host checks the screen against any edit checks that must be performed, updates the user's display and all the other actions that are required before the host abandons the terminal and then processes the information according to a procedure executing on the host.

Notice that the application that the user is running is actually executing on the host system. No processing of information takes place on the terminal. The host is responsible for data validation, preparing and formatting the information, the storage of the information and so on. In an environment with a number of terminals accessing the host, the overhead of this approach can have quite a significant impact upon resources.

Pros and Cons of Host-Based Environments

On the positive side, there are many operations that a host does that are well suited to its abilties. Massive database manipulations, extremely tight security and some distributed processing solutions are just a few of these. In situations where these abilities are widely in demand, a Host-based system will excel and be very beneficial to response times.

The stakes on security systems are going up every day. Microsoft is currently working toward a C-2 security rating on their Windows NT operating system and, by the time this book goes to press, will probably have attained it. It can be expected that other industry names, including Novell and IBM, may follow suit in the future. Microsoft's certification is expected to be approved in the very near future. This will help somewhat in the Local Area Network arena in the areas of system access control and perceived value as a secure environment.

On the downside, a host-based environment can be the source of an ever-growing resource requirement. This can require upgrades in both processing power and disk storage (DASD or Direct Access Storage Device) capabilities. There is usually an upper-end to the number of active sessions on the host at any given time. This is because a single system is doing all the processing work for an entire environment. These combine to present a 'wall' that must be avoided if the system is to continue to provide benefits to the user base.

Another drawback to the Host-based environment is the cost of the software that runs on the system. It's not unusual to spend more than $100,000 on a single software package. Software is typically priced based on either the expected user base, or the size of the CPU that will be running the software.

Personal Computers as Smart Terminals to the Host

As PCs became more prevalent, people wanted to move their terminals off their desks and begin using the more versatile PC to access the host. This is usually accomplished by installing a terminal emulation board in the PC and hooking it up to the same jack that the fixed function terminal was previously using. This emulation board provides an interface that the host would recognize without the need for any software changes, and it allows the user to use the PC for other jobs like printing, word processing and spreadsheet handling.

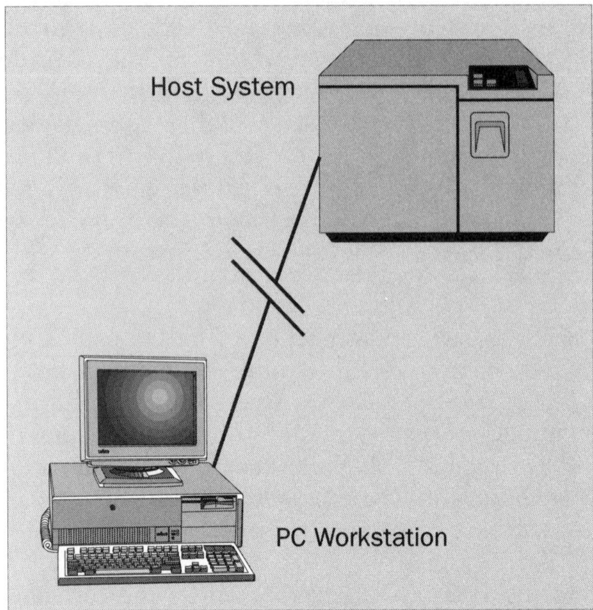

PCs and the interface software allow users to download files and information sets to the local system for use in other packages. This was the first basic implementation of **Distributed Processing** at a Personal Computer level. It also began to relieve the host of the additional processing that was required to refine the information in its databases, in order to get the required results. The negative impact of this technique is that the actual download process can be a significant drain on the communications bandwidth for the host network. When a download is underway, other users of the system are sure to notice if the download is of any significant size.

Pros and Cons of PCs as Terminals

The main point here is that PCs can be used to offload some of the processing requirements from the host system. Printing, formatting, re-calculation and presentation of the information returned from the host can all be accomplished using the PC, rather than the host. In addition, PCs allow users to do things that aren't feasible on host systems, such as WYSIWYG word processing.

The downside is that the PC is still used to function largely in the capacity of the terminal it replaced. The added functionality of multiple sessions, local printing and possibly file downloading is an advantage, but there is a limit imposed on the functionality offered by the PC as it must still pretend to be a fixed function terminal. Additionally, an unmanaged PC network with access to host information can reduce the security of information as it is possible to download, store and remove the information onto floppy disks.

Local Area Networks (LANs)

In the early 1980's, the Personal Computer became a popular desktop productivity tool. The PC offered the ability to process information reasonably quickly, going by the standards of the time. One of the biggest initial goals of the LAN was the ability to share printers. A side benefit of the LAN became the ability to increase the disk space available to connected systems. A server could be established to provide added hard disk space to all of the workstations on the network.

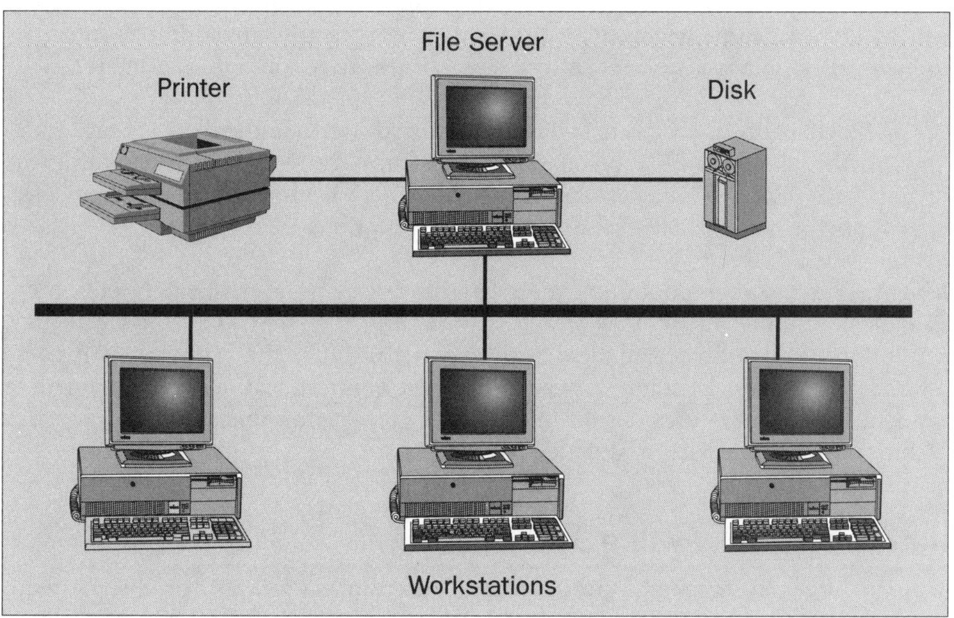

LANs are very cost effective and provide quite a lot of connectivity for the office and campus settings. Wide area networks (WANs) provide some capability to branch out into remote areas, but are somewhat more difficult to administer. With most LANs, you can also provide electronic mail, file sharing, printer sharing and common backup capabilities, all of which are advantageous to the average user.

Today, the demands, made by users upon the information retrieval systems that are currently employed, are growing at an alarming rate. Network-aware applications have begun to make users aware of the benefits of shared databases, network services and many other facets of a shared computing environment that make everyday life easier.

By using Access, you allow the database subsystem to take care of the different aspects of this sharing process for you. Concerns about record locking, transaction processing and so on are all managed for you, allowing you to focus on the application and what it needs to accomplish.

Pros and Cons of Local Area Networks

The cost savings that are available by implementing a Client/Server solution in offices can be tremendous, because a single, better quality printer can now serve several workstations. The added disk space is an added benefit, often used to store documents used by many different people. In addition, more and more network-aware applications are being introduced on the market today.

On the down side, LANs can become bogged down because of network traffic, although this depends heavily on the type of applications that are running on the network. Word processing and spreadsheet applications tend to wear less heavily on the network than do database applications.

Debugging a network communications problem can be a challenge. Tools are available that can help in this area, but they are often not available until an installation becomes more mature and begins to obtain the necessary support materials and tools. In many cases, a network communications problem will go undetected and merely cause the overall network communications to slow due to communication retries and failed conversations.

Distributed Processing Systems

In many larger systems, the processing of information is split, or distributed, between the system components most efficiently able to handle a particular job. In some cases, an installation may rely on smaller, individual host systems to work with physically separated areas. For example, if a bank has five large field offices around the city, rather than each terminal or workstation having a connection back to the host directly, it may be that a mini computer installed at each of the locations would make sense.

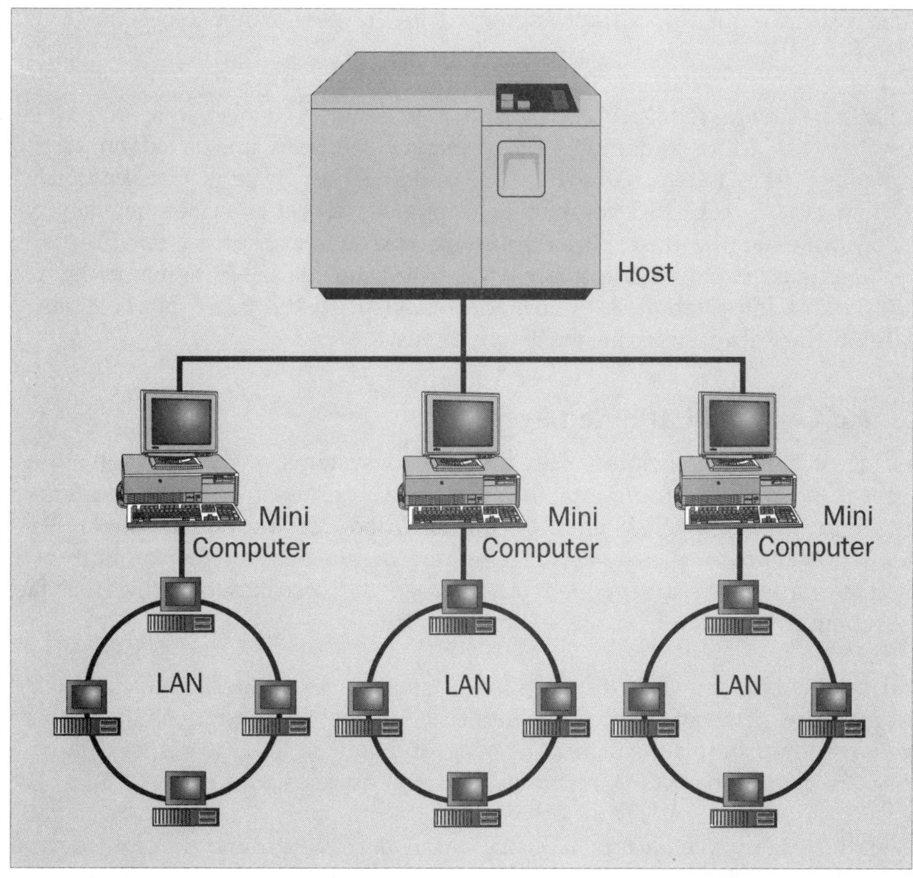

In this figure, mini computers are shown as the distributed hosts. In some larger computing environments, these distributed hosts may be individual mainframes linked to an overall host mainframe. The size and type of the system will vary depending on workload, throughput requirements, processing needs and storage requirements.

There are several benefits available to the designer of distributed systems. Of these benefits, two are of primary concern: response time and fault-tolerance. Response times can be boosted because the users are working with a local system. There is less traffic so the system will be able to afford more time to each task being managed. Secondarily, functions supported by the local system can continue in many cases even if the host goes down. Transactions can be queued up for a time and then submitted to the host when it becomes available again.

Distributed systems ideology comes into play when you also look into Client/ Server systems. More and more, Client/Server solutions are called on as intermediate steps between the PC user and the host system. Gateways to the host, some that are ODBC compatible, provide a direct interface between a client system and the host. Other solutions turn a server-based database into a Data Warehouse, holding information extracted and possibly summarized from the host. This information is then made available to the client applications without further impacting the host operations.

Pros and Cons of Distributed Systems

The biggest benefit associated with distributed systems is that of fault tolerance. By placing processing power in a multitude of different locations rather than a single processing host, the likelihood of the entire network of systems going down is not very high. If the architecture of the application is such that transactions are queued up between the distributed CPUs, this facet can become a key factor in the system's value.

It's also worth noting that for distributed systems to be designed correctly, there is a new level of complexity involved during the design of the system. Data synchronization, information sharing and fault-tolerance planning are among the topics that come into play in this environment.

One of the prohibitive factors in using mini- and mainframe distributed hosts is cost. The added cost of these systems can be prohibitive and may cause other facets of the network to be compromised, in order to help make up some of these costs.

Enterprise, or Workgroup Networks

None of the systems we have considered so far are 'Client/Server', but simply ways of passing information and sharing network resources.

However, with the introduction of Peer-to-Peer networks by Artisoft and Microsoft, it became possible to share information directly between two systems even more easily than in the LAN systems where common printer and disk services were the goal. With Peer-to-Peer networks, you can establish your PC system as both a 'Server' and a 'Client' or a workstation on the network. This means, with sufficient rights, other users can access information directly from your system.

The application that requests information of the Server is called the Client, and the application providing the information back to the Client is called the Server.

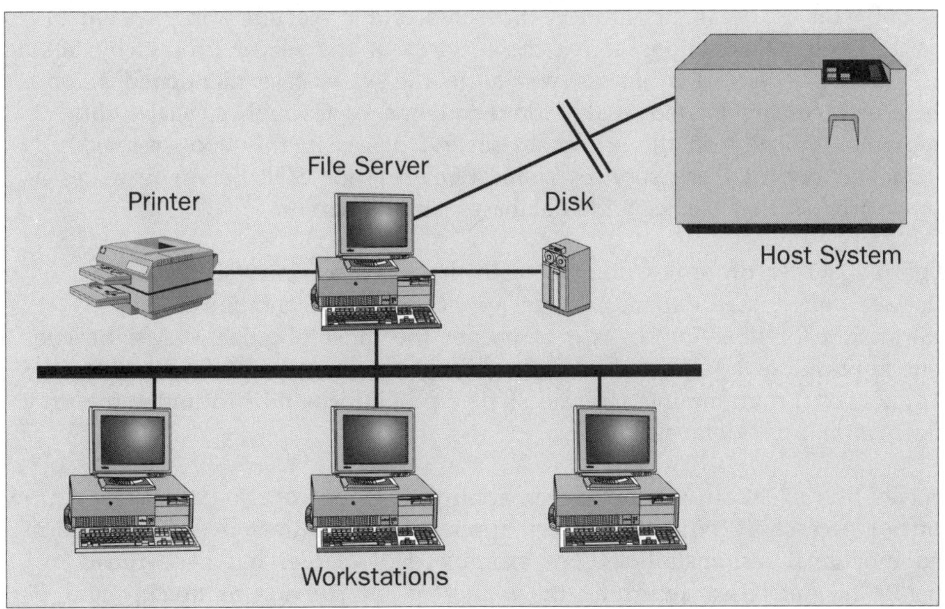

Network Operating System (NOS) technology has also become more comprehensive with improvements to its abilities. Gaining access to another system's resources, assuming you have the appropriate rights, is becoming very easy. Security is greatly enhanced since the NOS is taking on more responsibilities in the areas of user authentication and validation. In addition, the concept of 'Server Processes' has become a significant part of these more advanced networks.

With Novell's Netware Loadable Module (NLM) support, a developer can write an application that actually runs on the server and can be accessed by the users of the workstations or their software. This is one form of a Server Process. The NLM is loaded by the person designated as the system administrator and can provide access to database services, file services, printer management as well as to applications on the network. NLMs are complex to develop and require a great deal of testing, as they are loaded at the operating system level on the network server.

Microsoft and IBM went in another direction with their development of LAN Manager, LAN Server and Windows NT Server. When you create server processes in these environments, you don't have to create applications that only run as a server process as is the case with an NLM.

Instead, you create an application that runs under the operating system of your choice. Other workstations access the services of the server process by talking to it with pre-defined protocols, just as in the NLM case mentioned before. These services are loaded at the command line or through special utility programs, typically on the server. In several places in this book we've mentioned one of these services called SQL Server. SQL Server provides a server process that works with databases on the server.

Typically, server processes don't actually have a user interface. The user interface you do see depends on an application's presentation of the information for you. In the case of one of the most popular NLMs, Btrieve, your application talks to the services through a set of pre-defined APIs (Application Programming Interfaces) that put information to and retrieve information from database files.

Usually, the client drives the server, controlling what operations are performed, but not necessarily how. The server application is optimized for its platform and functional responsibilities. For example, SQL Server has been tuned to operate on databases, returning the requested information as quickly and efficiently as possible to the requesting application.

In a Client/Server system, both the client and server portions of an application are optimized to do what they do best, whether it is the presentation of information or the manipulation of it. Implementing a Client/Server solution is an exercise in design, test and re-design. It will often be that an optimal solution can only be designed once the application is in beta test and you can see how information is actually flowing across the network. You can then determine if further processing should be shifted to the client or server portions of the solution.

Pros and Cons of Enterprise and Workgroup Networks

The major thrust, and the biggest advantage of networking today, is the power that users now have at their beck and call. This manifests itself in the ability to easily share information between LAN workstations, the ability to allow other users to share resources on the LAN and the ability to access a LAN remotely using standard modems as communications devices.

One of the biggest detrimental perceptions of the LAN environment has been that of security. It may be surprising to know that the ability of workstations to easily share information can be a detrimental to the system as well. As more and more LAN users open up their systems and resources, the responsibilities of network administrators increases in line with the volume of network traffic, and control over resources and access rights becomes a major issue. As we mentioned earlier, this is being addressed by the next wave of operating systems that are on the horizon. Windows '95, Windows NT Server and the NT Workstation all address the issue of security and control over resources.

Definitions of Client/Server Computing

There are several interpretations of what Client/Server solutions entail today. One of the better examples is that of a file cabinet and the one specific file that is in demand:

Suppose you ask your assistant for a specific file related to one of your major customers, the Roganstetis Corporation. In a typical, non-Client/Server environment, the analogy would be that your assistant would wheel the entire file cabinet system down the hall to your office.

You would then be free to open each drawer, browse through its contents and eventually locate the file you want. It may be located at the end of the files because of the alphabetical sorting, and then again perhaps not, depending on the format of the index. The file cabinets would then be wheeled back down the hall to their original location. You can see a few problems in our somewhat comical example:

1. The act of moving the file cabinets would be substantial. The effort with the cart and actually moving the data back and forth is obviously not the most efficient way of accomplishing the task at hand.

2. The need for you, the client application, to sort through the information looking for what you need, is not a good use of your time. You should be presented with the file (or record) you need, not all of the other files in the system.

In a typical non-Client/Server LAN database application, this is exactly what's happening. Since no intelligence on behalf of the server is used, all the information processing must be done by the client application. Essentially, the whole file is returned just to get the one record you're interested in. The records must be sorted and searched for the specific item or items needed.

Now consider a Client/Server implementation of this same scenario. When you request the file you need, the single folder containing the information you need is delivered. The only thing to be transported is the contents of that record:

This is true of a well-implemented Client/Server application. The server is able to process and return **only** the information you request. There is no need to process the results further to glean the information you are looking for.

The ultimate goal for enterprise systems is to be able to access information to which you have rights, without regard to where it resides, how it is accessed or what tool it is that you employ to work with it. This is the main goal of the Microsoft's chosen direction of 'Information at your fingertips'. The premise is that the average software user should only specify what he needs to work with and be able to have the system determine how to get it, work with it and update it.

There are many people defining what a Client/Server system is all about or is supposed to accomplish. We've summarized below three basic definitions, pieced together from various sources at Microsoft (as well as other authorities on database design), to help us define where the responsibilities and expectations may lie.

A Technical Definition of Client/Server Computing

The technical definition focuses on the computational divisions that are made. These divisions include how the processing is split up, which components perform certain tasks and so on. A basic technical definition would be as follows:

'Client/Server computing is the division of tasks between individual processes, located on single or multiple devices, known as servers and clients. This division of tasks is made so that specialized hardware, software or shared data can be located on a server to be utilized by one or more clients in an economical and efficient manner.'

A Business Definition of Client/Server Computing

When a business unit must justify or explain its goals in moving to a Client/Server environment, a more results-oriented definition often comes into play:

'Client/Server computing is an architecture that allows information processing to be performed more effectively by distributing software processing. This results in more end-user productivity, shorter development times and lower costs.'

The shorter development times are derived from the fact that the client components can be built with mainstream, PC development tools including Microsoft Access, with any of the suite of development languages and platforms currently available, as well as any of the specialized tools such as ODBC for accessing information.

> *It should be noted that there are currently many heated debates in the computer community regarding the validity of the assumptions concerning reduced costs for PC software development. Many people feel that PC projects are prone to an ever-growing schedule. It's easy to understand why: people's expectations of PC software are growing exponentially as they use more and more powerful applications in their daily work. Be sure to scope your applications and timelines carefully to help in avoiding this problem.*

A Programmer or Developer's Definition of Client/Server Computing

Typically, a programmer's desires lie in working with the latest and greatest technologies. This includes seeing how computers can work together in the most simplistic fashion. It also includes exploring the fruits of moving traditional systems to a more leading edge environment. A developer's definition of Client/Server computing has been said to be, quite simply, 'The Really Fun Stuff!'

Why Consider a Client/Server Solution?

Aside from being the industry's direction and the source of a whole flurry of buzzwords, why would you want to consider moving to a Client/Server environment?

Client/Server offers a combination of benefits that can be quite compelling. Probably first and foremost is that, with PCs, users are able to utilize more presentation, manipulation and informational tools against their information. If you combine this fact with the mainframe's ability to work with and store enormous information bases, you have a combination of actual data and manipulation tools that make the information more valuable to the end users.

In the early part of this chapter, we outlined what each scenario, from host-based systems to enterprise-wide systems, is good at and not so good at. In the Client/Server world, you optimize on these traits and use the positive pieces of a given architecture. For those items of functionality not readily provided by a given paradigm, the developer looks to other toolsets. Client/Server lets you optimize your environment to get the most out of your processing resources.

With Client/Server environments, you can focus hardware dollars where they make most sense, from the applications' point of view. In many cases, servers are far out-classing workstations in terms of processing power, resources and capabilities. If you use this to your applications' advantage, you can gain some very significant increases in your return, to set against the investment made in the system.

Fully integrated servers are providing a wide variety of capabilities to the client applications. These include:

- Database services
- Host connectivity, through both gateway access and data warehousing
- Messaging and workflow services

As mentioned earlier, Client/Server software divides the functional requirements of your system. Here's a diagram to help explain where certain basic responsibilities lie:

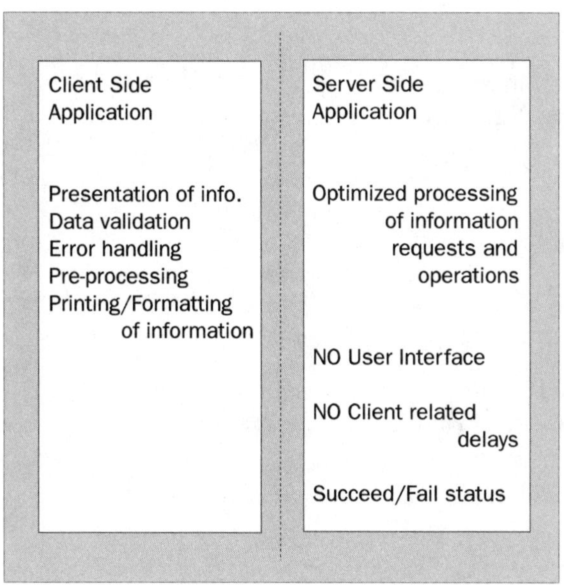

Client Side
Application
Presentation of info.
Data validation
Error handling
Pre-processing
Printing/Formatting
of information
Server Side
Application
Optimized processing
of information
requests and
operations
NO User Interface
NO Client related
delays
Succeed/Fail status

These areas are outlined in more detail in the following sections of this chapter.

Client Software Design Goals

When you are determining how a client software component should be designed and built, there are several different considerations to keep in mind. To optimize the architecture and get the most out of your development dollars, consider the areas of User Interface and Functionality, which are outlined below.

Client-Side User Interface

The client software should be responsible for **all** user interfaces that are to be presented. This means that if the user is prompted with a dialog box for information, an input screen to enter data or any other informational aid for the user, all of these must be handled by the client application.

If at all possible, you should design your application so that status information is presented to the user for all operations. General guidelines call for an hourglass cursor for operations over three seconds and a message box or other indication of progress for times in excess of 10 seconds. These are, of course, only guidelines and you should modify them as appropriate, for your user base.

In traditional systems, many users have grown used to checking their hard disk drive light for activity as an indication that a process was running. Remember that, with network applications, the disk drive light is not lit. Providing feedback on the screen may be the only thing that keeps a user from rebooting their system the first time they execute a longer process.

Client-Side Functionality

When you design what is to be done by the client software, you should include all processing in the following areas:

- Error handling
- Data validation
- Status monitoring

Error handling must not only include the errors returned from Access, but also those generated by the server application. Remember that, in some cases, it may be desirable to retry an operation before notifying the user of a potential problem. This may be the case in a 'Record Locked' situation or if a timeout is received from a lengthy operation.

Various servers will return different error messages and codes. When you develop your application, you'll need to know the codes that you can expect and how to work with them when they are encountered.

As you are designing the application, you should make sure that once a server process is called, in all cases it is able to complete its task with the information you provide. You should avoid the case where the server is forced to request additional information from your application once the process has been initiated on the server. The optimum use of the server is to submit the request, allow it to operate on the request at full, uninterrupted speed and then return the results to your application.

Data validation must include a check on the information entered on the form or being processed by the server operation. All fields should be reasonably checked for correct format, valid date or other value ranges and so on. The goal is to make a server operation fail only for unforeseen problems, not problems that can be controlled by the client application.

You should note that this might involve copying validation data from the server at the beginning of a session for lookups and validation, rather than going to the server each time you need to verify a value.

Server Software Design Goals

The server side of the equation provides the highly optimized modules, or 'Server Processes', for the client application to use. Examples from Microsoft include the Exchange Server (electronic mail), SQL Server (database) and the SNA Server(host access), to name but a few. Other vendor solutions are available from Oracle, Sybase, Borland and many others.

Server-Side User Interface

The only user interface anticipated for a server application would be for the server-based utilities that are required to run the application. All daily use of the system should be free from user interface. The reasons for this are purely response-based.

If the user is allowed to enter information directly into the server, the application will be waiting on the user to complete its task. A server application is optimized to take the information or service request and run with it until completion.

Besides maintenance interface, no user interface should be required for the server application.

Server-Side Functionality

Functionally, the server should be prepared to take the information given it and work with it until its natural end. This should be either a success or failure, with the status and any associated information being returned to the calling application. This applies not only to the actual server application, but also any routines or procedures that you may develop and call from your client application. Each routine should be able to fully execute its operation without further intervention.

This applies to server processes and the programs you design for them to execute. For example, if you have a stored procedure running on the server, you'll need to ensure that it can process the information passed to it, providing feedback to the calling application.

Factors That Help to Determine Likely Client and Server Components

Now that we've outlined the underlying assumptions and ideas behind a Client/Server system, how do you apply these to an application and determine where you may want or need to divide it between the Server and Client components?

When you design a system for a Client/Server environment, you'll need to consider many factors. We've outlined many in this chapter and they include the following:

- **Where is the host located in relation to the user base?**

  If the host is remotely accessed by the user base, it may make a great deal of sense to break functionality into local and remote components. This can optimize the users' environment, providing improved usability. Advantages that we've outlined include enhanced throughput and fault tolerance.

- **What are the user's system capabilities?**

  If the computers in place on the desktops are lower-end systems, you can optimize your application by trying to move all major processing functions to a server application. This allows the functions to perform at server speed, returning the information to the user at a much faster rate, while still allowing the workstation to perform additional, local work with the information.

  If computers on the desk top are more powerful, say 386-33 to 486-33, you will want to consider a split workload between the workstation and the server. Since these systems are able to process information reasonably well, all sides will benefit if you reallocate some of required processing to the PCs. You'll lessen the demands on the server's processing time, resulting in increased capabilities. You'll also increase the user's control over the application as more of the processing will be taking place on the local system.

  If you have a system where the desktop computers are very well equipped, as may be the case with systems with significant hard drive space, RAM and processor speed, you can shift the majority of the application processing to the workstation. This frees up your server processes to be truly focused on the task of working with the Email system, database or other operations that you've set the server up to handle.

What is the network traffic prior to installing the application? What is the expected level of traffic that will be produced by the application?

If the network bandwidth is already stressed, you will want to carefully design what information is being passed between client and server components.

If you want to decrease traffic, you'll have to consider the average requests for information. If the requests are for reports that include much of the database, the differences you'll see with a Client/Server system will be minimal. This is because most of the database will be passed across the network regardless of where it is processed.

If, on the other hand, your system is largely a query-and-respond type of system, you can drastically decrease network bandwidth requirements in the Client/Server environment. If designed correctly, your application should only be passing a qualified request for information to the server process. The server works through the request and returns a validated result set for you.

Will users of the system include remote, off-LAN users?

If you have a user base that will be using your system across remote services, including such examples as Remote Access Services for Windows NT, PC Anywhere and others like them, you'll have to design this fact into your software.

If you consider these environments to be a very slow network, you'll be on track in your design efforts. In a slow network installation, as in a congested network traffic environment, you'll want to minimize the traffic across the network. Highly optimized Client/Server applications can take an application that performs poorly over a remote connection and bring it into the realm of an easily usable application. In cases where the queries and processes are designed properly, the actual response time differences between the remote user and the local user can be minimal, with only a small overhead in time difference.

In one such application, the response times over a remote connection to do a significant search and retrieve operation on a database of over 1,000,000 records impacted the remote workstation by only three to five additional seconds. This type of remote response, on a query that required under five seconds in a local user mode, is considered as very reasonable.

As you design your systems, try to determine the time frame that will satisfy your users' requests for information. For instance, in many cases, if information is being submitted to a central office for later use, it may be that the information can be sent to a server process. This server process is then responsible for sending the information to the central office for processing.

Since the user doesn't require that the information be immediately available to the central office, the server process can take the time to optimize the information transfer. Perhaps an after-hours exchange of information can occur or the information can be bundled with other submissions and submitted as a larger batch all at once.

In any event, in a case such as this, the client application is able to continue with its work, even though the information has not actually been physically moved to the central office computer system. This has been called 'near real-time' or 'real-enough time' processing. It provides the information transfer required, but allows the transfer of information to occur at a somewhat different pace than in real-time processing.

Implementing 'Mainframe Server' Applications

In many cases, the biggest problem when implementing a LAN-based solution in an established computing shop is the existence of a legacy system. For example, suppose an existing accounting system is in place and functioning well, but is mainframe-based. While the accounting department is very happy with the system, other people would like to be able to pull reports on, and possibly modify, the information in the system.

In these cases, you'll want to consider a couple of different avenues for providing further automation:

1 Check into the availability of an ODBC gateway product for your host environment. If an ODBC gateway exists, it may be possible to attach the legacy system's tables directly to your Access application. While this is a very powerful tool and can boost the capabilities of the Access system immediately, consider carefully the implications of this type of environment.

   The positive side of this type of application solution is that information is always up to date. An application can allow changes and updates to the host, if the host security system will allow this to happen.

A warning about this approach is in order. If you provide an ad-hoc query and update capability to the host system through the ODBC gateway, you may find that a report related query generated from several systems simultaneously will result in the host system being taken to an unacceptable performance level. In addition, the security implications of an unguarded ODBC gateway into your database are a real concern.

2 Create a middle-man type of server process. This can be accomplished by setting up a system where the accounting data is periodically retrieved and made available to the user. This can be done as an attached table, giving users the ad-hoc query capabilities of an Access environment while still protecting critical host processing requirements.

This is an up and coming field of database design and is often referred to as 'Data Warehousing' as mentioned earlier in this chapter. The information that users are able to access is set up on a summary and/or detail basis from a server database system. The server is set up to automatically refresh its tables on a periodic basis, assuring that the information is current. This Client/Server setup is ideal for an Executive Information System (EIS) solution.

In cases where a host system is in use and the target of the automation is not to displace it, consider the host a very capable server. Its processing capabilities are beneficial and can be put to good use in your systems.

An Overview of Microsoft's SQL Server

Microsoft's SQL Server was one of the first and most comprehensive Client/Server database products on the market. It now shares the marketplace with competitors from Sybase, Oracle and Borland. In this section, we'll review some of the different aspects of the server and how they can be used in your applications. We'll also briefly cover how you install necessary programs in the server, making it compatible with ODBC and the Jet engine.

This section largely pertains to Microsoft's product, but the capabilities, methods and basic concepts are still applicable to the other industry participants. You may find syntactical differences between the various flavors, but consultation with the appropriate documentation should sort out any problems that you encounter.

Installation Requirements

When ODBC works with dynasets, snapshots and attached tables, it works through a series of stored procedures on the server, if the server supports this capability. These procedures are actually created in real-time when the link to the database table is initiated.

ODBC is the standard SQL-based cross platform connectivity tool and thus doesn't use stored procedures for all target database systems. Some drivers, such as the one developed for Microsoft's SQL Server, will generate stored procedures as mentioned above, but the driver will use SQL statements for the majority of its functionality.

You may notice that, if there are cases where your system doesn't close the connection to the database, these temporary stored procedures remain on the system. This happens when your application encounters an error and terminates abnormally. This usually occurs quite a lot when you are in development mode, but shouldn't occur when your application is in production.

In order for ODBC to be able to create these stored procedures and accomplish other tasks on the server, you must first install a series of supporting stored procedures. When ODBC is installed, it includes the **INSTCAT.SQL** script file. You must install this on your server prior to using ODBC to access it.

The easiest way to install the script is with the ISQL for Windows utility provided by Microsoft SQL Server. From the query window, select File and then Open. Select the **INSTCAT.SQL** script file from the open file dialog box.

Run the script and you'll receive a series of messages indicating the progress of the procedure. Once loaded, the script gives ODBC access to data type conversions, the ability to manage dynamic stored procedures, version and configuration information for the server and support for database join and union type operations.

If you run an ODBC query without first setting up these scripts, you'll receive an error message indicating that your catalog stored procedures are out of date. If you receive this message, run the `INSTCAT.SQL` **script against the server.**

You should contact your server and ODBC driver vendor for specific guidelines regarding the use of `INSTCAT.SQL` with your system.

Using Stored Procedures from Access

In the last chapter, we briefly covered some of the benefits of stored procedures. In addition, a quick overview of the types of conversions that are required to change simple queries into stored procedures was presented. Once you've created stored procedures to accomplish your tasks, there are two basic ways to use stored procedures from within your Access Basic code:

- Pass-through queries
- Dynaset and snapshot creation or Recordset definition and initialization

Pass-Through Queries

Pass-through queries are created when you select SQL Specific, Pass-Through from the Query menu. The standard QBE grid is changed into a basic SQL editing window and any query you have defined is changed into its corresponding SQL statement:

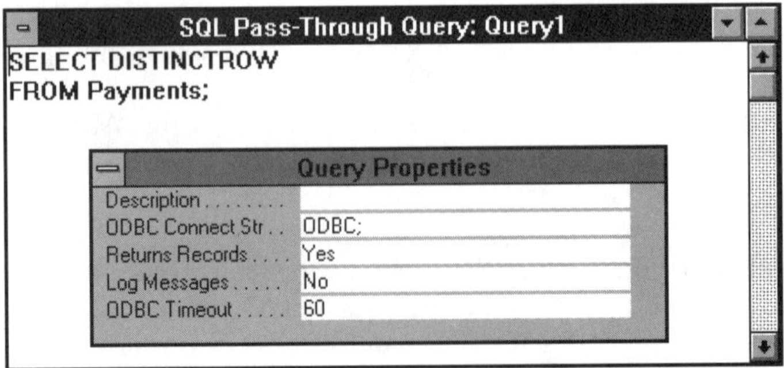

Pass-through queries are unique in their interaction with the server process. When you create a normal Access query, it is processed through ODBC or the Jet database engine. The query is translated into appropriate commands which directly access the underlying database. With a pass-through query, the complete instruction you have provided is given to the server untouched and translated there.

Pass-through queries are quick to execute because of this lack of translation. However, you should keep in mind that you are taking the responsibility for understanding the subtle rules, syntax requirements and other aspects of working with your specific database server. If you pass an invalid statement to the server, the call will fail and you will need to debug the statement to find the problem.

In our figure, we've also included the properties for the query. You'll notice a couple of important things denoted here. Perhaps the most consequential item is the Returns Records property. Pass-through queries are not only fast ways of requesting information from a database server, but also an excellent way of sending update information to the server where no records are being returned.

By default, Access expects to receive information from the server when a query is successful. If you are sending information to the database server in an update only mode and you probably don't expect any information back from the query, set the ReturnsRecords option to 'No'. This will prevent Access from generating an error when no rows are returned.

In Visual Basic, the equivalent to the 'Returns Records = No' property is using the `ExecuteSQL` method. In the case of VB, the number of rows affected by the call is the only return value.

You will have to experiment with the ODBC Timeout property in your query. The value of this property will depend on the reaction time of the server you are accessing. This value, specified in seconds, will determine when Access will intervene with a timeout dialog box after you submit the query.

Remember that, while in development, your tables may be quite small. If you are creating a system that will be working with increasingly larger databases, you made need to set this value larger to allow for the increased processing time. In addition, if the query will be impacting more than one database table, will include a large join or some other multi-faceted operation, then this value may need to be increased again. It is probably better to make the time longer than expected to allow for database growth.

Dynaset/SnapShot Creation or Recordset Definition and Initialization

When you create a recordset, you typically provide the name of the table from which you want to create the recordset. You can also specify the name of the query in the place of the table name. In addition, you can specify a stored procedure to call as a method of setting up the recordset. The syntax for this is outlined in the following example:

```
Dim MyDB As Database
Dim MyQuery As QueryDef
Dim MyData As Recordset
Set MyDB = CurrentDB
Set MyQuery = db.CreateQueryDef("")
MyQuery.Connect = "ODBC;"
MyQuery.SQL = "sp_GetMyTable"
Set MyData = MyQuery.OpenRecordset(DB_OPEN_SNAPSHOT)
```

> **Leaving the name of the `QueryDef` blank allows you to establish an unnamed, temporary query that can be used by your application. When the database connection is closed, the `QueryDef` is discarded automatically by Access.**

If you have a query that is a pass-through, it will automatically create a snapshot type of recordset for you. This is because Access has no way of determining where the information you requested came from. Remember that the SQL statement or stored procedure you specify is not interpreted by Access, Jet or ODBC. The results are returned to the recordset as a read-only snapshot. If you need to update records in this results set, you'll have to update them manually. You would probably have to accomplish this using another query. The update query can be one that updates the values as needed but doesn't return rows.

For example, if our stored procedure mentioned above, **sp_GetMyTable**, returned a set of records that we planned to send updates to, we could create a second pass-through query to manage the updates. This query would include parameters that are processed by the server stored procedure:

```
...
Dim MyUpdQuery As QueryDef
Dim MyNewName As String
...
```

```
'The code here retrieves the value to be contained in
'"MyNewName" and places it in the MyNewName variable.

Set MyUpdQuery = db.CreateQueryDef("")
MyUpdQuery.Connect = "ODBC;"
MyUpdQuery.SQL = "sp_UpdateMyTable @NewName = '" & MyNewName & "'"
Set MyData = MyUpdQuery.OpenRecordset(DB_OPEN_SNAPSHOT)
```

When you pass values to SQL Server, either need to pass them in the order defined by the stored procedure, or by specifying the name of the parameter and using the '@' sign before the variable name as shown above.

In many cases, you'll want to update a number of rows in the underlying table and then update your recordset. You can accomplish this by adding additional stored procedures for the update tasks. Consider a situation where a set of records is first retrieved from the database for review and editing by the user. As changes, additions and deletions are made to the database, the second stored procedure, separate from the one used to return the original record set, is called to make the changes:

```
/* Delete the requested row, but first copy it to a */
/* backup table                                     */
Create Procedure sp_DelRow (@RowID as Integer)
        as
           Select * INTO DeletedRows where MyTable.RowID = @RowID
           Delete from MyTable where RowID = @RowID
```

When the user deletes a row from the table, you could call the **sp_DelRow** stored procedure, then re-call the original query, MyQueryDef, to update your recordset to reflect the change in the database. This would somewhat mimic the look and feel of a dynaset type interface to the database, as changes would be visible immediately.

As an alternative, you can make a small change to the **sp_DelRow** stored procedure and to the calling convention that you use. If you change the stored procedure to select records from the database as a result of the stored procedure, you can cut in half the number of calls that you'll have to make to the server:

```
/* Delete the requested row, but first copy it to a */
/* backup table                                      */
Create Procedure sp_DelRow (@RowID as Integer)
        as
          Select * INTO DeletedRows where MyTable.RowID = @RowID
          Delete from MyTable where RowID = @RowID
          Select * from MyTable Order By RowID
```

Now, when you make the call to delete the record, you return the updated recordset. You can pass the stored procedure name as a parameter to the **OpenRecordset** method call:

```
...
MyQuery.SQL = "sp_DelRow @RowID = " & MyRowID
Set MyData = MyQuery.OpenRecordset(DB_OPEN_SNAPSHOT)
...
```

This has the effect of re-initializing the recordset based on the results of the **sp_DelRow** stored procedure. Since we're deleting the record in the stored procedure and then doing a **SELECT** on the table, the results will be the complete recordset less the record to be deleted, all accomplished in one call. Using this technique, you can take one step toward optimizing your application and the network traffic that it generates.

> **If you have a situation where you don't necessarily need to update the user's data set after an operation, you won't need to use this type of update consolidation. The reason for this is that with this technique, you will cause the user to wait for the update and refresh operation unnecessarily. Consider using only the update query without the refreshing of the recordset in those cases.**

Microsoft strongly discourages you from using the Snapshot and Dynaset objects. The objects are provided largely for backward compatibility and are not the optimum method of accessing the tables. In almost all cases, an attached table accessed through queries will be faster, offer more capabilities and generally provide more benefit to your applications.

If you have existing Access systems that use these methods and objects, you should consider migrating them to use the new recordset methods, objects and capabilities. More information on attaching tables is provided in Chapter 9, as well as information about converting database tables from one database provider to another.

Using Views Defined on the Server

When you create systems with a variety of users and associated security levels, all of whom require the information in your tables, you can create views on the server that provide only the information and access that you define. For example, a data entry person working on timesheets might be allowed to enter timesheet information into the system, but wouldn't be able to see information on salaries, employee personnel information and other information that is confidential.

Another use of views is to use them to make a 'virtual' table. The view consists of a definition that can outline how a join is to work and what information is to be returned. The view sets up these parameters so that, to the user of the view, it appears to simply be another table. In actuality, the view may contain values from several tables, joined in a manner that makes sense.

You may notice some parallels here to the Access query definitions. That's because a query is really a view in SQL terminology. In Access, you can specify a query as a table source in almost all instances. To Access, the query looks and operates the same as an actual table would with few exceptions. This is true in SQL as well. You can attach a view to your Access database, you can execute stored procedures and **SELECT** statements against it, or any of the other things you would expect of a table. Exceptions to this rule include the fact that a query that uses aggregate expressions is not updateable.

There is one caveat to using views. When Access uses a view, it doesn't, by default, use any predefined indexes This prevents Access from opening anything other than a Snapshot type of object as the content of the view. However, by specifying which field is unique you can instruct Access to create an updateable recordset as follows:

```
Create Unique Index MyViewIndex On MyTableName(MyField)
```

To create this query, select Query, New and then New Query. Next, select the SQL button or SQL from the View menu. Enter the statement in the SQL window, deleting the 'Select DistinctRow' that Access places in the window for you. When you run the query, the index will be created.

When you issue the statement to create the index, Access doesn't actually index the view. Instead, Access simply remembers that you've defined `MyField` to be a unique field in the view. Access will use that field as its unique identifier and will allow you to create updateable references to the view.

Managing SQL Server Connections

When you establish a session using ODBC and SQL Server, a logical connection is established to the server. If you think of a session as a pipeline to the server, you'll have a good picture of what we're talking about:

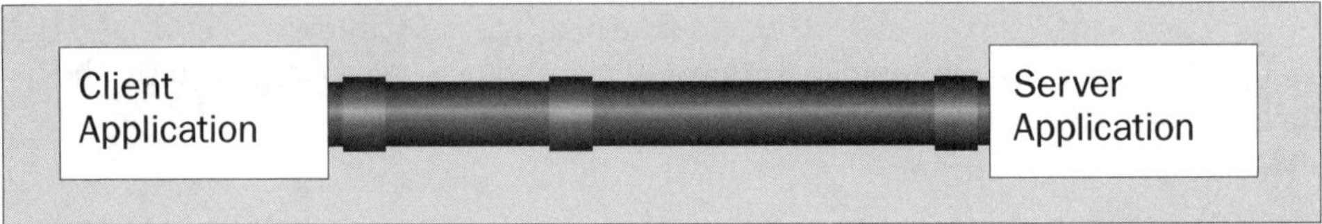

While the pipeline can handle information in both directions, depending on the server you are using, it may be that only one operation can be carried out at a time. For example, you may need to submit a request for information, retrieve all information associated with the request (or cancel it) and then issue another request to update or get more information.

Typically, this is not something that you worry about at an application level. Both ODBC and Jet are configured to know which servers support multiple conversations per channel and which require a completed set of results prior to additional requests being received. SQL Server requires that requests be fulfilled prior to issuing a new request. Jet and ODBC handle this by establishing a new connection if you need to gain access to the server during the time that results are pending on the current connection.

While this automatic management of connections is nice, you must remember that many products are moving toward a 'per-connection' licensing arrangement. Microsoft's SQL '95 product, for example, grants 15 connections per workstation license. The server product itself is purchased separately, with workstation licenses being provided as needed or in bundled packages. While 15 connections per workstation may sound substantial, consider that each of the following requires at least one connection:

- Open queries
- Operations within a transaction
- Dynasets (or Recordsets opened as dynasets)
- `SELECT` statements

Remember that a new connection is only established if results are pending on the current connection. If no other information is flowing on the current connection, it will automatically be used for the next request.

Optimization Of Connections

You should be aware of how you are defining your calls to the server application. Remember that if you issue an `OpenRecordset` call, you'll be establishing a new connection. If you can retrieve all values from that call prior to the next call, a new connection will not be required.

By default, Access only retrieves a reasonable number of rows from the results set of your query. Further information is obtained as needed when you work with the recordset. You can force Access to retrieve all values by issuing a 'Top 100 Percent' query. Setting the Query's TopValues property to 100 will return all values and force Access to flush the buffer, thus retrieving all values.

Note that this is less of an issue with SnapShot type objects because all data is retrieved at the time the call is made. The TopValues property can, however, help in the management of connections for other types of connections to the underlying tables:

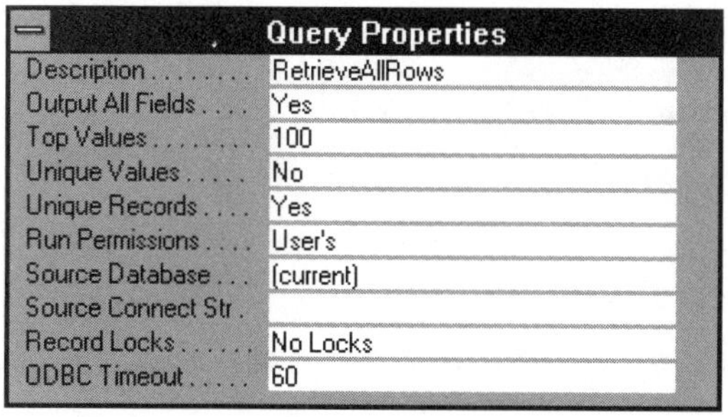

Query Properties	
Description	RetrieveAllRows
Output All Fields	Yes
Top Values	100
Unique Values	No
Unique Records	Yes
Run Permissions	User's
Source Database	(current)
Source Connect Str	
Record Locks	No Locks
ODBC Timeout	60

You can accomplish the same results as the 'Top XXX Percent' query by specifying the **MoveLast** method immediately after your call returns:

```
...
MyQuery.SQL = "sp_DelRow @RowID = " & MyRowID
Set MyData = MyQuery.OpenRecordset(DB_OPEN_SNAPSHOT)
MyData.MoveLast
...
```

This forces Access to go to the end of the Recordset, flushing it out of the buffer. You should take note that if your underlying recordset is small, this step is unnecessary and it's recommended that you make the results set as small as possible for performance reasons. However, if you have a need to return a larger data set, this technique can help you flush the connection more quickly than waiting for Access to retrieve the information in the background.

An additional point to consider is that 100 rows is a magic number for Access. If the results set returned to your application contains more than 100 records, a second connection is required to maintain the pointers to the records. If you can limit your record requests to less than 100 records, you can potentially cut your connection requirements in half.

Options for Optimizing ODBC

As you fine tune your application, you may find it necessary to review your configuration settings in the ODBC section of the **MSACC20.INI** file. These settings control many different aspects of the behavior of ODBC. For complete details on these options, check in the Access help system under the heading 'MSACC20.INI'.

Of special note are the following settings:

- QueryTimeOut
- LoginTimeout
- ConnectionTimeout

These options specify the values, in seconds, that determine when ODBC will fail a connection or operation.

Setting these values too low may cause unnecessary failures for longer queries or under busy network conditions. It's difficult to suggest specific parameters due to the fact that networks vary so widely depending on configuration, usage levels and so on. Your best bet is to experiment with these values to find the setting that covers the situations that you encounter.

ConnectionTimeout will cause a user's connections to be closed after the time period has expired. The connections are dynamically and transparently restored when the user resumes work and needs information from the server process.

The default values for these options are:

- QueryTimeOut: 60 seconds
- LoginTimeout: 20 seconds
- ConnectionTimeout: 600 seconds

Considerations in a Client/Server Environment

There are some different things that you can do or should at least consider when establishing a Client/Server system that can help in either performance or functionality of your system. These items don't fall under any specific heading elsewhere in this chapter and are presented here as food for thought.

Multi-Database/Multi-Server Joins

Some database systems allow multiple databases to reside under their control. SQL Server falls into this category, allowing a Device/Database/Table relationship for objects that are under its control:

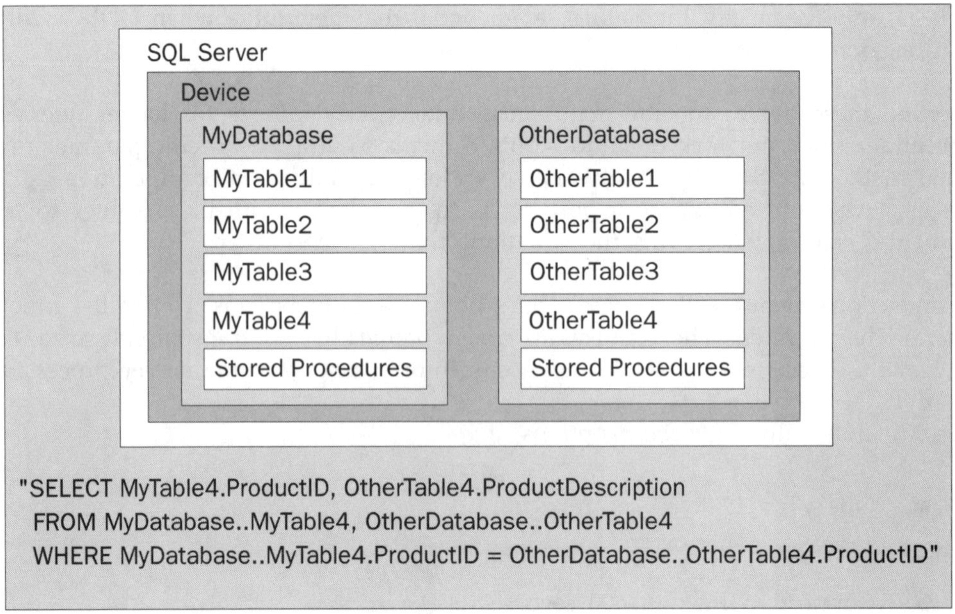

Creating joins that span databases, servers or database types forces Jet to accomplish at least part of the join locally, decreasing the benefit of the server process. The result is that Jet retrieves one set of values locally and then works with that set against the other data values. Visually and functionally, this works fine in your application. The impact this will have upon your system is focused on the performance of your application. Significant negative performance impacts can be expected in this type of installation.

You may want to circumvent the need for the join by defining a view that accomplishes the same thing. This way, when Jet opens the table, the view will manage the join of the tables. The restrictions on this work-around are generated by the server you are using, along with the requirement that all of the data to be included in the join is managed by that same server process. Joins across more than one type of database system (for example dBase and Access or dBase and FoxPro) will always result in this type of locally administered and processed join.

Setting Up Data Entry Forms

When a form is bound to a table, a recordset is established linking the form to the underlying table. The default mode for this operation is a browse-type of function where the user can navigate the database by going up and down the recordset. As we mentioned earlier, this type of recordset or dynaset is the most costly in terms of overhead.

There is a very important setting that you can establish to help alleviate the impact a form has on the system where the underlying table or view is stored on the server. This is the DefaultEditing property. By default, forms generally open with `DefaultEditing=AllowEdits`, which holds open at least one connection to the underlying recordset. If you set the DefaultEditing Property of the form to Data Entry, Access will only show a blank record and not forge a connection to the table or view. The user can then append records as needed:

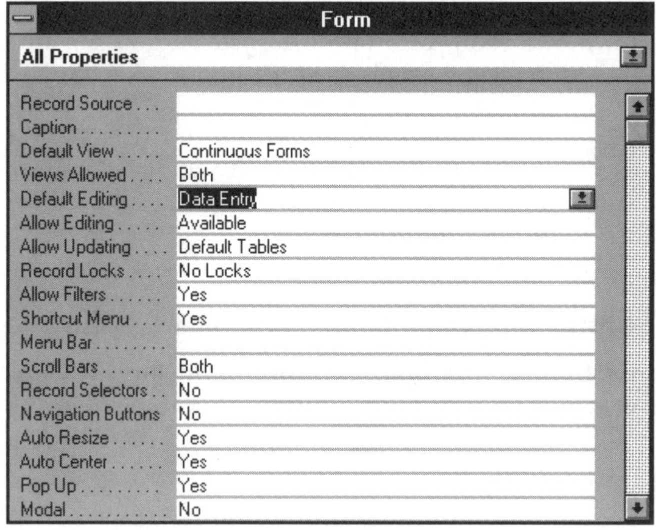

Other records can be reviewed by establishing a filter, but by default, the form will operate in append-only mode. This allows Access to set up the dynaset without regard to the existing data. In this mode, Access doesn't have to establish and maintain positioning information, providing a significant speed increase.

One additional method of decreasing connection usage is to make forms Read-Only with Edits Unavailable. This will allow Access to proceed without active update connections to the table.

Using Local Access MDBs for Lookup Information

When you use a database server with your Access system, you may find that you are continually looking up different bits of information used, for example, in list boxes. In these cases, consider creating a routine that will download the information to a local database, placing it in a native Access table. Change your list boxes to use the local table. You'll probably see a significant change in performance for the better. In addition, you'll be doing your part to limit network traffic.

This technique works rather well in environments where you have other static information that you are constantly referring to. Alternatively, if you are working with tables and need to make changes, you may want to bring the information down to a local table on your system. You can make the changes there and then re-submit the whole table of information to the host for processing.

Once again, as you develop your Client/Server applications, be sure to consider not only **how** a process is completed, but **where** and **what** method and/ or system is best suited for the operation.

Helpful Technologies in a Client/Server Application

There are several different technologies covered in this book that can help you along the way in Client/Server development. These items include NetDDE, OLE and MAPI.

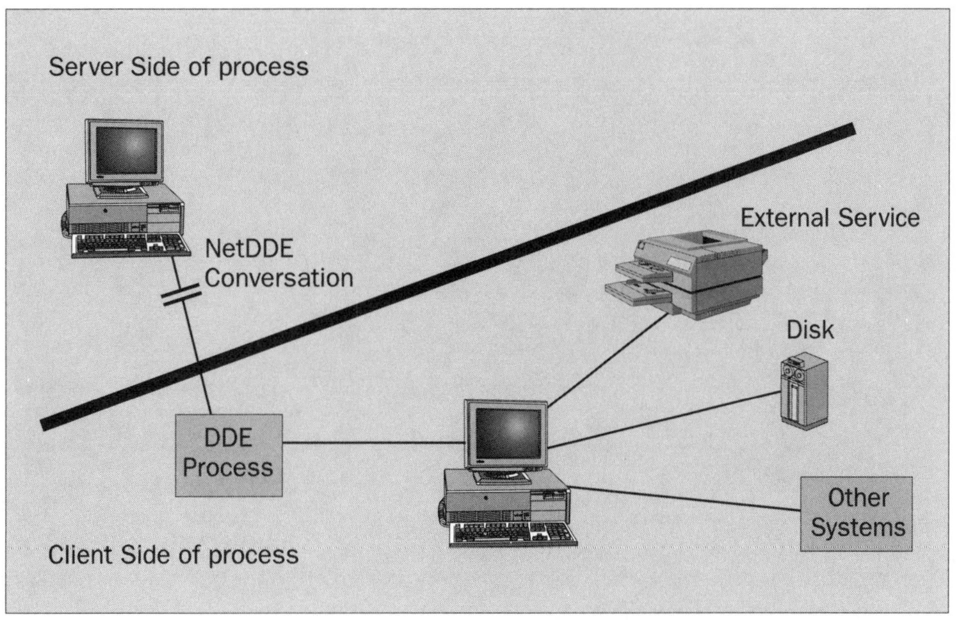

NetDDE

NetDDE allows you to connect to a remote application. You can then send and receive information to and from the remote application. If you don't have a back-end server process for a specific procedure, you can create a DDE server. This server can take messages passed to it and act accordingly, retrieving data, processing a request or it can take some other action as appropriate. This still falls under the category of Client/Server applications as once the request for information, action and so on, is sent to the DDE server, the operation is performed on the DDE server system, not the client computer.

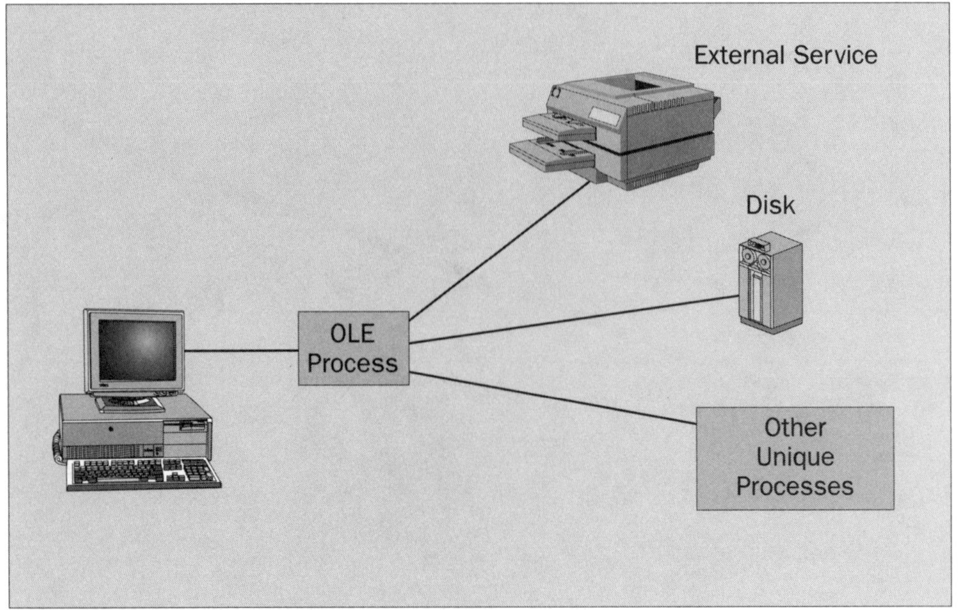

OLE

While OLE doesn't currently support a 'NetOLE' standard, you can still use an OLE object as a local server to accomplish a given task. As an example, you may want to create an OLE server application that only knows how to work with a specific, outdated server. In this case, your core Access application can call this OLE server, passing in information about the needed operation. When the OLE application receives the request, it can format it, add other formatting information to create a command and so on. When the host returns the information, the OLE server takes over the request, returning the re-formatted values to the client application.

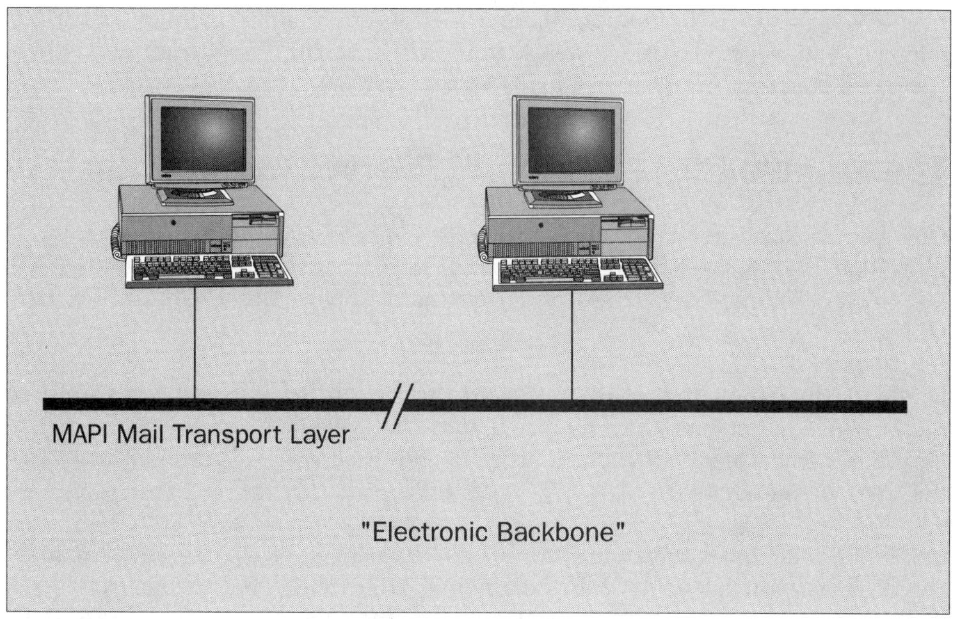

MAPI

Although not discussed until a later chapter, Microsoft's Messaging API, or MAPI, provides some significant Client/Server capabilities. We'll go into this more in the next chapter that details how to mail-enable your application.

There is a paradigm shift that you should consider when thinking about the mail system. Instead of only a messaging transport layer, it's really becoming more of an information, or data transport layer. You can send a wide variety of objects including transactions, email messages and records, relying on the server product to get your request through. The MAPI transport layer can become an electronic backbone for your information systems.

If you keep these technologies, along with the other items mentioned earlier, in mind as you develop your systems, you will have the knowledge and tools you need to design optimum Client/Server systems.

The Sample PIM as a Client/Server Application

Our sample application provides the perfect means of testing out different ideas you may have had about migrating to a Client/Server environment. The PIM includes three basic tables, the Contacts, Company and Projects information tables.

Before starting with the migration effort, be sure to backup the **CONTACTS.MDB** file if you have entered any live data into the system. Next, create a copy of the MDB named **CONTSQL.MDB**; this is the file that we'll experiment with in this part of the chapter.

Using the techniques covered in previous chapters, migrate these tables to SQL Server. Once you have, rename the original tables and attach your newly created SQL tables. You should end up with the table listing that looks like the figure that follows:

Remember the final step: renaming the newly-attached tables to the original table names. This removes the prefix of 'dbo_' and will allow your forms and queries to operate with the attached tables without any changes to code.

If you review the database structure that results on the server, you'll notice that the OLE Object fields in Access map to an Image type field in SQL Server. The translation between the types is handled by Access through Jet or ODBC.

More information on data type conversions is presented in Chapter 10, along with information about the Upsizing Wizard. The Upsizing Wizard provides a somewhat automated migration path from Access to SQL Server.

When you work with attached tables in this manner, you are really not operating in a Client/Server environment. While it's true that the tables reside on and are managed by the SQL Server, there is very little, if any, automation that is being cooperatively managed by the server and Access. In this case, Access requests the information in the tables from SQL, processes the information in the table and then submits this updated record back to SQL for storage. Remember, for an application to be truly Client/Server, you should expect more than simple disk I/O processing from the server application.

Migrating a query from Access to SQL Server is straight-forward and will begin to show more advantages for your application by moving the processing onto the server. To install an Access query in SQL Server, select the Query tab from the database dialog box. Select the query you want to work with and select Design.

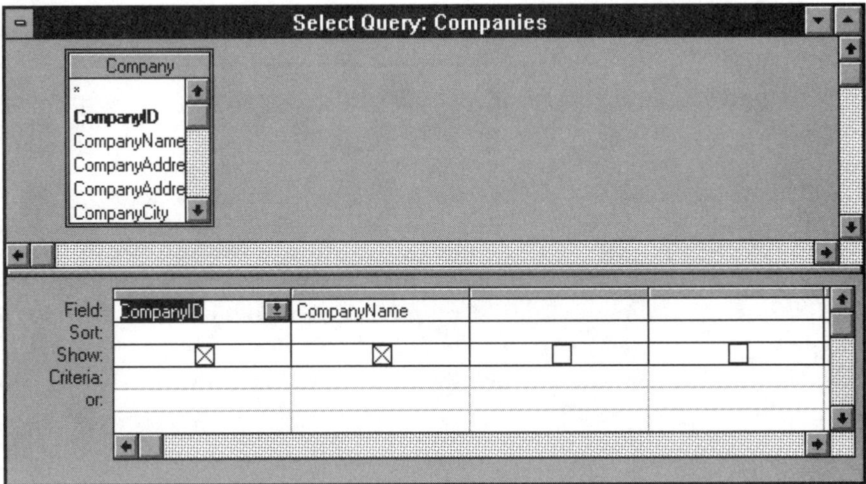

Next, select the SQL button, or choose SQL from the View menu:

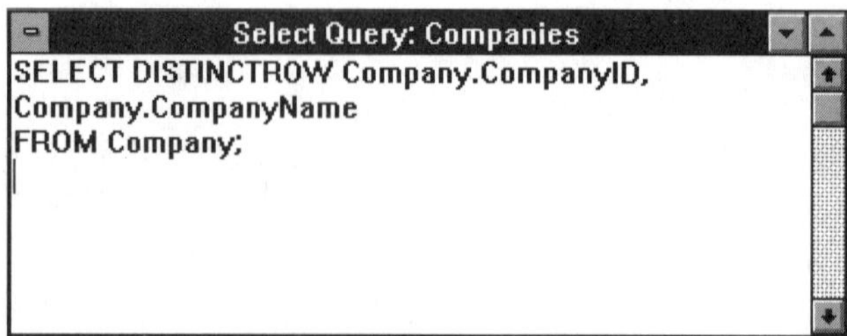

This provides you with the basic syntax that you can use for a view or `SELECT` statement to use against SQL tables. However, there will be some differences. Things will vary slightly from server to server, but as an example, with Microsoft's SQL Server, the DistinctRow option is not offered. You'll need to investigate using the `Distinct` keyword instead.

You can then use this to create your view on the server. For example, for the information shown above, the statement to create the view would be:

```
Create View MyView
as Select CompanyID, CompanyName from Company
```

This view definition assumes that the current database has a table named Company *and that* CompanyID *and* CompanyName *are columns in that table.*

To make the new view available to your application, you will include it as an attached table just as you did previously for the exported tables. When you attach the query, you can access it just as you do any other table, provided you have sufficient access rights to the view.

The software developers at Microsoft who worked on Access went out of their way to implement this compatibility. Since you can specify query and table names interchangeably in your queries, forms and other controls, this operation is straightforward. You won't have to change your forms or any of the rest of the functionality that makes up your application as long as you name the newly attached table with the same name as the original query.

Once the query to create the view has been created on the server, it will be compiled. This optimizes it and will help in the speed of execution. When SQL compiles the query, it examines the underlying table structure to determine the best way of retrieving the requested information. This execution plan is then followed each time the view is referenced.

You may notice a slower response time the first time a query or view is accessed. This can be due to a number of things, including network traffic. However, it is more likely that SQL is either compiling the query, or is caching it for future use. Subsequent uses of the query will yield better performance.

Comments and Suggestions

In this chapter, we've covered a lot of different ideas for using Client/Server technologies to tune up your application. If you combine this information with that in previous chapters covering other technologies, upsizing techniques and customizing capabilities for Access, you'll have some powerful tools in your development arsenal.

In the next chapter, we'll cover how you can integrate messaging into your application. Messaging transport layers offer an interesting alternative as a means of moving more than just messages between two points and we'll show how this can be put to work in your applications.

CHAPTER 14

Creating Mail-Enabled Applications

The user demand for access to the Information Super Highway is revolutionizing the availability of information in the world today. For too long, the idea of electronic mail has been restricted to messages between colleagues, but now with products such as Lotus Notes, and the impending release of Microsoft's Exchange, electronic mail is taking on the shape of a major information distribution system.

What's Covered in This Chapter

In this chapter, we'll introduce you to the different ways you can implement electronic mail in your application. We've included information on using the **`SendObject`** method, along with details of mail-enabling your application. With these details, you'll be able to provide your user base with some very interesting functionality, including the following:

- Provide access to the post office address book and allow the user to select a name or names to which to send a message
- How to attach files to mail messages
- What message classes are and how they can be used in your application

Applying this information to your application, you can provide a seamless interface between your applications and the mail system.

Chapter 14

How This Chapter Impacts Our Application

This chapter adds a new function set to our application. We'll be implementing 'send mail' functionality from within the application, as well as a message browser. The browser will provide an 'in-box' for the user of the system without the necessity of exiting the system.

We'll also cover how to designate special messages that are used only by your application, but are sent over the same mail subsystem. Using this technique, you can enable 'private' messaging between specific applications.

Introduction

Electronic messaging is traditionally a separate, standalone application that allows a user to enter, read and file messages. Typical implementations of these environments include Microsoft Mail, Novell's Office, Lotus' cc:Mail, as well as many others. As can be expected in a highly competitive marketplace, there are varying degrees of standardization. Three overall standards have emerged as mainstream options.

- Microsoft's Mail system uses the 'Messaging Application Programming Interface' (MAPI).
- Lotus Development's cc:Mail product uses 'Vendor Independent Messaging' (VIM) as the interface specification.
- Novell uses 'Message Handling Service' (MHS). This standard was one of the original specifications and was originally widely implemented in WordPerfect Corp.'s Office product line and Novell's electronic mail offerings.

In addition, an emerging specification, but as yet not a widely implemented standard, is the 'Common Mail Calls' (CMC) specification. This specification's aim is to provide a single, industry-standard mail calling convention.

The systems that are currently on the market, as of the writing of this book, generally use a store-and-forward type of methodology. When a message is submitted to the system, it's stored in a protected location. This is often a subdirectory structure or common database maintained by the mail system. No action is taken on the message until the recipient or some other human-based process interacts with it.

In the upcoming Microsoft Exchange product, the mail is part of a high capacity client server system. When messages are submitted to the system, they can be acted on by server processes, rules, routing and replication between systems. These functions happen independently, without intervention, as server processes.

In the following sections, we'll outline how you can put some of these specifications to work for you.

Some Background on Messaging

Office environments require that people be able to share information. This is evident in the networking systems that are coming on the market such as Windows for Workgroups, Lantastic and Novell's lower-end network products. These products allow information sharing on a peer-to-peer level and are becoming quite popular because of that fact.

More and more, applications are also sharing information. This sounds obvious at first, but carefully consider the possibilities. With network and client server implementations, it's easy to understand how this information is readily available and shared between users of the system. This is not as evident where you are only connected to a peer via a Wide Area Network or, even more commonly, only by electronic mail.

Sharing of information can take the form of passing a note from one desk to another, or it can be more sophisticated, ranging from Voice and Electronic Mail to entire databases of information. When actual transaction, database or processing information is to be sent between two different locations, the requirements for fault-tolerance are increased dramatically. If a database update doesn't arrive at its intended destination, the update will not be made, with obvious possible side effects on the reliability of the information in the database.

Electronic Information Transfer - the Electronic Backbone

Messaging has traditionally been an over-looked way of moving information around the network where fault-tolerant is an issue. With messaging, you have the luxury of sending your request to the other function and being guaranteed that it will get there 'soon'. The timing for delivery depends on the underlying mail system's configuration, the network conditions and many other factors.

In the case where you need to send specific information from one person to another and want to make sure it arrives at your intended destination, the use of the electronic mail option is worth investigation. If you decide to send a message directly from one system to another, as might be the case with a DDE, NetDDE or other direct connection method, you are responsible for handling any network errors that may prevent the message from getting through. If you can, using a mail-based transfer can provide a fault-tolerant way of moving data across a wide area.

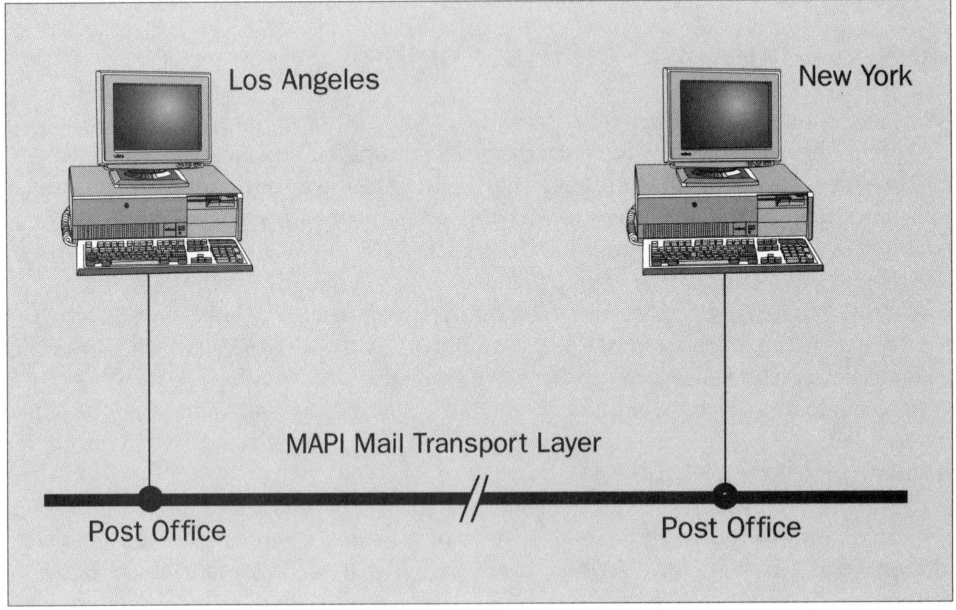

The technique used by the mail system is what makes the connection between locations and workstations so fault tolerant. When a workstation submits a message to the system, a post office puts the message in a message store. From the message store, the message can be bound for any of several different destinations:

- Another mailbox located on the same system
- A mailbox on another postoffice, but locally attached
- A mailbox on another postoffice, accessed remotely over a Wide Area Network (WAN)

- A mailbox on another postoffice, accessed remotely over dial-up lines
- A mailbox on another mail system, possibly requiring a gateway and/or conversion between unlike systems

In each of these cases, except the last one, the Microsoft Mail system will deliver your message to the destination mail box and you can be assured of an accurate delivery, with all associated information intact. The difference with the last item is that it's likely that message types and message attachments will be altered in the translation process. This happens because, in other systems, the message type has no meaning. It's not used by the other systems to route or handle messages.

With attachments, if you send a message out on the Internet, for example, you may find that it becomes UUEncoded. UUEncoding is a standardized method of changing an item from its original, possibly binary form, into a text representation of it.

This allows the message to be transmitted as text across the many diverse networks as needed. On the receiving end, it's expected that the message will be decoded, which works very well in most cases. The problem with this approach occurs when you are expecting a specifically formatted message with data and instead receive a message with what will appear to be a jumbled mess.

You'll need to keep these points in mind if you'll be designing systems that may be sending mail to external, foreign systems. If this is a requirement of your software, you'll need to consider creating a decoding routine for attachments. In the case of the message types, you may be able to simply designate a specific user's mailbox to receive all incoming messages. Setting up an 'Incoming Messages' mailbox may remove the requirement to have the message types defined. You'd be able to assume that anything coming in to that mail box will be something that needs to be processed by your application.

The Future of Messaging

In the coming 12-18 months, the features, capabilities and applications that are reliant upon mail will be changing drastically. If you look at Lotus Notes, you can already see a major shift from using electronic mail simply as a means of leaving notes around the offices to a system that is capable of wide-area use.

The current wave of enthusiasm over the inherent capabilities of the connectivity options offered by Internet providers is not going to change. This, coupled with Microsoft's commitment to messaging, is going to bring sweeping changes, for the better, to the industry as a whole.

Microsoft's Exchange product will begin integrating messaging at the operating system level for the first time. In prior releases of Windows, the messaging application may have been included in the disk set with the operating system, but the new approach implements mail as just another service. This puts your mail browser on a par with File Manager, Print Manager and other services like them.

With Exchange, the information we're providing here will still function properly. The calls currently supported by MAPI's version '0' product will be compatible with the MAPI release 1.0 coming out concurrent with the Exchange product. If you would like more information on the MAPI specification, be sure to check Microsoft's Internet service 'Microsoft.COM' as well as CompuServe's Microsoft Knowledge Base (MSKB) and Workgroups Forums (MSWGA).

Implementing These Examples Using the VIM Specification

While this chapter focuses on the Microsoft MAPI specification, you can implement many of the techniques found by setting up your system slightly differently. There is a DLL available that provides a translation between MAPI and VIM calls. The `MAPIVIM.DLL` file is available with several Microsoft applications as well as on CompuServe (Go MSWGA) and other on-line services.

To install the translation layer, examine your `WIN.INI` file. Find the `[Mail]` section if possible. If the section doesn't exist, you need to manually create it to follow the guidelines provided here.

The translation is implemented when you specify the following entries in your `WIN.INI` file:

```
[Mail]
MAPIDLL=<Windows>\SYSTEM\MAPIVIM.DLL
MAPI=1
```

When a call is made to load mail, the `WIN.INI` is searched first to determine what mail subsystem to make available to the application. If this entry is found, the `MAPIVIM.DLL` translation layer will be loaded instead of the `MAPI.DLL`.

> **Note that if you need to support both MAPI and VIM on your system, you'll need to alternate commenting and uncommenting out this line, by placing a semicolon in front of the line.**

Using Different Types of Messages

When you send a message, you establish what's referred to as a **Message Type** or **Message Class**. This class determines a number of different things about how the message will be processed, including whether the user will see it in their standard inbox:

> *Message class and message type are synonymous and are used interchangeably in this chapter. As you develop mail applications, you'll see references to both terms in the documents that you'll be using for assistance.*
>
> *In reality, the difference is that a type is a broad class of messages, as shown in the next table, while a message class refers to a specific, fully qualified instance of a message type, including its unique identifier.*

There are two different message classes that are available in a typical mail installation:

Inter-Personal Messages - IPM prefix	These messages are typically sent between individuals. In your current messaging system, it's likely that these types of messages are currently in use. IPM messages appear in a user's inbox and can be accessed by double-clicking the new message icon.

Inter-Process Communications - IPC prefix

These messages are provided as a means of sending information between two automated processes. This is how you can send data back and forth between applications without the mail client application becoming confused about what to do with the information.

IPC messages don't appear in the Microsoft Mail 3.x inbox. These messages must be processed by another application and can't be activated by the default mail client provided with Microsoft Mail.

Message types are indicated in the `MessageType` property of the `MAPIMessage` structure. Message types are string values and are generally of the following format:

```
IPM.WroxPress.RevAccess
```

or

```
IPC.WroxPress.RevAccess
```

Message types are case sensitive. One of the causes of errors in retrieving messages that you expect is that the letter-case of the specified message class doesn't exactly match the message type you are specifying. Message classes and types are the foundation for the mail system and its ability to handle your messages correctly, and so a legitimate identification of the class is imperative.

You can see examples of custom messages defined to the mail client software in the `MSMAIL.INI` file. In the `[Custom Messages]` section, the message classes are defined, along with what can be done with the message and how it will be viewed by the user.

```
[Custom Messages]
IPM.Microsoft Schedule.MtgReq=3.0
;;;;SchedMsg.DLL;;1111100000000000;;;;
IPM.Microsoft
Schedule.MtgRespP=3.0;;;;SchedMsg.DLL;;1100100000000000;;;;
```

```
IPM.Microsoft
Schedule.MtgRespN=3.0;;;;SchedMsg.DLL;;1100100000000000;;;;
IPM.Microsoft
Schedule.MtgRespA=3.0;;;;SchedMsg.DLL;;1100100000000000;;;;
IPM.Microsoft Schedule.MtgCncl=3.0
;;;;SchedMsg.DLL;;1100100000000000;;;;
```

In the examples shown in the previous listing, the different messages generated by Schedule Plus 1.0 are shown.

Schedule Plus allows you to manage your schedule by using a calendar and making entries in the calendar. If you want to schedule a meeting, Schedule Plus will send messages to each of the meeting participants requesting their attendance. Electronic mail is used to send these meeting requests and their associated responses.

However, it's important to note that the software product is not important for this explanation. Schedule Plus was chosen simply due to its large installed base since it's distributed as part of Windows for Workgroups.

These messages comprise the following different messages that can be expected in the inbox:

Message	Meaning
IPM.Microsoft Schedule.MtgReq	Meeting request message.
IPM.Microsoft Schedule.MtgRespP	Meeting request positive response, e.g. 'Yes I will attend'.
IPM.Microsoft Schedule.MtgRespN	Meeting request negative response, e.g. 'I will not attend'.
IPM.Microsoft Schedule.MtgRespA	Meeting request tentative response, e.g. 'I might attend'.
IPM.Microsoft Schedule.MtgCncl	Cancellation of a previously scheduled meeting.

These are just some of the message classes you may have defined on your system. Others include how fax messages are handled, how to work with help desk service requests and any others that may be used by utilities on your system.

Since message classes are the key to processing the message, all message classes must be unique on a given client workstation.

Sending Information Using MAPI

Using the mail system from within Access can take on many different looks and approaches. The different and most commonly used ways that you'll want to send messages are highlighted in the Messaging menu options of the PIM sample application:

File Menu

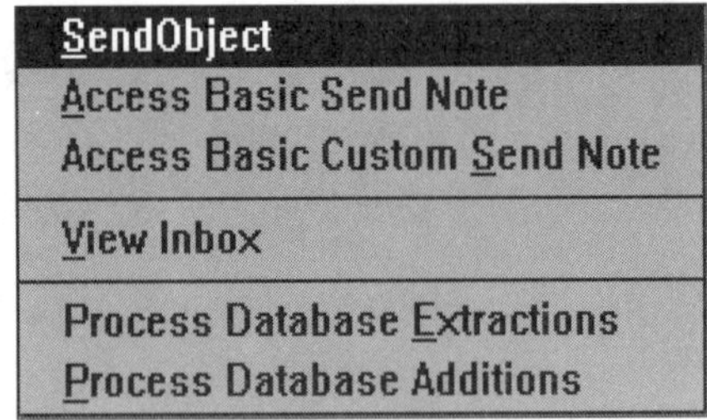

Messaging Menu

First, Access offers the ability to send the output from the current object as a mail message, formatted in such a way that Access can easily import the information. This is done by using the standard Access Send... command from the default File menu.

Next, you can create a standard text mail message by calling the MAPI functions to present the dialog and send the message. This allows your application to present an interface for creating a message that your users are comfortable with and already know how to use. In addition, it allows the MAPI subsystem to gather up the information required to send the completed message. This approach is the same as when using the common dialog functions offered by Windows and reviewed briefly in the chapter on working with wizards.

Third, you have the option of creating a message from within your application. This can take the form of the Send... command, or can be more elaborate and create a message that is only processed by your application. This is done by establishing one of the message types mentioned above.

Finally, you can implement a true custom message along the lines of the **Microsoft Electronic Forms Designer**. The Eforms Designer allows you to create custom 'compose and read' forms for managing a message class. Once defined, you can distribute the forms for your user base to use in working with the class of message.

Eforms Designer is actually provided as a set of libraries for Visual Basic, it is possible to convert them to work with the Access Basic environment. Future mail products from Microsoft will include wizard-type capabilities for creating basic electronic forms and will continue to provide extended capabilities from within Visual Basic for Applications.

While the Eforms Designer kit is outside the scope of this book, you can learn quite a lot about it, along with sample code and applications by visiting Microsoft on the Internet or in the MSWGA forum on CompuServe. More than ten different workgroup applications are available, each including source code, for your use and modification.

Using File, Send... to Send an Object

Perhaps the easiest way to send information from the system using MAPI is the Send command found on the default File menu and is also provided under the File menu on the PIM main menu. We've referenced the original File menu's Send... method in the PIM's main menu to more easily show how to implement these capabilities.

It's important to understand that, with the standard Send... method, you'll be sending the output from whatever is currently in focus. Specifically, if you search for a name using the PIM, and then select Send from the File menu, you'll be sending the output from the currently displayed form. The table is not sent, unless you are in a table at the time you select Send.... It's only what is currently active in Access.

If you are sending a recordset object, either by sending the output from a form or by sending the results of a query or table browse, you'll be prompted for an output type. This is the format that the information will be placed in so that it may be read at the recipient's system:

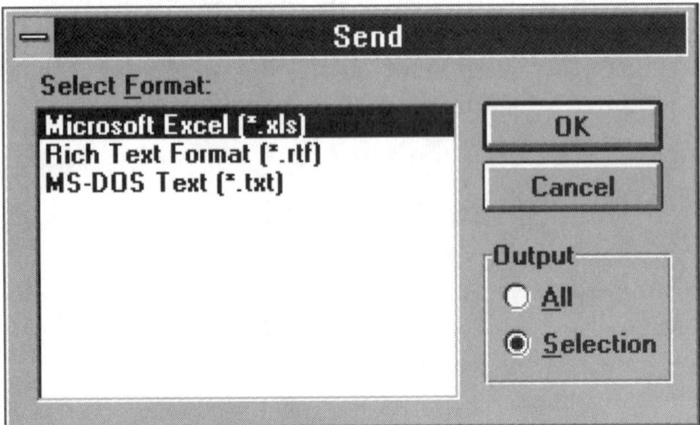

Select the format to which you need to export the data and select OK. If you have selected a record or records in a table view, the Output frame will be enabled, allowing you to send only the select row(s) or the entire table. Once you indicate how to format the information, the standard send note dialog box is shown, allowing you to specify typical options, addressee information, additional attachments and so on:

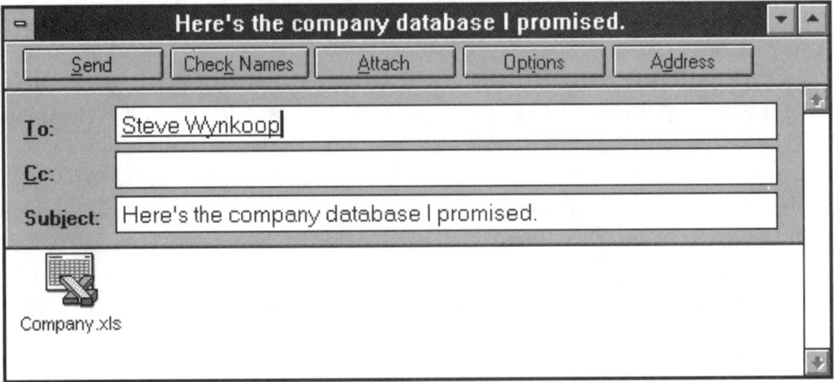

Notice that the information has been inserted as an attachment and Access has used a 'best guess' at what the file may relate to when it named the object. In addition, if you selected a recognizable export format, an appropriate icon will be provided. The easiest output format for re-use by Access on the receiving end is the Excel format.

You can also use this method to send code from modules. If you find yourself in need of a way to share code examples with a colleague of yours, simply go into the routine you need to send them. Select File, Send from the menu. The module will be attached to the mail message as a text file and you'll be able to send it off right from Access.

Enter addressing information, subject and so on, before clicking on the Send... button. The mail message will be sent, from within Access, and it will be delivered to the destination you specified.

What Information is Sent?

An important note is that if you are currently on a form and select File, Send..., Access is going to send all visible output on the form to the destination you specify. It's important to understand this if you have information on the form that doesn't relate to a bound table. In these cases, Access will still export not only the database information, but also the other fields on the form. If you export in Excel format, Access will be able to indicate what fields are not database-related. If you review the exported information, you'll find that, for each unbound item represented, the column is shaded indicating that the information was indirect information.

Using SendObject to Send Information Objects

As we showed in the previous section, using MAPI to send messages is quite straight-forward, but you'll probably find that you'll come across instances where you require more programmatic control over the information that is sent. You may also find that you don't want, or need, to bother the user with prompting about where to send an item, what to attach to the mail message and what type of format to use for the item.

In these cases, you can use the Access Basic **SendObject** function. With **SendObject**, you specify all of this information from within Access Basic. If you do leave out a piece of information that is required, MAPI will step in and ask the user to clarify that item. This can be helpful, for example, if you want to completely set up the message for the user, but then allow them to select the destination for the message.

In our sample PIM, we've implemented the **SendObject** capabilities in the Messaging menu. The first item, **SendObject**, shows how these functions work. The following diagram shows how the menu item is declared:

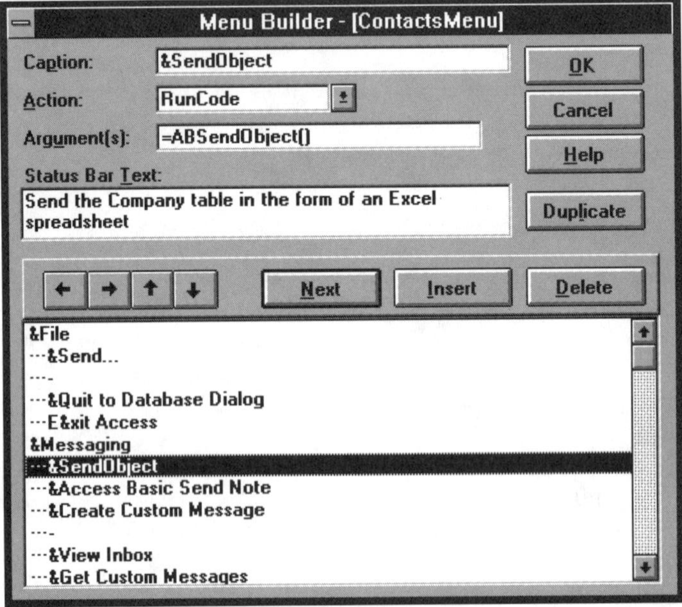

When the **ABSendObject** function is called, it will send two copies of the Company table to the destination you set up.

Be sure you change sRecipient in the ABSendObject function before you use this function. It must be a valid, distinct user. There must be no vague user name specified, by which we mean that if you have a John Smith I and John Smith II, you can't specify John Smith. When MAPI resolves the name, it must be unique without further prompting.
If you don't specify a unique name, the Send Note dialog will be shown and you will have to specify the name to send the message to.

The routine first automatically sends a message to the destination specified in **sRecipient**. The second message is sent after first prompting you for the recipient by using the standard Send Note dialog box:

```
Function ABSendObject ()
    'send an object, using MAPI, from Access to
    'another system - this routine is hardcoded
    'to send the company table.

    Dim sRecipient As String
    sRecipient = "Steve Wynkoop;"

    'This example specifies the user to send the object to.
    MsgBox "Sending message to: " & sRecipient & "..."
    DoCmd SendObject A_TABLE, "Company", A_FORMATXLS, sRecipient, ,   ⏎
        , "Here's the company database I promised.", , False

    MsgBox "Message sent.  You will be prompted for the recipient for ⏎
        the next message."

    'This example doesn't specify the user.
    DoCmd SendObject A_TABLE, "Company", A_FORMATXLS

    MsgBox "Second message sent."

End Function
```

We've added message boxes along the way to indicate where we are in the process of sending the messages. Here's a summary of the information you can provide with the **SendObject** method of **DoCmd**:

ObjectType Use the Access intrinsic constants of **A_TABLE**, **A_QUERY**, **A_FORM**, **A_REPORT** or **A_MODULE**. These are the items that allow you to take this next step from the File, Send... option presented first in this chapter. They allow you to specify not only the output from the current object, but any object that appears in the system.

ObjectName This is a string expression indicating the name of what you're going to send. In the case of a form, use the form name, for a query or table, use the query or table name, etc.

OutputFormat

You'll recall from the File, Send... function, that you can select one of three different output formats for information in the system. These are represented by the **A_FORMATXLS**, **A_FORMATRTF** and **A_FORMATTXT** intrinsic constants. Remember, if you're sending this information to a system that will be importing it into Access, it's probably best to use the **A_FORMATXLS** option.

To, CC, BCC, Subject and MessageText

These are all string expressions. In the case of the addressees (To, CC, BCC), you can specify more than one name by placing a semicolon between names. Note that BCC, or Blind Carbon Copy, recipients may not be supported by your system. Microsoft Mail version 3.x doesn't support BCC. It is, however, part of the upcoming Exchange product line.

EditMessage

This 'true' or 'false' option indicates whether you want the user to be presented with the Send Note dialog box, filled out to your specifications here, prior to sending the message. If this option is not specified, it defaults to 'false'.

If you want the user to be prompted for the recipient information, as is the case in our second example, you can leave the recipient information blank. MAPI will present the dialog box prompting the user for the recipient information automatically. If the recipient information provided is not valid, the message is not sent. In our example, you'll also receive an error message indicating that the recipient was not valid:

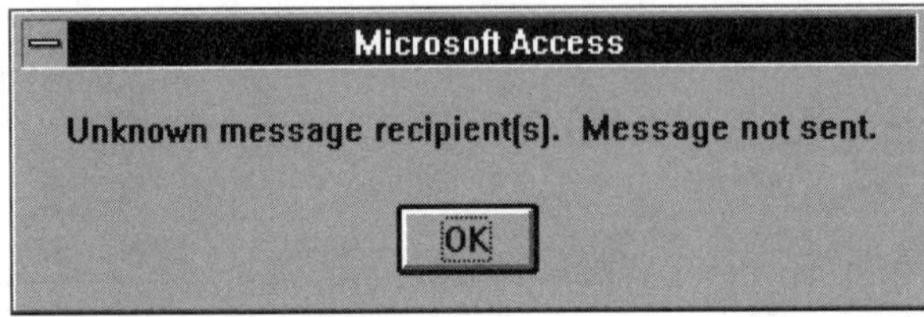

If your application is going to be sending messages automatically, as in our example, be sure that you have valid recipient information. In addition, be sure that you implement an error handling call at the beginning of each subroutine or function that will be sending or receiving messages.

Using Access Basic and MAPI to Send Mail

The next functional step in sending messages within Access is not addressed by built-in functions. When you make the decision to add more robust messaging capabilities to your system, you'll be working with MAPI directly. In this section, we show how you can use MAPI to add functionality to your Access application that looks, feels and operates exactly as it does in the mail client software for Microsoft Mail 3.x.

First, there are a series of items that must be established whenever you're going to work with a MAPI-type interface. In our sample PIM application, the MAPI Library module contains the definitions, declarations and constants that we'll be using with MAPI:

```
Type MAPIMessage
    Reserved As Long
    Subject As String
    NoteText As String
    MessageType As String
    DateReceived As String
    ConversationID As String
    Flags As Long
    RecipCount As Long
    FileCount As Long
End Type
```

The **MAPIMessage** structure contains the basic elements of the message. This includes the subject, the text of the message, number of recipients for the message and several housekeeping items. Note the **MessageType**; this is the string that contains the IPC or IPM message class that we discussed earlier in this chapter. This is the field that we can use to help filter out messages when it comes time to automate the processing of incoming messages.

In terms of the mail message structure, the **MAPIMessage** is the 'header' record, referring to recipients and attached files or objects in a one-to-many relationship:

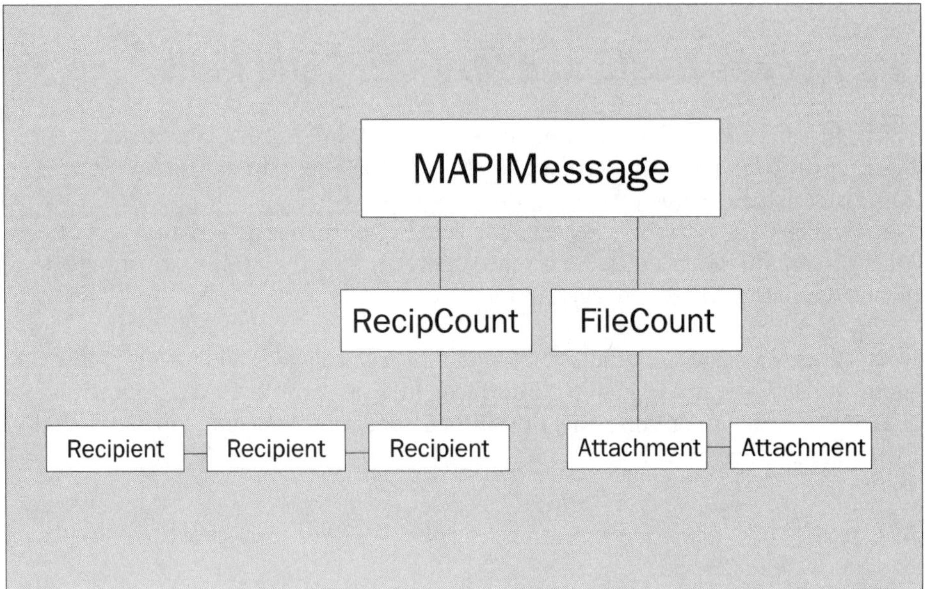

The **RecipCount** maintains the number of related recipient structures associated with this message. Each recipient structure contains all information necessary to properly address the message to the destination specified:

```
Type MAPIRecip
    Reserved As Long
    RecipClass As Long
    Name As String
    Address As String
    EIDSize As Long
    EntryID As String
End Type
```

Notice that there is no 'CCRecipient' structure. This is because you define a recipient to be either a CC or To recipient in the **RecipClass** field of the **MAPIRecip** structure. Four different types of users can be represented by the **MAPIRecip** structure, as outlined here:

MAPI_ORIG = 0 This represents the originator of the message if you are creating a message to be sent. If you are reading in existing messages, the structure will contain the originator of the message.

MAPI_TO = 1 This is the name of the primary recipient or recipients for the message. In the typical Send Note, this corresponds to the "TO:" field.

MAPI_CC = 2 This is the name of the CC recipient or recipients.

MAPI_BCC = 3 Blind Carbon Copies are not directly supported by the current implementation of MAPI and the mail client. This option will allow you to establish a recipient as if he had appeared upon the CC listing, but the other recipients won't know that he has received a copy. Setting this value will cause a MAPI error. It is provided here to support future versions of the mail client and MAPI.

The remaining structure, which rounds off the core of the MAPI required structures, is the attachments record. Each instance of this record contains an identifier telling what file should be attached to the message, along with other information items that pertain to the file:

```
Type MAPIFile
    Reserved As Long
    Flags As Long
    Position As Long
    PathName As String
    FileName As String
    FileType As String
End Type
```

The position refers to the location in the message at which the attachment will appear. This is a number of characters from the beginning of the `NoteText` for the message.

IMPORTANT: Before you can attach a file to a message, you must have at least one character in the `NoteText`. If you are not sending any text in the message itself, place a space in the `NoteText`. If you don't, MAPI will not send the attachment with the message.

The actual calls to the MAPI system are made through the Windows API and are established with declarations, which are also defined in the MAPI Library module. While we won't go into each of these calls, most of the calls you'll need in your systems are defined for you in this module. The following table represents a summary of the most commonly used calls:

MAPILogon This function allows you to logon to MAPI. It returns a session ID that you'll be providing to all other calls to the MAPI DLL functions. The Session ID is a variable of type Long and should be declared globally to all functions that will be using it.

MAPILogoff When you logoff from MAPI, you drop the session that you specify in the logoff command. If you find yourself getting Too Many Sessions error messages from the MAPI layer, you'll need to be sure that you're successfully logging off the system. In our examples, we've forced the issue somewhat because when we logoff, we log off the first 10 sessions that are running against MAPI. There will be more detail on this in the **DoMAPILogoff** function description.

MAPISENDMAIL This function takes the recipient structure, attachments and message structure to send the message as requested.

MAPIResolveName This function performs the task of validating all recipients specified in the recipient structure. If a name is not unique, a dialog box is provided, allowing the user to select a specific name.

Each of these is described in more detail as they come into use in the upcoming sections.

Adding Basic Compose Note Functionality To Your System

Our application has implemented the Send Note functionality in the **SendMailBasic** function. The Messaging menu has been set up to call the function as the starting point for adding the Send Note to our application.

Logging On to a New MAPI Session

Before you can work with any MAPI functions, you must first establish a session. When you do, MAPI will make sure that you're already logged in. On the logon function call, you specify whether you want the standard logon dialog box displayed if a logon is necessary:

```
DoMAPILogon = MAPILogon(0&, "", "", MAPI_LOGON_UI...
```

If you have requested the logon user interface and the user is not currently logged on to a valid mail session, a login dialog box is displayed. In our sample application, the **DoMAPILogon** function handles the logon process:

```
Function DoMAPILogon () As Long
    'Logon to MAPI if needed. If the gMAPISession is other
    'than 0, simply exit, returning success.

    Dim iStatus As Long

    On Error GoTo DoMAPILogonErr

    If gMAPISession = 0 Then
        'There is no current session.  Establish one, requesting
        'the logon user interface if a logon is required.

        'Return values are shown in the global constants, but
        'should return SUCCESS_SUCCESS.
        DoMAPILogon = MAPILogon(0&, "", "", MAPI_LOGON_UI, 0&, ⮰
            gMAPISession)
    Else
        'The user is already logged on and a valid
        'session ID is set up.
        DoMAPILogon = SUCCESS_SUCCESS
    End If

    Exit Function

DoMAPILogonErr:
    MsgBox Str$(iStatus & " MAPI error encountered.")
    Exit Function

End Function
```

The global variable **gMAPISession** is set up by this routine. If it is zero coming into the routine, we attempt to establish a new session. As mentioned earlier, by specifying **MAPI_LOGON_UI** in the **MAPILogon** call, we allow MAPI to provide the familiar login dialog box:

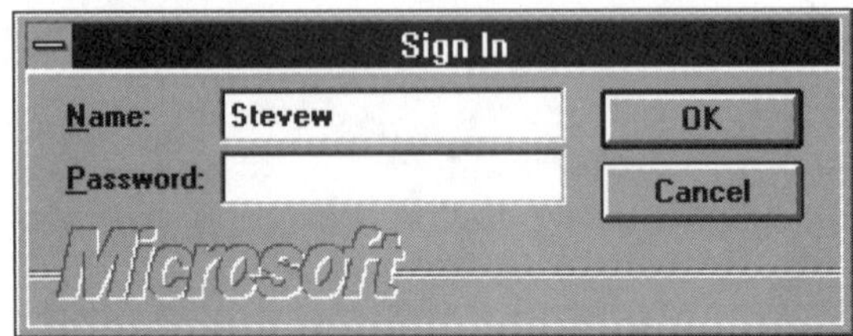

Once the user enters the name and password, control returns to our routine. Note that if the user presses Cancel, an error is returned to our login routines. Since we're returning the status back to the original calling procedure, we can check that a valid session was established. If not, we display an error message indicating that the session could not be established either because of an error or because the user pressed Cancel during the login process. The message returned by the login process will provide feedback on what caused the problem:

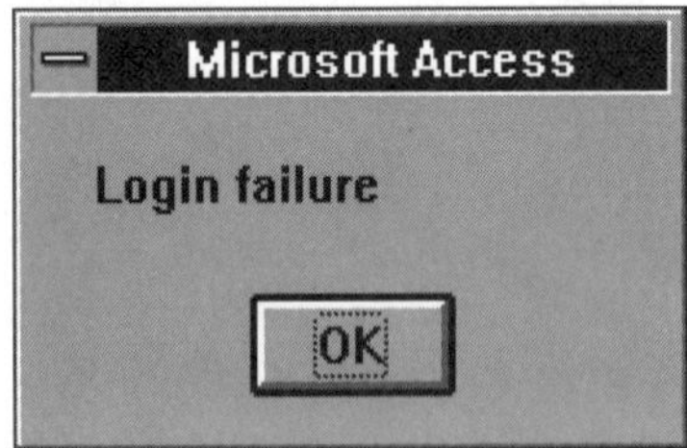

If you are automating the logon process and don't want to prompt the user for sign in information, you can specify the user name and password as the two parameters represented by empty quotations in our example. We'll go into additional detail about this option later in our discussion of automating the process of sending data between mailboxes.

Logging Off of MAPI Sessions

As you work with MAPI sessions, it's very important that you logoff from sessions that you are finished with. When a session is established with MAPI, it is not shut down when your program terminates or when a procedure goes out of scope. Instead, you must manually log off, terminating the session. If you don't logoff, you'll eventually receive a Too Many Sessions error message when you attempt to log on:

In our sample, the DoMAPILogoff routine handles shutting down the session and logging off MAPI:

```
Sub DoMAPILogoff ()
    'Logoff of MAPI, releasing our session

    '-----------------------------------------------------------------
    'NOTE:
    'This routine will clear ALL sessions currently open
    'and using MAPI.  This will include products like Mail,
    'schedule plus and others that use MAPI.  If you run
    'into problems, you can limit the scope of this routine
    'so that it only works with Session IDs that you are using
    'in your program.
    '-----------------------------------------------------------------

    'Clear all sessions, including any left open during
    'development or testing.

    Dim lSession As Long
    Dim iStatus As Long

    'if we get an error, it's probably due to an invalid session
    'or other expected error.  Ignore it and try the next
    'session number
    On Error Resume Next

    'loop through the first 10 sessions, shutting
    'them each down (logging off) as we go.
    For lSession = 1& To 10&
        'Specify the session to attempt to logoff
        iStatus = MAPILogoff(lSession, 0, 0, 0)
    Next

    'Set the session back to 0 so we know that there
    'is no valid session in other areas of the system.
    gMAPISession = 0

End Sub
```

As mentioned in the routine, if you find that your application is logging you off not only your Access connections, but also Mail, Schedule Plus or other connections, you may want to remove the counter loop. The counter is used to logoff the first 10 connections to the MAPI service. This will help during your development efforts as connections tend to stack up in the background when your application shuts down with an error.

Forcing these connections to close can alleviate the problem of too many sessions as mentioned earlier. Its impact on other software is just a side-effect of this cautiousness. In any case, with a production system, remove this loop, logging off only the session or sessions that you are directly responsible for.

Implementing MAPI's Send Note in Your Application

Once you have implemented the login and logoff functionality, you can call these functions to support the sending of a standard mail note. The **`SendMailBasic`** function has been referenced on the Messaging menu shown within the PIM. **`SendMailBasic`** logs onto mail using **`DoMAPILogon`**, calls up the Send Note dialog box and then logs off mail using **`DoMAPILogoff`**:

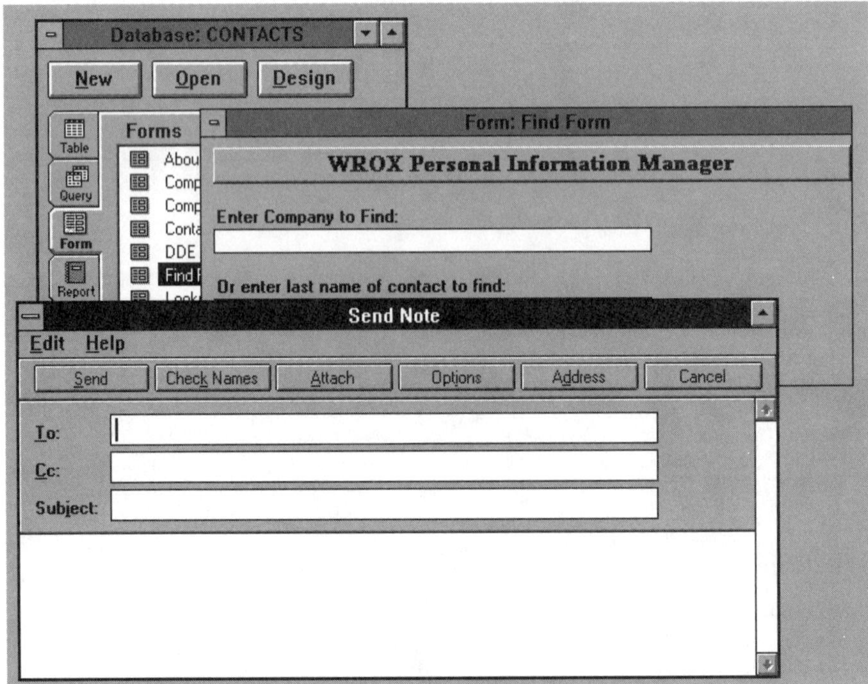

The following code listing shows the functions used to implement the Send Note in the application:

```
Function SendMailBasic ()
    'This function simply calls the MAPI functions
    'to prompt the user for login, addressee information, etc.
    '
    'This is the most basic of mail-enabling routines because
    'we're allowing MAPI to handle all aspects of the creation
    'of the message.

    On Error GoTo SendMailBasicErr

    Dim iStatus As Long
    Dim tMessage As MAPIMessage
    Dim tRecips As MAPIRecip
    Dim tFiles As MAPIFile

    'make sure we're logged on.
    iStatus = DoMAPILogon()
    If iStatus <> SUCCESS_SUCCESS Then
        MsgBox GetMAPIErrorText(iStatus)
        Exit Function
    End If

    'next, call up the dialog box.  Since we're not specifying
    'basic information and we are requesting the standard dialog box
    'by specifying MAPI_DIALOG, the result is the presentation of
    'the standard send note dialog box.
    iStatus = MAPISENDMAIL(gMAPISession, 0&, tMessage, tRecips, tFiles, ↵
        MAPI_DIALOG, 0&)
    If iStatus <> SUCCESS_SUCCESS Then
        MsgBox GetMAPIErrorText(iStatus)
        Exit Function
    End If

    'logoff of mail, release our session
    DoMAPILogoff

    Exit Function

SendMailBasicErr:
    MsgBox Error$
    Exit Function

End Function
```

The first thing we do in this function is to setup the error handler and variables that we'll need in the rest of the routine. We're also referencing the types we discussed in the last section. The error handler will simply display a message indicating a problem and exit if it is called.

If you develop applications that operate in a MAPI environment, placing this functionality in all your applications is a good idea. This way, if users of your systems need to send mail, they'll not need to switch out of Access to do so.

Implementing a Custom Send Note for Messages

There may be cases where you don't want to use the MAPI Send Note to send messages from your applications. In these cases, you can create a form and pass the values into the structures manually. This is the next evolutionary step in creating a custom mail handler. With this step, you're removing your use of the MAPI transport level's user interface, with the possible exception of the login dialog box:

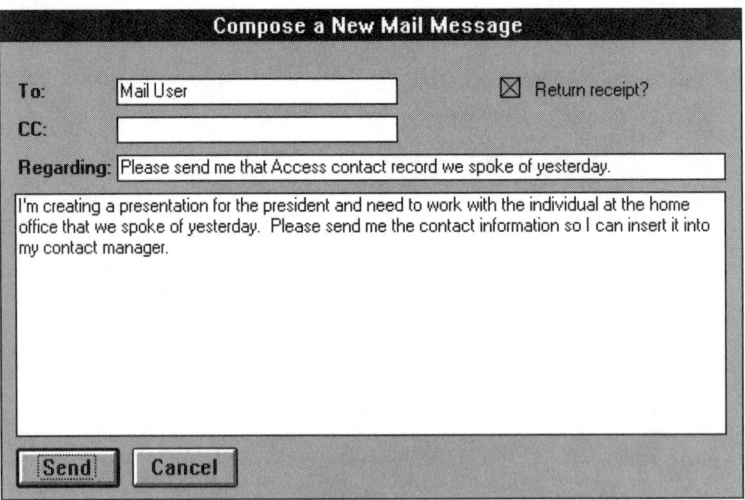

In our sample, we've provided the user with a means of enter a TO and CC user, along with the subject and message text. We've also set up a check box to allow selection of a return receipt for the message.

The underlying message handling routines are generic and allow you to specify the form that contains the message you want to send. The only constraint on this is that you must name your controls as indicated in the table shown opposite:

Display Name	Control Name	Description
To:	txtTO	The destination recipient of the message. The name must be fully qualified and unique on the mail system.
CC:	txtCC	List a carbon copy recipient if needed. The name must be fully qualified and unique on the mail system.
Regarding:	txtSubject	The subject of the message.
(text box)	txtNoteText	The text content of the message.
Return Receipt	chkReturnReceipt	Flags whether to send the message when a return receipt is requested.
Send	cmdSend	Button initiates the **SendMessage** process. This control name is not important to the message and can be changed in your forms.
Cancel	cmdCancel	Button unloads the form. This control name is not important to the message and can be changed in your forms.

The Cancel button is coded with the standard **DoCmd Close** function. This shuts down the form when we've finished using it. The form is accessed from the Messaging menu with the Access Basic Custom Send Note. The menu definition for this option calls the **StartCustomSendNote** function that displays our form.

The code behind the Send... button is quite straightforward. Its only task is to call the **SendMessage** function. Once back from the function, we display a quick message box telling the user that the message was sent:

```
Sub cmdSend_Click ()
    'Gather up the information on the form and
    'send out the message.

    Dim iStatus As Long

    'Call the routine
    iStatus = SendMessage(Me)

    'Let the user know we're done with the process
    If iStatus = SUCCESS_SUCCESS Then MsgBox "Message sent."

End Sub
```

The keyword ME is used to refer to the current form. By passing in the reference to ME, the SendMessage function can access the controls on the form directly.

The work of preparing the message to be sent is carried out in the **SendMessage** routine. **SendMessage** is responsible for verifying the contents of the form and for placing them into the proper structures, **MAPIMessage**, **MAPIRecip** and **MAPIFile**:

```
Function SendMessage (WhatForm As Form) As Long
    'This procedure is called by our custom send not to
    'send out a message using the requested
    'form to get the information needed.

    'If no recipient is specified, exit the routine with a message.
    If IsNull(WhatForm!txtTO) Then
        MsgBox "You must specify a destination address in the TO: field. "
        WhatForm!txtTO.SetFocus
        Exit Function
    End If

    'Set up our variables
    Dim iStatus As Long
    Dim tMessage As MAPIMessage
    Dim iNumRecips As Integer
    Dim tFiles As MAPIFile
    Dim iNumFiles As Integer

    'Make sure we're logged on.
    iStatus = DoMAPILogon()
    If iStatus <> SUCCESS_SUCCESS Then
        MsgBox GetMAPIErrorText(iStatus)
        Exit Function
    End If
```

```
'------------------------------------------------------
'Establishing recipients
'------------------------------------------------------

'Check to see if 1 or 2 recipients specified.
If Not IsNull(WhatForm!txtCC) Then
    '2 recipients; TO and CC
    iNumRecips = 2
Else
    'only the TO recipient was specified.
    iNumRecips = 1
End If

'Set up our structure
ReDim tRecip(1 To iNumRecips) As MAPIRecip

'fill in the structures as needed
tRecip(1).Name = WhatForm!txtTO
tRecip(1).RecipClass = MAPI_TO

'If applicable, set up the CC addressee
If Not IsNull(WhatForm!txtCC) Then
    tRecip(2).Name = WhatForm!txtCC
    tRecip(2).RecipClass = MAPI_CC
End If

'Update the message header with the number of recipients
tMessage.RecipCount = iNumRecips

'------------------------------------------------------
'Establishing attached file counts
'------------------------------------------------------
tMessage.FileCount = 0

'------------------------------------------------------
'Establishing the actual message
'------------------------------------------------------
If Not IsNull(WhatForm!txtSubject) Then
    tMessage.Subject = WhatForm!txtSubject
End If

If Not IsNull(WhatForm!txtNoteText) Then
    tMessage.NoteText = WhatForm!txtNoteText
End If

If WhatForm!chkReturnReceipt Then
    tMessage.flags = MAPI_RECEIPT_REQUESTED
End If

'------------------------------------------------------
'Send the message
'------------------------------------------------------
```

```
    SendMessage = MAPISENDMAIL(gMAPISession, 0&, tMessage, tRecip(1), ↵
        tFiles, MAPI_LOGON_UI, 0&)
    If iStatus <> SUCCESS_SUCCESS Then
        MsgBox GetMAPIErrorText(iStatus)
        Exit Function
    End If

    'logoff of mail, release our session
    DoMAPILogoff

End Function
```

As with our previous routines, the first thing we do is make sure we have a valid session. If not, we call the MAPI logon routines. Once we've established the **gMAPISession**, we refer to it later to send the message.

In setting up the variables' declarations, we've left out one of the variables that must be set up. The **tRecip** structure is not defined because we must first determine how many recipients there are going to be for the message.

> **For our sample, you're limited to only one TO recipient and one CC recipient. Therefore, the number of recipients in our sample is one or two. In your applications, you may need to have more recipients than outlined here. In that case, you'll need to set the iNumRecips variable to reflect the total number of recipients, both TO and CC.**

Once it's been determined that there are either one or two recipients, we **ReDim** the **tRecip** structure. This allows the structure to be grouped in memory and will make it possible to pass this to the send mail routines later in the function. For each name that is defined, establish the following:

Variable Name	Value or Possible Values	Description
tRecip(x).Name	Name of the recipient	The name of the recipient or CC recipient. This name must be unambiguous on the user's mail system.
tRecip(x).RecipClass	**MAPI_CC**, **MAPI_TO**, **MAPI_BCC**	The type of recipient. Can be specified as a carbon copy (CC), primary (TO) or blind carbon copy (BCC) recipient.

> *You should use the constants* **`MAPI_TO`**, **`MAPI_CC`** *and* **`MAPI_BCC`** *for these values. This will make it easier to maintain at a later date should these values change for future versions of MAPI.*

The counts in the message header for both the recipient count and attached file count must be updated. These values are maintained in **`tMessage.RecipCount`** and **`tMessage.FileCount`** respectively. We also need to setup the subject, contained in **`tMessage.Subject`**, and the actual text portion of the message, contained in **`tMessage.NoteText`**.

The remaining step allows you to establish the return receipt. The **`tMessage.Flags`** field will allow you to request a receipt on the mail message. Setting the Flags item to **`MAPI_RECEIPT_REQUESTED`** will cause the receiving system to generate a return receipt for you.

On the actual **`MAPISENDMAIL`** call, we pass in our session ID, the structures we've set up and a flag that indicates that the standard mail message dialog box shouldn't be shown. If you're curious what your message will look like just before it goes out, you can change the **`MAPI_LOGON_UI`** to **`MAPI_DIALOG`**. The message will be displayed just as if you'd typed it in.

> **With the standard mail client, if you designate a message to have a return receipt, the message is automatically flagged as high-priority. When you are setting the return receipt flag in this manner, the message retains its priority, but still delivers the return receipt back to the originator. Don't be concerned if you don't see the red exclamation mark next to the message in the inbox.**

Assigning Attachments to Your Messages

If you are attaching files to your messages, you will be doing so in the **`tFiles`** structure. As with the recipients, you must first determine the number of files that will be attached. In the following listing extract, assume that three files will be attached:

```
...
'-------------------------------------------------
'Establishing attached file counts
'-------------------------------------------------
tMessage.FileCount = 3
ReDim tFiles(3) as MAPIFile

tFiles(1).PathName = "C:\AUTOEXEC.BAT"
tFiles(1).Reserved = 0&
tFiles(1).Position = -1
tFiles(1).FileName = ""
tFiles(1).FileType = ""

tFiles(2).PathName = "C:\CONFIG.SYS"
tFiles(2).Reserved = 0&
tFiles(2).Position = -1
tFiles(2).FileName = ""
tFiles(2).FileType = ""

tFiles(3).PathName = "C:\CONFIG.BAK"
tFiles(3).Reserved = 0&
tFiles(3).Position = -1
tFiles(3).FileName = ""
tFiles(3).FileType = ""
...
```

When you pass in the send command, the command will be identical. The number of files specified in the header will allow MAPI to walk down the structure of files and pull the ones to attach into the message. In this case, the message would have the three files attached to any text message created from elsewhere in the routine.

Since the **FileType** is a simple text field, if you are sending information between systems to be automatically processed, you can use this field to indicate the type of data being presented. This can help narrow down the exact nature of the data prior to your working with it in your application.

Creating Messages of a Custom Message Type

The only additional thing you need to do to create a message of a special class or type is to update the message header. If you set the **MessageType** field in the message header to the message class you've chosen, the message will be handled appropriately:

```
tMessage.MessageType = "IPM.Wrox.PIMData"
```

> **We've established a global variable, `gMessageClass`, that allows you to designate a message class to use for sending, retrieving and inbox functions. Set this variable to the message class you want to work with and all functions will work accordingly.**

As a reminder, if you designate a message as being an IPM message, it will be sent to the inbox of the standard Microsoft Mail 3.x client software. IPC messages are not shown in the inbox and are intended specifically for program to program communications. When we discuss the process of reading in messages, we'll explain where you can specify all of or a part of the message class as a means of limiting what messages are retrieved from the system.

Using MAPI to Send Database Information

Now that we've gone through the different ways you can send a message in Access, we want to consider how to send information from one system to another. This will be done without user intervention beyond possibly logging in or providing recipient information.

Probably the best way to transfer data is the method used by the **`SendObject`** function. The information is exported to a common format and then sent in that manner. When the receiving system gets the message, the data can be saved to disk and imported into the application.

To accomplish this without user intervention, we'll be using the **`TransferSpreadsheet`** action with the **`DoCmd`** function. This action allows us to export the file to a temporary file on disk. In the demonstration program, we're hard coding the file and path to be **`C:\WROX\MAPIOUT.XLS`**. The **`MAPIExport`** function creates the export file and calls the **`SendMessageNoForm`** function. **`SendMessageNoForm`** is identical to **`SendMessage`**, used in the last section, apart from two exceptions.

First, all parameters are not form driven, but specified in the call to the function. This allows us to complete the operation programmatically. The second difference is that we can specify a file name as a parameter. This is where we'll tell MAPI to pick up the temporary file that we've just created.

Note that our **MAPIExport** routine selects all fields from the **Company** table except the **CompanyID**. Since we don't know what **CompanyIDs** are already in place on the receiving system, our **CompanyIDs** may conflict with the unique index on the ID. By leaving the **CompanyID** out of the select statement, we allow Access to provide a new **company ID** on the receiving system.

If you attempt to use the **TransferSpreadsheet** action to import a table with duplicate IDs, you'll receive an import error.

```
Function MAPIExport ()
    'This function extracts a portion of the database,
    'using a query, and sends it off to another system
    'for processing.

    'We'll use the TransferSpreadsheet action of the
    'DoCmd function to send the spreadsheet out to a file.

    Dim iStatus As Long

    DoCmd TransferSpreadsheet A_EXPORT, 5, "MAPIExport",⏎
        "C:\wrox\mapiout.xls", True

    iStatus = SendMessageNoForm("Steve Wynkoop", "", "Export of ⏎
        Companies in Arizona", " ", "C:\wrox\mapiout.xls", True)
    If iStatus <> SUCCESS_SUCCESS Then
        MsgBox GetMAPIErrorText(iStatus)
        Exit Function
    End If

    'Remove the file from disk
    Kill "C:\wrox\mapiout.xls"

    MsgBox "Database extract successfully sent."

End Function
```

The MAPIEXPORT macro selects the records from the table, allowing us to create the export data set.

> The `TransferSpreadsheet` action will not overwrite an existing file. Be sure that you pick a unique file name and path for your temporary file. In the last few statements of the function, we use the Access Basic `KILL` command to remove the file from disk, preparing the system for the next export.

We won't present the entire listing for **SendMessageNoForm** here; instead, here's a look at the differences between it and **SendMessage**.

Look into the SendMessageNoForm Function

The calling protocol for the function has changed to allow the parameters. The function declaration is:

```
Function SendMessageNoForm
    (
    sTO As String,          The primary destination of the message
    sCC As String,          The CC recipient
    sSubject As String,     The subject line
    sNote As String,        Any additional text needed
    sFileName As String,    The name of the file to send
    iReceipt As Integer)    True or False controls receipts
As Long
```

As with **SendMessage**, the status is returned to the calling routine. Once executed, the user is prompted, if needed, to enter their logon information. The file is exported, attached to the message and the message is sent. The final step requires the user to be logged off and our MAPI session to be closed.

Another difference in the new **SendMessageNoForm** is that we're working with files for the attachment process. Here's the portion of code that sets up the file structure:

```
'-------------------------------------------------
'Establishing attached file counts
'-------------------------------------------------
If IsNull(sFileName) Then
    tMessage.FileCount = 0
Else
    tMessage.FileCount = 1
End If
```

```
If tMessage.FileCount = 1 Then
    ReDim tFiles(1) As MAPIFile
    tFiles(1).PathName = sFileName
    tFiles(1).Reserved = 0&
    tFiles(1).Position = -1
    tFiles(1).FileName = ""
    tFiles(1).FileType = ""
End If
```

This establishes the filename as specified in the parameters. Since we're always going to be passing in a filename to the routine, you could hardcode the `FileCount` to '1'. We've left it in this way to show only the changes between this and the other `SendMessage` routine.

The remaining changes pertain to variable naming. When we were referring to the fields and controls on the form, we were using **WhatForm!<control>**. With this implementation, the control and variable references must be changed to use the parameters passed on the function's command line.

When the routine has completed, we display a message box indicating procedural success.

Using Access Basic and MAPI to View Messages

The first step in retrieving messages is simply to look at the inbox to see what messages are available. To demonstrate how this can be done, we've established a simple inbox viewer. The viewer is accessed from the Messaging menu by selecting the View Inbox option:

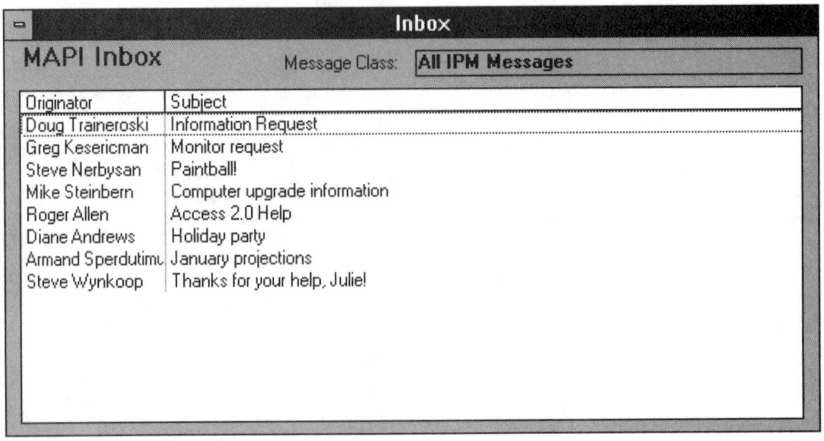

Inbox

MAPI Inbox   Message Class: All IPM Messages

Originator	Subject
Doug Traineroski	Information Request
Greg Kesericman	Monitor request
Steve Nerbysan	Paintball!
Mike Steinbern	Computer upgrade information
Roger Allen	Access 2.0 Help
Diane Andrews	Holiday party
Armand Sperdutimu	January projections
Steve Wynkoop	Thanks for your help, Julie!

In our simple inbox example, we're displaying a list box bound to the Message table. When you select the View Inbox option from the menu, the **ViewInbox** function queries your MAPI inbox, pulling down all messages in the system. The **ViewInbox** routine first clears the table of all existing information to prevent duplicates in the table when you next run the inbox viewer.

> **Note that ViewInbox doesn't clear the table on termination. In a production system, this would be a good idea just to prevent a listing of messages from being accidentally accessed. In our examples here, we've left the entries in the table to allow you to investigate the actual values contained in the message structure.**

The process of populating the table requires two steps. First, the message queue is initiated by reading the first message. You access the first message by using the **MAPIFindNext** function. The following code listing shows what is provided by the **ViewInbox** function:

```
Function ViewInbox ()
    'Query the inbox for messages on the system.
    'When messages are retrieved, place the message ID, originator,
    'subject, date sent in the Message table.
    Dim iStatus As Long

    'First logon to the MAPI subsystem
    iStatus = DoMAPILogon()
    If iStatus <> SUCCESS_SUCCESS Then
        MsgBox GetMAPIErrorText(iStatus)
        Exit Function
    End If
```

The first section of the routine logs on to the MAPI session. This uses our standard **DoMAPILogon** function that returns the status from the call. If we succeed here, we'll continue on to set up the tables for our messages:

```
    Dim db As Database
    Dim tb As Table
    Set db = CurrentDB()
    Set tb = db.OpenTable("Message")

    'Remove any remnants of old messages
    db.Execute ("delete * from Message")
```

Remove all records from the table. This will prevent duplicate records from appearing in the inbox listing. If you're interested in keeping older message information, you may want to consider deleting the message information into another table prior to copying it. This is helpful if you're going to implement a foldering or other message archival system. Be sure to copy the MessageID to the new table as it is the unique identifier that relates back to the message:

```
'Declare the message-related variables
Dim NumRecips, NumFiles As Integer
Dim sMessageID As String
Dim tOriginator As MAPIRecip
Dim tMessage As MAPIMessage
ReDim tRecips(1) As MAPIRecip
ReDim tFiles(1) As MAPIFile

'Initiate the process by doing a FindNext
iStatus = MAPIFindNext(gMAPISession, 0&, gMessageClass, sMessageID, ↵
    0, 0, sMessageID)
If iStatus <> SUCCESS_SUCCESS Then
    MsgBox GetMAPIErrorText(iStatus)
End If
```

Initiate the process of reading messages by getting the first message in the queue. Note that we're passing in a message type established by the **gMessageClass** global variable. We'll investigate in a later section how to use the message type to limit the types of messages that are returned to your application:

```
'If there are messages to process, loop through them to see
'what's available.
Do While iStatus = SUCCESS_SUCCESS

    'Read the current message, the header information
    'for the message was returned by MAPIFindNext
    iStatus = MAPIReadMail(gMAPISession, 0, sMessageID, 0, 0, ↵
        tMessage, tOriginator, tRecips(), tFiles(), NumRecips, ↵
        NumFiles)

    'Add the message information to the table.
    tb.AddNew
        tb!MessageID = sMessageID        'unique id for the message
        tb!NumRecipients = NumRecips
        tb!NumFiles = NumFiles
        tb!Subject = Left$(tMessage.Subject, 50)
        tb!MessageType = tMessage.MessageType
```

```
            tb!DateReceived = tMessage.DateReceived
            tb!Originator = tOriginator.name
        tb.Update

        'read the next message.
        iStatus = MAPIFindNext(gMAPISession, 0&, gMessageClass, ↵
            sMessageID, 0, 0, sMessageID)

    Loop
```

This loop walks through the messages returned by the calls to **MAPIFindNext** and **MAPIReadMail**. These routines get a message header and then the associated message. As each message is retrieved, key information about it is stored in the Message table. The message table serves as the source of information for the Inbox form as well as a good place to start your research into what is going to make up the different messages that you're working with.

Message type, originator information and many other items are stored for anyone particular message. If you find that you need more information on the messages, you can add a field to the Message table. In addition, you need to add a line in this section of code that will assign the appropriate value to your new field.

```
    DoMAPILogoff

    'Show the form that will display the messages
    'available.
    DoCmd OpenForm "MAPIINBOX"

End Function
```

The final steps of the routine log the user off mail and open the inbox form. The form contains a list box that is bound to the Message table. The first column, which is not displayed on the form, contains the **MessageID**. The **MessageID** is used to retrieve the message from the system for manipulation or display.

In our example, if you double click on a message, a form is displayed that allows you to review the text of the message. The routine to display the message is basic and uses the **MessageID** from the Message table to retrieve the information into the read form. The code logic in the **DblClick** event of the list box that assigns the values to the new read form is shown next:

```
sMessageID = lstInbox.value

iStatus = MAPIReadMail(gMAPISession, 0, sMessageID, 0, 0, ↵
    tMessage, tOriginator, tRecips(), tFiles(), NumRecips, NumFiles)

DoCmd OpenForm "Read"

Forms![Read]![txtFrom] = tOriginator.name
Forms![Read]![txtSubject] = tMessage.Subject
Forms![Read]![txtNoteText] = tMessage.NoteText

DoMAPILogoff
```

The Message ID used to retrieve the message is associated with the **Value** property of the list box. We assign the Message ID to the **sMessageID** variable and then use the variable in the **MAPIReadMail** call. Once the information is returned from the call, we open the Read form and place the information into the various fields as needed:

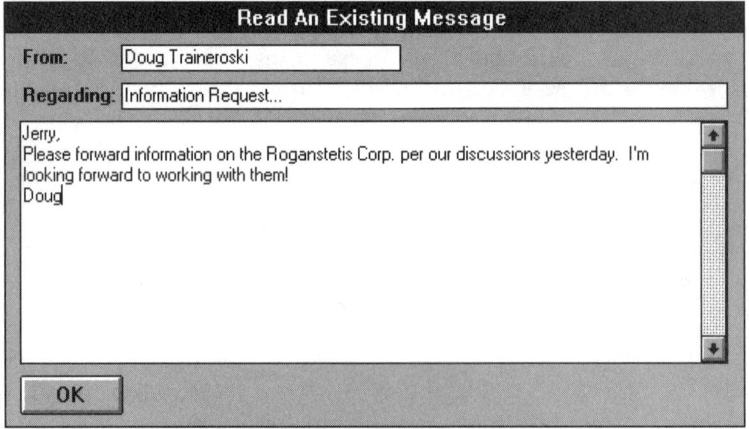

The Read form allows you to scroll around a form to see the text of the message, the originator of the message and the subject. When you press OK, the code behind the button will issue a **DoCmd Close** as in our other examples.

In our example, we log on and off within each routine. You'll find this to be somewhat tedious for a production application, but while you're developing, you'll want to make sure you are properly logging off each MAPI session that you establish. In the sample, we log off as a precautionary measure to allow you to stop a program at any point and see what is happening.

In your own systems, you should establish a global variable that contains the session ID for the current MAPI session. If the session is 0, a given routine will know to logon. Otherwise, you can use the same session number across your functions. Be sure to add code to the Form_Unload event that will log your user off the MAPI subsystem; this prevents the Too Many Sessions error we spoke of earlier.

Using Custom Message Classes

Now that we've investigated sending messages and viewing messages in the inbox, it's a natural step to begin putting this information to more use in our application. The first step is to set up a way that you can weed out messages created by your application from the other messages being created in the system.

The easiest way to do this is to set up a custom message class that you can use in your messages. Remember, if you're only going to be sending messages between applications, consider using a prefix of IPC for your messages. This will keep the message from appearing in the user's inbox in the mail client software.

To test this process, you'll make temporary changes to two different procedures. First, on the send message side, you need to modify the **SendMessageNoForm** procedure:

```
'--------------------------------------------------
'Establishing the actual message
'--------------------------------------------------
If Not IsNull(sSubject) Then
    tMessage.Subject = sSubject
End If

If Not IsNull(sNote) Then
    tMessage.NoteText = sNote
End If

If iReceipt Then
    tMessage.Flags = MAPI_RECEIPT_REQUESTED
End If

tMessage.MessageType = "IPC.Wrox.Test"
```

The final line, specifying the **MessageType**, will create a new message type on your system. You'll notice that, if you watch the outbox, the message will show up, but once it is sent, the message will not appear in the mail client inbox. In fact, if you run the inbox viewer from the Messaging menu within the PIM, the message will not be displayed.

In order to view the message by the inbox viewer, you need to make a change to the **MAPIFindNext** function calls. You may remember that, in our previous section, we mentioned that the message type we passed in to retrieve all messages was a blank type. When you don't specify a type, MAPI assumes that you want all messages of type IPM:

```
'Initiate the process by doing a FindNext
    iStatus = MAPIFindNext(gMAPISession, 0&, "IPC.Wrox.Test", ⏎
        sMessageID, 0, 0, sMessageID)
    If iStatus <> SUCCESS_SUCCESS Then
        MsgBox GetMAPIErrorText(iStatus)
    End If
```

When you specify the message type to be retrieved by the inbox, the next time you view the inbox contents, you'll be able to see your custom message. If you take a moment and browse the actual table contents, you'll see that the message class of **IPC.Wrox.Test** is shown and no other messages were returned.

> **If you have trouble retrieving the custom message in your code, be sure to check the case of the different letters in the class definition. The message class is case-sensitive and both the MAPIFindNext call and the original Send Note call must match exactly.**

Using the IPC message class not only allows you to filter messages, but also allows you a new level of security. This is afforded to you because a user would have to know the message class, including case, to retrieve a message of your new type.

Unbundling Message Attachments

So far, we've shown how to send standard Email messages, messages with attachments and how to query the inbox. Next, we need to programmatically do something with an incoming message. This will allow us to bring in the company record(s) produced by the **Process Database Extractions** function.

When we created the message, we placed the attachment's file name and other information in the **MAPIFiles** structure. As we retrieve the message containing the file, we'll need to reverse this process and retrieve the file and its contents. The **ProcessDatabaseAdditions** function allows us to walk down through our inbox, processing all messages that have attachments:

```
Function ProcessDatabaseAdditions ()

     'Query the inbox for messages on the system.
     ...
```

The code that appears in the top portion of this function is identical to the **ViewInbox** function. It has been removed here for brevity.

```
     ...

     'If there are messages to process, loop through them to see
     'what's available.
     Do While iStatus = SUCCESS_SUCCESS

         'Read the current message, the header information
         'for the message was returned by MAPIFindNext
         iStatus = MAPIReadMail(gMAPISession, 0, sMessageID, 0, 0, ↵
             tMessage, tOriginator, tRecips(), tFiles(), NumRecips, ↵
             NumFiles)

         'Add the message information to the table.

         If NumFiles > 0 Then
             'since there is a file attachment, import it.
             MsgBox "Importing " & tFiles(0).PathName & "..."
             DoCmd TransferSpreadsheet A_IMPORT, 5, "Company",     ↵
                 tFiles(0).PathName, True
             MsgBox tFiles(0).PathName & " imported.  Will remove ↵
                 message from system."
             iStatus = MAPIDeleteMail(gMAPISession, 0, sMessageID, 0, 0)
             If iStatus <> SUCCESS_SUCCESS Then
                 MsgBox "Unable to delete message. " & Chr$(13) & ↵
                     GetMAPIErrorText(iStatus)
             Else
                 'Remove the file from the temp subdirectory
                 Kill tFiles(0).PathName
                 counter = counter + 1
             End If
         End If

         'read the next message.
         iStatus = MAPIFindNext(gMAPISession, 0&, gMessageClass, ↵
             sMessageID, 0, 0, sMessageID)
```

```
    Loop

    DoMAPILogoff

    MsgBox "All information has been retrieved.  " & Str$(counter) & " ⏎
        database update(s) processed."

End Function
```

This function shows how you can loop through the messages until you find a message with an attachment. Once you do, if you retrieve the message using **`MAPIReadMail`**, MAPI will place the file for the attachment in the Windows temporary subdirectory. The fully qualified path and file name will be stored in the **`tFiles(x).PathName`** variable, where x is the number of the attachment. Attachment numbering is zero-based, so the first attachment will be **`tFiles(0).PathName`**.

Using the **`TransferSpreadsheet`** action, you can import the spreadsheet and update the Company table. The **`TransferSpreadsheet`** action is used here in the same way as in the **`MAPIExport`** routines, with the only difference being that we specify an import operation rather than an export.

The final step in bringing in the file is to remove the temporary file from the temporary directory. If you don't remove the file, you'll notice a number of files accumulating in the temporary Windows subdirectory. Once you exit Windows, you can generally remove these files.

An important note about removing files from the temporary subdirectory in Windows: if you have had to reboot your system, or if an application was forced to exit in a non-standard fashion, be sure NOT to delete the files in the temp directory. In many cases you may be able to recover some information from these files in an emergency.

While our process only imports the first attached file, it's a simple step to extend this functionality to provide access to additional attachments. In addition, if you create a custom record format, you can transfer single records or other items using this technique, the same programming methods apply. The following figure shows the flow for the process of working with an attached data item:

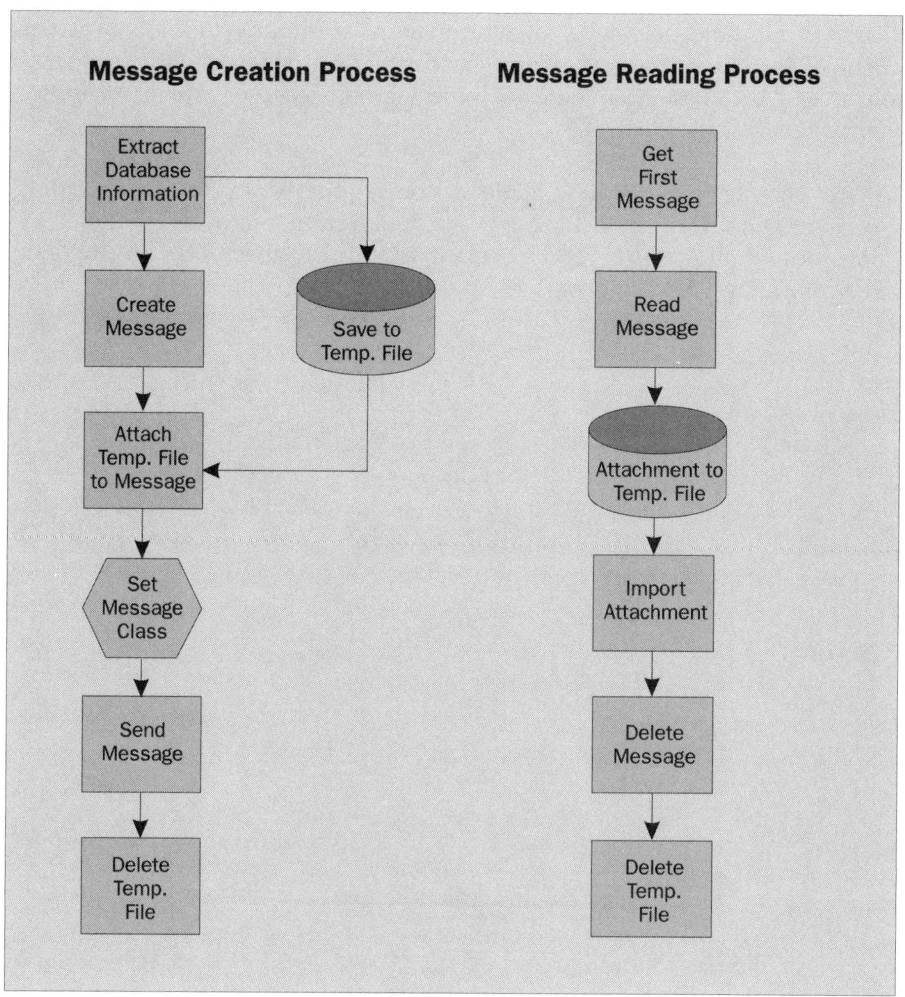

Comments and Suggestions

In this chapter, we've investigated many different means of using MAPI in your applications with varying levels of complication. These start with the most basic implementation, using the **`SendObject`** methods, and go all the way to creating custom message classes to transfer program data behind the scenes.

MAPI brings a whole new level of fault-tolerant communications between not only people, but also processes. The next time you are faced with a decision on how to get the data from here to there, perhaps a look at a MAPI-based transfer system is in order.

In the next chapter, we'll review some of the requirements for implementing multi-user systems. Record locking, system requirements and suggestions, along with other information on several different techniques that you can implement in your applications are all a part of the next chapter.

CHAPTER 15

Application Development Considerations

No matter what the size of the application, security should be of prime importance to you and your client. When you consider that the information in your database could be of a confidential nature, together with the concept of information sharing across applications, platforms and other more physical boundaries, simply locking the office when you leave at night is no longer good enough. Data must be protected, and Access has the tools to accomplish just this.

What's Covered in This Chapter

In this chapter, we'll be covering topics that range from general network implementation considerations to security in your applications. When you develop applications for distribution, you add a level of complexity to the planning of these applications. Networked, multi-user applications involve considerations for record locking, security, file locations and much more. This chapter includes these topics, along with information about adding the finishing touches to your application. These include:

- System optimization
- Security
- Database encryption

This chapter also includes several techniques that you can apply to your applications in order to improve its 'security rating'.

Chapter 15

How This Chapter Impacts Our Application

As you've seen in the last chapter about the MAPI interface, the menu system provides an excellent way to include features that are not form dependent. In this chapter, we'll be covering any considerations that may be pertinent to using the PIM in a network installation.

Introduction

Throughout this guide, we've covered many different aspects of application development in Access. In this chapter, we'll cover some additional items that don't really fall under the heading of a separate chapter, but are important in the designing of a networked, multi-user system.

Optimizing Access in a Networked Environment

When you move your Access system to a network, multi-user environment, there will be several new considerations that you'll need to be aware of. Some of these items, especially those pertaining to performance, will also apply to an Access application running on a network, even if it is only used by one person at a time.

Some of the variables that need to be considered in an environment such as this are:

- Will the application be used by more than one person?
- What type of security do you need to establish for the system?
- Will the databases be used by applications other than Access?
- How will the application be implemented to optimize network performance?

Using Multiple MDBs to Optimize Performance

One of the most straightforward things you can do to optimize performance on your systems is to separate the code from the database tables. By using attached tables, you can execute commands against the tables without modifying your program code. For our PIM application we'll split it up into two databases **`PIMCODE`** and **`PIMDATA`**:

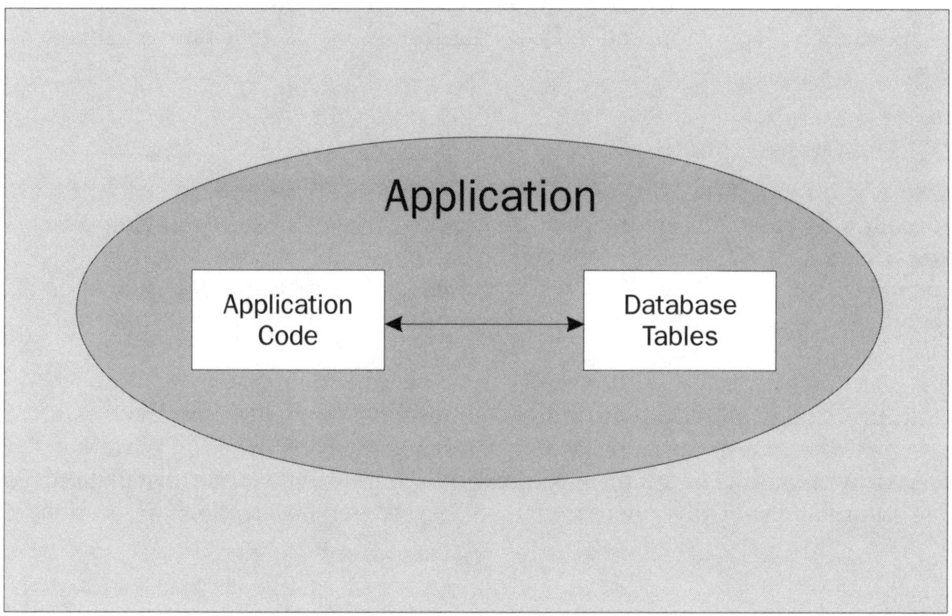

Database modules should reside on the user's local system wherever possible. This will give easy, ready access to the Access basic code, add-ins, queries and forms that make up the application. This also has the added benefit of decreasing network traffic as you'll only be transferring table information across the network. The performance gain can be substantial using this type of model.

Modifying the Database

There is yet another benefit to this type of implementation. A typical project life cycle includes many modifications to functionality, especially those items covering reporting, queries and new forms to view data. If you have the data and supporting application in one database, you'd have to import updated routines every time a change was made.

Instead, if you've separated the code and database, you can replace the code database at will. The connections will remain valid, and the functionality will be updated. The database containing the tables will not be changed unless there is a need to update the structures of the tables, which is a much less common occurrence.

You'll also now be able to assign independent security levels to the code and data portions of your application. We'll discuss more on that later in this chapter.

Split Database Problems

There is a downside to this, which is that you'll be potentially distributing an application to many different desktop systems. Instead of just allowing users to share a common installation of Access, you'll have to manage a wider implementation of the executables and modules. The footprint for Access is not insignificant, requiring disk space on systems that may already be tight on space.

If you do have a problem with the disk space requirements, you may want to implement the system with the Access Developer's Toolkit Setup Wizard. It takes away a great deal of the overhead of a full-blown Access installation. For more information on this alternative, see the chapter on creating applications for distribution.

Temporary Tables in the Code

There is one additional consideration when you're dividing up your system. You should place all temporary tables, or tables that hold values specific to a user, in a table that is maintained in the **PIMCODE** database. This will prevent temporary table naming conflicts and will allow you to have work tables that are only used on a temporary basis.

In our PIM, the Message table is an example of this. While we are moving it to the **PIMDATA** database for our examples, it would be worth considering leaving it local as the Message table will contain messages specific only to that user. If the table is shared, messages from multiple users could be placed in the table, making it somewhat difficult, if not impossible, to use.

An easy way to think about this model is:

'If it's information in the system, it's in the **PIMDATA** database. If it pertains to how that information is used, it's in the **PIMCODE** database'.

Where to Locate Your Database Modules

Generally, when you decide to implement a system to be used by more than one person, you need to share data more than the actual program code that comprises the application. If this is true, it will be very important to break apart your application and move the tables to a separate MDB.

You'll probably be developing an application in a single MDB. During the time you're developing the application, this certainly makes sense and puts the different component parts in a central location. In the production application, you will be moving those tables to a separate MDB. The following steps are required to accomplish this.

1. Backup your original database
2. Create a database to hold the new tables
3. Copy the database tables from the original database to the new one
4. Delete the tables from the original system
5. Attach the tables to your original database

Before you begin, be sure to make a backup copy of the existing application .MDB. You'll probably want to copy it to a new file rather than back it up off your system. This is because you will want to have ready access to it if you need to check on some aspect of the conversion. Creating a new database is simple and something that you're familiar with from other phases of the project. Create the new database using a meaningful name that will help you associate it with the application.

> **You may want to consider naming both the code and database tables with the same prefix in their file names. For example, consider '`PIMCODE.MDB`' and '`PIMDATA.MDB`'. This will make it easier to associate the appropriate files when you're viewing the subdirectory.**

You can achieve this database split in one of three ways:

- Copy and delete
- Copy and paste
- Export

Starting with Copies of the Databases

Probably the easiest and most concise way of migrating the system to the distributed format is to copy your original file twice. This means that you'll copy it once to an MDB that will become your Code database, and once to an MDB that will become your Data database.

From File Manager, or at the DOS level, copy **CONTACTS.MDB** to **PIMCODE.MDB** and **PIMDATA.MDB**. We'll use these two files for the examples in these sections.

Once the files are copied, open **PIMCODE.MDB**. When you do, press and hold down the shift key to prevent the opening search dialog box from opening:

It may be helpful to write down the names of the tables in the system, ready for when you attach the tables from the **PIMDATA.MDB** database.

Before you delete the tables, you'll have to delete the relationships that have been set up between the tables, otherwise Access won't allow you to delete them. Go to the relationships window from the Edit menu and delete the joins between the Company, Contacts and Projects tables, and then delete each of the tables from the listing.

> **You need to be aware that you can't attach to an external query. All queries will need to remain in the PIMCODE database.**

You can then delete all of the queries, forms and other non-table objects from the **PIMDATA** database, and you'll have completed the set up of the database split.

Using Cut and Paste to Move Tables

Rather than producing two copies of the database and then removing half the objects from each, you can simply move the table to a new .MDB file using Windows' Cut and Paste technology. This can be useful if you have enough system resources to run two copies of Access. If this is not the case, the process can become somewhat tedious because you end up switching between databases every step of the way.

Load the PIM database on one side of your screen and load your new database on the other side. This will allow you to see what's happening on both systems. Click on the table you want to copy on the PIM database and select Edit, Copy. Next, click on the database window on the new database and select Edit, Paste.

> *Be sure that you don't open the* ***CONTACTS.MDB*** *exclusively or you'll get an error message telling you that you can't paste the table because it's already open.*

You'll be prompted to supply a table name and other information about the table you'll be inserting:

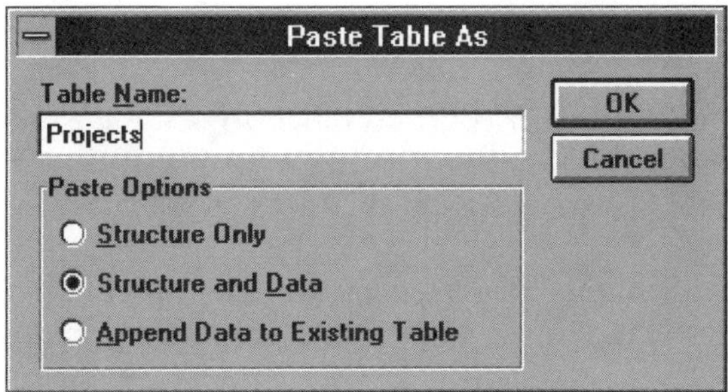

You have the option of copying in just the table structure, or the structure and the associated data in the table. If you're converting a system from development into production and the information in the table is largely testing information, select Structure Only. This will give you a clean table in the new database.

You should be aware that this method of table creation is the only way to re-initialize a counter field in a table. Copy the table, and paste it into the same database with the Structure Only option. Use an append query to move the records (excluding the counter field entries) from the original table to the new one, and then delete the original. The records in the new table will now appear with consecutive counter field entries.

You also have the option of adding the information to an existing table in the target database. This function is not really pertinent to what we're doing here, but can be useful if you're trying to copy information from one table to another.

If you are unable to run two copies of Access simultaneously, you'll have to close the `CONTACTS.MDB` database and then open the `PIMDATA.MDB` database to perform the cut and paste operation. When you've pasted the information into the `PIMDATA.MDB` database, close it and return to the `CONTACTS.MDB` database. This accomplishes the same thing as having two copies of Access running at the same time.

There is a significant drawback to doing your system split in this manner. Any relationships that you've defined are not transferred. You'll have to redefine them in the new database before they'll be in effect. If your relationships are extensive, this factor may prevent you from seriously considering this method of exporting.

Exporting Tables between Access Databases

You can also use the Access Export routines to send the information from one Access system to another. Use the File, Export... menu option to select each table that you want to export to the `PIMDATA.MDB` database.

You'll be prompted for the type of export, and you should be sure to select Access... as the destination. The next dialog box will prompt you for what type of Access object you'd like to export. From these choices, you can select any object in the system. Select Tables from the drop down list box to show the various tables available:

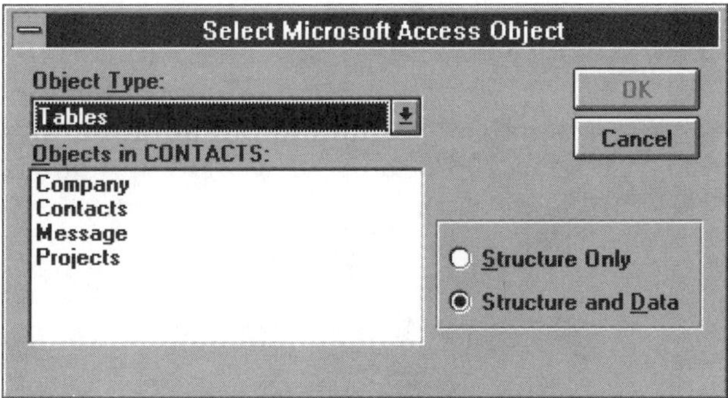

As with the Cut and Paste method mentioned above, you have the option of exporting the structure only.

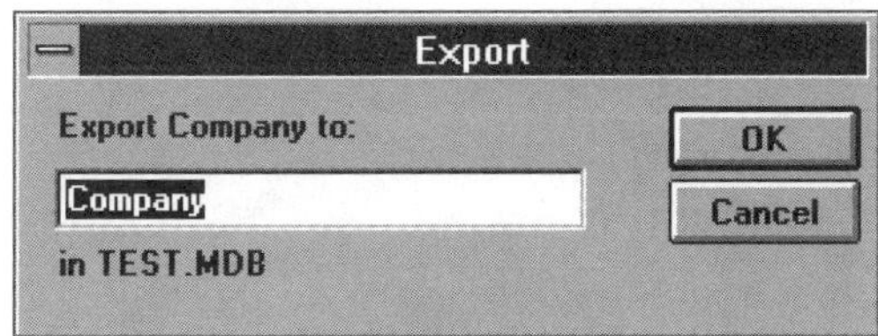

You'll be prompted for the name of the table to export to in the destination database. Access will default to the existing name, but you can override it in this dialog box. If you do override it, be sure you write down the name of the object in the original database and the name of the table in the new one. You'll need this information later when you attach the table to the code database.

If you specify the name of a table that already exists in the target system, you'll be prompted to confirm overwriting the table:

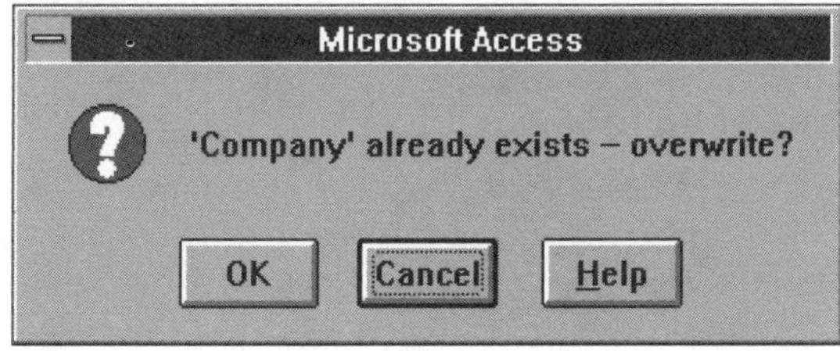

The difference between this and the cut and paste method is largely the fact that you can't append to information in the target system. If this is a requirement, consider using the cut and paste method outlined in the previous section.

The Final Step: Attach the Tables and Test

The final step is to attach each of the tables to your **PIMCODE.MDB** database. This will create the tables with the same names, but spanning the two different database files. The icon beside each file will be updated to reflect the fact that the table is an attached table:

Be sure to run your application at this point. Be sure that all functions operate successfully and that all queries are returning the information you would expect. If you experience any problems, remove the attached tables and change to the **PIMDATA.MDB** database. If you run your application from within that database, it should function correctly. If not, correct the problem and restart the process. Remember, if you change something in the **PIMDATA.MDB** database, you'll need to copy the **PIMDATA.MDB** file to the **PIMCODE.MDB** file to incorporate the changes there.

Using the Attachment Manager When Databases Are Relocated

After you've tested the application and you've confirmed that the system works in the new environment, you'll probably be copying it onto a network drive. When you do this, Access will lose track of the attached tables. You can update these attachments using the Attachment Manager. If you don't update the connection, the first time you attempt to run the application, Access will generate an error message indicating that the file couldn't be found:

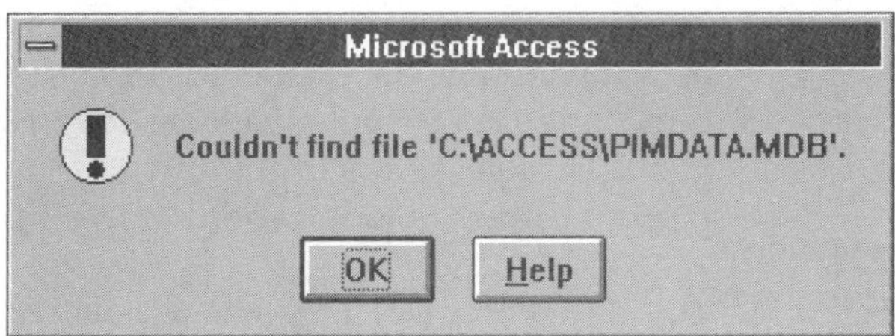

Select the Attachment Manager from the Add-Ins menu. You'll be presented with a list of all attached tables and their original locations:

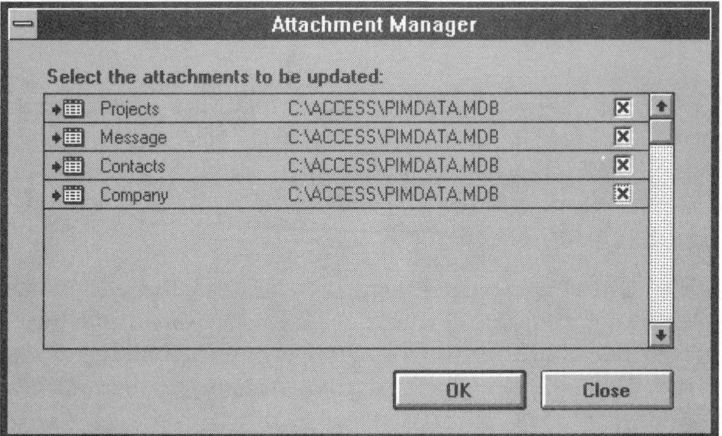

When the form is first displayed, the check boxes next to each item are not selected. Check each one that you need to update. In our example, you'll need to check each box. Press OK and you'll be prompted for the new location of the database. If the Attachment Manager is successful at updating the file locations, a dialog box is displayed indicating that success.

Network Drive Conditions

If you are placing the data files on a network drive, be sure that the following conditions are met:

Drive letter mappings	All users should refer to the drive with the same drive letter. In other words, you'll be creating much more work for yourself if Mary considers the network drive F: and John refers to it as drive G:. This will mean that the attachments need to be set up individually on each system. If you have the same drive mappings available for your user base, you'll be able to distribute the code module to each person without modification.
Network access rights	The different users of your system will need read and write access to the directory containing the database. If this is not granted, they will not be able to access the database in a mode other than read only. There is no indication from Access that a table is read only, other than the fact that it will not allow database updates and insertions.

Note that when you first specify a new table to attach, the Attachment Manager attempts to use that path to update the other items you've selected. If this process is unsuccessful, you'll be prompted to select the location of the database that was not found. This will continue until all attachment locations have been updated.

A warning is in order as it relates to your testing of the new system. If you only copy, not move, the database to the production area and then do your testing, the database attachments will still work, even without updating them. This is because they will refer back to your system and will successfully attach to your local database files.

It's a good idea to test your application on a system that doesn't have the development environment installed on it. As a second best alternative, you can move all files from your development area to another temporary subdirectory. This will ensure that anything that is pointing back to your system will come up as an error when you are testing, allowing you to correct it to point to the correct location.

Where to Locate Code Modules

Once you've moved the database tables out of the **PIMCODE.MDB** database, you can remove everything apart from the tables from the new **PIMDATA.MDB**.

Once you've removed everything, apart from the tables, you should compress the database to free up any space possible. Close the database, but stay in Access and from the File menu, select Compact Database.... You'll be prompted for the database file to compact and the output file name. You can select a different file name or you can overwrite the source file.

Note that when compacting a database you must have enough memory on your system for the old database and the new database even if you opt to overwrite the old one.

Once the operation has completed, you can go into File Manager to see the results. The difference should be substantial as the space taken up by forms and code modules can be significant. In many cases, a 50% or better decrease in the size of the database can be expected.

Using Record Locking in Your Applications

When you implement a system that allows more than one person access to a common database table or tables, you need to be able to protect the contents from individual simultaneous updates. That is, you can't have more than one person updating the same record at the same time.

Types of Record Locking

Record locking is like a library system. When you check out a book, you give the library your library card number so it knows who has the book. While you have the book checked out, no one else can read it. When you return the book, other people can read it or check it out themselves.

Record locking is much the same. Depending on how you set up Access, you can allow one of three things (see the following table).

Type of Locking	Library Analogy	Access Implementation
Exclusive Access	No one else can get . into the library while I'm in there looking around	No other users can access the same database while you have a database open in exclusive mode. This is the default mode in which databases are opened.
All Records	When I select a book, no one else can take any other book until I'm done.	Access places a table lock on the table containing the record you are editing. No one else can work with the table until you release this lock by updating the record.
Edited Record	The book I select is the only book that no one else can read until it's returned. All other books, and the library, will be open for business.	Only the record you are working with is locked against another user's access. All other information in the system is editable by another user with appropriate rights.

Configuring Access' Record Locking Options

You set up your application database using the Options... choice in the View menu. The Multiuser/ODBC option in the Category list box allows you to set various options that relate to ODBC connections. These settings are in addition to the settings and configuration options that you establish in the **MSACC20.INI** configuration file and the ODBC Manager in the Control Panel for Windows.

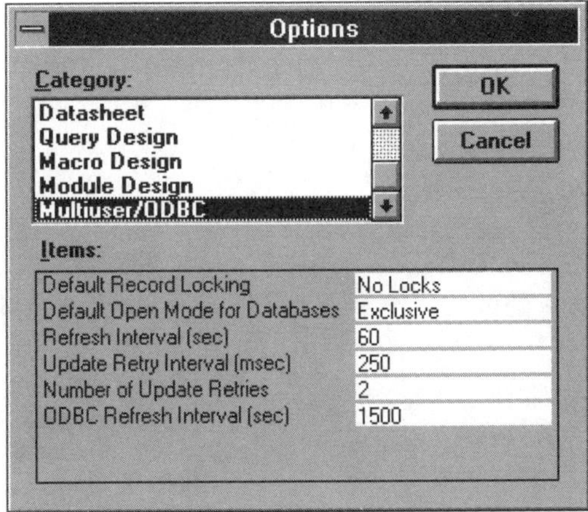

The specific item we're interested in is the Default Record Locking option. The default is No Locks but, in a multi-user installation, this will probably be unacceptable. In a situation where no locks are used, when you save a record back to the database, you'll get a message indicating that the source information has changed if another user or process has modified the record:

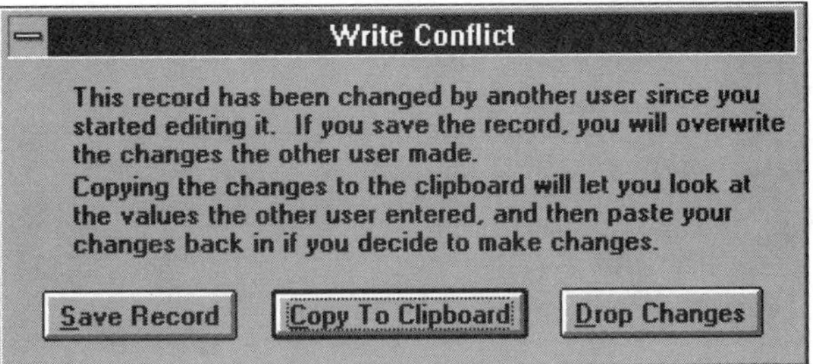

If you select Save Record, your version of the information is saved over the other version of the record. This basically overwrites any work completed by someone else. The other two options, Copy to Clipboard and Drop Changes, allow you to either temporarily save your work or discard your changes respectively. Chances are you'll end up re-entering your work after you've determined what else was changed on the record.

In order to avoid this problem, set Default Record Locking to Edited Record. Rather than calling up a record, making changes to it and saving it back only to find out it has been changed by someone else, you'll be notified immediately if someone else has the record open.

Microsoft Access
Couldn't update; currently locked by user 'Admin' on machine 'STEVEWHOME'.
OK
Help

The big difference here is that your process will wait on the other process that has the record locked. While it's locked, your application will attempt to re-save the record. You establish the number of times that the save is re-tried and the interval of time between retries in the Option dialog shown earlier.

Set the Update Retry Interval to a slightly higher value, and increase the Number of Update Retries if you find your application running into sharing problems. The first option would be to increase the number of retries.

Remember, while the system is working to update the record, the user only sees an hourglass. It's probably best to increase the retries in the hope of getting through rather than the time between attempts.

Opening a Database in Exclusive Mode

When you open a database, you have the option of opening it in exclusive mode. If you do, other users will not be able to open the database regardless of their security rights. This is a helpful option when you are the administrator for a system and it is time to compact the database or do some other operation requiring exclusive control of the database.

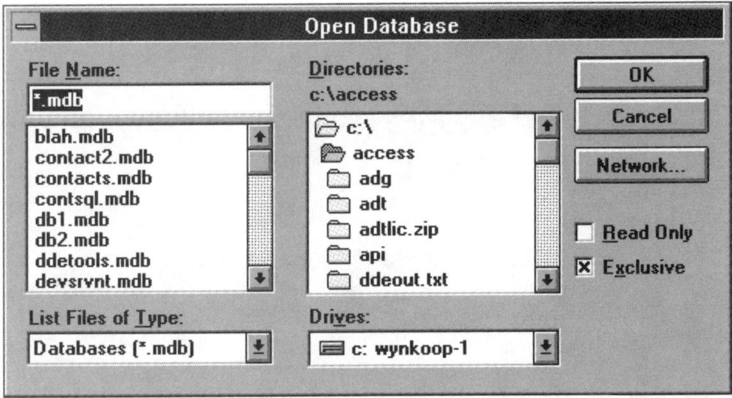

Access' default mode for opening a database is to use the exclusive option. You can change the option in one of three ways. The first and most obvious is to de-select the checkbox on the Open Database dialog box. This opens the database in shared mode allowing other users to gain access to the database.

To change the default mode you can update the Multi-User/ODBC options. The Default Open Mode... option allows you to determine what the default behavior will be for this item. The two options are Shared and Exclusive.

The final way you can control the open mode of a database is by specifying the parameter to share the database on the command line for Access:

```
c:\access\msaccess.exe pimcode.mdb
```

If you start Access and specify a database on the command line, Access will open the database in Shared mode by default. If you don't want this to happen, you can specify the **/excl** command line switch:

```
c:\access\msaccess.exe pimcode.mdb /excl
```

If you need to run a macro when the database is loaded, you can use the **/x** switch, and specify a macro to run. By using the **/excl** and **/x** switches together, you'll be able to start Access and run a maintenance routine automatically. The routine can be assured that there will be no other people using the database when it's opened in exclusive mode.

If you attempt to open a database opened in exclusive mode, Access will display a dialog box indicating the problem.

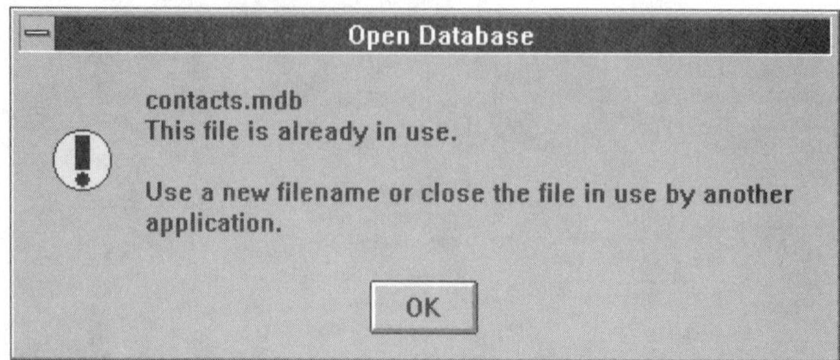

What to Do If Records Are 'Stuck' in a Locked State

It may be that, even after everyone using your application exits, records remain locked. This can happen if a user who is editing a record shuts off his system, experiences some sort of program error and is exited out of Access, or some other type of error that causes Access to shut down unexpectedly. If this happens, you can unlock those records manually.

The first thing you must do is to make sure anyone that uses the application has exited the application. They should exit Access completely and remain out until this operation is completed.

In the directory containing the data files, there is a file with an extension .LDB and with the same filename as the .MDB file. The .LDB file contains information about all of the locks held against the database.

If you erase this file, the locks will be removed. The file contains no data, only information about the locks. Removing the file will not cause any other problems with the database, so after you've removed the file, the users will be able to return to the application and continue working.

Using Record Locking in Your Access Basic Code

The options in the previous section apply largely to forms that are bound to the underlying database table. If you have an Access Basic application, the methods for managing record locking are somewhat different.

After you've opened a recordset, you have the ability to control the way that locking is handled. Two different locking methodologies are implemented in

Access and you select which to implement for your recordset.

Pessimistic Record Locking

Pessimistic record locking tells Access to assume the worst in deciding when to lock a record. When a record is accessed, the page containing the record is locked. Since pages often contain more than one record, the impact of this type of lock can be significant. If you use pessimistic locking, you should try not to have any user intervention during the time the lock is held against the database. This will prevent unnecessary delays in releasing the record while the user works with the information.

An example of where you might want to use pessimistic record locking is where you have a database that is reasonably small requiring frequent updates to the information. Since the database is small and records are updated frequently, the chances of getting conflicting updates goes up.

Optimistic Record Locking

Optimistic locking tells Access to hope for the best. This means you are hoping that no one has changed the record you are editing since you opened it and so it will be safe to write the record back to the table. Optimistic locking locks the page containing the record you're updating only at the time the record is updated in the file. During edits, the record and the page it is on are left unlocked.

It will be likely that optimistic locking is the choice for most table accesses. This will be especially true in an insert-intensive system, and one where users are not likely to be updating the same record at the same time.

Using the LockEdits Property of Recordsets

You establish record locking methodologies by setting the LockEdits property for recordsets. This property has two values, true and false.

```
...
Set DB = CurrentDB()
Set TB = DB.CreateRecordset("Company")
TB.LockEdits = True
...
```

If you set the LockEdits property to 'true', optimistic record locking will be used. Setting the value to 'false' implements pessimistic locking.

We've provided a sample testing routine in the **CONTACTS.MDB** that you can run from the immediate window. Open the Company table in datasheet mode and edit the record with a company name 'Test'. Change the information in any field except the company name. Don't move off the record, but instead, minimize the datasheet. Now choose the AB Code module, then select Design. Once the module window is open, you can select View, Immediate Window to get the debugging window opened for you. Type LockDemo and press Enter. You should receive the message shown below, indicating that the record is locked by another session:

Microsoft Access
Error # 3188 Couldn't update; currently locked by another session on this machine.
Pessimistic locking test.
OK

Note that if the record is being edited on another machine rather than on your own machine you will get a slightly different error message with a different error number, similar to the one below:

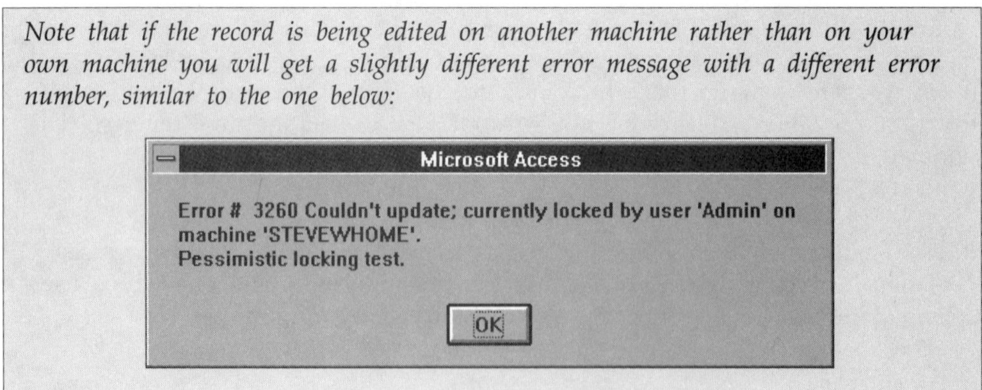
Microsoft Access
Error # 3260 Couldn't update; currently locked by user 'Admin' on machine 'STEVEWHOME'.
Pessimistic locking test.
OK

You should experiment with the **LockDemo** subroutine to learn more about how the locking process works:

```
Sub LockDemo ()
    'This routine shows how to implement locking
    'and what the effects of locking will be
    'on your program code.
```

```
    'Set up our variables
    Dim db As Database
    Dim RS As Recordset
    Dim tPhase As Integer
    Dim sError As String

    On Error GoTo LockDemoErr

    'Open the database and recordset
    Set db = CurrentDB()
    Set RS = DB.OpenRecordset("Company")

    'Select the companyname index so we can search on it
    RS.Index = "CompanyName"
    RS.Seek "=", "test"


    'First, test Pessimistic locking

    RS.LockEdits = True     'Pessimistic locking

    For tPhase = 1 To 2 'tPhase tells us whether to continue

        If Not RS.NoMatch Then
            'attempt to update the record
            RS.Edit
            RS("CompanyName") = "Test Update"
            RS.Update

            'now set it back
            RS.Edit
            RS("CompanyName") = "Test"
            RS.Update
        Else
            'there must be a record with a companyname
            'of "Test"
            MsgBox "Please add a company with a name of 'Test'"
            RS.Close
            db.Close
            Exit Sub
        End If

AfterLock1:

        RS.LockEdits = False    'set for Optimistic locking

    Next tPhase

    MsgBox "All updates were successful."

    Exit Sub
```

```
LockDemoErr:
    sError = "Error # " & Str$(Err) & " " & Error$
    sError = sError & Chr$(13)

    If tPhase = 1 Then
        sError = sError & "Pessimistic locking test."
    Else
        sError = sError & "Optimistic locking test."
    End If

    MsgBox sError

    If tPhase = 1 Then
        Resume AfterLock1
    Else
        Exit Sub
    End If

End Sub
```

The first sections of the procedure establish our variables and error handling. Opening the database and the Company recordset is also handled early in the procedure.

Once the recordset is open, we select the **CompanyName** index. This will allow us to use the **Seek** method to search for the test record.

> **When you create an index in Access' table design mode, it is titled with the name of the field it is indexing.**

Using the **Seek** method, we look for the 'Test' company. The next step, **RS.LockEdits=True**, turns on the pessimistic record locking. The **tPhase** loop tries to update the record. You'll notice that with Pessimistic locking there is a delay while Access tries to lock the page containing the record. This delay is the item that you configure in the Multi-User/ODBC options mentioned earlier.

If there is an error, the error handler is called. The message box generated includes the error number and message, along with which type of locking was in effect at the time of the error.

When the update has completed the first pass, or when the error handler returns control to the routine, we set **RS.LockEdits=False** to enable the optimistic locking. The same updates are then performed using this option.

With optimistic locking, you'll see a nearly immediate response from the locking failure. This is because Access knows that you've already changed the record. Since the change has already been entered, the update needs to be committed to the database table as soon as possible. This fails when Access determines that this update can't be saved.

Recovering from a Lock Situation

When you try the above example you can note the error number and then modify your error handler to retry the operation for your user.

Instead of relying on the Access retry mechanisms, your application could handle this functionality. This would allow you to establish the number of retries and the message received by the user during this process. The code to do this would be look something like this:

```
Sub ErrorHandlerTest ()
    'Test the error handler to catch
    'locked record errors.
    Dim ErrCount As Integer
    Dim MaxErrorCount As Integer

    MaxErrorCount = 5
    ErrCount = 1
    ...
    ...
MyErrorHandler:

    ErrCount = ErrCount + 1
    If Err = 3188 And ErrCount < MaxErrorCount Then
        txtStatusLine = "Retrying operation..."
        Resume
    Else
        sError = "Database table is locked "
        sError = sError & "by another user or process.  "
        sError = sError & "Please retry the "
        sError = sError & "operation again later."
        MsgBox sError
        Exit Sub
    End
    ...
    ...
End Sub
```

As an added benefit you can tell your users that you're retrying the operation. Placing a status line on the form and updating the control with a message will help reduce the number of 'My computer's not doing anything' calls to your desk.

Remember, if you have a transaction around certain updates, you'll need to rollback the transaction if the lock situation occurs. In the case of a complex operation, this will make the ability to retry the operation all the more important.

What Happens on an ODBC Lockout

When you receive an error from an ODBC update operation, the error number and message will probably be somewhat different. You should change your error handler to check for errors in the range 3146 to 3299. These are generally the errors that will be returned by the server.

These error numbers are those generated by SQL Server. If you are using a different server product, be sure to check the documentation to determine what values you can expect to see returned.

When an ODBC error is generated, the ODBC error, along with the Access error, is returned to the `Error$` system variable. You can locate the ODBC error by searching for the pound sign in the string. This will allow you to show or research the cause of the error. Errors generated by ODBC generally have a cascading effect and so generate Access errors. You'll need to get the ODBC error to completely understand the source of the Access error message.

Implementing Security in Your System

Once you begin implementing a system that is used by several different people, you'll often run into a requirement to 'lock down' the system. If the information is confidential or if different people have different rights on the system, Access' security model will help you to control their access to the tables and information in the system.

Once security is enabled on an Access system, all users will be prompted to sign in to Access when the program is started. This 'sign in' includes a user name and password and will be used to determine the rights associated with the user.

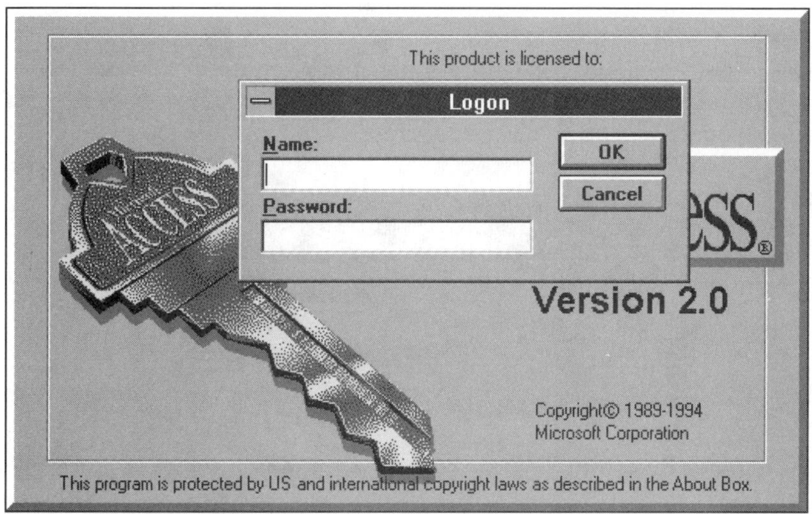

By default, there are two accounts that are set up. The Admin account, with rights to all aspects of the Access system, and the Guest account, with only limited rights to objects in the system.

How to Turn on Access' Security Management

When you first implement Access, security is not enabled. You enable security by establishing a password for the system and setting up workgroups. From the main menu bar, select Security.

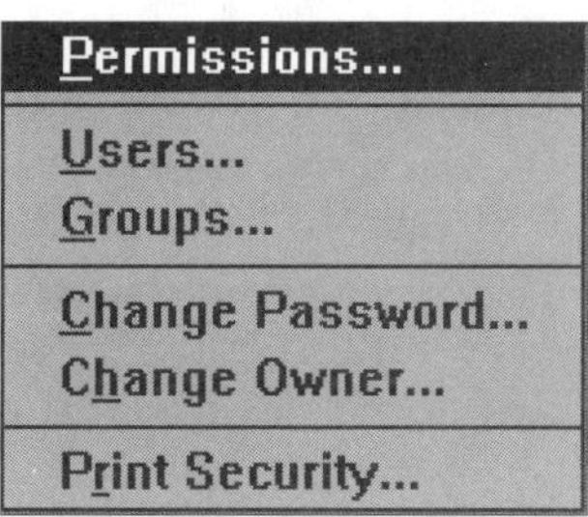

Creating Security Groups

You should first establish the Groups that are associated with the Access environment. Select Groups... from the menu and a dialog box will be displayed that allows you to define the various groups for your system:

When you select New, you'll be prompted for the name and a personal ID for the group:

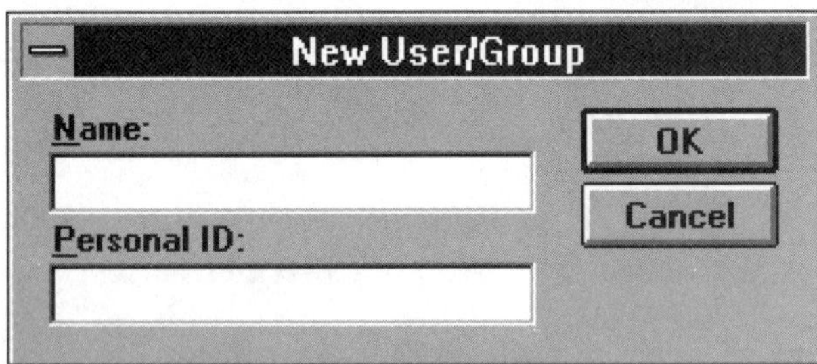

The **Name** and **Personal ID** must be unique for your Access installation.

> **It is very important that you write down the group name and Personal ID that you use to define it. If you don't have this information, you'll be unable to recreate the account later if you need to.**
>
> **The Personal ID is case sensitive and must be at least 4 characters long. Be sure to keep a note of the exact case and spelling for the Personal ID.**

Groups are used to more easily assign user rights to the various people that will be using your system. Try to think of the various responsibility sets, levels of involvement and 'political rankings' of your user base as you define groups.

If you can define groups to cover a majority of the users in your system, you'll be able to rely on the groupings to manage any future changes to the security. If you don't set up some groups and assign your users to those groups, then you'll have to change each user's account individually, which could be a lengthy and manually intensive job.

Creating Users

Once you've defined the various groups you'll be using, you need to define the users of the system. From the Security menu, select Users.... The next dialog box will be shown, allowing you to add users and associate them with a specific group or groups:

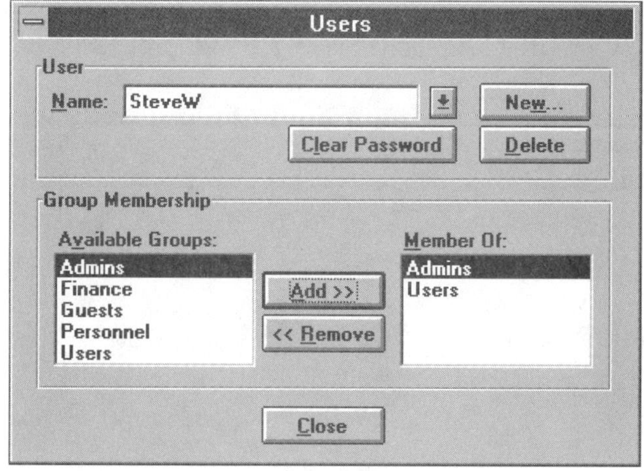

When you create a new user, you'll be prompted with the same dialog box as the new Group definition outlined in the previous section. You'll need to provide a Personal ID to use when creating the account. Again, it's very important to write down this Personal ID. It will be required if you ever need to recreate the database permissions in the future.

Once you've defined the user, you can do several things. One of the more common things you'll probably need to do is to clear the password on the account. This will be helpful in those cases when a user forgets his password and can no longer access the system.

Once the user logs in with the blank password, he'll be able to update the password by using the Security menu options.

The remainder of the options allow you to define what groups a user belongs to. You select the groups by clicking on the left-hand pane and then selecting the >> or >> buttons just as you do in the various wizards in the Access system.

Assigning Access Rights to Users and Groups

After you create the users and groups for your system, you establish rights for them. Before you start this function, you'll probably want to print the report listing the various users and groups. From the Security menu, select Print Security... to view or print the report listing users, groups or both.

C:\ACCESS\CONTACTS.MDB Friday, December
Security Information

Users

User Name	Groups that User Belongs To
admin	Admins, Users
guest	Guests
SteveW	Admins, Users

Groups

Group Name	Users that Belong to Group
Admins	admin, SteveW
Finance	
Guests	guest
Personnel	
Users	admin, SteveW

You can establish the different rights that you'll be granting users or groups in the system by selecting Permissions...from the Security menu:

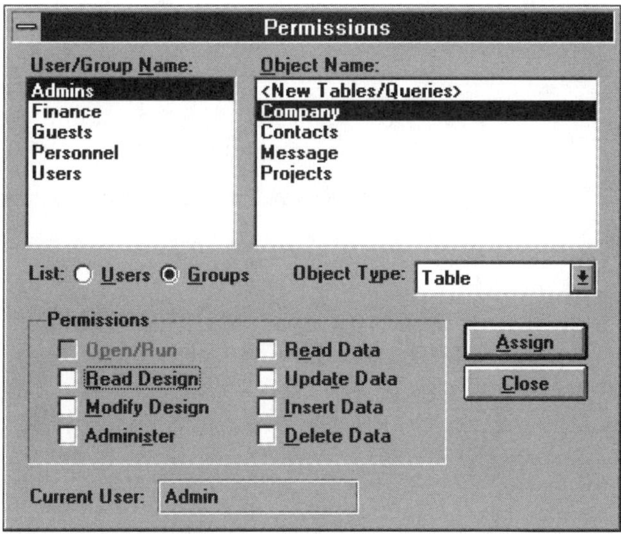

First, select the type of names that you want to work with: Users or Groups. It's highly recommended that you make all security assignments possible against groups. This will make later updates to security rights much easier to administer. When you tie access to a specific user, you'll always have to remember what that user had access to. If you tie security to a group, you just make changes to the group if a user changes or additional people need the same level of security.

Remember, you establish users and groups on a system-wide level. The same users and groups are used by all databases in the system. However, when you apply the security rights, you assign rights on a database-by-database level. You need to open the database you want to control and then work with the different security options.

Notice on the Permissions dialog box that you select the Object Type that you want to work with. The following objects can be controlled in your systems:

Object Type	Permissions
Database	Open/Run, Read Design
Table	Read Design, Modify Design, Administer, Read Data, Update Data, Insert Data, Delete Data

Continued

Object Type	Permissions
Query	Read Design, Modify Design, Administer, Read Data, Update Data, Insert Data, Delete Data
Form	Open/Run, Read Design, Modify Design, Administer
Report	Read Design, Modify Design, Administer, Read Data, Update Data, Insert Data, Delete Data
Macro	Read Design, Modify Design, Administer, Read Data, Update Data, Insert Data, Delete Data
Module	Read Design, Modify Design, Administer

The various permissions that you assign to objects are outlined in the table shown in the Access help file. Search on the topic 'Permissions Command' to locate these items. These permissions are selected by marking the check boxes next to each option.

Once you've selected the options for the current object, press the Assign button to save the permissions. Remember, if you're assigning permissions for each object individually, you'll need to press Assign after each object you establish. If you don't, the security assignments are not saved. Access will warn you if changes are made that have not been saved.

After you've established all security rights and permissions, you should print out a copy of the security assignments again. File the report in a safe place. If you need to re-assign user rights in the future, the report will prove to be an invaluable tool.

Using Other Applications to Access Tables

Traditional database systems have been proprietary in the way that you access the information they maintain. Today's systems are moving toward a more open format, allowing many different types of applications to access the information. Everything from your word processor to your spreadsheet and more, now have full access to the information in your databases.

Since ODBC and Jet are open standards, you'll also have to consider other applications that may be accessing your database tables. Excel, Word, Visual Basic and others now support connecting directly to an Access database file to retrieve information. This can become a consideration in those cases where your application and database tables are widely distributed. The Access security layer can help with this challenge.

After you've enabled Access' security layer, people using applications outside your control will also have to enter a password. For example, if you have someone trying to access your tables from Excel's external data capabilities, they'll have to know the user ID and password as well. When the first attempt is made to access the information in the database, the user will receive an error message indicating that access was denied:

After this message is acknowledged, a login screen is provided for the user. He is prompted for the username and password that should be used in the login process:

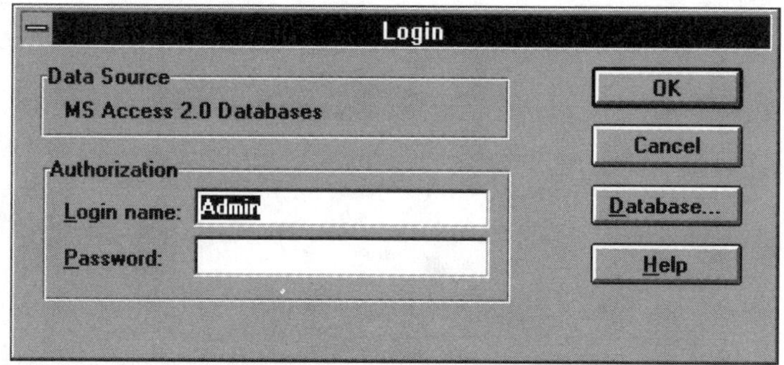

Once the user signs in, he will be able to have the same controlled access that he'd be granted if using the system from within Access. This can be an extremely important factor with the open standards of today's database systems. Consider carefully how you grant access to your database objects. Be sure you put a plan in place before you start distributing the database to many desktops.

> **If you plan to implement security before distributing your application, be sure that the setup wizard includes the SYSTEM.MDA file. This will transfer the rights to the databases that you're distributing.**

Encrypting or Decrypting Databases

If you are concerned about someone 'breaking into' your database by attempting to view it with other tools, you can encrypt it. When you encrypt the database, Access scrambles the underlying database information in such a way that only authorized users can access it.

If you attempt to look at an encrypted database with anything but an authorized viewer all you'll see is garbage. An authorized viewer uses the standard API provided to access the database. Application examples include Word and Excel. Unauthorized viewers might include trying to view the file with Windows Write or a DOS-based editor.

To encrypt or decrypt a database, select Encrypt/Decrypt... database from the File menu. This option is only available when no databases are open, and the database in question isn't currently being used by another user or process. You must have exclusive access to it.

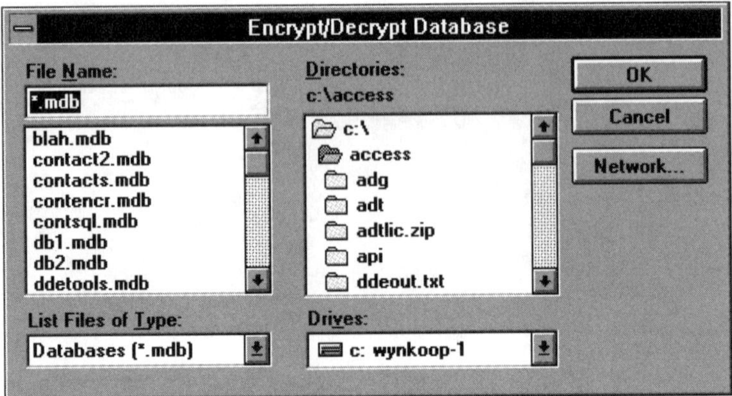

Once you've selected a database, Access will be able to determine whether it is already encrypted. If it is, Access assumes you want to decrypt the database. You'll be prompted for the file name of the new file to be created. This is the name that will be used for the newly encrypted or decrypted file. The name you provide can be the same as the source file. Access will attempt the operation against the database, and, if successful, will overwrite the original file with the newly created file. If the operation is unsuccessful, Access will not modify the original file.

With the increasing use of electronic, unsecured means of moving information around, encrypting and decrypting the database is a great option. Consider encrypting a database that you are distributing to users in remote locations, databases that you are sending over the Internet or any other databases where sensitive information can fall into the wrong hands.

Implementing Application-Enforced Security

In addition to the capabilities outlined here, you may want to implement application-based security. By this we mean security that is enforced by your application, not by the system. To do this, you'll need to set up a login process and global security variables.

In addition, you'll need to establish a database table that contains the different logins and their associated security levels. In the `SAMPLES.MDB` database, the Login Test form shows a sample implementation of a security login and user right validation routine:

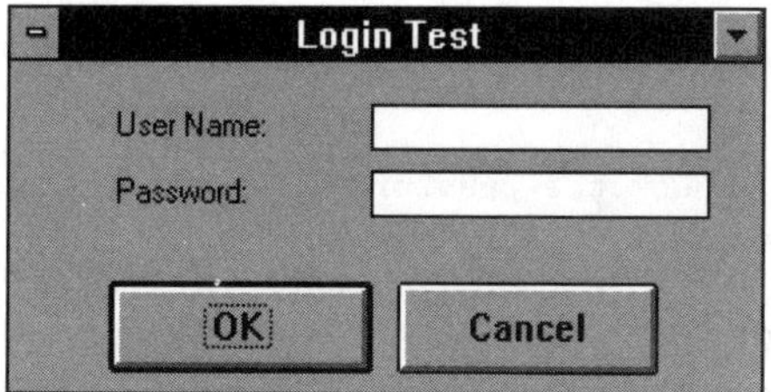

Once a user enters a name and presses the OK button, the `cmdOK_Click` event code will check the information provided against the Logins table. The user name and password are looked up first. If a match is found, the security level determines which of three message boxes is displayed.

> **You should set the Input Mask of the Password field to 'Password,' which tells Access to display asterisks for each character entered in that field. This is a good security measure and prevents someone from looking over the shoulder of another user to learn his login user ID and password.**

Here's a look at the **cmdOK_Click** code:

```
Sub cmdOK_Click ()
    'Attempt to "log in" to our system, look
    'up the user name and password in the
    'logins table.

    'Set up our variables
    Dim DB As Database
    Dim RS As Recordset
    Dim sMessage As String

    'Open the connection to the database
    Set DB = CurrentDB()

    'Get the recordset to lookup logins against
    Set RS = DB.OpenRecordset("Logins")

    'Select the index and search on it.
    RS.index = "UserID"
    RS.Seek "=", txtUserName

    'Did we find it?
    If RS.NoMatch Then
        'not found
        MsgBox "You are not authorized to use this system."
        Exit Sub
    Else
        'found, now check the password
        If RS("Password") <> txtPassword Then
            MsgBox "The password you supplied is incorrect."
            Exit Sub
        End If

        'The information supplied was correct.
        sMessage = "Welcome to the system" & Chr$(13) & Chr$(13)
        sMessage = sMessage & "You are authorized to use the system." &
Chr$(13)
        Select Case RS("Level")
            Case "1"
                sMessage = sMessage & "You are a supervisor."
            Case "2"
```

```
                sMessage = sMessage & "You are a normal user."
            Case "3"
                sMessage = sMessage & "You are a guest." & Chr$(13)
                sMessage = sMessage & "You can only view information." &
Chr$(13)
                sMessage = sMessage & "No changes will be allowed. "
        End Select

        'Tell the user what we know about them
        MsgBox sMessage

    End If

    'close our connections
    RS.Close
    DB.Close

End Sub
```

We've implemented the lookup against the logins table, showing the user what level of access he will be allowed. This makes it possible for your application to control user access. Of course, the downside to this approach is that your code will need to check the user's access level in the various procedures and functions that you develop. You'll need to determine what security levels you want to allow and how they will affect the functions you are developing.

The Logins table is quite simple. It provides for the user ID, password and a security level. The User ID field is indexed and is what we use to look up the user's sign in:

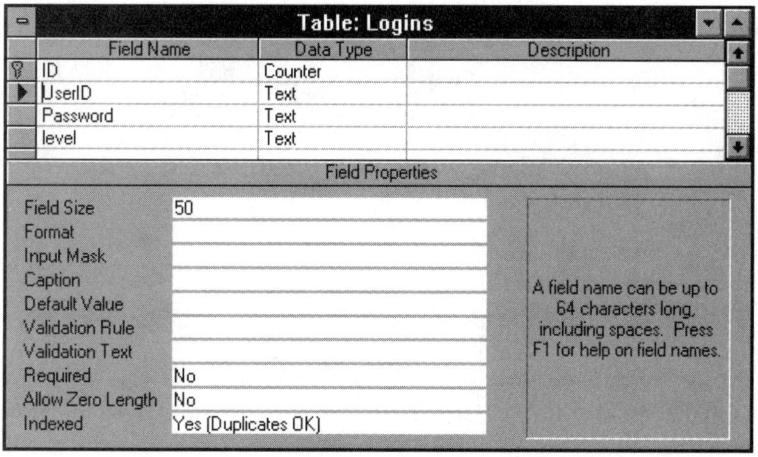

Table: Logins

Field Name	Data Type	Description
ID	Counter	
UserID	Text	
Password	Text	
level	Text	

Field Properties

Field Size	50
Format	
Input Mask	
Caption	
Default Value	
Validation Rule	
Validation Text	
Required	No
Allow Zero Length	No
Indexed	Yes (Duplicates OK)

A field name can be up to 64 characters long, including spaces. Press F1 for help on field names.

When the user is validated against the database, one of four messages is displayed. If the user is not found, access should be denied altogether:

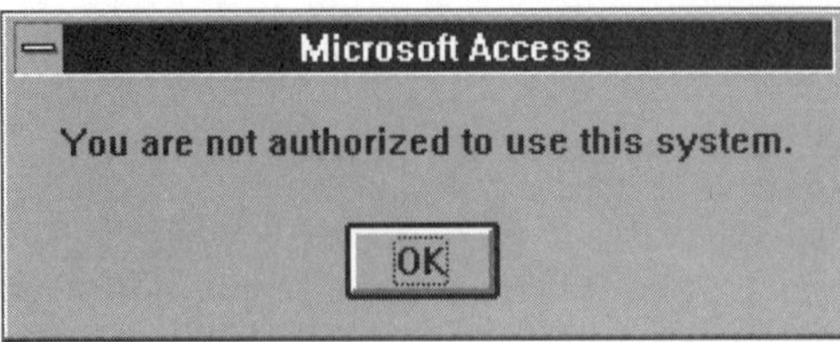

If the user is a valid user, one of the following message boxes is displayed:

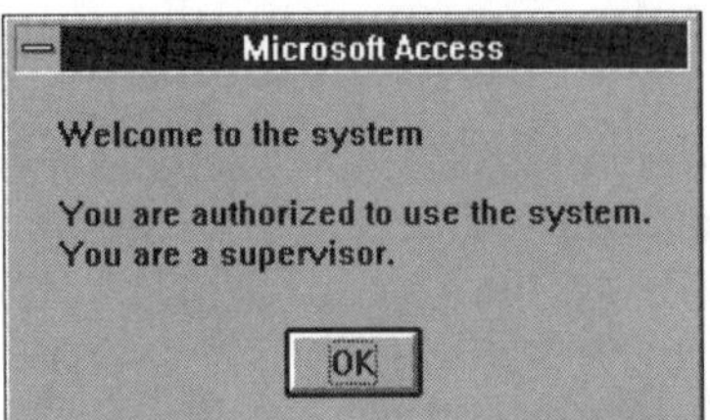

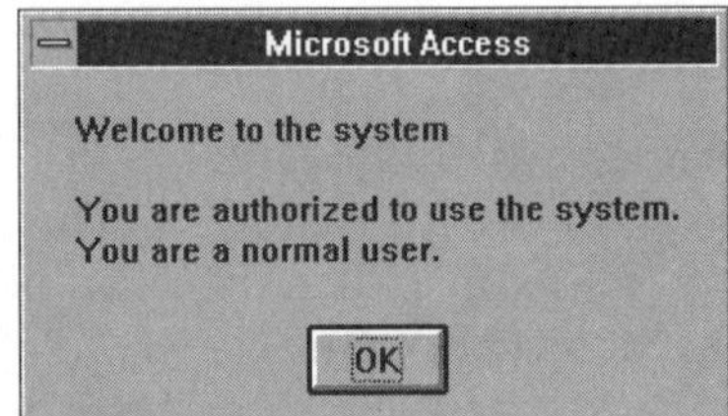

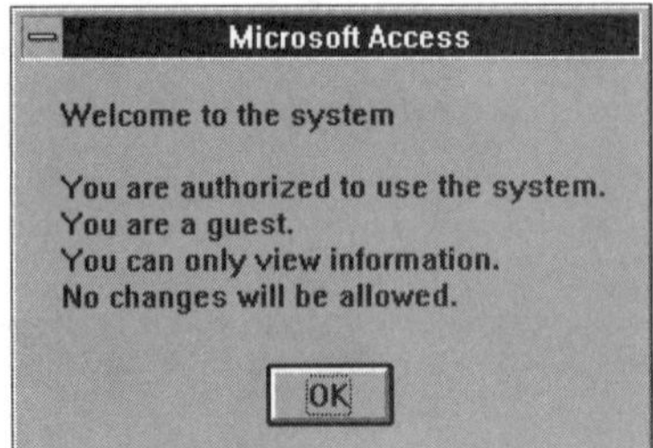

At this point, your application can continue execution and manage menu items, a form's display attributes and other items that you need to control in your application.

Managing System Security with Access Basic

We've covered the different aspects of managing security using the menu system within Access. You can also manage users, groups and permissions with Access Basic, allowing you to write the programs that will control what users can do with your software systems. Most of the following code can be found in the Security Management module in the **SAMPLES.MDB** database. To run any of the procedures, view the immediate window and type in the name of the procedure.

The security object hierarchy is set up in a similar way to the data access objects. The structure contains information about Owners, Groups and Users. Control over the access that is available to the various Access objects in your application is something that you can manage with Access Basic code.

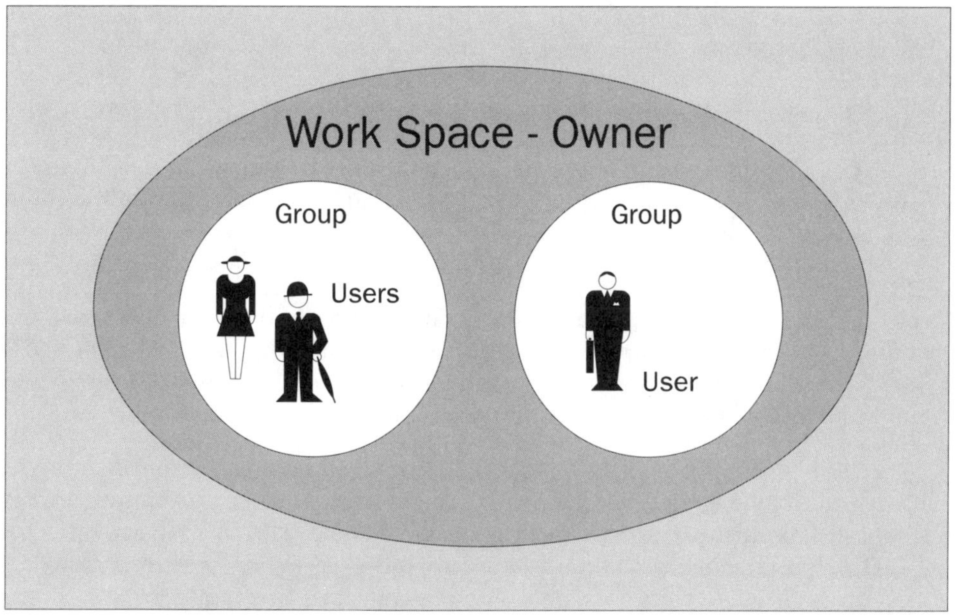

The highest level security object is the Workspace. The Owner is defined at this level, and this can be set at run time as long as the user making the change is the current owner of the database.

Passwords and PIDs

When you establish owners and users for databases, you'll also be able to assign a password. The password is modified by updating the Password property of either the User or Workspace objects.

Creating an Account and Setting an Initial Password

You initially set the password when you create a new user or establish an owner for a workspace. The code sample below shows how to establish a new user, John Smith, and assign him a password of 'DROWSSAP':

```
Dim MyUser as User
Dim MyWS as Workspace
Set MyWS = DBEngine.Workspaces(0)

Set MyUser = MyWS.CreateUser("John Smith")
MyUser.PID = "WROX"
MyUser.Password = "DROWSSAP"
MyWS.Users.Append MyUser
```

Notice that you first use the **CreateUser** method for the workspace to initialize the user structure. You then set up the user by establishing a password, a PID and user name. The **Append** method inserts the user object into the specified workspace, effectively saving the new user and allowing him to gain access to the system.

Note that passwords are case sensitive. It may be helpful to determine a standard for your passwords and enforce it at the program level. For example, 'all passwords will be lower-case' will help eliminate phone calls from users who like to mix case as they type in their password.

You'll recall from the discussion about setting security using the built-in Access functions that you must specify both a password and a PID, or Personal ID. The PID helps establish a unique pointer to the user in the system. Passwords can be up to 14 characters in length and the PID can be from 4 to 20 characters in length.

PIDs are used by the User and Group objects. You'll use the PID, in either case, as the unique identifier for the object.

Changing a Password on an Existing Account

Once an account is established, you may want to provide users of your system with the ability to update their own password. Often you'll establish a default password for the user and then allow him to update the password to a value that he prefers.

The **NewPassword** method, which applies to the User object, allows you to change the existing password. When you call the method, you'll use the format:

```
user.NewPassword OldPassword, NewPassword
```

For example, if we want to change John Smith's password from 'DROWSSAP' to 'PASSWORD', we can use the following code:

```
Dim MyWS as Workspace
Set MyWS = DBEngine.Workspaces(0)
MyWS.Users("John Smith").NewPassword "DROWSSAP", "PASSWORD"
```

You must be logged in as the user whose password you are trying to change or you must be a part of the Admins group. Otherwise, the command will fail, indicating that you don't have sufficient rights.

You can remove the password from the account by specifying the old password, and an empty string, "", for the new password.

You should record this information as new users are created to ensure your ability to re-create the user at a later date if needed. If you re-create the user with a different PID, even though the user name is the same, Access will work with it as a completely new user. The previously assigned security options will not be used.

Working with the Database Owner

You can control the database owner from Access Basic as well. Setting the owner requires that you establish a reference to the **Documents** collection. The Documents collection contains all of the different objects in your database, ranging from the tables to the modules.

The Documents object collection is a part of the Containers object collection. The reference to the object that allows you to set owner information is:

```
DBEngine.Workspaces(0).Databases(0).Containers(0).Documents(0).Owner
```

You can't reference this object directly: Access can't resolve the database reference without it being assigned to a variable. The code sample below shows how you can first inspect, and then set the owner for the current database.

```
Sub testowner ()
    'This subroutine tests the current owner,
    'and then sets it to "New Owner"

    Dim MyDB As Database
    Dim MyWS As WorkSpace
    Dim MyDoc As Document

    Set MyWS = DBEngine.Workspaces(0)
    Set MyDB = MyWS.Databases(0)
    Set MyDoc = MyDB.Containers(0).documents(0)

    MsgBox "Current owner is '" & MyDoc.Owner & "'"

    MyDoc.Owner = "New Owner"

End Sub
```

If you run the routine above against your database, the owner will be changed to 'New Owner', possibly preventing you from accessing the database. Be sure to change the reference to 'New Owner' to a user name that is meaningful to your system.

In the `SAMPLES.MDB` database, the `MyDoc.Owner =` line has been commented out to prevent accidentally changing the owner of the database.

We first display the name of the current owner for the database. Next, we set the owner to 'New Owner'. You must be the current owner of the database, or a member of the Admins group, to change the owner of a database. In addition, the user name you specify must be a user that already exists in the system.

Working with Groups

Groups are used to control logical segments of your user community. Groups allow you to establish rights for the group and then to assign rights to users by adding them to the group. Once a user becomes a member of a group, he inherits the rights of the group(s) to which he belongs.

Working with Existing Groups

In Access Basic, you can work with the groups by referencing the object as part of the workspace. The example below will list all groups in the current database:

```
Sub ListGroups ()

    'Routine to list groups in the current workspace
    Dim MyWS As WorkSpace
    Dim GroupCount As Integer

    Set MyWS = DBEngine.Workspaces(0)

    Debug.Print ""
    Debug.Print "All groups in the current workspace"
    Debug.Print "-----------------------------------"

    For GroupCount = 0 To MyWS.Groups.Count - 1
        Debug.Print MyWS.Groups(GroupCount).Name
    Next GroupCount

    Debug.Print "-----------------------------------"
    Debug.Print "End of listing of groups"

End Sub
```

The **Count** property of the Groups collection contains the total number of groups in the system. Remember that collections are zero based, so you'll start with element 0.

Creating New Groups

There are two different ways to use the **CreateGroup** method from within Access Basic. The first option creates a new group in the system, setting it up to be referenced by users that will be added later. The second provides the means of adding users to a group that is already defined on the system. Each of these will be reviewed here.

You can create new groups in Access by invoking the **CreateGroup** method of the Workspace object. **CreateGroup** allows you to establish the name and PID of the group. The code sample shown next indicates how to add a new group to the current system. Once added, this example calls the **ListGroups** procedure from the last section to show the list of all groups in the system:

```
Sub AddGroup ()
    'This subroutine adds a new group, "TestGroup"
    'and then calls ListGroups to show the
    'list of all groups in the system.

    Dim MyGroup As Group
    Dim MyPID As String
    Dim MyGroupName As String

    'Change this value to the group name you want
    'to create
    MyGroupName = "WROX Press"

    'create the group, append it to the workspace
    Set MyGroup = DBEngine.Workspaces(0).CreateGroup(MyGroupName, "WROX")
    DBEngine.Workspaces(0).Groups.Append MyGroup

    ListGroups

End Sub
```

When you're ready to assign users to groups, you'll also use the **CreateGroup** method. Instead of using the method associated with the workspace, you'll be using the method that is related to the user object:

```
Sub AddUserToGroup ()
    'This routine adds a user to an existing
    'group

    'You'll need to change the user name and group
    'name below to be pertinent to your system

    Dim MyUser As User
    Set MyUser = DBEngine.Workspaces(0).Users("SteveW")
    MyUser.Groups.Append MyUser.CreateGroup("WROX Press")

    ListGroupsForUser

End Sub
```

You set up the User object with the reference to the user you need to work with. Then, using the **CreateGroup** method, you use the Groups collection's **Append** method to add the user to the group. **MyUser.CreateGroup** passes the reference to the **Append** method, creating the relationship between the user record and the associated group.

The **ListGroupsForUser** routine loops through all users in the system, listing the groups to which they are associated, if any. It's a good indication of the success or failure of programmatic attempts to add users and/or groups to the system. The code includes two loops, working with the users names first, then with the associated groups:

```
Sub ListGroupsForUser ()
    'Routine to list groups for users in the system

    Dim MyWS As WorkSpace
    Dim GroupCount As Integer
    Dim UserCount As Integer

    Set MyWS = DBEngine.Workspaces(0)

    Debug.Print ""
    Debug.Print "List groups for users"
    Debug.Print "------------------------------------"

    'determine the number of users...
    For UserCount = 0 To MyWS.Users.count - 1

        'print out the user's name
        Debug.Print MyWS.Users(UserCount).name

        'determine the number of groups...
        For GroupCount = 0 To MyWS.Users(UserCount).Groups.count - 1

            'print out the groups associated with the user
            Debug.Print "      " &
MyWS.Users(UserCount).Groups(GroupCount).name
        Next GroupCount

        Debug.Print ""

    Next UserCount

    Debug.Print "------------------------------------"
    Debug.Print "End of listing of groups for users"

End Sub
```

Comments And Suggestions

In this chapter, we've covered several different topics that help put some of the finishing touches on your application. Real-world applications face the real-world implications of user security and prevention of unauthorized tampering with information.

Access provides some good tools to manage the groups, users and overall access to the database tables. We've investigated each of these and explained how they can be used to lock down the security for your application.

CHAPTER 16

And Finally, How About...

As with all developmental projects, at the end of the day, you must tidy up all the loose ends, answer any nagging questions and finally present the finished project. Here is our 'end of the day' presentation.

What's Covered in This Chapter

In this chapter, we'll be discussing some extra information that didn't seem to fit in any of the other chapters. Some of these things are helpful only in certain circumstances and we'll try to provide information on what those circumstances may be.

Some of the things we'll cover are:

- Creating a Dynamic List of Reports
- Hiding the Database Window
- Using IIF
- Using Domain Functions

We've implemented some of these in the **SAMPLES.MDB** and our PIM database but haven't specifically talked before about how they are used.

Chapter 16

Creating a Dynamic List of Reports?

In the **CONTACTS.MDB** database, we offer the user the option of selecting from any report installed in the database. We do this by directly querying a hidden system table that contains the names of the reports. Before we begin explaining how this example works, you'll need to turn on system tables in the tables listing. To do this, select Options... from the View menu, calling up the Options dialog box:

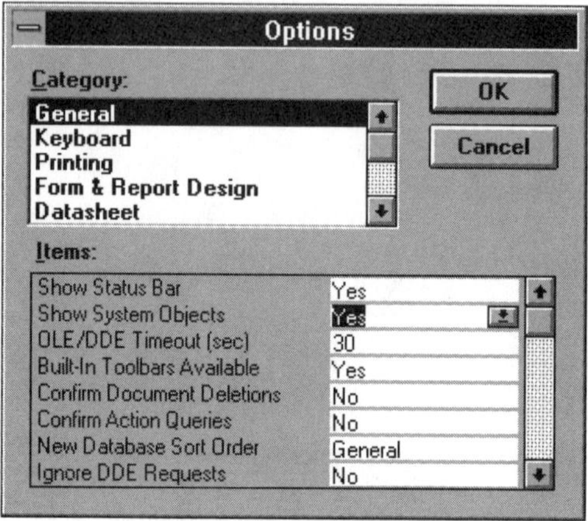

Locate the Show System Objects entry in the General category and change the entry to a 'Yes'. Once you've set this option, Access will display the system tables in the Table dialog box. You can then create queries, forms and other tools that reference these system tables.

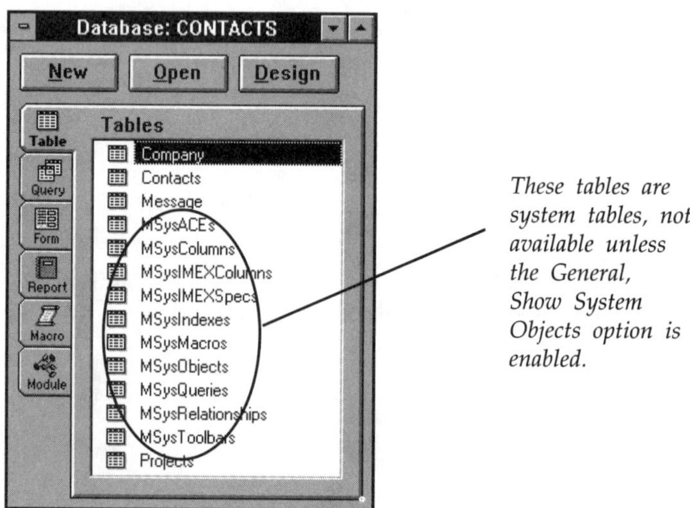

These tables are system tables, not available unless the General, Show System Objects option is enabled.

Now that you've enabled the system tables, we can investigate how to accomplish a dynamic listing of reports and allow the user to select and run a report from within an application. Of course the key to our problem is the need for the list to be dynamic and not hard-coded. In the **CONTACTS.MDB** database, the form that accomplishes this is the Sample Reports form. The form is quite straight-forward; it presents a list of available reports and a Quit button:

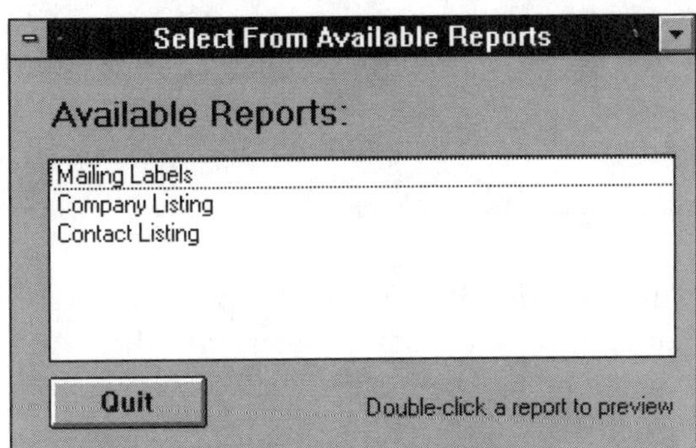

The following two key controls are on the form, allowing for the list box and its functionality:

lstReports This is the list box that displays the report names.

cmdQuit The Quit button, closing the form at the user's request.

In addition, we've added a caption to the form and we've turned off all scroll-bars, navigation keys and the maximize button. For consistency, the background has been set to gray.

The code behind the Quit button is pretty standard, unloading the form when the user has completed his work with the reports:

```
Sub cmdQuit_Click ()
    'close the form, returning to the
    'calling application

    DoCmd Close
End Sub
```

When the form loads, the list box automatically refreshes its contents by calling the query List Reports. This query extracts all entries in the MSysObjects table that have a type of -32764. There wasn't any magic in determining which number to retrieve for the Type field. You simply take note of the reports you have defined and scan the table for rows with the report names in the Name column:

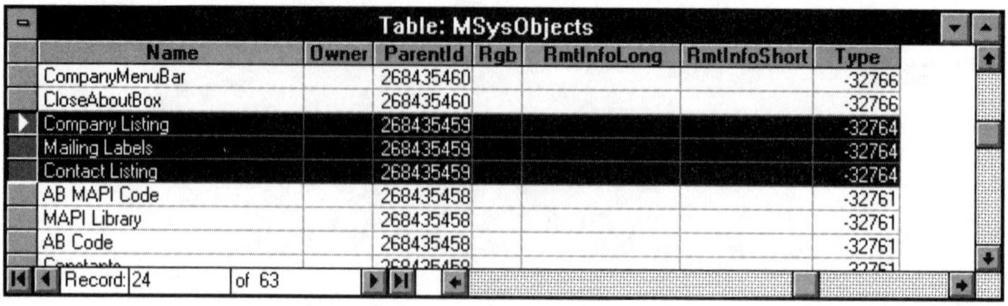

Table: MSysObjects

Name	Owner	ParentId	Rgb	RmtInfoLong	RmtInfoShort	Type
CompanyMenuBar		268435460				-32766
CloseAboutBox		268435460				-32766
Company Listing		268435459				-32764
Mailing Labels		268435459				-32764
Contact Listing		268435459				-32764
AB MAPI Code		268435458				-32761
MAPI Library		268435458				-32761
AB Code		268435458				-32761

Record: 24 of 63

The Type field is a unique identifier for the type of object. Since you know all of the reports by name, you can quickly determine that Access uses a type of -32764 as the designator for a report.

You can use this same technique to determine the type identifier for other objects in your system. The following table shows some of the more common objects and their related type:

Object Class	Type
Query	5
Table	1
Modules	-32761

Be sure that you look for an object that you know the name for. The entries that indicate databases, tables and so on, are system values, not the values that represent those types of objects. When in doubt, add a single entry for each type of object in the system. Name it MY<OBJECT>, for example MYTABLE, and you'll be able to easily locate it and determine what type of object it represents.

If we take this information and create a new query that extracts only the information pertaining to reports, we'll have the source of information that we need for the list box:

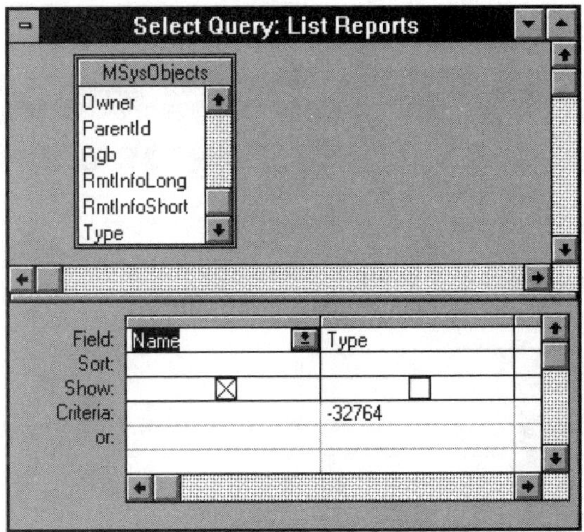

Note that Type *should not be displayed, so clear the check box in the* Show *property for the field. In the* Criteria, *enter the object type ID we discovered in the steps above.*

Now that you've created the necessary query, you can return to the Options dialog box and set the Show System Objects option to No. The query will still be able to work with the table, but the tables used by the system will no longer be shown in the table listing. The major benefit of this is that you won't subject yourself or your users to unnecessary listings of tables in the dialog box. This can be a benefit if you have newer users on the system that may become confused if they see several tables that they had not expected.

Returning to the form design, set the list box's Row Source Type to Table/Query and set the Row Source as shown below:

```
SELECT DISTINCTROW [List Reports].[Name] FROM [List Reports];
```

This will return only the Name field from the query. This expression was built with the Expression Builder, hence the **DISTINCTROW** entry. If you're entering the statement directly, you can leave out the **DISTINCTROW** option and it should have no effect on this operation since all report names must be unique in the system:

List Box: lstReports

All Properties

Name	lstReports
Control Source	
Row Source Type	Table/Query
Row Source	SELECT DISTINCTROW [List Reports].[Name] FROM [List Reports];
Column Count	1
Column Heads	No
Column Widths	
Bound Column	1
Default Value	
Validation Rule	
Validation Text	
Status Bar Text	
Visible	Yes
Display When	Always
Enabled	Yes
Locked	No
Tab Stop	Yes
Tab Index	0
Left	0.2 in

If you have problems displaying information in the form's list box, be sure to check the Row Source Type property. It must be set to Table/Query in order for the Row Source to work correctly.

If you have a problem with the Name field, try placing it in square brackets as shown. Name is an often-used property for objects in the system and may cause a naming conflict if the square brackets are not used to designate it as a variable.

The final step is to allow the user to double-click a report on the list and have the report previewed on screen and potentially printed. The On Dbl-Click property for the lstReports control will allow us to trap the double-click event.

First, set the property to [Event Procedure] by requesting the assistance of the code builder, then create a code module that will preview the requested report. You may remember from earlier chapters that the .Value property of a list box contains the value of the selected row. Using this information, we can determine which report was requested.

Place the following code in the DblClick event for the lstReports control:

```
Sub lstReports_DblClick (Cancel As Integer)
    'Run the requested report
    On Error Resume Next
    DoCmd OpenReport lstReports.value, A_PREVIEW

    'Return to the form...
End Sub
```

You'll need to set up the **On Error...** statement because, if the user presses *Es* or otherwise cancels the operation, he will receive an error message from Access indicating that the Access Basic code was not able to complete. With the error handler enabled as in this case, when an error is encountered, the program will simply continue with the next step in the module.

Using the **OpenReport** keyword, **DoCmd** opens the specified report. We're specifying the **A_PREVIEW** intrinsic Access constant so that the user has a chance to look over the report results prior to printing the report. For more information on the constants that are available for this command, search Access help for OpenReport.

The last step is to add the item to the custom menu that we're using throughout the PIM.

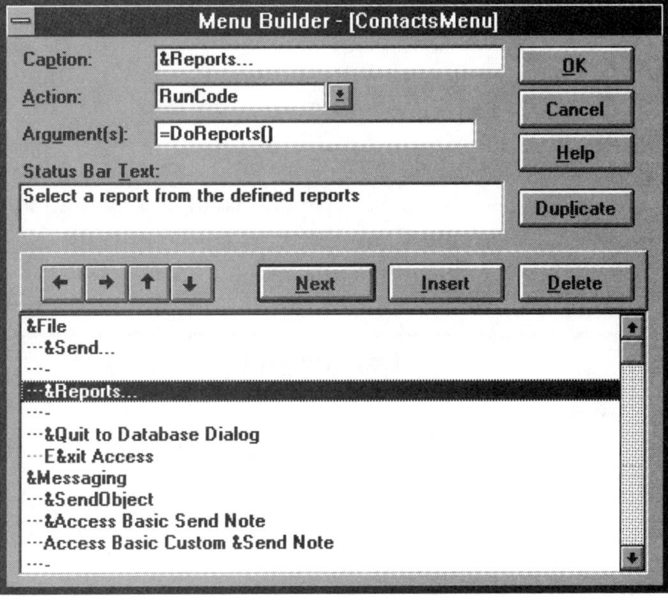

Add the Reports... option to the File menu in the ContactsMenu custom menu. This will enable the option while the user is in the main search screen of the PIM. The new option should be separated from the Send and Quit... options by a separator bar.

If you implement this on a menu bar available at all times on the system, the user can print reports at any time. In addition, since the list is dynamic, the user will see new reports appear on the list whenever they are added, all without having to change the program to support the new reports.

Making a Function Available to a User, Regardless of the Current Database?

If you have a situation where you want to make a particular function, form, report or other option available to a user at all times, you can use a feature of the macro subsystem called AutoKeys. The AutoKeys capabilities allow you to modify the functionality of the keyboard handler, substituting what you want to happen when a particular key or keystroke combination is pressed.

For example, suppose you wanted to make the WROX.INI File Manager available at all times by pressing *Ctrl-F1*. You can use AutoKeys as follows to give this functionality to your users.

From the Macro sheet, select the Macro Name button from the toolbar or select Macro Names from the View menu. This will open a new column along the left side of the macro sheet called Macro Name.

When you assign macros through AutoKeys, you specify a keystroke as the macro name. The Action is what will happen when that keystroke is pressed. In the example above, we're trapping on the *Ctrl-F1* combination. Here's how the keystrokes are designated to AutoKeys:

Keystroke	Description
{F1}	Any function key
^{F1}	Ctrl+Any function key
^A or ^4	Ctrl+Any letter or number key

Continued

Keystroke	Description
^{DELETE} or ^{DEL}	Ctrl+Del key
^{INSERT}	Ctrl+Ins key
{DELETE} or {DEL}	Del key
{INSERT}	Ins key
+{F1}	Shift+Any function key
+{DELETE} or +{DEL}	Shift+Del key
+{INSERT}	Shift+Ins key

The syntax for the keys is the same as that for `SendKeys`. Here's an overview of the different keys available:

Key	Code	Key	Code
Backspace	{BACKSPACE} or {BS} or {BKSP}	Break	{BREAK}
Caps Lock	{CAPSLOCK}	Clear	{CLEAR}
Del	{DELETE} or {DEL}	Down Arrow	{DOWN}
End	{END}	Enter	{ENTER} or ~
Esc	{ESCAPE} or {ESC}	Help	{HELP}
Home	{HOME}	Ins	{INSERT}
Left Arrow	{LEFT}	Num Lock	{NUMLOCK}
Page Down	{PGDN}	Page Up	{PGUP}
Right Arrow	{RIGHT}	Scroll Lock	{SCROLLLOCK}
Tab	{TAB}	Up Arrow	{UP}
F1	{F1}	F2	{F2}
F3	{F3}	F4	{F4}
F5	{F5}	F6	{F6}
F7	{F7}	F8	{F8}

Continued

Key	Code	Key	Code
F9	{F9}	F10	{F10}
F11	{F11}	F12	{F12}
F13	{F13}	F14	{F14}
F15	{F15}	F16	{F16}

You designate these keys as the keystroke that you want to capture. So, for our example of calling up the .INI file manager, you want to set the *Ctrl-F1* combination to call the ini_entrypoint() function, just as you have it defined in the **MSACC20.INI** file. This will allow users to select the option from the Add-in menu, or by pressing the now-magical *Ctrl-F1* combination.

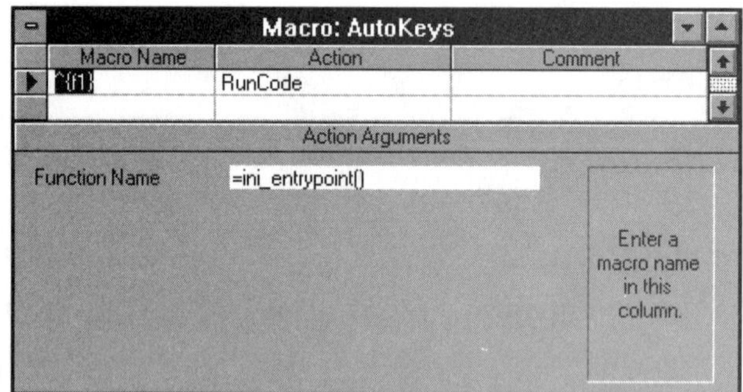

Notice that you have only one line per keystroke that you want to capture. If you need to activate more functionality than can be accomplished on the single line, you'll need to use the **RunCode**, **RunMacro**, **RunSQL** or **RunApp** actions to call additional functions.

Returning to a Specific Record?

There are many cases where you'll want to find a record, look up additional information about the record in the table, then return to the original record for updates or further action. Typically, you can re-search for the record based on the original search criteria, but there is no guarantee that you'll be returning to the exact same record from whence you came. Access supports a bookmark property that can be set and queried to allow you to both mark a position in the table and return to your mark later, after other operations have been concluded.

Suppose you want to look up the first occurrence of John Smith in your database, and then compare it to other John Smiths to see if they are duplicates. Here's an example piece of code that you could use to accomplish this:

```
Sub SmithTest ()

    'This example shows how you can use the
    'bookmark property of a table to return to an
    'original location

    'Set up our variables
    Dim MyDB As Database
    Dim MyRS As Recordset
    Dim MyBookMark As String

    'Initialize a database and recordset connection
    Set MyDB = DBEngine.Workspaces(0).databases(0)
    Set MyRS = MyDB.OpenRecordset("Contacts", DB_OPEN_DYNASET)

    'locate the first record
    MyRS.FindFirst "LastName = 'Smith'"
    If Not MyRS.NoMatch Then
        'set our bookmark, let the user know
        MyBookMark = MyRS.BookMark
        MsgBox "First Name (at bookmark): " & MyRS("FirstName")
    End If

    'loop through the recordset, looking for other
    'Smith records
    Do While Not MyRS.NoMatch
        MyRS.FindNext "LastName = 'Smith'"
        If Not MyRS.EOF Then
            'let the user know we've found one
            MsgBox "First Name (walking through table): " & MyRS("FirstName")

            'do some work...

        End If
    Loop

    'all set, return to the original
    MsgBox "Out of loop.  Returning to original record..."
    MyRS.BookMark = MyBookMark

    'confirm that we have the right one
    MsgBox "Back to First Name of: " & MyRS("FirstName")

End Sub
```

The bulk of the important work is done just after the **FindFirst** to locate the first Smith on file. Once we have the record we're looking for, we make a copy of its bookmark property. This is what we use to return to the record.

We then loop through the remaining records until there are no more matches. Once we've run out of Smiths, we want to return to the original record. To do this, we simply set the bookmark property of the recordset back to what it was when we had the correct record. Access moves us instantly back to where we started.

Our example is relatively straight-forward. The only thing that you'll need to be aware of in your applications is that not all data sources support the bookmark. These vary depending on circumstances on your system, the type of database, and so on. You can determine from your subroutine whether a specific record set supports a bookmark by checking the BookMarkable property of the recordset. If this property is true, you'll be able to work with bookmarks. If it's false, make sure you're opening the recordset as a Dynaset. If you continue to have problems, consult your database interface documentation for additional information. In addition, Access' on-line help system offers additional information. Search on the keyword 'Bookmark'.

Hiding the Database Window When My Application is Running?

In many cases, you'll want to have your application take control of the user's desktop while the application is running. This entails clearing the database window from the desktop at the initiation of the program and showing it again on termination of the program. You would probably use a macro to accomplish this. For example, you could create two macros as shown below:

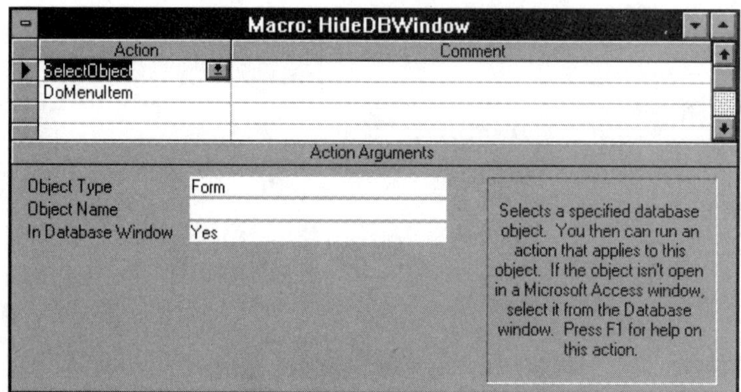

When the HideDBWindow macro is run, it will first select the database window and then hide it. This will remove it from the active desktop. In the PIM database we've set up the initial form, the Opening form, to call this macro in the On Load event:

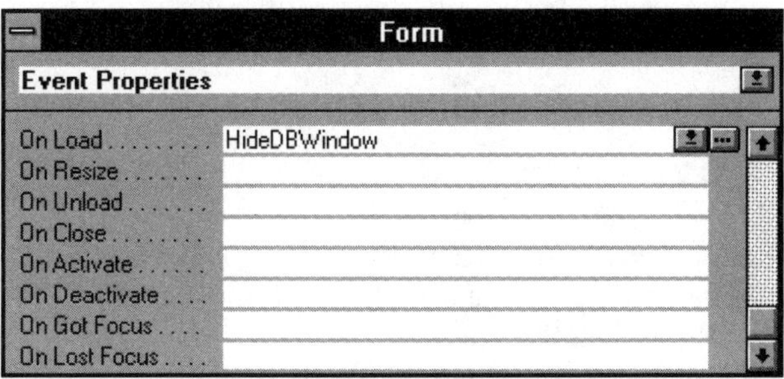

Whenever the form is loaded, which happens as a default whenever the application is started, the database form is hidden and won't clutter the desktop for our application. Also, this affords some level of security as the users won't be able to gain access to the database window quite as easily.

You can modify the **`cmdQuit`** option of the Find Form to leave Access altogether. Instead of **`DoCmd Close`**, use **`DoCmd Quit`**. This will unload the database and exit Access. While you're developing, you'll want to use the **`Close`** option. You won't want to be constantly exiting and re-starting Access while you're making changes to the system.

If you return users to the Access environment, rather than exiting the system, you'll need to UnHide the database dialog box. The procedure is the same except that you'll be specifying the UnHide action in the macro.

Some Interesting Language Elements

Access Basic provides a wide range of capabilities as part of the Basic language. In this section, we'll present an overview of some of the lesser-known, but nevertheless very useful, options.

Chapter 16

Using IIF() to Analyze Information

If you find that you need to analyze a value and take one of two actions based on that value, **IIF()** may be just the tool to accomplish your task. **IIF()** allows you to specify a test to be performed and it allows you to specify two different results based on the results of the test.

Here's the syntax for the command:

```
<variable> = IIF ( <test>, <true value>, <false value>)
```

The test is evaluated, returning either a 'true' or 'false'. Based on this value, the appropriate value is returned as a result of the function call. Note that **<test>** can call another function or can be a mathematical equation that resolves to a result of 'true' or 'false'.

In typical Access Basic code, this could be expressed with an IF statement, much like that shown next:

```
If Value = 20 Then
    MsgBox "The value is 20"
Else
    MsgBox "The value is NOT 20"
End If
```

With **IIF()**, you can shorten the series of statements and accomplish the same thing with a single statement:

```
MsgBox IIF(Value = 20, "The value is 20", "The value is NOT 20")
```

If the Value equals 20, the string 'The value is 20' is returned to the **MsgBox** function, displaying the appropriate message. If not, the indication that the value doesn't equal 20 is returned and displayed. **IIF()** is a function and, as such, you'll need to assign the results of the statement to a variable appropriate to the type of result returned, whether it be a string, numeric value, variant and so on.

> IIF() is equivalent to the Excel =IF() function and the Lotus @IF function.

Selecting a Response With Choose

If you have a situation where you need to select one of several different results based on a given value, you can use the **Choose()** function. This function accepts one value as the test value, much like the **IIF()** function covered in the previous section. The difference between **Choose()** and **IIF()** is that **Choose()** allows you to specify more possible results. Here's the syntax of the **Choose()** function:

```
<variable> = Choose(<test>, Value1 [, Value2] [,ValueN] ... )
```

For example, suppose you have a customer classification that determines a discount rate for a customer. If the value ranges from 1 to 3, and is used to represent a discount percentage, you could use the following routine, located in the Misc Functions module of the **SAMPLES.MDB** database:

```
Sub ChooseTest ()

    'This subroutine tests the the Choose() function.
    'The routine determines and calculates a discount
    'based on iCustLevel, a customer classification.

    'Value ranges from 1 to 3
    '1 - offer a 10% discount
    '2 - offer a 30% discount
    '3 - offer a 50% discount

    Dim cPrice As Currency
    Dim iValue As Integer
    Dim iCustLevel As Integer

    iCustLevel = 2
    cPrice = 100

    iValue = Choose(iCustLevel, 10, 30, 50)

    cDiscount = (iValue / 100) * cPrice

    cPrice = cPrice - cDiscount

    Debug.Print cPrice

    'cPrice now represents the total
    'discounted price for the item.

End Sub
```

If you run this routine from the immediate window, you'll see that the result is $70.00, indicating that the customer enjoys a 30% discount from the starting price of $100.00. You can specify up to 14 different return values for the function, making it an attractive way to process multiple choice type comparisons. To accomplish the same thing with an **If...ElseIf...End** If structure would require significantly more lines of code to create.

> **The `Choose()` function is much like the older `On <variable> GoSub` statements available in the true Basic language.**

Using Domain Functions

There are several functions that are created to work against an entire set of data, much like some of the functions that are used to manipulate tables or recordsets. Domain functions allow you to do many different things some of which can save you many hours of time in programming. The format of the Domain function syntax is consistent across functions:

```
<Variable> = <Function>(<Expression>, <Domain> [,<Criteria>] )
```

For example,

```
cResult = Dmax("[Item Cost]", "Sales")
```

In most cases, you don't need to specify the criteria for a given function.

Here's a summary of the different domain functions and their purpose:

Function Name	Description
Dfirst(), Dlast()	Look up the first or last record in a set
Dlookup()	Find a value in a set
Dcount()	Count the records in the set
Dsum()	Calculate the total of the values specified in the set
Dmin()	Calculate the minimum value in the specified set

Continued

Function Name	Description
Dmax()	Calculate the maximum value in the specified set
Davg()	Calculate the average value in the specified set
DStDev()	Calculate the standard deviation for the values for a sample population
DStDevP()	Calculate the standard deviation for the values in the specified population
Dvar()	Calculate the estimated variance for the sample population
DVarP()	Calculate the estimated variance for the population

These functions are often used in reporting, but are also available in your Access Basic procedures as mentioned here. In most cases, you can specify a calculation for the **<Expression>** portion of the statement. For example, you could specify the following to calculate the total cost of all sales in a sample table:

```
cResult = Dsum("[Item Cost] * [Item Quantity]", "Sales")
```

The domain functions are very flexible and can greatly speed up your efforts in working with data sets that require analysis of this type. For more information on a specific function, search Access' on-line help for the specific function you are interested in.

Where Do You Go From Here?

We've covered quite a lot of ground in this book and hope that it provides some of the answers to the questions you're going to encounter as you develop applications that use these advanced technologies.

There are excellent reference sources that provide an ongoing, updated source of information to support your development efforts. The Beginner's Guide to Access 2.0, also available from Wrox Press, is a good primer to the user interface and other aspects of the development environment and the forthcoming Beginner's Guide to Access Basic provides a solid grounding in using Access Basic in your applications. Beyond this, SmartAccess is a great monthly newsletter, which provides constantly evolving information on the latest news from Microsoft about the Access product line.

For technical education, consider attending Microsoft's TechEd conference. This conference is no sales and all technical information. You'll be able to attend lectures on a wide range of subjects related to not only Access but the whole Microsoft product line. For more information on this, contact Microsoft Inside Sales.

CompuServe provides an excellent resource for your development efforts. The Microsoft Knowledge Base, MSKB, allows you to search on any topic and retrieve white papers, sample code and so on, on almost any conceivable topic. The MSACCESS forum offers not only demonstration forums, but also peer assistance and is a useful place to find tools that can help in your development efforts.

Remember, the best way to learn, though, is to experiment. Some of the excitement comes because computers and software present such a rapidly changing environment. Constant newer and better versions, with even more changes on the horizon.

Have fun with Access and always push the limits!

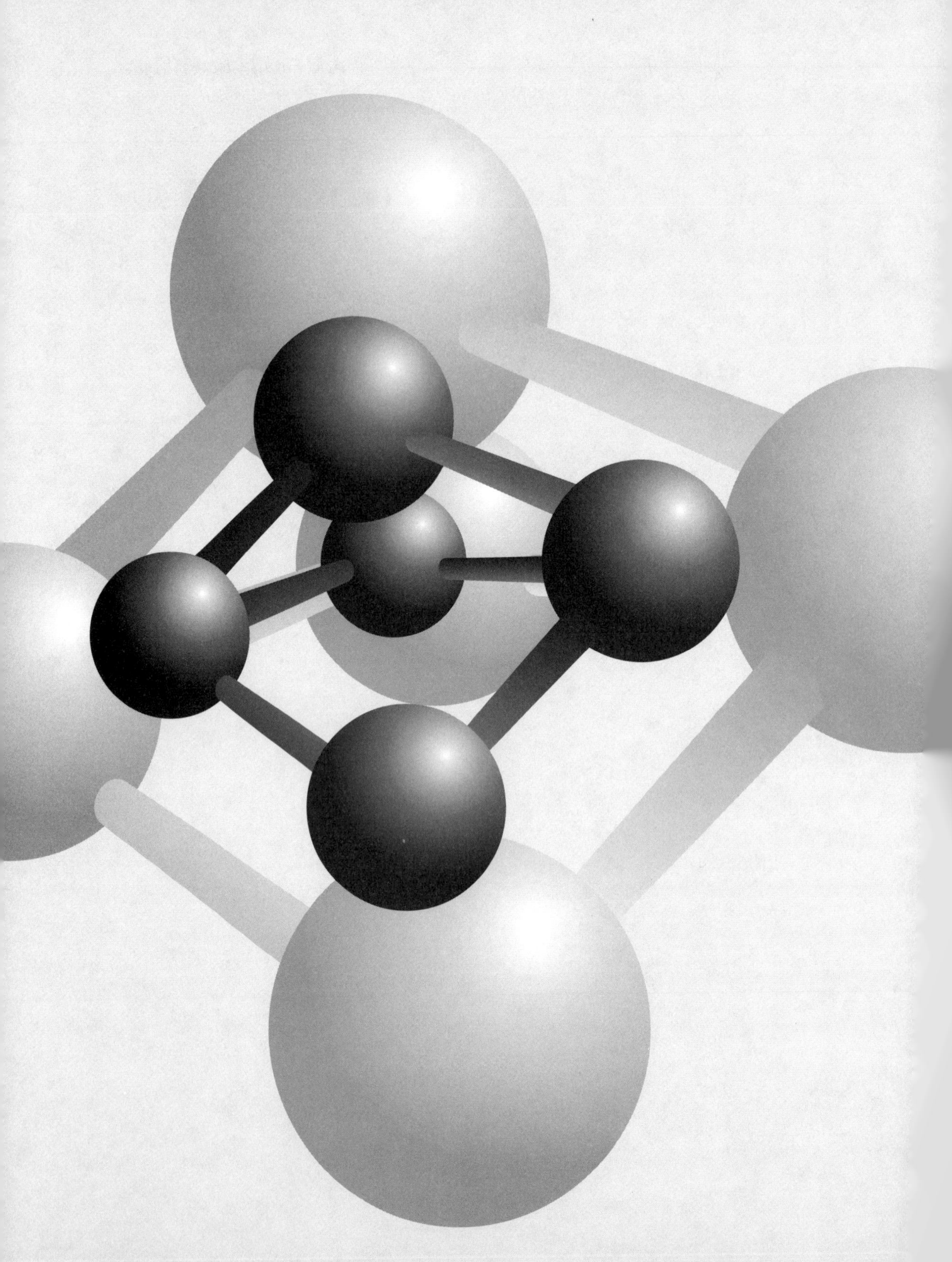

Appendix A

Using The Sample PIM

Introduction

In many different areas of this book, we talk about a Personal Information Manager or PIM. This PIM is provided as a way to demonstrate features that range from OLE integration to custom menus and mail functionality.

In this appendix, we will be covering the use of the PIM and explaining the relationships between the tables that support it. This information will be presented from a more user-oriented perspective than in the other, more technical portions of this book.

Overview

The PIM is largely centered around three tables. These tables are:

- Contacts
- Company
- Projects

Relationships between the tables allow for relational integrity. Each table has an ID for each entry made, and an ID of the related table to enable the lookup functionality that is used to relate the tables.

When you first start the PIM, you're presented with an opening copyright screen. This simply presents the startup information, and is responsible for removing the database window from the user's desktop.

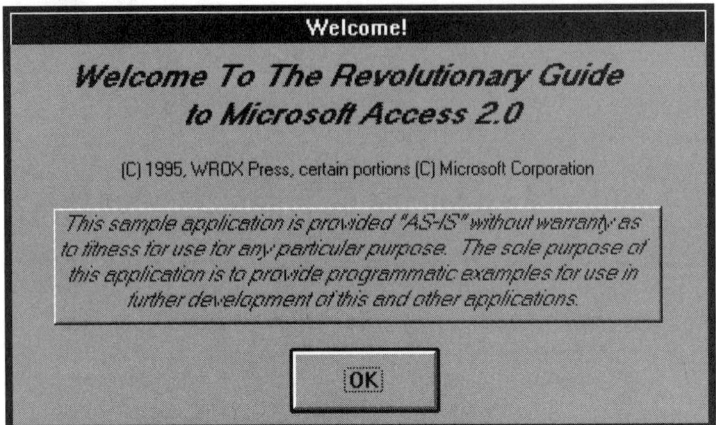

After you select OK, the opening dialog is removed and the search form is displayed. You can enter a company or individual's name to search for, or you can add a new contact from this form:

To load the CONTACTS.MDB database without starting the PIM application, you can press and hold down the Shift key while selecting the database to open. This will load the application without starting the AUTOEXEC macro.

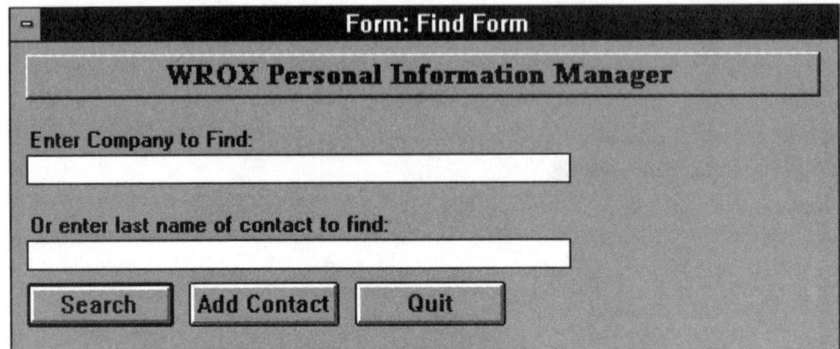

In the next sections, the layout of the tables and the use of the individual features of the system is covered. Note that specific details on how items and options are implemented are not covered in this appendix. Please refer to the technical section in the different portions of the book for more information.

Using the Menu System

Once the application has started, a new menu system is put into place. The menu bar offers three different options; File, Messaging and Help:

The File menu offers four different options. Each of these is described in the upcoming sections.

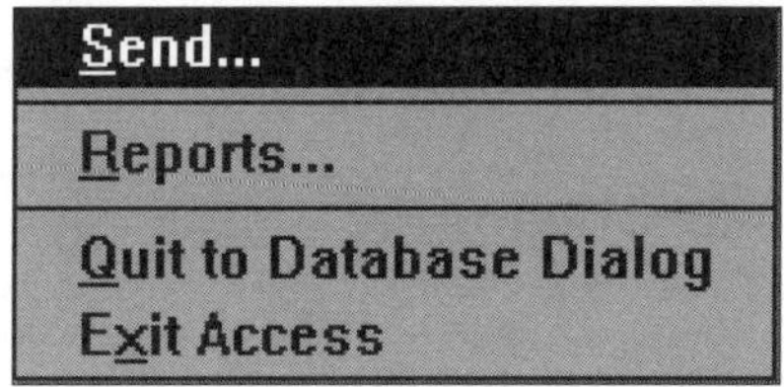

File, Send...

Using File, Send will allow you to send the output from the current form using the Mail subsystem. Access will take the various fields that are displayed at the time you request the option and will send the information to the destination that you request.

This option presents the most simple, straight-forward option for sending an object using electronic mail.

File, Reports...

Selecting the Reports... option presents a dialog box that allows you to choose a report that you want to run. The dialog box will automatically show any and all reports in the system, including reports that are added as the system is used:

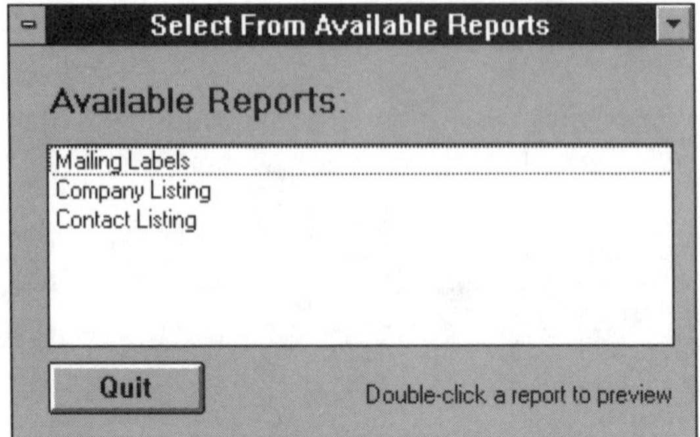

To run a report, double-click the report's entry on the list. If more entries exist than will fit on the screen, a scroll bar will appear, allowing you to move up and down the list to make your selection.

When you run a report, it will be run first in preview mode. To print the report, select the Printer icon on the button bar of the preview screen.

To add a report to the options shown, simply add it to the database. You can use all the standard tools to create the report. Once the report has been saved in the database, it will automatically be listed on the report selection screen.

To exit the screen without selecting a report, click the Quit button. You will be returned to the calling application, which in this case means wherever you were in the PIM when the Reports... option was selected.

File, Quit to Database Dialog

When your application offers the user a choice to exit, you must take into account whether the user will be exiting from the system, or only closing the current database. If the user is only closing the database, they may want to do other work.

In those cases where you simply want to exit to the database dialog box, you can select the Quit to Database Dialog option. This will allow you to stay in the **CONTACTS.MDB** database to create additional reports or do other modifications to the system.

File, Exit Access

If you're finished working in Access entirely, this option will close the current database and return you to the Windows Program Manager.

The Contacts Table

The Contacts table contains information on the specific individuals in the system. Contacts are the people that you deal with and are the hub of the system. Contacts relate to companies, and contacts relate to projects.

You can have multiple contacts per company and you can also have multiple projects per contact. However, you can't have multiple companies for a given contact, nor can you have multiple contacts responsible for a specific project.

Here's the layout of the Contacts table:

Field Name	Data Type	Description
ContactID	Counter	Unique contact ID
CompanyID	Number	Reference to the related company
Prefix	Text	Mr., Mrs., etc.
FirstName	Text	First name for the contact
LastName	Text	Last name for the contact
Suffix	Text	Dr., PHD, etc.
Address	Text	Address for the contact (street address)
City	Text	The contact's city
State	Text	The contact's state
ZipCode	Text	Zip code (postal code) for the contact
Country	Text	Country where the contact resides (for this address)
WorkPhone	Text	The work phone number
HomePhone	Text	Home phone number
FaxNumber	Text	Fax phone number
ReferredBy	Text	Who referred the contact
Note	OLE Object	Misc. notes about the contact. Implemented with Word as the editor (OLE2)

The Company Table

The Company table provides information on companies that have contacts in the system. You'll recall from the previous section on contacts that contacts are related to companies, and this is based on CompanyID.

Field Name	Data Type	Description
CompanyID	Counter	The unique ID for the company
CompanyName	Text	Name of the company
CompanyAddress1	Text	Address, line 1
CompanyAddress2	Text	Address, line 2
CompanyCity	Text	City where the company resides
CompanyState	Text	The state where the company is located
CompanyZip	Text	Zip code (postal code) for the address
CompanyCountry	Text	Country for this address
CompanyPhone	Text	Phone number for the company
CompanyFax	Text	Fax phone number for the company
CompanyNotes	OLE Object	A word object that allows the user to take notes on the company

Since the relationship to the projects table is indirect, there is no means of identifying projects within a company without first determining what contacts work for a given company. With that information, you can write a report that will detail all projects for a given company.

For more information, and an example of this, consider the Company, Contacts and Projects query:

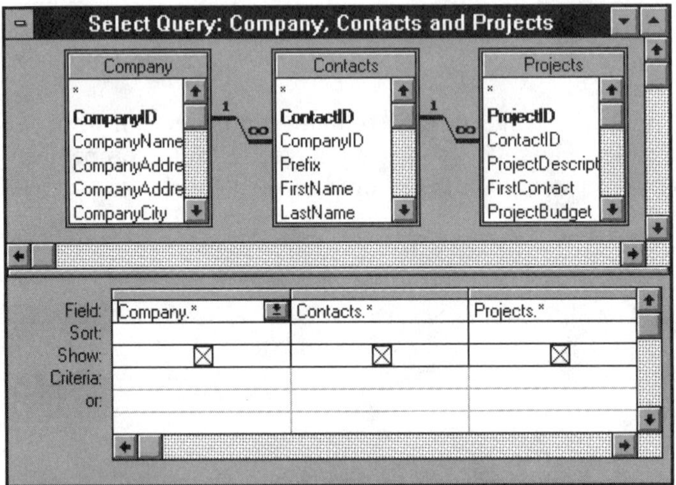

This query incorporates the different tables and relationships to produce a recordset that is a superset of all of the information in the various tables. Using this query, you can create reports or other materials that require a broad view of the system information.

The Projects Table

The Projects table contains the information on the projects that are proposed, underway or completed for a given company. The diagram shown next provides the background information on the table structure:

Field Name	Data Type	Description
ProjectID	Counter	Unique ID for the project
ContactID	Number	Reference into the contact database
ProjectDescription	Text	Description of the project
FirstContact	Date/Time	Date of first contact
ProjectBudget	Number	Total customer budget for project
ProjectHours	Number	Estimate of number of hours
ProjectNotes	Memo	Free-form text about the project
AccountManager	Text	Name of the account manager for the project
ProjectManager	Text	Name of the project manager for the project

The information provided will give you a good basic project overview, including financial information, and information about who is responsible for the project, both at account manager and customer contact level.

Relationships Between the Tables

We've established relationships between each of the tables as necessary to ensure information integrity in the system. The relationship starts with the Company table and includes the Contacts table and the Projects table:

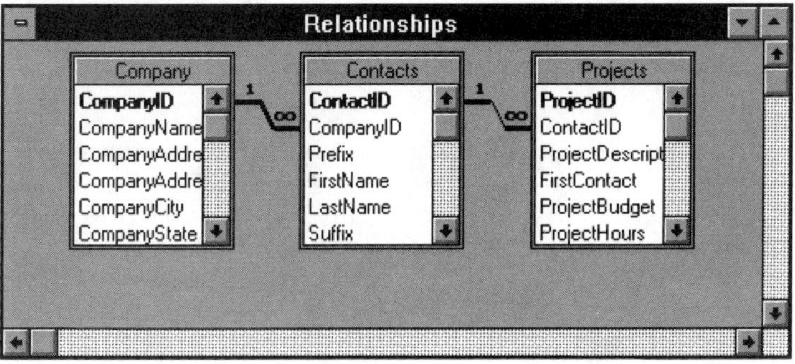

We're enforcing cascading deletes from a given point in the chain to the remaining portions of the relationship. Put more simply, if you delete a company record, all associated contacts are deleted, as are all related projects. If you delete a contact record, associated project records are removed.

For more information on how each relationship is set up, please refer to the chapters on data integrity, referential integrity and cascading database actions.

The Contact Details Form

Once you've found a contact that you want to work with, you'll be presented with the Contact Details form. This form allows you to select a related company and enter information about the individual contact and other related materials:

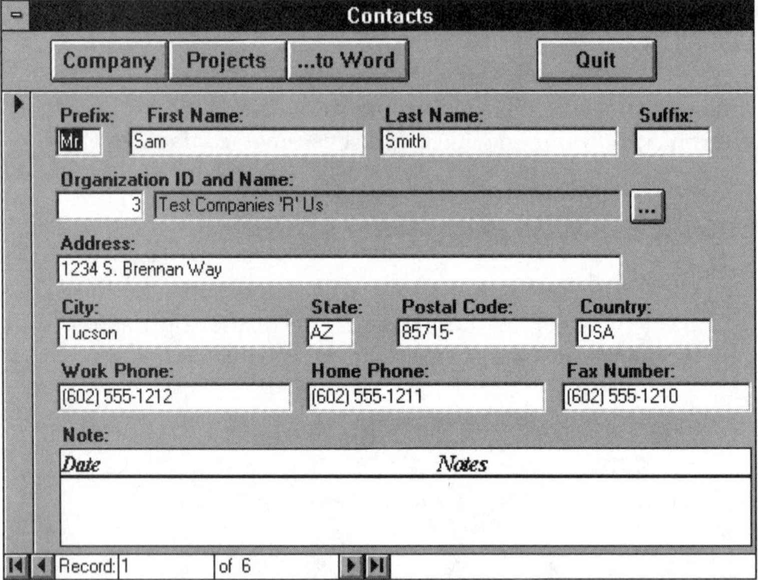

The different features of the form are described next.

The Company Button

The Company button allows you to call up the Company Details form. This form will contain all the specific information about the company associated with this contact record. Note that when you use the Company button, you'll only be working with the company associated with this record; you will not be able to browse the entire Company table. This is done to make it easier to determine the company relationships to other information in the system. It also helps to prevent any confusion about which company is being worked with and what contact it relates to.

The Projects Button

When the Projects button is selected, the project form(s) that relate to this contact will be shown. When the projects are displayed, they will be limited to those projects that relate to this contact only. If no projects are on file, you'll be able to add one if needed.

The ...To Word Button

If you want to send the information from the current contact to Word, you can use the ...To Word button. When the button is selected, Word is activated and the contact information is sent to Word to be included in a form letter, report or other system in which Word's textual formatting is useful.

> **If you do not have Word loaded, Access will attempt to load it on demand to complete the request. If Word is not on your path, it will not be able to load automatically. Be sure to add the Word subdirectory to your path to enable Access to send information automatically to it.**

The following information and format is sent to Word for your use.

```
02-14-1995



Mr.  Sam  Smith
1234  S.  Brennan  Way
Tucson,  AZ  85715  USA

Dear  Sam,
```

You can change this information and its formatting by modifying the underlying Access Basic program. Please review the DDE chapter for more information.

The Quit Button

Selecting the Quit button will exit the form to either the Search form or the Contact Details form, depending upon how you arrived at this form.

The Company Details Form

When you are setting up a company to be referred to by contacts, you'll be using the Company Details form. The form allows you to enter full company name and address information:

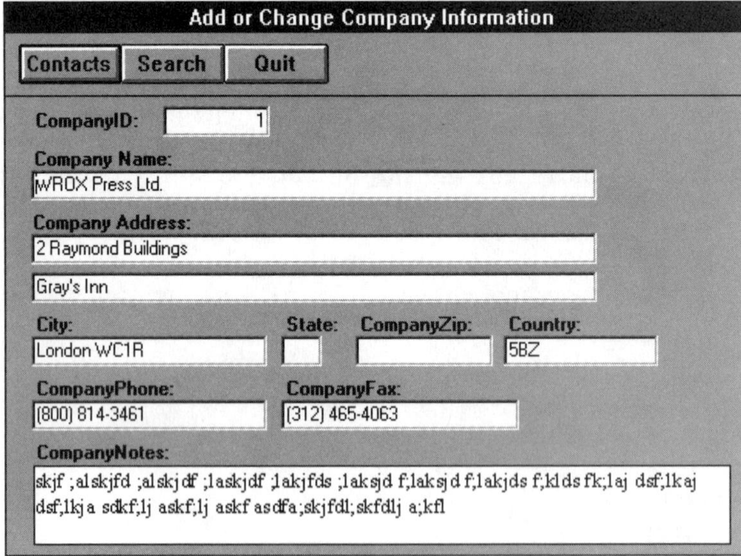

Note that the Company Details form does not have any provision for assigning a contact to the account. You must establish the link between the company record and the contact record from the contact record.

The Contacts Button

If you select the Contacts button, the Contact Details form will be displayed. It will show only those accounts for the company you were working with when you pressed the Contacts button.

You can use the navigation keys in the Contact Details form to move between records in those cases where there are multiple contacts per company.

The Search Button

Pressing the Search button returns you to the opening search screen. From here, you can start a new search or exit from the system.

The Quit Button

The Quit button will unload the Company Details form, returning you to the form or routine that initially called the form. Usually, you'll be returning to one of two places; the Search form or the Contact Details form.

The Project Details Form

The Project Details forms is how you manage the different projects that are assigned to contacts. Like the Company form, it allows you to work with those projects that relate to the current contact only. You can't generally browse through all project records with the form if it's loaded from within the application:

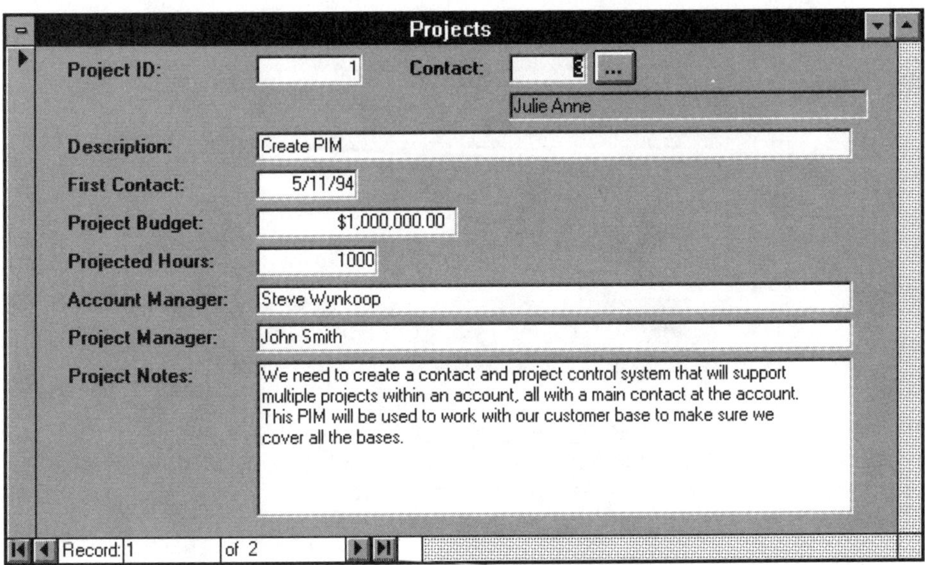

The form allows you to make the changes to the Projects table, using Access' default settings to save the information as you move between entries. Notice the ellipses button, '...' on the form. This button will call up a selection dialog box allowing you to choose a contact name from the table of contacts.

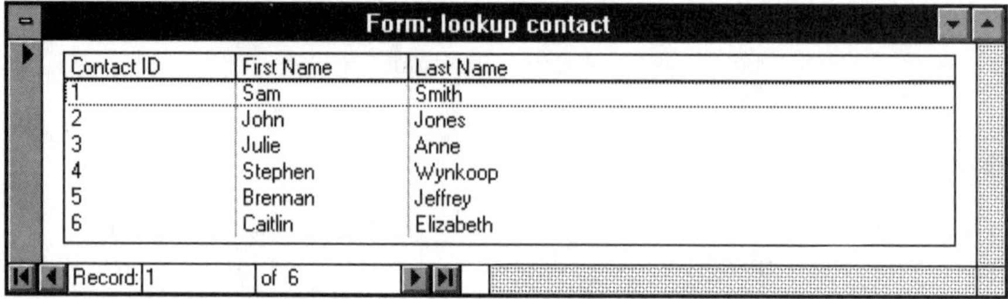

You can scroll around the list and find the name you want to assign to the project record. Once you've found it, double-click on the line. The Contact ID will be updated in the Project Details form for you automatically.

Reports Included in the System

There are three reports in the system as it is originally provided with this book. The reports that are available from the Reports... menu option include:

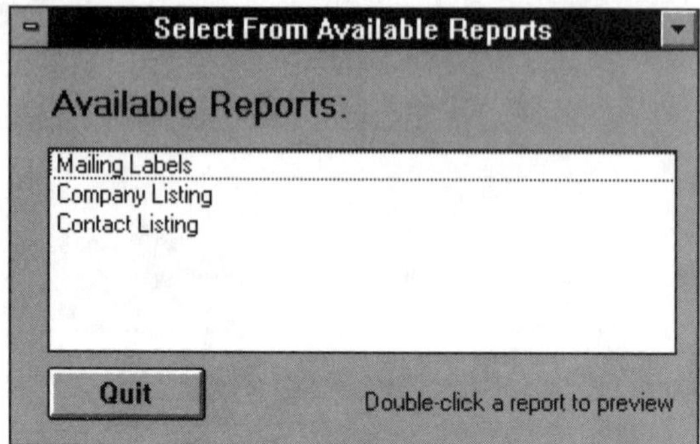

While basic in nature, these reports show how you can set up additional reports and begin using them right away. As mentioned before, any reports you add to the system will also be shown in the report selector, accessed from the menu.

Mailing Labels

The Mailing Labels created by the system will be 3-across labels showing the address information for each record in the database:

Ms. Caitlin Elizabeth Marvelous Literay Productions, Inc. 9735 E. Sunrise Sunset Drive Tucson, AZ 85718-	Mr. Brennan Jeffrey Marvelous Literay Productions, Inc. 9735 E. Sunrise Sunset Drive Tucson, AZ 85718-	Ms. Juli Marvelo 9735 E Tucson
Mr. John Jones Marvelous Literay Productions, Inc. 9735 E. Sunrise Sunset Drive Tucson, AZ 85718-	Mr. Stephen Wynkoop Test Companies 'R' Us 12331 N. Test Center Drive No. Phoenix, AZ 85574-	Mr. San Test Co 12331 N No. Ph

You can adjust the settings in the report if you are using different label stock or would like to modify the information that is shown on the labels.

Company Listing

The Company Listing report provides one line of output for each company in the database. The entire company record is printed, except for the notes field:

Company Listing

15-Feb-95

ID	Name	Addressl	Address2	City	State	Zip	Country	Phone	Fax
4	Anom Guild	221115 N. Blah Bl		S. Yammervi	FL	12311-			
2	Marvelous Literay	9735 E. Sunrise Su		Tucson	AZ	85718-	USA	(602) 798-6268	
13	Test	test	test	test	TS				
14	Test Companies 'R'	12331 N. Test Cen		No. Phoenix	AZ	85574-	USA		
3	Test Companies 'R'	12331 N. Test Cen		No. Phoenix	AZ	85574-	USA		
1	WROX Press Ltd.	2 Raymond Buildi	Gray's Inn	London WC1			5BZ	(800) 814-3461	(312)

Contact Listing

The Contact Listing report provides one line on the report for each contact in the system. The report is similar to the Company Listing in that it shows all detail about a given account except for the notes field:

Contact Listing

15-Feb-95

Prefix	First Nam	Last Name	Suffix	Address	City	State	Zip	Country	Work	Home	Fa
Ms.	Julie	Anne	Ph.D.		Tucson	AZ	85718-				
Ms.	Caitlin	Elizabeth									
Mr.	Brennan	Jeffrey									
Mr.	John	Jones									
Mr.	Sam	Smith		1234 S. Br	Tucson	AZ	85715-	USA	(602) 555-	(602) 555-	(60
Mr.	Stephen	Wynkoop		2035 N. Ro	Tucson	AZ	85748-				

About the Mail Enabled Options

The specifics of using the mail options are covered in depth in the chapter on mail-enabling your application. There are, however, several things that you'll need to consider before you decide to use the features.

There is a bug in MSMail 3.x that occurs if you are low on memory. If you find that you are getting error messages when you try to load the client software, check to see how many other applications you may have running. If you have several, you should try loading the client software with only Access running.

However, you will have to exit Windows and return if you receive these error messages. Otherwise, when you try to re-load the client software, the mail software may hang just after presenting the menu bar.

Microsoft Mail 3.x Required

First and foremost, you'll need to have Microsoft Mail installed and running on your system. With the upcoming release of the Microsoft Exchange mail server, it's still too early to predict how complete the compatibility of these options will be with the new platform. When you begin moving to the Exchange environment, be sure to re-test your application thoroughly.

The examples may produce unexpected results if you decide to use the VIM mapping DLL. Inconsistencies between mail systems may prevent you from using this compatibility layer for your application development work. The VIM mapping layer is meant more for standard Email type implementations, not directed calls to MAPI that exploit some of the features that we've covered here.

About The Microsoft Mail 3.x Remote Client

If you are using the Microsoft Mail 3.x Remote Client, you may find that it dials immediately upon submitting a data packet to the system. This is a known short-coming of the current mail product. You may want to batch your exports and send them as one transmission. This may be the case if you need to optimize your transmissions for long distance charges. In this case, you'll want to create your own batches of information.

Save your information into a table during processing. Once you've completed the work for the day, you can export one or more tables and attach them all to the same message. When the message is submitted, all tables will be sent at once.

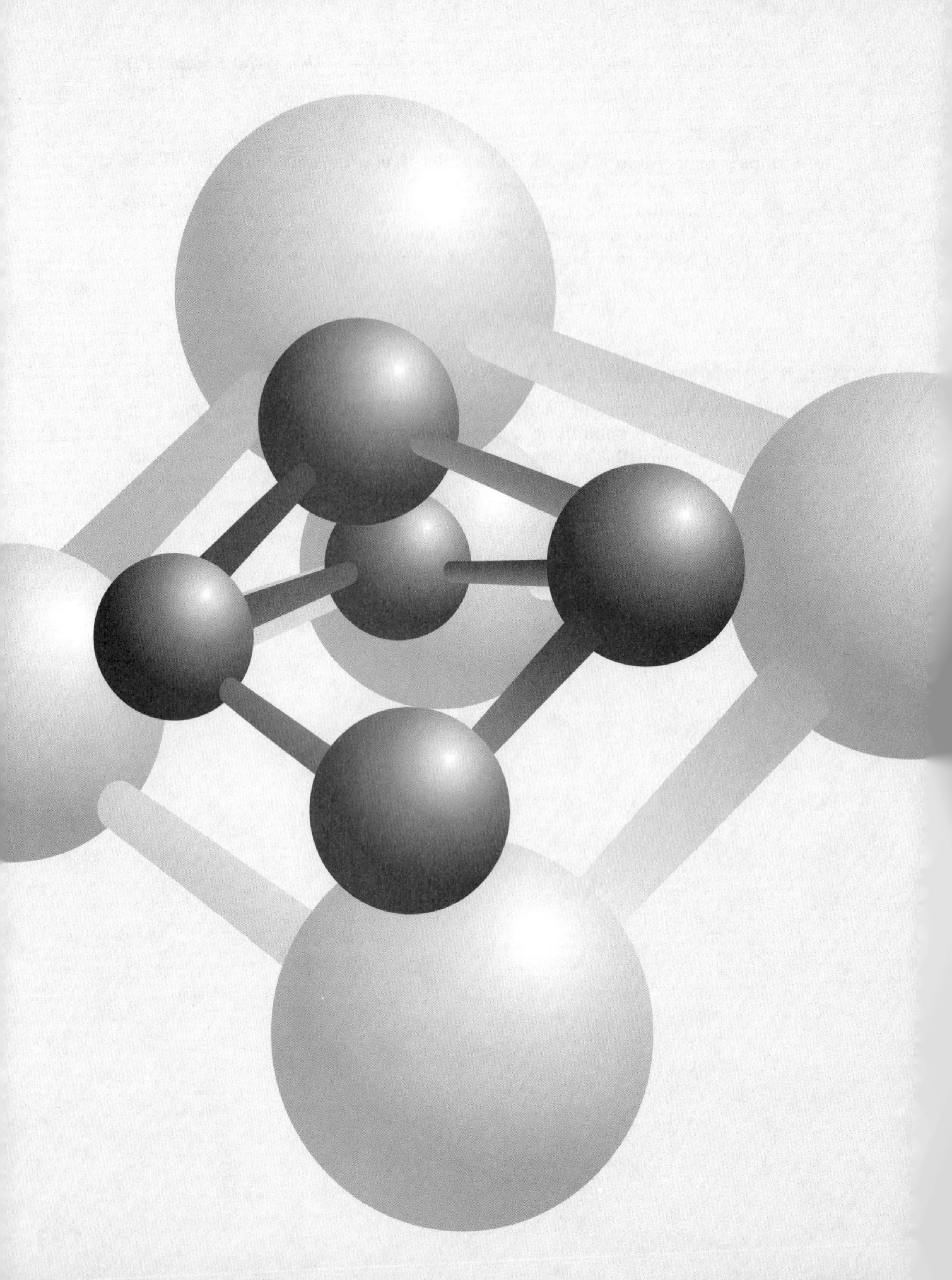

Dynamic Data Exchange Access Topics

If you need more detail or an example use of any DDE or NetDDE related function, consult the Access help files, under 'Using Microsoft Access as a DDE server', 'DDE' or information exchange

The System Topic

SysItems — Returns the items that are available at the System level. Will return available topics like **SQL**, **TABLE** and **QUERY**.

Formats — Lists the available file formats supported by the installation of Access.

Status — Returns the status of the server application; can be either Busy or Ready.

Topics — Lists the topics available, includes currently open databases, system tables and so on.

Appendix B

The TableName and QueryName Topics

All Returns all information associated with the query or SQL command. The 'All' topic also returns column names.

Data Returns all information, less column names, associated with the query or SQL command.

FieldNames Gets a listing of the field names for the current item. Tab delimited.

FieldNames;T Returns the same information as FieldNames without the ';T', with one exception. Where FieldNames returns a single row of column names, adding the ';T' to the query makes Access pass back a second row corresponding to the Type of each column. The types are enumerated and are outlined in the on-line help file for Access. Search under 'DDE Server' for more information.

SQLText, SQLText;n Returns or sets the text associated with the SQL query. Specifying ';n' and replacing 'n' with a value forces Access to return the SQL statement in 'n' sized chunks. This is useful in presenting the string for a user; you can use this option to prevent the SQL statement from wrapping unexpectedly in a list box.

FieldCount Returns the number of fields in the table or database query.

Navigational Topics

NextRow, PrevRow, FirstRow, LastRow Selects data from a particular row. NextRow, on a new connection, returns the first row in the result set. When using NextRow and PrevRow, if there are no more records (end of file, beginning of file), the calls will fail.

Converting Access 1.1 to 2.0

If you're currently using Access 1.x, or if you have systems that use the Access 1.x format, you'll need to consider converting those databases to the newer Access 2.0 format and capabilities. After the conversion process, you'll encounter many benefits and a few things that have changed, creating a pit-fall or two.

In this appendix, we'll provide more information about the conversion process, how you go about completing the conversion, and any considerations that you should be aware of before you move to the new format and capabilities of Access 2.0.

Introduction

You may have noticed that Access 2.0 will allow you to open Access 1.x files, but certain restrictions have been placed on those connections to the older formatted files. If you use Access 1.x files with version 2.0, you'll first be presented with a warning that you can't modify certain properties of a 1.x database:

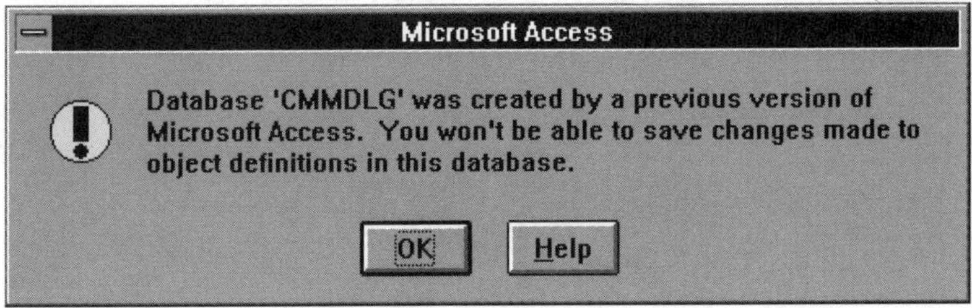

If you click on the OK button, you'll still be able to use the database, but you will be restricted from altering any of the object definitions and from creating new objects, at least until the database, and each of the objects contained in it, is converted to the new version 2.0 format.

If you assume that all will go perfectly the first time you run through the conversion, you're probably going to be a bit disappointed. With the large number of changes to the Access world that occurred with the release of version 2.0, you need to plan and test your migration carefully, making sure that all components transfer as you expect:

- Be sure to backup your existing database, prior to making any changes in format, functionality and so on.
- Using a copy of the production system, run the conversion. Test the results by checking the import and/or conversion error tables. Make sure that objects are converted as you expect and that the functionality of the system is maintained after the update.
- Test the new system, preferably running in parallel with the original system. This will make sure that no changes have been overlooked.

If you keep these items in mind, and run through the sections outlined next, you should find the upgrade process a bit easier. If all else fails, divide the system up for the process. Move the procedures and reports first, attach the existing 1.1 database tables, then run your system. Convert the tables as the last phase of the upgrade. This will help narrow down any problems that you may encounter.

Menu Changes: DoMenuItem

In Access 2.0, menus have changed. In order to accommodate users of the 1.x systems, the **DoMenuItem** now has an added argument. The argument, when set to **A_MENU_VER20**, indicates to Access that the 2.0 menu structures should be used. The syntax for the **DoMenuItem** is now:

```
DoCmd DoMenuItem menubar, menuname, command [,subcommand]
[,version]
```

The default entry for the version parameter is **A_MENU_V1X**, and when these commands are converted, Access will still be using the version 1.x menu system. You must physically open the macro and add in the version parameter, **A_MENU_VER20** to update these commands.

By default, Access uses the database version to determine the default menu system to use and therefore, if you create a new **DoMenuItem** command without specifying a version, Access will assume the parameter. However, you are advised to implicitly demand a version, as implied parameter values can cause problems when porting the application over different machines.

Menu Changes: SendKeys

In general, you'll want to begin phasing out the use of **SendKeys** in applications. **SendKeys** were implemented as a way of completing operations on the system where it was not possible to programmatically manipulate them. Since, as of Access 2.0, you can work with objects, methods and properties at a much lower level with Access Basic, the requirement for **SendKeys** has been greatly diminished. If you are continuing to use **SendKeys**, or if you'll be leaving it in place until after the conversion, there are a few items that you should be aware of that may impact your ability to use those options without modification.

If you use **SendKeys** to run menu options and respond to dialog boxes, you'll have to test your commands for compatibility with the new version of Access. When you are ready to convert your system, carefully consider the new options available to you with the **Data Access Object Model** and other new features of Access. You will probably find that most, if not all, of your **SendKeys** requirements have been addressed with specific commands, statements, methods or definable options.

Security

For example, if you are using the security options that Access has to offer, review the chapter on managing security with Access Basic. Using these new techniques, you'll be able to take better advantage of the upgraded security sub-system as well as the new options that are now available.

Environmental Settings

Consider using the **`GetOption`** and **`SetOption`** methods to set environment settings. These methods allow you to manipulate the Access environment and control many different things. Many different classifications of objects can be set using these methods. These include:

- General
- Keyboard
- Printing
- Form & Report Design
- Datasheet
- Query Design
- Macro Design
- Module Design
- Multiuser/ODBC

For more information on each of these areas of options, review Access' on-line help and search for 'options: setting'. Each of the options is explained in detail, including defaults and available settings.

Before You 'Convert Database...'

Before you begin the conversion process, there are several things that must be considered. Of utmost importance is the task of backing up your database file at regular intervals. This will give you a fall-back position should you have any unexpected problems during or after the conversion process.

Multi-User Systems

If you are going to be converting a multi-user system, you'll need to make sure you've exclusive access to the system from the time you begin the process to the time you have completed the update and any associated changes that are required to the system. For this reason, it's highly recommended that you run a 'dry-run' of the conversion process one or more times, against a test database, to make sure that all components convert as you'd expect.

Unfortunately, getting sole use of a production system may require that the conversion process be carried out in the off-hours of operation. You'll also want to allow plenty of time to test the system once it's been converted.

Permission Changes

Permissions can't be set on an Access 1.1 database. The permissions model has been re-written and requires the re-initialization of the system database in order to create appropriate permissions for objects.

The System Database

The system database, **SYSTEM.MDA**, has been modified to support the new security features of Access. While Access can use an older version of the **SYSTEM.MDA** file, you'll want to convert the system file as well if you're going to be using the security features.

To create the new 2.0 version of the file, you'll need to re-create all users, groups and permission assignments in the 2.0 version of the database. It's a good idea to then use the database documentor to print a report of the database, its associated security assignments and so on, all prior to upgrading the system to the new 2.0 format.

Visual Basic

If you are sharing databases between Access and other development environments, be sure that you work with the developers of the other systems during the upgrade. With Visual Basic 3.x, you'll need to upgrade the Jet database engine. As of this writing, an update to the Jet engine is imminent and a Compatibility Layer is currently available. The Compatibility Layer provides a layer of translation between the version 1.x calls and the 2.x implementation. In most cases, this will serve your needs nicely.

In any case, if you're updating a shared database, be sure that all software has been examined and tested against the new format of the Access 2.0 database. You will probably want to leave the Visual Basic-shared application databases as the last items to be converted.

Note that this presents a good opportunity for making changes to your Access environment. Typically, a Visual Basic application will not use too many queries in its data retrieval. If this is the case, this is a great time to break the code, reports, macros and so on, away from the underlying database tables.

You should remember that this helps to optimize the Access environment, and can really be of benefit later when you need to update the code surrounding the information. Once you break apart the database and code, you'll be able to attach the 1.x tables to the 2.x code. This will leave the information formatted for Visual Basic, but still allow you to begin reaping the benefits of the new environment.

Repair and Compact the Database

The final step in the conversion process is to repair and compact the database. These steps will sweep through the database and update any erroneous information, notifying you of any problems found.

Repairing the Database

When you repair a database, Access works through each of the indexes and makes sure they are valid and working with the correct information. You can also use the command to attempt to fix a corrupt database.

Repairing the database will ensure that all pointers and data appear to be correctly saved in the tables that make up the database. Running the Repair option is much like running **CHKDSK** or **SCANDISK** prior to backing up the system. You simply want to make sure all is in order.

Benefits and Changes with Access 2.0

There are some great features that become available to you in the new Access 2.0 environment. It may be that no one single item will present the requirement for conversion; when you take into account the enhancements overall, you'll probably find that for maintainability, updated functionality and usability, Access 2.0 is a good upgrade to move to.

Speed in the new version has improved dramatically in many cases. New Rushmore Technology is used to accomplish searches, often significantly reducing search/seek time. For more information, including information on how the new Rushmore capabilities can be optimized, search on-line help for 'Rushmore'.

Many other items have changed in this latest release of Access. These include the items shown in the next sections.

Customizable Toolbars

In Access 1.x, you could create toolbars that were maintained in the Utility add-in database. In Access 2.x, this is not supported. As noted in the User Interface chapter, you can now modify any toolbar in the system, as well as creating your own. In addition, with full access to custom menus, you'll probably find that custom toolbars of the type implemented in version 1.x are no longer required.

You can assign macros and functions to toolbar buttons, and you can then determine when the toolbar is shown and what functions it will perform. To modify toolbars, select Toolbars... from the View menu:

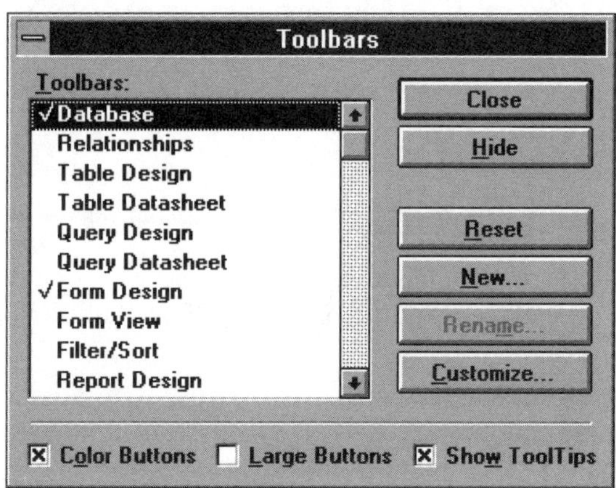

You'll then be able to modify the appearance, location and attributes of the toolbar as needed.

Spotting a New Record

A common practice in Access 1.x was to inspect the return from **`IsNull`** to determine whether a new record is being inserted.

With the newer event procedures in version 2.x, you'll be able to use the **`BeforeInsert`** and **`AfterInsert`** events. These events allow you to inspect the information in the record being added. This can happen either prior to it being added to the table, or immediately after it's added and before another operation is completed.

Empty vs Zero Length vs Null Strings

Empty strings are now distinguished from Null string values. In version 1.x, if a string were empty, it would also be considered to be Null. The new property, **`AllowZeroLength`**, will prevent an empty string from being saved, but will pass a null string.

If you have an Access 1.x database and have converted it, you'll notice that Access adds a new property. This property is called **`V1xNullBehavior`** which determines whether strings should be treated as they were in version 1.x, or whether they should be treated as Access 2.x strings. If this property is set to 'true', which is the default, Access will convert zero-length strings to Null.

The property is accessed via the **Database Object's Properties Collection**, using the following syntax:

```
MyDB.Properties.V1xNullBehavior
```

You can both set and retrieve the value of the property. Once you've converted a database, you may want to reset the value to 'false' to turn on the version 2.x behavior with Nulls.

Hiding Columns in Views

If you need to hide a column from a datasheet view, you'll now have to update the ColumnHidden property of the control. Previously, if you set the visible property, the control wouldn't be shown on both the form and the datasheet view.

An example of this might be a case where you define a sub-form that is to be used as a datasheet view to a parent form. If you want a field to be on the sub-form, but not visible to the user, update the new property. Note that if the sub-form is shown in a mode other than datasheet, the field will not be visible.

Improved Validation Rules

When you convert a database to the new 2.x format, validation rules are also converted. In most cases, the rules will transfer without a problem. Exceptions to this include the following cases:

- Domain functions
- User-defined functions
- References to other Access objects like forms, tables and queries
- Aggregate functions
- Field-level validation can't refer to other fields
- Record validation will allow references to fields within the record

While these may seem somewhat restrictive, the new rules were developed for good reasons. Validation is now enforced at the database engine level. This means that if the database is being updated by any function, be it a form, query, user input or whatever, the validation will now be performed on the information.

> *You should note that if you have validation rules incorporated in your forms, these rules will still function and will be applied. Forms-level validation occurs in conjunction with the validation performed at the table and field level.*

Conversion Problem Documentation

If Access encounters a problem during the conversion process, a new table is created in the destination system. The table will be named ConvertErrors and will contain information about the problems that were encountered. The format of the table is as follows:

Field	Description
Error	Description of error encountered
Field	What field in the table caused the error
Property	What property caused the error
Table	The name of the offending table
Unconvertible Value	What property value caused the error to occur

After converting your system, you should always look for this table to make sure the existing validation rules were successfully incorporated into the new system. If a rule does cause a problem and is placed into this table, the entire rule was abandoned during the conversion process. You'll need to enter the rule manually against the new table or correct the source table and re-convert the database.

New Access Basic Reserved Words

With the release of version 2.0, several new additions were made to the Access Basic reserved word list. These are outlined below:

CompactDatabase	Container	CreateDatabase
CreateField	CreateGroup	CreateIndex
CreateObject	CreateProperty	CreateRelation
CreateTableDef	CreateUser	CreateWorkspace
CurrentUser	Document	Echo
Field	Fields	FillCache
GetObject	GetOption	GotoPage
Group	Idle	Index
Indexes	InsertText	Move
NewPassword	Object	OpenRecordset
Parameter	Property	Quit
Recalc	Recordset	Refresh
RefreshLink	RegisterDatabase	Relation
Repaint	RepairDatabase	Requery
SetFocus	SetOption	TableDef
TableDefs	Workspace	

If your 1.x programs used these key words in procedures, you'll need to make sure you change them to differ from the new reserved words list.

New Property Names

In addition to the new reserved Access Basic words, there are several new property names introduced with version 2.x. If you're referring to variables with these names in your code or other areas of your system, you'll need to either change the reference to a different variable name, or place square brackets around the name, distinguishing them from the reserved words:

Version 1.x	Version 2.0
ControlName	Name
FormName	Name
OnInsert	BeforeInsert
OnMenu	MenuBar
OnPush	OnClick
Scaling	SizeMode
UpdateMethod	UpdateOptions

For example, if you're referring to the Name field in a table, you'll need to specify `MyTable.[Name]` instead of the previous method of simply specifying `MyTable.Name`.

New Reserved Words in SQL

With the enhancement of the SQL subsystem came the addition of several keywords that relate to the SQL language. You'll need to review your code to make sure you have not used these in a manner that will conflict. Again, if you have, you can either update the code, or place square brackets around the keyword:

All	Any	Counter
Database	Date	Double
Exists	Foreign	Full
Ignore	Index	Integer
Key	Match	OLEObject
Outer	Partial	Percent
Single	SmallInt	Some
TimeStamp	Top	Values
Varbinary	VarChar	YesNo

Object Names Containing a Backquote

You can no longer have objects that have a backquote (`) character in their name. This change is fairly dramatic because you won't be able to open, import or convert the object using version 2.x. You'll need to first change the name of the object and any references to it from within queries, Access Basic code and so on, before being able to convert, import or open the object with version 2.x.

System Tables - Access Using DAO

In version 1.x of Access, you could gain access to the system tables using standard functions. You'll now need to use the Data Access Objects layer to work with these objects. Direct manipulation is no longer supported.

If you have code that relies on direct interaction with these objects, you'll need to update it to take advantage of the DAO.

How to Convert Your System

Before you begin the process of converting a version 1.x database to the new 2.x format, make sure that you have read and understood the other sections in this appendix. This will prepare you for any problems that the basic conversion that is offered by Access may throw up.

Remember that it is essential for you to make regular backups of your database throughout the conversion process. This will allow you to recover any normally unrecoverable situations, simply by reverting back to the last backup.

You begin the conversion process by using the Convert Database... option from the File menu. This option is only available when the application doesn't have a database loaded. When you select this option, the following dialog box will appear on screen:

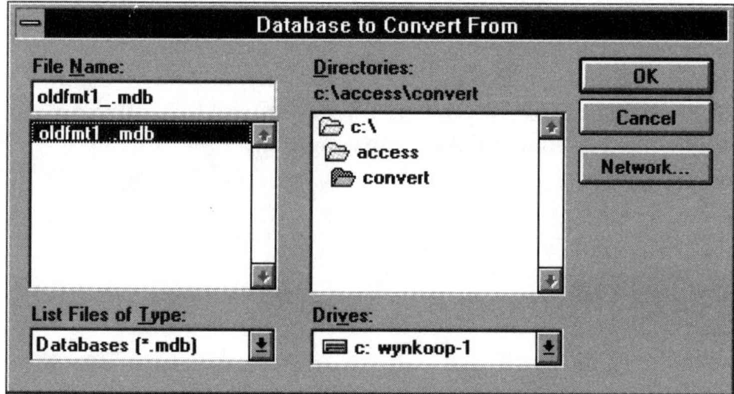

Select the database to convert and select OK. Access will then prompt you for the destination file and directory. You must specify a database that is different from the source for the operation to continue. Access will then convert your 1.x database to the 2.x format, by following a very simplistic set of rules, placing the new database in the directory you specified, with the appropriate name.

During the conversion process, Access will also compact the database.

As a final step in the conversion, you should go into the database and open and save all tables. You don't need to add information to the tables. Simply going into the table will cause Access to optimize the table, enabling better access times when the tables are interrogated in the future. This is also true for all the queries in the database. Run all queries except the delete/archive-type queries. This will ensure that all aspects of the system have been optimized as much as possible by Access.

Comments and Suggestions

While the conversion process is well-implemented when moving to version 2.x of Access, you'll need to carefully consider the different things we've mentioned here as part of the conversion process. For additional information, check the Access User's Guide and the **ACREADME.HLP** file that is located in your Access directory.

Access 2.0 is a highly optimized, full-function database system, as you've come to learn from your experiences in the development cycle. There are many reasons to complete the conversion process, many of which enhance your control over the application development, implementation and support process. You'll find that the benefits quickly out-weigh the costs in moving down the conversion path.

APPENDIX D

The Table Wizard

The Tables On Offer

This section shows the different table designs that are shipped with Access. You can add new tables and their related fields, making them available to the wizard for future table definitions. Below is a listing of all the tables that you can ask the Table Wizard to create:

Accounts
Artists
Authors
Book Collection
Category
Classes
Contacts
Customers
Deliveries
Diet Log
Employees
EmployeesAndTasks
Events
Exercise Log
Expenses
Fixed Assets
Friends
Guests
Household Inventory
Investments
Invoice Details
Invoices
Mailing List
Music Collection
Order Details
Orders
Payments
Photographs
Plants
Products
Projects
Recipes
Reservations
Rolls of Film
Service Records
Students
StudentsAndClasses
Suppliers
Tasks
Time Billed
Transactions
Video Collection
Wine List

Appendix D

The Fields On Offer

The following fields are available from within the Table Wizard. You can select any of these, in any combination, as you use the wizard to create your tables. As noted in the chapter, you can also add fields and their associated types and masks if you need additional types of fields.

In the cases where `Caption` is blank, the `FieldName` is used in the table. The table below lists the various fields available. The next section details how each `FieldTypeName` is implemented and what its associated input mask is:

FieldName	Caption	FieldTypeName
AccountID	Account ID	ID Field
AccountName	Account Name	Indexed Text 50
AccountNumber	Account Number	Text 50
AccountType	Account Type	Text 50
Action		Text 255
ActionItems	Action Items	Memo
Activity		Text 50
ActorID	Actor ID	ID Field
ActressID	Actress ID	ID Field
ActualCost	Actual Cost	Currency
Address		Text 255
AdvanceAmount	Advance Amount	Currency
AerobicOrAnaerobic	Aerobic Or Anaerobic	Text 20
AlternativePhone	Alternative Phone	Phone Number
AmountPaid	Amount Paid	Currency
AmountSpent	Amount Spent	Currency
Aperture		Text 50
AppraisedValue	Appraised Value	Currency

Continued

FieldName	Caption	FieldTypeName
ArrivalDateTime	Arrival DateTime	General Date
ArtistID	Artist ID	ID Field
AssetName	Asset Name	Indexed Text 50
AuthorID	Author ID	ID Field
AuthorizedBy	Authorized By	Text 50
AvailableSpaces	Available Spaces	Short Integer
BeginningValue	Beginning Value	Currency
BillableHours	Billable Hours	Single Float
BillingDate	Billing Date	Short Date
Birthdate		Short Date
Birthplace		Text 255
BookCollectionID	Book Collection ID	ID Field
BuyorSellDate	Buy or Sell Date	Short Date
BuyorSellPrice	Buy or Sell Price	Currency
CaloriesBurned	Calories Burned	Short Integer
CaloriesPerServing	Calories Per Serving	Short Integer
Camera		Text 50
CategoryID	Category ID	ID Field
CategoryName	Category Name	Indexed Text 50
CheckedIn	Checked In	Yes/No
CheckinDateTime	Checkin DateTime	General Date
CheckNumber	Check Number	Short Integer
CheckoutDateTime	Checkout DateTime	General Date

Continued

FieldName	Caption	FieldTypeName
ChildrenNames	Children Names	Text 255
City		Text 50
ClassID	Class ID	ID Field
ClassName	Class Name	Indexed Text 50
Clear		Yes/No
Color		Text 30
ColorFilm	Color Film	Yes/No
Comments		Memo
CommonName	Common Name	Indexed Text 50
CompuServeID	CompuServe ID	Text 50
Confirmed		Yes/No
ContactID	Contact ID	ID Field
ContactName	Contact Name	Indexed Text 50
ContactTitle	Contact Title	Text 50
ContactType	Contact Type	Text 50
CopyrightDate	Copyright Date	Short Date
CostPerPerson	Cost Per Person	Currency
Country		Text 50
CountryofOrigin	Country of Origin	Text 50
CoverType	Cover Type	Text 30
CreditCardExpDate	Credit Card Exp Date	Short Date
CreditCardName	Credit Card Name	Text 50
CreditCardNumber	Credit Card Number	Text 30
CreditCardType	Credit Card Type	Text 30
CurrentLocation	Current Location	Text 255

Continued

FieldName	Caption	FieldTypeName
CurrentValue	Current Value	Currency
CustomerID	Customer ID	ID Field
DateAcquired	Date Acquired	Short Date
DateDelivered	Date Delivered	Short Date
DateDeveloped	Date Developed	Short Date
DateFertilized	Date Fertilized	Short Date
DateHired	Date Hired	Short Date
DateJoined	Date Joined	Short Date
DateLastTalkedTo	Date Last Talked To	Short Date
DateofDeath	Date of Death	Short Date
DatePlanted	Date Planted	Short Date
DatePromised	Date Promised	Short Date
DatePruned	Date Pruned	Short Date
DatePurchased	Date Purchased	Short Date
DateRepotted	Date Repotted	Short Date
DateSold	Date Sold	Short Date
DateSubmitted	Date Submitted	Short Date
DateTaken	Date Taken	Short Date
DateUpdated	Date Updated	Short Date
DateWatered	Date Watered	Short Date
Deductions		Short Integer
DeliveryID	Delivery ID	ID Field
DepartmentName	Department Name	Indexed Text 50
DepartmentNumber	Department Number	Short Integer

Continued

FieldName	Caption	FieldTypeName
DepositAmount	Deposit Amount	Short Date
DepositDue	Deposit Due	Currency
DepreciationMethod	Depreciation Method	Text 50
DepreciationRate	Depreciation Rate	Single Float
Description		Memo
DestinationAddress	Destination Address	Text 255
DestinationCity	Destination City	Text 50
DestinationCountry	Destination Country	Text 50
DestinationPostalCode	Destination Postal Code	Postal Code
DestinationState	Destination State	Text 50
DevelopedBy	Developed By	Text 50
DietLogID	Diet Log ID	ID Field
DietType	Diet Type	Text 50
DirectorID	Director ID	ID Field
Discontinued		Yes/No
Discount		Single Float
DistanceTraveled	Distance Traveled	Text 30
DuesAmount	Dues Amount	Currency
DuesPaidDate	Dues Paid Date	Short Date
EditionNumber	Edition Number	Long Integer
EmailAddress	Email Address	Indexed Text 50
EmailName	Email Name	Indexed Text 50
EmployeeID	Employee ID	ID Field
EmployeeTaskID	Employee Task ID	ID Field

Continued

FieldName	Caption	FieldTypeName
EmrgcyContactName	Emrgcy Contact Name	Text 50
EmrgcyContactPhone	Emrgcy Contact Phone	Phone Number
EndDate	End Date	Short Date
EndTime	End Time	Long Time
EstimatedCost	Estimated Cost	Currency
EventID	Event ID	ID Field
EventName	Event Name	Indexed Text 50
EventType	Event Type	Text 50
ExerciseLogID	Exercise Log ID	ID Field
ExerciseType	Exercise Type	Text 50
ExpenseID	Expense ID	ID Field
ExpenseType	Expense Type	Text 50
Extension		Text 30
FaxNumber	Fax Number	Phone Number
FertilizeFrequency	Fertilize Frequency	Text 50
FilmExpirationDate	Film Expiration Date	Short Date
FilmID	Film ID	ID Field
FilmSpeed	Film Speed	Text 20
FilmType	Film Type	Text 30
FilterUsed	Filter Used	Text 50
FirstName	First Name	Text 50
FixedAssetID	Fixed Asset ID	ID Field
Flash		Yes/No
Flowering		Yes/No

Continued

FieldName	Caption	FieldTypeName
Format		Text 50
FreightCharge	Freight Charge	Currency
FriendID	Friend ID	ID Field
Genus		Text 50
GiftGiven	Gift Given	Text 255
Grade		Text 30
GramsCarbohydrates	Grams Carbohydrates	Short Integer
GramsFat	Grams Fat	Short Integer
GramsProtein	Grams Protein	Short Integer
GroupName	Group Name	Indexed Text 50
GuestID	Guest ID	ID Field
HealthProblems	Health Problems	Memo
Hobbies		Text 255
HomePhone	Home Phone	Phone Number
HourlyRate	Hourly Rate	Currency
HoursSinceLastSrvc	Hours Since Last Srvc	Short Integer
HoursSleep	Hours Sleep	Single Float
HouseholdInvID	Household Inv ID	ID Field
Ingredients		Memo
Instructions		Memo
Instructor		Indexed Text 50
Insured		Yes/No

Continued

FieldName	Caption	FieldTypeName
InterestEarned	Interest Earned	Currency
InvestmentID	Investment ID	ID Field
InvoiceDate	Invoice Date	Short Date
InvoiceDetailID	Invoice Detail ID	ID Field
InvoiceID	Invoice ID	ID Field
ISBNNumber	ISBN Number	Text 50
ItemName	Item Name	Indexed Text 50
ItemType	Item Type	Text 50
LaborHours	Labor Hours	Single Float
LastMeetingDate	Last Meeting Date	Short Date
LastName	Last Name	Indexed Text 50
Length		Text 50
LensUsed	Lens Used	Text 50
LightPreference	Light Preference	Text 50
Location		Text 255
MailingListID	Mailing List ID	ID Field
Major		Text 50
MajorInfluences	Major Influences	Memo
Make		Indexed Text 50
Manufacturer		Text 50
MaximumPulse	Maximum Pulse	Short Integer
MembershipStatus	Membership Status	Text 30
MiddleName	Middle Name	Text 30

Continued

FieldName	Caption	FieldTypeName
MilesSinceLastSrvc	Miles Since Last Srvc	Short Integer
MilligramsSodium	Milligrams Sodium	Short Integer
MobilePhone	Mobile Phone	Phone Number
Model		Text 50
ModelNumber	Model Number	Text 50
MovieTitle	Movie Title	Indexed Text 50
MusicCollectionID	Music Collection ID	ID Field
NationalEmplNumber	National Empl Number	Personal ID Number
Nationality		Text 50
NeedDaycare	Need Daycare	Yes/No
NextServiceDate	Next Service Date	Short Date
Nickname		Text 30
Note		Memo
NumberAttending	Number Attending	Short Integer
NumberofServings	Number of Servings	Short Integer
NumberofTracks	Number of Tracks	Short Integer
NutritionalInformation	Nutritional Information	Memo
OrderDate	Order Date	Short Date
OrderDetailID	Order Detail ID	ID Field
OrderID	Order ID	ID Field
OrganizationName	Organization Name	Indexed Text 50
OstetatiousProse	Ostetatious Prose	Memo

Continued

FieldName	Caption	FieldTypeName
PackageDimensions	Package Dimensions	Text 50
PackageWeight	Package Weight	Text 50
Pages		Short Integer
ParentsNames	Parents Names	Text 255
PartsReplaced	Parts Replaced	Memo
PaymentAmount	Payment Amount	Currency
PaymentDate	Payment Date	Short Date
PaymentID	Payment ID	ID Field
PaymentMethod	Payment Method	Text 50
PaymentTerms	Payment Terms	Text 255
PercentAlcohol	Percent Alcohol	Single Float
PersonID	Person ID	ID Field
PhoneNumber	Phone Number	Phone Number
Photograph		OLE Object
PhotographID	Photograph ID	ID Field
Pick-upDateTime	Pick-up DateTime	General Date
Pick-upLocation	Pick-up Location	Text 255
PlacePurchased	Place Purchased	Text 50
PlaceStaying	Place Staying	Text 50
PlaceTaken	Place Taken	Text 50
PlantID	Plant ID	ID Field
PledgeAmount	Pledge Amount	Currency
PledgePaidDate	Pledge Paid Date	Short Date
PostalCode	Postal Code	Postal Code

Continued

FieldName	Caption	FieldTypeName
Prefix		Text 20
PrevServiceDate	Prev Service Date	Short Date
PricePerUnit	Price Per Unit	Currency
PrintSize	Print Size	Text 50
ProblemDescription	Problem Description	Memo
ProducerID	Producer ID	ID Field
ProductID	Product ID	ID Field
ProductName	Product Name	Indexed Text 50
ProjectDescription	Project Description	Memo
ProjectID	Project ID	ID Field
ProjectLead	Project Lead	Text 50
ProjectName	Project Name	Indexed Text 50
Promised-byDate	Promised-by Date	Short Date
PublisherName	Publisher Name	Indexed Text 50
PurchasedAt	Purchased At	Text 50
PurchasePrice	Purchase Price	Currency
PurposeofExpense	Purpose of Expense	Text 255
Quantity		Double Float
QuantityOnHand	Quantity On Hand	Short Integer
QuantityReserved	Quantity Reserved	Long Integer
Rating		Text 20
ReceivedBy	Received By	Text 50
RecipeDescription	Recipe Description	Memo

Continued

FieldName	Caption	FieldTypeName
RecipeID	Recipe ID	ID Field
RecipeName	Recipe Name	Indexed Text 50
RecordingLabel	Recording Label	Text 50
ReferenceNumber	Reference Number	Text 50
ReferredBy	Referred By	Text 255
Region		Text 50
ReorderLevel	Reorder Level	Long Integer
Required-byDate	Required-by Date	Short Date
ReservationDate	Reservation Date	Short Date
ReservationID	Reservation ID	ID Field
RestingPulse	Resting Pulse	Short Integer
Review		Memo
Room		Text 50
RoomNumber	Room Number	Text 50
Salary		Currency
SalePrice	Sale Price	Currency
SalespersonName	Salesperson Name	Text 50
SalesTax	Sales Tax	Currency
SampleSoundClip	Sample Sound Clip	OLE Object
SampleVideoClip	Sample Video Clip	OLE Object
SectionNumber	Section Number	Short Integer
SecurityName	Security Name	Indexed Text 50
SecuritySymbol	Security Symbol	Text 20
SecurityType	Security Type	Text 50

Continued

FieldName	Caption	FieldTypeName
SerialNumber	Serial Number	Indexed Text 50
ServiceCharge	Service Charge	Currency
ServiceDate	Service Date	Short Date
ServiceRecordID	Service Record ID	ID Field
ServingInstructions	Serving Instructions	Memo
SharesOwned	Shares Owned	Double Float
ShelfNumber	Shelf Number	Long Integer
ShipAddress	Ship Address	Text 255
ShipCity	Ship City	Text 50
ShipCountry	Ship Country	Text 50
ShipDate	Ship Date	Short Date
ShipName	Ship Name	Indexed Text 50
ShippedFrom	Shipped From	Text 50
ShippedTo	Shipped To	Text 50
ShippedVia	Shipped Via	Text 50
ShipperPhoneNumber	Shipper Phone Number	Phone Number
ShipperTrackingCode	Shipper Tracking Code	Indexed Text 50
ShippingCost	Shipping Cost	Currency
ShipPostalCode	Ship Postal Code	Postal Code
ShipRegion	Ship Region	Text 50
ShipState	Ship State	Text 50
ShipVia	Ship Via	Text 50
ShutterSpeed	Shutter Speed	Text 50
SocialSecurityNumber	Social Security Number	Personal ID Number
Source		Text 50

Continued

FieldName	Caption	FieldTypeName
Species		Text 50
SpouseName	Spouse Name	Text 50
StartDate	Start Date	Short Date
StartTime	Start Time	Long Time
State		Text 50
Status		Text 30
StudentClassID	Student Class ID	ID Field
StudentID	Student ID	ID Field
Subject		Text 255
SubjectAddress	Subject Address	Text 255
SubjectName	Subject Name	Indexed Text 50
SubjectPhone	Subject Phone	Phone Number
Suffix		Text 20
SupervisorID	Supervisor ID	ID Field
SupplierID	Supplier ID	ID Field
SupplierName	Supplier Name	Indexed Text 50
SweetOrDry	Sweet Or Dry	Text 20
TaskDescription	Task Description	Memo
TaskID	Task ID	ID Field
Taxable		Yes/No
TempPreference	Temp Preference	Text 30
Term		Text 30
Thank-youNoteSent	Thank-you Note Sent	Yes/No
TimeBilledID	Time Billed ID	ID Field

Continued

FieldName	Caption	FieldTypeName
TimeExercised	Time Exercised	Text 30
TimeTaken	Time Taken	Long Time
TimeToPrepare	Time To Prepare	Text 50
Title		Text 20
TotalCalories	Total Calories	Short Integer
TotalDue	Total Due	Currency
TrainingLocation	Training Location	Text 50
TransactionDate	Transaction Date	Short Date
TransactionID	Transaction ID	ID Field
TransactionNumber	Transaction Number	Long Integer
Type		Text 30
UnitPrice	Unit Price	Currency
Units		Short Integer
UnitsInStock	Units In Stock	Long Integer
UnitsOnOrder	Units On Order	Long Integer
Variety		Text 30
Vegetarian		Yes/No
VideoCollectionID	Video Collection ID	ID Field
Vineyard		Text 50
Vintage		Long Integer
Vitamins		Text 255
WateringFrequency	Watering Frequency	Text 50

Continued

FieldName	Caption	FieldTypeName
WhichMeal	Which Meal	Text 50
WineListID	Wine List ID	ID Field
WineName	Wine Name	Indexed Text 50
WineType	Wine Type	Text 50
WorkoutDate	Workout Date	Short Date
WorkPhone	Work Phone	Phone Number
Year		Short Integer
YearReleased	Year Released	Short Integer

Field Types Provided By The Table Wizard

The following table shows the different fields provided by the table wizard and their associated Mask, together with whether they are Primary Key fields or whether they are indexed.

Where a field type has more than one mask, it's due to the fact that it supports more than one country format. For example, a phone number or personal ID are formatted differently depending on the country code. When Access selects the mask to use, it will supply a `CountryCode` that specifies which format to use. For example, for the United States, the `CountryCode` is '1'. This applies to items like Phone Numbers and 'Personal ID Numbers':

Field Type Name	Mask	Primary Key	Index
Byte		No	No
Currency		No	No
Double Float		No	No
General Date		No	No

Continued

Field Type Name	Mask	Primary Key	Index
ID Field		Yes	Yes
Indexed Long Integer		No	Yes
Indexed Short Integer		No	Yes
Indexed Text 50		No	Yes
Long Date		No	No
Long Integer		No	No
Long Time	09:00:00 >LL	No	No
Medium Date	99->L<LL-00	No	No
Medium Time	09:00 >LL	No	No
Memo		No	No
OLE Object		No	No
Personal ID Number	000-00-0000	No	No
Personal ID Number	000 000 000	No	No
Personal ID Number	0 00 00 00 000 000	No	No
Personal ID Number	00000000	No	No
Personal ID Number	>LLLLLL00L00L000L	No	No
Personal ID Number	000.00.000.000	No	No
Personal ID Number	000000-0000	No	No
Personal ID Number	000000	No	No
Personal ID Number	000000 00000	No	No
Personal ID Number	00000000	No	No
Personal ID Number	99.000.000C->a	No	No
Personal ID Number	00.000.000-0	No	No
Personal ID Number	000 000 000	No	No

Continued

Field Type Name	Mask	Primary Key	Index
Personal ID Number	0-0000-00000-00-0	No	No
Personal ID Number	0000.00.000	No	No
Phone Number	!(999) 000-0000	No	No
Phone Number	!(999) 000-0000	No	No
Phone Number	(9) 00.00.00.00	No	No
Phone Number	(009) 900 00 00	No	No
Phone Number	000-000 00 00	No	No
Phone Number	(9999) 00090009	No	No
Phone Number	00-000 00 00	No	No
Phone Number	00 00 00 00	No	No
Phone Number	!(99999) 999 000 000	No	No
Phone Number	!(999) 000-0000	No	No
Phone Number	(0009) 999-9999	No	No
Phone Number	000-000 00 00	No	No
Phone Number	(999) 000 0000	No	No
Phone Number	99999-0000999	No	No
Postal Code	00000-9999	No	Yes
Postal Code	>L0L 0L0	No	Yes
Postal Code	00000	No	Yes
Postal Code	00000	No	Yes
Postal Code	00000	No	Yes
Postal Code	0000	No	Yes

Continued

Field Type Name	Mask	Primary Key	Index
Postal Code	>LL00 0LL	No	Yes
Postal Code	000 00 >?<??????????????	No	Yes
Postal Code	0000 >?<???????????????	No	Yes
Postal Code	00-000	No	Yes
Postal Code	00000	No	Yes
Postal Code	0000	No	Yes
Postal Code	00000-000	No	Yes
Postal Code	0000	No	Yes
Postal Code	00000	No	Yes
Postal Code	0000->LL	No	Yes
Short Date	99/99/00	No	No
Short Integer		No	No
Short Time	00:00	No	No
Single Float		No	No
Text 20		No	No
Text 255		No	No
Text 30		No	No
Text 50		No	No
Yes/No		No	No

INDEX

Symbols

A

D

N

O

P

X

The Revolutionary Guide to Visual C++

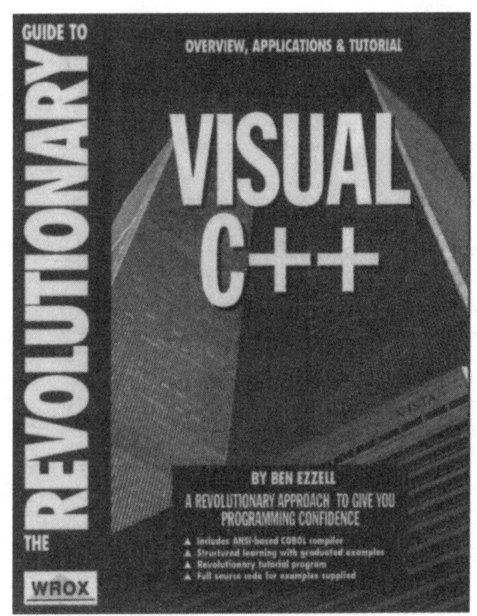

Building on your knowledge of C, this book is a complete guide to writing C++ applications for Windows using Microsoft's Visual C++ compiler. We focus on the Microsoft Foundation Class (MFC) and show you how it can be used to produce professional looking programs. A truly comprehensive guide to all the Visual C++ tools.

Ben Ezzell ISBN 1-874416-22-2
$39.95 / C$55.95 / £37.49

The Revolutionary Guide to OOP using C++

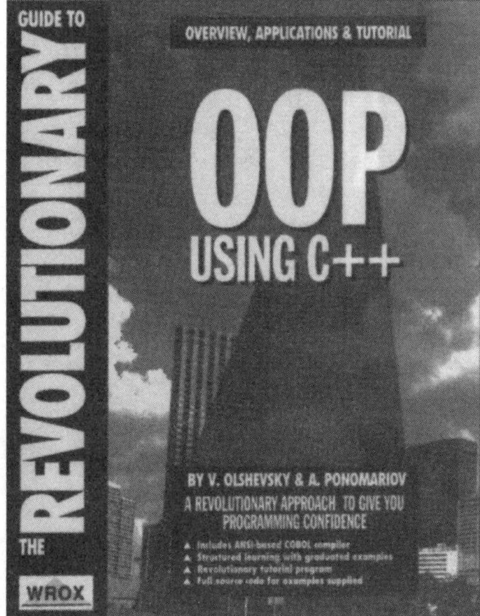

Benefit from the authors' years of experience using C and C++ in some of the most complex and demanding programming environments around today. This book aims to ease the difficulties in making the transition from C to C++, and will show you the power of object-oriented C++.

V. Olshevsky and A. Ponomarev ISBN 1-874416-18-4
$39.95 / C$55.95 / £37.49

The Revolutionary Guide to Assembly Language

Take the Challenge. Learn how to design, develop and debug powerful assembly language routines. Take control of your system and increase the power of your high level programs. Why learn unnecessary information when you can accomplish the task with expert assistance. "At £35.00, it's worth every penny!" (Syd Anderson, The Association of C and C++ Users).

Vitaly Maljugin et al. ISBN 1-874416-12-5
$39.95 / C$55.95 / £34.95

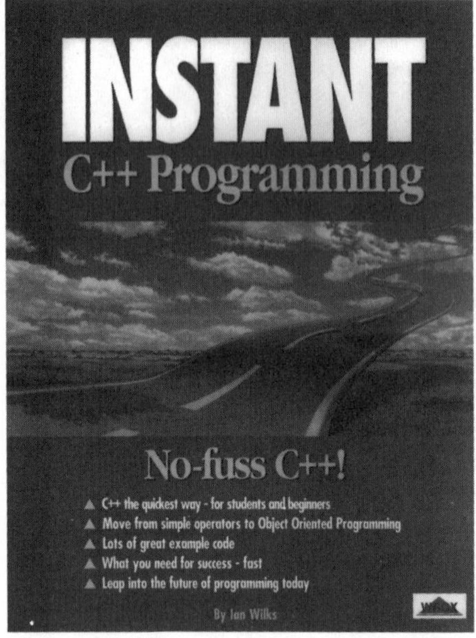

Instant C++ Programming

If you want a swift route to proficiency in C++, this no-nonsense, fast-paced tutorial teaches you all you need to know in an instant and gets you writing programs from day one. The book is ideal for the programmer moving to a new language. Lots of example code and self-check exercises enable you to quickly become proficient in C++ and then move to object-oriented programming.

Ian Wilks ISBN 1-874416-29-X
$19.95 / C$27.95 / £18.49

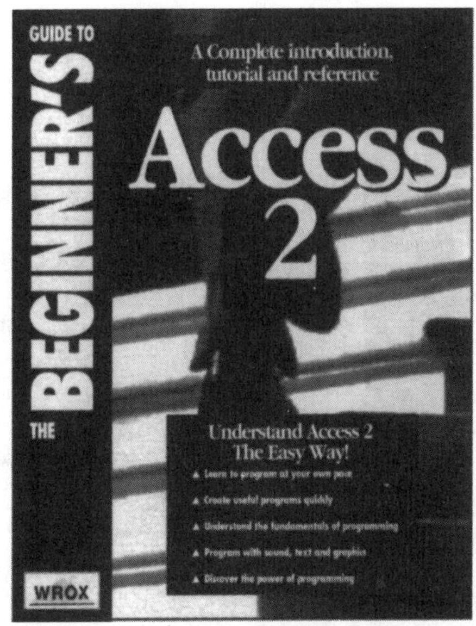
THE BEGINNER'S GUIDE TO
A Complete introduction, tutorial and reference
Access 2
Understand Access 2 The Easy Way!
Learn to program at your own pace
Create useful programs quickly
Understand the fundamentals of programming
Program with sound, text and graphics
Discover the power of programming
WROX

THE BEGINNER'S GUIDE TO
A Complete introduction, tutorial and reference
OOP in C++
Understand OOP in C++ The Easy Way!
Learn to program at your own pace
Create useful programs quickly
Understand the fundamentals of programming
Program with sound, text and graphics
Discover the power of programming
WROX

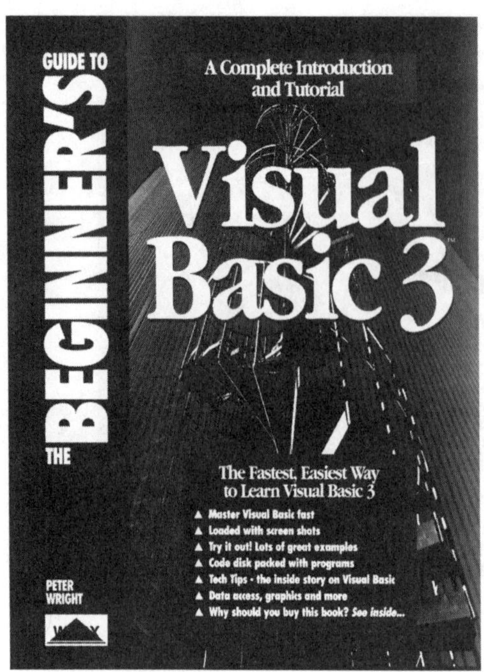

The Beginner's Guide to Visual Basic 3

If you're a beginner to programming, this book is the place to start. We'll show you how easy, fun and powerful Visual Basic can be. If you're familiar with another language, you'll learn how Visual Basic does things in terms you'll understand. Along the way, you'll get all the background information you need on Windows Programming to help you develop really professional applications.

Peter Wright ISBN 1-874416-19-2
$29.95 / C$41.95 / £27.99

The Beginner's Guide to C++

The ideal start for the newcomer to the world of programming languages, this Beginner's Guide contains comprehensive coverage of the language syntax. You'll master procedural programming in easy stages, and then learn object-oriented programming - the essential programming methodology of the future.

O. Yaroshenko ISBN 1-874416-26-5
$24.95 / C$34.95 / £22.99

Notes

Notes

Notes

Notes

WIN FREE BOOKS

TELL US WHAT YOU THINK!

Complete and return the bounce back card and you will:

- Help us create the books you want.
- Receive an update on all Wrox titles.
- Enter the draw for 5 Wrox titles of your choice.

FILL THIS OUT to enter the draw for free Wrox titles

ıme ______

dress ______

______

______

______ Postcode/Zip ______

ɔupation ______

ʌ did you hear about this book ?

Book review (name) ______

Advertisement (name) ______

Recommendation

Catalog

Other ______

ʼre did you buy this book ?

3ookstore (name) ______

Computer Store (name) ______

ʌail Order

)ther ______

What influenced you in the purchase of this book ?

- ☐ Cover Design
- ☐ Contents
- ☐ Use of Color
- ☐ Other (please specify)

______

How did you rate the overall contents of this book ?

- ☐ Excellent
- ☐ Good
- ☐ Average
- ☐ Poor

What did you find most useful about this book ?

______

What did you find least useful about this book ?

______

Please add any additional comments. ______

______

______

What other subjects will you buy a computer book on soon ?

______

What is the best computer book you have used this year ? ______

Please do not put me on your mailing list ☐

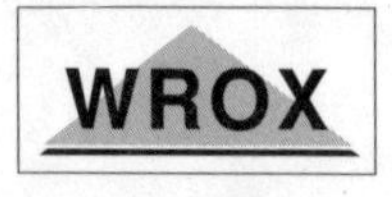

WROX PRESS INC.

Wrox writes books for you. Any suggestions, or ideas about how you want information given in your ideal book will be studied by our team. Your comments are always valued at WROX.

Free phone from USA 1 800 814 3461
Fax (312) 465 4063

Compuserve 100063,2152.
UK Tel. (4421) 706 6826 Fax (4421) 706 2967

Computer Book Publishers

NB. If you post the bounce back card below in the UK, please send it to: Wrox Press Ltd. Unit 16 Sapcote Industrial Estate, 20 James Road, Tyseley, Birmingham B11 2BA

NO POSTAGE NECESSARY IF MAILED IN THE UNITED STATES

BUSINESS REPLY MAIL

FIRST CLASS MAIL PERMIT#64 CHICAGO,IL

POSTAGE WILL BE PAID BY ADDRESSEE

WROX PRESS
2710 WEST TOUHY AVE
CHICAGO IL 60645-3008
USA